From the Bahamas in the north to Curaçao in the south, more than thirty million people share a common history . . .

1492—The Spanish arrive in the Caribbean.

1508—Juan Ponce de León leads an expedition to Puerto Rico—and founds towns near Camparia (now San Juan) and at San Germán.

1511—The Arawaks, with the help of the Carib, rebel against the Spanish conquistadores but are defeated and eventually become extinct.

1511—Cuba is colonized.

1625—The Dutch, British, and French begin to take control of Spain's Caribbean colonies.

1794—Toussaint Louverture leads the Haitian slave revolt.

1802—Napoleon invades Saint-Domingue.

1804—Haiti is proclaimed independent.

1838—Slaves are emancipated in the British islands.

1902—Pelée erupts, killing all 30,000 inhabitants of Saint-Pierre.

1933—Batista y Zaldívar becomes dictator of Cuba.

1948—Cuba holds its last free election.

1962—Jamaica and Trinidad receive independence.

1983—Grenada is torn by civil war.

1986—President Duvalier flees Haiti with his family.

1999—Supporters of Haitian ex-president Aristide press for his reelection amid governmental chaos and political assassinations.

JAN ROGOZIŃSKI is a freelance writer specializing in historical and technical subjects. He holds a Ph.D. in social and cultural history from Princeton University. Mr. Rogoziński lives in Florida.

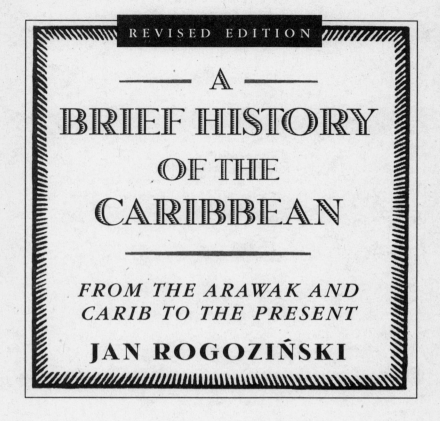

REVISED EDITION

A
BRIEF HISTORY
OF THE
CARIBBEAN

*FROM THE ARAWAK AND
CARIB TO THE PRESENT*

JAN ROGOZIŃSKI

A PLUME BOOK

FOR PAUL FRANCIS HAUCH

in caritate sincera sempiternaque

―――∞∞∞―――

PLUME
Published by the Penguin Group
Penguin Putnam Inc., 375 Hudson Street, New York, New York 10014, U.S.A.
Penguin Books Ltd, 27 Wrights Lane, London W8 5TZ, England
Penguin Books Australia Ltd, Ringwood, Victoria, Australia
Penguin Books Canada Ltd, 10 Alcorn Avenue, Toronto, Ontario, Canada M4V 3B2
Penguin Books (N.Z.) Ltd, 182–190 Wairau Road, Auckland 10, New Zealand

Penguin Books Ltd, Registered Offices: Harmondsworth, Middlesex, England

Published by Plume, a member of Penguin Putnam Inc. This is an authorized reprint of a hardcover edition published by Facts On File, Inc. For information address Facts On File, Inc., 11 Penn Plaza, New York, New York 10001.

First Plume Printing, September 2000
10 9 8

℗ REGISTERED TRADEMARK—MARCA REGISTRADA

The Library of Congress has catalogued the Facts On File edition as follows:
Rogoziński, Jan.
    A brief history of the Caribbean: from the Arawak and the Carib to the present /
Jan Rozoziński. —Rev. ed.
    p. cm.
Includes bibliographical references and index.
ISBN 0-8160-3811-2 (hc.)
      0-452-28193-8 (pbk.)
    1. West Indies—History. I. Title.
F1621.R72   1999
972.9—dc21   98-51304

Printed in the United States of America
Original hardcover design by Evelyn Horovicz

CONTENTS

PART FOUR
THE ABOLITION OF SLAVERY AND THE CHALLENGES OF FREEDOM

PART FIVE
POVERTY AND PROGRESS IN THE CARIBBEAN SINCE 1914

LIST OF TABLES

LIST OF MAPS

PREFACE

The following pages provide a descriptive and analytical history of the Caribbean islands. From the Bahamas in the north to Curaçao in the south, more than 30 million people share a common history and similar patterns of development. In recent years, the Caribbean sometimes has been more widely defined to include the mainland of Central America from Mexico down as far as French Guiana. However, the islands and the mainland really form two separate regions. These two geographic zones are endowed with very different natural environments, and they have followed divergent paths since the Spanish conquest.[1]

In recounting the history of the islands, this book focuses on the interrelated evolution of the economy, political institutions, and social forms. The Caribbean enjoys a rich intellectual, cultural, and religious life. A full appreciation of these aspects of its history would have required a much longer work.

The region's long and complex story is best understood from the inside looking out—from a point of view that begins with the islands rather than seeing them as an extension of the United States, Europe, or Africa. At the same time, the reader deserves a self-explanatory narrative, so that events are comprehensible without the use of reference books. When these must be mentioned, I have defined technical terms and identified non-Caribbean institutions and events. For example, in mentioning a treaty transferring sovereignty over an island, the text cites the signatory powers and date of signing. For many centuries, the islands formed part of large empires ruling over several continents. I describe these imperial institutions with special attention to the ways in which they evolved in the special circumstances of the Caribbean.

MANY TRADITIONS, A SHARED HISTORY

Islands are different. The seas serve both as a barrier and as a highway. Island peoples are intensely attached and loyal to their birthplace. Yet, as economic needs dictate, they easily move to other islands or to the mainland—but always intending to return to their homeland. A strong sense of local particularism or even nationalism is especially characteristic of the Caribbean. The islands are scattered across a very large sea. Until the invention of the steamship and the airplane, the strong easterly trade winds and currents made it easier to sail from Europe to Barbados than from Cuba to Barbados. Moreover, the islands also enjoy a variety of landforms and climates that make each different from its neighbors.

Rule by four major (and several minor) European empires increased the region's natural diversity. Island cultures were therefore more varied than in either North America (primarily northern European and Protestant) or South America (mainly Hispanic and Roman Catholic). Each empire imposed its own language, religion, habits, and prejudices on the governed. Their very different political systems also have left a lasting imprint. The Spanish tried to govern their empire from Europe. The British (at least before 1810) allowed the whites on each island to make their own laws. These distinctions were less sharp in practice than in theory. Simply because Spain was far away, it often left island élites alone to govern themselves. But the colonial centuries did leave different traditions—of one-man rule in one case, of parliamentary politics in the other.

Each of the islands has its own cultures and traditions. But they also share certain experiences that are different from those of the mainland. Since they supplied the same agricultural commodities to a world market, all have been affected by the same worldwide economic trends. With rare exceptions, all were once slave societies, to an extent never seen before or since. Their peoples thus practice similar social forms and habits, although sometimes with different names. While the island peoples have had the same experiences, they sometimes have had them at different times. Jamaica and Cuba both became major producers of sugarcane, grown by black slaves. However, Jamaica developed into a plantation society in the 18th century, Cuba during the 19th.

FROM COLONIES TO SOVEREIGN NATIONS

Given their intense insular patriotism, all islanders consider political independence a decisive event—perhaps the most decisive—in their history. About half of the islands, with perhaps 90 percent of the population, now are independent. Like the abolition of slavery, self-rule came to the islands at different times. Haiti and the Dominican Republic have governed themselves since the 19th century. Cuba became independent when American troops withdrew in 1902. Guadeloupe and Martinique (with their dependencies) gained more local autonomy in 1946, when each became a province or *département* within the French Republic. Puerto Rico became an Associated Free State or Commonwealth in 1952, and the U.S. Virgin Islands also gained control over local affairs in 1968. In 1954, the six Dutch islands became self-governing territories associated with the Netherlands, although discussions about their eventual independence continue.

Most of the former British colonies also have become sovereign states since 1962. The drive for independence began with the formation of labor unions and trade associations, supported by the British Labour Party and often led by men who had served abroad during the First World War. Since most islands depended on one or two major export crops, the Great Depression of the 1930s was severe. Demonstrations, strikes, and riots were frequent throughout the British Caribbean between 1935 and 1938. Other islands also suffered violence and political oppression. Rafael Trujillo imposed a police state on the Dominican Republic, while a civil war ended Gerardo Machado's attempt to establish one-man rule in Cuba. Nevertheless, a British commission chaired by Lord Moyne found much to blame in the Crown colony form of government. It called for stronger labor unions, increased self-government, and universal adult suffrage.

After World War II, the British authorities encouraged the formation of a West Indies federation that included 10 of their colonies. But the federation enjoyed little popular support, and Jamaica and Trinidad withdrew and received independence in 1962. An attempt to create a smaller federation among the colonies in the Lesser Antilles also failed, and Barbados gained self-rule in 1962. Most of the remaining British colonies also became independent in the 1970s and 1980s. Anguilla, Montserrat, the British Virgin Islands, the Cayman Islands, and the Turks and the Caicos remain Crown colonies, enjoying a measure of internal self-government.

Some states remained under European rule until recently. But the United States long has been the main economic influence in the region. From the 1880s, American capital had a major role in developing the sugar industry in Cuba, Puerto Rico, and the Dominican Republic. The United States remains the region's largest trading partner—except for Cuba, which trades mainly with the Soviet Union.

The United States also intervened politically in several Caribbean states earlier in the century. For humanitarian reasons and to prevent interference by one of the warring European states, President Woodrow Wilson purchased the Danish Virgin Islands in 1917. He also sent American troops to occupy the Dominican Republic (1916–1924) and Haiti (1915–1934). In addition, the United States also intervened in Cuba on several occasions between 1906 and 1934. These American efforts failed in their avowed purpose: to establish honest, stable, and democratic governments. Thus the United States generally has taken a hands-off approach since the 1930s. However, it did send troops to intervene during civil wars in the Dominican Republic (1965) and Grenada (1983).

As they face their sixth century since Columbus irrevocably joined them to the Old World, the Caribbean nations may be judged a political success. Except in Haiti and Cuba, every island regularly holds elections, the winner takes office, and the loser retires—tests of democracy not met in most of the world.

The Caribbean islands continue to seek a secure economic base. Cane sugar made them the wealthiest colonies in the world during the 18th century. But the industry disappeared before World War I from several of the islands in the Lesser Antilles. Since 1945, it also has declined in importance on the larger islands, except for Cuba. At the same time, the population has continued to soar as health care has improved, and unemployment has been high.

Efforts to find a substitute for sugar have enjoyed only mixed success. Several islands, especially Puerto Rico, that introduced manufacturing and processing industries before the mid-1970s have suffered from economic stagnation. A few governments have tried to manage the economy on the former eastern European model—Cuba since 1959, Jamaica during the 1970s, and Grenada under the Bishop regime. Their efforts failed to increase and probably hindered economic growth. Without local industry, most nations continue to pay for imported oil and industrial products with lower-value agricultural products. Thus they suffer from chronic trade deficits and must depend on tourism to earn foreign currencies.

The island peoples face economic and social challenges directly linked to their history. In the Caribbean, Europeans created a plantation society unlike almost any other in human history. They settled the islands, invested large amounts of capital, and introduced sophisticated technologies for one purpose only. They replaced the extinct native peoples with hundreds of thousands of African slaves and drove them to grow sugar.

Although planters also developed other crops (notably coffee), all of the major islands were true monocultures by the middle of the 17th century. Sugar provided 80 percent or more of their exports, and many had to import food and other necessities. The sugar industry remained profitable into the 19th century. But almost all the profits were taken and remained in Europe. The islands were peopled to support one industry. That industry is no longer significant, and islanders must find alternative ways of making a living. The task for island leaders is difficult—but not impossible. A nation's history does not determine later events, and the future remains open.

For several centuries, a few white masters and many black slaves made up the societies of the sugar islands. Issues involving race thus are unavoidable in any study of Caribbean history. Over time, racial relations have taken many complex forms. In place of the stark division into two races found in some other parts of the world, island societies developed an elaborate network of shades and hierarchies. Because white laborers were few, slaves were everywhere and did every kind of work. Racial and ethnic blending began at an early period, and some members of racially mixed groups became wealthy and—especially on the French islands—owned slaves.

Precisely because they have played a crucial role throughout the history of the islands, it is essential to use meaningful and consistent language to describe racial relations. Throughout this book, I use the terms *black, white,* and *colored* with the meanings traditionally ascribed to them by the peoples of the islands. *Black* (French *noir;* Spanish *negro*) refers to persons perceived as being of African origin. *White* describes persons accepted by their neighbors as of European origin. *Colored* (*gens de coleur, gente de color*) refers to those perceived to be of mixed race, usually of mixed African-European descent. (Because the native Indians largely died out during the 16th century, alliances between Indians and other races were relatively rare.) Eighteenth-century authors—particularly those writing about Jamaica and Saint-Domingue—often present elaborate and complex systems of color coding with as many as eight, 10, or even 16 categories. However, ordinary folk probably did not make these distinctions between small variations in whiteness.

Following most recent literature about the Caribbean, I use the term *freedman* to designate any male or female person of black or mixed ancestry who attained the legal status of non-slave. By the end of the 18th century, some sources distinguish between "free coloreds" and "free blacks." But these latter terms were not used consistently on the various islands.

During recent years, some in the United States have adopted the term *African-American* and prefer it to *black* and *colored*. However, a historian of the islands cannot use the analogous term "African-Caribbean." This new word would obscure a basic and important distinction. As used in the islands, African referred only to African-born slaves. The term *creole* indicated those—both black and white—born and raised in the region.[2] To make the same distinction, a writer using the term *African-Caribbean* would have to call black immigrants "African-born African-Caribbeans." Those traditionally called coloreds presumably would become "native-born African-Caribbeans of African-European ancestry." The islanders already have given us useful terms with positive connotations. Thus there seemed to be no reason to follow this new American coinage, which would have greatly lengthened the book.

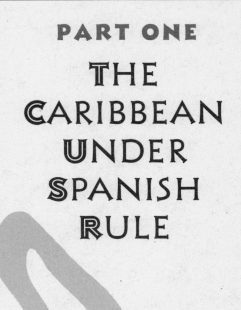

PART ONE

THE CARIBBEAN UNDER SPANISH RULE

CHAPTER 1

THE ENDURING ENVIRONMENT AND THE FIRST ISLANDERS

Taken together, the Caribbean islands create a kind of long narrow chain, almost 2,500 miles long but never more than 160 miles wide.[1] Running roughly north of and parallel to Central and South America, they enclose a body of water we call the Caribbean Ocean or Sea. The Caribbean can be distinguished from and is somewhat more salty than the Atlantic. But it is not a closed sea, and strong currents provide a constant interchange with the larger oceans.

On a map, this long group of islands seems to form a bridge between North and South America. The historical reality has been more complicated. Merchants, planters, and job-seekers always have moved from one island to another or to the mainland. Until the end of the 19th century, however, the islands were colonies of four major European empires that sought to monopolize their resources. Thus the rivalries and the frequent wars of their foreign rulers sometimes hindered this natural flow of trade and migration.

Altogether, thousands of islands rise from the Caribbean. They range in size from uninhabitable rocks and tiny cays to Cuba, which is among the world's largest islands, comparable in size to Sicily and slightly larger than Ohio. During the five centuries since their discovery by Columbus, their rulers have assigned the islands to various political and administrative divisions, and several have changed hands many times. Geographically, however, all of the islands fall into four major groupings—the Greater Antilles, the Bahamas archipelago, the Lesser Antilles and the southern islands along the South American coast. These groups have different physical characteristics, and each island's natural resources have strongly influenced its economic and political fortunes.

THE GREATER AND LESSER ANTILLES, THE BAHAMAS

The four larger islands of Cuba, Jamaica, Hispaniola, and Puerto Rico are known as the Greater Antilles. All are long and relatively narrow and generally lie more or less from west to east. Just above the Greater Antilles, more than 700 small islands and cays form the Bahamas group (which geographically includes the Turks and Caicos). To the east of Puerto Rico, the Lesser Antilles seem to trace a semicircle or arc that runs from the Virgin Islands in the north to Grenada in the south. Geographically and climatically, the Lesser Antilles actually fall into two groups. The larger inner arc is composed of mountainous volcanic islands. The smaller outer arc—Anguilla, Barbuda, Antigua, and the eastern half of Guadeloupe—is much lower in height. These are primarily formed of limestone, and have a dryer climate, characteristics that also are shared by Barbados to the south.

Trinidad, Tobago, and the three arid islands of Aruba, Bonaire, and Curaçao form a fourth grouping. The weather patterns of the Curaçao islands, located just off the coast of South America, are very different from those affecting other Caribbean islands. Although they sometimes were politically affiliated with the Lesser Antilles, Trinidad and Tobago are an extension of the South American mainland and share its climate.

Mountainous Islands and Flat Islands

Except for the Bahamas, almost all of the Caribbean islands represent the peaks of mountains that rise from the floor of the ocean, thrust up by enormous pressures under the earth's surface during two separate eras in the distant past. According to geological theories, these pressures deep below the surface of the planet cause the continents to move very slowly over long periods of time. The earth's crust is composed of large rigid sections, known as *plates,* that move alongside one another. One of these plates more or less coincides with the Caribbean Sea, with its outer edge being marked by the arc of the Lesser Antilles. It moves very slowly eastward relative to the North American plate, which in turn is tending toward the west. The boundary where these two plates meet in the Caribbean islands suffers from recurring volcanic activity as well as serious earthquakes.

In geological terms, the oldest islands are the Greater Antilles and the eastern or outer arc of the Lesser Antilles. Volcanic activity created both of these groups some 70

Table 1. **THE CARIBBEAN ISLANDS** *(Reading from Northwest to Southeast)*

Island	Size (square miles)	Highest Point (feet)	Estimated Population 1995–1997
GREATER ANTILLES			
Cuba	42,827	6,142	11,000,000
Jamaica	4,411	7,405	2,616,000
Hispaniola	29,530	10,417	14,500,000
Haiti	10,714		7,336,000
Dominican Republic	18,816		8,052,000
Puerto Rico	3,435	3,494	3,900,000
Cayman Islands	96	49	36,000
BAHAMAS GROUP			
The Bahamas	4,566	320	276,000
Turks & Caicos	169		14,600
LESSER ANTILLES			
U.S. Virgin Islands			105,000
St. Croix	84	1,526	51,500
St. Thomas	28	1,300	49,500
St. John	20		31,500
British Virgin Islands		1,700	19,000
Tortola	24		
Anegada	13		
Virgin Gorda	9		
Anguilla	35	180	11,000
Saint-Martin/Sint Maarten	13	1,391	40,000
Saint-Barthélemy	10		5,100
Saint Eustatius	8	1,801	2,600
Saba	5	2,900	1,200
Saint Kitts	68	3,793	42,000 ⎫
Nevis	50	3,232	⎭
Antigua	108	1,322	64,000 ⎫
Barbuda	62	72	⎭
Montserrat	32.5	2,435	(see page 308)
Guadeloupe	657	4,813	412,000
Martinique	421	4,582	403,000
Dominica	305	4,666	67,000
Saint Lucia	233	3,120	150,600
Barbados	166	1,109	259,000
Saint Vincent	133	3,868	119,000 ⎫
Grenadines	17		⎭
Grenada	120	2,756	96,000
Trinidad	1,864	3,087	1,131,000 ⎫
Tobago	116	1,874	⎭
CURAÇAO GROUP			
Aruba	73	548	88,000
Bonaire	111	791	14,200
Curaçao	171	644	150,700

to 50 million years ago.[2] The Greater Antilles thus represent the peaks of three chains of volcanic mountains that were thrust up and extended east from the mainland. The first of these mountain ranges ran east along what are now the northern coasts of Cuba and Haiti. A middle and much longer chain of volcanoes created the Cayman Islands. It then continued east along the southern coast of Cuba (the Sierra Maestre) and through the central regions of Haiti (the Cordillera Central) and Puerto Rico (El Yunque), finally coming to an end at what today is known as the Virgin Islands. A third and southernmost chain created the Blue Mountains of Jamaica and then extended along the southern coast of Haiti.

While Central America and the Greater Antilles were rising from the sea, similar volcanic forces created the Andes Mountains. Branches of this great South American chain continue north and east to make up the Caribbean coast range. The highest peaks of one branch of this coastal mountain range form the islands of Aruba, Bonaire, and Curaçao just north of the mainland. Another branch stretches north from Colombia and Venezuela to Trinidad and Tobago, and perhaps to Barbados.

This age of great earth movements was followed by a quieter era—dated by geologists between the Middle Eocene and the Middle Miocene epochs. Volcanic activity died down. The sea again covered parts or all of the islands. Great deposits of sediment, such as sandstone and limestone, were laid down as the bodies of marine animals decayed. And some of the older islands—especially those along the outer rim of the Lesser Antilles—were flattened out and never again became active volcanoes. After several million years had passed, a second great period of mountain building took place during the late Miocene and Pliocene epochs. The four islands of the Greater

Volcanic islands: Vapor vents, Saint Lucia. Volcanic vents and hot sulfurous springs cover an extensive area near the coastal town of Soufrière. During the 18th century, the island exported sulfur dug from the springs, which also were used for medicinal baths.

Antilles again arose above the sea. And new volcanoes—several are still active today—created the inner arc of mountainous islands in the Lesser Antilles.[3]

The Bahamas group (including the Turks and Caicos) includes more than 700 small islands, innumerable rocks and cays, and hundreds of reefs lying only a few feet below the surface. Strictly speaking these islands and reefs are not found within the Caribbean Sea. And, unlike the Caribbean islands proper, they were not formed by volcanic eruptions. Instead they represent the highest points of the Bahamas Banks, two shallow blocks of rocks covered by limestone and sand that at various points in the ancient past probably rose above the water to form one landmass. Many of the Bahamas stand only a few feet above the water, with the highest hills—on Cat Island—reaching some 300 feet. Although their land surface taken together is close to that of Jamaica, only 22 are inhabited.

The Trade Winds Bring Endless Summer

The Caribbean islands are uniformly warm, and all—including those that receive little rain—also are humid. Except for the most northern of the Bahamas, the islands lie south of the tropic of Cancer. Moreover, they are surrounded by waters that are warm throughout the year. Because they are located within this warm sea, temperatures on the islands do not vary greatly with the seasons. Throughout the year, the average temperature ranges from around 78° Fahrenheit in the northern Bahamas to 80° in the south near Curaçao. Rarely is the difference between the warmest and coldest months greater than 8°.

Indeed, daily variations in temperature usually are much greater than any seasonal change. Differences of 15° between day and night temperatures are common, and changes of 20° or more have been recorded. Throughout the year, the air temperature is at its coolest immediately before sunrise. It rises quickly to reach its highest point about noon, and then begins to fall off during the late afternoon. Relative humidity always is high, although this also varies during the day. Generally, humidity reaches a peak of more than 90 percent at dawn and falls as temperatures increase during the day. But the humidity never falls below 50 percent and rarely below 70 percent.

The pleasant climate of most islands is mainly due to the constant trade winds. During periods of lull, the constant heat and humidity can become unbearable. Some relief can be gained by moving to the higher elevations. On average, the temperature falls by about 1° for every 300 feet in height. Some of the higher plateaus in the Greater Antilles thus enjoy a climate more suitable for temperate than tropical crops.

The northeast trade winds, originating in the Bermuda-Azores high-pressure cell, are the prime "weather machine" of the Caribbean and the Gulf of Mexico. Month in and month out, the northeasterly trades (that is, coming *from* the northeast) blow at a steady 15 to 25 knots, varying no more than a compass point in any direction. Beginning at the latitude of Bermuda, the winds shift toward the north and east in a clockwise rotation. They then form the southwesterly trades that prevail at that latitude back across the Atlantic to England, France, and northern Spain. Because of the easterly trades, the Caribbean islands and parts of the Central American coast enjoy generally pleasant weather. However, summers are hot and rainy, with the end of summer (July through October) forming the dangerous hurricane season.

The ocean currents join the winds in carrying ships west through the Caribbean and then north up the coast of North America. Sometimes reaching a velocity of 5 knots, Atlantic waters move westward through the channel between Cuba and the Yucatan Peninsula until they turn northward in the Gulf of Mexico. Powered by the tropical sun, they sweep along the Cuban coast and squeeze through the 90-mile strait between Cuba and Florida, powering the great Gulf Stream along the American coast and back toward Europe.

Volcanic islands: Mont Pelée, Martinique. At 4,700 feet, Mont Pelée towers above the small village of Saint-Pierre. An eruption in 1902 destroyed the original Saint-Pierre, the island's largest city. The areas bare of vegetation mark the course of the 1902 lava flows.

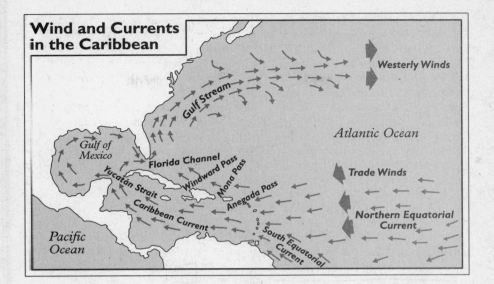

Tropical Islands and Desert Islands

As they travel across the warm waters of the South Atlantic and the Caribbean, the trade winds become extremely humid and can produce very heavy rains when they are cooled. Generally speaking, this cooling can occur in two different ways, either through orographic effects—which are determined by the height of an island—or though convection—which is influenced by its size.

Orographic effects occur when the moisture-rich trade winds rise to pass over a high point on an island. As the trades rise, they become cooler, their moisture content condenses, and rain is produced. Even a relatively small island can cause this effect, but it increases with the height of the land. On average, low-lying islands thus receive less than half as much rain each year as mountainous ones. Moreover, especially on the larger islands of the Greater Antilles, the rain is heaviest at the top and on the windward (north and east) side of high mountains. As the winds descend on the leeward side, they have already lost most of their moisture. For this reason little rain falls on the southwestern coasts of many islands.

On the larger islands, such as the Greater Antilles, rain also is caused by convectional air currents. These are created because the land heats up and cools down more rapidly than water. When the air over the island becomes hotter during the morning and early afternoon, it rises and creates a powerful updraft or "convection." As the air rises, it also becomes cooler, and its moisture content condenses to form clouds. These clouds in turn cool the land, ending the upward flow of hot air. Toward mid-afternoon, the clouds may cool off enough to bring sudden and usually very heavy rains.

Since the temperature is essentially the same, the natural vegetation and the types of crops that can be grown on each island depend on the amount of rain it receives. For the reasons described, average precipitation can vary considerably in different regions of one island, depending on the location of mountain ranges. In general, however, mountainous islands receive more rain than flat islands, and smaller islands receive less than larger islands. For example, because of their size, the Greater Antilles generally are moist, although low-lying Cuba gets less rain than mountainous Jamaica. In contrast, the small, flat islands and cays of the southern Bahamas normally receive less than 25 inches of rain per year.

In the Lesser Antilles, similarly, the islands in the outer arc generally are arid compared with those in the inner arc with their volcanic mountains. Extremely dry conditions are found in the three islands (Aruba, Bonaire, and Curaçao) off the Venezuelan coast. In this region, the trade winds are least effective during the summer, when they produce rain on the other islands. On these islands, the brief "rainy season" actually occurs during the winter rather than during the summer.

The amount of rain received by each island is thus affected by its height above the sea and by its size. Except for the northern Bahamas and the Curaçao group off the Venezuelan coast, most islands tend to experience two distinct seasons each year— a dry season (usually from February to April) and a "rainy season" (from May or June to October or November). During the summer, troughs of low pressure, accompanying shifts in the global wind patterns, arise in the eastern Caribbean and move west. These unsettled periods, known as easterly waves (or "waves in the easterlies"), can bring overcast weather and occasionally very heavy rains.

The Deadly Power of Hurricanes

Sometimes, especially during the late summer, one of these easterly waves develops into a hurricane. For reasons that to this day we do not completely understand, a powerful upward current of air arises. This air current sets up a circular area of extremely low pressure that spirals inward (counterclockwise in this hemisphere) around the storm's calm center, or "eye." Although the heaviest damage is near the center of the storm, adverse weather may extend over an area 600 miles in diameter. Generally hurricanes bring very heavy rains; as much as 18 inches in one 24-hour period have been recorded. Except at the eye, wind speeds are severe. Velocities of 75 miles or more are common, and gusts near the center of the storm can exceed 200 miles an hour.

Hurricanes affecting this region arise in the eastern Caribbean or in the eastern Atlantic off the coast of Africa. Their course is totally unpredictable, but most tend to travel slowly westward, at about 10 miles an hour, across the Lesser Antilles and Greater Antilles. Next they may curve to the northeast or north, either striking the southeastern coast of the United States or dying out in mid-ocean. Only Trinidad and the three islands off Venezuela—far to the south of a hurricane's normal path—are safe from their destruction.

On average, eight hurricanes occur each year, but many do not touch land. Overall, 174 hurricanes were severe enough to be mentioned in local records between 1492 and 1800. Although they happen in every month except May, more than 80 percent hit during August, September, and October. Since they occur haphazardly, hurricanes may pass by an individual island for decades. But when they do hit, they can cause extraordinary damage.

In October 1780, for example, a hurricane—probably the greatest storm known to us—ravaged Barbados, Saint Lucia, Martinique, Dominica, Saint Eustatius, Saint Vincent, and Puerto Rico. During its savage passage, it killed well over 22,000 people and totally destroyed large British and French naval fleets as well as hundreds of merchant vessels. No instruments existing at the time could measure the force of its winds. But maximum gusts must have been well in excess of 200 miles per hour, since raindrops stripped the trees of their bark.

THE CARIBBEAN ENVIRONMENT: RAIN FORESTS AND CACTUS

Until the 20th century, all of the island peoples made their living from agriculture. Thus the resources of the islands—soil, water, and climate—both provided the potential for and also placed limits on growth. In fact, the history of individual islands often is the story of how successfully their settlers came to terms with the natural potential available to them.

Beginning with Columbus, visitors to the islands have remarked on their lush, dense vegetation, which at first often hindered settlement. But appearances are deceiving. The environment of the islands is quite fragile. Because of the moist, warm climate, chemical weathering occurs rapidly, and soil erodes easily and massively. In hilly areas, even natural forests are subject to severe erosion during the heavy rains of the summer wet season. And erosion can dramatically increase when the forests are removed for cultivation. In the upland regions of Puerto Rico, Jamaica, and especially of Haiti, centuries of erosion have totally destroyed some areas, which are no longer able to support life.

Even before they were cultivated, the soil in most of the islands was not very fer-

Tropical islands: El Yunque rain forest, Puerto Rico. As the trade winds rise to pass over high mountains such as El Yunque, they produce heavy rains on the windward (north and east) sides. This is a true rain forest with three levels of evergreen leaves, the highest or canopy layer reaching 120 feet.

Desert islands: Small cabins (said to be former slave huts) on Curaçao. Low-lying islands do not break the flow of the northeast trade winds, and they thus receive little rain. The three flat islands of Aruba, Bonaire, and Curaçao are especially arid.

tile. In the rain forests, most of the nutrients are contained in the vegetation itself, and the soil is relatively sterile. In upland areas, the heavy showers tend to leach minerals and organic matter deep into the ground, where they can be reached only by the roots of trees and shrubs. Once the trees are cut, the soil is exhausted quickly and requires heavy use of fertilizers to produce crops.

It is precisely because their soils are relatively poor that most of the islands originally were covered by forests rather than by grasslands. Even today, a great variety of vegetation can be found on each island. Overall, there are six main types of natural environment—tropical rain forests, seasonal rain forests, dry forests, savannah, thorny woodlands and cactus scrub, and mangrove swamps—with the prevalence of each type depending on the amount and frequency of rain an island receives.

Tropical Rain Forests   The rarest and most lush environment, tropical rain forests occur only in regions that receive 80 or more inches of rain and are wet at least 10 months of the year. Throughout the islands, these areas are found primarily in lowland areas on the windward side of high mountains. Two or three levels of constantly green vegetation block the sun, with the highest leaf canopy rising as much as 120 feet about the ground. As the temperature falls at higher levels (above approximately 3,000 feet), the tall rain forest merges into the mountain (or montane) forest, even more thickly covered with ferns and mosses.

Seasonal Rain Forests[4]   These receive 50 to 80 inches of rain during seven to nine humid months. Originally they covered most of the lowland districts and are still found on the leeward sides of the Greater Antilles. During the early centuries, several species had significant commercial value, including cedar and some trees used to make dyes, such as logwood. Only two layers of leaf canopy are found, and many trees lose their leaves during the dry season. At higher elevations in Cuba and Hispaniola, these seasonal rain forests merge into grasslands containing extensive forests of pine trees.

Dry (or Tropical Deciduous) Forests   These grow in regions with between 30 and 50 inches of rain and five to seven humid months. While frequently merging into the seasonal rain forest, the dry forest can be recognized by its more open nature. Trees rarely are more than 30 feet high, do not form a continuous canopy, and lose their leaves during the dry season. Since the ground is not shaded, it often is filled by a dense thorny brush, which is extremely difficult to pass through.

Savannah   Flat dry grasslands containing scattered scrub trees originally occurred only in areas of seasonal drought and hard, coarse soils in Cuba, Hispaniola, and the northern Bahamas. Man-made savannahs are found now on most islands, where they have been created by burning the dry forest or seasonal rain forest.

Thorny Woodlands and Cactus Scrub   These are found in areas with less than 30 inches of rain and only three to four humid months. Occurring on the dry leeward coasts of many islands, they cover much of the Bahamas and the three arid islands off Venezuela. Although only six or seven feet high, often they are almost impenetrable.

Mangrove Swamps   Originally encircling the more humid windward coasts of most islands, some species of mangrove swamps can tolerate salt water. Above the waterline, coastal areas were covered by low dense thickets of salt-tolerant plants such as seagrape and sometimes by palm trees.

Island Animal Life

Until the invention of modern steamships, the history of the islands was continuously influenced by the strong flow of the trade winds and currents more or less from east to west. Because of these winds and currents, it is much easier to move through the Caribbean from Venezuela than from Florida. And, as far as we know, virtually all plant, animal, and human life did migrate from east to west—from the northern coast of Venezuela to Trinidad, up through the lesser Antilles and Virgins, and then across the Greater Antilles to Puerto Rico, Hispaniola, Jamaica, and Cuba.

When Europeans reached the islands in 1492, they found relatively little animal life. Apparently, few of the larger species had been able to cross the water from South America. Among wild animals, a variety of small mammals was found only on Trinidad, which is closest to the mainland. These included the sloth, anteater, tiger cat, racoon, and a small deer. On the other islands, the only mammals, other than bats, were various rodents, including the large and tasty hutia, which reminded the Spanish of a rabbit. One kind of frog and a wide variety of reptiles also thrived, including the caiman, crocodiles (found only in Cuba), several snakes, and many lizards, such as the giant iguana.

The native peoples added very few domesticated animals over the years. The Carib kept Muscovy ducks, and the Arawak may have raised guinea pigs as well as small dogs (called *alco*), which did not bark. The Spanish themselves introduced many European plants and animals, some of which thrived and became major export crops. The most important of these are cane sugar, cattle, pigs, chickens, goats, donkeys, and horses.

THE ARAWAK AND THE CARIB

When the Spanish reached the islands in 1492, they found three major groups of people. All had come to the islands from South America in the relatively recent past. Small groups commonly referred to as the Ciboney (or Siboney) lived on the northwestern tips of Cuba and Hispaniola. The island Arawak dominated the Bahamas, the Greater Antilles, and Trinidad. The Carib were found on the Virgin Islands, many of the Lesser Antilles, and the northwestern tip of Trinidad. The Arawak, the first native group they encountered, told the Spanish that they had come after the Ciboney and were being chased by the Carib—and most archaeologists believe this story to be true.

The history of these native peoples is inherently fascinating: they play an important role during the first decades of European settlement and they have left us much of their material technology and a few descendants of mixed blood. But their story cannot be summarized easily and is largely conjectural. Since none of these peoples had a written language, we must rely on Spanish accounts and archaeological evidence.

The three major groupings of Indians are linguistic, with each group speaking similar and mutually comprehensible languages. Various scholars have distinguished a number of separate cultures, and they have given various names to these subgroups. However, none of these systems is generally accepted—except possibly for the use of Lucayan for the Arawak inhabiting the Bahamas.

Because of the importance of marine protein in their diet, all of the native peoples tended to live near or along the coasts. The least advanced and probably the oldest group were the Ciboney. By 1500, they primarily lived in rock shelters and caves along the northwest coasts of Cuba and Hispaniola. Small family groups apparently survived by collecting shellfish, wild fruits, and herbs as well as by hunting or culling fish, turtles, and reptiles (such as the iguana). Like all of the native peoples, they wore few clothes and painted their bodies, and their only implements were chipped and ground stone tools. Thus their sites reveal no evidence of cultivated plants, pottery, domestic utensils, or weapons.

Conuco Agriculture and Its Survival Today

In contrast to the Ciboney, the Arawak and Carib carried more advanced ways of life with them from their original homeland in the Amazon basin. The Arawak and Carib were in frequent contact, and both peoples used essentially the same material technologies. They farmed, hunted, and fished in comparable ways and used similar methods to make canoes, build huts, weave cloth, and make pottery. There do seem to have been significant differences in their social and political organization and in their religious beliefs, although these differences may have been exaggerated by some of the first Spanish observers.

Both peoples brought from South America a system of raising root plants known as *conuco*. This method produces large amounts of starch and sugar with relatively little effort, and it also is well suited to the fragile soil of the Caribbean islands. Toward the end of the dry season, the Indians first burned off the forest or brush. This released nutrients into the soil, which was then heaped up into mounds, more or less knee-high and some three to six feet across. Using pointed sticks, the women placed in these mounds cuttings from several types of root plants. The most important of these was the bitter yuca (called *manioc* in Brazil). Since its roots are poisonous, they are shredded or grated and drained of their juices before being baked into a kind of flat, unleavened bread known as *cassava*. A sweet form of yuca and yams or sweet potatoes also were grown and eaten boiled or baked.

The bitter yuca provided the Arawak and Carib with an abundant and constant supply of starch and sugar. The yuca is ideally suited to the islands. Because the *conuco* mounds provide drainage and prevent erosion, it can be grown on both in lowlands and on slopes. The plant grows in almost any soil, resists winter droughts and summer hurricanes, and can be stored (in the form of cassava bread) for months. Moreover, since the mounds require only modest weeding and can be harvested continuously, there is little urgency about work in the fields. While the crops become less abundant with time, the same mounds can be used for up to 10 or 15 years. For all of these reasons, yuca later became one of the main foods of the African slaves, and it continues to be very widely grown throughout the Caribbean by peasant farmers.

Yuca and yams were the main crops. In addition, the mounds also produced several other types of plants, including arrowroot, peanuts, peppers, and gourds. And the Indians also grew smaller amounts of seed plants, such as tobacco, corn (maize), beans, and squash. For variety these could be supplemented by local fruits, including the pineapple, the guava, and possibly the cashew.

Fishing and hunting provided additional protein. The native peoples mainly hunted the hutia, the iguana, and several kinds of birds (pigeons, doves, and parrots), and they sometimes ate snakes, worms, spiders, and insects. The seas were much richer than the land, providing many varieties of shellfish, crabs, and fish as well as large marine mammals such as the manatee, or sea cow. The Arawak and Carib also caught many types of waterfowl, and they especially relished the eggs and flesh of the giant green turtle, which can weigh as much as 1,500 pounds. By contrast, freshwater fish were of comparatively less importance. Whether meat or fish, most of what they caught was placed with vegetables such as the sweet yuca into a pepper pot, a bowl left on the fire to simmer continuously.

The Gentle Arawak

The Spanish described the Arawak as peaceful, gentle, hospitable, friendly, and ceremonious. No doubt individual Arawak suffered pain and unhappiness, but the islands of the Greater Antilles and the Bahamas probably did form a kind of tropical paradise. As Carl Sauer has noted, the *conuco* method "would have been a competent agricultural system without yuca. With this great staple it was productive as were few parts of the world."[5]

Because of the climate, there was little need for elaborate housing or artificial heat. With their food needs so easily met, the Arawak had the leisure to design and make pottery (by the coil method), baskets, woven cotton clothing, simple stone tools, and elaborate stone sculptures. Both men and women painted their bodies and ornamented them with jewelry made of gold, stone, bone, and shell. Gold was especially prized. Although the island Arawak did not mine gold, they recognized its natural form and collected usable amounts from riverbeds. These nuggets were pounded into smooth plates and then shaped into ear and nose rings, necklaces, and masks. Gold ornaments later proved their undoing by attracting the attention of the Spanish, who enslaved the Arawak to obtain more of the precious metal.

When they were not hunting or fishing, the Arawak spent much of their leisure time in games. These included a kind of ball game (something like European soccer) that was played on rectangular courts found in almost every village. Informal feasts and dances also were frequent, sometimes in connection with games. And the village chiefs organized more solemn festivals on religious and ceremonial occasions. If anything, dances were even more common among the Carib, who accompanied them by drinking alcoholic beverages made from fermented corn, sweet potatoes, cassava, and pineapple juice. In later years, many Arawak also drank routinely, but some authorities believe that they did not use alcohol before the Spanish conquest. Both peoples also enjoyed tobacco, which they rolled into a kind of primitive cigar and also took as a nasal snuff.

The Arawak had organized systems of religion and government. They believed that good and evil spirits inhabited both human bodies and also many natural objects. They sought to control these spirits through their priests or shamans as well as by capturing them in icons or statues called *zemis,* sometimes made of gold.

To the first Spanish explorers, the Arawak political system seemed very similar to their own. Each island was divided into provinces ruled by paramount chiefs known as *caciques* (five or six in Hispaniola, perhaps as many as 18 in Puerto Rico). The provinces were in turn allocated into districts ruled by sub-chiefs and villages governed by headmen. While the village headmen are said to have exercised despotic powers over their own villagers, the caciques' rule seems to have been looser or even merely ceremonial. In either case, chiefs and headmen owed their authority, at least in part, to their possession of superior *zemis* that contained the most powerful spirits.

Arawak ceremonial ballpark, Puerto Rico. The Arawak played a ball game (something like soccer) on these rectangular courts found in almost every village. This park, which includes paved walks and plazas outlined with colored stones, may also have been used for religious ceremonies.

The Warlike Carib

Government was more decentralized among the Carib, perhaps because they did not possess *zemis*. Each village was independent, and one or more war chiefs were elected for each island. Carib men spent their time hunting, fishing, and practicing their military skills, while women did the other work. Both the Arawak and the Carib divided up tasks among the genders, but the division was far more rigid among the Carib.

In both cases, women maintained the *conucos,* prepared food, wove cloth, and made household baskets and pottery. But Arawak women were relatively equal in many areas, and they were not segregated before marriage. Virginity was not considered desirable; indeed, Arawak men preferred sexually experienced wives. By contrast, Carib men lived together in communal houses and kept their wives in separate huts. They treated their wives as servants, who had to dress and feed their husbands, clean their houses, and carry all burdens in addition to working in the fields.

Carib men were experts in building and managing boats. They also were fearless warriors, who almost always defeated the Arawak and even had some success against Europeans. Although their skills were excellent and they considered war the highest art or game, battles actually took up only a small percentage of their time.

Because the Carib fought attempts to enslave them, the Spanish described them as bloodthirsty savages. Indeed, the English term *cannibal* is derived from their Spanish name (*caribal*). But human meat had no place in their regular diet. Cannibalism was practiced as part of a religious rite in which their captors tortured, killed, and ate the bravest warriors taken in a battle. The Carib's reputation for violence and cruelty almost certainly is exaggerated. When the French and British settled the Lesser Antilles in the 1630s, the Carib initially were friendly and provided food to the starving adventurers. They turned hostile only after they were attacked by the Europeans.

THE CARIBBEAN DISEASE ENVIRONMENT

Millions of tourists come to the Caribbean islands each year to rest and relax from their everyday cares. They are convinced, correctly, that their trip will improve their physical and spiritual health. Until this century, however, most Europeans believed, again correctly, that the islands were one of the least healthy places on Earth, that they were the proverbial "white man's graveyard." For four centuries, the Caribbean's semitropical climate provided an ideal environment for microbes and a deadly environment for humans.

The earth's winds and currents make the Caribbean a natural highway both for persons and for parasites traveling from Europe and Africa to the Americas. The port cities of the islands provided a meeting place for the diseases endemic to three continents. Here Europeans and their African slaves gave each other diseases against which the other race had no immunity. As many as a third of both races died during their first two years on the islands—often of different diseases.

Humans and microbes coexist, and they adapt to one another over time. As a disease becomes broadly endemic within a society, changes or adjustments in the human immune system may result in genetic immunity. Total immunity usually is acquired only through actual contact with a disease. However, when a disease is endemic, a group develops a partial or relative immunity so that the disease affects it in a less virulent form. Most individuals suffer though a mild case in childhood and thus acquire the antibodies needed to protect them from further infection as adults.

Prior to the 15th century, the peoples of Europe and Africa rarely mingled, and the indigenous peoples of the Americas existed in total isolation. A distinctive disease environment developed on each of these continents. The people developed relative immunities to some—but not all—of the diseases endemic among them, which thus became relatively mild or "childhood" illnesses.

Until Europeans and Africans arrived, a host of illnesses—including smallpox, measles, typhus, yellow fever, malaria, tuberculosis, and pus infections—were totally unknown in the Americas. The native peoples were not immune to these diseases. Thus they died in staggering numbers when Europeans and African slaves introduced them. The Spanish enslaved the natives and wanted to use them as laborers. Within a decade, they accidentally exterminated them. When Columbus touched land in 1492, the Caribbean islands were home to at least a quarter-million Arawak and Carib Indians—perhaps as many as 6 million, according to some archaeologists. Within 20 years, almost all were dead.

Europeans and Africans have roughly the same tolerance for diseases endemic on both continents—smallpox, diphtheria, whooping cough, measles, mumps, and influenza. Although these diseases originated in Africa, Africans are more likely than whites to suffer from yaws, leprosy, and intestinal worms. They also are more susceptible than Europeans to bacterial pneumonia, tuberculosis, and tetanus. By contrast, most West Africans are at least partially immune to two diseases—yellow fever and *falciparum* malaria—found only in Africa.

Africans coming to the Caribbean fared better than European colonists. Most islands were decidedly unhealthy for whites, who today form only a small minority—5 percent or less—of their population. Europeans coming to the islands brought their own diseases with them. They also were exposed to yellow fever and *falciparum* malaria, two deadly African fevers to which they did not have natural immunity. Only in this century have physicians begun to understand the complex ways in which these two diseases are transmitted. Until about 1900, the causes of both diseases remained a mystery, thus increasing the fear and horror they incited.

Yellow fever and malaria are among the diseases carried by mosquitoes. Both travel from one victim to another through the insect, and neither passes directly from human to human. The pattern of transmission is from human to mosquito to human—and back to mosquito. However, the mosquitoes carrying malaria and yellow fever belong to separate species with distinct habits. Thus they spread the two diseases in somewhat different ways.

Falciparum malaria was endemic on some islands but not on others. Primarily a rural disease, it quietly winnowed children and immigrants. Over the centuries, it killed as many or more victims than yellow fever, but its ravages often passed unnoticed. Yellow fever, the other great killer, is dramatic in its onset and terrible in its ferocity. Yellow fever was not endemic to the islands, but it sporadically visited all of them with devastating effects. Primarily an urban disease, yellow fever suddenly descended upon a crowded port city or the packed tents of an invading army. Over the course of a few weeks or months, many—half or even more—of the citizens or soldiers died horrible deaths. Then the plague disappeared, sometimes returning in a few years, sometimes not for decades.

Falciparum *Malaria*   One of the oldest and most widespread of diseases, malaria is an infection by one of four species of the *Plasmodium* parasite (protozoa). It is normally transmitted to humans by the bite of the female *Anopheles* mosquito, widespread throughout both Africa and the Americas. As the tiny mosquito feeds on human blood with a lancet smaller than the head of a pin, the malaria parasites rapidly enter the liver and multiply. They then break out into the bloodstream and feed on the victim's red blood cells.

Two types of malaria afflicted the Caribbean islands, making its peoples shake with fever and ache with pain. Europeans brought *Plasmodium vivax*. This milder form rarely is deadly. But it leaves its victims weak and anemic and thus can contribute to death from other causes. *Plasmodium falciparum*, a much more severe form, is a tropical disease endemic in West Africa but not in Europe. African slaves brought it to the islands during the 16th century, and it later reached the American mainland.

Before the 1840s, when quinine became available in a purified form, *falciparum* malaria was a major killer among newly arrived adult Europeans. At least 25 percent—sometimes as many as 75 percent—of whites died following their first encounter with the disease. Malaria also killed Africans, but whites died more rapidly and in greater number. West Africans, who lack certain hemoglobin determinants, are almost totally resistant to *vivax* malaria and they enjoy a relative immunity to *falciparum* malaria. Victims (black or white) surviving *falciparum* malaria acquire partial immunity. But they remain infested with the parasite for life, and they thus pass it on when bitten by an anopheline mosquito.

Anopheline mosquitos breed in profusion in standing water, with some species preferring dank, stagnant swamps. Since mosquitoes cannot survive there, this disease did not exist on the relatively dry islands of Barbados, Saint Kitts, and Anguilla; it was rare in the Bahamas, Antigua, and Saint Vincent. But malaria was endemic in the more humid islands of the Greater Antilles (Cuba, Jamaica, and Hispaniola), as well as on Guadeloupe, Martinique, Dominica, Saint Lucia, Grenada, Trinidad, and Tobago.

Yellow Fever   A mosquito also carries yellow fever from human to human. The *Aëdes aegypti* mosquito (formerly called *Stegomyia fascinata*) has an eccentric lifestyle that makes yellow fever primarily an urban disease. This mosquito is a domestic pest that flourishes in the company of humans. It breeds only in standing water, and it favors water kept in open containers with solid sides and flat bottoms, such as cisterns or water casks. It cannot fly very far, only a few hundred yards at most. *Aëdes aegypti* and the virus need a closely packed population to supply the blood that is their food. Thus those threatened by the disease could escape it both by rigidly quarantining the sick and also by immediately leaving the infected area.

The yellow fever virus affects some victims lightly—especially children—and they may show few visible symptoms. Nonimmune European adults suffer a terrible death, but fortunately one that comes swiftly. After a brief period of remission, the disease reappears and involves the kidneys. Fever increases, causing extreme prostration, frequent vomiting, and jaundice (the yellow skin giving the disease its English name). As the disease progresses, its victims suffer internal hemorrhage and vomit blood (hence the Spanish name *vomito negro,* "black vomit"), delirium, coma, and death. There is no cure for yellow fever. Even with care in a modern hospital, the death rate in severe cases approaches 50 percent. In earlier centuries, 75 percent or more died among those encountering the disease for the first time.

The death rate from yellow fever was much higher among whites than among blacks. Since the disease is endemic in West Africa, many West African peoples have developed a relative immunity. They can become infected with yellow fever, but their power to resist and survive the virus's effects is much greater than that of whites or Indians. In contrast, Europeans almost never acquired immunity to yellow fever before coming to the islands.[6]

Whether the illness is mild or severe, it leaves its victims with total lifelong immunity, and survivors are safe from further symptoms. Indeed, their blood will not support the disease, and they cannot act as carriers. In the Caribbean, once an epidemic finished its course, the virus ran out of nonimmune hosts. It died out—often for many years—until an infected individual reintroduced it into a population.

Yellow fever thus was never endemic to the islands. But it visited and revisited them all with devastating effects. Africans brought both the yellow fever virus and *Aëdes aegypti* to the New World. The mosquito remained, but the virus died and was periodically reintroduced to a nonimmune population. Invariably epidemics were associated with slave ships newly arrived from Africa. Port cities crowded with European sailors, businessmen, and immigrants supplied nonimmune hosts. The packed tents of soldiers provided the mosquitoes and the virus with an ideal environment. Thus invasions during wartime set off several of the worst epidemics.

For more than 300 years—from about 1600 to the end of the 19th century—malaria and yellow fever had a major influence on the life of the islands. Over and over again during these centuries, they struck down thousands of white settlers. On several occasions, these diseases literally determined who would control the region by destroying an invading fleet or army. Indeed, these diseases often were—as the following chapters document—the creole population's best defense against invading armies of nonimmune Europeans.

Because both the malaria parasites and the yellow fever virus require masses of nonimmune hosts, they probably spared the sparsely settled Spanish islands during the 16th century. These fatal microbes were present by 1598, when yellow fever and other diseases killed most of a British army that had taken and planned to occupy San Juan, Puerto Rico. After 1625 they continued to ravage northern Europeans trying to settle the Lesser Antilles and Jamaica. In 1655, the French landed 1,500 men at Saint Lucia. A few months later, only 89 remained alive. During some years after the British captured Jamaica in 1655, the death rate among new settlers was almost as staggering.

At all times the islands were fatal for new arrivals. The creoles, who caught relatively mild cases in childhood, thus acquired immunity to yellow fever and malaria. But the death rate was extraordinary among healthy young Europeans. One-third to one-half of the indentured servants arriving during the 17th century did not live to complete their five- to seven-year term of bondage.

The toll was as great 200 years later. From 1817 through 1836, 12 percent of white troops in Jamaica died of disease each year on average, compared to a death rate of only 3 percent among black troops. The entire regiment had to be replaced every eight years. If individuals quickly succumbed, the death rate was even higher among the compact ranks of troops fresh from Europe. During their invasion of Saint-Domingue (1793–1797), the British sent some 20,500 soldiers to occupy that island. About 12,500 died, mostly of malaria and yellow fever.

Perhaps because there often is a significant interval between the mosquito bite and the onset of illness, physicians were extraordinarily slow to identify the causes of malaria and yellow fever. Carol Finlay of Havana correctly identified *Aëdes aegypti* as the species carrying yellow fever in 1881, and Ronald Ross described the complex life cycle of the *Plasmodium* parasite in 1898. During the early 1900s, public health authorities accepted their findings. Killing the mosquitoes stopped the spread of the two diseases, which became rare by World War I.

Aëdes aegypti was easily exterminated because it needs to live close to humans. The American army occupying Havana eradicated the pest in 1901 by treating standing water with oil and requiring that all home supplies be kept in mosquito-proof containers. Within a year yellow fever no longer originated in that city. Other Caribbean countries also adopted anti-mosquito measures with marked success, and the last case of yellow fever among European troops at Port Royal, Jamaica, occurred in 1904.

Humans could not as easily get rid of the indigenous *Anopheles* mosquito. But malaria killed fewer victims from the 1840s, when a purified form of quinine became widely available both as a prophylactic and as a treatment. Improved sanitation and public health measures also indirectly reduced the urban mosquito population. Public authorities provided Kingston, Jamaica, with water flowing through filtered pipes in 1871, and they built a street sewage system by 1895.

Improved shipping also helped to eradicate malaria and yellow fever. Wooden ships take in water from leaks on the keel, providing many damp refuges for insects. Pests are less likely to infest steel ships, which are comparatively water-tight. And water condensed from steam replaced stagnant casks. By the 1890s the governors of Jamaica and several other islands began to tout their healthy climate, although tourism did not develop as a major industry until the 1920s.

CHAPTER 2

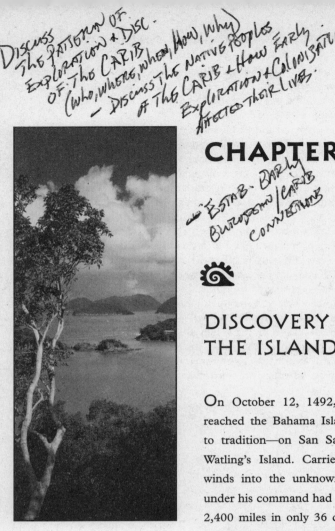

DISCOVERY OF THE ISLANDS

On October 12, 1492, Christopher Columbus reached the Bahama Islands, landing—according to tradition—on San Salvador, today known as Watling's Island. Carried by the easterly trade winds into the unknown, the three small ships under his command had made a smooth voyage of 2,400 miles in only 36 days. Believing that some 2,500 miles (rather than 7,500) of ocean separated China and Japan from Europe, Columbus thus sought to sail to the Indies by a westward passage. When he reached the Bahamas, he was convinced that he had achieved his goal, and he continued to claim the islands as part of Asia until his death in 1506.

The history of the Caribbean islands is strongly affected by their geographical situation and by the environmental qualities discussed in Chapter 1. And until recently their history also has been closely tied to events in Europe. Columbus is said to have "discovered" America, and that statement is largely accurate. Columbus was not the first person to cross from the Old World to the New. But, by returning to Spain, he became the first to make the Americas widely known to Europeans, who now entered the region in force.

THE ISLANDS UNDER THE RULE OF CHRISTIAN MONARCHS

The Caribbean was the first part of the New World to be reached by Columbus. Moreover, Europeans ruled the islands longer than most other parts of the Americas. Until the 1960s, many islands were directly attached to European states as political and economic dependencies. And their peoples, or at least the ruling groups, often considered themselves to be Europeans even though they had been born in the islands.

When Columbus discovered the Americas, Europe was only beginning to emerge from its medieval past. During the next few centuries, both technology and the ways in which Europeans viewed the world changed dramatically. Thus the history of the islands largely is the story of adaptation to developments in Europe or, in later centuries, in the United States. Europeans—to take one example—imposed slavery on the islands. Later, when European governments turned against slavery, they forced island planters to free their bondservants.

🌞 DID COLUMBUS DISCOVER THE AMERICAS?

For almost five centuries, there was agreement that Christopher Columbus discovered the Americas. More recently, there have been some who quibble with the traditional view. Human beings, it is said, already lived on the Caribbean islands when Columbus arrived, their ancestors having emigrated from Siberia thousands of years before.

For those that would deny the title to Columbus, a *discoverer* is simply the first person to see or to find out about something—whether a place, an event, or a natural phenomenon. However, if the word has only this very limited meaning, then no one ever has discovered any place. It cannot be proved that a particular person was the first to arrive; it always is possible that someone else may have been there first. The best that can be said is that every place was discovered by an unknown man or woman back in the dim recesses of time.

However, as historical dictionaries document, the verb *discover* long has had a more precise meaning. The word signifies not only finding something but also revealing, disclosing, and exposing to others whatever has been discovered. In this sense, Columbus did indeed discover the Caribbean islands and the Americas. Columbus was clearly not the first to go to the Americas. He probably was not even the first European to pay a visit. But he was the first to go there and make his findings widely known.

The discovery of the Americas by Christopher Columbus is one of the germinal moments in human history. For thousands of years, Europeans, American Indians, and Africans had been going their separate ways. Suddenly, they were linked together in intimate contact, with enormous consequences. Because Columbus found the Caribbean islands and then made his discovery widely known, the Arawak peoples died out through exposure to diseases against which they had no natural defenses. For Africans, the result was equally momentous, as more than 9 million were transferred as slaves to the Caribbean as well as North and South America during the next three centuries.

At just about the same time that Columbus discovered America, Portuguese explorers passed around the Cape of Good Hope into the Indian Ocean. In dedicating the *General History of the Indies* to Emperor Charles V in 1552, Francisco López de Gómara described the Iberian seafarers' discovery of the ocean routes to the West and East Indies as "the greatest event since the creation of the world, apart from the incarnation and death of Him who created it." Just over two centuries later, Adam Smith, the pioneering political economist, stated virtually the same thing when he wrote: "The discovery of America and that of a passage to the East Indies by the Cape of Good Hope are the two greatest and most important events recorded in the history of mankind."

Even in this age of space travel, many may believe that López de Gómara and Adam Smith were far from wrong. Prior to the Spanish and Portugese voyages of discovery, the various branches of mankind were dispersed and isolated. Europeans knew nothing about the human societies that waxed and waned in the whole of the Americas as well as in the greater part of Africa and the Pacific. Africans and Asians were equally ignorant about Europe. For their part, Americans had no knowledge of Europe, Africa, and Asia. It was Columbus and the Portugese pioneers in the Indian Ocean who linked up, for better and for worse, the widely separated branches of the human family.

Before leaving on his first voyage, Columbus negotiated with Queen Isabella of Castile the terms of a contract in the form of a royal grant (*capitulación*). In the event that he succeeded, the Crown would grant Columbus hereditary nobility and the title of admiral, make him viceroy of the mainlands and islands he reached, and give him one-tenth of the profits taken from them. The privileges granted to Columbus were unusually generous. But the *capitulación* itself was a traditional device through which the Crown delegated specific royal powers to the leader (*adelantado*) of an expedition. Most of the conquistadores who followed Columbus into the Americas solicited and operated under these contracts. Normally, the expedition's leader combined most of the administrative authority of a governor with the powers of a military captain-general.

Queen Isabella believed that she could delegate such great powers to her captains because the lands of pagan peoples were hers by right of conquest. A legitimate monarch did not invade the territory of another Christian ruler without just cause. But monarchs were obligated to bring under their rule territories occupied by pagans (or Christian heretics). By right of conquest, the ruler owned everything in these territories. And he or she could in turn distribute this conquered property to various sub-

"An Indian Cacique of the Island of Cuba, addressing Columbus concerning a future state."
Columbus reached Cuba on his first voyage in December 1492.

jects in whatever ways seemed most likely to facilitate settlement by Christians or the conversion of the present inhabitants.

In theory, a Christian monarch was not a tyrant, because she or he exercised control in accordance with the law and followed legal procedures. The monarch was above all others, but could not act capriciously. The monarch's actions were limited by the laws and customs of the realm, by divine and natural law, and by the obligation to take counsel with experts (secular and religious) and with those affected by her or his decisions.

In actual practice, royal powers were also limited by financial resources and by the small number of officials available to carry out decrees. Particularly in the case of Spanish America, royal authority was restricted by the technology of the day. Local officials had a great deal of latitude in applying royal decrees simply because it literally took months and even years for such orders to reach the Americas from Madrid.

Columbus Rules the Caribbean

Guided by the Lucayo Indians, Columbus sailed south from the Bahamas to Cuba, and spent six weeks exploring its northern coast. By December 6, 1492, he reached the northeastern tip of a second large island, which he named Isla Española (Anglicized as *Hispaniola*). On Christmas Day, his flagship, the *Santa Maria*, was grounded on a sandbank and destroyed. Leaving behind 39 men at the first European settlement of Navidad, Columbus sailed back to Spain. To impress the queen, his two remaining ships carried some gold nuggets and six Lucayo. His return elicited popular excitement as well the applause of his monarch, who granted him the rewards promised in his contract.

Judging by its small size, the queen and her counsellors had viewed Columbus's first voyage as a kind of tentative exploration that might open up trade with the East. They rapidly prepared a second and much larger expedition to establish a permanent foothold on the islands he had reached. In September 1493, Columbus—now an admiral of Spain—again sailed, this time in command of 17 ships. In addition to perhaps 1,500 men, 1,200 of them armed soldiers, his fleet carried horses, sheep, cattle, and hogs, as well as European plants such as wheat, barley, grapes, and sugarcane.

On this second voyage, the admiral steered further south and made landfall on Dominica. Turning west, he passed through and named the entire chain of the Lesser Antilles—Santa Maria de Guadalupe, Santa Maria de Montserrate, Santa Maria la Antigua, Santa Maria la Redonda, Santa Cruz, San Juan Bautista (Puerto Rico)—before arriving in Hispaniola in November 1494. Here he remained for almost 17 months until March 1496.

Columbus again sought to stake out Spanish claims against those of Portugal or other nations. This time he also intended to establish permanent settlements under his control. Above all, he wanted gold. In these latter aims, he was largely unsuccessful. Finding Navidad deserted and its men killed, he founded the city of Isabella in an unhealthy and poorly located site on the northwest coast and put it under the command of his brother Bartholomé. He then sailed away for six months, discovering Jamaica and exploring along the southern coast of Cuba.

Neither Christopher nor Bartholomé Columbus could rule the new colony. Both alienated the Spanish by demanding that they work. And Columbus also disrupted the production of food on the native *conucos* by forcing each Indian to dig up a set amount of gold. Many Indians died, and those that rebelled were harshly punished. When Columbus sailed for home in March 1496, Hispaniola was in poor condition. Food was in short supply and the natives were much diminished in numbers. Many settlers had returned to Spain with complaints about his rule.

The Encomienda: Indian Slavery

The admiral remained in Spain until May 1498, while the Crown sought to regulate the sorry affairs of the colonies and to encourage their development. Up to this point, the settlers theoretically were Columbus's salaried employees, although seldom paid. One royal decree authorized the distribution (*repartimiento*) of land, all legally owned by the Crown. Individual settlers were expected to work the land, build dwellings, and remain on it for four years. In return they received the use of their property in perpetuity and could sell it, give it away, or will it to their family. This decree was repeated by Emperor Charles V in 1513, and it later became one basis of land ownership in the Greater Antilles. However, when Columbus returned on a third voyage to the islands in 1498, it was distorted to justify the virtual enslavement of the Indians.

During his absence, Columbus again left his brother Bartholomé in charge as *adelantado*. In August 1496, Bartholomé transferred the capital from Isabella to the new city of Santo Domingo, located on the southeast coast in a productive region with a good harbor. The administrative capital of the Spanish Empire until 1526, Santo Domingo was a natural destination for ships following the easterly trades from Europe and the Lesser Antilles. Thus it proved an excellent base from which to explore South America during the next 50 years, and it remained economically important until the 1560s, when a change in sailing routes made Havana the preferred port.

Bartholomé's efforts to rule the settlers were even less successful than those of his brother. Perhaps half of those remaining in Hispaniola joined a revolt led by Francisco Roldan, who set up an independent administration in the southwest. Instead of working, the Spanish squatted on the Indian communities and lived off their labor. In May 1498, Columbus returned on his third voyage with a modest fleet of six ships. Sailing through the passage between Trinidad and Venezuela, he landed in Santo Domingo in August to face Roldan's revolt. To placate the rebels, he distributed to them not land but Indian communities. Individual settlers could legally force "their" Indians to work without wages in a kind of semi-slavery or serfdom, known in Spanish both as *repartimiento* and as *encomienda*.

The institution of Indian *encomienda* dominated Spanish America for centuries. Strictly speaking, it was illegal. Moreover, it tended to create a dangerous group of overpowerful subjects, independent of the Crown. Despite its reservations, the royal government believed it had to allow the Indian *encomienda* to make the colonies profitable. The initial groups of settlers did not go to the Americas to work, and the economy could not survive without Indian labor. Thus Queen Isabella confirmed the practice in 1502–3 with certain limits, and Charles V again regulated it by the laws of Burgos in 1512.

The Formation of Royal Government for the Indies

While Christopher Columbus was a superb navigator, his direct rule of the Indies did not prove successful. Beginning in 1499, Queen Isabella acted in three ways to take back the powers she had delegated to the admiral. She appointed Francisco de Bobadilla as "royal governor and judge of all the islands and mainland of the Indies." At the same time, the Crown began to license other expeditions under new leaders. Finally, the queen created the Casa de Contratación (Board of Trade), the first of two councils in Spain charged with commissioning and overseeing both these royal officials and adventurers in the Indies.

In approving Columbus's second voyage to the Indies in 1493, the queen assigned Juan Rodriguez de Fonseca (1451–1524), her chaplain and archdeacon of the Cathedral of Seville, to coordinate preparations. From then until his death in 1524, Fonseca effectively was in charge of government in the Indies, making or approving appointments and royal orders to the colonies. Seeking to increase overseas revenues, Fonseca set up a disciplined organization at Seville, which was formalized in 1503 as the Casa de Contratación. For more than two centuries, this powerful bureaucracy regulated emigration and trade, collected revenues due to the Crown, and supervised all expenditures authorized by the Crown or the Council of the Indies.

The Settlement of Hispaniola

For the first royal governors of the Indies, the queen chose two experienced administrators. Both were also officers in hybrid military/monastic orders that had developed to reconquer Spain from the Moors and that now managed large properties. When Francisco de Bobadilla (d. 1502), commander of the Order of Calatrava, arrived in Hispaniola in August 1500, he found a full-scale civil war in progress. Carrying out the queen's orders, he immediately arrested the Columbus brothers, sending them back to Spain in chains. During the next two years, Bobadilla restored order to the island and substantially increased the production of gold by offering incentives to individual entrepreneurs. All minerals were held to be royal property, and each mine was worked under royal license. Bobadilla initially may have set the Crown's share at 50 percent of output, but he apparently forgave payment of some of the first royalties.

Under this system of monopoly licenses, which became the standard in Spanish America, gold soon was produced in some quantity, perhaps as much as 600 pounds in 1501 alone. Only estimates are possible because a hurricane sank most of the fleet leaving for Spain in July 1502, taking with it Bobadilla, his records, and all of the gold he had collected. Hispaniola was now a going proposition, and his successor laid out the new city of Santo Domingo on a grander scale on the west bank of the river.

It was Brother Nicholas de Ovando, commander of the military order of Alcantara, who finally established royal control over Hispaniola. Arriving in April 1502 with a fleet of 30 ships and 2,500 settlers (including the first women and children), Ovando ruled the island until 1509. He imposed strict discipline upon the settlers and treated the natives with great harshness. Spanish troops now conquered the rest of the island, treacherously murdering the chiefs (*caciques*) of the western regions at a banquet. Their communities were broken up, and the Arawak became serfs. Most were assigned to individual settlers as workers in the fields or gold mines. But the *encomienda* grants were made at Ovando's pleasure, and he reserved the right to transfer Indians to those settlers who got the most work out of them.

Under Ovando's severe rule, Spanish Hispaniola enjoyed a brief era of prosperity. The number of residents soared from perhaps 300 in 1502 to as many as 8,000 to 10,000 in 1509. To bring these settlers under his jurisdiction, Ovando founded 15 towns. Food production rose, with the number of cattle increasing rapidly. And, by reducing the Crown's share from 50 to 20 percent, Ovando encouraged entrepreneurs to increase gold production, which reached its peak in 1509.

By that year, however, the very harshness of Ovando's regime had helped to kill off the native peoples, on whose labor Hispaniola's prosperity was based. An official Spanish census in 1509 counted only 60,000 adult Indians, and another in 1518 found as few as 11,000. With the approval of the royal government, the settlers raided the Bahamas and even the Lesser Antilles, bringing their inhabitants back to Hispaniola as slaves. And they also began to import black slaves, at first from Spain or from the Canary Islands and then from West Africa. Neither effort provided enough labor to maintain gold and food production. Moreover, the mines on Hispaniola now began to fail. Very little gold was produced after 1515, and all mining virtually ceased by 1519.

In 1509 Ovando retired, and King Ferdinand restored the governorship of the islands to Diego Colón, Christopher Columbus's only legitimate son. To control Colón, the Crown also sent Miguel de Passamonte as royal treasurer reporting directly to Juan de Fonseca in Seville. Disputes soon arose over Colón's authority to distribute Indians to the settlers in *encomienda,* to approve town councils, and to appoint the governor of Puerto Rico. To resolve these, the king sent three judges, who arrived in 1512, to form an *audiencia,* or royal appellate court, the symbol of royal justice since the Middle Ages.

The Conquest of Cuba, Jamaica, and Puerto Rico

By the end of Ovando's reign, the settlers were ready to undertake new conquests. Ruthless adventurers with money made in gold mining staked their new fortunes by outfitting expeditions. They found ample recruits among their less prosperous neighbors, who were eager to try their luck again in a new colony. The Crown also sought gold, and its agents licensed each expedition against a share of the spoils.

Overall, the occupation of other islands followed the pattern set in Hispaniola. The expeditionary forces marched quickly through the island, terrorizing the natives and crushing any rebels. A brief gold rush drew in thousands of Spaniards, who divided up the natives in *encomienda.* After only a few years, with the natives dead and the mines exhausted, the colonists moved on, leaving behind their cattle and pigs to take over an empty landscape.

In July 1508, Governor Ovando authorized Juan Ponce de León to lead an expedition to Puerto Rico. Ponce founded towns near the richest pockets of gold at Camparia (now San Juan) and at San Germán, whose *vecinos* (male citizens) divided up the Indians. Some historians believe that Ponce treated the natives less harshly than most other Spanish conquistadores. Nevertheless, early in 1511, the Arawak rebelled with the help of more warlike Caribs, who had entered the island from Saint Croix. Ponce and his troops brutally crushed the rebellion. But the gold was quickly exhausted, and the Carib continued to raid the coasts. By 1518, most of the colonists drifted back to Hispaniola or moved on to Cuba or Panama. Replaced as governor by a protégé of Diego Colón at the end of 1511, Ponce moved on to discover Florida (Paschua Florida) on Easter Sunday, 1513.

Because of his dispute with the Crown, Diego Colón rushed to appoint Juan de Esquivel as governor of Jamaica, with Pánfilo de Narváez second in command. Earlier, both had played a leading part in brutally putting down Indian rebellions in Hispaniola. Their occupation of Jamaica began in 1509 near St Ann's Bay, where they founded Sevilla Nueva. Since they did not find gold, they gave out the Indians to settlers who intended to sell their crops to expeditions exploring the mainland. Horses, cattle, pigs, and goats were brought in and soon increased prodigiously in the absence of natural predators. Within 10 years, nearly all the natives were dead. In 1519, most of the remaining colonists followed the royal governor, Francisco de Garay, on an expedition to Mexico. A few remained to raise and hunt cattle for sale to passing ships.

The Spanish Crown largely abandoned Puerto Rico and Jamaica. After Hispaniola, the most important settlement was Cuba, which was first colonized in 1511. In that year, the king approved a contract between Diego Colón and Diego Velázquez de Cuéllar, one of the two captains in charge of Ovando's treacherous 1504 massacre of native chiefs. Velázquez landed in the northeast to capture a party of Arawak under the cacique Hatuey, who had earlier fled Hispaniola. (Hatuey has since become an adopted national hero in modern Cuba.) Western Cuba was conquered by Pánfilo de Narváez and other Spaniards from Jamaica, whose march through the island was marked by unprovoked massacres of Indians. Within a year the entire island was under Spanish control. Events in Cuba followed the same course as in Hispaniola and Puerto Rico. In 1512, significant amounts of gold were found in the central mountains. Settlers rushed in from Hispaniola and the mainland, and Velázquez founded seven towns, disbursing the entire native population in *encomienda*. Once again, most Indians died within a decade, although small groups did survive in the Sierra Maestre and on some of the offshore islands. As in Jamaica, the native population was supplanted by cattle and especially pigs, whose numbers increased at an extraordinary rate.

By 1519, the Cuban gold placers were exhausted and most of the towns deserted. Ignoring the superior harbor at Havana, Velázquez maintained the capital at Santiago on the southeast coast. Western Cuba was largely abandoned by the restless, gold-seeking Spanish. Its population dropped precipitously in November 1519, when Hernán Cortés—after quarreling with Governor Velázquez—sailed for Mexico, taking with him 600 men, 16 horses, and many of the Cuban hogs to supply meat and breeding stock. Those settlers that stayed lived by herding semi-wild cattle and horses on open-range ranches.

The Spanish in Panama and the Lesser Antilles

Between 1502 and 1512, invasions from Hispaniola subdued Puerto Rico, Jamaica, and Cuba. Beginning in 1499, what today is known as Panama and the northern coast of Venezuela were visited by several expeditions that combined exploration, trade, looting, and slave hunting. Most were tentative until 1509 when the Crown authorized Alonso de Ojeda to take the northern coast of Colombia and gave Central America to Diego de Nicuesa. Both expeditions were routed by the Indians, but a few survivors grouped themselves at Darien, where Vasco Nuñez de Balboa seized power.

A comparatively humane leader, Balboa was the first to cross the Isthmus of Panama to the Pacific Ocean in 1513. He lost power in the same year, when the Crown sent out Pedro Arias de Ávila (called Pedrarias) as royal governor. Under Pedrarias, who beheaded Balboa in 1519, the Spanish ferociously ransacked the peninsula for gold, killing virtually all the native population in the process. When Pedrarias stepped down as governor in 1529, the few settlers left in the city of Panama (founded in 1519) had to import Indian slaves from other regions.

Several of the excursions to the mainland apparently touched on various of the Lesser Antilles. An expedition under Alonso de Ojeda is known to have discovered Bonaire, Curaçao, and possibly Aruba in 1499. Columbus himself landed on Martinique during his fourth and last voyage in 1502. But the Spanish did not attempt to settle these islands.

King Ferdinand and leaders such as Cortés and Pedrarias were interested only in gold. Hispaniola, Puerto Rico, and Cuba all saw perhaps 10 years of furious activity and were abandoned when their gold was exhausted. Since the Lesser Antilles had no gold at all, they were ignored. In the words of Diego Colón, these were "useless islands" (*islas inutiles*). Their population was seen only as a source of slaves to replace the Indians who had died out on Hispaniola.

In 1511, King Ferdinand authorized slaving expeditions to the Lesser Antilles and the Curaçao group. Enslavement of the Carib was justified, the king said, because they were cannibals who refused to obey the Spanish. By 1520, the northern or Leeward Islands from the Virgins to Barbuda were depopulated except for Saint Kitts and Nevis. To the south, the Spanish also removed to Hispaniola the inhabitants of the Curaçao group, Barbados, Saint Lucia, and Tobago. On the remaining islands, the Carib retreated to the mountainous interiors, where they resisted with some skill.

By the 1570s, the Spanish had virtually forgotten about the Lesser Antilles. Between 1525 and 1540, a few hundred Indians were transferred back to Curaçao to work on the land. Then the Curaçao group also was abandoned until the 1620s, except for occasional visitors from Venezuela. As Carl Sauer suggests, "The political geography of the West Indies is starkly simple: the French, English, and Dutch colonies of the seventeenth century occupied islands that had been emptied of their natives early in the sixteenth century in order to keep Española going. To a great extent the North European successors were able to live off the Spanish livestock that had replaced the Indians."[1]

The Extermination of the Arawak

The Spanish Crown abolished Indian slavery in 1542, and it outlawed the *encomienda* system of semi-slavery in 1550. In South America, where substantial numbers of Indians had survived, Spanish settlers resisted these laws and continued to demand forced labor for centuries. In the Greater Antilles, the royal decrees had almost no significance simply because most of the Arawak had died out decades earlier. The few survivors on each island grouped themselves into one or two villages. Here they often intermarried with runaway slaves and gradually lost their ethnic and cultural identity.

There can be no question that the Spanish occupation totally destroyed Arawak society and led to the extinction of the Arawak race. Although the subject has been studied in depth for more than 80 years, what is less certain is how many Indians were killed or why they died. After analyzing all the competing theories, Lynn McAlister concluded that "No one knows how many Indians inhabited the Western Hemisphere in 1492 and, indeed, the problem has generated one of the liveliest controversies in American ethnohistoriography."[2]

The problem of an accurate count began with the first settlers. Almost as soon as the islands were taken, some Spanish observers harshly criticized the way in which their contemporaries were treating the Indians. Among the most consistently outspoken of these critics were members of the Dominican religious order. As early as 1511, for example, Antonio de Montesinos, a Dominican preaching before the governor, officials, and citizens of Santo Domingo, told his distinguished congregation that they would burn in hell because of their mortal sins against the Indians.

☀ THE ARAWAK AND CARIB

The Arawak have disappeared from the face of the earth, leaving behind only a few words and possibly some culinary customs. Slave raids during the early 1500s destroyed the Indian population of the Bahamas. On Hispaniola, a group owned by Diego Colón rebelled in 1522 under the leadership of the cacique Enrique. After a struggle of 15 years, this group was allowed to establish an independent village at Boya, where some individuals of mixed blood may have lived as late as 1798. In Puerto Rico and Jamaica, a few Indians still survived in 1600, but none are mentioned a century later. Several Indian villages maintained themselves in isolated parts of Cuba as late as 1900. Perhaps 200 Indians still lived in the Trinidadian village of Arima before World War II. Although referred to as Carib, most probably were of Arawak origin.

In the lesser Antilles, the Carib resisted the Spaniards, who avoided their islands. But they too welcomed and merged with runaway slaves, forming the maroon communities known as Black Carib. Those on the island of Saint Vincent surrendered to British troops in 1796 (see page 170) and were transported to Rattan Island, off the coast of Honduras. More than 40,000 of their descendants—still ethnically and culturally distinct from their neighbors—now live in Honduras, Belize, and Guatemala. In the Caribbean itself, Carib villages survive only on the island of Dominica.

The Dominicans found their greatest spokesman in Bartholomé de Las Casas, the famous "Apostle to the Indies," who joined their religious order in 1522. Las Casas had arrived in Santo Domingo in 1502 with Governor Ovando. He participated in the conquest of Cuba in 1511 and acquired a large *encomienda* of Indian serfs, which he gave up in 1515. For the next 50 years he dedicated his life to the defense of the Indians, preaching, writing tracts, and lobbying the royal government.

He was a firsthand observer almost from the beginning. The unanswerable question is whether he exaggerated his charges. While other early Spanish observers reported that about 1 million Indians lived on Hispaniola, Las Casas wrote that between 3 and 4 million were present in 1492. Early anthropologists thought his estimates were incredible; more recent scholars tend to accept them. Since it was the most heavily populated island, most studies assume that the total Indian population was roughly twice that of Hispaniola. Assessments of the number of Indians throughout the Caribbean thus range from a low of 225,000 to as high as 6 million. All are simply educated guesses based on conflicting assumptions about how many people the Indian system of *conuco* agriculture could support.

How and why the Arawak died is even less certain than their original numbers. Traditionally, the "Black Legend" of Spanish settlement (especially favored by Protestants) asserted that the colonists wantonly tortured the Indians and literally worked them to death. Las Casas and other contemporary critics, who stress the brutality of individual masters, provide evidence that can be used to support the Black Legend. Taken as a group, however, the Spanish did not want to kill off the Indians. They wanted to make them work. But even relatively benign masters may inadvertently have hastened their death by herding the Indians together, especially at gold mines in the center of the islands. Here the Arawak were both exposed to new diseases and also cut off from the sea, which supplied their main source of protein.

It is said that the Europeans and especially their animals destroyed the native *conucos*. This was not generally true, since there is no evidence that cassava was ever in short supply. But cassava and yams supply only starch and sugar. They do not provide protein, animal fat, and salt—all of which are absolutely necessary to sustain life. Thus, even though they were well fed, the captive Arawak were malnourished and susceptible to sickness.

Isolated for thousands of years, the Arawak did not have natural immunity to the diseases carried by Europeans or Africans, including influenza, smallpox, measles, malaria, and the common cold. These diseases, which elsewhere were endemic childhood illnesses, spread rapidly and killed men and women of every age. Since the women of childbearing age died, demographic losses could not be made up by an increased birthrate after the plague was gone.

Another mystery is why the Arawak did not fight against the Spanish, even though they vastly outnumbered their captors. The mountains and dense scrub of the Greater Antilles are a natural environment for guerrilla warfare. And the weapons carried by the Spanish—especially their single-shot, smooth-bore muskets—were clumsy, slow, and inaccurate. During the 18th century, runaway black slaves (known as *maroons*) easily defeated professional solders with far better guns. While isolated rebellions did occur, most of the Arawak apparently let themselves be enslaved without resisting.

Many contemporary observers protested the fate of the Arawak, and the settlers may have doomed the Indians through their ignorance of disease and diet rather than through deliberate sadism. Nevertheless, the extermination of the Arawak was a crime. And, as Brother Antonio de Montesinos told Diego Colón in 1511, it also was a sin. Indeed, according to the teachings of Christianity espoused by the Spanish, their sin was equally damning whether they killed 225,000 or 6 million.

CHAPTER 3

PIRATES FIGHT FOR SPANISH GOLD

From the 1530s, the Caribbean formed only a minor part of a vast Spanish empire, whose heart was in upland Mexico and Peru. On the mainland, Spanish adventurers finally found the untold riches—in gold and especially in silver—that the islands could never provide. Henceforth, the islands were important only because Spanish treasure fleets had to pass by them on their way to Seville. For more than two centuries, the Caribbean played a crucial role in commerce, but solely as the highway that carried treasure from the mainland to Spain.

The rulers of other European states envied the wealth of Spain's monarch and allowed their subjects to plunder it. Piracy became an accepted business in many French and British ports, with the Dutch joining in after 1599. Thousands of pirate ships attacked Spanish shipping and ports in the Caribbean and along the coast of Central America. The greatest booty was taken by Sir Francis Drake, who captured an entire year's yield of Peruvian silver in 1573.

To protect its treasure fleets from pirates, Madrid imposed a system of economic regulation that endured until the 1750s. Spain closed its American empire to outside trade, and it limited trade with Europe to two yearly convoys. Under this restrictive system (the famous Laws of the Indies), Spain paid little attention to its island possessions. It fortified the ports used by the treasure fleets but did little to defend the other cities in the Caribbean.

THE COCKPIT OF EUROPE

For more than two centuries, Spanish rulers claimed that all of the Americas were their property because Columbus had sailed under the authority of Queen Isabella. By virtue of conquest, the Crown was said to possess all political, judicial, and religious authority, own all property, and retain all powers of taxation throughout the Indies. Anyone of any nationality entering the Americas must obey the royal laws. In theory, only Spaniards could move to or trade with the colonies, and all goods had to be brought over from Spain in the annual fleets of licensed Spanish ships.

Rulers of other states soon resented Spain's claim to a monopoly over the Indies. Francis I of France reportedly asked where in Adam's will did the first man leave the Indies exclusively to the Spanish king. But the Dutch, British, and French did not begin to plant colonies in Spain's island world until about 1625. Seizing territory involved expensive problems of governance and defense. Spain's enemies preferred to weaken the Spanish economy and kingdom by licensing (or ignoring) pirates and "privateers" who seized Spanish ships on the high seas. Until the 1620s, piracy was the most common—and probably the most effective—form of warfare in the Americas. Since the Caribbean formed the narrow choke point through which passed all of Spain's trade with the Indies—including the great silver fleets—it inevitably bore the brunt of foreign attacks.

In seeking to maintain a total monopoly over all the Americas, the Spanish government ironically permitted, or even invited, its enemies to invade its American empire. The Spanish Crown focused its attention on Europe, and it depended on the Americas primarily as a source of treasure to support its European wars. The Spanish government showed little interest in Cuba, Jamaica, and Hispaniola after the discovery of gold and silver in Mexico and Peru. The Spanish Crown built great forts to defend the route of its treasure fleets. It left the other settlements to fend for themselves, even to the point of deliberately depopulating them. Spanish settlers on the islands were poor and ill-defended by the cumbersome colonial government—both overcentralized and overcomplicated. They fell easy prey to the buccaneer raids that brought death and devastation for the next two centuries.

The Spaniards Discover a Mountain of Silver

During these centuries, Spanish rulers had a number of goals—not always articulated and sometimes contradictory—for their American kingdoms. Above all else, they wanted to maintain ownership by preventing others either from occupying their overseas territories or from dominating them economically. The Spanish government also wanted and desperately needed revenue for the royal treasury in Spain.

Most of the first settlers had one aim only: to make quick fortunes by finding gold and other precious substances. If gold could not be found, they would attempt to become lords over Indian serfs. Between 1520 and 1550, some Spanish adventurers did achieve these goals. Driven by their dreams of personal glory, great military captains conquered the native empires of the Aztecs and Incas, carving out a great empire for Spain that stretched from Arizona to Argentina.

In the conquest of Central and South America, the Greater Antilles played a major role as a staging area and source of supplies and fresh meat. In 1519, Hernán Cortés sailed from Cuba with an expedition that captured the Aztec capital of Tenochititlán in 1521. From this city, renamed Mexico by its conquerors, his lieutenants quickly took over the remainder of the Aztec Empire. During the same years, Spanish forces operating from a forward base in Panama followed the Pacific coast of South America to Peru. By 1533, the forces led by Francisco Pizarro had occupied Cuzco, the capital of the Inca Empire. Following the Inca road system, Spanish expeditions soon occupied Colombia, Chile, and Upper Peru (now Bolivia).

In Mexico and Peru, Spanish adventurers and their king finally found the wealth they had been seeking, although it largely took the form of silver rather than gold. Given the available technology, Spanish miners could profitably take gold ore only from high grade surface ores. The gold ore available through existing methods usually was fully exploited within 10 to 20 years. Thus the mines in Santo Domingo, Cuba, and Puerto Rico largely were played out by the end of the 1520s. Similarly, the output from mines in Central America dropped off sharply in the 1550s.

But the diminishing gold quickly was replaced by immense amounts of silver from enormously rich veins in Peru and Mexico. In 1545, explorers discovered what was literally a mountain of silver at San Luis de Potosí in Upper Peru. Other major strikes were made in the 1530s in central Mexico (at Taxco) and in the 1540s and 1550s in northern Mexico (at Zacatecas, Guanajuato, and Pachuca). For about a hundred years, from the 1530s to the 1620s, silver production continuously rose. Altogether, the Casa de Contratacióon in Seville registered 16,887 tons of silver and 1,813 tons of gold as legally imported from the Americas between 1501 and 1650. Almost as much may have been smuggled out as illegal contraband.

Given the changes in the purchasing power of money, the value of this immense hoard cannot be precisely stated. However, the king's share—perhaps 40 percent of the total registered amount—became absolutely essential to the Spanish monarchy. American silver provided as much as 20 percent of all royal revenues at the end of Philip II's reign (1556–98). Although royal receipts dropped dramatically after 1620, this reduced amount of treasure still provided Philip IV (1621–65) with perhaps one-tenth of his funds.

Moreover, unlike many other taxes, the American treasure took the form of ready cash on hand. Thus the government of Philip II could pledge the treasure as security in borrowing from German and Genoese bankers. During the last third of the 16th century, these loans allowed the Spanish Crown to assemble the Great Armada that invaded England in 1588, send mercenary soldiers to crush the rebellion in the Netherlands, and subsidize the Catholic forces in France. The government borrowed lavishly against the arrival of the next treasure fleet. Seeing to it that the fleet arrived safely became its overriding concern.

FRENCH AND ENGLISH PIRATES INVADE THE CARIBBEAN

Almost from the beginning, the sailors of other nations began to attack Spain's treasure fleets and American colonies. Operating out of a series of different bases, pirates remained a threat for many generations. At first they sailed from Europe itself, easily following the trade winds to and from the Caribbean. For more than 150 years, until the final collapse of Spanish power in the 1670s and 1680s, Spanish ships and ports provided the main prey in the Caribbean. The Spanish, with the only settlements in the region, remained the traditional victims—although by 1600 their towns had been

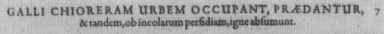

French pirates capture, plunder, and burn Havana in 1555. ("Galli chioreram urbem occupant, praedantur, et tandem, ob incolarum perfidiam, igne absumunt.") *Pirate bands continued to loot Caribbean ports during the next three centuries.*

raided so often, later pirates sometimes found slim pickings.

During the 16th century, pirates sailed almost continuously from ports in western England and northern France, where entire cities became dependent upon their infamous trade. The number of voyages to the West Indies rose and fell. But French and English captains (often with crews from several nations) left virtually every year, during times of truce as well as during hostilities. All sought booty. But many also were strong, even fanatical Protestants (many followers of Jean Calvin, called Huguenots in France), who added hatred of the Catholic Spanish to their greed for loot.

Norman French Corsairs

The French, who were almost continuously at war with Spain until 1559, were the first to attack Spain's Caribbean ports. As early as 1522 and 1523, naval squadrons belonging to Jean d'Ango of Dieppe in Normandy managed to seize four ships carrying back to Spain Montezuma's fabled treasures and other riches seized by Cortés in conquering Mexico. In 1537, another of d'Ango's fleets captured nine ships carrying silver from Peru.

These hauls were taken near the Azores. But their extraordinary richness encouraged French captains to invade the Caribbean itself during the 1530s. By the mid-1550s, as many as 30 French ships raided the Indies each year, virtually controlling the seas and repeatedly pillaging coastal towns on Hispaniola, Puerto Rico, and Cuba. The climax of their campaign came in 1555, when the French corsair Jacques de Sores captured Havana itself and burned it to the ground.

The 1559 peace treaty ending hostilities in Europe brought little respite to the Spanish colonies in the West Indies. As France was torn by religious civil wars during the next half-century, the government was too preoccupied and too weak to make the effort needed to stop pirate ships operating out of Normandy. Individual French ships and small squadrons continued to ply the Caribbean into the 1620s, operating as both privateers and smugglers. Indeed, Norman French pirates may well have outnumbered those from other nations even during the Anglo-Spanish war that broke out in 1585.

The Carrera de las Indias

In response to these pirate attacks, the Spanish government created a system of annual convoys, with warships protecting merchant vessels sailing to and from Seville. In 1503, the Crown had required most ships to use the one port of Seville. From an early stage, many ships sailed in groups as security against increasing pirate attacks, and the convoy system reached its final form in the 1560s. In 1564, the Spanish Crown ordered that all ships must sail in two armed fleets for New Spain (Mexico) and Tierra Firme (mainland Central America). The Mexican fleet (called the *flota*), which included any ships bound for the Greater Antilles, was supposed to leave in April. The Terra Firme fleet (the *galleones*) was to sail in August. Both were assigned a naval escort. Usually two galleons accompanied the *flota*, and eight were assigned to the Terre Firme fleet—the famous *armada de la guardia de la carrera de las Indias*.

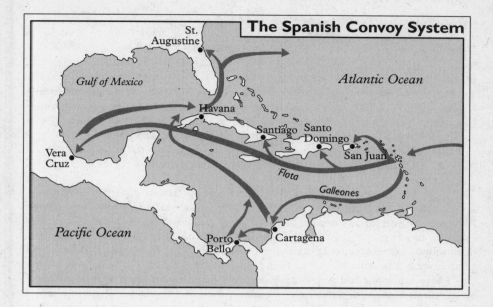

Each year the two fleets left Seville (although rarely on schedule), caught the northeasterly trades just south of Spain near the Azores, and followed them to Dominica or another island in the Lesser Antilles. Here their routes divided. Ships from the Terre Firme fleet proceeded either to Cartagena or to Nombre de Dios or (after 1598) to Porto Bello (Portobelo) in Panama. To the waiting gelleons in these ports, the great treasures from Peru arrived after an overland journey from the Pacific across the narrow neck of Panama.

The other fleet proceeded north to Vera Cruz (Veracruz) or to the nearby port of San Juan de Ulúa to pick up the cargoes brought along the treasure trail leading down from the Mexican highlands. To beat the hurricane season, both fleets reassembled in Havana in the late spring or early summer. In one great convoy, the heavily laden ships made their way through the narrow channel between Florida and the Bahamas until they reached the Carolinas and could catch the westerly trades across the Atlantic back to Seville.

The convoy system succeeded in its main goal, that of protecting the silver fleets. For more than two centuries, when Spain was so frequently at war with the northern maritime powers, the corsairs—both licensed and freelance—sought to capture the source of its power. Year after year, they prowled the broad channel between Cuba and the Yucatan as well as the narrower Florida Strait, ready to seize any unfortunate ship that might be separated from its fellows by a storm or accident. Almost never, however, were their arduous efforts rewarded. Occasionally, a pirate or privateer might cut off one or two merchant ships. But a royal galleon, heavily armed and carefully guarded, was taken on fewer than a dozen occasions. On only three occasions (in 1628, 1656, and 1657) was the entire treasure fleet taken, each time by a large squadron of enemy warships.

THE MILITARY WEAKNESS
OF THE SPANISH CARIBBEAN

While the Spanish government succeeded in protecting its treasure ships, it did little to protect the cities on the islands. And, given the fragmented and ineffective nature of Spanish local government, the islands could do little to defend themselves. Spanish officials did not form a chain of command in the military sense. Because of the juridical and legalistic nature of Spanish government, every group of officials in practice became an independent agent. There was no central command post for the entire Caribbean, and the various local authorities often did not even cooperate with each other.

In response to dozens of French raids, colonial governors began to fortify important ports and to organize militia companies to defend them. But the poor and sparsely inhabited Antilles colonies could afford little, and only Santo Domingo had a reasonably complete set of permanent works by 1560. In the following decades, the Crown gradually began to use taxes from the mainland (called the *situado*) to defend the Caribbean, which was so vital to the entire Americas.

Pedro Menéndez de Avilés deserves credit as the Spanish leader who began the royal fortresses at major Caribbean ports. Menéndez, first appointed captain-general of the *armada de la carrera* in 1554, took out the Indies fleets in 1555, 1560, and 1562, bringing each safely back to Spain. His experience convinced him of the crucial importance of the lands along the Bahama Channel. In 1565, as *adelantado,* he led an expedition to Florida, wiping out a French colony and establishing a Spanish base at Saint Augustine. In the following year, he toured the islands and left soldiers and guns at Santo Domingo, San Juan, and Santiago de Cuba. As governor of Cuba (1568–1572) he ordered new defenses for Havana. However, these were not constructed until the 1580s, after a series of devastating raids by Britain's greatest sea raider.

Sir Francis Drake

While the French alternatively traded with and pillaged isolated towns and merchant vessels, the richest hauls now went to the English. The glory of taking the king's treasure at Panama fell to the famous English captain Sir Francis Drake. During a period of 30 years, Drake and his teacher, John Hawkins, made no fewer than seven voyages to the Spanish Main. Scholars dispute the purpose of Hawkins's voyages in the 1560s. But Drake's goal in the early 1570s was clear: to seize the Peruvian silver, which each year was brought by mule train across the isthmus from Panama to Nombre de Dios.

During his first two voyages in 1570 and 1571, Drake spied out the coast of the Spanish Main and made friends with the *cimarrones,* African slaves who had run away from their Spanish masters. In January 1573, following several failed attempts, Drake finally succeeded in taking the Peruvian silver, after joining forces with the Norman Huguenot Guillaume Le Testu. Le Testu was killed during the struggle, but the Anglo-French pirates captured the mule train just north of Nombre De Dios. Although they had to leave behind 15 tons of silver, the pirates made off with gold worth the enormous sum of 100,000 pesos.

In 1577 Drake led a small fleet through the Straits of Magellan (at the tip of

South America), probably intending to attack Panama from the east. Off the coast near Valparaíso, the British seized the Spanish ship *Cacafuega* carrying another rich treasure. Drake then sailed east around the world, returning to England in 1580. This was his last great haul in the New World. In 1585–86, this time carrying royal orders, Drake returned and ransacked Santo Domingo and Cartagena. But he did not capture any treasure, and the ransom paid by the two cities did not cover his costs. In 1595, a fleet of 27 ships captained by both Hawkins and Drake tried to repeat the earlier successes. This time, Drake's good fortune totally failed him. San Juan was guarded by the new fort of El Moro, both Hawkins and Drake died during the siege, and the fleet returned without booty.

English Piracy Becomes Big Business

Drake's fantastic hauls in 1573 and 1578 aroused feverish enthusiasm in England and are still remembered today. Over the years, however, the economy of the islands suffered greater damage from the dozens of other English privateers who flocked to the Caribbean during the Anglo-Spanish War. Especially during the 1590s, certain ports in the west of England, such as Weymouth and Southampton, gave themselves over to

El Moro Fortress, San Juan, Puerto Rico. To protect its treasure fleets from pirate attacks, Spain built large fortresses guarding the ports of Havana, San Juan, Porto Bello, Cartagena, and Vera Cruz. Begun in the 1580s, this massive fort was completed nearly two centuries later.

the business of fitting out privateer ships and disposing of their cargoes. No less than 100 private warships sailed from these ports each year. Not all went to the Caribbean, but at least 10 to 20 did each year.

No one was able to repeat Drake's seizure of royal treasure. At all times, few pirates actually gained great heaps of gold and jewels. Most seized merchant cargoes. Captured slaves were taken into small ports along the coast of Hispaniola or Cuba. Since the pirates sold these slaves at a price well below the official tariffs, they found eager buyers on the Spanish islands. The pirates then brought back other booty to their base ports in England and France and sold it for cash. Although less fabulous than the treasure of the Andes, their hauls were impressive. By a conservative estimate, the owner of a privateer ship could expect a 60 percent return on the capital invested, even after deducting the shares of the crew and captain.

Although convinced of the need to fortify the major ports, the Spanish Crown did little until 1585, when Drake attacked and easily captured Santo Domingo and Cartagena. Finally, stung to action, Philip II in 1586 sent out the Italian engineer Juan Bautista Antoneli, who devoted the next 20 years of his life to the defenses of the Caribbean. At Havana and San Juan, Antoneli sketched the works for the immense forts—both popularly known as El Moro—that ultimately came to dominate the entrances to the two harbors. Fortifications also were designed for San Juan de Ulúa, Porto Bello, and Cartagena.

Many years and large sums of money were needed to complete these defenses. The great forts at San Juan and Havana, as we see them today, were not completed until the 18th century. Moreover, the Crown sought primarily to protect the ports essential to the defense of the silver fleets. Two galleys unsuccessfully were stationed for a time at Santo Domingo, Cartagena, and Havana. Otherwise, the smaller cities and rural areas in the Caribbean effectively were left to their own, totally inadequate, devices. Constant pirate attacks on shipping and coastal cities increased the poverty of the islands, as the insecurity of life along the coasts forced their inhabitants to move inland to isolated farms.

The First Dutch Attack, 1599–1609

The Dutch were remarkably slow to enter the Caribbean. From 1568 to 1609, the seven northern provinces forming the United Netherlands fought a long and often savage war against the king of Spain, their hereditary overlord. During these years, Dutch corsairs attacked enemy (and neutral) shipping in European waters. But only rarely did a Dutch ship venture to the Spanish Main. The majority of marauders during these years were British and French, and regular Dutch traffic began only in the years 1593–94.

Dutch attacks on the islands suddenly and dramatically increased when the Spanish government in August 1598 imposed a general embargo on Dutch traders in the Iberian Peninsula. Two products in particular drew them to the Caribbean. The first of these was high-grade salt, previously taken from the east coast of Portugal and absolutely necessary to their enormous trade in herring. The second was tobacco, which was beginning to become popular throughout western Europe. A substitute for Portuguese salt was found near the tip of the Araya Peninsula on the coast of Venezuela. About one-third of a mile inland from Araya Bay lies an inexhaustible natural salt pan, four to five miles long and one to two miles wide. From March 1599 to December 1605, a minimum of 768 Dutch vessels sailed to Araya to load up with salt.

While the large salt hulks lay at anchor in Araya Bay, some of their crews ranged throughout the Caribbean in armed pinnaces and sloops brought over on the mother ships. Together with other Dutch pirates and smugglers, they robbed and sank Spanish coastal shipping, sweeping it from the seas by 1606. They also traded widely with the Spanish colonies throughout the area for hides, ginger, tobacco, and sugar. To a lesser extent, French smugglers also used the protection provided by the Dutch salt hulks, and British merchants reentered the West Indian trade in 1602 for the first time in more than 30 years.

In response to this invasion, the Spanish government, which literally was bankrupt, decided it could not afford to send ships to police the Caribbean. Instead it took the drastic measure of destroying the crops the aliens wanted or even depopulating the regions most likely to trade with the enemy. At the end of 1605, a Spanish fleet from Lisbon swept through the region, seizing the salt ships at Araya and other smugglers and killing their crews. Steps were taken to stop the inhabitants of Cuba from trading with the enemy. In Venezuela tobacco growing was prohibited for 10 years. Most drastically, armed force was used to depopulate northwestern Hispaniola. These measures forced the tobacco trade to shift eastward to Trinidad and the Orinoco River, until this trade also was suppressed in 1612.

The Guyana Connection

The years from 1606 to about 1620 saw a brief lull in foreign incursions into the Spanish Caribbean. English privateering became illegal piracy when the Peace of London with Spain was signed in December 1604. Whatever his other faults, King James I was the first English king to shun privateering totally, issuing no commissions of his own and outlawing British captains who took commissions from other princes. Dutch efforts in the region also fell off after a 12-year truce was concluded in 1609, reopening access to Portuguese salt.

A few Dutch smugglers continued to visit the Greater Antilles, as did a small number of English and French pirates. In 1598, the Treaty of Vervins ended 70 years of almost continuous war between France and Spain. However, by a secret restrictive article added to the treaty, the two governments agreed that the peace applied only in Europe and did not extend south of the tropic of Cancer and west of the meridian of the Azores. "Beyond the lines," French and Spanish ships might attack each other and take fair prize as in open war. Despite this clause, French piracy probably did decline after 1605. Most of the cities in Cuba and Santo Domingo or along the Spanish Main had been raided so frequently that they now offered pirates little to plunder.

The Spanish respite in the Caribbean was brief. During the first two decades of the 17th century, several English and Dutch treasure-hunting and tobacco-planting expeditions headed for the Wild Coast, the region stretching south from Trinidad and the Orinoco delta to the Amazon. Spanish colonists believed that a rich Incan kingdom existed inland from the Wild Coast. Its fabled capital was ruled by El Dorado, called the "gilded one" because he covered his body with gold dust before bathing. Several major expeditions attempted to discover this city of gold. Antonio de Berrio established the first Spanish colony in Trinidad in 1592 as a base for his explorations on the mainland. Similarly, Sir Walter Raleigh, the English statesman and adventurer, led expeditions up the Orinoco in 1602 and again in 1616.

Particularly after 1612, when the Spanish banned the Trinidad tobacco trade, other Dutch and English adventurers tried to establish tobacco plantations along the Wild Coast. Because of the harsh environment, most failed within two or three years or were destroyed by Spanish and Portuguese forces. But tobacco prices remained high, and the failure of the Guyana expeditions indirectly contributed to the settlement of the Lesser Antilles by the English, French, and Dutch.

CHAPTER 4

SPAIN'S CARIBBEAN COLONIES

The kings of Spain claimed absolute authority in their American dominions. Here they considered themselves free of any constitutional constraints limiting their power in Europe. Obviously the kings could not rule the Americas in person. (Indeed, they never went there.) Over the years, they thus delegated various of their powers to different officials and administrative bodies. Despite the absolutist claims of the Crown, the great distance between Seville and the Americas ensured that these officials enjoyed a great deal of latitude or even autonomy in interpreting royal laws.

Spain's laws closing its empire to foreign trade hindered economic growth. As Table 2 indicates, the population of the islands stagnated. The Crown virtually abandoned the Antilles, and most Spaniards coming to the Americas preferred the mainland. Havana became a major port for the Spanish fleet. Otherwise the few isolated settlers remaining on the islands had to become self-sufficient cattle ranchers and smugglers.

FORMS OF GOVERNMENT IN THE SPANISH EMPIRE

During the first 25 years of settlement, significant steps were taken to enforce royal powers. The Crown established the Casa de Contratación to supervise and control all movement of persons and goods. It sent out royal governors and treasurers to each of the territories as they were conquered. In 1511, it established in Santo Domingo an appellate court—the *audiencia*—to resolve conflicts between local officials. Between 1520 and about 1560, these institutions were modified to handle the vast new territories conquered in Mexico and Peru. The laws and institutions thus established remained in effect for more than two centuries, until reforms were introduced by the Bourbon kings in the 1760s. Under the protection of these laws, a system of society and ways of life developed in Spanish America that differed significantly from those of the British or French colonies.

The Spanish concept of governance was juridical rather than political. Spanish officials primarily thought of government as a system of laws. In this view, the king's duty was to embody in regulations appropriate to a specific province the ideal and universal laws of God and of nature. For this reason, the government of the Spanish colonies differed from current practices in major ways. Councils or groups of officials made important decisions, and there was no "separation of pow-

Table 2. **POPULATION ESTIMATES FOR THE SPANISH ISLANDS, 1570–1673**

	Total	Whites	Slaves	Free Non-Whites
Cuba				
1570*	17,550	1,200	—	15,000**
1610	20,000	—	—	—
1662*	30,000	—	—	—
Hispaniola				
1570*	35,500	5,000	30,000	—
Puerto Rico				
1530*	3,039	368	1,523	—
1570*	11,300	1,000		10,000**
1673	1,523	820	667	304
Jamaica				
1570*	1,300	300	1,000	—

*The estimated "Total" includes Native Americans for the years indicated: Cuba—1570 (1,350) and 1662 (3,500); Hispaniola—1570 (500); Puerto Rico—1530 (1,148) and 1570 (300). (In 1570, Spanish sources mention a small but unspecified population of Native Americans on Jamaica.) For 1673, the data for Puerto Rico include the township of San Juan only.

**Figure includes both slaves and non-whites.

SOURCES: Salvador Brau, *Historia de Puerto Rico* (San Juan: Editorial Coqui, 1966), 70–71 (1530); Lyle McAlister, *Spain & Portugal in the New World*, 131 (1570); Angel Rosenblat, *La población indigena y el mestizaje en América*, 2 volumes (Buenos Aires: Editorial Nova, 1954), I:218–19 (1610, 1662, 1673).

ers." These bodies made regulations, administered them, and acted as a court to consider disputes about their application. Every colonial council had a delegated rather than an independent authority. Thus it always was possible to appeal from its decisions to the Crown. Moreover, there was no real distinction between local and central government. Every town council—like every governor—acted under powers delegated by the king.

The Council of the Indies and the Casa de Contratación

Under the Crown, the chief body for ruling the colonies was the Royal and Supreme Council of the Indies, set aside as a permanent committee of the Council of Castile in 1511 and transformed into a sovereign court in 1524. Until it was abolished in 1834, the council theoretically enjoyed absolute authority, and every aspect of colonial life fell within its jurisdiction. It appointed the highest judicial, military, and administrative officials (including bishops), prepared most of the laws governing the Americas, saw to it that officials enforced these laws, and sat as a supreme court to judge appeals from the highest courts in the colonies.

Although the Casa de Contratación, created in 1502, legally was subordinate to the Council of the Indies, it was largely autonomous in economic matters. For more than two centuries, the Casa controlled all trade with Spanish America. This immensely powerful bureaucracy registered, licensed, and supervised all immigration to the Indies as well as all ships and merchandise to and from the New World. It suggested and supervised the laws relative to navigation and commerce, served as a court for all cases involving trade with the Americas, and collected duties on exports and imports. In return for a monopoly granted in 1543, the merchant's guild (*consulado*) of Seville worked closely with the Casa in organizing and unloading the fleets. Henceforth, virtually all trade with the colonies had to be funneled through the congested and inadequate port facilities at Seville. In many matters, a local governor was responsible first to the Casa and then to the Council of the Indies.

The *Audiencia* of Santo Domingo

In the American colonies, the Casa de Contratación and the Council of the Indies primarily dealt with governors, the highest courts (*audiencias*), and town councils. Colonial government was complicated because the Crown kept adding new levels of officials. Originally each island or region was ruled by a royal governor, with the first governor being the leader (*adelantado*) of the expedition that conquered the territory. Over the centuries, the Crown tended to limit the autonomy of local governors. In 1511, the king thus created the *audiencia* of Santo Domingo (which became permanent in 1524).

An *audiencia* was a kind of permanent committee. The governor—in Santo Domingo given the title and powers of a military captain-general—presided over its meetings. He was joined by a varying number of judges (*oidores*), three in the case of Santo Domingo. Under the Council of the Indies, an *audiencia* exercised judicial, administrative, and legislative powers. As the highest provincial court, it handled civil and criminal cases for the town in which it was located, and it also heard cases on appeal from lower courts. As the regional council, it prepared laws on local matters and helped supervise subordinate officials. In the interim between two governorships, it wielded all royal authority in the colony. From 1535, the captain-general and *audiencia* of Santo Domingo nominally were subordinate to the viceroy of New Spain in matters of defense. Because Mexico City was so far away, however, they generally communicated directly with the Council of the Indies.

At first the *audiencia* of Santo Domingo governed all of the Americas. After the appointment of a second *audiencia* for Mexico City in 1528, Santo Domingo retained jurisdiction over the Caribbean islands, Florida, and the settlements on the northern coast of Venezuela. Its *audiencia* thus had jurisdiction over Puerto Rico, Cuba, Jamaica, and (until 1662) Trinidad. In theory, the *audiencia* was both the supreme court of appeal and the regional council responsible for supervising government throughout the islands. As such, it always had the right to send out special judges who could overrule the decisions of local authorities. Over time, however, the *audiencia* increasingly found it difficult to exercise these powers. Under the onslaught of French and English corsairs, the governors of Cuba and Puerto Rico also began to deal directly with the Council of the Indies. Symbolizing this change, the council granted both governors the military powers of a captain-general.

Town Government

For most people in Spain's American colonies, the most important instrument of royal power was always the town council or *cabildo*. In medieval and early modern Spain, men and women participated in politics not as individuals but as members of corporations. In Spanish America, the most important of these corporations was the municipality or town.[1] Neither the Spanish Crown nor the settlers could conceive of any other way of organizing society. Unlike those living on the English and French islands, most Spanish colonists lived in towns from the very beginning.

A town included more than just the urban center. The area under its authority included all of the surrounding countryside up to the boundaries of the next town. In Puerto Rico, for example, the entire island was legally divided into the two townships of San Juan and San Germán until 1752, when Ponce was founded. Even though some colonists might spend most of the year on a farm or ranch, the population of each town included registered male citizens (*vecinos*) who owned a certain amount of property, as well as their families, black slaves, and Indian dependents.

Under the supervision of the royal governor and *audiencia,* each town was administered by a city council (*cabildo*) made up of four to 12 councillors (*regidores*) and two municipal magistrates (*alcaldes ordinarios*) appointed by the *regidores.* The founder of the city named the first councillors, and these usually appointed their successors. In a few cases during the first years of settlement, some town councils were democratically elected by all *vecinos.* By the 1600s, however, the position of town councillor had become—as was also the case in Europe—a lifetime and hereditary position. In most cases, the council effectively was controlled by a few of the wealthiest creole families. However, the office of councillor was usually not sold by the king, as sometimes happened in the wealthier mainland colonies.

The Islands Suffer from the Convoy System

While it protected the American silver fleets, the Spanish system of annual convoys created powerful monopolies that prevented economic growth on the islands. The system gave great powers to the merchant guilds (*consulados*) in Seville, Mexico City, and Lima. Their representatives controlled the annual fairs in Porto Bello and Vera Cruz, where prices were set for European goods and arrangements were made for their distribution throughout the Americas. As the years passed, these merchants found less and less room for cargoes to or from the Antilles.

The annual fleets provided only a precarious lifeline between the Caribbean islands and Europe. Even when they brought goods to the Antilles, the system tremendously increased prices of imported goods. Taxes were only a small part of the problem. More fundamental was the series of high markups inherent in the entire monopoly system. Moreover, the system began to falter altogether after 1623, and both the number and tonnage of ships fell at least 50 percent by 1650. The fleet system continued for the rest of the century, though not on an annual basis. But tonnage remained at a fraction of former levels, and legal trade virtually ceased during the War of the Spanish Succession (1701–14). Although Spain's new Bourbon dynasty permitted a somewhat looser system of licensed ships, it did not decree free trade until 1765. From that year, with only slight restrictions, any Spanish captain of a Spanish ship might trade at any time between numerous ports in Spain and the Antilles.

The economic situation in the islands was bleak. Years might pass between arrivals of ships from Spain, and trade between the islands almost ceased during the second half of the 17th century. After about 1620, the inhabitants of each of the islands had to become self-sufficient. Urban life declined, and most of the population, living on isolated cattle ranches, governed themselves with little interference from representatives of the Crown. Although conditions may have improved somewhat earlier in Cuba, the economy and the pulse of civilized life did not really revive until the 1760s.

THE NATURAL RESOURCES OF THE ISLANDS

To purchase manufactured goods and foods not grown on the islands, their inhabitants had to produce products they could export profitably. In the days of sail, the Caribbean was very far away from Europe in time as well as in distance. On average, the passage from Seville to Havana or Panama lasted 75 days or a little more. The return voyage to Spain took 65 days from Havana—the closest port to Europe—and as long as three months from Trinidad. To this direct distance must be added the months that ships might spend in Havana while they waited for the yearly fleet to assemble. Thus, to be profitable, any product for export had to be something that grew easily in the Caribbean, that Europeans wanted but could not produce as cheaply themselves, and that was neither perishable nor so heavy or bulky that the long trip back to Seville ate up all the profits.

Since it is rare, imperishable, and highly valuable for its weight, Mexican and Peruvian silver clearly met all of these tests. Unfortunately for the islanders, their mines were played out by the 1530s. In choosing among possible export crops, the inhabitants of the Caribbean have found that while the tropical environment is kind to some plants and animals, it is also deadly for others.

Cattle Ranches Flourish in the Caribbean

Spanish colonists at first tried to introduce into the islands the plants and especially the animals with which they were familiar at home. Certain European animals immediately took to the region, which lacks any natural predators. The tough Spanish pig multiplied at an incredible rate. Cats, chickens, goats, and Spanish cattle also took readily to life in the Indies. Horses were more fragile and slower to multiply, but they also were widespread by the 1530s. Only sheep did not find the heat and humidity of the Antilles congenial.

For almost three centuries, until the end of the 18th century, most of the inhabitants of the Spanish Caribbean—both black and white—earned their living through subsistence farming and as open-range cattle ranchers. Cattle and hogs provided meat for the towns. Further, their hides and fat (tallow) found a ready market in Europe both through legal exports (when these were possible) and through sales to foreign smugglers.

Throughout the Greater Antilles, the land was divided up into great cattle estates—although local laws also provided for smaller land grants (called *estancias*), which could be located next to or even within cattle ranches. In the absence of royal laws, rights to land generally were distributed by the *cabildos,* or town councils, usually for a small charge. Most of these grants were not approved by the king until much later (as late as 1778 in Puerto Rico). However, they were given de facto legal approval in 1574 by a magistrate of the Santo Domingo *audiencia,* who was reviewing the administration of an outgoing Cuban governor.

Sugar Is Introduced to the Islands *Columbian Exch.*

The conquest of the Antilles and South America brought about a transfer of plants and animals as well as of peoples. The Spanish and Portuguese sent samples of native plants back to Europe. Some now are widely grown in Europe, Asia, and Africa—including tobacco, corn (maize), potatoes, tomatoes, red peppers, and even yuca. Tobacco at first provided a valuable export, but the Americas soon lost their monopoly over its production. By the 1650s, tobacco had been carried from the Americas to Europe, Asia, and Africa. Henceforth, it was grown everywhere from Sweden and Siberia in the north to the Cape of Good Hope in the south. But due to Spanish regulations, tobacco provided a commercial crop only in Cuba prior to the 19th century. Although they ultimately came to enjoy corn, yams, and yuca, Spanish colonists tried out many types of European plants in their efforts to find a valuable export crop. Most did not flourish. Seed crops, such as wheat and barley, are not successful in the Tropics, where they tend to mildew and run to stalk instead of head. Grapes and olive trees later were carried to parts of South America and Mexico, but they cannot be grown successfully in the Caribbean. Other crops did adapt well on the islands as well as on the mainland. These included bananas and all forms of citrus trees (oranges, lemons, and limes) as well as various garden vegetables from cabbages to garlic.

Ultimately, the most successful European import was sugarcane, which found ideal environmental conditions in the Antilles. On some of the islands taken from the Spanish by the British and the French, sugar became virtually as good as gold during the late 1600s. However, sugar plantations largely disappeared from the Spanish Caribbean (except for Cuba) in the 1570s. They were destroyed by the trade monopoly enforced through the convoy system, and sugar did not again become an important crop until trade policies were changed at the end of the 18th century.

If the Spanish government had not subordinated the immediate interests of the Antilles to the trade regulations of a large empire, sugar certainly would have flourished there. The Greater Antilles and Trinidad provide an ideal environment for sugar and became major producers in later centuries. It is true that a sugar plantation requires considerable technical skills, substantial capital to build mills, and large amounts of labor. But European demand was growing during the 17th century, and capital was available. Sufficient labor could have been acquired by opening up the African slave trade. Moreover, Spanish planters long had grown sugar successfully in the Canary Islands, using techniques similar to those that later succeeded in Jamaica and Saint-Domingue.

Sugar was brought from Europe to the Caribbean with the very first Spanish expeditions. Columbus carried cane from the Canaries to Hispaniola in 1493, and sugar again was planted in 1503 under Governor Ovando. Although these initial attempts failed, a wealthy surgeon had built a mill using the best available technology by 1517, and Santo Domingo exported sugar to Europe in 1522. Progress was rapid at first, and King Charles V encouraged the industry with loans, tax exemptions, and experts from the Canaries. By the late 1530s, 34 mills already were in operation, most located along the coast just west of Santo Domingo. And efforts were made—again with royal loans—to expand the industry to Puerto Rico and Jamaica.

The sudden collapse of the Caribbean sugar industry in the mid-1570s almost certainly is tied to the development of the annual convoy system. Most of the newer and larger ships were now carrying silver bullion from Mexico and Peru, and only a diminishing number of the smaller (and thus more expensive) freighters continued to call on Santo Domingo. Moreover, sugar now could be produced more cheaply on the mainland, especially in Brazil, which was ruled by the Spanish Habsburgs from 1580 to 1640. Brazilian sugar production boomed after 1570, flooding the Iberian market.

THE SLAVE TRADE BEGINS

Until the 19th century, sugar and black slavery were linked together. Almost all sugar plantations were worked by slaves, and the brief sugar boom from 1530 to 1570 thus saw the origins of the slave trade. Spain's Mediterranean cities and the Canary Islands imported African slaves, and blacks—both slave and free—took part in the first Spanish expeditions. In 1513, the government began to grant licenses to bring slaves directly from Africa. It legalized the trade partly to forestall Portuguese smuggling and partly because of requests by Dominican friars on Hispaniola, including Bartolomé de Las Casas. The Dominicans suggested that white and black slaves be imported to prevent the extermination of the Arawak.

Until the 1590s, the slave trade was carried out through individual licenses, although sometimes a monopoly was granted for a number of years. The Casa de Contratación granted or sold licenses to import a specific number of sales at a set fee per slave. From 1595 to 1640 (with brief interruptions), a series of Portuguese merchants purchased a monopoly over the slave trade, known as the *asiento*. In return for annual payments, the king granted these merchants the exclusive right to bring slaves into the Americas, and the latter in turn sold licenses to shippers. Until the 1560s, Santo Domingo was the main slave market for the islands. Under the *asiento,* all slaves first had to be taken to Cartagena.

Under the license system, the Crown collected a large fee for each slave, and it also limited the total number of slaves brought over each year. As a result, slaves became very expensive, and planters on the islands could not compete for legal imports with richer buyers on the mainland. We cannot measure the precise number of slaves imported under the *asiento* system, particularly since many other slaves were smuggled into the islands by foreign merchants and pirates. But it is known that slaves never outnumbered owners as dramatically as later became the case in the British and French colonies. As the economy stagnated during the 17th century, slavery also declined in importance. From the 1570s, free blacks and coloreds outnumbered whites on all the Spanish islands.

Given the sparsity of evidence, it is difficult to judge how well slaves were treated. However, slave revolts began early. Black slaves aided an Arawak revolt on Hispaniola in 1519. Three years later, some 40 slaves owned by Diego Colón held out for some months before being caught and executed, and in 1527 another revolt occurred in Puerto Rico. In later years, when large parts of the islands were only sparsely settled, flight into the deserted countryside apparently became more common than revolt. Judging by the enactment of harsh local laws, substantial numbers of runaway slaves existed in Hispaniola, Cuba, and Jamaica. These runaways were called *cimarrones*—a word which was later corrupted to *Maroons* on the British islands.

The Emergence of Havana, Cuba

Santo Domingo remained the administrative capital of the Spanish Antilles. From the 1560s, however, Havana became the most important settlement in the Caribbean because of its vital importance in protecting the treasure fleets carrying American silver to Spain. In July 1519, Cortés, who was quarreling with the governor of Cuba, ordered a subordinate to reach Spain by sailing directly north from Vera Cruz through the Bahama Channel; in this way he avoided any contact with officials in Santiago or Santo Domingo. This route soon replaced the Windward Passage as the ordinary route for ships sailing from Mexico and Panama to Seville.

Havana effectively became the capital of Cuba under Hernando de Soto, who used the island as a base to support his invasion of Florida in 1538. The permanent residence of the governors from 1550. Havana soon became the only major city on the island. For more than two centuries, Havana owed its importance to its domination of the old Bahama, or Florida, Channel, through which passed all legal shipping from the New World to Spain. The Gulf Stream, the strongest ocean current in the world, carries ships through the Bahama Channel at up to 10 kilometers per hour. Thus only a little over two months was needed to complete the entire passage from Mexico to Seville. Moreover, the harbor at Havana is one of the finest in the world. Its spacious anchorage is deep enough for the largest vessels, and a promontory along the western shore of the harbor mouth provided an excellent location for defensive fortifications.

Since Vera Cruz does not have a natural harbor, ships left Mexico for Havana as soon as possible. There they refitted for the ocean voyage, and waited—often for months—for other vessels to join the one annual convoy or *flota* to Seville. From the 1560s, the Crown also designated Havana as the assembly point for all ships from Terre Firme (Central America). The fleets now totally bypassed Santo Domingo and Santiago de Cuba, and these lost their commercial importance.

Because the law made Havana the main port for convoys to Seville, Cuba was somewhat more prosperous than the other islands. The fortunes of Havana itself rose and fell with the annual convoys. Moreover, the city's role as an international port also opened the island to trade both with Europe and with other islands. Because land communications were very difficult, most industry was confined to regions near Havana or on the coasts. From the 1550s, immigrants from the Canary Islands established tobacco farms, which produced a very high quality tobacco much esteemed by the state monopoly in Seville. Cuban tobacco is a sensitive plant, and the need to ensure a high-quality product gave the industry a relatively democratic nature. Most farmers worked the fields beside their families, although the more prosperous might own a slave or two.

As early as the 1590s, some holders of *estancias* (small farms) received state loans to build sugar mills near Havana. But only small amounts of sugar were produced for more than a century. Cargo space was limited, freight charges were very high, and tobacco received preference as cargo on the annual trade convoy to Spain. Moreover, because of the inefficient *asiento* system, slaves were expensive and in short supply. Sugar harvests increased after 1700, but they did not really take off until the British conquered the island in 1762.

Hispaniola, Puerto Rico, and Jamaica

For two centuries, Hispaniola suffered from many buccaneer attacks. As on other Spanish islands, economic life reached its lowest ebb during the second half of the 17th century, when inter-island trade almost disappeared. An energetic governor, Alonso de Feunmayor, completed the building of the cathedral and erected walls and forts around Santo Domingo between 1533 and 1556. Hunkered down behind its walls, the capital survived as a "city of lawyers" dealing with the legal work of its *audiencia*.

Almost all of the other 15 cities established under Governor Ovando were totally forgotten by 1605. That year, to curb smuggling by Dutch ships, the captain-general was ordered to burn the remaining towns in the western part of the island. The inhabitants were removed by military force to the Santo Domingo region, and their cattle ran wild. The deserted region was left wide open to invasion first by buccaneers and then by the French, who in 1697 gained formal control of the western third of the island, henceforth called Saint-Domingue.

With the extinction of the sugar industry after 1600, plantations and slaves also disappeared from Puerto Rico. Through intermarriage and more casual contacts, the population became predominantly colored. Away from the fortress at San Juan, Puerto Rico's few thousand inhabitants raised cattle on open-range ranches and grew crops for their own subsistence. From 1651 to 1662, not a single ship arrived at the island.

Jamaica largely escaped royal control because of the special position of the Columbus family. In 1536, the family gave up its rights under the 1492 contract granted by Queen Isabella. In return, the Crown gave Christopher Columbus's grandson the titles of duke of Veragua and marquis de la Vega and possession of Jamaica. According to the royal grant, the Columbus family received all royal revenues and powers, "supreme jurisdiction [only] remaining to us and nothing else."[2] Until 1640, the family continued to collect taxes, but it otherwise took no interest in the island, which fell under the corrupt misrule of a series of petty local tyrants.

Under the absentee rule of the Columbus family, Jamaica was isolated from the rest of Spanish America, and all contact between the island and Spain ended in 1634. When the pirate William Jackson plundered Spanish Town (the only urban settlement) in 1642, he found 400 or 500 houses, five or six churches, and one Franciscan monastery. His description of the island's fertility indirectly encouraged the British invasion and conquest in 1655.

Trinidad Goes Its Solitary Way

During the 16th century, Trinidad served the Spanish as a source of Arawak slaves. The Carib had begun to raid the island even before the Spanish conquest and had established camps on the northern coast. In response to Spanish and Carib slaving attacks, the Arawak moved their villages inland, where fishing was difficult and the soil was less fertile. Overall, as in the Greater Antilles, the Spanish invasion led to a severe drop in the Arawak population.

The Arawak and the Carib now began to resist further Spanish encroachment, and their attacks probably contributed to the failure of Spanish attempts at colonization in 1532–34 and in 1569. It was not until 1592 that a permanent settlement was established at San José de Oruña (Saint Joseph). The city's founder, Antonio de Berrio, planned to use it as a forward base for expeditions searching the neighboring mainland for El Dorado, the mythical city of gold. Since it had not authorized De Berrio's act of possession, the Spanish Crown ordered him to leave the island. He refused, and the government was powerless to evict his followers. This initial act of rebellion presaged Trinidad's isolation from the main centers of Spanish settlement during the next two centuries.

A second town soon was established near the present capital of Port of Spain (Puerto de España). But the Governor continued to reside in Saint Joseph until 1754 and shared his powers with the town's council (*cabildo*). Both supposedly were answerable to higher authorities at Santo Domingo or (after 1662) on the mainland, but they had virtually no contacts with these distant courts.

Since Trinidad was not situated on a shipping route useful to the empire, there was no Spanish market for its products. No Spanish ship arrived in Trinidad for 20 years after its settlement in 1592. In 1613, because of the growing presence of foreign ships in the area, the Crown ordered that one ship a year should go to the island with the convoy for New Spain (Mexico). However, trading contacts continued to be rare and intermittent, especially after the entire convoy system began to break down in the late 1600s. Spanish ships again failed to visit Trinidad from 1702 to 1716.

Few Spaniards lived on Trinidad until reform governments in Spain began to encourage settlement in the 1770s. During the 17th century, the number of male householders (*vecinos*) rarely exceeded 100, largely consisting of free blacks and coloreds. These normally lived on their farms, and Saint Joseph consisted of a few mud huts roofed with thatch. At the beginning of the century, the settlers were able to sell small amounts of tobacco to Dutch, English, and French merchants. But this industry could not compete with the English colonies in North America, and it was harmed by Spanish efforts to end the contraband trade.

Throughout the colonial period, the settlers at Saint Joseph relied on food produced by the Indian villages. Four *encomienda* villages existed during the 17th century. But most Indians continued to live in independent communities outside direct Spanish control. In 1687, the Spanish government introduced Capuchin missionaries, who gathered several thousand Indians into a number of settlements. Complaints by landowners, who wanted labor for their cocoa plantations, led the Crown to abolish the missions in 1713 and the *encomienda* in 1716. Henceforth, *corregidors,* responsible to the governor, acted as magistrates in the native villages and organized the distribution of Indian workers to Spanish landowners.

For three centuries, Spain treated the Caribbean islands as mere way-stations along the route of their treasure fleets. The Spanish government did not develop the economies of the islands, and it repressed all attempts by their minuscule creole populations to trade with foreign nations. These Spanish policies were intended to keep other nations out of the Caribbean, but they actually facilitated French, English, and Dutch settlement. During the 17th century, Spain permanently lost the Lesser Antilles, Jamaica, and the western third of Hispaniola (which became the French colony of Saint-Domingue). A British fleet easily took Trinidad in 1799, and Santo Domingo fell in 1802. Spain retained Cuba and Puerto Rico. But these islands could not prosper until after the 1760s, when Spanish reformers finally abolished the restrictive "Laws of the Indies" imposed under Queen Isabella almost three centuries earlier.

PART TWO

NORTHERN EUROPEANS COME TO STAY

CHAPTER 5

THE DUTCH EMPIRE

After pillaging Spain's empire for 150 years, northern Europeans finally planted permanent colonies in the 1620s. They concentrated first on the smaller, still unoccupied islands of the eastern Caribbean. After 1650, they moved west into the Greater Antilles. The success of these expeditions often depended on events in Europe. In particular, islands often changed hands during wars in Europe, as local forces or naval expeditions seized control. Until the 1700s, European events directly affected the islands, but the latter did not in themselves cause wars between European states. The Caribbean was only one of many areas in which Europeans were interested, and some Dutch merchants initially considered them valuable mainly as the gateway to Spanish America.

Since wars between European rulers decided who controlled the islands, historians often treat each nation's expeditions separately. But the settlement of the islands was an international movement.[1] During the first half of the 17th century, all of the new colonies depended on Dutch traders, and the merchants that funded the settlements had interests in many regions. Mariners from all the northern European states (who usually were Protestant) worked together against the Catholic Spanish until at least the 1650s. Pirate ships sailing from any of the Atlantic ports were manned by crews of mixed nationality—Norman French, British, Dutch, and even Scandinavian.

In the same way, the first settlers cooperated in order to survive, and sometimes divided up small islands amicably.

Governments played only a limited role in the initial settlement and economic development of the islands. The first colonies were established by individual adventurers, often acting for groups of merchants. Governments were not directly involved in settling the islands for two important reasons. Their rulers were more interested in European adventures, and they literally had no money to spend on foreign colonies. European rulers during the 17th and 18th centuries were chronically short of the revenues needed to obtain their goals, and were content to leave exploration and settlement to private enterprise.

Just as Queen Isabella drew up a contract with Columbus, so did other European governments give adventurers exclusive licenses to exploit specific parts of the world in return for a share of their profits. In France and the Netherlands, the state usually granted a monopoly to a joint-stock company, such as the Dutch West India Company. In England, the Crown often granted monopoly rights to looser merchant groups or to noblemen acting as agents for individual merchants. But in no country did the Crown put up its own cash, and it rarely provided ships and settlers for expeditions.

NORTHERN EUROPEANS CREATE SEVERAL TYPES OF COLONIES

During the first half of the 17th century, merchant groups in France, England, and Holland continued to sponsor pirate attacks on Spanish shipping. But they also began to plant their own colonies, which were intended to accomplish a variety of goals. Some expeditions had as their aim the creation of trading posts where goods could be stored for sale or for later transport to Europe. Their owners did not make any attempt to bring over European settlers to these colonies—the major examples being the Dutch colonies of Curaçao and Sint Eustatius. Other colonies were established as plantations where precious metals might be mined or tropical products grown for sale in Europe. Only a few colonies deliberately were founded as settlements for European immigrants. Often these were planted by dissident groups, such as the Pilgrims and Puritans of New England, who wanted to create alternative societies.

In the Caribbean, most of the English and French colonies—Saint Christopher, Barbados, Martinique, and Guadeloupe—were settled as tobacco plantations. Jamaica and the Dutch islands initially were meant to be trading posts, bases from which to carry on privateering and to trade with Spanish America. Some of the trading posts later developed into plantations; the Dutch islands provided salt while Jamaica produced sugar. But none of the islands taken over by northern Europeans became a place of settlement that attracted thousands or even millions of European immigrants, as the British North American colonies did.

The Dutch Open Up the Caribbean to Northern Europeans

The Dutch entered the Caribbean in force in the 1620s, and English and French colonists depended on their help in the settlement of the Lesser Antilles. A massive influx of Dutch raiders swept Spanish shipping from the seas in 1618, and Dutch attempts to conquer Brazil in the 1620s and 1630s tied down Portuguese and Spanish resources. This Dutch invasion thus provided a shield behind which the French and the English were able to plant settlements in the region.

The Dutch also helped the English and French to create the plantation society based on sugarcane that dominated the islands during the following centuries. The Dutch remained the main carriers of products in the Caribbean until the end of the century. During the first years of the new settlements, when their inhabitants often come close to starvation, Dutch traders took their crops in return for food and tools. Finally, Dutch merchants transformed the entire society of the English islands by helping to introduce the cultivation of sugar, by providing the African slaves needed to produce it, and by marketing and popularizing the crop in Europe.

Viewed from Amsterdam, however, the islands were only one area in which Dutch commerce was expanding. During the 17th century, the Netherlands led all other European nations combined in manufacturing, commerce, and finance capitalism. Citizens of this tiny state owned at least half of the world's total stock of shipping, and Amsterdam was the world center of international trade through which passed goods and products from every part of the globe. Building on their domination of European commerce, the Dutch now sought to expand into the "rich trades" in luxury goods. During the first decades of the 17th century, they entered and soon dominated trade with the Far East, Africa, and the Caribbean, as well as (during some periods) the Mediterranean and the Levant.

In all these regions, Dutch merchants came both to trade and raid. Their efforts succeeded in part because of the close collaboration between the Dutch government and the nation's merchant elite. The Dutch state set up, promoted, and protected—through war if necessary—a variety of cartels, organizations, and joint-stock companies, including the powerful Dutch East India and West India Companies. Backed by the power of their government, Dutch traders followed two contradictory policies, in neither case allowing conventional morality to interfere with business. When a variety of competitors existed, they called for "freedom of the seas" and opposed any restrictions other governments might place on trade. Carefully avoiding political entanglements, they succeeded by undercutting competitors. By contrast, in areas far from Europe or major European colonies—most successfully in Ceylon and Indonesia—they sought a total monopoly over luxury goods, such as spices, tobacco, or sugar. In these areas, they set up forts from which they controlled the native populations and ruthlessly drove off or sank ships from other nations.

In the Caribbean, Dutch traders initially followed both of these policies. As the Spanish were their enemies in Europe, they sank Spanish ships without mercy and pursued illegal or contraband trade with the Spanish colonies. Yet they took a more friendly attitude toward the fledgling (and much weaker) French and British colonies, providing them with essential supplies and at times financing their industries. At first the Dutch were often the only available carriers. After 1650, despite the complaints of their home governments, many French and English planters continued to prefer Dutch traders simply because these gave them better terms.

The relative sophistication of Dutch finance and insurance meant that they could offer planters loans with lower interest charges and for longer terms. Because Dutch ships were smaller and better designed, their freight rates were cheaper, and they could sell European goods at lower prices. Since tariffs and freight charges were lower, French and English planters often made a larger profit on sales to Holland. Some also believed that Dutch captains took better care of their cargoes. In the 1650s, however, England and France turned on the Dutch and drove them from the region during several wars. The Dutch were allowed to retain only six small conquests—three tiny Leeward Islands (Sint Maarten, Sint Eustatius, and Saba), and a larger but semi-desert group (Aruba, Bonaire, and Curaçao) off the coast of Venezuela.

The Dutch West India Company

In the 1620s and 1630s, large fleets employed by the Dutch West India Company (WIC) dominated the Caribbean. During these decades, the company was an instrument of war, although one that also sought to conduct war profitably. With the ending of the 12-year truce in 1621, Spain and Portugal (united under the Habsburg Crown between 1580 and 1640) again were at war with the Republic of the Netherlands. Until 1648, while the armies of the two states fought in Europe, their navies battled throughout the world. The Republic set up the West India Company in 1621 primarily to carry this war into the Caribbean through piracy and conquest. Although permitted to engage in trade and to set up colonies, the company at first subordinated these activities to its naval and military ambitions.

As chartered in 1621, the WIC largely resembled the East India Company (founded in 1602), although its management was less centralized. The state assigned the WIC a 25-year monopoly in every territory not already given to its older sister—the Atlantic, the west coast of Africa, and the Americas. In its structure, the company combined public and private powers. Like a private corporation, it sold stock listed on the Amsterdam exchange. At the same time, it was set up, supervised, and guaranteed by the States General, which provided continuing subsidies. In cooperation with the state, overall management was administered by five chambers representing different regions, and these in turn elected the Heren XIX—a central governing board with 19 members.

Until 1624 the company left the Caribbean to the small-scale raiding of independent corsairs, who often were allied with English and French captains. In that year, it launched large-scale attacks with three ambitious goals: to occupy the Portuguese sugar plantations in Brazil, to conquer the Portuguese slave stations in West Africa, and to seize the treasure fleets that carried Peruvian and Mexican gold from Havana to Seville. In all these efforts, the company ultimately failed after enjoying astounding initial victories.

In 1624 the company captured Bahia, the chief town in northeast Brazil, but lost it again the following year to a joint Spanish-Portuguese armada. In 1630 it took Pernambuco (Recife) and Olinda, and its forces controlled a large area of sugar plantations by 1637. To supply Brazil with West African slaves, an expedition from Pernambuco in 1637 captured the Portuguese fortress at Elmina. Other company forces further overran Angola, Axim, and the island of São Tomé. The Dutch now controlled both the international sugar trade and the Atlantic slave trade. However, in 1645, the Portuguese Catholics rose up in a devastating revolt. They soon swept the Dutch out of most of their Brazilian territories, although the company retained the fortress of Recife until 1654.

Brazil represented the company's most important adventure. But its fleets also scoured the Caribbean, both plundering merchant shipping and seeking to capture the Spanish treasure fleets. Small Dutch fleets returning from Brazil were present throughout the 1620s and 1630s, and the company sent major expeditions to the region in 1625 and again between 1628 and 1635. On land, the great Spanish fortresses built since Drake's invasion in the 1580s held, and the company's forces failed to take El Moro in San Juan during a five-week siege in 1625. Although they devastated Spanish shipping, the company's fleets took too little plunder to pay for their enormous cost.

The company's greatest victory in the Caribbean came in 1628 and was never repeated. In September of that year, ships captained by Piet Heyn managed to trap the entire Mexican treasure fleet in Matanzas Bay off Cuba. Heyn's men took an enormous treasure in gold, silver, and goods estimated at 11 million guilders—enough to pay the cost of the entire Dutch army for eight months. Because of this one haul, the company in 1629 paid its shareholders a cash dividend of 70 percent.

Until 1635, the company continued to mount large and costly expeditions to pillage Spanish settlements and shipping in the West Indies. Overall (and including its Brazilian campaigns), the company by 1637 had sent out over 800 ships manned by some 67,000 sailors. From its point of view, their take was meager, and its shares sank to record lows on the Amsterdam exchange. However, the company's attacks—together with those of smaller fleets of Dutch, English, and French pirates—did succeed in destroying Spanish commerce and communications. Between 1625 and 1635, Dutch maritime forces changed the balance of power in the Caribbean, making it possible for Dutch traders to control most of the region's commerce for decades.

Sint Maarten, Sint Eustatius, Saba

While it engaged in the struggle to control Brazil and the West African slave trade, the West India Company also continued to look for a secure source of salt, of particular interest to its Zeeland branch. During the 1630s, their need for salt led Dutch traders to occupy three tiny islands, closely grouped together at the northern tip of the Leeward chain. All three are very small and relatively infertile. Saba and Sint Eustatius form part of the inner or volcanic arc of the Lesser Antilles. Indeed, Saba is simply the rocky remains of an extinct volcano rising abruptly from the sea to a peak almost 3,000 feet high. On Sint Eustatius, a large plain extends between volcanic hills to the northwest and Quill, another but more attractive extinct volcano, 1,800 feet high. Sint Maarten, part of the outer or limestone arc of islands, is comparatively flat. However, it also is arid and lacks an adequate water supply.

⚙ WINDWARD OR LEEWARD—IT DEPENDS ON WHOM ONE ASKS

Visitors wonder why the Dutch Windward Islands—Aruba, Bonaire, and Curaçao—are located in the midst of the British Leeward Islands. The prevailing trade winds tend to blow more or less from the east to the west—during some months from southeast to northwest. In English and American usage, *windward* denotes the direction or side from which the wind blows. In this meaning of the word, every Caribbean island is thus leeward of those

---

to its east and windward of all those to its west. For its own administrative convenience, the British government arbitrarily divided its colonies in the Lesser Antilles into the Leewards (in the north) and the Windward Islands (in the south). In Spanish, French, and Dutch, the meaning of *windward* is the opposite of English usage. Thus the Dutch, viewing the map from Curaçao, call their northern possessions the Windward Islands (Bovenwindse Eilanden, the "islands before the wind").

The desire to exploit the salt pans on the Araya Peninsula of Venezuela had led the Dutch to invade the region in 1599. After the renewal of war in 1621, construction of a new Spanish fort effectively closed off Araya. From the mid-1620s, the Dutch found alternative sources on Sint Maarten and on Tortuga Island, near Venezuela.[2] Spanish countermeasures made it difficult to keep Tortuga open. Thus the company in 1631 sent a fleet to occupy Sint Maarten, possibly unaware that some 14 French families already lived on the other side of the island. The salt flats on Sint Maarten proved to be of extremely high quality, and the island soon attracted hundreds of Dutch, French, and English ships. According to one source, Sint Maarten's salt paid most of the cost of the company's 6,000-man garrison in Pernambuco.

The Spanish Council of the Indies took the Dutch occupation of Sint Maarten seriously. In June 1633, the annual Panama fleet stopped at the island, landing 1,300 soldiers who easily overcame the company's 80-man garrison. The Spanish fleet left behind a force of 250 soldiers, who remained in place for the next 15 years. In 1644, this garrison bravely beat off a Dutch attack led by Peter Stuyvesant, during which the governor of Curaçao—and later of New Amsterdam—lost a leg.

With peace imminent in 1648, the Spanish withdrew from Sint Maarten. A few Dutch and French civilians stayed on the island, and the governors of Dutch Sint Eustatius and French Saint Kitts sent troops to defend their nation's claims. In March 1648, the leaders of the two groups negotiated a settlement dividing Sint Maarten along customary boundaries, with the Dutch retaining the valuable salt pans.[3] During the 18th century, residents of both parts of the island also developed cattle ranches and sugar plantations.

Unlike the other Dutch colonies, Sint Eustatius was settled as a tobacco plantation. In 1635, a company of merchants sent out two ships to Saint Croix. Finding that the island already was occupied by the English, 50 colonists chose to stay at Sint Eustatius. On the ruins of a former French fort (possibly built in 1627) overlooking the bay, they erected Fort Orange (Oranjestad). During the 18th century, Sint Eustatius flourished as a free port, from which the French and British islands illegally imported goods to avoid their government's tariffs.

In 1640, several Dutch planters from Sint Eustatius built a small fort on the southern coast of Saba. Agriculture never flourished, and Saba's few inhabitants survived by fishing, shipbuilding, and making shoes. Since its people owned few slaves, Saba remained one of the rare Caribbean islands with a predominantly white population.

Curaçao

Aruba, Bonaire, and Curaçao form the southern end of the Lesser Antilles. Because of their location, they are all extremely arid. Although Curaçao produced some sugar during the 18th century, the island owes its importance to its site just off the coast of Venezuela and its excellent harbor (present-day Willemstad). The Spanish reconquest of Sint Maarten in 1633 left the West India Company without a secure source of salt. Since the late 1620s, Dutch ships returning from Brazil had stopped at Bonaire and Curaçao to take on salt, and the Heren XIX apparently were misled about the value of the pans on these islands. They also hoped that Curaçao would serve as a military base from which to monitor and plunder the Spanish treasure fleets.

With the help of a state subsidy, the West India Company sent six ships to seize and hold Curaçao—which it considered "a suitable place where we can procure salt, hard-wood and other items, and from where we can infest the enemy in the West Indies." The Dutch forces easily overran Curaçao in July 1634 and occupied Bonaire and Aruba in 1636. The conquerors transferred the few Spanish colonists and their Indians to the mainland, and Spain, occupied during these years with the war in Brazil, could not launch an effective counterattack.

During the next 20 years, the island proved to be an expensive liability for the company, which seriously considered abandoning it. As long as the war lasted, trade with the Spanish mainland colonies was practically nonexistent. During the 1640s, Curaçao served as a base for company forces raiding coastal settlements in Puerto Rico, Cuba,

Mounds of salt sparkle in the sun, Bonaire. The Dutch initially settled Sint Maarten (1631), Curaçao (1634), and Bonaire (1636) to secure a safe supply of salt. Sea water was pumped into a series of ponds. The water evaporated, leaving rough salt crystals like those shown.

and the mainland. Peter Stuyvesant, the island's only famous governor, similarly led an abortive attack against Sint Maarten in 1644. After the loss of Brazil, the Heren XIX made Stuyvesant governor of New Amsterdam in 1645, and he ruled both colonies from North America until New Amsterdam became English New York in 1664.

The Dutch Colonies after 1648

As the West India Company's fortunes waned, it gradually gave up its commercial monopoly, at first for a fee. It allowed individual traders—Dutch, Jewish. and later Portuguese—to carry salt (1633) and to trade with Brazil (1638), Curaçao (in the 1640s), and later West Africa (1734). In 1646, the directors accepted the failure of the company's grandiose schemes. They reorganized it as a commercial organization that would supply slaves and goods to the colonies of other powers, relying for protection on the Dutch state. With these more modest goals, the company was rechartered in 1647. When it became bankrupt in 1674 during the Third Dutch War, the state reorganized it under the same name, and it survived until 1799 as the administrator of the Dutch colonies and as a slaving company of some importance. The Republic now focused its main efforts on the East India Company, which continued to provide a profitable outlet for Dutchmen with an ambitious and aggressive spirit.

Curaçao, created as a war base, began to make a profit for the company only after the conclusion of peace with Spain in 1648. The Treaty of Muenster recognized the Dutch colonies in the Americas but expressly prohibited trade with the Spanish islands or mainland. However, the Dutch were now the principal carriers in the Caribbean, and trade with the British and French colonies in the Lesser Antilles flourished from the 1640s. Some merchants operated directly from Amsterdam, bypassing Curaçao. But the company largely controlled the supply of West African slaves, and Curaçao now became an enormous slave depot.

From 1662, Spain allowed Dutch merchants to ship slaves through Curaçao into its American colonies, and they enjoyed a virtual monopoly until 1689. Although it remained illegal, the Spanish government also tolerated commerce in other goods from 1654. Dutch ships called on Cuba and Hispaniola, and Curaçao became the main depot for an extensive trade with Venezuela and Peru until 1713. Contacts with the mainland again declined during the 18th century, but Curaçao and Sint Eustatius remained prosperous ports for trade with the islands. Dutch ships carried goods and slaves legally to the Danish Virgin Islands, and they also illegally smuggled them into the British and French colonies. Throughout these years, Aruba and Bonaire—where the salt pans proved unprofitable—served mainly to support commerce through Curaçao. The company maintained Aruba as a vast cattle ranch, and it grew corn on Bonaire to feed the slaves passing through its depots on Curaçao.

CHAPTER 6

SETTLEMENT OF THE LESSER ANTILLES

With the outbreak of the Thirty Years' War (1618–48), a brief truce in Europe's dynastic wars ended. Spain's enemies were glad to see their subjects menace the source of Spain's wealth, and new waves of Dutch, British and French marauders descended on the Caribbean. This time, they intended to stay.

Many influences came together during the 1620s to help the northern European settlements survive and succeed. In Britain and France, the first expeditions directly grew out of the privateering voyages of the preceding 50 years. Ships were available with crews that knew the islands well, and the profits from pirate voyages also provided merchants with the capital to fund settlements. Pirate raids had impoverished the Greater Antilles, and Spanish efforts to end smuggling had only made things worse. The way was open, and tropical products, such as tobacco and sugar, fetched high prices. Few investments at home were as profitable, and young men could be induced to leave Europe to find work.

The pursuit of economic gain was the paramount reason for the settlement of the Caribbean, which was facilitated by the naval weakness of Spain. As always, individual colonists had variable, complex, and obscure motives. A desire for fame and honor clearly drove many leaders, and economic and religious nationalism also were a significant influence with some. Old habits die hard, and the decline of the Spanish Empire probably is more obvious now than it was at the time. All of the northern European colonists thus tended to join together in their hatred of Spain.

From the 1650s and 1660s, the French and English governments imposed greater controls on the various trading posts and plantations under their flag. Both government needed to supply their colonies with settlers and money. They wanted their colonies to repay these expenses by producing products for sale in Europe. Both wanted to keep control over their colonies and ensure that they traded only with the homeland. Until the late 1800s, they enforced a system of economic regulations—sometimes called mercantilism—that kept out foreign imports through high tariffs. However, neither could totally enforce these rules. Both British and French colonists happily smuggled in foreign goods through Dutch Sint Eustatius or Danish Saint Thomas.

TOBACCO AND SUGAR

The first French and English settlements were established in the early 1620s to grow tobacco. During the 1590s, most of the tobacco entering England had been taken by pirates from captured Spanish merchant ships. Since quantities were small, prices rose dramatically, reaching 90 shillings a pound in 1598 and averaging 40 to 60 shillings from 1600 to 1613. Its high price made tobacco one of the most lucrative commodities, and many merchants wanted to secure their own exclusive source of supply. Thus the cultivation of tobacco provided the main incentive for the settlement of the Lesser Antilles. In fact, English merchants sponsored the settlement of Saint Kitts and Barbados for tobacco farming. And tobacco also encouraged the creation of French colonies on Saint Kitts, Martinique, and Guadeloupe.

Unfortunately, tobacco is a weed that will grow anywhere, and the tobacco boom in the Caribbean was short-lived. By 1629 exports from Virginia (founded in 1607) reached 1.5 million pounds, and the high prices even encouraged production in England itself. Supply quickly outstripped demand from the late 1620s. Prices fell drastically to a few pennies a pound, and they remained depressed until the end of the century. All the colonies suffered a severe setback, until tobacco was replaced by sugar as their main crop. Barbados became the richest colony in the 1640s because its planters were the first to introduce sugarcane.

BRITISH COLONIES
IN THE LESSER ANTILLES

By 1623, the Dutch West India Company had driven Spanish ships from the seas. As usual, the islands bore the full force of these attacks, to the extent that towns along the southern coast of Cuba could not deliver their products to Havana. The absence of Spanish forces removed the fear that they would slaughter the colonists during their first months on an island.

Many English captains already were familiar with the Caribbean islands. Since

Columbus's second voyage, ships from Europe usually had followed the trade winds to the outer islands of the Lesser Antilles, halting there to make needed repairs and obtain fresh meat and water. By the 1620s, many captains had established regular bases on some of these islands, where they might stay for several months while they launched raids against the Greater Antilles. The southern or Windward Islands were occupied by hostile Carib, who annihilated at least three English attempts at settlement between 1605 and 1614. But pirates maintained camps throughout the Leewards, where fewer Carib lived—especially on Saint Kitts, Nevis, and on several of the Virgin Islands, including Virgin Gorda and Saint Croix.

Saint Kitts

On January 38, 1624, Thomas Warner, accompanied by fewer than 20 "gentlemen adventurers," landed on the small island of Saint Kitts and founded the first permanent English settlement in the Caribbean. A Suffolk gentleman of limited means and large ambitions, Warner in 1620 joined an ill-fated expedition to the Amazon. Leaving in 1622, before the colony failed, he sailed through the Lesser Antilles until he came to Saint Kitts, which he judged to be "a very convenient place for the planting of tobaccoes which ever was a rich commodetie." Back in England in 1623, Warner gained the financial support of a syndicate of English merchants led by Ralph Merrifield and Maurice Thomson, launching his adventure early in 1624.

Under Warner's control, the adventurers first killed or drove off a small group of Carib and then planted tobacco. A hurricane destroyed their first crop in September

The tomb of Sir Thomas Warner, Saint Kitts. Thomas Warner founded the first permanent English settlement in January 1624 and governed Saint Kitts until his death in 1649. From Saint Kitts, parties of settlers established colonies on Nevis, Montserrat, and Antigua.

1624, but another crop was ready by the next summer. In the spring of 1625, Warner's party was joined by the crew of a disabled Norman privateer under Urbain du Roissey and Pierre Bélain d'Esnambuc. With their help, Warner defeated a force of Carib who sailed to the island to avenge the massacre of the preceding year. From the beginning, the two groups divided the island between them, with the English receiving the center and more mountainous sector, and the French inhabiting the two extremes. In 1625, Warner returned with the first tobacco crop to England, where he obtained a royal commission naming him governor of Saint Kitts, Nevis, Barbados, and Montserrat.

Barbados: The Carlisle Grant

Saint Kitts soon was surpassed by Barbados, which was permanently settled in 1627 and grew at a very rapid rate. Barbados is larger and was not occupied by the Carib. Moreover, it lies 100 miles to the east of the other islands so that any hostile force had to approach it by sailing against the strong trade winds. For these reasons, Barbados is the only island in the Lesser Antilles that was never taken by a hostile naval force

As on Saint Kitts, a syndicate of merchants sponsored the settlement of Barbados. The dominant partner was Sir William Courteen, an Anglo-Dutch trader with many interests in Amsterdam and along the Wild Coast in South America. Between 1627 and 1629, Courteen's group poured money and men into the island—carrying over, according to one estimate, more than 1,500 people at a cost exceeding 10,000 pounds.

Two merchant syndicates now had set up tobacco plantations in the Lesser Antilles, but neither had a clear title. Following Spanish precedent, all lands the French or the English acquired in the West Indies were deemed possessions of the Crown. Both groups thus sought to purchase a member of the court nobility who could secure a proprietary grant from the king. The Merrifield (Saint Kitts) syndicate bought the support of the bankrupt James Hay, earl of Carlisle. The Courteen group (Barbados) purchased that of William Herbert, earl of Pembroke. After a sordid story of intrigue and backroom dealings, Carlisle's grant was upheld in February 1629, and the Merrifield group thus ended up in control of both Saint Kitts and Barbados. The Crown confirmed Sir Thomas Warner as governor of Saint Kitts and the other Leewards, an office he held until his death in 1649.

Barbados: The First Sugar Boom

The royal privilege to Carlisle (as well as the abortive grant to Pembroke) was a revival of a kind of "feudal" grant no longer found in England itself. In return for a small yearly payment, the proprietor received both ownership of all land and all governmental powers. He appointed the governor and judges, and he could make laws with the assent of the freeholders. In 1641, the Civil War in England cut the island off from its proprietor (and his merchant backers). Until then, his governor apparently acted in a harsh and unpopular way, ruling through an appointed council and arbitrarily levying heavy taxes and fees.

Because of the Pembroke-Carlisle dispute, Barbados until 1641 was divided between two groups of settlers, who made the first "starving years" worse by burning each other's crops. As on other islands, many new settlers died in transit or during their first year. An unspecified "plague" also killed off perhaps 1,200 whites on Barbados between 1647 and 1650.

Table 3. **BARBADOS POPULATION ESTIMATES, 1635–1684**

	Total	Whites	Slaves
1635*	1,227	1,227	—
1639*	8,707	8,707	—
1655	43,000	23,000	20,000
1684	68,743	21,941	46,802

*For 1635 and 1639, figures include only adults age 14 years or older.

SOURCE: Richard S. Dunn, *Sugar and Slaves* (New York: Norton, 1973), 55, 87.

Despite these political and economic difficulties, the first colonies of Saint Kitts and Barbados initially attracted a rush of settlers. Barbados had 10,000 white settlers by 1640, and the governor had distributed virtually all of the island's land. The population doubled again by 1655, leaving Barbados more densely populated than most regions in England or Europe. For the first two decades these settlers experimented with various crops, looking for a product they could export at a profit. Most at first planted tobacco. When the price of that crop fell drastically, some switched to sea-island cotton, and others tried indigo and ginger. During the 1640s, the largest planters finally found in sugar a crop that not only paid their bills but that made them the richest men in English America by the 1680s.

Traditionally, the Dutch receive credit for introducing to the French and English islands both the sugar plant and the technical expertise needed to grow it. From 1630 to 1654, the Dutch West Indies Company occupied the Pernambuco region of Brazil. And Pernambuco planters introduced both the plantation system and the technology—three-roller mill and copper furnace pots—later used on Barbados. However, the Barbados planters were eager students, and several went to Brazil to see for themselves how the system worked. What the Dutch did provide was a ready market for the product and the large loans needed to create and maintain a sugar plantation. The success of the first sugar crops in the early 1640s set off a frenzied boom. By 1647 most of the large planters had switched to the new crop, and production, land prices, and the demand for labor soared. Until about 1710 Barbados was the main sugar producer in the Caribbean, and it soon caught up with and even overtook Brazil in the world market.

Successful sugar planting required large estates. For Barbados the optimum probably was about 200 acres. Although smaller estates continued to exist, many were now combined into large plantations. At first most of the workers on the sugar estates were white indentured servants. Some planters probably preferred African slaves, who were widely used in Brazil, but these were in relatively short supply during the 1640s. The number of both white and black servants probably continued to increase until the 1660s. But black slaves made up the overwhelming majority of the population by the 1680s. (See Table 3.)

As a result of the sugar boom, Barbados was the first Caribbean island to develop the plantation society later found on the smaller Leeward Islands and Jamaica and Saint-Domingue. A few big planters owned the best sugar acreage, reaped most of the profits, and dominated island politics. Perhaps one-fourth of all white males could

Drax Hall, Barbados. James Drax, a planter of Anglo-Dutch lineage, helped to build the first sugar mill on Barbados during the 1640s. Constructed before 1700 as a copy of an English manor house, Drax Hall was totally unsuited to the Caribbean climate.

vote under a 10-acre property qualification. But the smaller planters deferentially elected their betters to the important offices on the island.

Colonists in Bondage

The colonists who created cane estates on Barbados during the 1640s and 1650s were at least moderately well-off in the home country. Below this élite, most of the settlers came over as indentured servants. The landowner paid for a servant's passage to the island and provided him (for most were very young men) with food, clothing, and shelter. In return he worked, usually in the fields, for three to five years. Only at the end of this term did he receive wages, called "freedom dues." Initially in the form of land, later in a set amount of sugar, these provided him with the chance to become an independent farmer or laborer.

Contemporaries often compared indentured servants to slaves, and their status fell somewhere between freeman and slave. During the term of his contract, a servant was the property of his master and could freely be sold or given away. He could not run away, marry without his owner's permission, and was usually not allowed to engage in commerce. At the same time, he could (unlike an African slave) own personal property, sue, and testify in court. He further was protected by the terms of his indenture and the island's apprenticeship laws, and he might apply to a local magistrate if he was grossly mistreated.

While the indentured servant's condition may seem barbarous today, temporary servile status as an apprentice or servant was a normal part of growing up in 16th-century England. Indentures, of course, were not limited to the Caribbean islands. Most of those immigrating to the southern colonies in North America also came as servants.

At first most of the servants in the West Indies came over voluntarily, drawn by the hope of acquiring their own land. During the 1640s and 1650s, some were kidnapped, and "Barbadosed" took on the same meaning that "Shanghaied" has today. After the English Civil War ended, captives from Cromwell's expeditions to Ireland and Scotland were forcibly brought over between 1649 and 1655. But fewer criminals entered the islands as servants than were sent either to British America or later to Australia.

Fewer indentured servants came to Barbados or the Leewards after 1660, although some continued to go to Jamaica throughout the 18th century. On most islands, African slaves now did most of the hard field work and formed the majority of the population. Alarmed by this trend, the island legislatures from the 1670s unsuccessfully tried to encourage white immigration. They required planters to bring in indentured servants and sometimes subsidized their cost. Most also passed laws requiring better treatment of white servants. Masters had to give servants a minimum amount of food and clothing, and they needed a magistrate's permission to flog them.

In the early days, working conditions were brutal, and some owners cruelly punished shirkers. Antagonism was increased by religious differences between Irish Catholic servants and Anglican masters. Discontented servants regularly burned cane fields on Barbados and planned an armed uprising there in 1649. In the Leewards, Irish Catholic servants similarly cooperated with invasions by the Spanish and the French, and an outright rebellion took place on Saint Kitts in 1689.

The Origins of African Slavery

It was the combination of sugar and tropical diseases that made the Caribbean islands into colonies populated almost entirely by African slaves. The introduction of sugar to Barbados between 1640 and 1645 did not in itself make African slavery inevitable. European laborers can grow sugar, and white labor produced much of the sugar grown in Barbados into the 1650s. Indentured servants stopped coming during the 1660s, because the islands became deadly for whites. The African slaves sold by the Dutch in the 1640s introduced several diseases to which whites have no immunity. Whether colonists came from Europe or Africa, they faced a new disease environment in the islands, but blacks fared less badly than whites in adjusting to this new climate. As a general rule, about one out of three slaves died during the first two years in the islands. As many as three out of four white settlers perished soon after arrival.

Indentured servants began to avoid Barbados both because its planters gained a reputation as cruel masters and because emancipated servants often could not find satisfactory work. A servant's meager "freedom dues" were not enough to set up a sugar estate. As planters increasingly trained their slaves in most forms of skilled labor, white wage earners could not compete. During the mid-1600s, moreover, black slaves were becoming cheaper than white servants, since the price of Africans fell while English wages were rising. But the main obstacle to European immigration—now and for two centuries to come—was the Caribbean's reputation as a white graveyard. Why go to Jamaica or Martinique, where an indentured servant faced a high risk of a horrible death? By opting for North America instead, British laborers chose a region with a better disease environment than Europe.[1] Unlike those going to Jamaica or Barbados, they could at least expect to survive their years of voluntary slavery and become independent workers or farmers.

Barbados Goes It Alone

The English Civil War that began in 1642 freed the Barbados planters from their proprietor and temporarily made them independent of the home government. Governor Philip Bell consolidated and expanded the island's independent executive and judicial system. The legislative assembly (first called together in 1639) gained the power to make new laws, abolishing those of England. Under Governor Bell, it sought to remain neutral in the Civil War afflicting the home country. Above all, whatever their private beliefs, the planters wanted to maintain free trade with Amsterdam. They argued that the Dutch offered better prices, brought in superior goods, and offered longer credit.

The death of the king and the establishment of the Commonwealth government (1649–1660) of Oliver Cromwell ended this truce between Barbados's Cavaliers and Roundheads—the names given to the Royalist and Parliamentary factions. With the fighting over in England, members of both factions came to the islands, some with money to purchase estates. A long series of plots and counterplots ended with the victory of the Cavaliers. In May 1650, the assembly declared its loyalty to the late king's exiled son and adopted a program of free trade with Holland and Hamburg.

The Navigation Acts

Barbados's free-trade policy ran headlong into the mercantilist goals of the Commonwealth government, which sought to destroy the Dutch commercial monopoly. Cromwell's government responded in October 1650 by prohibiting trade with four colonies—including Barbados and Antigua—that had recognized the exiled Charles Stuart as king. In October 1651, the Council of State extended these rules by the Navigation Act. This established the mercantilist and exclusionary policies that regulated trade with the North American and Caribbean colonies until after 1776. Primarily directed at the Dutch, the act proclaimed that all imports into England or its colonies must be brought in on ships that were built, owned, and captained by British subjects. European products could be imported into the colonies only on ships sailing from England, its colonies, or the country where the goods were produced.[2]

To enforce its rule over Barbados, the Commonwealth government sent a fleet under Sir George Ayscue. Led by Lord Francis Willougby—who had leased Carlisle's rights and also acted as governor—the planters reinforced the island defenses. By the time Ayscue arrived in October 1651, his fleet could blockade but not take the island. After three months, this stalemate was broken in January 1652 when both sides accepted articles of surrender generally favorable to the islanders. The Barbadians accepted a new governor appointed by the Commonwealth. In return, they gained liberty of conscience, local control of taxation and justice, and restoration of free trade with the Dutch. The home government latter reneged and tried to exclude Dutch traders, but Barbados retained political autonomy.

The restored monarchy was as determined as the Commonwealth to control colonial trade, and it passed additional and even stricter Navigation Acts in 1660 and 1663. These laws effectively required the islands to deal only with England. They provided that the trade of British colonies, both import and export, must be carried in British ships.

The most important products (including sugar and tobacco) could be sent only to England or to other English colonies. Goods not of English origin first had to be brought into England and then reshipped to the colonies. Another law, enforced until 1678, required the planters to buy their slaves from the monopolistic Royal Africa Company.

Passage of these acts ended one era of English colonialism in the islands and, indeed, throughout British America. In economic matters, successive English governments now sought to bring the colonies under centralized control. By the outbreak of the Second Dutch War in 1665, the government had excluded most Dutch ships from the English islands. The resulting increase in transportation costs helped to bring an end to the first golden age for sugar planters. In September 1663, moreover, the government forced Barbados to accept a 4.5 percent tax on all goods exported from the island. In return, the Crown permitted the planters to retain significant control over local finance.

The economic effect of the Navigation Acts has been debated. Caribbean planters lost access to foreign buyers operating through Amsterdam. At the same time, they gained a protected market in England, with prohibitive tariffs set against foreign sugars. However, most historians agree that the islands were harmed by the 4.5 percent export tax, which in practice was paid by the individual planter. The island legislatures sought to end this hated tax until it was repealed in 1798.

Saint Kitts, Nevis, Antigua, and Montserrat

The first settlers on the other Leewards came from Saint Kitts. Thomas Warner, governor until 1649, successfully promoted immigration to Saint Kitts, and the best land soon was taken. Servants who had completed their term of indenture readily moved to neighboring islands and even to English America. In 1628, Anthony Hilton, a relatively wealthy planter, led a group of 150 settlers to Nevis, first obtaining the title of governor from the earl of Carlisle. According to tradition, the first immigrants from Saint Kitts arrived on Montserrat and Antigua in 1632.

All of the English Leewards legally were under the authority of the earl of Carlisle's lieutenant governor at Barbados. But the great distance separating them from the larger island made them virtually independent colonies. Each island had its own deputy governor and assembly, who were jealous of any outside authority. As on Barbados, conflicts during the English Civil War led to greater local control.

After the monarchy was restored in 1660, the English government tried but failed to impose a federated system of government. In 1664, the assemblies of the four islands made the same bargain with Charles II that the Barbadians earlier had agreed to. In return for self-government and confirmation of their land titles, they granted the Crown a 4.5 percent tax on all exports. To their disappointment, however, the king placed them under the governor of Barbados.

The Leeward colonists resisted their subordination to Barbados, their main economic rival. Moreover, federation soon proved ineffective during the Second Dutch War, when French naval forces seized and plundered Saint Kitts, Antigua, and Montserrat. These defeats convinced the London government that it needed to separate the northern islands from Barbados. In 1671, Charles II tried to create one unified government, with one governor-general and one General Assembly for the four Leeward islands. Despite the continuing French menace, however, the planters on each island remained intensely jealous of their own independence. Since they refused to grant revenues, the General Assembly seldom met, although it survived on paper until 1798.

Table 4. **BRITISH LEEWARD ISLANDS POPULATION ESTIMATES, 1678**

	Total	Whites	Slaves
Antigua	4,480	2,308	2,172
Saint Kitts	3,333	1,897	1,436
Montserrat	3,674	2,682	992
Nevis	7,370	3,521	3,849

SOURCE: Dunn, *Sugar and Slaves,* 127.

While each of the four northern Leeward islands has a distinctive personality, they are all much smaller than Barbados. Each also presented problems to settlers. Like Barbados, Antigua is generally flat with higher volcanic hills along the Leeward and southern coasts. The island is quite dry, but it possesses exceptionally fine harbors. English Harbor, now restored and renamed Nelson's Dockyard, became the British fleet's home port during the 18th century. Saint Kitts, Nevis, and Montserrat represent the upper slopes and cones of volcanoes. The hillside fields are difficult to clear and erode easily, and Nevis is generally arid. None of these three has a natural harbor.

Settlers on these four islands repeated the history of Barbados 50 to 60 years later. Throughout the 17th century, most settlers were small tobacco and cotton farmers, and society had a rough-hewn frontier quality. Except on Saint Kitts, larger sugar plantations were developed toward the end of the 17th century. But the industry really began to expand only with the Treaty of Utrecht in 1714, when the French part of Saint Kitts passed to England.

War and a lack of money held back the introduction of sugar on the Leewards. Until the 1660s, most colonists were former servants who lacked the capital to purchase milling equipment or slaves. English investors tended to focus on wealthier Barbados. After the Restoration in 1660, efforts to create plantations were thwarted by the destructive wars with the French, Carib attacks, and the general slump in the sugar industry. Except for Saint Kitts, all were thinly settled for several decades, and planters tended to rely on white servants rather than black slaves. (See Table 4.) Many of the settlers were Irish—with Irish settlers forming 70 percent of the white population on Montserrat in 1678.

The British Virgin Islands and Anguilla

Under the law of 1671 separating the Leewards from Barbados, the English government gave the governor of the Leewards authority over Anguilla and the Virgin Islands. The small populations of these islands could not support a representative assembly, and a deputy or lieutenant governor and six-man advisory council represented the Crown. Although their arid climates discouraged planters, the British government kept them for military reasons. An enemy with a base on these islands would have easy access to Barbados and the British Leewards.

British forces took the Dutch colony on Tortola—the most important of the Virgins—in 1665 and 1672. The governor of the Leewards again occupied it during the

Nine Years' War (1688–97) and forcibly resisted Danish efforts to expand from Saint Thomas. Into the 18th century, Tortola and the other British Virgins mainly served as bases for pirates and smugglers, and visitors described their people as lawless, immoral, and riotous. Although planters grew some cotton for export, the government in 1710 and 1735 rejected requests for a separate government. With the sugar boom of the 1750s, the white and slave population grew as cane plantations were introduced on Tortola. In 1773, the Crown finally conceded a representative assembly to the free-holders of Tortola, Spanish Town (Virgin Gorda), and Josh Vandyke. In return, the islanders granted the 4.5 percent export tax levied in the other Leeward islands.

Anguilla, north of Saint Martin (Sint Maarten), is flat and built of limestone. Like the Virgins, it receives little rainfall and is covered by spare dry woodlands. Because it is too arid for sugarcane, Anguilla's population lived from fishing and salt making. Already investigated by the Dutch in 1631, the salt ponds attracted British settlers after 1650. A few planters also grew tobacco and tried to make rum. As late as 1774, how-ever, fewer than 400 planters with some 2,000 slaves inhabited the island.

THE FRENCH IN THE LESSER ANTILLES

French pirates, who had long attacked Spanish shipping and cities, founded perma-nent camps from the early 1600s on Tortuga, Hispaniola, and several of the Lesser Antilles. In 1625, more peaceful colonists settled Saint Kitts, which until 1669 remained the political capital of the French Antilles. In 1635, colonists from Saint Kitts landed on Martinique, while another group from France settled Guadeloupe. From these first colonies, French settlers slowly spread south into the Windwards, and they also moved west to Hispaniola. Although both islands remained independent pirate kingdoms for a long period, French governors planted the flag on Tortuga in 1628 and on Hispaniola in the 1660s.

French and English colonization began at the same time, and both nations claimed many of the same islands. But the French colonies grew more slowly than the English. Until after 1713, the sugar industry on the French islands lagged behind that of the English partially because it lacked workers. As Table 5 indicates, the French sim-ply did not move to the islands in large numbers. Fewer indentured servants (known in French as *engagés*) went to Martinique or Guadeloupe than to Barbados, and the French also imported fewer slaves. In 1665, when the French and the Dutch went to war against the English, the latter outnumbered them by more than three to one.[3]

Like the English, the French colonies developed out of the piracy of the preced-ing century, and they similarly sought to profit from high tobacco prices. However, the first French colonies were not settled by individual merchant groups. They were cre-ated under state guidance by two powerful prime ministers, Richelieu in the 1620s and 1630s and Colbert in the 1660s. Richelieu believed that individual settlements needed protection, and the French government created several companies with monopolies in this region. However, these official companies proved to be economic failures. Since the companies could not provide either needed provisions or slaves, the colonists ignored their representatives. Instead they sold their tobacco and other prod-ucts to Dutch traders, who dominated Caribbean commerce during these years.

The first years were marked by economic hardship, political conflict, and even

Table 5. **POPULATION ESTIMATES FOR THE FRENCH ISLANDS, 1664–1699**

	Total	Whites	Slaves	Free Non-Whites
Martinique				
1664	15,401	2,681	12,704	16
1696	20,066	6,435	13,126	505
Guadeloupe				
1670	8,696	1,227	5,267	47
1699	10,111	3,687	6,076	349
Saint-Domingue				
1681	6,648	4,336	2,312	—

SOURCES: Orlando Patterson, *Slavery and Social Death: A Comparative Study* (Cambridge, Massachusetts: Harvard University Press, 1982), 480–81; Guy Lasserre, *La Guadeloupe: Etude géographique* (Bordeaux: Union Française d'Impression, 1961), 284.

civil wars. The governors ruling each island for the company tended to act as independent rulers. Often nobles of high rank with strong and dominating personalities, these governors frequently clashed with each other and with the less submissive colonists on their islands. During the 1650s, the French government simply gave up and sold the islands to their governors. In 1664, Colbert again imposed French control, and the islands for the first time became directly subject to the king.

Saint-Christophe

The small northern island of Saint Christopher/Saint-Christophe was the mother colony for both the French and the British. When the British captain Thomas Warner arrived on Saint Kitts in January 1624, he may have found a small French party already there. Early in 1625, these pioneers were joined by a pirate crew led by two Norman nobles, Urbain du Roissey and Pierre Bélain, sieur d' Esnambuc. Finding that Saint-Christophe produced excellent tobacco, Esnambuc decided to settle down and proved to be an energetic and popular leader. He returned to France with a valuable cargo and approached (through Roissey's relatives) the powerful cardinal de Richelieu. Impressed by Esnambuc, Richelieu created the Compagnie de Saint-Christophe, granting it a monopoly for 20 years over Saint Kitts, Barbados, and the neighboring islands.

Four ships carrying 500 passengers left Normandy in February 1627. On their arrival in May, Esnambuc and Thomas Warner—acting as representatives of their governments—divided Saint Kitts among the two parties. The first years proved difficult, and the Compagnie de Saint-Christophe soon ran out of funds. Most of the first colonists died, the French and English quarreled, and a Spanish fleet forced both groups to flee the island in October 1629.

This dismal beginning did not discourage Cardinal de Richelieu, who decided to expand the French colony to other islands. In February 1635, the Compagnie de Saint-Christophe was folded into a new and more powerful Compagnie des Isles d'Amerique. The Crown gave the new company both possession and full lordship over virtually all the Lesser Antilles. (Its possessions thus overlapped those granted to the earl of Carlisle in 1627.) In June 1635, some 500 men landed on Guadeloupe under the leadership of Charles Liénard, sieur de l'Olive. Esnambuc believed that l'Olive had stolen his plans. When he heard of the Guadeloupe expedition, he angrily led his own small group of 150 settlers to Martinique the following September.

Guadeloupe and Martinique

French settlers worked for decades to settle Martinique and Guadeloupe. Much larger in size than Saint Kitts, both had significant Carib populations, and both contain difficult terrain. Along the northern coast of Martinique, Mont Pelée rises more than 5,000 feet from steep hills. Still an active volcano, Pelée erupted in 1902, killing the 30,000 inhabitants of Saint-Pierre. Since it lies to the leeward of these high mountains, the plain covering the southern part of the island is arid. Given Martinique's harsh landscape, plantations developed slowly. However, Fort-de-France, built over a large enclosed bay on the leeward side of the island, soon became a major port. The first stop for French ships following the trade winds from Europe, it was from 1669 the seat of the governor-general and the political capital of the French Antilles.

Two separate islands, divided by the narrow Rivière Salée, make up Guadeloupe. The dividing line between the inner volcanic and the outer limestone arcs of the Lesser Antilles runs between these two islands, which thus offer totally different environments. The western island, called Basse-Terre, is mountainous with fertile soil and ample water. Running parallel to the west coast, a mountain ridge rises almost 5,000 feet. It is dominated by Mont Soufrière, a volcano that erupted in 1956 and is still unstable. By contrast, the eastern island, called Grande-Terre, is flat and arid with brackish water. The French under l'Olive soon moved to Basse-Terre, and sugarcane was not planted in Grande-Terre until the 18th century.

🐚 WHY SO MANY ISLANDS HAVE A TOWN NAMED BASSE-TERRE

Basse-Terre ("low land") seems an inappropriate name for the mountainous island making up the western half of Guadeloupe. French sailors used the word to mean "protected," and it is equivalent to the English "leeward." Thus all towns named Basse-Terre (Basseterre) are located on the inner or Caribbean coasts and often on the southern side of an island. In contrast, the first settlers gave the name Capesterre ("headland") to towns along the Atlantic or "windward" coast.

Internal Conflicts and Carib Wars

Civil wars and wars with the Carib devastated Guadeloupe and Martinique until the 1660s. On Guadeloupe, the Carib initially aided the French, providing them with food during their first nine months on the island. However, in January 1636, the governor attacked the Carib in order to steal their provision grounds (conucos). The resulting war lasted until June 1640, when a new governor defeated the Carib during a 30-hour battle. The colonists on Martinique also warred with the Carib, and the latter retired to their strongholds on Dominica and Saint Vincent. Reciprocal massacres continued until the French signed a peace treaty in 1660.

Political turmoil also disturbed the young colonies, with Guadeloupe especially torn by conflict. Under the charter of the Compagnie des Isles, the Crown named a governor-general over the governors of particular islands. A civil war now broke out between the two rivals for this office. In February 1638, the king appointed Philippe, sieur de Lonvilliers de Poincy, a captain in the royal navy and a high officer in the Knights of Malta. During the next 21 years, de Poincy proved to be a strong military leader, but he often acted for his own benefit. In 1645, he refused to step down when the Crown sent out a new governor-general. De Poincy won out only after two years of civil war, during which the governors on each island took sides.

The French Attack
the Carib in the Windwards

This period of anarchy and Dutch control of shipping contributed to the failure of the Compagnie des Isles d'Amerique during the 1640s. To regain their capital, the directors sold each of the islands to its governor, who became its proprietor and hereditary lord. In September 1649, Charles Houël purchased Guadeloupe and the smaller islands around it. The following September, Esnambuc's nephew, Jacques Dyel Du Parquet, bought Martinique as well as the company's claims over Saint Lucia, Grenada, and the Grenadines. Acting for the Knights of Malta, de Poincy in May 1651 acquired the French rights on Saint-Christophe and Saint-Martin (Sint Maarten) as well as the company's claims over Saint Croix, Saint Barthélemy, and Tortuga.

🌞 THE POINCIANA TREE,
FLAMING GLORY OF THE TROPICS

The royal poinciana (*Poinciana regia*) is among the world's most colorful trees with its great masses of blossoms in tones of scarlet or orange. This flamboyant (as it is often called in the Tropics) was introduced to the Caribbean from Madagascar. It is named in honor of Philippe de Poincy, royal governor of the French Antilles, because its flowers resemble the scarlet robe worn by de Poincy as a Knight of Malta.

The new proprietors aggressively extended the territories under their rule. De Poincy pushed north from Saint Kitts. At his direction, an expedition took Saint Barthélemy and another drove a small Spanish force from Saint Croix. Meanwhile, the lords of Martinique and Guadeloupe sought to drive the Carib out of the islands to the south. From Guadeloupe, Houël occupied the Saints and Marie Galante and in 1653 dispatched an expedition to Grenada. His troops massacred all the Carib on the island, 40 of whom jumped to their deaths from a cliff often called the Morne des Sauteurs (Leapers' Bluff).

In 1654, Du Parquet similarly dispatched a punitive expedition to Saint Vincent. To save this island—one of their last refuges—the entire Carib community mounted a concentrated attack. Those on Saint Lucia rose up and massacred the small French settlement, while some 2,000 warriors temporarily overran Martinique. Four years later, a new governor of Martinique organized a general slaughter of the Carib remaining on that island. In 1660, de Poincy and Houël finally signed a treaty—accepted by the British governors of Saint Kitts and Montserrat—reserving Dominica and Saint Vincent to the Carib. The small number of Carib left on these two islands generally remained at peace with the French, who sometimes instigated their raids on the British colonies.

The French Islands
Come under Royal Control

Independent rule by proprietors ended soon after 1661, when Louis XIV assumed power as king. Needing tax revenues to support his expensive European wars, Louis put the economy under the control of Jean-Baptiste Colbert, his finance minister. Colbert enacted laws—similar to the English Navigation Acts—that excluded foreign imports and encouraged French exports. For Colbert, the immediate threat was Dutch control of world trade, and he sought to increase his control over the French colonies. In his view, the colonies existed for, and were the exclusive property of, the home country. Their interests must be subordinated to those of France.

The situation in the West Indies was totally unsatisfactory to Colbert. Hundreds of Dutch ships visited the main port at Martinique each year, gathering up tobacco and sugar for sale in Amsterdam. Thus the colonies, which had been chartered and subsidized to make a profit for France, actually returned nothing to the home country. Colbert distrusted private enterprise and preferred large monopolistic companies under governmental regulation. In April 1664, the Crown chartered the Compagnie des Indes occidentales (West Indies Company)—based on the Dutch West India Company—and gave it a monopoly over all Atlantic shipping. The king also repurchased the rights of the existing proprietors and replaced them with royal governors.

The new company did succeed in taking over trade with the islands and in removing Dutch merchants through military action. However, it lost large sums of money during the Second Dutch War and through its own financial mismanagement. In 1670 Colbert opened West Indian commerce to all French nationals, while continuing to forbid entry to foreigners. In 1674, the Crown liquidated the overambitious company. The islands now became part of the royal domain, legally provinces of France itself.

France governed its colonies directly from Europe. French planters paid lower taxes than English colonists. But they also lacked the representative assemblies that made laws for many British islands. The French Ministry of the Marine appointed the military, administrative, and judicial officials for each colony. A governor supervised military affairs and the many courts, while an *intendant* controlled the civilian administration and finance. *Conseils supérieurs*—appointed by the governor—claimed the right to discuss and register laws. Saint-Domingue had two such *conseils,* reflecting the geographical divisions that effectively made it three colonies rather than one (see page

118). Not until 1788 did the French Crown create representative assemblies with limited powers for Martinique and Guadeloupe—but not for Saint-Domingue.

Although the islands were under direct royal rule, the government did not subordinate their interests to those of the homeland. In political and economic matters, the French Crown was less absolute than it liked to claim. In practice, the Crown had to balance the interests of organized groups at home (for example, sugar refiners and shippers) against the competing aims of planters and merchants on the islands. It could not impose its will by force and gave up trying to enforce unpopular laws. Caribbean planters often got their own way in commercial matters, and they largely controlled government on the islands themselves.

THE VIRGIN ISLANDS

Rising from the sea 40 miles east of Puerto Rico, a group of more than 100 small islands and cays represents the culmination of the mountain chains forming the Greater Antilles. All are relatively mountainous, and only Saint Croix has an extensive plain. Because of their small size, the Virgins are relatively dry or even semiarid, and droughts frequently cause serious water shortages.

In 1493 Columbus called the largest island Santa Cruz and named the northern group after Saint Ursula and the 11,000 virgins martyred at Cologne by the Huns. The Spanish left the Virgins uninhabited, and informal occupation by other Europeans began in about 1600. Pirates, privateers, and smugglers coming from Europe set up camps on several of the islands. Here they could obtain fresh water and food while planning expeditions to the major Spanish colonies in the Greater Antilles. The smaller islands remained pirate bases for a long time. But Saint Croix also attracted planters from the 1620s, and sugar plantations developed there and on Saint John during the 18th century. Saint Thomas is less fertile, but it has an excellent harbor and commands the Anegada Passage, a major channel between the Atlantic and the Caribbean. Thus it mainly served as a depot for Dutch and Danish traders carrying slaves from West Africa.

Saint Croix under the Dutch, British, and French

In about 1625. separate parties of British and Dutch planters occupied Saint Croix. The Dutch, governed by the West India Company, occupied the harbor at Christiansted, while the British took the southwestern shore, near Frederiksted. By 1645, the British settlers had driven out the Dutch, who migrated to Sint Maarten and Sint Eustatius. The Spanish authorities did not welcome a large British colony so close to San Juan, Puerto Rico. In August 1650, Spanish troops attacked and expelled the British.

De Poincy, the French governor at Saint Kitts, took advantage of this opportunity to add to his empire. He sent soldiers to expel the Spanish garrison, and he bought Saint Croix (as well as Saint Kitts) for the Knights of Malta in 1651. De Poincy spent large sums on the Saint Croix colony. However, the island proved unhealthy, and a drought burned up the cane fields. In 1696, Governor Bertrand d'Ogeron de la Rivière evacuated the remaining inhabitants and resettled them in his colony at Saint-

Domingue. The French abandoned their claim to the island in 1713, and its ownership reverted to the Knights of Malta. In 1733, the latter sold it to the Danish West India Company, which already occupied Saint Thomas.

The Danish West India Company

Dutch planters unsuccessfully tried to settle Saint Thomas from the 1640s onward. Permanent occupation began under the Danish West India and Guinea Company, chartered by Christian V of Denmark-Norway in 1671. This venture was modeled after the Dutch West India Company and was given broad powers in Africa and the Americas. Its sponsors believed they could gain substantial profits by carrying slaves to Saint Thomas for resale throughout the West Indies.

Like the Dutch, the Danish company functioned as a commercial venture and attracted few European immigrants. Few Danes ever came to the Americas, and the Danish islands economically formed part of the Dutch Empire. From 1685 to 1718, Denmark also allowed an Africa company chartered by the duke of Brandenburg-Prussia to sell slaves on Saint Thomas.

Like its Dutch and French rivals, the Danish West India Company rarely made a profit, and it went out of business in 1754. Except for the slave trade, the company gave up its monopoly rights at Saint Thomas in 1724, permitting ships of all nations to trade there on payment of small export and import taxes. Since this era, Saint

Table 6. **DANISH VIRGIN ISLANDS POPULATION ESTIMATES, 1686–1835**

	Total	Whites	Slaves	Free Non-Whites
Saint Thomas				
1686	633	300	333	—
1720	4,752	565	4,187	—
1775	—	—	3,979	500
1803	—	—	5,968	—
1835	14,022	3,520	5,298	5,204
Saint Croix				
1742	2,080	174	1,906	—
1755	10,220	1,323	8,897	—
1792	—	—	22,420	—
1803	—	—	27,161	—
1835	26,681	1,892	19,876	4,913
Saint John				
1728	800	123	677	—
1739	1,622	208	1,414	—
1787	2,383	167	2,200	16
1803	—	—	2,598	—
1835	2,475	344	1,929	202

SOURCES: Paterson, *Slavery and Social Death*, 482; William Boyers, *America's Virgin Islands: A History of Human Rights and Wrongs* (Durham, North Carolina: Carolina Academic Press, 1983), 40, 48, 53 (1835).

Thomas has been described as a "free port." (Saint Croix received the same privileges in 1831.) Ten years later, the company also opened the slave trade to all Danish subjects in the West Indies. Nevertheless, its losses continued, and the Danish king purchased all of the shares held by private investors in 1754. The three islands became Crown colonies, directly subject to royal governors.

Although the company itself failed, the islands developed as major sugar producers. Cane and cotton plantations developed from the 1680s on Saint Thomas. To encourage their expansion, the company settled Saint John in 1717 and Saint Croix in 1735, offering tax exemptions and subsidies to attract planters. The sugar industry rapidly developed on both islands and prospered throughout the 18th century. By the 1830s, a few hundred planters—most not Danish—controlled several thousand slaves.

From the beginning, merchants at Saint Thomas welcomed ships of all nations. Its excellent harbor soon served as a refuge both for merchant ships chased by pirates and for corsairs selling their loot. Collusion with pirates was most obvious during the 1680s. Buccaneers chased from Jamaica by a reforming governor sought new havens to the north. They received a warm welcome from Adolph Esmit, who seized the governorship from his brother in the autumn of 1682. Esmit's obvious collusion with buccaneers caused an international incident the following year. The governor refused to turn over a pirate ship to a British man-of-war and even fired a cannon at the British ship. Subsequent Danish governors were less blatant in their support, but buccaneers continued to call on Saint Thomas for several decades.

CHAPTER 7

THE BUCCANEERS OF JAMAICA, SAINT-DOMINGUE, AND THE BAHAMAS

French, English, and Dutch companies planted commercial colonies on several of the Lesser Antilles during the 1620s and 1630s. From 1655, northern Europeans moved west into the Greater Antilles. Here the British conquered Jamaica, while the French occupied the western third of Hispaniola, which they renamed Saint-Domingue. In contrast to Barbados, Hispaniola and Jamaica prospered through piracy rather than by growing sugar. Initially settled by buccaneers, these islands remained pirate havens until almost 1700, attracting thousands of men who chose a life of adventure over drudgery on the sugar plantations of Barbados or Martinique.

Jamaica and Hispaniola were ideally located to be centers of piracy. Port Royal in Jamaica, with its strategic location in the center of the Caribbean Sea, provided a perfect base for strikes against Spanish shipping and raids on ports in Cuba and Central America that guarded the Spanish treasure fleets. The northwestern coast of Hispaniola and the island of Tortuga are situated between two straits—the Windward Passage and the Mona Passage—that carry merchant shipping from Europe or North America into the Caribbean.

Until the 1690s, pirates openly operated out of a series of havens, first out of Tortuga and Hispaniola and then, after 1655, from Port Royal in Jamaica. After they were chased from these bases, many carried on their trade from the Bahamas during the following century. All of these pirates traditionally are known as buccaneers. Strictly speaking this name is not accurate. It initially referred to groups of men who caught the wild cattle and hogs that were abundant on both islands. However, British settlers expanded the meaning of *buccaneer* during the 1660s, and it is now used to refer to any pirates based in the Caribbean rather than in Europe.

🔥 THE BUCCANEERS—FROM HAITIAN COWBOYS TO SEA-ROBBERS

Pirates cruising from Caribbean havens are known as *buccaneers.* Derived from the French *boucanier* ("barbecuer"), this word originally referred to cattle hunters who illegally camped in western Hispaniola (modern Haiti). According to a colorful legend, the hunters gained their name from the special type of grill, or *boucan,* on which beef was smoked to preserve it for sale or for later use. (The hunters borrowed the word as well as the method from the local Indians. Spanish colonists called the same smoking process *barbacoa,* and it is the Spanish word that has passed into English as *barbecue.*)

After they occupied Jamaica, English settlers began to use *buccaneer* to refer to pirates operating from Port Royal as well as Tortuga Island and Hispaniola. The name was universally adopted after 1684, when Alexander Exquemelin's best-selling pirate tales were translated into English as *The Bucaniers of America.* There is a certain logic to using the same name for the hunters and the pirates. While some pirates were never hunters, many hunters practiced piracy at one time or another. Nevertheless, other languages continue to reserve "buccaneer" for the Hispaniola hunters. French authors call the Caribbean pirates *flibustiers* ("freebooters"), the Dutch refer to them as *Zee-roovers* (sea rovers), and the Spanish prefer *corsarios* (corsairs).

THE BUCCANEERS ON HISPANIOLA

The natural environment of Hispaniola and Jamaica also made these islands ideal pirate bases—while hampering governmental control and the development of plantations. Rugged mountains and hills cover both islands. These mountain chains run more or less from west to east, hindering transportation and communications across the islands from north to south. Although long stretches of their coasts are hazardous to shipping, landings are possible in many locations. Governments based on the coasts could not control the fertile central valleys, which provided a haven for pirates and for runaway slaves. Because of their mountainous terrain, both islands receive abundant water. Dense forests of tropical hardwood trees initially covered the fertile sections, and it took planters decades to cut down these woodlands and plant cash crops such as sugar.

The climate of the islands provides cattle and pigs with a favorable climate, plenty of food, and no natural predators. As early as the 1530s, escaped or freed animals had multiplied into vast herds covering Cuba, Jamaica, and Hispaniola. Around 1600, many Spanish colonists made their living from these wild cattle and hogs, selling their hides, meat, and fat to French or Dutch smugglers and pirates. To stop this illegal industry, the governor of Santo Domingo burned the homes of the settlers in northwestern Hispaniola and ordered them to move to Santo Domingo (see page 43).

This evacuation program of 1605 backfired against the Spanish government. The illegal hide trade continued, and the now empty land soon began to draw outsiders. Presumably some of the Spanish cattle-hunters escaped the 1605 roundup, and they soon were joined by free spirits and beachcombers of many nations and races. Hunting bands and settlements maintained themselves through the hide trade on Hispaniola until well into the 1670s.

At some time, perhaps long before 1600, the island of Tortuga—far removed from the main Spanish port of Santo Domingo—became a stopover for smugglers and pirates. A multinational settlement developed that was perhaps the earliest independent European community in the new world, owing allegiance to no king and trading with every nation. In the 1630s, it gained strength through a curious alliance with the leaders of the Puritan party opposing the royal government in England.

PURITAN PIRATES ON PROVIDENCE ISLAND

While the first British colonists struggled to survive on Saint Kitts and Barbados, another and more daring group entered the western Caribbean, the heart of the Spanish Empire. Chartered by the Crown in 1630 and sponsored by the principal Puritan politicians of England, the Providence Company planted settlements on three islands. Toward the end of May 1631, its men established bases on Providence (Santa Catalina) and Henrietta (San Andreas), less than 250 miles from the strategic town of Porto Bello. In the same year, it extended its claims to include Tortuga Island and sent Anthony Hilton to act as its governor. Hilton, a persuasive rogue who founded the first colony on Nevis in 1628, had been chased away by the Spanish the following year, leaving behind large debts in Saint Kitts.

The company advertised its intention to create a godly commonwealth such as the one in Massachusetts. But both of its colonies—well placed to harass the Spanish but badly located to trade with other British settlements—devoted themselves to piracy. Some settlers on Providence and Tortuga did try farming. Since they sold their hides and tobacco to Dutch traders, the Providence Company did not receive a return on its investment. The company wholeheartedly endorsed piracy after suffering Spanish raids on Providence and Tortuga in 1635. The settlers on Providence drove off a Spanish fleet, and the colony survived for another six years. But Spanish forces quickly overran Tortuga, hanged the male residents, deported the women and children, and razed the settlement. Although the Spanish troops soon departed, the Providence Company abandoned Tortuga. But the pirates, once again without any ties to a European government, soon drifted back to the island.

In reprisal for these Spanish attacks, the king granted the Providence Company the power to commission privateers. Piracy, long secretly practiced from Providence, now became the company's main purpose. Goaded by increasing attacks on Spanish ships and cities, the governor of Cartagena launched a larger and more carefully planned attack that occupied Providence in May 1641 and carried its male residents to captivity in Spain.

The Providence Company went bust and abandoned both Providence and Tortuga, but it continued to issue privateering commissions for some years. In July 1642, Captain William Jackson, armed with letters of reprisal, sailed from England with three ships and recruited four more at Barbados. For the next three years, Jackson's fleet cruised the Caribbean, plundering several cities. In 1643, his forces easily seized Villa de la Vega (presently known as Spanish Town), the principal settlement on Jamaica. Jackson extracted from it a miserable ransom of only 7,000 pieces of eight. But the island was fruitful, and Jackson's men liked it so much that many of them deserted and remained with the Spaniards after the fleet sailed. Moreover, Jackson's account of his raids, which stressed Spanish weakness, helped to persuade Oliver Cromwell to launch the 1655 campaign that added Jamaica to the English dominions in the West Indies.

THE WESTERN DESIGN AND JAMAICA

The English conquest of Jamaica in 1655 was the one result of a failed campaign to capture the entire Caribbean from Spain. England itself was torn by a civil war from 1642 to 1649 between supporters of King Charles I and various factions associated with Parliament. Ultimately the army seized power under the leadership of Oliver Cromwell, who executed the king in 1649 and ruled supreme until his death in 1658. Cromwell's government sought both to expand abroad and to bring the English dominions under one centralized rule. It conquered Ireland in 1649 and Scotland in 1650, sending captives to the Caribbean colonies as indentured servants. In 1651, it sent a fleet to bring the existing English colonies in Barbados and the Leewards under its control, and it passed the Navigation Act to prevent their trading with the Dutch. Until that time, the planting of colonies had been almost entirely a matter of private initiative. But from then on, trade and national finance became dominant considerations, and settlement concerned the nation's government as well as individual merchants.

In 1654, Cromwell's government and his ministers conceived a grandiose scheme called the Western Design. Convinced of Spanish weakness, they sought to take over the entire Caribbean, even though the two nations were then at peace. The government hurriedly assembled a fleet and an army of 2,500 men, placing them under the command of Admiral William Penn—father of the founder of Pennsylvania—and General Robert Venables.

Late in January 1655, the expedition arrived in Barbados. There its commanders spent 10 weeks recruiting additional soldiers, including perhaps 3,500 men from Barbados and at least 1,200 more from Saint Kitts, Nevis, and Montserrat. Having decided to make Hispaniola their first target, the commanders besieged Santo Domingo. Although the British forces outnumbered the city's defenders at least 10 to one, they were hopelessly defeated. In all, the army made two attempts to reach Santo Domingo. But the landings had been made 40 miles from it, and the walls were never reached. The untrained and undisciplined soldiers taking part in this disastrous campaign lacked food, weapons, and medicine. Moreover, Penn and Venables—who were not on good terms—frequently quarreled, and the fleet took little part in the siege.

The British commanders feared Cromwell's wrath if they returned without a prize. They thus decided to turn against Jamaica, which they knew to be thinly populated and weakly garrisoned. On May 10, 1655, 38 vessels with some 6,000 men cast anchor at Passage Fort, at the western end of the present Kingston Harbor. Opposition was useless, and the invaders easily took the small Spanish forts. The British allowed the Spanish colonists to leave the island but confiscated their lands and all of their possessions. General Venables gave the governor a week to consider these terms of surrender. Led by Cristóbal Arnaldo de Ysassi, many Spaniards instead freed their own slaves and fled north to the mountains. There the Spanish colonists held out for five years while they waited for reinforcements from Cuba and Mexico.

In their fierce resistance, the Spanish formed an alliance with escaped slaves, who controlled the region northeast of Spanish Town, still called Juan de Bolas after one of their chiefs. On June 27, 1658, a new British governor, Edward d'Oyley, finally defeated an invading Spanish army in a pitched battle near Río Nuevo—east of Saint Ann's Bay on the northern coast. The former Spanish governor held out for two more years in the mountains until Juan de Bolas went over to the British side. In May 1660, the last Spaniards sailed away to Cuba, according to tradition, from a pleasant beach at Runaway Bay. However, a small number of slaves (called *Maroons*) retained their independence, making their new headquarters at Nanny Town on the northern slopes of the Blue Mountains.

THE BRITISH SETTLEMENT OF JAMAICA

During the 1700s, Jamaica became an immensely wealthy producer of sugar. During the first 30 years under the English flag, however, it was a second Tortuga, offering hospitality to generations of pirates drawn from Europe and throughout the Caribbean. Despite the government's efforts to promote agricultural development, few acres were cleared and put under cultivation during the 17th century. Establishing a sugar plantation required large amounts of capital and labor, and most of the first settlers had little money and few slaves. Thus there really were two Jamaicas from 1655 to 1689—an agricultural colony of small farms and cattle ranches and the wealthy buccaneer capital of Port Royal.

The proprietary system used to plant Barbados and the Leewards now was discredited. Cromwell's government ruled Jamaica under martial law, and Charles II (after the Restoration in 1660) retained the island as a Crown property. Both governments sought to develop the island as a source of tropical products. They encouraged white settlement by guaranteeing settlers British citizenship and by offering generous grants of land. Under Sir Thomas Modyford, governor from 1664 to 1673, most of the best

Table 7. **JAMAICA POPULATION ESTIMATES, 1661–1673**

	Total	**Whites**	**Slaves**
1661	3,470	2,956	514
1673	17,272	7,768	9,504

SOURCE: Dunn, *Sugar and Slaves*, 155.

farmland along the south-central coast was distributed, much of it in large allotments.

Despite the government's offers, the population of Jamaica grew very slowly during the 17th century. (See Table 7.) Due to the introduction of tropical diseases such as malaria, Jamaica was an unhealthy place during these years. In addition to soldiers and settlers from England, many white servants and poor planters from overcrowded Barbados and the Leewards moved to Jamaica, searching for better opportunities on a bigger island. Most died during their first year of residence. The mortality rate among the soldiers was very high, and immigrants from other islands fared little better.

Altogether, perhaps 12,000 white settlers came to British Jamaica during its first six years, but the population in 1661 was only 3,470. It increased more rapidly under the Modyford administration but fell again toward the end of the century. The earthquake of 1692 damaged the entire island and wiped out Port Royal. A severe malaria epidemic took many lives, and a French invasion almost captured the island in 1694.

Jamaican planters had only begun to clear the thick tropical forests by 1713, when a general European peace finally allowed agriculture to take off. The first 60 years proved to be a harsh winnowing process. Only a few of the men arriving during the first decades survived. But those that did endure founded dynasties that became immensely wealthy during the 18th century. As on Barbados, as the number of white settlers shrank, the survivors took over their property and imported African slaves. Few white servants wanted to go to Jamaica, and black slaves outnumbered their masters almost seven to one by 1700. Most of the best land henceforth was held in very large estates. The gulf between large and small planters had grown very large, and the chief sugar planters dominated local offices. Most of their property still lay fallow, and sugar production remained low until the 1720s. However, the stage had been set for the rapid development of a classic plantation society during the 18th century.

Jamaica's Planters Gain Control Over Local Government

During the Restoration period (1661–89), the Jamaican planters succeeded in gaining control over local taxation as well as the power to initiate laws regulating property and slavery. As in Barbados and the Leewards (and later in British America), the planters took British government as their model. Thus they claimed for their assembly the same powers enjoyed by the British House of Commons. Since the West Indian colonies were regarded as Crown property, they were not immediately subject to the Parliament in England. The Crown delegated administrative and military authority to a royal governor. The king also appointed the judges and the governor's council, generally on the governor's recommendation.

Planters in all the colonies opposed the Navigation Acts and the Royal Africa Company's monopoly over slave imports. But the major constitutional issues came down to control of taxation for local defense and the general purposes of administration. In Jamaica, several governors gained temporary control by manipulating conflicts between the planters and the buccaneers, Nevertheless, the planters ultimately won on the main point and did not grant a permanent revenue to the king.

The commission issued to the first royal governor in 1661 permitted him to convoke an assembly. The first elections were held two years later, beginning the assembly's often stormy career that lasted until its suppression in 1866. Under the royal instructions, it could initiate laws for the colony, but such laws had to be approved within two years by the Crown as well as by the governor and council. For the next 28 years, a series of governors struggled to control the assembly. The main issue was the grant of a permanent revenue to the Crown similar to the 4.5 percent export duty in Barbados and the Lesser Antilles. A compromise was reached in 1689, when the Glorious Revolution brought William II to the throne of England. The new government, which needed the Jamaica customs revenue, confirmed the constitution as it existed in 1661. For the next two centuries, the large planters controlled local taxation and largely governed the island according to their own views.

THE BAHAMAS

The Bahamas group was uninhabited after the Arawak died out in the 1520s, victims of Spanish slaving expeditions and disease. Its many islands and cays first were settled by Bermudians, fleeing religious conflicts during the British Civil War. During the 1640s, Bermudians belonging to the Puritan faction planted the first permanent colony in the Bahamas, and the two groups of Atlantic islands remained closely associated until the Bahamas became a pirate haven in the 1680s.

British sailors stranded by a hurricane had landed on Bermuda in 1609, and the Crown granted the island to the Somers Islands Company in 1615. The small island enjoyed a short period of prosperity based on tobacco and fishing, and its population grew to more than 2,000 by the 1620s. As in Barbados, conflicts between the proprietors and settlers marked Bermuda's early years. The Somers Company was controlled by the earl of Warwick and other men with Puritan views, who preferred colonists of their own persuasion. But the majority of the islanders, who apparently supported the Royalist and Anglican cause, sought independence from the company's rule. In 1632 the Somers Company appointed Captain Philip Bell, previously governor of Bermuda, as governor of their new colony on Providence Island. Bell led about 100 Bermudians to the Bahamas. (After the Spanish closed down Providence in 1641, Bell became the governor of Barbados.)

Puritans continued to form a minority in Bermuda after the outbreak of the Civil War in 1642, and members of that sect made several attempts to settle in the Bahamas. In 1647, Captain William Sayle, a moderate Puritan, traveled to London, where he founded the Company of Eleutherian Adventurers. Although it never actually received a charter, the company enjoyed support at high levels and wrote an elaborate constitution. The following year, Sayle led some 80 adventurers from Bermuda and founded a settlement, probably at Spanish Wells.

Plantation crops do not flourish in the arid climate and thin soil of the Bahamas. Sayle's colony was not a success, and only a few settlers remained at Eleuthera, eking out a miserable livelihood from occasional shipwrecks. Tiny communities also may have existed at Exuma, Inagua, and in the Turks and Caicos, part of the Bahamas until 1848. As Bermuda continued to be overcrowded, other expeditions ventured into the Bahamas. About 1666, one of these groups colonized Sayle's Island, renaming it New Providence in memory of the Puritan colony destroyed in 1641. By 1671, New Providence had become home to 900 settlers, who established an assembly and asked Jamaica to confirm their choice as governor.

Agriculture never has prospered in the Bahamas. But the islands are strategically placed next to both the Windward Passage and the Florida Strait leading to the Gulf of Mexico. Thus New Providence soon became a major center for British pirates. In 1670, Charles II, ignoring previous grants, gave the Bahamas to six of his Lords Proprietors of Carolina. If the settlers looked to their new lords for aid, the latter sent them only a succession of incompetent, corrupt, and ineffectual governors. From the 1670s, when the government of Jamaica tried to curb the pirates of Port Royal, the proprietary governors of the Bahamas happily sold the buccaneers commissions as privateers.

In 1684, Spanish forces retaliated by attacking New Providence and sacking the main settlement (called Nassau from 1695). Some of its inhabitants returned in 1686, and the island once again became a pirate haven. Particularly after the outbreak of war with France in 1689, British pirates based at Tortuga reestablished themselves in the Bahamas. Its inhabitants welcomed the buccaneers' trade, and several of the proprietary governors openly helped them. Not until 1718 was a serious effort made to suppress their activities.

PIRATE SOCIETY IN THE CARIBBEAN

For the next 50 years, hungry, adventurous, or criminal men from the established colonies in the Lesser Antilles constantly replenished the pirate bands. Failed planters, disgruntled former servants, runaway black slaves, petty criminals, and religious and political malcontents all drifted north and west to the thinly populated islands of Puerto Rico, Hispaniola, and Jamaica. A party of men merely had to find a boat and follow the prevailing winds and currents. When they arrived at the larger islands they found these inhabited mainly by enormous herds of wild cattle descended from the flocks abandoned by the Spanish in the 1530s and 1540s. Some joined the cow hunters who made their living by selling smoked meat and hides to passing ships. Others turned to piracy, using small boats against Spanish merchant and treasure ships sailing past their coast.

The Pirate Kingdom of Tortuga

Many hardened pirates gathered on the island of Tortuga, which remained virtually an independent pirate kingdom until the end of the 17th century. After the Spanish destroyed the Providence Company's Tortuga settlement in 1635, British and French buccaneers soon returned to the island, from which they attacked merchant ships of many nations. But the two groups quarreled, and the French on Tortuga asked de Poincy (the French governor-general at Saint Kitts) to send them a governor.

In response, de Poincy sent 50 Huguenots and other troublesome settlers under the command of Jean Le Vasseur in 1642[2]. A Norman nobleman and a professional military engineer, Le Vasseur forced his followers to construct an impregnable fortress or citadel on the summit of a steep crag. From this citadel armed with two dozen cannon, Le Vasseur defied his French patron and beat off repeated Spanish attacks. Ruling as a cruel and greedy king over the buccaneers, Le Vasseur collected a share of their plunder and taxed the hides brought into Tortuga from Hispaniola. For a dozen years, he reigned in barbaric splendor. Finally, in 1653, he was killed by a treacherous lieutenant, whose mistress he had appropriated.

Le Vasseur's death did not end pirate control over Tortuga. A Spanish force in January 1654 defeated the new governor sent by de Poincy. However, with the approach of Cromwell's fleet in 1655, the Spanish deported the French and withdrew their own troops back to defend Santo Domingo. As soon as the coast was clear, the buccaneers poured back in greater strength than before.

D'Ogeron in Saint-Domingue

For the next 10 years, the French and the British, now occupying Jamaica, continued to dispute control of Tortuga. Beginning in 1665, Tortuga and the western third of Santo Domingo were brought under the French flag by Bertrand d'Ogeron de la Rivière. As governor for the new French West Indies Company, d'Ogeron's instructions ordered him to impose some order at Tortuga and settle farmers along the western coast of Hispaniola. During the next 10 years, d'Ogeron skillfully accomplished both of these goals.

Since they formed the colony's only defense, d'Ogeron could not expel the buccaneers. Instead he transferred those on the mainland to Tortuga. Through his energetic efforts—and sometimes at his own expense—d'Ogeron replaced the pirates with more peaceful colonists from France. By 1681, perhaps four thousand settlers lived on the French section, centered around the town of Port-de-Paix, opposite Tortuga. (See Table 5, page 78.) The small Spanish colony still living in the eastern half of Hispaniola could hardly challenge their possession, especially as the mountainous central part of the island separated the two groups.

As on other islands, tobacco initially formed the main cash crop on Saint-Domingue. The government encouraged sugar planting after 1697, when the Treaty of Ryswick tacitly recognized French occupation. The industry took off after 1713, when slaves became available through Jamaica. Saint-Domingue then underwent a spectacular boom, as planters created hundreds of sugar estates on its virgin soil. By 1740, these estates produced more sugar than all the British islands taken together.

D'Ogeron and his successors were less successful in controlling the pirates of Tortuga. Henceforth, these were primarily French in nationality and generally did not seize French shipping bound for Saint-Domingue. But their raids against Spanish and British shipping actually increased during d'Ogeron's administration. The Tortuga buccaneers of the 1660s and 1670s—men such as François l'Ollonais and Michel le Basque—are still famed for their daring and their cruelty.

The Buccaneers Come to Port Royal

In 1657, Governor d'Oyley, seeking help against the Spanish, invited the British buccaneers at Tortuga to transfer their headquarters to Jamaica. Spanish settlers soon were thrown off the island. The buccaneers remained for decades. By 1665, more than 2,000 buccaneers regularly sailed in a dozen large ships from Port Royal, a small spit of land at the south of Kingston Harbor. Most were desperate men, accustomed to living at sea and with no trade save burning and plundering. Electing their own captains, they followed men—such as Henry Morgan—whose missions promised enormous rewards. They obeyed royal laws only when these were backed by stronger and faster frigates.

On his restoration in 1660, Charles II officially ended the war against Spain begun by Cromwell in 1655. But violence continued to rage "beyond the line" in the Indies. In naming Sir Thomas Modyford governor of Jamaica in 1664, the king instructed him to control piracy and forbade him to commission privateers. Nevertheless, pirates openly flourished at Port Royal during the next two decades. Governor Modyford and other Jamaicans shared in their profits. Prominent merchants bought whatever the pirates brought in, and planters belonging to the island's assembly and governor's council sponsored their voyages.

Jamaica also depended on the pirates for protection against foreign enemies. In times of war, the buccaneers, licensed as privateers, were the only available defense against enemy attack. Neither the French in Tortuga nor the British in Port Royal could suppress their own pirates unless they could be sure that the other side would do the same. During the Anglo-Dutch Wars (1652–74), it would have been simple for the pirates to find a new base in Dutch Curaçao. Piracy could not be suppressed until all nations turned against it. But that did not happen until the end of the 1720s.

CHAPTER 8

WAR AND PIRACY, 1665–1720

The Second Dutch War (1665–67) marked the end of one era in Caribbean history and the beginning of another. Until that point, northern Europeans generally had worked together to plunder the Spanish possessions in the Caribbean. From 1665 to 1815, England and France fought a long series of wars to gain colonies and to control world trade. The Spanish Empire, now terminally weakened, often sat out most of these conflicts but still suffered from the pirate raids that accompanied them.

Both Britain and France placed a high value on the Caribbean islands, and they sent large naval fleets and soldiers from Europe to attack each other's colonies. During these almost constant wars, several of the islands were conquered and reconquered many times—only to be restored to their original owners at the final peace conference. These were true world wars, and the islands were only one chip in a massive poker game played for high stakes. They often were traded back for gains on other continents.

For islanders, the wars between 1665 and 1713 were almost wholly destructive. Both French and British colonists took advantage of them to destroy rival sugar producers. They were especially eager to steal slaves from the enemy, and these wars often resembled nothing more than enormous reciprocal slave raids. Moreover, this half-century of international war provided an environment in which piracy flourished. Neither Britain nor France could keep a navy permanently in the islands. Both used the pirates during times of war. When peace came they found it impossible to disband their now unwanted allies, who continued to pillage the sea-lanes. Until the 1720s, there were two parallel societies in the Caribbean. Planters, merchants, and slaves peacefully grew sugar and other tropical products for sale in Europe. The buccaneers attacked the ships connecting the islands to Europe and bringing slaves from Africa.

THE SECOND DUTCH WAR, 1665–1667

In contrast to modern wars, the Second Dutch War was purely a commercial struggle, instigated by English merchants suffering from Dutch competition and monopoly. Hostilities began in West Africa, where English forces in 1663 captured most Dutch strongholds along the slave coast. In retaliation, the Dutch dispatched a fleet under one of their greatest admirals, Michel de Ruyter. De Ruyter retook the forts and brought his fleet across the Atlantic early in 1665. There he attacked English merchant ships off Barbados, Nevis, and Montserrat, effectively destroying that season's export crops.

From Jamaica, Governor Thomas Modyford suggested that the government turn the Port Royal buccaneers against the Dutch naval bases in the region. The Crown agreed that Modyford should use the pirates "to dispossess the Dutch from Curaçao and their other plantations." This, the first inter-island war, began with a pirate raid against Sint Eustatius, Saba, and Curaçao. Modyford gave a privateer's commission to Edward Morgan, uncle of the more famous Henry Morgan, who gathered 10 ships and 500 pirates. Morgan promised them their pay in plunder, and the king provided only gunpowder and shells. In the event, however, the pirates were unreliable allies, who preferred not to fight regular troops.

Morgan's fleet easily defeated the small garrison guarding Dutch slave pens on Sint Eustatius and Saba. Meanwhile another group of Jamaican pirates looted the Dutch settlements on Tobago. However, the pirate crews refused to go on to Curaçao, which they knew to be more heavily armed. The English sent out a second privateer fleet in January 1666 under Edward Mansfield and Henry Morgan, both of whom later became notorious pirate chiefs. Again, the crew choose not to take on the Dutch forts at Curaçao. Instead they turned south against the weaker Spanish, looting Providence Island and the colonies along the coasts of Honduras and Mexico.

French Troops Pillage the Leeward Islands

The war began with quick English victories, but the Dutch soon gained their revenge through their French allies. Dutch privateers attacked English shipping throughout the region, while French pirates raided the coast of Barbados. The French colonists also seized the English part of Saint Kitts, which the two nations had shared since 1627. The English governor of Saint Kitts had brought over militia from Nevis and also hired some of the buccaneers from Sint Eustatius. Fearing these preparations, the French in April 1666 decided to strike first and soon forced humiliating terms of surrender on the English. English plantations were devastated, more than 8,000 planters _eft with their slaves, and the rest took an oath of allegiance to the French Crown. In July 1666 a hurricane off Martinique sank most of the eight English ships carrying 1,000 men sent from Barbados to retake the island.

The French and English governments now sent men-of-war from Europe to aid their colonies. Local forces supported by regular French troops took Antigua and Montserrat in December 1666 and in February 1667. On both islands, many indentured servants—primarily Irish Catholics—aided the invaders. On Antigua, the French were also assisted by Carib from Guadeloupe, Dominica, and Saint Vincent. The war ravaged plantations on both islands, and the French seized hundreds of slaves. Only Nevis escaped, and it took in the white refugees from neighboring islands. The tide of battle turned in May 1667, when a fleet from England defeated a mixed Dutch-French armada off Nevis. The English soon recaptured Antigua and Montserrat, but they could not take the strongly fortified French positions in Saint Kitts.

The Treaty of Breda (1667) restored all colonies to their previous owners with one exception: Tobago passed from the Netherlands to France. Nevertheless, the war is significant because it set the boundaries between the French and English colonies until 1763. It also marked the end of Dutch ambitions in the region. The war proved a mortal blow to the Dutch West India Company, and the English and French now rigidly enforced restrictions against Dutch traders.

In the Caribbean, the Second Dutch War seriously disrupted economic growth, ended a century of Anglo-French cooperation, and fostered piracy. All the islands suffered from the disruption of trade and heavy taxation, and several English colonies had been ruined. The French did not hand back Saint Kitts until 1671, and they kept the captured slaves and other war booty. The English had to rebuild Saint Kitts from scratch, and Antigua had been devastated from end to end. The material damage could be repaired. However, the violence of the fighting in the Leewards left behind lasting bitterness, creating a tradition of antipathy between French and English colonists.

Henry Morgan and the Port Royal Buccaneers

During the 1660s and 1670s, thousands of pirates made their homes at Port Royal and Tortuga, with smaller groups operating out of other bases, such as Saint Croix, the Virgin Islands, and Curaçao.[1] The French and English governments had recognized the buccaneers by granting them commissions during the Second Dutch War. After the war ended, they went back to attacking Spanish shipping and ports. Of all the pirates, the most infamous was the Briton Henry Morgan, who led three notorious raids between 1667 and 1671.

During the Second Dutch War, Morgan commanded a ship in the 1666 expedition that took Providence Island. When the Spanish captured and killed Mansfield shortly afterward, the buccaneers elected Morgan as their "admiral." The next year, fearing an invasion from Cuba, Governor Modyford commissioned Morgan to capture Spanish prisoners. Collecting 10 ships with 500 to 700 men, he pillaged Puerto Principe in Cuba and then turned against the Spanish Main. There Morgan took by storm the fortified and well-garrisoned town of Porto Bello and held it for 31 days against successive attacks. Seeing that his forces could not drive out Morgan's men, the governor of Panama agreed to an enormous ransom of more than 100,000 pounds.

The Porto Bello raid obviously exceeded the terms of Morgan's commission. And the buccaneers under his command acted with horrible cruelty, torturing their prisoners to discover where they had hidden their treasures. Nevertheless, Modyford soon commissioned him to lead another expedition against Cuba. In January 1669, Morgan almost lost his life when the pirates on board accidentally blew up his flagship during a drunken party. Escaping with most of his officers, Morgan nevertheless sacked the Cuban towns of Maracaibo and Gibraltar, destroyed three Spanish ships waiting to intercept him, recovered a considerable treasure, and again exacted a heavy ransom from the Spanish authorities.

Henry Morgan Sacks Panama

For his third and final raid in 1670–71, Morgan assembled about 2,000 buccaneers in 36 ships and again turned them against Panama. Recapturing Providence Island, he then seized the castle at the mouth of the Chagres River, slaughtering its garrison of 300 men. With some 1,400 buccaneers, he ascended the Chagres over difficult terrain. Appearing before Panama in January 1671, Morgan again defeated a much larger force than his own and took the city.

However, Morgan's behavior after the battles somewhat tarnished the glory of this victory. Morgan's men sacked Panama, torturing and slaughtering its inhabitants. While the buccaneers enjoyed drunken orgies, the captain and crew of a Spanish galleon escaped and sailed away with much of the captured loot. Enough remained to enrich all the participants. But, on returning to Chagres, Morgan cheated the other members of the expedition out of their fair share. Morgan escaped with a few ships to Jamaica, leaving the rest to find their own way home.

In July 1670, England and Spain signed the Treaty of Madrid. For the first time Spain officially recognized British holdings in the Caribbean, and both nations agreed to prohibit piracy against the other. Since Morgan had raided Panama after the signing of this treaty, the British arrested him and Governor Modyford, taking them to London. There Morgan gained the favor of Charles II, who knighted him in 1674 and sent him back to Jamaica as lieutenant governor. Morgan was now 39, immensely rich, and the owner of a plantation of 6,000 acres. He spent the next 14 years in drunken idleness. By his death in 1688—ousted from his offices for incoherence—he was so immensely fat that he no longer could move from his hammock.

Although their raids now were totally illegal, other pirate captains continued to sail throughout the 1670s, and their stolen cargoes remained welcome in Port Royal. Not until 1682 did a new governor, Sir Thomas Lynch, finally convince the Jamaican assembly and council to enforce the laws. Even then, other islands and other ports continued to welcome their trade, and the pirates simply moved on.

The earthquake of 1692, during which Port Royal sank under the sea, was a fitting punishment for the sins of that new Sodom. But it did not mark the end of the British buccaneers. From the 1680s, pirate ships found new havens with more friendly governors in the Danish and British West Indies and finally in the Bahamas. After again serving their king as commissioned privateers (during the War of the Spanish Succession, 1701–1714), thousands of buccaneers settled in the Bahamas, which became their last haven during the great era of pirate terror.

THE THIRD DUTCH WAR, 1672–1678

Despite the hostility between their colonists in the Caribbean, England and France joined against the Netherlands in the Third Dutch War. This war marked another attempt by England and France to abort Dutch supremacy in world commerce and shipping. It was decided by land and sea battles in Europe, and the islands suffered comparatively little damage. Since the English withdrew from the war in 1672, Dutch and French forces fought the main battles in this region.

Both the Netherlands and France considered the islands extremely important. Their sugar was increasingly valuable, and they also provided a base for trade with the Spanish mainland. Seeking total conquest of their enemy's colonies, both nations sent large armadas carrying soldiers from Europe. However, European troops could not take fortified bases. Local pirates (and merchant vessels commissioned as privateers) again proved the most effective weapon.

When the war began in July 1672, the French and English seized the Dutch forts on Sint Maarten, Sint Eustatius, and Saba as well as the Dutch bases on Tortola and Virgin Gorda. However, the West India Company held on to the Curaçao islands, and two massive French expeditions against Curaçao in 1673 and 1678 failed disastrously. During the 1673 French attack on Curaçao, the French governor-general wanted to use Bertrand d'Ogeron and the Tortuga buccaneers. But d'Ogeron and his fleet disappeared in bad weather off the northern coast of Puerto Rico. Without their help, the Dutch at Curaçao repulsed the royal warships. The second French expedition in 1678 proved an even greater disaster. Seven large warships and three belonging to buccaneers ran aground on a hidden reef near Bonaire, drowning more than 500 sailors. Before this abortive attack on Curaçao, however, the French fleet did take Tobago.

Two large armadas sent from Holland also met with disaster. In July 1672, soldiers from a fleet commanded by Admiral de Ruyter were defeated with large losses at Cul de Sac in Martinique. In 1676 a second expedition temporarily regained Tobago and Sint Maarten but failed to take the buccaneer colony at Saint-Domingue.

After the war, the Dutch regained the small islands of Sint Maarten, Sint Eustatius, and Saba in the Leewards. The British retained Tortola and Virgin Gorda, and the French kept (but did not settle) Tobago. The Dutch state now permanently ended its involvement in West Indian commerce. The enormous expense of its failed campaign against Martinique in 1673 bankrupted the original West India Company, which was dissolved in 1674. However, individual Dutch merchants continued to trade successfully from Curaçao and, in later years, from Sint Eustatius.

SAINT-DOMINGUE BECOMES THE PIRATE CAPITAL

For a decade after the Treaties of Nijmegen (1678–79), the European states officially were at peace. But piracy on a large scale continued to plague the region. Since the English finally denied them Port Royal, pirates from many nations now gathered on Tortuga and Saint-Domingue. There Louis XIV of France followed a duplicitous policy. Although refusing royal commissions to freebooters, he permitted Governor de Pouançay to issue privateering licenses under his own name. As usual, Spanish ports provided the most lucrative targets, but the pirates also seized Dutch and British ships.

In 1683, buccaneer captains from Tortuga attacked Vera Cruz, the Spanish treasure port on the coast of Mexico. Plundering its houses, churches, and convents, they seized a fortune, which they later divided into more than 1,000 shares, each containing 800 golden pieces of eight. Enraged by this attack, the Spanish briefly went to war, until the French government agreed to the Truce of Ratisbon (August 1684) pledging peace in the West Indies as well as in Europe.

The following year, England and France similarly promised not to encourage buccaneering expeditions against each other's colonies. Despite these solemn treaties, pirates from Tortuga in 1685 looted Campeche, Nicaragua, gaining a large booty. The European nations were not yet ready to end their toleration of pirates. Without permanent naval garrisons in the islands, they still depended on privateers as their first line of defense in time of war.

THE NINE YEARS' WAR, 1688-1697

In yet another reversal of alliances, England, Holland, and Spain (and many other European states) now fought France. Louis XIV declared war on Holland in November 1688. England joined the anti-French alliance in May 1689, after William III replaced James II on the throne. (For this reason, some histories call this "King William's War.") Battles in Europe again decided the war, but it soon spilled over into the colonies. The Dutch no longer took an active role in the Caribbean, but both the British and the French launched expeditions that caused extensive damage.

As in the previous war, both sent warships from Europe, and the French also enlisted the Saint-Domingue and Tortola pirates. The 1695 attack on Cartagena was, after Morgan's rape of Panama, among the largest of pirate raids. Both regular forces and privateers again caused heavy damage in the Leewards. And they also carried the war west into the Greater Antilles. For the first time since the English conquest in 1655, Jamaica and Hispaniola suffered devastating raids.

Early in 1689, the French destroyed the Dutch settlements on Sint Eustatius, and they once again occupied the English part of Saint Kitts. Irish Catholics on Nevis, Antigua, and Montserrat rebelled in support of the deposed king, James II. Thus English prospects in the Leewards looked bleak. They were saved by the leadership of Christopher Codrington, governor-general of the Leeward Islands. Codrington managed to head off the Irish rebellion, and retook Saint Kitts and Anguilla in June 1690. Determined to put an end to the French presence on Saint Kitts, Codrington packed the French settlers off to Saint-Domingue and distributed their lands to British settlers.

In March 1691, Codrington, who wanted to force the French out of all the Leewards, then invaded Guadeloupe. There the English razed French sugar plantations and burnt the principal towns, but Codrington had to withdraw when his naval support suddenly pulled out. In 1693, an English invasion of Martinique came to a similar end. Codrington's troops quickly took most of the island and destroyed its plantations. But they again had to withdraw, devastated by disease while besieging the fort at Saint-Pierre.

For the first time in many years, the larger islands of the Greater Antilles also suffered major war damage. On Hispaniola, both the French and the Spanish tried to conquer or destroy each other's colonies. In 1690 French settlers and buccaneers burned the Spanish settlement of Saint Iago. The following year, in revenge, a strong Spanish force burned the port city of Cap-Français, massacred whatever men they could find, and carried off the women, children, and slaves to Santo Domingo.

To replace the governor of Saint-Domingue—killed in this raid—the French Crown turned to Jean Du Casse, himself a leading buccaneer captain. Taking advantage of the 1692 earthquake, Du Casse sent French buccaneers to pillage and to steal slaves from plantations along the coast of Jamaica. In June 1694, Du Casse personally led a fleet of 22 ships that ravaged Jamaica's southern coasts at Port Morant, Cow Bay, and Carlisle Bay, burning 50 sugar plantations and capturing some 1,300 slaves.

While Du Casse pillaged Jamaica, the British planned to attack Saint-Domingue while a Spanish army marched across the island from Santo Domingo. In July 1605, this joint expedition took the northern coast, destroyed Cap-Français for a second time, and thoroughly plundered the capital at Port-de-Paix. Once again, an outbreak of disease halted a successful invasion, and the British fleet withdrew.

The Sack of Cartagena

Du Casse prepared a counterattack on Santo Domingo. But the French king instead decided to take Cartagena, the main port for the Spanish treasure fleet carrying silver from Peru. Obedient to his orders, Du Casse assembled more than 700 buccaneers on seven ships. In March 1697, these joined 13 royal warships brought over from France by their admiral, the arrogant and dishonest Jean-Bernard Desjean, baron de Pointis.

Before the combined fleet sailed, de Pointis gave his word that the men could divide any loot in equal shares, following pirate custom. Only after a savage battle was the French force able to take Cartagena, which the Spanish had heavily fortified since Drake's conquest in 1573. Its defenders finally surrendered, when the French admiral agreed to spare civilians and their homes. Working rapidly, de Pointis's regular soldiers collected gold and silver worth perhaps 20 million French *livres*. They then prepared to sail for France.

Du Casse, who had to live with the buccaneers in Saint-Domingue, demanded that de Pointis honor his word and give them their promised share of the loot. When de Pointis refused, Du Casse managed to restrain the pirates until the royal fleet could leave. He promised to present their claims and gain their share from the French courts.

At first the buccaneers also prepared to sail home. But four of the seven captains decided that gold in hand was better than Du Casse's promise. Heading back to the prostrate city, the buccaneers ruthlessly sacked Cartagena, until its inhabitants agreed to pay them another 5 million *livres*. Much more than the destruction of Port Royal, the pirates' final departure for Saint-Domingue marks the end of their reign. Henceforth, individual pirate ships might take individual merchant or treasure ships. But the sack of Cartagena in 1697 represents the last time that a joint force of buccaneers in many ships sailed home with immense booty from a looted port.

THE WAR OF THE SPANISH SUCCESSION, 1702–1714

The Treaty of Ryswyck in September 1697 ended the Nine Years' War. All sides again returned the colonies they had taken, and they tacitly recognized the French colony of Saint-Domingue governed by Du Casse. Only five years later, in May 1702, Austria, England, and the Netherlands declared war on France and Spain. The allies fought mainly to prevent the uniting of the French and Spanish Empires. The French royal house of Bourbon now occupied both thrones because Charles II of Spain had willed his kingdoms to Philip V, Louis XIV's grandson. As one of their war aims, the British sought the right to trade with the Spanish mainland. They particularly coveted the *asiento*, the contract to import slaves into the Spanish colonies.

Only France and Britain sent troops to the Caribbean. In this region, privateering raids had continued even during the brief peace after 1697. The war simply continued the hostilities between the two empires that had begun in 1665. Initially, both sides hoped to take colonies from the other, and each sent a fleet to the region in 1701. However, tropical diseases soon killed so many of their crews that both navies accomplished little. Local forces again proved more effective than imported troops, and the war turned into a series of destructive raids in the Leewards. The British wanted to destroy their economic rivals and to steal their slaves. The French, outnumbered by English colonists, needed help from the Saint-Domingue pirates. The buccaneers only sought booty.

Under Christopher Codrington Junior, governor of the Leeward Islands from 1699 to 1704, the English won the first battles. In July 1702, Codrington seized the French portion of Saint Kitts. The next year, he invaded Guadeloupe with 3,600 troops and inflicted great damage during a two-month campaign. Although Codrington could not defeat the French troops on the island, his men totally ruined the enemy's sugar plantations.

Unable to send a navy from Europe, the French government sought revenge for these raids through an alliance with the Saint-Domingue pirates. In 1706, the king put the local forces under the command of Pierre Le Moyne, sieur d'Iberville, a famous French-Canadian soldier and seaman of great ability. Iberville was ordered to seize Barbados and Jamaica with the aid of the buccaneers, and he planned the expedition as a classic pirate raid. Iberville and his associates outfitted the ships, and the king sent only 600 soldiers. The Crown expected the buccaneers and French colonists to do most of the fighting, and it offered them the majority of any booty that might be taken.

Iberville and his pirate allies harshly revenged the earlier English raid on Guadeloupe. In February 1706, they plundered Saint Kitts, systematically stripping and burning every plantation beyond the reach of the British cannon. They then turned on Nevis. There the English planters quickly surrendered under humiliating terms. The French seized all of their property (except for their houses and clothes), including 3,187 slaves. The English also promised to catch and hand over another 1,400 slaves who had escaped to the hills. With both islands in ruins, the British government in 1711 gave out £28,000 to the planters on Saint Kitts and distributed another £75,000 among the sufferers on Nevis.

Rebellion in Antigua

Iberville died in Havana soon afterward, but French buccaneers continued to raid the British islands. In July 1712, a privateer squadron (estimated at 3,500 men) threatened Antigua and then took Montserrat, carrying off 1,200 slaves. During these years of danger, the Leeward Islands certainly needed a strong governor. The royal army and navy could not protect them against French privateers, and the wealthy planters commanding the local militia had refused to fight at Nevis. However, Colonel Daniel Parke, appointed governor of the Leewards in 1706, was the wrong choice.

Governor Parke soon earned the hatred of the planters, especially on Antigua, where he usually resided. He apparently made too many reforms too quickly, and he also was greedy and possibly demented. His assailants shot at the governor several times in 1708 and 1709, wounding him in the arm. In December 1710, after Parke took control of the local regiment, armed rebels surrounded his house and demanded that he leave for Nevis. In the ensuing tumult, the rebels murdered Parke and brutally killed or wounded most of the 70 soldiers guarding him. None of the participants was punished. When the Crown tried to investigate the rebellion, no Antiguan would testify, and the new governor could not punish the entire colony.

THE BUCCANEER REPUBLIC IN THE BAHAMAS

The buccaneers again had proved the most effective force, and this war also strengthened pirate control of the Bahamas. In 1703 and 1704, a joint French-Spanish force raided New Providence and destroyed the small settlement there. The surviving inhabitants took refuge in the woods or fled to the smaller out islands. By 1714, only 200 families still lived in the entire Bahamas group, and the pirates totally dominated New Providence.

This Bahamian era of piracy was brief. In the 1680s, pirates began to move to Nassau. After 1713, they were joined by thousands of former privateers who had lost their livelihood with the peace of Utrecht. But these pirates went into the trade not to fight but to gain easy money by looting merchant ships. Their easy pickings ended in 1718 with the appointment of Captain Woodes Rogers as first royal governor of the Bahamas.

A man of strong character and a skilled captain, Woodes Rogers was, like many of the pirates, from the west of England and had served as a privateer. During the War of the Spanish Succession, he became famous by sailing around the world, taking as prizes the Manila treasure fleet of 1709 and more than 20 other galleons. Because Rogers lacked a strong fleet of his own, he cleverly turned the pirate captains of the Bahamas against one another. He granted an amnesty to pirates willing to surrender. And he paid prizes to former pirates who captured those still at large and brought them into Nassau to be hanged. By 1720, most of the remaining buccaneers sought less dangerous waters, usually in the South Seas.

During their brief reign of terror during the 1710s, several pirate captains gained lasting fame. As their double-crosses indicate, most were greedy robbers without scruples. Partly because they often did not work well together, none carried out large raids or gained the enormous wealth of earlier buccaneers such as Henry Morgan. Unlike some of their predecessors, few pirates now hesitated to attack ships flying the flag of their own country, as long as they appeared to be easy targets.

Some of these last buccaneers were superb navigators who could sail out of sight of land for months. Although based in the Bahamas, they brought terror from one end of the globe to the other. They sought their prey throughout the Caribbean, along the Atlantic coast as far north as Maine, and even marauded across the Atlantic to West Africa and the South Seas. Their exploits became famous in their own day because they were eagerly covered by the new popular newspapers and novels, including Daniel Defoe's *Robinson Crusoe* and his *General History of the Pyrates*.[2]

☀ BLACKBEARD—PIRATE CRUELTY REACHES NEW LOWS

Since Daniel Defoe published the *General History of the Pyrates* between 1724 and 1728, his colorful work almost never has been out of print. Defoe artfully combined fact and fiction in narrating the lives of the pirates operating in Bahamian waters. The most notorious of these brigands is Edward Teach, alias Blackbeard. To straightforward reporting of Teach's adventures, Defoe added lurid stories portraying him as a monster. Later authors picked up Defoe's tales and even embellished them, creating the Blackbeard portrayed in numerous novels and movies.

Defoe's Blackbeard is vile beyond belief. Ranting into battle, he wore 12 pistols and several cutlasses in a special belt. A physical giant with an enormous appetite, he was said to have had 14 wives and to have drunk enormous amounts of rum long after his crew had passed out. This legendary Blackbeard enjoyed torturing his victims and sometimes his crew. In one trick, he supposedly made his ship into an imitation hell by closing up the hatches and burning brimstone until the seamen almost suffocated.

The real Edward Teach was a big strong man. When finally cornered in 1719, he reportedly went on fighting for several minutes after receiving five musket shots and numerous sword wounds. He certainly did commit piracy and then went on to cheat his crew out of their share of the booty. But there is no evidence that he ever murdered or tortured either his captives or his men or that he raped his wife or other women.

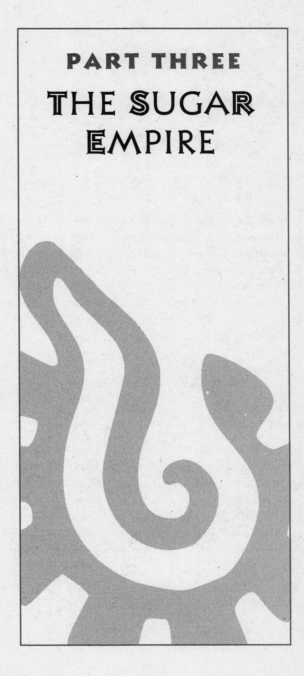

PART THREE
THE SUGAR EMPIRE

CHAPTER 9

SUGAR RULES THE ISLANDS

Following the Treaty of Utrecht (1713) and the end of the War of the Spanish Succession, the Caribbean enjoyed almost 80 years of relative peace and prosperity. The economy—especially the sugar industry—grew rapidly. Today, the islands supply only a small fraction of Europe's sugar. During the 18th century, however, the islands—as shown in Table 8—produced 80 to 90 percent of the sugar consumed by western Europeans. The European homeland always wanted more sugar, and the British and French planters increasingly grew nothing else.

THE COLONIAL EMPIRES IN 1713

A century after northern Europeans established their first settlements, the decaying Spanish Empire still retained Cuba, Puerto Rico, and the eastern part of Hispaniola (Santo Domingo). In 1713, the main centers of French and British occupation remained the Lesser Antilles. There the French controlled Martinique and Guadeloupe, and the British ruled Barbados, Saint Kitts, Antigua, Montserrat, Nevis,

Table 8. **SUGAR PRODUCTION IN THE AMERICAS, 1741–1824**
(Annual Averages in Tons)

	1741–1745	1766–1770	1820–1824
French West Indies	64,675	77,923	47,658
British West Indies	41,043	74,452	147,733
Brazil (Portuguese)	34,000	20,400	—
Virgin Islands (Danish)	—	8,230	23,000
Surinam (Dutch)	9,210	6,800	—
Cuba (Spanish)	2,000	5,200	50,384

NOTE: For possessions other than British, data available only for some years during the period reported.

SOURCES: Richard Sheridan, *The Development of the Plantations to 1750* (Aylesbury, England: Ginn and Company, 1970), 22 (1741–1770); David Watts, *The West Indies: Pattern of Development, Culture and Environmental Change since 1492* (Cambridge: Cambridge University Press, 1987), 287–288 (1820–24); Franklin Knight, *The Caribbean: The Genesis of a Fragmented Nationalism* (New York: Oxford University Press, 1978), 241 (Haiti/Saint-Domingue, 1820).

and the British Virgins. In the Greater Antilles, the British occupied Jamaica, and the French held the western third of Hispaniola (Saint-Domingue). During the 18th century, Britain and France rapidly developed these larger islands, which became their most important colonies by the 1750s.

Only the Windward Islands remained largely uninhabited by Europeans until after 1763. Dominica and Saint Vincent both retained large settlements of Carib, whose ownership had been guaranteed by a treaty in 1660. Expeditions from the French and British Leewards tried to settle Saint Lucia and Saint Vincent from time to time, but the other side usually drove them off. French settlers from Martinique did set up plantations on Grenada, which produced significant amounts of sugar by the 1760s as well as coffee and cocoa. Further south a few Spanish colonists clung to survival on Trinidad, while Tobago (nominally under French control) had only a small population.

The Non-Spanish Islands
Give Themselves Wholly to Sugar

All of the Caribbean islands became integrated into the tropical plantation system during the 18th century. On the British islands sugar became virtually the only crop, and a true monoculture developed. The French islands enjoyed a somewhat more diversified economy, but sugar was their main and most important product. The plantation system reached out to dominate the economies even of islands that grew no sugar. At the far north, the Bahamas remained unsettled because they were unsuited to sugar. To the far south, the Dutch retained the Curaçao islands as outposts of trade to Latin America through Venezuela. But everything between Curaçao and the Bahamas was dominated by the plantation system. The Danish Virgin Islands and the Dutch Leewards—Sint Eustatius, Saba, and half of Sint Maarten—served as free ports selling slaves to the British and French islands. As the sugar industry flourished, sugar plantations also came to dominate Danish Saint Croix.

The very success of the sugar islands retarded development of the Windwards. Sugar plantations require large amounts of capital. British Jamaica and French Saint-Domingue did not reach full development until the 1750s, and there was little money to spare for the smaller Windwards. Moreover, the shipping schedules were tied to the needs of the sugar islands, especially during times of war. Captains were loath to go to the remoter territories, such as Grenada or even Guadeloupe, which had to send their crops to Martinique for pickup.

Europeans Consume More and More Sugar

Overall, the four centuries from 1550 to 1950 saw a sharp increase in per capita sugar consumption, and prices generally rose until the 1820s. Particularly during the 18th century, Europeans of all classes increasingly drank tea, coffee, and cocoa, and ate processed foods, jams, and candy. With the exception of the French, consumers in northern Europe always have eaten more sugar than those living in Mediterranean regions, with the British having the greatest capacity for sweets. Thus the sugar habit grew throughout northern Europe during the 1600s, and it increased most rapidly in England.

Over the longer term, prices generally rose until the 19th century. Nevertheless, sugar went through a series of boom and bust periods with serious effects on the islands. Prices soared to new records after 1645, when the revolt against the Dutch devastated Brazilian plantations. Planters on Barbados enjoyed profits of 40 to 50 percent a year during the 1650s, and they rapidly expanded production. By 1661, a glut had developed on the European market, and prices eventually fell by as much as 70 percent. They remained depressed until about 1690 and then rose again until a minor slump in the 1730s.

With constantly rising demand, the market again rose from the mid-1740s. Planters on the British islands did especially well during times of war (1748, 1756–1763). Although they never again equaled those on Barbados in the 1650s, profits were generous. They soared again during the Napoleonic wars from 1791 to 1815, when the price of sugar on the London market reached its all-time high. From the 1840s, both prices and profits began to fall dramatically. European governments subsidized the beet sugar industry, Cuban production soared, and the British Empire found new sources in Asia.

The Mercantilist System during the 18th Century

The French and British governments both sought to make their colonies—the most important sugar producers—benefit the mother country. Both forbade islanders from importing or exporting goods on ships not owned by their own subjects. At home, both placed prohibitive duties on any kind of sugar imported from a foreign nation or its colonies. To protect domestic sugar refiners, both also taxed imports of semi-refined (clayed) sugar at a much higher rate than the raw product (muscovado).

Despite their shared "mercantilist" philosophies, the French and British regulations also differed in important ways that significantly affected the economies of their islands. Neither government followed a totally consistent policy over the years, since both had to please many constituencies with divergent interests. In general, however, the British government followed a high tax policy to increase its own revenues. The French government collected lower taxes and mainly sought to increase its exports to other countries.

🏛 THE BRITISH CRAVING FOR SWEETS

Sugar consumption in Great Britain continuously increased for several centuries, in one of the most dramatic changes in eating habits known to human history. In 1700, on average, Britons used a mere four pounds of sugar each year to sweeten their drinks and food. By 1750, per capita consumption had doubled, and it doubled again by 1800, reaching 18 pounds a year. Consumption doubled yet again in the 1840s, after the British government removed import taxes on sugar. The British passion for sweets peaked in the early 1960s. During those years, each Briton, on average, devoured more than 110 pounds of sugar each year—amounting to almost a third of a pound every day of the year.

The British government always burdened consumers with high import duties on tropical products—especially sugar, tobacco, and tea—that had to be brought into the British Isles. The import duties first imposed on sugar in 1650 continued to rise until 1705. Moreover, planters on Barbados and the Leewards (but not Jamaica) also paid a 4.5 percent duty on all their exports.[1] But the French government primarily wanted to increase France's exports rather than to raise revenues. It thus emphasized the sale of tropical products, especially sugar, to other European countries. From the 1660s, the government organized its empire to encourage commercial growth with the main benefits accruing to French merchants. From 1717 it did away with taxes—except for a 3 percent tax on all colonial exports—on sugar reexported from France.

In 1739 the British government also eliminated duties on sugar exported directly from the West Indies to Europe. Nevertheless, French West Indian sugar remained cheaper than British products, and French sugars dominated the Amsterdam and Hamburg markets during times of peace throughout the 18th century. Thus the British islands primarily shipped their sugar to the large protected market in England. Because of the tax laws, British planters were restricted to making raw sugar, but they were guaranteed high prices.

Because the French planters made more clayed sugar, they also had an abundance of molasses, a byproduct of the claying process. Throughout the 18th century, British North American merchants purchased inexpensive rum from the French islands, as well as molasses for their rum distilleries. As a result, British planters lost the American market. To placate planter interests, the Parliament in 1733 placed prohibitive duties on sugar, molasses, and rum imported from non-British islands. British customs officials did little to enforce this Molasses Act, and American merchants openly and brazenly violated it until the 1760s. When the British government did attempt to prohibit French rum and molasses through the 1764 Sugar Act, it infuriated American merchants and shippers. This act became a major grievance leading to the American Revolution of 1776.

The Profits and Power of the Sugar Lords

The Caribbean colonies justified mercantilist theories by supplying sugar and other staples in return for North American provisions and European manufactured goods. By the early 1770s, Jamaica, Barbados, and the Leewards thus supplied about 24 percent of all goods imported into Britain and took 13.4 percent of all British exports. The direct duties on sugar were only a small part of the revenues Britain and France took from the islands. Sugar and slaves were lucrative trades, and most of the profits went to the homeland. Payments to absentee landlords, commissions, freight, insurance, and other charges took the greater part of the income of the islands.[2]

European states invested nothing to finance, govern, and defend their Caribbean colonies. On the contrary, the plantations largely financed themselves after the first investments in the 1600s, and their profits found a permanent home in Europe. Moreover, the sugar colonies were at the heart of a complex "triangular trade" that indirectly returned revenues to the mother country considerably in excess of official customs taxes. By this system of trade from Europe to Africa to America (and then back to Europe), as Basil Davidson notes,

> three separate profits were made and taken, all high and all in Europe: the first profit was that of selling consumer goods to the slavers; the second derived from selling slaves to the planters and mine-owners of the Americas; while the third (and biggest) was realized on the sale of American and West Indian cargoes in Europe. It was largely on the steady and often stupendous profits of this circuitous enterprise that France and England would ground their commercial supremacy.[3]

But neither sugar nor slavery in itself tells the entire story. European consumers paid high prices that covered all taxes and all the costs of producing sugar (as well as any profit to the planters). Thus the sugar and slave trades supported many European interests—from wealthy merchants, refiners, and shipowners through prosperous insurers and lawyers down to humble grocers. Many, both then and now, have exaggerated the total profits from sugar and slavery, which formed only a fraction of Europe's gross national product. The important point is that British and French statesmen considered sugar and slavery essential to the national economy. Capital put into these trades brought in much higher profits than alternative investments, and they thus increased national income and government revenues.

Even if they had wanted to, governments could not ignore sugar merchants and slavers, who were concentrated in several large cities. In France, the three great ports of Nantes, Bordeaux, and Marseilles dominated the French slave trade and supplied most of the sugar and coffee consumed in Europe during the 18th century. Given the steady rise both in sugar prices and the volume of consumption, the French sugar trade soared throughout the 18th century. Despite wartime interruptions, the total value of French sugar imports increased fivefold—from 15 million *livres* in 1730 to 75 million in 1790. Thus these ports became much richer than the rest of France. The French government felt it had to maintain its hegemony over one of Europe's largest trades. It protected its Caribbean colonies, even if this meant (as in 1763) abandoning North America and India.

A few large cities also captured the sugar and slave trades in England. London, with an estimated 180 refineries by the 1780s, dominated sugar refining, followed by Bristol, Liverpool, and Glasgow. Liverpool became the world's leading slave port, eclipsing Bristol and London in the 1740s. These British merchants joined with West Indian sugar planters to form one united "West India Interest." Shared profits and needs bound together wealthy absentee planters, merchants, manufacturers, bondholders, agents of colonial governments, and military officers serving in the West Indies. In addition to creating formal associations, the West Indians formed a close social circle, bound together by family and marriage ties as well as lasting friendships.

In England, the "West India Interest" was able to express its concerns through a large and generally united voice in Parliament. Seventy West Indian merchants and absentee proprietors purchased seats in Parliament from 1730 to 1775. The leading planter families of Jamaica, Saint Kitts, and Antigua sat throughout the century. Taken all together, the 1766 Parliament held "forty members who are either West Indian planters themselves, descended from such, or have concerns there that entitle them to pre-eminence."[4] While the Parliament also represented competing interests and industries, the West Indian bloc had no difficulty making its concerns known to the government.

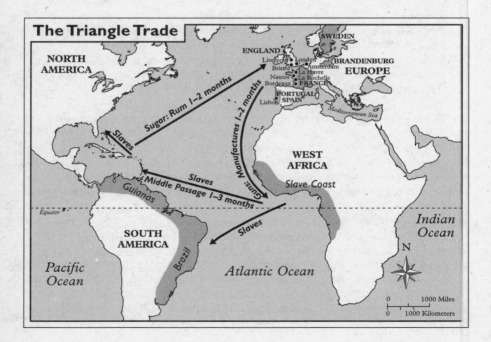

⚙ DID THE PROFITS FROM CARIBBEAN SLAVERY FUND·BRITAIN'S INDUSTRIAL REVOLUTION?

The transition from an agricultural economy to one based on manufacturing occurred first in Great Britain. In his influential 1944 study *Capitalism and Slavery,* Eric Williams (later the prime minister of Trinidad) argued that the profits from Caribbean sugar plantations paid for Britain's industrial development. Williams believed that the profits from the triangular trade between Africa, the Caribbean, and Great Britain "fertilized the entire productive system of the country." He also asserted that these profits were directly invested in the technological changes known as the Industrial Revolution.

For a time, historians adopted this "Williams Thesis," but it now is seen to be overstated. The profits from slavery represented less than one-half of 1 percent of Britain's annual income. While the British and North American economies might have developed more slowly, the Industrial Revolution still would have occurred without the Caribbean slave plantations.

THE VARYING FORTUNES OF THE ISLANDS

During the 18th century, as sugar dominated the islands, planters adopted one relatively uniform plantation system. Innovations often began on Barbados and then spread north to the Leewards and west to Jamaica and Saint-Domingue. Despite the wars between their two nations, French and British planters were willing to learn from each other. Although they used relatively uniform agricultural methods, the pace of economic development varied—because of each island's different resources, the policies of England and France, market fluctuations, wars, and natural disasters. At one extreme were the small, intensively cultivated estates of Barbados, at the other the vast holdings of Jamaica and Saint-Domingue.

Natural resources partially determined which regions formed part of the fabled sugar empire. Sugarcane grows best when heat and water are plentiful year-round. An ideal climate provides a predictable 60 to 70 inches of rain per year, with no prolonged droughts. These conditions are common along the coasts of the larger islands in the Leewards. By contrast, rainfall is highly localized in the Greater Antilles because of their high mountains. Here different parts of the same island can receive from 20 to 200 inches a year. In the drier areas, cane could not be profitably produced without irrigation.

Cane grows well both in the volcanic soils found on Guadeloupe and Martinique and also on the limestone soils of geologically older islands like Barbados. However, the soil rapidly loses fertility after trees are removed, and cane itself further takes minerals out of the soil. The productivity of older plantations quickly falls unless the cane fields are heavily fertilized—during the 18th century through the application of animal dung. New plantations always enjoyed an advantage that was accentuated by improvements in technology over time.

Planters on the smaller islands of Barbados and the Leewards initially could produce more cheaply than Jamaicans because of their easterly location and because of the high ratio of coastline to landmass. Since the prevailing winds are from the east, ships carrying goods from Europe and slaves from Africa reached Barbados and Martinique several weeks before arriving at Jamaica or Saint-Domingue. Similarly, ships carrying sugar from Barbados to Europe could tack north against the easterlies. In contrast, ships leaving Port Royal in Jamaica had to sail downwind south of Cuba to catch the Gulf Stream through the Florida Passage and up the Carolina coast. Simply because the voyage took longer, Jamaican sugar cost more than Barbadian sugar by the time it reached Liverpool.

Until the 19th century, plantations along the sea also enjoyed a cost advantage. Even milled sugar is quite heavy. Most of the best sugar land was near the coast, so that barrels of sugar could be rolled to the beach and carried in small boats to seagoing vessels. Inland plantations on Jamaica and Saint-Domingue either had to produce more efficiently or enjoy smaller profits. Ultimately, Cuba surpassed all the other islands when railroads opened up access to its interior provinces during the 19th century.

Barbados and the British Leeward Islands

Each island enjoyed its Golden Age at slightly different eras. Sugar planters on Barbados enjoyed the highest profits ever during the 1650s and 1660s. Planters in the Leewards naturally tried to follow Barbados's lead. However, a lack of capital and slaves held back the development of cane estates, and French invasions depopulated the islands during the War of the Spanish Succession. After 1713, Barbados maintained and even expanded production, but it soon was surpassed by the Leewards.

Table 9. **BRITISH LEEWARD ISLANDS POPULATION ESTIMATES, 1724–1834**

| | 1724 | | 1834 | |
	Whites	Slaves	Whites	Slaves
Anguilla	360	900	350	2,000
Antigua	5,200	19,800	1,980	23,350
Saint Kitts	4,000	11,500	1,612	15,667
Montserrat	1,000	4,400	330	5,026
Nevis	1,100	6,000	700	7,225
Virgin Islands	760	1,430	447	4,318

NOTES: For 1724, the Virgin Islands estimate includes Virgin Gorda and Tortola only. Under 1834, the estimates for Anguilla refer to 1790.

SOURCES: Alan Burns, *History of the British West Indies* Second edition, revised (London: Allen & Unwin, 1954), 461 (1724); Noel Deerr, *The History of Sugar*, 2 volumes (London: Chapman & Hall, 1949–50), II:279 (1834); Elsa Goveia, *Slave Society in the British Leeward Islands at the End of the Eighteenth Century* (New Haven: Yale University Press, 1965), 203 (Anguilla, 1790).

By the 1750s, these small islands were producing three times as much sugar as Barbados, and Saint Kitts was the richest colony in the British Empire by 1776. Sugar prices then fell, but the islands enjoyed a final burst of prosperity during the first decades of the 19th century.

Sugar estates totally dominated Barbados and the British Leewards, which developed into extreme examples of monoculture. By 1770, sugar products counted for 93 percent of Barbados's exports and more than 97 percent of exports from the Leewards. Cane was planted on every possible piece of land, and the islanders depended upon outside sources for food, clothing, building materials, and draft animals.

Sugarcane exhausted the natural fertility of the soil, but planters managed to increase production by using better technology and more slaves. Although they used relatively primitive mills and distilleries, Barbados planters introduced many innovations that became standard throughout the islands. These included planting the cane in holes, the heavy use of animal manure or dung, and construction of windmills to power their mills. Intense human labor was needed to dig cane holes and to carry dung to each plant. The planters devoted more and more slaves to each acre, and the number of slaves constantly rose. Partially because they were hard driven and received inadequate amounts of imported food, slaves on Barbados and in the Leewards died at a rapid rate.

Only the wealthiest could afford to buy sugar estates with their heavy investment in machinery and slaves. A few families owned virtually all the land. By 1750, 74 families on Barbados owned 305 of the 536 cane estates. An even smaller number of families—often living in England—controlled the Leewards, where consolidation of estates and concentration of ownership increased throughout the 18th century. On Nevis, perhaps the most extreme case, planters consolidated the hundred sugar plantations existing in 1719 into less than three dozen a century later. Some families among this sugar aristocracy, especially on Barbados and Antigua, were descendants of the original settlers. Most were newcomers (many Scots) who bought estates as an investment or came to the islands as merchants or lawyers and bought up the estates of failed owners.

With their soil devoted entirely to cane production, Barbados and the Leewards could not support a white population. The planters trained their slaves as managers, slave drivers, bookkeepers, and domestic servants. There was no work for wage laborers, and white settlers preferred to immigrate to British North America. Thus the

Table 10. **BARBADOS POPULATION ESTIMATES, 1712–1834**

	Total	Whites	Slaves	Free Non-Whites
1712	54,498	12,528	41,970	—
1757	80,417	16,772	63,645	—
1786	79,115	16,167	62,115	833
1833–1834	100,242	12,797	80,861	6,584

SOURCES: Dunn, *Sugar and Slaves*, 87 (1712); Deerr, *History of Sugar*, II:278 (1757); Jerome S. Handler and Arnold A. Sio, "Barbados," *Neither Slave nor Free: The Freedmen of African Descent in the Slave Societies of the New World*, edited by David Cohen and Jack Greene (Baltimore: Johns Hopkins University Press, 1972), 218–219 (1786–1834).

white population stagnated or (in the case of Montserrat and Nevis) fell while the number of black slaves soared. The Leewards had virtually no white population at all. (See Table 9.) Here slavery reached its most extreme state, with the slaves outnumbering the small number of estate employees 15 or even 20 to one.

Barbados, the original British colony, retained a substantial white population—with one white for every four slaves. (See Table 10.) But only a small number of whites shared in the profits of the sugar industry. Many poorer planters had emigrated to Jamaica in the 1660s, and the more ambitious continued to leave. Those that remained lived in squalid poverty. By 1834, three-fourths of the whites remaining on Barbados belonged to the class known as "Redlegs" (because of their sunburned legs). Most earned a marginal living by fishing or by planting a few acres.

Jamaica and Saint-Domingue

Jamaica and Saint-Domingue—as Table 11 shows—became the world's main sugar producers during the 1740s. Both had an abundance of good land and ideal climates, but their greater size actually held back settlement until the 18th century. By 1750, Jamaica became the greatest sugar producer in the British Empire, a position it retained until the 1830s. Saint-Domingue, ultimately the richest of all the sugar islands, developed in two stages. Many cane estates were created in the 1720s and 1730s along the coastal region. By the 1740s, these produced more sugar than the British islands taken together. To increase production, French engineers then built an elaborate series of irrigation systems in the central province that ensured Saint-Domingue's dominance of the sugar trade until 1791. Other tropical crops also flourished. Coffee, indigo, and cotton thus represented about one-third (by value) of Saint-Domingue's exports in 1770.

Jamaica   Wars, Maroon raids, and low sugar prices held back Jamaica's settlement until the 1720s. The French devastated the island in 1692, and Barbados con-

Table 11. **SUGAR PRODUCTION OF SELECTED CARIBBEAN ISLANDS,** 1741–1770 *(Annual Averages in 1,000 U.S. tons)*

	1741–1745	1766–1770
Saint-Domingue*	42.4	61.3
Jamaica	15.6	36.0
Antigua	6.2	10.7
Saint Kitts	7.3	9.7
Martinique	14.2	8.8
Saint Croix	—	8.2
Guadeloupe	8.1	7.9
Barbados	6.6	7.8
Grenada	—	6.6
Cuba	2.0	5.2

*Saint-Domingue became Haiti in 1804.
SOURCE: Sheridan, *Development of the Plantations to 1750*, 23.

t.nued to attract most of the available capital and slaves. Jamaicans could make their fortunes more rapidly as buccaneers and smugglers or by raising cattle and cutting logwood. The government gave out large grants of land to potential sugar planters, but few developed their estates at this time. Only 70 sugar estates existed in 1675, most of them along the easily defensible southern coast near Kingston.

The Jamaican sugar industry began to flourish in the 1740s. Treaties with the Maroons in 1738 and 1739 ended their raids (see page 158), British traders began to bring in many more slaves, and sugar prices remained high after 1748. Jamaica increasingly became a colony of large sugar estates. As in the Leewards, a very small population of white planters, estate managers, and other professionals controlled a population of black slaves that outnumbered them at least 10 to one. In 1758, 18,000 whites supervised 180,000 slaves, and 455 sugar plantations produced 24,000 tons of sugar. (See Table 12.)

This plantation economy, almost wholly devoted to sugar produced by black slaves, expanded rapidly during the next 25 years. By 1775 fewer than 19,000 whites ruled over 193,000 slaves. Both the size of the average plantation and output per slave had increased dramatically. Jamaican sugar exports, produced on 775 much larger plantations, had doubled to more than 40,000 tons.

Historians at one time believed that the British West Indies's economy suffered a severe decline after 1763. Supporting this interpretation was the natural inclination of the planters to exaggerate their difficulties and hide their profits from the British Parliament. Studies by present-day economic historians have now shown this interpretation to be false. The planters' private accounts indicate that Jamaica and the other British colonies remained prosperous until the 1820s. The planters were hurt by the American Revolution, but prosperity soon returned. Sugar consumption grew rapidly in Great Britain after the duty on tea was reduced in 1786, and a slave rebellion in 1791 eliminated exports from Saint-Domingue. The Napoleonic wars opened new markets on the continent, and Britain officially reopened the islands to United States shipping in 1793. Prices on the London market boomed, reaching the highest level ever recorded in March 1815.

Sugar planters significantly increased production by improving their mills, introducing superior varieties of cane and grasses, growing more food crops, and using more dung. By 1806, 859 estates—even larger and much more productive than in 1775—produced more than 80,000 tons of sugar. While the slave population had increased by 50 percent since 1775, sugar exports had doubled, and Jamaican coffee production also boomed.

Table 12. **JAMAICA POPULATION ESTIMATES, 1730–1834**

	Total	Whites	Slaves	Free Non-Whites
1730	82,183	7,658	74,525	—
1758	198,300	17,900	176,900	3,500
1775	216,000	18,700	192,800	4,500
1800	340,000	30,000	300,000	10,000
1834	376,200	20,000	310,000	46,200

SOURCE: Patterson, *Slavery and Social Death*, 477.

Saint-Domingue   The natural environment divides Saint-Domingue (and present-day Haiti) into three distinct provinces, whose citizens communicate with each other as well as with France by sea. The western end of Hispaniola is shaped something like a capital U lying on its side. The two arms of the U (called the North and South Provinces) are continuations of the great mountain chains that stretch from Central America through Cuba and on to Puerto Rico. The central sector (known as the West Province) also is mountainous, but it is cut by several major river valleys.

Sugar plantations rapidly developed in the 1720s and 1730s in the lowlands along the northern coast. The region south and east of Cap-Français possessed rich soils and adequate rainfall. Moreover, planters could ship their harvest through the island's largest city and political capital.

The central or West Province, with its capital at Port-au-Prince, developed more slowly. To grow cane, planters first had to construct a sophisticated irrigation system using surface water. Parts of the province then enjoyed an abundance of fertile soil. But some of the best land received little rain because it lay within a rain-shadow to the leeward (west) of high mountain ranges. Beginning in the 1730s, French engineers constructed an elaborate system of reservoirs, diversion dams, levees, aqueducts, and canals. Altogether, more than 100,000 acres were brought under irrigation by 1791. Although the cost of these projects was huge, they quickly paid off. With irrigation, some plantations became the most productive in the Caribbean. From the 1740s to 1791, Saint-Domingue's planters produced almost as much cane (much of it in a semi-refined or clayed form) as the British West Indies put together.

The South Province, the bottom arm of the U, was the last to develop. Using irri-

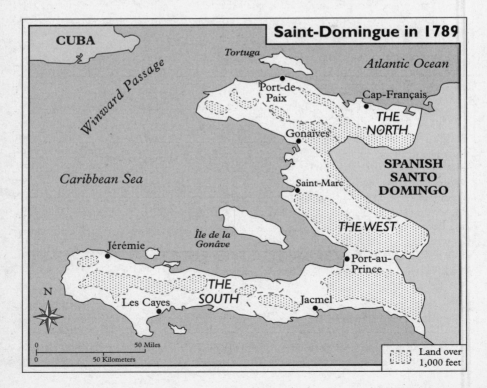

Château Murat, Marie-Galante. French planters constructed island "big houses" in the baroque and rococo styles. A great slave rebellion (1791–1804) destroyed the French plantations on Saint-Domingue (today Haiti). This estate house survives on Marie-Galante, near Guadeloupe.

gation, planters created substantial sugar estates on the coastal Les Cayes plain. Elsewhere in this region, coffee provided the main product from the 1730s. This crop was grown on many, comparatively smaller, estates in the hills, some owned by colored freedmen. Only a few small towns—Jérémie, Les Cayes, and Jacmel—served the area.

Guadeloupe and Martinique

Tobacco remained important on Guadeloupe and Martinique until about 1660, when the French tobacco monopoly switched to Virginia leaf. These islands developed cane estates more slowly than Saint-Domingue. Thus they had fewer inhabitants, both white and slave, and planters were more likely to reside on the island. Fort Royal (today Fort-de-France) was the political capital of the French Antilles, while Saint-Pierre (destroyed by a volcanic explosion in 1902) was a major commercial center and the first stop for slave ships from Africa. Thus both islands served the French Empire as trading posts more than as producers of tropical products. Both islands had a significant number of free coloreds (see Table 18 on page 165), but they were less affluent than on Saint-Domingue. More free coloreds worked as artisans or retailers in the towns, and fewer owned plantations and slaves.

The Windward Islands

By the Treaty of Paris in 1763, Great Britain gained control of Saint Vincent, Dominica, Grenada, and Tobago. Britain returned Saint Lucia to France, but British forces reoccupied the island in 1778 and 1794. (See page 141.)

La Pagerie, Martinique. This estate was the birthplace of Marie-Rose Tacher de la Pagerie, later Empress Josephine, first wife of Napoleon Bonaparte. Pictured is La Pagerie's massive stone kitchen, now a museum. A hurricane destroyed the plantation big house in 1766.

Table 13. **WINDWARD ISLANDS POPULATION ESTIMATES, 1763–1832**

	Total	Whites	Slaves	Free Non-Whites
Dominica				
1763	8,090	1,718	5,872	500
1788	16,648	1,236	14,967	445
1805	26,449	1,594	22,083	2,822
1832	19,225	791	14,387	4,077
Saint Lucia				
1765	13,717	2,397	10,270	1,050
1789	21,778	2,198	17,992	1,588
1825	18,595	1,194	13,530	3,871
Saint Vincent				
1763	5,263	695	3,430	1,138
1787	13,603	1,450	11,853	300
1825	22,239	1,301	18,114	2,842
Grenada				
1753	13,426	1,262	11,991	173
1771	27,872	1,661	26,211	—
1829	28,732	801	24,145	3,786

SOURCES: Watts, *West Indies,* 316, 318; Patterson, *Slavery and Social Death,* 479.

Thousands of British and Scots adventurers descended on the islands, hoping to repeat the success of planters in Barbados, the Leewards, and Jamaica a century earlier. They quickly cleared the forests, built mills, and imported thousands of new Africans.

The newly established sugar plantations flourished for 20 years on Saint Vincent and Grenada. But they were devastated by rebellions in 1795. (See page 170.) The Black Carib held Saint Vincent for six months, while rebel slaves controlled Grenada for more than a year. By the time British military forces reoccupied the islands, the rebels had killed many white settlers and sacked their plantations. It was even more difficult to subdue rebellious slaves on Dominica. The island's mountainous terrain allowed runaway slaves to establish Maroon communities, which the British could not eradicate until 1814. Because of these disturbances, some planters left Saint Vincent, Dominica, and Grenada. Most moved on to Saint Lucia and Trinidad, which were comparatively tranquil and contained large areas of unoccupied land.

THE SPANISH ISLANDS

From 1713, the British and French islands followed Barbados in adopting sugar as their main or only crop. Yet the islands ruled by Spain long remained *hacienda,* or rancher, societies, not unlike those later found in the western United States. Here vast herds of cattle roamed open ranges between isolated towns. Governmental regulation rather than a lack of natural resources hindered the development of sugar estates in the Spanish colonies. Under the Laws of the Indies, Spain limited trade to two convoys a year. Only Spanish ships could trade with her islands, but few Spanish ships called at their ports. Economic development thus became possible when the reforming Bourbon dynasty eased trade restrictions during the 1760s. Cuban planters now began to create cane estates, setting the stage for rapid growth during the 19th century. Change came more slowly to Puerto Rico and Santo Domingo, where large sugar estates were created only during the 20th century.

Cuba Comes under Spanish Control

During the 1600s, Havana had prospered as the main port of the yearly fleets that carried Mexican silver to Spain. Because of the port's strategic importance, its captain-general received political and military authority over the entire island. In fact, the captain-generals had little power in the countryside, especially in the central and eastern provinces. There local property owners governed through town councils (*cabildos*). The sharp contrast between prosperous western Cuba and the sparsely populated eastern provinces thus began early. Since the early 1600s, most Cubans have lived in the more prosperous west. All successful revolutions have begun in the lightly governed eastern provinces and then marched west against Havana.

Spanish efforts to reassert authority over the Americas began under the Bourbon dynasty, which replaced the Habsburgs in 1714. The Bourbons sought greater political and economic control because they needed colonial wealth to develop Spain's economy. Cuba and other relatively prosperous regions now lost the autonomy they had gained during earlier centuries. In 1729, all Cuban *cabildos* thus lost the authori-ty to distribute unoccupied land among local residents. To control smuggling, many municipal governments were brought under the army.

Cuba enjoyed modest economic growth after 1713 because of increased access to French markets. But the Bourbon government obstructed Cuban progress by placing commerce under state-sponsored monopolies. In 1717, it brought all tobac-co production under a royal monopoly (the Factoría de Tabacos), and it used the military to crush uprisings by tobacco farmers in 1717, 1723, 1729. Displaced farmers fled to new settlements east and west of Havana, and smuggled their crops out of the island.

In 1740, the Spanish government created a new monopoly with even greater powers. The Royal Company of Commerce (Real Compañía de Commercio) received total control over all trade between Spain and Cuba. The company bought Cuban sugar, tobacco, and hides at low prices, and it sharply marked up Spanish imports It made enormous profits at the expense of Cuban farmers. The monopoly hampered Cuba's commercial development, and Havana increasingly suffered food shortages.

The Cuban Sugar Boom Begins

The British conquest of Havana during the Seven Years' War (see page 149) trans-formed Cuba. The British controlled Havana for less than 11 months (1762–63), but their occupation eliminated all the obstacles to Cuban sugar development. Cuba was thrown open to free trade with Britain's American colonies. More than 10,000 ships entered Havana harbor—a port that had not seen more than 15 vessels a year during the previous 10 years. The British occupation freed Cuban planters from the restric-tions and high prices of the Royal Company. Above all, it gave them the labor they needed to expand production as British merchants brought in some 10,000 slaves—as many as would normally have entered in two decades. (See Table 22, page 201.)

Cuba had flourished during Spain's absence. Charles III, an "enlightened despot," was willing to make reforms that would continue commercial growth and increase the king's revenues. From 1765, the Crown gradually lifted all restrictions on trade between Cuba and the Spanish Empire. Beginning in 1789, it permitted both Spanish and for-eign slavers to bring in African slaves without restrictions or taxes, and it allowed unlim-ited cultivation and unrestricted sale of tobacco from 1817. In February 1818, Spain finally opened the island to ships of all nations. However, customs tariffs discriminated against island exports and foreign imports carried aboard non-Spanish ships.

The wars of the American and French Revolutions also benefited Cuba's sugar industry. The Anglo-Spanish war from 1779 to 1783 allowed North American mer-chants to visit the island. Trade with the United States—although still illegal—increased after 1783, and Cuba replaced the British colonies as America's main source of sugar. Cuban planters similarly profited from the 1791 slave revolution on Saint-Domingue, which removed that producer from the market.

Sugar prices remained at high levels for 60 years after 1762, reaching their peak in 1815. Allowed access to the world market, sugar planters rapidly expanded pro-duction. (See Table 8, page 108.) Ten thousand acres were devoted to sugarcane in 1761, 160,000 in 1792. The 100 primitive mills of 1763 grew to more than 1,000 in 1827, now larger and technically more advanced. As cane fields spread, planters cut down and burned the vast forests covering the island.

Santo Domingo and Puerto Rico

Efforts to develop Puerto Rico's agricultural potential began toward the end of the 18th century. The Crown sent a trusted representative, Marshal Alejandro O'Reilly, to tour the island in 1765. Based on O'Reilly's report, Spain bolstered the defenses of San Juan, reformed governmental practices, and allowed foreigners to sell slaves. A decree of 1778 welcomed skilled artisans and planters who professed the Roman Catholic faith and took an oath of allegiance to the Crown. The population tripled by 1800, and the local militia defeated a British army of 10,000 men that attacked San Juan in April 1797.

Table 14. **PUERTO RICO POPULATION ESTIMATES, 1765–1802**

	Total	Whites	Slaves	Free Non-Whites
1765	44,883	—	5,037	—
1775	71,260	29,263	7,487	34,510
1802	163,192	78,281	13,333	71,578

SOURCE: Watts, *West Indies*, 321.

Investors tended to favor Cuba, and they paid less attention to Santo Domingo (Hispaniola). Perhaps as few as 6,000 *vecinos* inhabited the entire colony in 1730. The situation improved somewhat after 1740. Ranchers found a ready market for beef in French Saint-Domingue, several ports were opened to foreign commerce, and substantial immigration began from the Canary Islands. By 1785, the total population had risen to about 125,000—one-third of those living under French rule in the western part of the island. Some 40,000 of these are described as "Spanish," or white, and about the same number were slaves.

Trinidad

Until the reforms of the 1770s and 1780s, Trinidad was neglected and undeveloped and had few contacts even with the neighboring mainland province of Venezuela.

Table 15. **TRINIDAD POPULATION ESTIMATES, 1777–1834**

	Total	Whites	Slave	Free Non-Whites
1777	1,410	340	200	870
1797	17,716*	2,151	10,009	4,474
1802	28,477*	2,261	19,709	5,275
1825	42,174*	3,214	23,230	15,003
1834	44,715	3,632	22,359	18,724

NOTE: "Total" includes Native Americans during the following years: 1797 (1,082), 1802 (1,232), 1825 (727).

SOURCE: Patterson, *Slavery and Social Death*, 479.

Cacao was the most important crop until 1725, when the coca trees were blighted, probably by a fungus. Some settlers left, and others were killed by disease, especially by a smallpox epidemic in 1741. A 1733 census reported 162 non-Indian adults, including 28 whites. The Arawak living on Trinidad fared somewhat better than those in the Greater Antilles, who quickly died off; some 2,000 Indians still lived on the island in 1777. From the 1780s, however, the rapid opening up of the island for plantation development brought about the virtual disappearance of Indian villages.

The lowest point in the colony's life was probably reached following the 1741 smallpox epidemic. In *The Loss of El Dorado,* the Trinidadian author V. S. Naipaul (1932–) quotes contemporary records that describe the *vecinos* of Saint Joseph living "in drunken isolation." A new governor in 1757 commanded its inhabitants to clean up the town, to build a meeting hall for the *cabildo,* and to keep its minutes in "a decent book, properly bound." As Naipaul recounts the incident, the citizens found excuse after excuse to not to comply with his orders.

> It would take them more than a year to clear the streets and fill the holes, if they had tools. They didn't have tools and couldn't afford to buy any; and there were no tools on the island anyway. . . . Orders will be given to Pedro Bontur, the only carpenter in the island, to make the chest for the records. . . . But his Excellency the Governor must provide the boards, the cabildo knowing no one on the island who can make them; and when opportunity offers, His Excellency must get the locks and hinges for the same from the Main, nothing of the kind being available here. Orders will be given for the papers of the cabildo to be properly arranged; and a book will be made when paper is available, the members of the cabildo not having a single sheet between them at the moment.[5]

CHAPTER 10

THE WORLD OF THE SLAVES

Sugar enriched many planters as well as their European creditors and suppliers—and sugar made slavery necessary. The labor of black slaves was the basis for life on the sugar islands from the 17th century. Economically, socially, and politically, slavery dominated the islands to an extent never matched in human history. By the 1750s, almost nine out of 10 men and women were slaves on all the islands where sugar was grown. Never before in human history had so high a proportion of a population been slaves.[1]

Slavery tended to change over time as the island economies developed. At first, most slaves worked as hands on cane estates. By the end of the 18th century, slaves did every conceivable type of task—thus creating an entire range of situations from total bondage to comparative freedom. Blacks condemned to gang labor on sugar estates had the least control over their own lives. White overseers and black drivers controlled every minute of their day. Slaves doing other sorts of work could exercise more initiative and set their own pace. The greatest autonomy was enjoyed by skilled craftsmen and slaves living in towns—for example, in the seaports of the Virgin Islands, Curaçao, or the Bahamas.

In the Caribbean slave societies, sugar and human misery went together. On an individual basis, some slaves may have lived decent lives—as good as or better than those of European laborers during the same centuries. Urban slaves and those on islands without sugar fared the best. Slaves endured the harshest labor and most rigid controls during the early years of development, as planters set up estates. During these years, life on the islands was brutal and rough for both owners and slaves. As their masters prospered, some slaves enjoyed better treatment, and governments strove to improve or "ameliorate" slave conditions from about 1770.

Overall, the sugar islands failed the most basic test of slave well-being—the ability to survive and multiply. Before about 1800, death rates among Caribbean slaves always were much higher than birth rates. Perhaps the most telling indictment of the sugar islands is the relatively happier fate of Africans carried to North America. While island blacks died out, the slave population rapidly multiplied in British North America and the United States. Since Caribbean slaves died without reproducing themselves, the sugar estates could operate only by constantly importing enormous numbers of new slaves. Moreover, the high death rate among slaves in the Caribbean does not tell the entire story. Millions more died while they were being brought across the Atlantic to the sugar islands. The slaughter started during the dread "Middle Passage."

THE SLAVE TRADE BOOMS DURING THE 18TH CENTURY

Except for the Spanish, all the colonial powers encouraged and were directly involved in the Atlantic slave trade.[2] Until the 1680s, the Dutch West India Company dominated Atlantic commerce, including the slave trade. The British and French then destroyed Dutch commercial power during the Second (1665–1667) and Third (1672–1678) Dutch Wars. Great Britain thenceforth flourished as the supreme slaving nation in the Atlantic world. Between 1690 and 1807, British traders exported some 2,500,000 slaves to the Caribbean and Spanish America. Envying British success, the French government tried to foster participation by its own nationals. But French entry into the slave trade was slow and ineffective. During the 18th century, French slavers exported from Africa only half as many slaves as British traders.

Because of the peculiar nature of the slave trade, European governments believed they needed to garrison fortified settlements and warehouses along the coast of West Africa. These forts provided a safe haven where their nationals received and stored slaves provided by African rulers and slave dealers. And the forts also protected them from attack by hostile European powers (especially, at first, the Dutch). These trading posts were enormously expensive, and private capital was not at first ready to enter the business. During the 17th century, the Dutch, French, British, and Danish governments thus set up privileged state companies for Africa. In return for maintaining the African forts, these were granted legal monopolies over the slave trade.

None of these monopoly companies made money or brought over enough slaves to satisfy the Caribbean planters, and all countries turned to free trade. The British government allowed the charter of the Royal Africa Company to expire in 1712. In France, a royal decree in 1716 largely opened the trade to all Frenchmen who fitted out their ships in any of five major ports. Further reforms effectively opened the slave trade to almost all French merchants by 1741. Moreover, the government further encouraged the trade by exempting slaves from certain export and import duties and collecting only a modest tax on slaves imported into its colonies.

The Major Slave Routes to the Caribbean

Under the free trade regime, the British and French slave trades dramatically expanded. At their high point in the 1790s, British traders, many headquartered in Liverpool, brought almost 50,000 slaves each year to the Caribbean. At first, they carried most slaves to Barbados. From 1720, Jamaica took the lion's share of British slave exports. The acquisition of the ceded islands and especially Grenada opened up new markets after 1763. Although British America also imported slaves, the Caribbean plantations were the main consumer of slaves. The 13 mainland colonies purchased only half as many slaves as the one small island of Jamaica.

After the Portuguese and the British, the French were the most important slave dealers. French slavers brought in about 150,000 slaves during the 17th century and more than 1 million during the 18th. However, the sugar plantations on Saint-Domingue consumed slaves so rapidly—especially after 1763—that French traders never met their needs. Between 1701 and 1810, French merchants supplied only two-thirds of the French West Indian market, with British, Dutch, and North American merchants making up the deficit.

French ships invariably stopped first at Martinique, their first landfall out of Africa. A few ships occasionally went to Guadeloupe, but most either sold their cargo on Martinique or continued on to Saint-Domingue. After 1730, Saint-Domingue became the preferred destination, receiving more than three-quarters of all French slaves in the 1780s. Before going on to Saint-Domingue, traders rested the slaves on Martinique or on one of the tiny islands nearby. After the deadly Middle Passage, most needed a few days of rest to regain the appearance of good health.

The Dutch, whose small and arid islands were only minor sugar producers, primarily brought in slaves for sale on the British and French islands and on the Spanish mainland. Although Dutch merchants lost their dominance of the trade during the 1680s, they remained highly competitive carriers. Dutch slave imports actually grew during the 18th century, but their cargoes now formed only a dwindling proportion of an immensely larger trade. Altogether the two West India companies carried about 225,000 slaves to the Caribbean and Spanish America, while Dutch free traders imported another 50,000 into the West Indies between 1734 and 1803.[3] Curaçao flourished as a slave depot into the 1720s. In later years, most Dutch slavers headed for Sint Eustatius to supply the French market.

The Danish West India Company also built forts and factories on the African coast. The company colonized Saint Thomas for use as a slave depot, and the Danish slave trade expanded after it purchased Saint Croix in 1733. Following the Dutch example, the Danish government abolished the company's monopoly in 1734, opening the trade to all Danish merchants. Saint Croix received substantial numbers of Africans for use on its own plantations. As a free port, it also developed into a major center for the interisland or secondary market in slaves. Generally, larger ships from Africa docked at Christiansted, while smaller vessels from the West Indies used the lesser port at Frederiksted.

Table 16. **ESTIMATED SLAVE IMPORTS,
BY IMPORTING REGION, 1601–1870** *(in thousands)*

	1601–1700	1701–1760	1761–1810	1811–1870	Total
CARIBBEAN REGION					**4,059.9**
British Islands					**1,664.8**
Barbados	134.5	180.4	72.0	—	386.9
Leeward Islands	44.1	142.4	159.5	—	346.0
Jamaica	85.1	263.8	398.5	—	747.4
Windward Islands	—	—	70.1	—	70.1
Trinidad	—	—	22.4	—	22.4
Grenada	—	—	67.0	—	67.0
Other	—	10.0	15.0	—	25.0
French Islands					**1,521.0**
Martinique	66.5	146.8	111.6	41.0	365.9
Guadeloupe	12.7	160.5	76.6	41.0	290.8
Saint-Domingue	74.6	308.7	481.0	—	864.3
Spanish Islands					**766.9**
Santo Domingo	—	—	6.0	—	6.0
Cuba	—	—	139.2	550.0	689.2
Puerto Rico	—	—	16.6	55.1	71.7
Danish Islands	4.0	20.0	33.0	0.2	**57.2**
Dutch Islands					**50.0**
SOUTH AMERICA					**4,879.1**
Brazil	560.0	959.6	931.8	1,145.4	3,596.8
Spanish colonies	292.5	271.2	167.6	—	731.3
Dutch Guiana	40.0	280.0	180.0	—	500.0
French Guiana	2.0	21.0	14.0	14.0	51.0
NORTH AMERICA					**455.7**
British/U.S.A.	28.5	170.6	177.4	51.0	427.5
French Louisiana	—	18.0	10.2	—	28.2

NOTES: Prior to 1760, small numbers of slaves were illegally smuggled into the Spanish islands. The British Windward Islands comprise Saint Vincent, Saint Lucia, Tobago, and Dominica. "South America" includes Mexico and Central America. "Dutch Guiana" consists of Surinam, Demerara, Berbice, and Essequibo.

SOURCES: Philip Curtin, *The Atlantic Slave Trade: A Census* (Madison: University of Wisconsin Press, 1969), 35, 40, 44, 85, 216, 234, 268–69; James Rawley, *The Trans-Atlantic Slave Trade* (New York, 1981), 100, 167.

The Slave Trade in Africa

The Africans brought to the Caribbean already were slaves in Africa, and they were sold to European traders by their African owners. Almost all came from western Africa, usually from tribes living within 200 miles of the coast. Over the centuries, the slave trade tended to move slowly down the coast of West Africa, from the Senegambian region down to the Congo and Angola. During the 1800s, Biafra and the west-central regions contributed the most slaves, with perhaps 10 percent coming from Mozambique on the eastern coast.

Slavery always was widespread in West Africa, often taking in one-third or more of the population. However, some scholars believe that African slavery during earlier eras usually involved smaller groups in face-to-face relationships. Thus, traditional African forms of slavery presumably were less harsh than slavery on Caribbean sugar estates.

In precolonial Africa, no one really was a free individual, and the family, kinship grouping, or lineage was the dominant political and economic institution. African kinship groups sought to assimilate newly bought slaves into their circle—although in a subordinate position or status. Over several generations, the descendants of these slaves might come to belong to the tribe. Many slave villages might then work under their own management, paying a tribute something like that owed by serfs in medieval Europe.

But only settled and assimilated slaves belonged to the tribe. Most new slaves were taken in war, kidnapped on raids disguised as wars, or convicted as criminals. Immediately after capture or trial, the new slaves' lives were forfeit, and their master could treat them as he liked. Usually the master tried to sell new slaves as far away as possible from the region where they were taken. This prevented them running away to their own kinship group.

Since African societies contained many slaves, an extensive internal slave trade had developed. When the Portuguese landed on the West African coast in 1450, they found that a complex system of trade routes already crossed the continent. Since the 600s, organized intercontinental slave trades had transported millions of Africans north and east to the slave-holding Islamic states. A northern route carried perhaps 7 to 10 million slaves across the Sahara to North Africa and Egypt. An eastern network took some 5 million slaves north to Egypt and the Middle East, or across the Red Sea to Arabia.

After the Europeans arrived, Africans continued to control the supply of slaves to the transatlantic trade. Because they had no immunity to malaria and yellow fever, Europeans (and North Africans) literally could not live in West Africa.[4] Moreover, African warriors were equal or superior to Europeans, and their weapons were as effective until the end of the 19th century. European traders visited the slave coast at the sufferance of its African rulers. They did not create trade networks. They simply set up forts along the coast that tapped into the routes of Africa's already existing slave trade.

African slave dealers charged high prices in trade goods. As more and more slave ships came to the West African coast, prices rose sharply during the 18th century. Obviously, selling prices could vary between widely separated African ports. Overall, the average price of a male slave probably doubled from about £10 in the 1700s to £20 in 1740. It then dipped before rising again in the 1780s, to an average of £25 on the Gold Coast.

European purchasers, who competed for supplies with both the internal and Middle East trades, had to take what African sellers offered them. Thus we cannot identify the precise origins of Caribbean blacks. European traders named slaves after the port where they purchased them, even though many had been captured hundreds of miles away. With rare exceptions, Europeans knew little about the political or cultural origins of the slaves they bought.

Because of the strong African demand, sellers tended to offer Europeans only the "least indispensable" slave.[5] African owners valued female slaves more highly than males. Thus fewer women than men showed up at slave markets, and the European slave traders mainly shipped adult males. Overall, European slavers carried twice as many men as women to the Americas, and children under 10 years of age made up less than 10 percent of their cargoes.

The Middle Passage

Slave traders often spent several months purchasing slaves at various ports. As soon as they accumulated their cargo, they sailed for the Americas with their captives on the notorious Middle Passage. Most followed a direct route due west to near the Ascension Islands and then turned north toward the West Indies and Martinique or Barbados. Tropical storms or the doldrums near the equator could delay the voyage, which might take as little as one month or as long as half a year.

As the trade boomed during the 18th century, slavers of all nations carried, fed, and treated slaves in similar ways. Slave ships tended to be small and narrow. Into their limited cargo space, their captains packed an average of 300 captives and a relatively large crew of 35 to control the slaves. On average they allotted each captive only half the amount of room afforded convicts, emigrants, or soldiers transported during the same years.

All traders used temporary platforms between decks to provide sleeping space. Male slaves, but not women or children, were shackled together in pairs—left leg to right leg, left wrist to right wrist. Some captains removed the shackles once the ship was at sea, others took them off during the day, and some left their captives chained throughout the voyage. Most fed the slaves on dried beans, rice, corn, yams, and palm oil—with meat a rarity.

The Middle Passage took a heavy toll of Europeans as well as Africans. All told, 13 percent of the slaves carried aboard French ships during the 18th century died before reaching the West Indies. And almost one out of five seamen sailing out of Nantes did not return to France. During the early years, outbreaks of smallpox, measles, or other highly communicable diseases caused astronomical death rates on some voyages. At all times, amebic dysentery and scurvy were the biggest killers. Contrary to legend, overcrowding or "tight packing" was not the major cause of death on board. Since the risk of dysentery increases with time at sea, the death rate instead rose with the length of the voyage, the quality of food and water during the passage, and epidemics and health conditions at the time of departure in Africa.

Slaves were expensive. Since they could not resell dead or diseased slaves, all captains had a strong economic motive to minimize losses. Most ships carried surgeons, but their medical efforts did the sick little good. Death rates dropped after 1750 because Europeans used faster ships, learned more about hygiene and diet, and introduced crude forms of vaccination against smallpox. On average, about 20 percent of the slaves died during the Middle Passage before 1700, compared with some 5 percent around 1800.

Although it killed fewer victims as slavers improved their techniques, the Middle Passage deserves the condemnation it has received. Whether it was caused by cruelty or by ignorance, even a 5 percent death rate (in 1800) is extraordinary among young adults during a two- to three-month voyage. Moreover, many additional slaves died on the way to the ships before leaving Africa. No precise accounting is possible. But as many as 8 million Africans may have died to bring 4 million slaves to the Caribbean islands.

THE UNIQUE NATURE
OF CARIBBEAN SLAVERY

Slavery is difficult to define precisely. Individual freedom, the logical opposite of slavery, is a modern concept. Before the 19th century, hardly anyone was free in our sense of the word. Ties and obligations, which they could not unilaterally dissolve, constrained most persons and limited their freedom of action. Every individual belonged to one or more communities and was bound by family traditions, village customs, obligations to lords, or craft regulations. Even today, it is questionable whether we can accurately describe as "free" the many men and women laboring at jobs they dislike in order to purchase food, clothing, and housing.

What made slavery on tropical plantations unusual was the master's total freedom of control over his or her slaves. In most agricultural societies, serfs were members of a village governed by communal traditions. Their lord usually could not interfere with the customary ways of doing things. By contrast, Caribbean sugar plantations resembled factories in a modern capitalist society. To meet the demands of the world market, the owner and his agents had to manage rigorously all steps of production. Until the end of the 18th century, most sugar estates used the "gang" system. The owner treated dozens or hundreds of slaves literally as units of production. He organized their labor from day to day and even hour to hour. And he used physical force to ensure that, like cogs in a well-oiled machine, the slaves performed their assigned tasks on time.

Slaves working on cane estates always suffered the harshest conditions and labored under the most rigorous controls. The very nature of the sugarcane industry

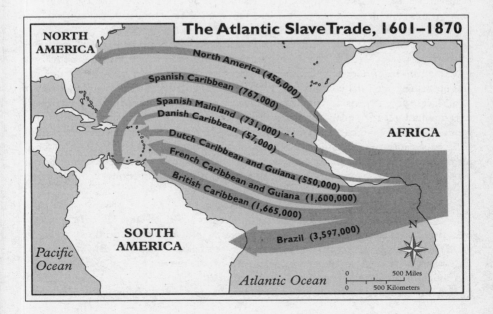

The Atlantic Slave Trade, 1601–1870

NORTH AMERICA

North America (456,000)
Spanish Caribbean (767,000)
Spanish Mainland (731,000)
Danish Caribbean (57,000)
Dutch Caribbean and Guiana (550,000)
French Caribbean and Guiana (1,600,000)
British Caribbean (1,665,000)
Brazil (3,597,000)

AFRICA

SOUTH AMERICA

Pacific Ocean

Atlantic Ocean

N

0   500 Miles
0   500 Kilometers

partially explains the master's need for total control. The weight and bulk of harvested cane are enormous compared to other grasses. (As a rule of thumb in the 18th century, planters needed 20 pounds of cane to make 1 pound of sugar.) Thus growers cannot export cane unless they first concentrate the sugar by milling it. In this process, machines squeeze out the cane juice, which then is boiled to evaporate excess water, producing crystalline sugar and a by-product called molasses.

Milling is crucial and must be done quickly. Laborers must cut sugar as soon as it is ripe and then take it to the mill within 24 hours or it will ferment. For this reason, immediate access to a sugar mill is essential. From the 1860s, most notably in Cuba, several dependent farmers (*colonos*) brought their cane to a large mill (*central*) owned by a dominant planter or corporation. During the 18th century, however, it was thought necessary for every plantation to have its own mill under the owner's total control.

A sugar plantation—a "factory set in a field"[6]—thus combined agriculture and manufacturing. It was a novel social, economic, and political organization that brought together large amounts of capital and human labor and combined them on tropical soils. To make a profit, a planter had to manage and coordinate a complex series of tasks. For the slaves, most of these tasks involved intense and monotonous labor.

Island Laws Give Planters Unlimited Power over Their Slaves

Planters, especially on cane estates, had to exercise close control over their slaves. At least through the 18th century, island laws granted them the unlimited powers they needed, and the courts seldom bothered with the relationships between slaves and masters. Since slavery now was rare in western Europe, the colonies had to develop new laws regulating slavery. The legislature of each British island made its own laws—with the consent of the governor and Crown—for and peculiar to that colony. Laws were harshest where slaves greatly outnumbered their owners (Jamaica) and less severe in islands without sugar plantations (the Bahamas).

French, Dutch, Danish, and Spanish islands in theory enjoyed less local initiative, since they were governed by royal laws. In 1685 the Crown proclaimed one single Code Noir (Black Code) governing the treatment of slaves in all French colonies. However, although it was drawn up in the mother country, French jurists based the Code Noir on practices and precedents in the Antilles. Thus, it was at least as oppressive in many areas as the laws passed by legislatures on the British islands.

All islands sought to protect the planter and not the slave. Whether British, French, Spanish, Dutch, or Danish, all courts savagely punished slaves who rebelled or struck their masters. In these cases, the penalties included slow death by torture or the loss of an ear, hand, or leg. Early slave codes also authorized mutilation for persistent runaways and for theft.

Except for the Spanish, slave codes treated the slaves as property and thus allowed planters to do as they pleased with their slaves. British slave laws often did not mention slave marriages, families, education, or religious conversion. The French Code Noir did recognize marriage and required slaves to be baptized. But slaves could not marry without their master's consent, and owners did not have to provide time off for religious education or worship.

The differences between these slave laws mattered little in practice. The sugar

THE WORLD OF THE SLAVES
THE WORLD OF THE SLAVES

planters and their agents dominated colonial society and controlled local affairs. London, Paris, Copenhagen, and The Hague sent governors to the islands under their flags. But these governors could act effectively only with the support of the colonial planters. On all islands, slavery was regulated by local courts and customary law.

The French Code Noir and Spanish colonial laws were more generous than British laws in their treatment of manumission (the gaining of free status). By prohibiting manumission without the owner's consent, the British colonies made it almost impossible to gain freedom. More slaves became free in the Spanish colonies, such as Cuba. Courts in these colonies frequently allowed slaves to own personal property, make contracts, and buy their freedom with their own savings. To a more limited extent, self-purchase also became part of the customary law in the French islands. French (and Spanish) courts also permitted marriage between white males and freed female slaves, whose children thus became free as well.

French law gave freed slaves full legal rights of citizenship. But British colonies usually denied freed slaves all legal privileges except that of a jury trial. Even if free, blacks and persons of color in British colonies could not vote or hold political office, and laws forbade them to enter certain trades. Thus freedmen were both more numerous and more powerful in the French colonies. They were especially influential in the South and West Provinces of Saint-Domingue, where they took a major part in the revolution of 1791.

The Harsh Life of a Field Slave

By the 18th century, sugarcane estates could not function without the labor of African slaves, who were bound to the soil by strict laws. The slave in turn became bound up in a rhythm of unceasing labor determined by the needs of the sugar plant itself. Work routines fell into a fixed and unvarying pattern. In a set sequence of steps, the slaves prepared and manured the soil, then planted, weeded, harvested, crushed, cured, boiled, and sometimes distilled the cane. As soon as they had completed one task, another demanded the attention of the planter and slaves.

Before land could be used for sugarcane, slaves with axes removed and burned the existing trees and brush. Once they cleared the land, owners laid out sugar plantations in patterns that made crop rotation easier, saved on transportation costs, and simplified slave management. Most planters divided their property into three to five large cane fields. Each year they harvested canes from one part of the land, with the other fields divided among growing canes and fallow. On the larger islands of Jamaica and Saint-Domingue, a sugar plantation usually took up about four times the amount of land given to cane. The cane mill and the boiling and refining houses occupied a central location in the middle of the fields. The remaining acres were taken up by food plots ("provision grounds"), grazing land, the planter's house, slave quarters, workshops, and animal pens.

The Plantation as Farm:
Planting and Harvesting Sugarcane

Planters generally harvested cane about 18 months after it was planted. They timed planting and harvesting to coincide with the island's rainy and dry seasons. During the rainy season—May/June to December/January—the slaves dug holes and dunged, planted, fertilized, and weeded the growing plants. During the dry season, from January to May/June, they harvested and processed the mature crop, cutting the canes and carrying them to the mill to be ground.

Sugarcane is propagated through cuttings from the tops of mature plants. Originally these were planted in long trenches. From the 1720s, most planters adopted holing to prevent soil erosion and conserve moisture. Using hand-held hoes, the slaves dug holes five to six inches deep and about five feet square. They then laid one or two cane tops in the center of each hole and covered them with about two inches of soil. As the plant sprouted and grew taller, the slaves filled the hole with mulch and dung until the field was level. During the following weeks, they weeded and thinned the growing plants and inserted new cuttings to replace any failing to grow. After five or six months, the canes were large enough to keep down the weeds.

This method of planting involved extremely heavy labor. Particularly on clay soils baked hard by the sun, holing is arduous work, and only the fittest of the slaves could endure it. Because the land was cut up by the cane holes, slaves had to spread dung by hand. Long files of slaves, usually women, carried the heavy dung baskets to the fields.

To spread out the harvest, planting was staggered over several months early in the rainy season. Cane planted in July was ready to be harvested 18 months later in January. Thus, the slaves performed one difficult task after another during the entire period from July through March. The heavy labor of holing, dunging, and weeding had barely ended, when it was time to begin cutting, hauling, and milling the mature cane.

Harvesting the cane was as difficult as holing. Using machetes, cutlasses, or long heavy "bills," the slaves chopped off the canes close to the ground. They then stripped the canes of leaves and cut them into shorter pieces three or four feet in length. These heavy bundles were then carried to the mills by the slaves, on pack animals, or in carts drawn by cattle or mules.

The Plantation as Factory: Sugar Milling and Refining

At the mill the slaves crushed the cane to remove the liquid or juice, which was boiled and clarified until it crystallized into sugar. As a final step, they might distill molasses (the residue remaining after the cane is clarified) into rum at the still house. The first step, crushing or milling the cane, used a vertical three-roller mill.[7] Wind, water, slaves, or cattle turned the middle roller. Through interconnecting cogs and teeth, it turned the two rollers on either side.

Two slaves fed the newly cut canes into this mill. One in front of the rollers inserted the canes. The other behind the rollers received the crushed stalks and passed them back to extract the rest of the liquid. The cane juice from the rollers ran off into a series of as many as seven copper vats of decreasing size. Slaves added lime water to the boiling cane syrup, and they removed the gross matter with a long-handled skimmer. From the last boiler, the liquid sugar was emptied into wooden troughs or coolers. If the boiling was successful, the liquid cooled into a mixture of crystals and molasses. After 13 or 14 hours, a plug at the bottom of each trough was removed, permitting the molasses to drain off.

This first stage of grinding and boiling produced a coarse brownish product known as *muscovado,* from a Portuguese word meaning "less finished." Many planters shipped the sugar in this state, but some went on to make a semi-refined grade known as clayed sugar. Slaves placed the muscovado into cone-shaped clay molds, and covered the top of each mold with a whitish clay. This helped to purge the sugar of molasses as the water drained down through the sugar toward a small hole in the bottom of the cone. Work in the sugar mill, where the constant heat of the fires raised the temperature above 120 degrees, was as difficult as field labor. It also called for considerable skill. The slave supervising the boiling operations had an especially demanding job. More than anyone else his judgment could mean the difference between a profit or loss.

African slaves harvesting sugar in Cuba, 19th century. ("Raza Negra-Negros de Guinea en Cuba.") Tools similar to those shown also were used during previous centuries. Field gangs often contained more women than men.

On most islands, cattle, horses, mules, or even the slaves themselves turned the sugar mill's rollers. On low-lying islands open to the trade winds, especially Barbados but also on Antigua, Saint Kitts, and lowland Guadeloupe, planters introduced windmills during the 18th century. Water mills primarily were found in the French islands. Many plantations on Saint-Domingue introduced water mills in the 1740s and 1750s. To a lesser extent, planters also built water mills on Guadeloupe, Martinique, and Jamaica.

Refining represents the third and last stage in sugar making. The raw product was reheated, and egg whites, white vinegar, or bullock's blood was added. This solution was clarified by the removal of scum, reboiled, and cooled in molds with a layer of wet clay to separate the crystals. Almost all sugar was refined in Europe or in North America. Some Martinique and Guadeloupe planters built their own refineries at the end of the 17th century, but the government forced them to close to protect the French refining industry.

Stone windmill, Saint Croix. One of dozens of windmills that provided power to grind sugarcane. Wind-powered mills were especially popular on low-lying islands (such as Barbados and Antigua) and along the windward coasts of Saint Croix, Saint Kitts, Nevis, and Guadeloupe.

Besides muscovado and clayed sugar, many plantations sold several liquid by-products of the milling process. They produced the coarsest—known as *garapa* by the Portuguese and *grappe* by the French—by collecting cane juice skimmed from the boiling syrup and allowing it to ferment. This produced an inexpensive but very strong liquor popular among slaves and poor whites. From the molasses left by the boiling and claying processes, the planters distilled a milder and smoother liquor known in French as *tafia* and in English as rum. All of the colonists enjoyed rum, but the British colonies in North America and the Caribbean formed the largest market. Thus the French sold most of their rum to foreigners, contrary to both British and French law.

Slave Gangs, Slave Tasks

During all periods, slavery was harshest on sugar estates under the "gang system." Sugar gangs enjoyed the least personal freedom, suffered the worst conditions, and endured frequent physical punishments. These slaves worked under close control at repetitive tasks, with each member of the gang doing the same work. Throughout the 1700s, planters rigorously standardized the gang system to increase production. Under the supervision of drivers, large gangs dug cane holes, weeded the growing plants, and cut mature cane. A long line of slaves moved down the field in order, urged on by the whips of the drivers. At other times—when the slaves carried dung baskets, cane, or grass on their heads—the gang marched in a file, with the drivers in the rear.

Many planters divided their field slaves into three or more gangs. They assigned slaves by age and strength, trying to match the strongest slaves to the hardest tasks. The drivers put mature men and women into the first or "great" gang, which they trained to do the hard work of holing and harvesting. The second gang—youths from 12 to 18 and elderly men and women—was given lighter field work. Children six to 12 went into the third gang, and the drivers put them to work weeding or gathering grass. Women as well as men formed part of the first gang. Indeed, more women than men worked in the fields. Since men held almost all the skilled jobs as drivers and craftsmen, women filled up the field gangs, even though men usually outnumbered women overall.

These gangs worked from dawn to dark, six days a week, and more than 300 days a year. Although they usually did not work on Sundays, owners expected field slaves to spend their spare time growing food on their provision grounds. The slaves marched to the fields about 5 A.M. in the summer and a little later during the winter months. They continued to labor until dusk, with two breaks to cook their meals. The normal workday thus lasted 10 to 12 hours. But it was much longer during the sugar harvest, when milling and boiling continued around the clock and slaves worked 16 or 18 hours a day.

The harsh gang system was most prevalent on the sugar estates. Slaves in towns or on smaller farms worked under the "task system." This meant that their owner or a driver assigned them a set amount of work to accomplish within a certain time limit. Artisans—carpenters, barrel makers, masons, bricklayers, spinners and weavers—always worked by the task. Moreover, tasking was employed in growing products other than sugar—including arrowroot, cocoa, coffee, long-staple cotton, pimento, rice, and lumber. Some sugar estates also switched from ganging to tasking during the late 18th century. On the British islands, tasking replaced ganging as part of a policy of "amelioration" that sought to keep slaves alive as prices for new slaves increased.

Field Slaves Must Fend for Themselves

On large plantations, owners and managers cared about the slaves only as laborers and only during working hours. After the day's gang labor was done, whites left the slaves to do as they pleased. In most cases, they expected the slaves to feed, clothe, and house themselves. As a result, estate slaves lived under miserable conditions, and they also had little contact with whites. These two facts are related. On a large cane plantation, eight to 10 whites managed hundreds of slaves. To these white managers, the slaves literally were faceless "hands" working in anonymous "gangs."

Field hands and most skilled slaves lived away from their owners in what often were miniature African villages. Estate slaves usually constructed their own houses out of straw and mud, thatching them with guinea grass, cane tops, or palmetto fronds, Rarely larger than 12 feet square, slave huts typically contained only two rooms, with dirt floors and without windows. Other than a few wooden bowls, a water-jug, and an iron pot for boiling their meals, most slaves had no furniture and slept on the floor.

These flimsy slave huts have disappeared without a trace. Old maps show that they often were set close to the sugar mill and within sight of the overseer's house. In the French West Indies, slave huts usually were constructed in a circle around a common open area. On some estates they were laid out in rows, with the huts of the headmen and drivers close to the more solid houses of the managers.

Estate owners also took little responsibility for slave clothing and food. In most colonies, laws required owners to give every slave clothes each year. On the British islands, these laws became more generous during the period of amelioration after 1770. But most owners simply gave out rolls of coarse cloth and expected the slave women to make it into clothes. As late as 1800, travelers described slaves—both male and female—as working naked or nearly so in both the fields and the sugar factories. For Sunday and holidays, slaves might dress up in better clothes that they had bought or made for themselves. House servants and town slaves were more decently dressed, though often barefoot.

The wholly inadequate housing and clothing of the field slaves contributed to their high death rate. Caribbean evenings and mornings can be quite cool, particularly in the winter months. West Africans have relatively little tolerance for cold. Already weakened by overwork and malnourishment, slaves easily fell victim to the "fevers" that killed so many.

More than anything else, however, plantation slaves suffered from a lack of adequate food. Planters used two methods to feed their estate slaves. Those on Barbados and the Leewards (and later Cuba) devoted all their land to sugar. To feed the slaves, they imported corn from North America and beans from England. On Jamaica, Saint-Domingue, Puerto Rico, and some of the Windward Islands, land remained more abundant. Here owners assigned the slaves "provision grounds" and expected them to grow their own food when they could.

Slaves often went hungry between June and September, the very months in which heavy work digging cane holes exhausted their energies. Many starved following hurricanes or during wartime naval blockades. At the best of times, a slave's diet was limited and monotonous. Most slaves lived on gruels or stews of cornmeal, rice, millet, and kidney beans ("pigeon peas"). To these they added the root plants—yams, potatoes, cassava, sweet potatoes—that formed the main diet of many West Africans. Some slaves also raised greens and fruit as well as hogs and chickens. However, they often sold both produce and animals, using their earnings to buy a few innocent pleasures, such as clothing, liquor, and tobacco.

Field slaves were seriously malnourished because they consumed little protein or fat. Planters rarely supplied fresh meat and fed their slaves from imported supplies of dried and salted fish, pork, and beef. Few slaves got as much as a pound a week, and the imported meat and fish often turned putrid before they received it.[8] A diet low in meat and fat condemned field slaves to poor health and low fertility. The lack of these essential elements led to high death rates—among newly born children and infants as well as adults. Planters did not deliberately set out to starve their slaves. However, most planters—especially during the 18th century—did not provide a diet that could maintain health or even an efficient workforce.

Overwork and underfeeding rather than deliberate cruelty were the main causes of high slave mortality. There is little reliable information about whipping and other punishments during the course of everyday life on rural estates. Occasional anecdotes describe cases of exceptional brutality, especially during the earlier years. In the British colonies at least, punishments apparently became less frequent and brutal toward the end of the 18th century. Most owners were sane enough not to deliberately destroy the expensive species of human machinery that provided their income. However, many planters—out of greed, carelessness, or mere stupidity—did allow their slaves to die of hunger and disease.

Slaves Take on Every Sort of Work

As the sugar islands prospered, their economies became more complex, and some planters became more polished. By 1800, slaves performed a wide variety of tasks. On some long-settled islands, probably less than half the slave population now lived on the sugar estates. Moreover, plantation records show that only about half of the slaves on rural estates actually worked as part of the field gangs.

☀ A DEADLY DIET

In the contemporary United States, where some are overfed, meat and fat often are regarded as harmful. In fact, both are absolutely necessary to life. Meat and dairy products are the only natural source of high-quality or perfect proteins that supply all the essential amino acids. These proteins build the muscles, blood, and internal organs as well as form enzymes and antibodies that sustain health and fight infections. For women, a lack of protein also can lower the age of menopause, inhibit ovulation, and increase miscarriages or stillbirths. Among men, a poor diet can lead to a loss of sperm mobility or even of sperm production. Fats also are essential to supply energy, to keep the body warm, to carry the fat-soluble vitamins (A, D, E, and K), and to help the body absorb other vitamins.

Throughout the islands, slaves did virtually any job that provided an income to their owners and that the free population could not or would not do. Since advanced schooling was not available, whites monopolized (at least for other whites) the "lettered" professions of accounting, law, medicine, and the clergy. Slaves performed virtually all other tasks. Many worked as domestic servants. Visitors frequently commented on the enormous staffs of servants maintained by Caribbean whites. In 1795, for example, the overseer on the Worthy Park estate in Jamaica assigned 36 slaves to serve six white persons.

In the towns as well as on the estates, slaves were responsible for every type of unskilled and skilled labor. In the ports, slaves worked as sailors and fishermen as well as dock hands. Slaves provided most of the internal marketing system. Slaves worked in many shops. Traveling saleswomen—called "higglers" or *revendeuses* (*révâdèz* in Creole)—carried provisions from the country to towns and also brought imported goods from the ports back to the rural estates. Town slaves commanded and often excelled at every kind of artisan skill—including carpentry, masonry, barrel making, cooking, baking, tailoring, hairdressing, performing, weaving, silversmithing, and cigar making.

The Ambiguous Life of Urban Slaves and Freedmen

It always is dangerous to generalize about the mysterious relationship between master or mistress and servants. Nevertheless, town slaves did enjoy more freedom and better treatment than field hands. A skilled artisan is a valuable property precisely because he or she can work without direction. Slave craftsmen and higglers often controlled their own time. Some were rented out and had a say as to who they worked for—or even who might buy them. Free persons of color supported themselves in many of the same ways as slaves. Thus the distinction between slavery and freedom eventually blurred in many towns.

Urban slaves also enjoyed better living conditions and thus lived longer than field hands. Since many were owned by poor whites and black freedmen, they were not luxuriously housed. But at least they slept under a solid roof, and they had access to a variety of fresh food and cotton clothing. Moreover, they could mingle at town taverns and dances with other slaves and sometimes with poor whites.

Freedmen and urban slaves could amass large sums of cash money. Rented slaves might keep tips above the contract price (legally under Spanish law). Higglers often controlled their receipts. In competition with other vendors, they charged that day's market price, kept the receipts, and settled up with their owners days or weeks later. On some islands, slaves controlled far more liquid cash than many sugar planters, who often were heavily in debt. After emancipation on most islands, former slaves, as well as freedmen, drew upon their cash hoards to buy thousands of acres from failed planters.

The Sugar Plantation as a Killing Machine

On all the sugar islands, death rates for black slaves were always higher than birth rates. Africans sold to Caribbean cane estates suffered a much harsher fate than those carried farther north to America. In contrast to the remarkable natural decrease (excess of deaths over births) in the Caribbean, the American slave population rapidly increased. Since the slaves in both cases came from the same regions of West Africa, this difference provides perhaps the harshest indictment of Caribbean slavery. In 1825, both the United States and the islands had an African population of about 2 million. But slave traders had carried (through 1810) about 3,500,000 slaves to the islands and only some 375,000 to British North America.

It sometimes is said that Latin or Roman Catholic countries enjoyed a milder or more humane form of slavery compared with the Dutch or English. The survival rates do not support this belief. African slaves fared as badly in the French colonies as in the British. In the Greater Antilles, it is possible to compare British Jamaica to French Saint-Domingue (today Haiti). From 1655 through 1807, Jamaica imported about 750,000 slaves. In 1834, only 310,000 slaves were freed. Saint-Domingue took in about 800,000 slaves prior to the slave rebellion in 1791. A census in 1789 counted only 435,000. The death rate was even higher on the smaller Leeward Islands. Although Barbados received 387,000 slaves, the planters only freed 81,000 in 1834. From 1635, Martinique imported 366,000 slaves; only 100,000 Africans remained in 1848, when the French abolished slavery.

The record is slightly better for Spanish Cuba and Puerto Rico. On these islands, the African population did not increase over time; but at least the slaves did not die off as rapidly as on the French and British islands. Cuba, for example, imported about 700,000 slaves from 1761 through 1870. The census of 1877 counted 480,000 Africans.[9]

Because the slaves died without reproducing themselves, the sugar estates could operate only by constantly importing new workers from Africa. A vicious cycle existed. The slave traders brought in new slaves, many of whom soon died—making it necessary to bring in yet more slaves to die. We could continue this catalog of human misery for every island (except the Bahamas and Curaçao). As with the extermination of the Arawak in the 1500s, the word *genocide* precisely describes the fate of Africans carried to the sugar islands as field slaves.

This "natural decrease" continued for some two centuries. Contemporary critics blamed cruel masters, poor food and housing, intense work schedules, disease, and the rigors of the Middle Passage. All of these worked together to make the tropical sugar plantation a true killing machine. Caribbean slaves suffered from both high death rates and low birth rates, and both factors hindered population growth. Very high infant mortality provided the most important check on the slave population. A low-protein and low-fat diet reduced births and also made adults more susceptible to disease.

There is an obvious connection between sugar plantations and high death rates. Slave deaths increased as agriculture intensified after 1700. At least in the British colonies, death rates fell toward the end of the century. Slavery thus was most deadly during the early years when planters rapidly developed sugar estates and introduced the factory-type discipline of gang slavery.[10] The population decline slowed in the older colonies as the economy matured and more slaves worked away from the fields.[11]

Overall, the natural decrease averaged about 3 percent per year in Jamaica and 4 percent a year in the Leeward and Windward Islands. By the 19th century, the African population fell only 1 percent a year or less in the older colonies. The French colonies may have had a worse record. Some planters on Saint-Domingue had to replace 10 percent of their hands every year.

African slaves (and white immigrants) died most rapidly during their first three years in the islands, when they were said to be undergoing "seasoning." During these first years, at least 15 to 20 percent died and sometimes as many as one in three. Already weakened by confinement and malnutrition during the Middle Passage from Africa, many perished from the sudden exposure to a new disease environment. Dysentery (the "bloody flux") killed many new arrivals. Others succumbed to tuberculosis, typhoid, and varieties of malaria and yellow fever to which they had not been exposed in Africa.

Slaves also died rapidly during their first years of life. Three out of every four babies died before the age of five. Thus, the effective birth rate was very low. Abolitionists and other critics accused planters of believing that it was "better to buy than to breed." Since both pregnant women and young children ate without working, these critics charged, planters did not encourage slave births. However, most planters probably favored births—at least in principle. Yet, as one planter said, despite all he did, "the children do not come."

Recurrent epidemics continued to kill off both creole slaves living past childhood and Africans that outlasted the seasoning process. A few lived into their sixties or seventies. But the average life expectancy, among those surviving infancy, probably was less than 40 years. A field hand's chance of survival to middle age finally began to increase after 1800. Second- and third-generation creoles adapted to the West Indian disease environment. When the slave trade ended in 1807, it brought a halt to epidemics introduced by the constant influx of new Africans. The number of creole slaves actually began to increase in Barbados by about 1810, in Jamaica from the 1840s. The development of natural immunities and better food probably helped the most—18th-century medical care the least.

🦎 WHY DID CARIBBEAN SLAVES PRODUCE SO FEW CHILDREN?

Modern historians suggest various reasons why Caribbean slaves had so few live children—the main reason the slave population fell each year. Few women of childbearing years were imported into the islands. Overall, African slave dealers sold fewer women than men to European traders. When they did put women on sale, they generally proffered only those who already were mature adults. After they arrived in the Caribbean, a poor diet and the physical stress of sugar planting reduced fertility among both men and women and also caused many stillbirths. West Indians retained the African custom of prolonged breast-feeding, which also reduces fertility. Lack of opportunity may also have prevented conception, since slave unions often were irregular and short-lived.

None of these modern explanations for low birth rates among slaves is fully convincing. One can easily understand why slaves died at a high rate, but the causes of low fertility remain something of a mystery. Perhaps slave mothers simply did not see much point in raising children solely to provide laborers for their masters.

CHAPTER 11

ENGLAND AND FRANCE STRUGGLE TO CONTROL THE ISLANDS

The great wealth of the sugar islands made them immensely valuable prizes during the world wars that pitted France against Great Britain from 1744 to 1783. The sugar estates now were much too valuable to destroy. Although England and France were at war during 16 of these 39 years, neither nation pillaged the other's Caribbean colonies. Both sides wanted to take the enemy's colonies intact. In sharp contrast to its policy during the 17th century, the British government thus ordered its invading armies to protect French plantations, and it gave generous terms to the islands it conquered. During all wars, French, British, and sometimes Spanish privateers destroyed thousands of merchant vessels, seriously disrupting trade with Europe and North America. Since many islands depended on imported food, the African slaves suffered greatly, and thousands died. But the cane estates themselves suffered little lasting damage.

During the War of the Austrian Succession (1740–48), the Seven Years' War (1756–63), and (in its international aspects) the War for American Independence

(1776–83), Great Britain and France fought to gain commercial and colonial supremacy throughout the world. Although the Caribbean certainly was a major theater of battle, these were true world wars, also fought in Europe, North America, Africa, and India. In Europe, the Franco-British contest over foreign colonies became entwined with continental wars of plunder that did not directly affect the Caribbean. The fortunes of war in Europe did influence decisions at the peace conferences. British statesmen in 1763, for example, gave up overseas gains in return for restoration of territories lost by their European allies.

During earlier wars between England and France, only one territory was permanently transferred.[1] In contrast, several islands changed hands many times during the 18th century. Saint Lucia probably holds the record for frequent changes of ownership. Although the island is mountainous with comparatively poor soil, Saint Lucia has in Castries one of the finest small harbors in the West Indies. Unlike those based in more distant Barbados and Antigua, British ships at Saint Lucia could watch the principal French base at Fort Royal, Martinique—less than 25 miles away. The island thus had strategic importance to the security of the French Islands. It was from Saint Lucia, for example, that Admiral Rodney sailed to win the decisive Battle of The Saints in 1782. British forces conquered Saint Lucia in 1762 and 1778, but returned it to France in 1763 and 1783 (Treaties of Paris and Versailles). The British took the island again in 1794 and 1796 and again returned it to France in 1802 (Treaty of Amiens). Retaken yet again in 1803, Saint Lucia finally was ceded to Britain in 1814 (Treaty of Paris).

However, even changes of flag did not deeply affect the society or economy of an island. Sugar dominated the economies of all the islands, and the planters in turn influenced local governments under both the French and the British. Some have argued that rule by one empire—either French or British—might have led to greater unity between the islands. This seems unlikely. An islander's loyalty is to his or her own homeland. The Leeward Islands—close neighbors under one flag—always resisted British pressures to form a federation. We may safely assume that Antigua and Martinique would not today form one country if the British had retained the latter in 1763.

THE MILITARY WEAKNESS OF SLAVE SOCIETIES

The wars between 1740 and 1783 did little damage in the colonies. However, the planters could not know this in advance. The British in particular were thrown into terror by any rumors that a French fleet had arrived. French attacks during earlier wars proved that even a small armed force could cause very great losses.[2]

To defend their ports and provide places of refuge during an invasion, island leaders hurriedly erected forts, some still extant. But the regular navies of England and France provided the main defense of the colonies. The islands were extremely vulnerable to attack because they had no local forces. Both Britain and France were reluctant to station large numbers of regular troops on the islands, since the planters refused to contribute toward their pay during years of peace. The island militias were very small, wretchedly trained, and almost wholly unwarlike.

With the growth of large estates worked by slaves, the number of white men able to join the militias had fallen. Guadeloupe was supposed to contain between 3,000 and 4,000 armed men, but not more than 1,600 appeared with weapons when the British invaded in 1762. To make up the gap, the militias included free blacks and mulattos, especially in the French islands. However, the planters generally did not trust their slaves with weapons and primarily used them as laborers. It was not until 1795 that the British government formed 12 West India regiments of black troops.

British and French Naval Strategies

Fleets sailing from Europe decided these wars, and the British and French developed different naval strategies. The West India Interest enjoyed substantial political influence in England. It insisted on squadrons of warships permanently stationed in the West Indies. Following the earthquake of 1692, the Crown rebuilt Port Royal's dockyard, and a second naval station was set up in 1743 at English Harbour in Antigua. In May 1757, the Admiralty decided to keep eight line warships at both stations, though it could not always fulfill this resolution.

Unlike the British, the French did not have permanent naval bases until 1784 and sent fleets from Europe for specific purposes. The British system probably was superior over the long run. Certainly British fleets dominated the Caribbean during the Seven Years' War. Britain's permanent fleets could not defeat major French expeditions, but they did command the seas during several months each year and interrupted French trade.

Caribbean bases contributed to British victory by allowing British fleets to stay in the region longer than fleets from France. To avoid the hurricane season, French ships intended to leave by October or November and return to Europe by the end of June. But large expeditions often were delayed in port and did not get off until the middle of January. In 1759 and 1762, French fleets thus arrived too late to prevent the British conquests of Guadeloupe and Martinique.

The French and British strategies both had advantages and disadvantages. French fleets arrived in the West Indies fresh from the dockyard and in good repair, whereas British ships quickly rotted under tropical conditions. Once they arrived in the region, however, the French fleets quickly ran out of food, while British ships could obtain provisions from the permanent naval stations. Because they had to carry their own supplies and provisions, French ships could stay in the Caribbean for no more than six months—or even less in the case of small frigates. Stores rarely lasted long in the Tropics, and some French fleets left early because their supplies had rotted.

French naval forces could purchase little food once they arrived. The French islands could not feed themselves in peacetime, and the British blockade hindered shipments from North America. Crews arriving from France immediately fell ill of yellow fever or malaria, often so severely that several squadrons could not sail. As soon as these epidemics began to subside, the food had run out, and it was time to go home. Thus, French squadrons sent to the West Indies took hardly one offensive measure between 1744 and 1763, even against British merchant ships.

Illness was the main killer during all the wars of the 18th century. Over and over, disease killed dozens of sailors and soldiers for every casualty in battle. After only a few days in port, men fresh from England or France began to sicken of yellow fever, malaria, and other tropical diseases. Any victory had to be won almost immediately, for a long siege led to staggering death rates. William Beckford was precise in September 1758, when he warned Prime Minister Pitt that—

> Whatever is attempted in that climate must be done *uno impetu;* a general must fight his men off directly, and not give them time to die by drink or disease; which has been the case in all our southern expeditions.[3]

THE "WAR OF JENKINS' EAR," 1739–1748

In October 1739, Britain began to war with the Spanish Empire, in what became known as the War of Jenkins' Ear. France joined the Spanish side by declaring war on England in March 1744. The War of Jenkins' Ear continued a centuries-old struggle between Britain and Spain. In this conflict, the British again sought both to force their commerce on the Spanish and to annex parts of their empire. In an ironic reversal of their traditional roles, however, the British now accused the Spanish of piracy.

The Spanish Crown had closed its empire to foreign merchants in 1502, opening colonial ports only to Spanish vessels licensed by the Casa de Contratación. Since these legal shipments were expensive, Spanish colonists in Cuba, Puerto Rico, and Santo Domingo eagerly bought cheaper slaves and goods smuggled from Jamaica. The Spanish responded by allowing Cuban and Puerto Rican privateers to seize British ships throughout the Caribbean.

The Queen Regent of Spain authorized the first Spanish privateering commissions in 1669, copying a British device previously abused by pirates such as Henry Morgan. Under these commissions, Spanish ships (called *guarda costas*) roamed the Caribbean, searching British ships for cargoes illegally acquired in Spanish ports. Like Henry Morgan, their captains were private men who paid themselves by seizing merchant ships as prizes and selling them in Spanish ports. Between 1714 and 1737, the *guarda costas* seized over 200 ships, and most were condemned by courts on the Spanish islands. A mini-war raged in Caribbean waters, with right and wrong on both sides. Jamaican smugglers made thousands of pounds each year through illegal trade with the Spanish islands. But the *guarda costas* seized both smugglers and innocent merchant ships legally passing a Spanish coast.

From 1713, Spanish and British diplomats continuously quarreled over the seizures by the *guarda costas*. For domestic political reasons, the British government drifted toward war in the spring of 1738. Captain Jenkins's ear provided the excuse it needed—as well as a name for the war. Jenkins was a master mariner of dubious reputation. In 1731, a *guarda costa* stopped his ship in open Caribbean waters and searched his cargo for contraband. The Spanish captain allegedly cut off one of Jenkins's ears. As Jenkins told the story, the dastardly Spaniard told him to take the ear to England as a token of the punishment awaiting British seamen who broke Spain's trade laws.

With war fever raging in 1738, Captain Jenkins appeared before a committee of the House of Commons. There he produced a piece of shriveled flesh said to be his severed ear. Although his enemies alleged that both Jenkins's ears were safely hidden under his wig, the opposition party took up his case. British merchants, eager to take new markets, joined in the call for war, and the government felt obliged to act.

Britain (and later France) fought the resulting war in traditional ways. Privateers based in the islands again proved their most effective weapon. The British also sent larger naval expeditions to conquer the Spanish colonies, but these failed as miserably as the British attack on Santo Domingo in 1655. A small squadron under Admiral Edward Vernon harassed the Spanish Main early in the war, seizing Porto Bello (November 1739) and Chagres (March 1740) and bombarding Cartagena. Vernon succeeded in these attacks by acting quickly before his men could fall sick of the fever.

A larger British fleet came to disaster in 1741. Its commanders—Vernon and General Wentworth—mistakenly tried long sieges during which most of their European and North American troops (some 15,600 men) died of tropical diseases. From March to May 1741, the Spanish repulsed a six-week siege of Cartagena. They had greatly strengthened the city's defenses after the French attack in 1697, and disease ravaged the British soldiers. Fewer than a third of the force lived to return to Jamaica.

After taking on fresh troops, the British fleet seized Guantánamo Bay in Cuba (July 1741), intending to march on Santiago. Sickness again killed most of the expedition (at least 208 officers died), and the fleet returned to Jamaica in November. Disease thwarted an even more ambitious plan to capture Panama City in March 1742, and a second attempt to take Santiago in 1748 also failed. The deputy governor of Anguilla led the only British land expedition that entirely succeeded. With some 300 soldiers, he captured the French part of Sint Maarten (Saint-Martin) and Saint-Barthélemy in 1744. The Anguillan militia also successfully repelled a small French force that attacked the island in July 1745.

The Treaty of Aix-la-Chapelle (1748) ended hostilities, and all parties returned their conquests. The treaty did not mention a principal cause of the war—the Spanish practice of searching British ships for contraband. The British and French confirmed the neutrality of Dominica, Saint Lucia, Saint Vincent, and Tobago. Both sides promised to reserve these islands for the resident Carib, and they agreed to remove their nationals from the small camps of squatters. The latter paid no attention, and French colonists continued to settle these islands. They were especially attracted to Dominica, located only a few miles between Martinique and Guadeloupe.

THE SEVEN YEARS' WAR, 1756–1763

After a brief and troubled truce, Britain and France in 1756 resumed their struggle for naval and commercial supremacy. The Seven Years' War was actually two wars—a European land war in which Prussia fought Austria and Russia, and a worldwide sea war between Britain and France. Friction between Britain and Spain continued, with Britain declaring war in December 1761. But Britain and France were the main rivals and the chief combatants both in the Caribbean and around the world.

The previous war began in the Caribbean. In this case, the major colonial rivalries between France and Britain centered on North America and the Indian subcontinent in Asia. As it went on, however, the sugar islands became valuable and vulnerable prizes in this worldwide war. Britain and France both sent larger forces to the West Indies than in any of their previous wars.

William Pitt, who directed the war for Britain from 1756 to 1761, sought nothing less than to destroy France as a colonial and extra-European power. His policies found wide support among both agricultural and commercial interests. Both India and North America formed extremely valuable parts of the British commercial empire. Merchants engaged in the American and Indian trades had great political influence in Britain.

The West India Interest also was wealthy and well-represented in Parliament. Unlike the East Indian and American interests, however, the West Indians initially did not want to annex French territory. British planters did not want to increase the number of sugar islands because this would reduce the price of sugar in the protected British market. As it turned out, the British subdued all of the Lesser Antilles in this war and annexed the neutral Windward Islands also. Both sides changed their attitude toward West Indian conquests during the course of the Seven Years' War. Britain launched major expeditions, and their commanders now had orders to annex the enemy's sugar colonies, not merely to pillage them. The French government also sent out large fleets, although these arrived too late to save their colonies.

Both sides thought of the sugar islands as valuable bargaining chips at the next peace conference. Early in 1756, the French navy conquered the important British naval base at Minorca in the western Mediterranean. In July 1758, British forces seized Cape Breton Island, whose great fortress, Louisbourg, was the key to French naval power in North America. Both governments wanted to recover these crucial bases, and the British looked for other conquests—such as the French islands—to trade during peace talks.

The British Occupy Guadeloupe, Martinique, and Havana

In contrast to the previous war, all British expeditions took their objectives. No major battles occurred in the West Indies until 1759, although British and French privateers again destroyed the other side's merchant fleet. At the end of 1758, now possessing Louisbourg, Pitt launched two attacks against the French islands. A British force captured France's slave factories in Africa, thus crippling the French slave trade. In January 1759, a naval force with some 5,000 soldiers unsuccessfully attacked Fort Royal (now Fort-de-France) in Martinique. Its commanders then turned against Guadeloupe, seizing Basse-Terre and besieging the French positions in the interior of the island.

During the siege of Guadeloupe, more than half the soldiers were sick within a month, and the British commander died late in February. His successor, Brigadier-General John Barrington, decided to adopt a divide-and-conquer strategy. Instead of attacking the main French positions, the British invaders plundered and destroyed outlying plantations. Members of the French militia deserted and came over to the invaders to protect their property, and the island surrendered on May 1. The French had sent a fleet, but when it finally arrived a few days later, Guadeloupe already had fallen.

To encourage surrender, Barrington offered the French planters very generous terms. The articles of capitulation granted the French access to British markets and imposed no new taxes. They guaranteed complete religious freedom, protecting church as well as secular property. The islanders retained the existing French laws, courts, and judges. Planters fighting for France could control their estates through attorneys. The articles even promised that the government would prevent British subjects from buying island properties before a peace treaty was signed.

Under these terms, the British conquest helped the Guadeloupe planters. They sold their sugar for high prices to British and North American merchants, who rushed in supplies and thousands of cheap slaves. The conquest also wiped out their enormous debts to French creditors, allowing them to borrow even more money from Antiguan factors.

During the second half of 1759 and through 1760, the conquest of Canada fully occupied the British forces. Troops from Canada easily took Dominica in June 1761. In November, Admiral George Rodney arrived at Barbados with more than 13,000 British soldiers. They turned against Martinique, taking Fort Royal in February 1762 after only three weeks of siege. Many of the Martinique militia deserted to save their estates, when the British commander, General Robert Monckton, offered them terms similar to those granted at Guadeloupe. The articles of surrender again maintained existing laws and taxes and confirmed the rights and properties of the religious orders.

The French rushed a strong squadron under Admiral Blénac to the Caribbean. Again, it reached the Caribbean too late to save Martinique. With Martinique gone, small squadrons quickly took Saint Lucia and Grenada. Although small French camps still existed on Saint Vincent and Tobago, the British now occupied all of the major French islands except for Saint-Domingue.

Throughout the war, British privateers had molested Spanish merchant shipping. Moreover, the Spanish government feared total British control of the Caribbean islands. Thus in 1761 it promised France to declare war before May 1762. The British government anticipated events by declaring war on Spain in January 1761 and fitting out a large expedition to take Havana.

Admiral George Pocock commanded the Havana fleet, which carried 15,000 soldiers under the command of George Keppel, the earl of Albermarle. Instead of taking the traditional route along Cuba's southern coast, Pocock surprised the Spanish by taking his armada through the dangerous Old Bahama Channel, north of the island. Moro Castle fell in August 1762, after a two-month siege. Some 5,000 troops died from fever or dysentery, while only 560 died in battle. The British force took enormous booty, including 12 ships of the line and nearly 100 merchant vessel. The total prize money reached the staggering sum of £750,000.

The Treaty of Paris

The conquest of Havana was the last major engagement in the Seven Years' War. With Britain victorious in the Americas and the European land war at a stalemate, it was time to negotiate a peace. The British had won more than enough prizes to trade against their losses and those of their Prussian ally. Which should they keep? Pamphlets thrashed out this question in the celebrated controversy of Canada against Guadeloupe. The West India Interest was divided, but many sugar planters now were converted to keeping at least some of the French islands.

In the end, this noisy debate probably did not influence the British ministers. By the Treaty of Paris in February 1763, France gave up most of her conquests in the Germanies. In return, Britain returned the French slave stations as well as Martinique, Guadeloupe, and Saint Lucia. The British kept Canada[4] as well as Grenada and the Grenadines and the formerly "neutral islands" of Dominica, Saint Vincent, and Tobago. They returned Havana to Spain, taking Florida in exchange. Spain also received Louisiana, which France ceded as some compensation for Spanish losses during the war. Even though it was still unsettled, the French negotiators had insisted on keeping Saint Lucia in order to defend Martinique and Guadeloupe. The British agreed to give up Saint Lucia in return for concessions in North America. Thus the British conquered in the islands in order to annex territory on the continent.

THE WAR FOR AMERICAN INDEPENDENCE, 1776–1783

The Treaty of Paris marks the high point of the old mercantile British Empire. Spain, Holland, France, and England had fought—almost since 1492—a fierce competition for sea power and colonial wealth. The sugar islands had been invaluable prizes of battle. Much of the fighting had taken place in the Caribbean seas, crossroads of the Atlantic trade. Now Britain was supreme in North America, free to expand territorially in India, and ready to absorb the commerce of Spanish America. Within 20 years, the British had lost the largest part of their overseas possessions, and their mercantile empire was gone. France and England now fought one more great war—the fifth since 1688—for colonial dominion. One last time, European navies fought for control of the wealthy sugar islands. This time the French won.

The French and Spanish Seek Revenge

The French and Spanish courts, both under Bourbon rulers, looked upon the peace of 1763 as a mere truce. Their chief ministers sought revenge and altered governmental policies to obtain it. Under the influence of the intellectual movement known as the Enlightenment, they reduced governmental regulations, restored state finances, and enlarged and improved their armies and navies. These enlightened ministers succeeded only partially in reforming French society and politics. However, even these partial reforms enabled the French to defeat Britain in the West Indies.

In France, the duc de Choiseul, as foreign minister and minister of the navy, rallied the nation in a campaign to rebuild the fleet. When royal funds proved inadequate, Choiseul turned to public fund drives. Private subscribers financed 15 ships of the line (the largest type), the most impressive being the 104-gun *Ville de Paris*. Choiseul also built a new naval station at Fort Royal on Martinique as a base for future military operations.

Choiseul's successors continued to build up a strong navy. By 1778, when France declared war on Britain, its navy had 78 ships of the line and 186 frigates and smaller craft. Compared to the British, many were better built, their gunners better trained. Although less efficiently manned, the Spanish fleet added 60 ships of the line to the combined force against England. The Royal Navy had as many ships. But some were not fit for sea, and many were tied down blockading the North American coasts. French and Spanish forces thus dominated the Caribbean for the first time in a century. Peace in Europe enabled the French government to concentrate all of its energies on the naval struggle with Britain.

In 1774, Louis XVI succeeded to the throne, and the comte de Vergennes became foreign minister. Vergennes sought war as eagerly as Choiseul, and the American Revolution gave him his opportunity. Although war would bankrupt the country, France began secret aid to the rebels in 1776. When the campaign ending at Saratoga (June to October 1777) proved that the Americans could win, the French government signed an offensive and defensive alliance in February 1778, declaring war on Britain in June. Spain entered the war in June 1779 when England refused to return Gibraltar.

France and Spain fought England to take the Caribbean islands.[5] The French ministers were indifferent to American independence, and the French navy mainly kept to the West Indies until the siege of Yorktown in 1781. The Spanish monarchy—openly hostile to all rebels—also sought territory in the West Indies. Spanish policy looked to the expulsion of Britain from both the Mediterranean and the Caribbean, long a base for British commercial infiltration into Spanish America. Spanish goals thus included the reconquest of Florida and even of Jamaica.

The British West Indies Fall to French Attack

Many West Indians favored the American cause and flagrantly traded with American ships. Nevertheless, their location tied the British islanders to the British navy—which now failed to protect them. The French blockade cut Jamaica and Barbados off from food and supplies, and thousands of slaves died of hunger and disease. Most of the other British islands suffered actual capture.

European troops rather than colonial militia again did most of the fighting. The weather strongly influenced British and French naval strategies. To avoid hurricanes, their fleets usually visited the Caribbean only from November through June or July. This shortened fighting season proved to be a wise precaution. The great hurricane of October 1780 (see page 10) destroyed those men-of-war that the French and British had left in the West Indies for guard duty.

The governor of Martinique gained the first French conquest by taking Dominica in September 1778. A strong French force under Admiral d'Estaing captured Saint Vincent and Grenada early in the summer of 1779. Only a brilliant British victory in Saint Lucia in December 1778 thwarted French domination of the Lesser Antilles. Acting quickly—before West Indian fevers destroyed his forces—the British commander landed soldiers from New York near Castries and successfully beat off a French counterattack.

The following season (winter 1779 to spring 1780) proved indecisive—although both sides dispatched large fleets commanded by their best officers. From March 1780, Admiral George Rodney commanded the British fleet, supported by a squadron under Admiral Samuel Hood. Rodney fought several inconclusive battles near Martinique in April and May. He also failed to intercept a Spanish armada that reached Martinique in June, carrying some 10,000 troops. The French and Spanish planned a joint attack on Jamaica or another major island. But their commanders waited too long. Disease—the islander's best defense against European invasion—ravaged the Spanish crews and troops, and the fleet retreated to Havana.

Admiral Rodney spent most of the next season (winter 1780–summer 1781) plundering the Dutch colony of Sint Eustatius. When Rodney took Statia in February 1781, the "Golden Rock" was at the height of its prosperity. Statia became a free port in 1756, when the Dutch abolished customs duties to compete with Danish Saint Thomas. At all times, its harbor provided a convenient haven where merchants and smugglers could trade during both war and peace. Its warehouses now became a vast depot for the guns and powder (largely French) used by the American rebels.

Great Britain declared war on Holland in December 1780, and Rodney seized defenseless Statia in February, along with Saba, Sint Maarten, and Saint-Barthélemy. With Statia, he took 150 merchant ships and an immense booty valued at 2 million to 3 million pounds—more even than the plunder seized at Havana in 1762. An ardent gambler, Admiral Rodney had fled to Paris in 1774 to avoid debtor's prison. He plundered Sint Eustatius so thoroughly that the island never regained its importance.

Rodney spent the next months supervising the sale of prizes at Sint Eustatius. While he delayed, a powerful fleet under the comte de Grasse, France's ablest commander, safely made its way to Martinique, took Tobago in May 1781, and then sailed north for the siege of Yorktown. In November 1781, after the British and French fleets had left the Caribbean, the governor of Martinique surprised the British during a storm, retaking Sint Eustatius and the other Dutch colonies.

The Battle of The Saints and the Treaty of Versailles

Cornwallis's surrender at Yorktown (October 1781) released the French fleet under Admiral de Grasse for a final season of naval war in the Caribbean. The following year began with continued victories for the French. It ended with the battle of The Saints, one of the few decisive sea battles in world history. Only Admiral Rodney's memorable victory saved her sugar colonies for Britain.

In January 1782, de Grasse's fleet captured Saint Kitts, Montserrat, and Nevis. The Saint Kitts planters surrendered when the French offered lenient terms, similar to those the British gave Guadeloupe during the previous war. However, a small British garrison boldly defended the fortress of Brimstone Hill against overwhelming odds for almost a month. The French held all the Leeward Islands, except Antigua, and most of the Windwards. The French and Spanish sea forces now planned an invasion of Jamaica. The outlook for the British planters was dark indeed when, on April 12, 1782, Rodney's victory over de Grasse suddenly turned the tables.

Rodney returned from England in February with a fleet that was—when joined with Hood's squadron—slightly stronger than that of the French. He took up his station at Saint Lucia and waited for de Grasse to act. At Martinique, de Grasse had collected a great convoy of transports with some 10,000 troops intended for the attack on Jamaica. Now he had to get them safely to the rendezvous at Cap-Français on the northeast coast of Saint-Domingue.

With Rodney in pursuit, de Grasse turned north from Fort Royal and found himself trapped in the narrow channel between Dominica and Guadeloupe. A group of small islands called Les Saintes (after which the battle is named) blocked progress to the north. With the wind blowing from the east, de Grasse's only open route lay to the

Brimstone Hill fortress, Saint Kitts. The sugar islands were tempting targets during wars between Britain and France. To protect themselves, planters constructed large fortresses. In 1782, a British garrison on Brimstone Hill held out for a month against a much larger French force.

south. The French fleet doubled back on its pursuers. Suddenly the wind fell off. Rodney's flagship, the *Formidable,* broke through the French line of battle, as did another of his fleet. Several British ships now could concentrate their fire on one of the scattered French vessels.

By nightfall, de Grasse had surrendered his flagship, the great *Ville de Paris,* and four other ships. The rest of the French fleet retreated. The French put off and finally abandoned the attack on Jamaica, whose inhabitants erected a statue to Rodney in Spanish Town. The Spanish force moved to Havana, taking New Providence in the Bahamas in May 1782. The British public reacted with pent-up hysteria to the Royal Navy's most decisive victory since the Seven Years' War.

With the combatants financially exhausted, peace negotiations now began. Britain, despite military defeat, was in a relatively strong bargaining position because of disagreements between her four opponents. Thus the Treaty of Versailles (February 1783) that recognized American independence also restored to England the French conquests in the Caribbean. France kept Tobago and regained Saint Lucia and its African slave forts, while Spain retained Florida (taken by troops from New Orleans in 1781). Tobago was a trivial prize after so much cost and loss of life. But the French ministers hoped that defeat in America meant the end of Britain as a great power. Without North America's resources to exploit, they believed that Britain soon would relapse into the position of a second-class power on the periphery of Europe.

CHAPTER 12

RUNAWAYS AND REBELS

Two different societies—European and African—occupied the islands throughout the slave era. Both existed to make sugar. But each led its own life, with owners generally leaving slaves to their own devices after working hours. Every planter or white employee knew he was vastly outnumbered by the slaves. Blacks exceeded whites at least 10 to one on most islands. The disparity was even greater in the countryside, where black slaves might outnumber white masters 50 to one. The slaves' working tools—machetes, axes, and even hoes—easily could become effective weapons. The very harshness of the slave codes shows that the planters distrusted and feared their slaves. Particularly on Jamaica, fears of slave rebellion were well founded.

There are few diaries or other firsthand accounts about the internal life of those—white or black—living on plantations. Some slaves doubtless accepted their condition and tried to make the best of the circumstances in which they found themselves. There were also many who refused to become the passive instruments of their owners' needs and whims. Although most rural slaves were grossly overworked and underfed, they resisted their owners' demands in many ways. Individual slaves frequently ran away, avoided work, or did it poorly. And groups of slaves—sometimes hundreds of slaves—

met together to plot their escape or even an uprising against the whites. Especially on Jamaica and Saint-Domingue, some runaways, called Maroons, created separate African communities that survived for many years. Others went even further and sought to kill the whites and destroy the entire plantation system. Hundreds of rebellions marked the entire slave era. But only the 1791 revolt on Saint-Domingue eventually succeeded in permanently freeing an entire island, renamed Haiti in 1804 to celebrate its liberation.

THE PLANTATION WORLD AND SLAVE RESISTANCE

Owners often complained that slaves refused to work consistently, regularly, and efficiently. Slaves dragged their feet, working at their own pace or pretending to be sick. Some ran away to the woods or, in later periods, to the towns. Despite almost inevitable recapture and savage flogging, most plantations always had one or more slaves absent without permission. Many went for personal reasons, to visit lovers or kin. Others ran away repeatedly, withholding their labor as a kind of—in modern language—spontaneous strike.

Theft by slaves also was a fact of life for planters. Many slaves stole food because they were hungry, but others stole as a form of aggression against their owners. Slaves might deliberately sabotage their owner's property by damaging machinery, setting fire to cane fields, or wounding and poisoning animals. A few slaves even attacked whites, although slave codes punished such assaults with painful forms of death. More careful slaves sought to kill a particularly hated owner or overseer by using poison. Planters on all the islands lived in fear of poison, and the French in particular believed that slaves often poisoned whites and other slaves.

Theft and their slaves' refusal to work harder reduced their profits, but plantation owners could survive defiance by individuals. As the slave codes recognized, coordinated resistance by groups of slaves was far more serious. The planters could blame individual acts of protest on the stupid or uniquely brutal management of one planter. Organized rebellion by slaves from several plantations represented a political statement against the entire system of slavery. If the rebellious group grew too large or powerful, the slaves could threaten the very lives of the planters. Planned permanent escape and revolution thus represented the most serious and feared forms of slave protest. The two were closely related, since many rebels sought to separate themselves from—rather than take over—white society.

The Maroons Create Independent Black States

Wherever slavery existed, there were runaways. When runaways banded together and sustained themselves in the wilds, they are called *Maroons*. The islands initially offered a natural refuge for runaways. Areas of dense brush and broken terrain marked every island, and high mountains dominate the Greater and many of the Lesser Antilles.

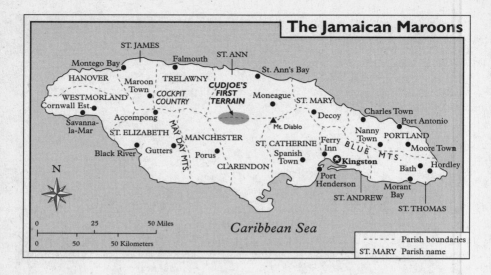

The Jamaican Maroons

Thus most islands sheltered Maroon bands during the early years of settlement. Runaway slaves formed bands on Cuba and Puerto Rico almost as soon as the Spanish imported Africans to replace the exterminated Arawak. During the 16th century, these Maroons joined in pirate and buccaneer attacks on Cuban cities. Rebel slaves also escaped and set up armed camps on Saint Kitts, Barbados, and Antigua during the first years of settlement.

These early Maroon communities usually disappeared as planters cut down the forests to create cane estates. Survival was never easy. To last for more than a few years, Maroons had to fight off white attacks, plant fields or *conucos,* and attract women. After about 1700, sugar plantations occupied all of the available land on the smaller islands, and the Maroons vanished. Organized Maroon communities survived only on the unsettled Carib islands of Saint Vincent and Dominica and in the mountains of Jamaica, Hispaniola, Guadeloupe, and Cuba.

The Jamaican Maroons   On the British islands, Maroon communities prospered only on Jamaica, which is heavily wooded, mountainous, and covered with broken limestone caves and "cockpits." A smaller Windward group (Nanny Town) formed soon after the British conquest in 1655. When the British took Jamaica, the Spanish colonists freed their slaves, some of whom fled to the mountains (see page 89). These Maroons ultimately settled on the northern slopes of the Blue Mountains, which rise to 7,000 feet. There they built their main camp, Nanny Town, on the brink of a 900-foot drop above the junction of two branches of the Río Grande.

A larger Leeward group (Trelawny Town) also existed in the western part of the island. In 1690, slaves in Clarendon Parish rebelled under the leadership of Cudjoe, a Coromantee warrior. Cudjoe's band ultimately found refuge in the terrible Cockpit Country—some 200 square miles of harsh sinkholes, jagged rocks, and dense vegetation. Both Maroon settlements survived by growing crops and hunting wild hogs. Their numbers grew to more than 1,000 by 1730, as more slaves escaped from the plantations.

As planters settled Jamaica's interior provinces, Maroon bands raided isolated

"Pacification with the Maroon Negroes, Saint Vincent." The Black Carib (descendants of the Carib and escaped slaves) defeated British efforts to drive them off the island. A 1773 agreement—modeled on earlier treaties with the Jamaican Maroons—granted the Black Carib autonomy.

frontier plantations, setting fire to the cane fields and carrying off food, cattle, and female slaves. Hostilities increased as the planters feared that Maroon successes would encourage a mass slave revolt. The British government sent two regiments of regular troops from Gibraltar in 1730, and the Jamaican legislature formed companies of freedmen and also recruited Mosquito Indians from Nicaragua. A fierce guerrilla war raged for eight years. The British finally succeeded in destroying Nanny Town in 1734. But its survivors temporarily joined forces with Cudjoe's

157

band. The black troops and Mosquito Indians systematically destroyed the Maroons' provision grounds, but they could not take Cudjoe's main settlements.

In March 1738, Governor Edward Trelawney finally signed a treaty that guaranteed the Maroons two homelands with more than 2,500 acres. In these territories, Cudjoe enjoyed complete jurisdiction except for the death penalty. In 1739, the Jamaican legislature signed a similar treaty with the Windward or Nanny Town Maroons.

A Second Maroon War broke out in the summer of 1795 that involved only the Trelawny Town Maroons, as Cudjoe's settlement was now called. As governor, the earl of Balcarres feared that French agents had spread revolutionary doctrines from Saint-Domingue to Jamaica. He led a large force of regular troops to destroy the Maroons' crops and threatened them with trained dogs imported from Cuba. Over 590 Trelawney Maroons surrendered and were exiled to the bitter cold of Nova Scotia. The British government finally transported the survivors to Africa in 1800.

Maroon communities on the French Islands   Stable Maroon communities also flourished on the French islands of Guadeloupe and Saint-Domingue. On Guadeloupe, Maroon bands with hundreds of members existed by the 1730s, and some communities survived until French slaves were freed in 1848. Saint-Domingue's rugged terrain favored runaways. By 1750 more than 3,000 escaped slaves lived in the mountainous no-man's-land between French Saint-Domingue and Spanish Santo Domingo. From their hidden villages, they harassed plantations in frontier districts throughout the 18th century. In 1752, a charismatic leader named Mackandal united the Maroon bands of Saint-Domingue and created a network of secret organizations among slaves on the estates. The planters believed that Mackandal planned to drive all the whites from the colony through the use of poison. Although he was betrayed, captured, and burned alive in 1758, other large bands continued to raid isolated plantations. The most famous band, that of Le Maniel, numbered 137 in 1784. As in Jamaica, the governor could not defeat Maniel's Maroons and had to negotiate a treaty protecting the estates from attack.

🖈 THE JAMAICAN MAROONS AS SLAVE CATCHERS

The Maroons retained their anomalous semi-independent status until Jamaica became independent in 1962. However, they preserved their own freedom only by agreeing to capture and return other runaway slaves and to assist in the suppression of slave rebellions. The Maroons kept their bargain, and the Jamaican government paid them £2 for each returned slave. In 1760, the Maroons captured Tacky, the leader of a major slave rebellion. As late as 1861, they also helped to suppress the Gordon riots. (See pages 164, 195.)

On the smaller islands, marronage became impossible after planters felled the forest. Slaves now fled by boat, often to the Spanish colonies or to the Carib islands of Saint Vincent and Dominica. The Spanish Crown frequently was at war with England during the 17th and 18th centuries. Thus it instructed colonial officials to receive

"A Family of Charaibes, drawn from the life, in the island of Saint Vincent." Another group of Carib—known as the Yellow Carib—maintained their separate racial identity and culture. A few dozen of their descendants may survive on Saint Vincent.

escaped slaves as free men—if they accepted baptism as Catholics and took an oath to the king. Puerto Rico became a haven for slaves fleeing plantations on the British Leeward Islands, Dutch Sint Eustatius, and the Danish and British Virgins. Over the years, thousands of slaves also fled from Saint-Domingue to the thinly populated Spanish colony of Santo Domingo, which welcomed them as ranch hands and dock workers. A smaller number of slaves fled from Jamaica to Cuba, and fugitives escaping from British Tobago to Spanish Trinidad also became free. In 1798, a general decree to all Spanish officials reaffirmed the freedom of fugitives reaching their colonies.

The Windward Islands, Saint Vincent, and Dominica—which international treaties reserved for the Carib—provided another haven for escaped slaves. Until the British occupation in 1763, a steady steam of runaways fled from Saint Lucia and Barbados to Saint Vincent, where they gradually absorbed the more pacific Carib. By 1763 more than 5,000 Black Carib formed an unusual community on Saint Vincent. The Black Carib were African and spoke a French dialect, but they had adopted the Carib political system, culture, and religion. On Dominica, north of Saint Vincent, a mountainous land with very high rainfall supported a dense virgin jungle. Here the Carib managed to maintain their ethnic identity, and the runaways formed separate black villages similar to those of the Jamaican Maroons.

African Slave Rebellions

The Maroons sought to separate themselves as much as possible from white society, although they had to trade with the plantations, especially for guns. Rebellious slaves sometimes went farther and sought to totally destroy the plantation system and kill the whites. Table 17 summarizes the available evidence about slave rebellions and lists both actual revolts as well as the conspiracies that the planters uncovered and crushed.[1]

Slaves rebelled much more frequently in the Caribbean than in the United States. The largest slave rebellion in the United States involved fewer than 500 slaves, and no rebellion seriously threatened white society. In the Caribbean, however, hundreds or even thousands of slaves joined in widespread violence on dozens of occasions, destroying plantations and killing their owners.

Caribbean slave rebellions followed a general pattern, with later colonies failing to learn from earlier experiences. The introduction of sugar plantations inevitably called up slave revolts. Whenever planters set up new cane estates, they imported thousands of slaves, most taken directly from Africa. Some of the newly arrived Africans refused to accept slavery. They either fled and set up Maroon communities or, when this was impractical, sought to exterminate their masters.

As the older colonies became settled after 1700, slave revolts became less frequent, except on Jamaica. Rebellions were rare on the smaller islands, such as Barbados, Antigua, and Saint Kitts. Cane estates entirely occupied their soil, and slaves did not have an interior into which to flee and create Maroon colonies. Many slaves were creoles born on the islands, and they understood the enormous power the white settlers could bring to bear to crush any rebellion. Among the larger islands, Jamaica holds the record for slave unrest prior to the Haitian Revolution of 1791–1804. Jamaica had more rebellions than all the other British colonies put together. More slaves participated in Jamaican revolts, which also did more damage, than in other colonies.

Slave revolts also were common in the Windward Islands after the British occupied them in 1763. Planters set up new plantations and imported thousands of slaves directly from Africa. Dominica, Grenada, and Saint Vincent all saw major rebellions as these newly arrived Africans resisted their captors. Slave rebellions reached their peak in 1795 because the revolutionary government in France encouraged them during its war with Great Britain.

In the same way, few slave revolts scarred the Spanish islands until the growth of the sugar industry after 1800. Slavery existed, but it took a mild form on the cattle ranches dominating Cuba, Puerto Rico, and Santo Domingo. From the end of the 19th

Table 17. **CARIBBEAN SLAVE REBELLIONS, 1522–1844**

Island	Conspiracy	Uprising	Number Involved	Comment
Antigua	1687		Dozens	Maroons seek to incite slave rebellions
		1701	Dozens	Coromantees, Christmas
	1729		Hundreds	Christmas, Crump Estate
	1735–1736		Thousands	Island-wide, Africans and some creoles
		1831	Thousands	Widespread unrest, arson
Bahamas	1734		Hundreds	General slave plot
		1830	Dozens	Exuma Island
		1832–34	Hundreds	Exuma, Eleuthera, Cat Island
Barbados	1649		Dozens	Simultaneous revolts by white servants
	1675		Hundreds	Coromantees
	1683		Dozens	Africans
	1686		Hundreds	Africans
	1692		Thousands	Creole elite as well as Africans
	1701		Hundreds	Africans and some creoles
		1816	Thousands	Bussa's rebellion
Cuba		1713		Santiago copper miners
		1729		
		1805		
		1809	Hundreds	Several provinces and Havana
		1825	Hundreds	Matanzas
		1826	Dozens	Guira
		1830–31	Dozens	Coffee estates
		1833	Several	Sugar estates
		1837	Dozens	Manzanillo
		1840	Dozens	Cienfuegos and Trinidada
		1841	Dozens	Havana
		1843	Hundreds	Several provinces
	1843–1844(?)		Hundreds	Conspiracy of La Escalera
Curaçao		1795	Hundreds	Led by Tula and Carpata
Dominica		1785–90	Thousands	First Maroon War
		1791	Hundreds	New Year's, Windward slaves
		1795	Hundreds	Colihaut uprising
		1802	Hundreds	8th West Indian Regiment mutinies
		1809–14	Thousands	Second Maroon War

Island	Conspiracy	Uprising	Number Involved	Comment
Grenada		1765	Hundreds	Revolt and Maroon actions
		1795	Thousands	Fédon's Rebellion; freedmen, slaves
Guadeloupe		1656	Hundreds	Almost all slaves on island
		1737	Hundreds	Revolt of Latulipe
		1789	Thousands	Tied to French Revolution
Jamaica		1673	Hundreds	Coromantees, Saint Ann's Parish
		1678	Hundreds	Saint Catherine's Parish
		1685	Hundreds	July, Guanaboa Vale
		1690	Hundreds	Clarendon, elder Cudjoe among leaders
		1730–40	Thousands	First Maroon War
	1742		Dozens	Coromantees, Saint James
	1745		Hundreds	Africans, Saint David's
		1760	Thousands	Tacky's Revolt, Coromantees
		1765	Dozens	Coromantees, Saint Mary's
		1766	Thousands	Westmorland
	1776		Thousands	Africans and creoles, Hanover Parish
		1791–92	Hundreds	Unrest after Haitian revolt
		1795–96	Hundreds	Second Maroon War
	1806		Dozens	Saint George's Parish
		1808	Hundreds	2nd W. Indian Regiment mutiny
	1815		Hundreds	Led by Ibos
		1822–24	Thousands	Widespread unrest, Hanover
		1831–32	Thousands	Christmas, "Baptist War"
Marie Galante		1789	Dozens	French Revolution
Martinique		1752		
		1789–92	Thousands	French Revolution
		1822		
		1833		
Montserrat	1768		Dozens	
		1776		
Nevis	1725		Dozens	Two executions
	1776			Williams
Puerto Rico		1527	Dozens	Africans

Island	Conspiracy	Uprising	Number Involved	Comment
Saint Croix	1759?		Dozens	Plot may not have existed
Saint-Domingue	1752–58		Hundreds	Mackandal unites Maroon bands
		1791	Thousands	French Revolution
Saint John		1733–34	Hundreds	Africans, slaves take island
Saint Kitts		1639	Dozens	French section of island
	1770?		Dozens	Plot probably did not exist
	1778		Dozens	Plan to liberate island
Saint Lucia		1795–96	Thousands	Brigand's War
Saint Vincent		1769–73	Thousands	Black Carib, First Carib War
		1795–96	Thousands	Second Carib War
Santo Domingo		1522	Dozens	40 African slaves
Tobago		1770	Dozens	Courland Bay
		1771	Dozens	Bloody Bay
		1774	Dozens	Queens Bay
	1801		Hundreds	Christmas, creoles
		1807	Hundreds	March on Government House
Tortola		1790	Hundreds	Pickering's estates
		1823	Hundreds	Pickering's estates
		1830	Hundreds	Lettsome slaves
	1831		Hundreds	Island-wide slave plot
Trinidad	1805		Hundreds	Plot among French slaves
		1837	Hundreds	1st West India Regiment mutinies

SOURCE: The references to rebellions on the British islands are based in part on Michael Craton, *Testing the Chains* (Ithaca: Cornell University Press, 1982), 335–339.

century, the number of cane estates rapidly increased in Cuba, bringing in immense numbers of African slaves. With sugar, slave revolts also became commonplace.

Until the 1770s, most rebellions involved newly imported Africans, who planned, prepared, and fought in African ways. Most were led by a powerful, charismatic leader who drew support from the large number of alienated and vengeful slaves. Members of Akan-speaking groups from the Gold Coast (modern day Ghana) were especially likely to rebel. Planters highly valued the strength and hardiness of these slaves, whom they called Coromantees. Several of the Akan peoples, including the Asante or Ashanti, had created warrior kingdoms that supplied slaves to the European forts along the coast. Coromantee warriors (themselves slave owners) retained their pride and military skills even after they were defeated in battle and sold to slave traders.

The goals of these African rebels were "restorist" rather than revolutionary. They did not seek universal freedom for all men. They wanted to recreate contemporary West Africa, as they remembered it. When marronage became impracticable, the rebels sought to destroy white society and replace it with an Akan-style autocracy. In the great Jamaican revolt of 1760, Tacky and his followers wanted to kill the whites and partition the island into small principalities. Their own slaves would grow crops (the Maroons also owned black slaves) for sale to white traders along the coast.

Savage punishment invariably followed all slave rebellions, whether large or small. The planters slaughtered many slaves during the initial stages of fighting. Colonial courts killed rebel leaders through slow tortures—by progressive mutilation, slow burning, breaking on the wheel, or starvation in cages. They then dismembered the bodies of the dead slaves, leaving their severed heads to rot in public places.

At least twice, these African slave revolts almost gained their ends. In 1733, slaves on the Danish island of Saint John captured the only fort, burned almost half of the plantations, and killed most of the whites. The rebels controlled the island for six months, defeating reinforcements from Saint Thomas as well as British Saint Kitts and Tortola. They were suppressed only when the French governor of Martinique sent two ships with 228 soldiers under an experienced commander.

An even more ambitious rebellion scourged Jamaica in 1760. Tacky, its main leader, was a Coromantee from the Gold Coast. He had as many as 30,000 followers who sought to kill all of the whites and bring the entire island under their rule. Their revolt began in April 1760 and spread to many of Jamaica's parishes. The Maroons honored their treaty and joined the Jamaican militia and British army in fighting the rebellion. But the forces of control only slightly outnumbered the rebel warriors. The latter held out until October 1761, and they were almost as bloodily effective as the more famous Haitian rebels of 1791–1804. Some 60 white persons and at least as many freedmen died. Five hundred slaves were killed or committed suicide, and as many were transported to Honduras. A contemporary historian estimated property damage at more than £100,000—perhaps as many millions in modern dollars.

SAINT-DOMINGUE IN 1789

Saint-Domingue was the most valuable colony in the world in 1789. Cane estates along the coastal plains produced 40 percent of the world's sugar, more than all the British colonies combined. Other tropical products also flourished, with the mountainous interior (rapidly developed since 1750) growing half the world's coffee. This one small colony provided 40 percent of France's foreign trade, and its 7,000 plantations also had substantial commercial links with the United States and the British and Spanish colonies. The planters complained that little of this wealth remained on the island. Although rich in land and pretensions, most colonists were heavily in debt to French merchants.

French law divided Saint-Domingue's inhabitants into three racial castes. In 1789, the island held about 31,000 whites, 25,000 freedmen (most of mixed race), and 435,000 slaves. All three groups were growing in number, with planters importing some 40,000 African slaves each year during the 1780s. Contrary to the British and Hispanic islands, however, racial caste and economic class did not neatly coincide. Both the whites and the *gens de coleur* (persons of color) comprised many competing groups, ranging from the very rich to very poor.

The highest ranks of white society included the top royal officials and the *grands blancs* (literally, "big whites"), who owned the largest and most prosperous sugar plan-

Table 18. **POPULATION ESTIMATES FOR THE FRENCH ISLANDS, 1750–1805**

	Total	Whites	Slaves	Free Non-whites
Martinique				
1751	79,386	12,068	65,909	1,413
1789	96,158	10,636	83,414	5,235
Guadeloupe				
1750	50,160	9,134	41,026	
1790	109,639	13,969	92,545	3,125
Saint-Domingue				
1754	191,352	11,540	117,411	4,911
1775	288,803	32,650	249,098	7,055
1789	490,108	30,831	434,429	24,848
1805	380,000	—	—	—

NOTE: The French colony of Saint-Domingue became the independent state of Haiti in 1804.

SOURCES: Patterson, *Slavery and Social Death*, 480–81 (1751–1789); Leo Elizabeth, "The French Antilles," *Neither Slave nor Free*, 148–151; Lasserre, *Guadeloupe*, 284, 297; James Leyburn, *The Haitian People*, revised edition (New Haven: Yale University Press, 1966), 321 (1805).

tations in the Caribbean. Next in status and wealth came the *petits blancs* ("little whites"), a widely diverse group that included self-made coffee planters, merchants, and artisans as well as soldiers, sailors, waterfront drifters, and criminals. More than on any other island, the *petits blancs* directly competed with the members of the large free colored community. Thus many—but not all—were strongly racist.

The free coloreds of Saint-Domingue were both more numerous and also more prosperous than those living on the Spanish, British, or even the other French islands. Most resided in the country, where they made up the rural police force and militia. Many worked as overseers on the estates of absentee white owners. Others became coffee and cotton planters, and they probably outnumbered white planters in the mountainous South and West Provinces. While not all freedmen were wealthy, those with money could buy slaves and land without any restrictions. In 1790 their spokesmen claimed that the coloreds owned a quarter of the colony's slaves and between a quarter and one-half of its productive land.

Despite the wealth of some freedmen, they had many grievances. French law had become increasingly racist since the 1730s as the colored population increased. The law now prevented freedmen from becoming priests, physicians, or lawyers. It also restricted them in many petty but irritating ways. Freedmen of mixed birth resented these restrictions because they tended to identify with their white ancestors. They typically despised the newly arrived slaves because of their African origins and customs. They copied white habits, and they looked for whiteness in their marriage partners.

The slaves, outnumbering whites and coloreds eight to one, formed the bottom of society. Nevertheless, as in other colonies, some slaves enjoyed a higher status than others. The great number of Africans arriving during the 1780s endured the hard work and poor food of the plantations. The creole élite of urban slaves and domestics—men like Toussaint Louverture—might enjoy a comparatively mild slavery under considerate or even indulgent owners.

The French Revolution and the Napoleonic Wars

Events in Europe during the French Revolution and Napoleon's First Empire (1789–1815) directly affected all of the Caribbean islands. The French Revolution began because the government was bankrupt—largely due to its wars with Great Britain. In May 1789, an advisory body called the Estates General met in Paris. Calling themselves the National Assembly, its members made radical changes in the laws and institutions governing France and its colonies. On August 4, 1789, they abolished the rights of the nobles and clergy, declaring that "all citizens, without distinction of birth, can be admitted to all ecclesiastical, civil, and military posts." Three weeks later, on August 26, the Assembly published the Declaration of the Rights of Man, which began "Men are born and remain free and equal in rights." Few members of the National Assembly thought of France's Caribbean colonies as they legislated for the homeland. But clearly, their decrees were inconsistent with a regime based on human slavery.

A Legislative Assembly took power in October 1791 and seized control of the king. France began to combat much of Europe—declaring war on Austria and Prussia (April 1792), on Great Britain and Holland (February 1793), and also on Spain (March 1793). A world war, involving all of Europe's colonies in the Americas, had begun. Hostilities lasted for 23 years until the final overthrow of Napoleon in 1815.

The most radical stage of the French Revolution began during the summer of 1792. King Louis XVI was overthrown in August 1792, and a National Convention, dominated by extreme revolutionaries, or Jacobins, took power in September. Under the leadership of Maximilien Robespierre, the Jacobins murdered the king and his family (January 1793). They then created the first totalitarian government and began a "reign of terror and virtue." Their rule was terrible but brief. On July 27, 1794, more moderate Jacobins turned on Robespierre. Assuming power as the Directory, they ruled until October 1799, when they in turn were overthrown by Napoleon Bonaparte.

The French Revolution Brings Civil War to Saint-Domingue

The revolution on Saint-Domingue began in 1788, when the king announced the forthcoming meeting of the Estates General. It ended 16 years later with the creation in 1804 of the black republic of Haiti. During the first stage (1788–91), whites fought whites, and whites also battled the colored freedmen. The black slaves looked on. Together with the legislative assemblies of Martinique and Guadeloupe, wealthy landowners from the North Province sent representatives to the Estates General in 1788. In June 1789, the National Assembly admitted six West Indian deputies—the first colonial representatives accepted by any European legislature. There they opposed the members of the Société des Amis des Noirs (Society of the Friends of Blacks), a newly formed club seeking the abolition of slavery.

The same landowners that had sent representatives to Paris also established assemblies on the island, one for each of the three provinces as well as a General Assembly meeting at Saint-Marc. As in France, however, the Haitian revolution became more radical during the summer of 1789, and these *grands blancs* lost control to other white factions. A virtual civil war existed by the spring of 1790, as these factions raised troops and fought for control of the assemblies and town governments. Except for the royal officials, all parties wanted to gain autonomy from France while maintaining slavery and a hierarchy of race on the island. Thus many whites refused to make any concessions to the colored freedmen. Only whites would share in the "liberty, fraternity, and equality" promised by the French Revolution.

Rebuffed by most white factions, some free coloreds also began to organize. In Paris, the coloreds, joined by the Amis des Noirs, demanded full legal equality. In May 1791, the National Assembly grudgingly granted full voting rights to colored men born of two free parents and otherwise qualified. Although it would have empowered perhaps 400 people, this decree infuriated the *petits blancs* factions. Toward the end of July 1791, the people of color in the West Province began to gather in armed bands, their patience exhausted. As disorder spread, some freedmen fortified their plantations and even armed their slaves. Wealthy coloreds returning from France initially provided leadership. Vincent Ogé (c.1750–91), one such figure, already had led an abortive colored revolt in 1790 near Cap-Français.

Governmental power had collapsed, and the whites and colored slave owners were divided into many warring factions. Yet no one expected the slaves to join the revolution. Suddenly, on the night of August 22, 1791, thousands of slaves near the city of Cap-Français rose up and took a terrible vengeance on their masters. Within 10 days, slaves had revolted throughout the entire North Province, leaving the whites in control only of Cap-Français and a few fortified camps in the western mountains. Within two months, rebel slaves killed 2,000 whites and destroyed 280 sugar plantations. Ash from the blazing cane fields rained down on the city of Cap-Français.

The Haitian revolution now became a many-sided struggle, with white, colored, and slave factions forming temporary alliances. The slave uprising was at first confined to the North Province. Sporadic slave uprisings in the other two provinces gradually died down by January 1793. In The West Province, André Rigaud (1761–1811) led the colored planters, who armed their slaves and gained control of the countryside, while a *petits blancs* mob controlled Port-au-Prince. In the South Province, the white planters generally maintained control.

French Slaves Gain Their Freedom

While these local factions fought for power, the revolution in France had become more radical. On April 4, 1792, the Legislative Assembly decreed full political and legal equality between all free men, both white and colored. To enforce its decrees, it sent a Revolutionary Commission with autocratic powers and 7,000 troops, who arrived at Saint-Domingue in September 1792.

Léger Sonthonax, who dominated the Revolutionary Commission, was a Jacobin closely associated with the Amis des Noirs. Sonthonax was convinced that Saint-Domingue's whites—whether *grands blancs* or poor townsmen—were royalists or separatists. He now allied himself with the colored militias as his French troops died of malaria and yellow fever. Establishing a Jacobin reign of terror, Sonthonax purged and deported his enemies, dissolved the colonial assemblies and municipal governments, and levied heavy fines and taxes on the towns and merchants. Sonthonax's despotism destroyed any remaining white military power in the North Province, and alienated white colonials throughout the island. Some of the coloreds, now in positions of power, persecuted their former persecutors.

Sonthonax initially did not intend to free the slaves. Indeed, he used the people of color to crush both rebel slaves and the island's whites, whom he believed to be counterrevolutionaries. To retain power, however, he was forced to end slavery in June 1793—the first abolition of African slavery anywhere in the world. On June 20, 2,000 sailors from the French fleet landed in Cap-Français to help its white citizens oust Sonthonax. While a fierce battle raged, Sonthonax promised freedom to all black warriors joining the republican cause. Taking up his offer, a large insurgent band attacked and burned the town during the night of June 20/21. More than 10,000 persons were killed, many of them whites. The surviving whites in the North Province fled to the United States, Cuba, Jamaica, and Puerto Rico.

While the French warred with each other, a Spanish army bore down on Sonthonax from the east. When war broke out in March 1793, a Spanish army of 14,000 men launched a two-pronged offensive towards Cap-Français and Port-au-Prince. As it advanced, many rebel bands joined its ranks. With the Spanish and their black allies closing in on his remaining bases, Sonthonax on August 29 decreed the abolition of slavery throughout the island. On February 4, 1794, the National Convention in Paris approved his act by unanimously abolishing slavery throughout the French dominions.

THE REVOLUTION ON GUADELOUPE AND MARTINIQUE

The French Revolution also exported political and social disorder to Guadeloupe and Martinique. Here, however, the white planters managed to maintain political control. In January 1793—frightened both by the Jacobin reign of terror and the massacre of whites in Saint-Domingue—their representatives placed both islands under British rule. On Guadeloupe and Martinique, the white planters succeeded in gaining the measure of autonomy Haiti's *grand blancs* had sought in 1789. Both islands enjoyed relative peace because they had fewer extremes of wealth and poverty. Thus the whites remained more united, while the free coloreds were fewer and less wealthy than on Saint-Domingue. (See Table 18, page 165.)

On Guadeloupe, the royal governor and the colonial assembly welcomed the constitution of 1789, which strongly guaranteed property rights. The *petits blancs* in the towns called for more radical changes. However, the assembly easily crushed their demonstrations, and they fled to France, Dominica, or Saint Lucia. Curiously, Marie Galante, perhaps seeking independence from its larger neighbor, chased out the royalist governor and adhered to the republican cause.

On Martinique, the French Revolution primarily pitted the planters against their *petit blancs* creditors in Saint-Pierre. Troops commanded by the governor and assembly blockaded the capital by land and sea throughout the autumn of 1790, finally taking it with the help of a volunteer militia from Guadeloupe. Most people of color sat out the revolution—some because the planters were their kin, others because the *petits blancs* were their commercial rivals. All factions supported slavery, and they united to crush small-scale slave revolts in 1790 and 1791.

The white planters thus retained power on Guadeloupe and Martinique. When the Jacobins dismissed the king in August 1792, the assemblies of both islands declared their loyalty to the Crown, thus effectively seceding from France. In October 1792, the Jacobins sent a revolutionary commissioner to regain control of the islands. Raising an army among the exiled republicans on Saint Lucia, the commissioner invaded Guadeloupe (January 1793) and introduced a Jacobin reign of terror. Some planters sent representatives to Britain, which had treated the islands well during an earlier occupation (1758–63). On January 17, 1793, planter envoys in London transferred their allegiance to the British Crown. The latter agreed to restore the islands to France, if the Bourbons regained the throne.

THE FIFTH CARIBBEAN WAR BETWEEN FRANCE AND GREAT BRITAIN

A British army invaded Saint-Domingue in September 1793, thus beginning the fifth great war with France for control of the Caribbean islands. British forces easily seized the French islands in the Lesser Antilles. But the invasion of Saint-Domingue became a costly disaster that dragged on until 1798. Altogether, the British government poured more than 10 million pounds and more than 20,000 soldiers into Saint-Domingue. Almost 13,000 men died—perhaps 1,000 in battle, the rest of malaria and yellow fever.[2] Tropical diseases played a major role in the British loss. But they were also defeated by the determined resistance of the insurgent generals, black and colored, who fought to preserve the freedom granted by France in February 1794.

British forces entered Saint-Domingue at the invitation of its remaining white planters. During the summer of 1792, 420 planters in London joined those from Guadeloupe and Martinique in transferring their allegiance to George II. The murder of King Louis XVI horrified the colonists, and many despaired of regaining their estates while the revolution raged in France. If the islands must be ruled from Europe, then the planters preferred British government to Spanish.

Prime Minister William Pitt's decision to intervene defies any simply explanation. The prime minister was no friend of slavery.[3] His motives probably were both defensive and aggressive. Some Jamaican planters feared that the rebellion in Saint-Domingue might encourage an uprising among their slaves—the most rebellious in the Caribbean. Conquest of the French West Indies also would serve traditional British goals. Even if Pitt did not intend to keep the French Caribbean, its occupation would be useful at the peace conferences. As it had during previous wars, Great Britain would use its navy to capture France's colonial empire, while leaving land battles on the continent to its European allies.

British troops invaded Saint-Domingue from Jamaica in September 1793. The white planters turned over the port cities and naval bases without a struggle, and many fought on the British side. By June 1794, the British forces had taken all the major ports and much of the South and West Provinces, and the Spanish and their black allies dominated the North Province. The French army controlled only Cap-Français and Port-de-Paix. Early in 1794, a British expeditionary force with 6,000 soldiers under Admiral Sir John Jervis and General Sir Charles Grey took Martinique

(February 20), Saint Lucia (April 4), and Guadeloupe (April 21). Since they already occupied Tobago, the British appeared on the verge of total victory in the French West Indies by mid-May 1794.

Suddenly the tide of battle turned against the British. In June, a French squadron landed troops on Guadeloupe under the command of Victor Hugues. As fanatical and bloodthirsty as Sonthonax but more effective, Hugues recaptured Guadeloupe in November. More than 1,200 white planters went to the guillotine at his order. Using Guadeloupe as a base, Hugues and the other commissioners sent from France encouraged rebellions in the French islands. They also sent agents to stir up the French-speaking free coloreds and slaves of Dominica and Grenada and the Black Carib of Saint Vincent, which Britain had occupied only since 1763.

French planters on Martinique managed to suppress Hugues's agents and remained under British rule. But serious slave revolts broke out concurrently on Saint Vincent, Saint Lucia, and Grenada. Pressed by the rebels—primarily black slaves joined by some free coloreds and Jacobin whites—the British had to flee Saint Lucia in July 1795. Joined by some African slaves, the Black Carib controlled almost the entire island of Saint Vincent for six months. On Grenada, the British army held only the fort at Saint George in February 1796. Under the leadership of Julien Fédon, a colored planter, the slaves established a virtual black republic. Even Jamaica itself was not immune, and July 1795 also saw the uprising of the Trelawny Town Maroons.

Simultaneous slave rebellions on so many different islands seriously challenged British rule in the West Indies. The British sent 17,000 troops to the Windward Islands in March 1796. This expedition ultimately did retake the French islands, but the black and colored rebels proved to be tough opponents. Those on Saint Vincent and Grenada surrendered only after offering sharp resistance, and some slaves on Saint Lucia held out for almost two years.[4] In contrast, British troops seized Trinidad (February 1797) and the Dutch islands without fighting, when Spain and the Netherlands came under French dominance.

TOUSSAINT LOUVERTURE
LEADS THE HAITIAN SLAVE REVOLT

Because of the slave revolts in the Windwards and Jamaica, Britain could not send reinforcements to Saint-Domingue, where yellow fever and malaria were annihilating its army. Quarrels between the British and the French planters also slowed their advance. In June 1794 the French National Convention finally recalled Sonthonax and gave command of the French forces to General Étienne Laveaux, a less divisive leader. Although disease, dissension, and the Windward rebellions weakened the British army, Toussaint Louverture (1743–1803) still deserves much of the credit for its defeat. Haitian independence became possible in May 1795 when Toussaint betrayed his Spanish allies and offered his services to the French under General Laveaux.

A creole slave from the North Province born François Dominique Toussaint, he adopted the name Louverture ("the opening") and organized a small band of loyal black followers.[5] With the outbreak of war, he entered the Spanish service and built up a force of some 4,000 black troops skilled in guerrilla warfare. When news arrived that the French Assembly had freed the slaves, he decided to cast his lot with the remnants of the French army. On May 6, 1794, Toussaint suddenly turned on the Spanish in Saint Raphael and slaughtered many as they came out of church after Mass.

An untrained but brilliant general, Toussaint effectively used both guerrilla tactics and frontal attacks against the British. By early 1795, he controlled much of the North and West Provinces. Two of Toussaint's lieutenants—Jean-Jacques Dessalines (1758–1806) and Henry Christophe (1767–1820)—especially distinguished themselves during these campaigns and later succeeded him as rulers of Haiti.[5] Moreover, Toussaint's victories inspired renewed attacks by André Rigaud, who commanded a force of several thousand colored and black troops in the South.

English forces had been driven back to four ports along the coast by June 1795, and the Spanish had retired to Santo Domingo. In July, the Spanish government officially withdrew from the war and ceded Santo Domingo to France (Treaty of Bâle [Basel]). The British sent another army under a new general, but Toussaint retained control of the North and West, while Rigaud kept the initiative in the South. In March 1798, General Thomas Maitland made one last attempt to hold the South Province, closest to Jamaica. When it failed, he sued for peace, signing a secret military and commercial treaty that treated Toussaint as an independent ruler. By October 1798, the last British troops had left Saint-Domingue.

As European power in Saint-Domingue collapsed, Toussaint and other black and colored generals fought for control. One by one Toussaint skillfully eliminated his rivals. In 1796, he defeated a plot by Rigaud and Villatte, the colored commander of Cap-Français. Although professing loyalty to the French government, he expelled its commissioners when they attempted to check his autonomy. By 1799, only Rigaud retained an independent power base.

With an army of 55,000 blacks, Christophe and Dessalines invaded the South in November. Because Rigaud had retained ties to France, an American fleet assisted their advance. Although his army contained black soldiers as well as whites, Rigaud's power rested on the colored planters, who distrusted the former slaves. The colored troops now fought as valiantly against Toussaint as they had against the British. At Jacmel, the defenders and their able commander, Alexandre Pétion (1770–1818), held out against savage attacks for six months.

When Jacmel fell, Pétion—and later Rigaud—escaped to France. To break the power of the colored forces, Toussaint appointed the brutal Dessalines to govern South Province. Despite Toussaint's earlier promises of no reprisals, Dessalines slaughtered thousands. Resistance was crushed, but Dessalines's brutality left a great bitterness among the people of color. Toussaint now controlled all of Saint-Domingue, but his experiences made him fear invasion from the Spanish part of the island. In January 1801, his forces invaded Santo Domingo, taking the capital after a triumphant three-week campaign.

Toussaint Louverture's New Order

Toussaint had won the war. Now he had to govern a devastated and impoverished country. Eleven years of civil war and invasion had destroyed Saint-Domingue's fabled prosperity. The cities were charred ruins, and war and neglect had devastated the elaborate irrigation systems. The island lacked both skilled technicians and laborers. Perhaps two-thirds of the whites and one-third of the colored freedmen had died or emigrated. More than a third of the 435,000 slaves had perished, and many of the rest had fled for safety to the mountains. Moreover, the civil war also had destroyed the traditions and the institutions of self-government. As C. L. R. James noted in his classic history of the revolution,

> For nearly ten years the population, corrupt enough before, had been trained in bloodshed and soaked in violence. Bands of marauders roamed the countryside. The only disciplined force was the army, and Toussaint instituted a military dictatorship.[6]

Toussaint's victory and the unification of Hispaniola posed in stark terms fundamental questions that have troubled Haiti ever since. The most important immediate problem was money. France, now ruled by Napoleon Bonaparte, was likely to invade its wealthiest colony. The export of tropical products grown on large plantations provided the obvious source of revenues to support an army. But any system of wages would make Haiti's sugar and coffee more expensive than crops produced on islands still under slavery. Moreover, few former slaves wanted to work on cane estates under any system. Prior to the revolution, the slaves had grown most of the island's food on their provision grounds. Now that they were free, they wanted to live as independent peasant farmers cultivating their own bit of family land. Freedom meant the right to control their own labor and keep the crops they grew with their own hands.

Toussaint sought to restore Saint-Domingue's prosperity by creating a centralized and authoritarian state based on forced labor. The constitution of July 1801 gave all power to Toussaint and granted him the right to name his successor. He controlled major appointments to the army, administration, and church. Each of the six provincial governors reported directly and only to him. Perhaps, given Napoleon's obvious ambitions, Toussaint had no choice. But his system gave Haiti a centralized and authoritarian government that has endured to the present.

Toussaint's constitution and subsequent decrees restored the plantation system under state control. Toussaint's government took over abandoned estates and rented them to revolutionary generals. Altogether, perhaps two-thirds of the land was state-controlled, and Toussaint also encouraged absentee white and colored planters to return to their estates. Half the profits went to the government, one-fourth to the owner, and one-fourth to the workers.

While whites and coloreds received key governmental and military posts, the former slaves were forcibly returned to the plantations. The blacks became subject to military discipline. A system of internal passports was introduced, and the army prevented workers from leaving the plantations. Dessalines, as inspector general, authorized physical punishment to keep them at work. Some plantations even purchased African slaves from slave traders. This system of "militarized agriculture" resembles modern socialism, and it borrowed from earlier decrees by Sonthonax, the Jacobin commissioner in Saint-Domingue.

Toussaint's policies stimulated a modest economic revival, but they also alienated his black followers. Some of Toussaint's own generals resented the return of white proprietors. In September 1801, Moïse, his adopted nephew and rumored successor, led a major revolt against the whites in the North Province. Toussaint quickly crushed the revolt, executed Moïse, and purged 2,000 of his followers. But he could not regain the trust of the population. To the newly liberated slaves, the work regimen imposed by the revolutionary state closely resembled the slavery they thought they had left behind. Some escaped to the mountains. Most were indifferent when French armies invaded the following year.

"Revenge taken by the Black Army for the Cruelties practised on them by the French." Napoleon Bonaparte sent more than 45,000 soldiers to reconquer Saint-Domingue (now Haiti). French troops acted brutally, and the former slaves tried to kill all whites remaining on the island.

Napoleon Invades Saint-Domingue

Napoleon became determined in 1801 to reestablish the French Empire in the Caribbean. The Peace of Amiens (October 1801) freed his hand by halting hostilities with Great Britain. In return for other concessions, Britain returned all French territories except Trinidad. Napoleon dreamed of a great western empire that would include Louisiana (returned by Spain in March 1801), Florida, and French Guiana as well as the West Indies. A prosperous Saint-Domingue was crucial to his plans, and he decided to restore slavery in the French Caribbean.

Commanded by General Charles Leclerc, Napoleon's brother-in-law, 20,000 soldiers, including many Swiss and Polish conscripts, reached Saint-Domingue by February 1802. Napoleon would lose 40,000 of his best soldiers before the French withdrew 22 months later. The French invasion thus repeated Britain's earlier defeat. But it also turned into a vicious war to the death between the races.

After destroying Cap-Français on February 4, Henry Christophe withdrew to the interior. The troops holding Santo Domingo and the South Province surrendered without resistance. By February 12, Leclerc held all the important coastal positions and launched an attack on the interior. His victories proved costly as Toussaint's generals fiercely resisted. Dessalines was especially effective in the South and West Provinces, where he killed the whites and burned towns and plantations. By the middle of April, half of Leclerc's soldiers were dead or sick of yellow fever. Suddenly, and somewhat mysteriously, first Christophe, then Toussaint, and finally Dessalines surrendered at the end of April. A month later Leclerc invited Toussaint to dinner. During the course of the meal, Toussaint was seized, bound, and hurried on board a ship for France—where he died in a freezing dungeon on April 7, 1803.

Leclerc's victory lasted barely five months. By mid-July, the yellow fever epidemic reached a peak. With fewer than 8,000 soldiers, Leclerc had to depend on Dessalines and Christophe to carry out his policies. At this crucial point, slavery and the slave trade were restored in Guadeloupe and Martinique (May 20, 1802), and Leclerc began to reimpose slavery in Saint-Domingue itself. Spontaneous revolts broke out across the island. The colored, who no longer trusted the French, increasingly joined forces with the black rebels. Leclerc replied with ruthless brutality, shooting entire brigades of black soldiers.

The black generals who had deserted Toussaint for Leclerc now swung back again to the opposition. Pétion (who had returned with the French army of invasion) and Christophe rebelled in the North, while Dessalines took the West. While he had served the French, Dessalines had eliminated many of his rivals. In late November 1802, the black and colored generals recognized him as leader of the resistance.

On the French side, General Rochambeau replaced Leclerc, who died of yellow fever on November 2. Reinforced by another 25,000 French troops, Rochambeau fought on for a year, acting with extraordinary brutality verging on genocide. Dessalines and Christophe responded with equal ferocity, determined to exterminate every white they could reach. In May 1803, Britain again declared war on France, shattering the Treaty of Amiens. British forces quickly retook Saint Lucia and Martinique, and they also captured Guadeloupe. Early in July, a British fleet blockaded Saint-Domingue and bombarded French positions on the coast. On November 30, the remaining French soldiers left Cap-Français accompanied by 18,000 refugees.

Saint-Domingue finally belonged to the black majority after 15 years of devastation. On January 1, 1804, Dessalines and his generals proclaimed Haiti's independence, choosing an aboriginal word (meaning "the land of the mountains") to replace the French name, Saint-Domingue. Dessalines became governor-general for life. In 1805 he had himself crowned emperor in imitation of Napoleon.

PART FOUR

THE ABOLITION OF SLAVERY AND THE CHALLENGES OF FREEDOM

CHAPTER 13

THE BRITISH COLONIES

Slavery dominated every aspect of life in the Caribbean islands. It made sugar plantations possible, shaped social and familial relations, and dominated the laws and politics of the islands. Thus the abolition of slavery represented a radical and dramatic change in island life. Great Britain was the first European state to permanently end slavery in its Caribbean colonies. Many Britons now felt that slavery was both cruel and economically inefficient. They believed that the slaves only needed freedom to become happy and productive. Unfortunately, freedom was all the abolitionists wanted to give the slaves. In 1846, Parliament adopted free trade and began to tax imports of West Indian sugar at the same rate as foreign sugars—which were cheaper precisely because they still were produced by slaves. Thus the British islands were forced to create entirely new societies while their incomes were rapidly falling. Many island governments failed this difficult test. From the 1860s, Britain thus abolished the island legislatures and ruled its colonies directly from London.

Table 19. **THE ABOLITION OF AFRICAN SLAVERY IN THE CARIBBEAN, 1792–1886**

Colonial Power	Slave Trade Outlawed	Slavery Abolished
Denmark	March 1792 (partial ban effective 10 years later); 1807 (total ban)	1848
France	February 4, 1794 (reimposed 1802 for Guadeloupe and Martinique); April 15, 1818	February 4, 1794 (reimposed 1802 for Guadeloupe and Martinique); 1848
Great Britain	1806 (bans sale to foreign colonies); March 25, 1807 (import of slaves into British colonies outlawed from March 1, 1808)	August 1834 (unpaid labor as "apprentices" required to 1838)
Holland	1814	1848 (Sint Maarten) 1863 (other colonies)
Spain	Formally banned in 1820. But illegal trade tolerated to Puerto Rico (until the 1850s) and Cuba (to 1865)	1873 (Puerto Rico) 1879 (Cuba; unpaid labor required to 1886)
Sweden	1824	1846

THE LONG ROAD TO FREEDOM

Until the 1780s, European statesmen and governments accepted slavery as inevitable and necessary. Through the labor of thousands of slaves, the island colonies produced extremely valuable exports of sugar and other tropical goods for European empires. Enormous amounts of capital invested in the sugar industry provided income to many Europeans and tax revenues for their governments. Since all European rulers agreed on the need for slavery, they let the planters rule their slaves and stood ready to help suppress slave rebellions. Events in Europe affected the islands, as we have seen, primarily when they led to international wars.

First in Great Britain and later on the continent, many Europeans came to believe that slavery was wrong and even evil. In most cases, they then forced abolition on island planters, who generally wanted to keep slavery. Even had they wanted to, the Caribbean whites could not abolish slavery until European governments turned against it. Except for Haiti and Santo Domingo, all of the islands were colonies, and their laws had to be approved by the European nation ruling over them. Beginning in 1792, European rulers began to force emancipation on their colonies. But the road to freedom was long. Almost a century passed before Caribbean slavery finally ended with its abolition on Cuba in 1886.

The Antislavery Crusade in Great Britain

The British Empire was the first to put a permanent end to slavery, and emancipation was a momentous event in the history of the British colonies. In 1833, the British islands were inhabited by many black slaves and a few slave owners, and there were only a relatively small number of black and colored freedmen. Crops grown by slaves formed the only export. No one knew whether crops grown by free-wage labor could compete with those from regions where slavery still existed—the French islands, Cuba, and Brazil. Haiti provided the only earlier example of black freedom, and abolition in Haiti had ruined a once buoyant economy and caused the massacre of many thousand whites. In abolishing slavery, the British government thus took a decisive step with unpredictable consequences.

Most historians now agree that this extraordinary act resulted from a profound change in the moral values of ordinary men and women. During the last quarter of the 18th century, antislavery sentiment suddenly spread throughout Great Britain. Intellectuals had long attacked slavery as uncivilized, unjust, and unproductive, but the abstract arguments of philosophers have little influence in themselves. Abolitionism prospered in Britain because it became part of a great religious revival associated with John Wesley's Methodist movement and the Evangelical reformers in the Anglican Church.[1]

The religious revival provided not only ideas but institutions that could bring pressure on the government. Methodists in Britain and North America—perhaps 300,000 strong by 1830—formed a vocal and highly organized pressure group. Moreover, compelled by their beliefs, Methodist and Baptist missionaries flocked to the British West Indies, where they began to convert growing numbers of black slaves. The black now was not only a brother—a fellow human—but also a born-again member of the same church.

The Struggle to End the British Slave Trade

Antislavery forces formed the Society for the Abolition of the Slave Trade in 1787. Given contemporary politics, they felt it would be easier to abolish the trade than to attack slavery head on. In abolishing slavery, the government would confiscate existing property rights, and laws passed by the colonial assemblies protected these rights. In contrast, Parliament alone had the power to regulate maritime commerce, and one law would thus end the slave trade.

The antislavery leaders thus began by asking supporters to send petitions against the slave trade. To their surprise, thousands responded, and Parliament received more than 100 petitions by the end of May 1788. William Wilberforce, a wealthy politician and close friend of the prime minister, William Pitt, became the chief parliamentary spokesman for the abolitionists. Because the number of petitions impressed the government, Wilberforce was able to accomplish a great deal, although later legends probably overstate his effectiveness.

Working behind the scenes with the king's ministers, Wilberforce initiated a series of parliamentary inquiries that brought out the horrors of the Middle Passage. To document its iniquities, Thomas Clarkson provided expert witnesses and accumulated massive data on all aspects of the trade—as well as collecting shackles, thumb screws, teeth chisels, and branding irons that vividly demonstrated its horrors. Between 1787 and 1794, Clarkson collected information showing that the slave trade was one vast graveyard both for the slaves and also for British sailors, who died even faster than the Africans.

George Cruikshank del.

Re-published from the Westminster Review, No. XXII, on the 1st Jan. 1830; by Robert Heward, at the Office of the Westminster Review, 2, Wellington Street, Strand, London. Sold there, and by Cowie and Strange, 55, Paternoster Row; and by all Agents of the Westminster Review.

STEREOTYPE.—Printed by T. C. HANSARD, 32, Paternoster Row, London.—PRICE ONE PENNY.

ART. I.—1. *Trial and Condemnation of Esther Hibner.* From the Morning Chronicle of April 11, 1829.

2. *Despatch of Mr. Secretary Huskisson to the Governor of the Bahamas, on the Subject of the Cruelties perpetrated by Henry and Helen Moss on a Female Negro Slave who died under the infliction, and the Application for Remission of their Punishment. Dated Downing Street, Sept. 28, 1827.* From the Anti-Slavery Monthly Reporter for April, 1829.

HISTORY tells of an individual, who believed he had travelled for seven years in foreign countries and there done many notable acts, when the truth was that he had dipped his head into a pail of water and taken it out again. Very much like this is the history of that metaphorical personage, the type of all that is foolish and deceivable in nations, in whom under one bestial appellation is concentrated the description of the ignorance and *gullibility* of the British community. Believing himself to be wise, it is impossible to tell the time when he became a fool. He said, 'I am rich, and increased with goods, and have need of nothing; and knew not that he was wretched, and miserable, and poor, and blind, and naked.' Puffed up with the idea that he was something and somebody, he winked and ran his head quietly into the endurance of such frauds, as could never have befallen anybody that was in the habit of walking with his eyes open, or was humble enough to conceive that he might possibly be made a dupe.

Not that the man positively would not take his fingers out of the fire when they were burning. On the contrary, nobody made more turmoil when he knew that he was hurt. But his coat might be taken off his back, by any body that would tell him a long story. He

"Slavery in the West Indies." An engraving by George Cruikshank on the cover of an abolitionist "penny pamphlet." To arouse public opinion against the slave trade and slavery, British abolitionists published millions of these inexpensive paper booklets from the 1770s.

Despite Clarkson's evidence, many in Parliament opposed the sudden interruption of a business long sanctioned by law. In April 1791, the Commons overwhelmingly defeated Wilberforce's first motion to introduce an abolition bill. The abolitionists only redoubled their campaign in the country. Pamphlets publicized the most telling evidence presented to the parliamentary commissions. Josiah Wedgwood sold 200,000 copies of a china medallion that showed a kneeling slave in chains with the inscription "Am I Not a Man and a Brother?" Over 500 petitions from regional abolition committees reached Parliament. A second crushing defeat of abolition would be politically dangerous. Prime Minister Pitt, in what many consider his most eloquent speech, carried both houses for gradual, not immediate, abolition.

THE RELIGIOUS ORIGINS OF ABOLITIONISM

Eighteenth-century Europe witnessed a religious revival that stressed the need for a personal relationship with God. In England, as well as in Germany and other nations, revivalism taught that believers expressed their spiritual rebirth through good works. The converted believed that God rewards the good and punishes sin and evil on this earth as well as in heaven. Thus they became convinced that abolishing slavery would ensure God's blessings, but continuing the sins of slavery and the slave trade would call down God's wrath.

After much debate, the Commons decided to end the British slave trade on January 1, 1796. But the Jacobin reign of terror and the war with France in 1793 discredited radical ideas. Pitt and other parliamentary leaders now gave only tepid support, and 1796 passed without an abolition bill. Some abolitionists charged that Pitt had lost interest because the British had conquered Dutch Guiana and Trinidad and were seeking to take Saint-Domingue from Toussaint Louverture's black rebels. Thousands of new slaves would be needed to restore Saint-Domingue's prosperity as well as to grow sugar on the rich lands of Britain's new colonies.

The majority of politically influential Britons had accepted the goal of abolition, but 14 more years of parliamentary maneuvering was needed to end the trade. The government first gained passage of the Foreign Slave Bill (May 1806), which prohibited the shipping of slaves to foreign colonies (like Cuba) or to Britain's new conquests, such as Trinidad. In 1807, Parliament finally abolished import of slaves into British colonies as of March 1, 1808, and imposed large fines on transgressors.[2]

The Illegal Slave Trade to the French and Spanish Islands

Abolition was much less popular on the continent than in Great Britain. In European countries the antislavery movement never became a religious crusade as it did in England. Only intellectuals and government officials joined groups such as the

French Société des Amis des Noirs. In Roman Catholic countries, most abolitionists were Protestants and the pope did not condemn the slave trade until 1839. Without pressure from Great Britain, therefore, most European countries would have continued to permit the slave trade.

Britain's abolition of the trade affected all the islands, since British ships had carried most slaves imported by the Spanish and French colonies. Following its victory in the Napoleonic wars, the British government tried, with varying success, to persuade other states to end the slave trade. The 1806 law ending the slave trade in newly conquered colonies applied to the Dutch West Indies as well as to the Danish Virgin Islands, captured in 1807.[3] Treaties with Sweden (1813) and the Netherlands (1814) confirmed the abolition of the slave trade to their Caribbean colonies.

It proved more difficult to suppress the slave trade in the French and Spanish islands. The British forced the defeated French to sign an 1814 treaty (confirmed in 1818), ending the trade. However, an illegal trade continued until 1831, delivering some 80,000 slaves to Guadeloupe and Martinique. The Spanish adamantly refused to conform to British demands, and continued to tolerate illegal traders. By a treaty in 1817, Spain agreed to end the slave trade in 1820. But Spanish officials refused to enforce laws passed under British pressure. The British navy ended the minor trade to Puerto Rico during the 1850s, after some 55,000 slaves entered that island. In Cuba, slave prices soared since illegal traders had to bribe governmental officials at all levels. But Cuba's growing sugar industry demanded slaves at any price. Until it was ended in 1865, the illegal trade brought in more than 500,000 slaves.

Slave Emancipation in the British Islands

The British Empire was the first to end slavery. The slaves gained their freedom sooner than those in the United States and without the enduring bitterness caused by the Civil War. Nevertheless, emancipation was not achieved without great difficulty, and 25 years passed between the end of the slave trade in 1808 and the abolition of slavery in 1833.

The British government was now committed to improving the conditions of the slaves. Sir James Stephen, the son of a leading abolitionist, managed Caribbean matters at the Colonial Office and relentlessly exposed abuses by the planters. After the American Revolution, the government did not want to force emancipation on its West Indian colonies. Instead it sought to persuade the planters to accept abolition through a series of major initiatives—slave registration (1815), amelioration (1823), and emancipation (1831).

The abolitionists sought slave registration both to prevent illegal imports and also to provide statistics proving that slaves were badly treated. Pushed by the British government, all the colonial legislatures by 1820 required masters to register their slaves. The five-year struggle to impose slave registration convinced the abolitionists that Britain must bring stronger pressures to bear on island legislators. In January 1823, they formed the Society for the Mitigation and Gradual Abolition of Slavery, whose name stated its goals.

The campaign to free the slaves repeated the tactics of the earlier crusade against the slave trade. The abolitionists set up local committees and solicited petitions from members of all parties, and especially from clergy. To whip up support, the Abolition Society published millions of pamphlets, won the support of newspapers, and sponsored public lectures across the nation.

Pressure from the Abolition Society forced Parliament to commit itself in May 1823 to eventual freedom. As an immediate goal, the government issued a series of Amelioration Proposals and began to press for their adoption by the colonial assemblies. These measures limited a master's control in many ways. New laws encouraged religious instruction and church marriages, restricted physical punishment, safeguarded a slave's private property, prohibited work (or markets) on Sundays, outlawed the breakup of families, and allowed slaves to testify in court under certain conditions. Despite their initial indignation, all island legislatures adopted at least some of the government's Amelioration Proposals. The legislatures of Barbados and Jamaica were the least willing to introduce these reforms, and the Jamaicans passed a Slave Act acceptable to the government only in 1831. During the 1820s, island assemblies also lifted the remaining restrictions on free coloreds, who could now vote and be elected to office.[4]

Violent Rebellions End Slavery in the British Islands

Abolitionists in Britain campaigned to end slavery, just as they earlier had pressed for an end to the slave trade. This time, however, the slaves themselves took an active role in the campaign. For the first time, slave revolts strongly influenced public opinion in Britain. Although they received freedom from the Crown in 1833, black slaves themselves played a major role in making abolition inevitable.

Slave rebellions significantly increased after 1815 on all the British islands.[5] Slaves rebelled both in the major sugar colonies and on the smaller islands. Unrest grew even in the Bahamas, which had no cane estates. Significantly, blacks no longer informed on conspiracies among their fellow slaves. During the 18th century, the planters usually heard about plots in time to arrest their leaders. From 1815 on, they stopped only one out of 14 major revolts. The masters' position was becoming untenable.

In 1816, a revolt ravaged Barbados, which had not known a slave conspiracy since 1701. Slaves on 70 of the largest estates suddenly rose up on Easter Sunday. Within a few hours, a third of the island was in flames. Many believed rumors that the British governor was bringing a "free paper" and that imperial troops would not march against them. Although only one white civilian was killed, the Barbados courts reacted with the usual ferocity. Fifty slaves died during the rebellion and 214 were executed after it was crushed.

On some—but not all—of the estates, slave unrest grew out of worsening conditions following the abolition of the slave trade. Slaves did not reproduce themselves, and the slave population thus fell temporarily when the trade ended. Since they had fewer hands, some masters forced their slaves to work harder. For example, cane estates shifted women, children, and colored slaves from domestic service to the field gangs. However, we can attribute only part of the unrest after 1815 to harsher treatment. The Jamaican rebellion in 1831 occurred when conditions were improving, and revolts also took place on islands without cane estates.

The extremely rapid spread of Christianity among the slaves also contributed to unrest—or so the planters complained. The established Anglican Church, which enjoyed a monopoly until 1754, had made little effort to convert blacks. On the islands taken from France in 1814, Roman Catholic clergy, who did baptize slaves, generally accepted slavery as licit. From the 1780s, dozens of Moravian, Methodist, and Baptist missionaries flocked to the West Indies. Most found it impossible totally to ignore slavery's manifest inhumanity. Moreover, their teachings emphasized spiritual rebirth in ways that increased a convert's self-esteem. Chapels with all-black congregations also provided black and colored deacons and preachers with a means of leadership. Several black deacons were at the head of the Jamaican revolt of 1831–32, often called the Baptist War.

These leaders gained the support of a large number of more ordinary slaves who could no longer endure slavery. Slavery remained intolerable even after amelioration laws limited a master's powers during the 1820s. Indeed, amelioration probably made revolution more likely: the right to assemble at black churches on Sundays made it possible for slaves from many estates to coordinate an uprising.[6] The slaves now had more to lose, and they wanted to keep their gains. Many rebel slaves believed that the king would soon grant freedom or had already given it. They feared that the planters would use force to take it away.

The African slaves who rebelled during the 1700s had wanted to kill their masters and restore the African communities they had left behind. The goals of the creole slaves in these rebellions were less extreme. They wanted to live in their own family groups on their own land. For most slaves, freedom now meant the right to live as self-reliant small peasants. They sometimes might work for a planter, but only for wages and only on their own terms.

Beginning in 1830, both British abolitionists and Caribbean slaves became increasingly impatient with the slow progress of the government's amelioration policies. But it was a Jamaican slave rebellion—and not the British antislavery movement—that finally brought slavery to an end. None of Jamaica's earlier slave rebellions matched the scale of this revolt. Led by the Baptist lay preacher Samuel Sharpe (1801–32), the uprising began on December 27, 1831. Before it was suppressed at the end of January, more than 60,000 slaves took part throughout an area of 750 square miles. More than 200 sugar estates in the northwestern parishes were burned and pillaged, the whites fleeing to Montego Bay and other coastal ports. Regular troops and militia put down the insurrection with the customary savagery, and 540 slaves and 14 whites died. The convicted leaders were members of the slave élite, and most were Baptists, including many black deacons. Blaming them for the revolt, incensed whites tore down the chapels of Baptist and Methodist ministers throughout Jamaica.

The Emancipation Act of 1834

News of the revolt and of its repression provoked outrage in Britain, and it especially energized groups, such as the evangelical churches, already recruited to emancipation. Missionaries who had fled Jamaica aroused audiences with graphic stories of the revolt. The new Parliament meeting early in 1833—the first after the Reform Act of 1832—received petitions signed by more than 1.5 million persons. Emancipation was ensured. Remembering the fate of Haiti, the government decided to compel the freed slaves to remain at work for a period of years. Justice also required that owners be compensated when the government seized property lawfully acquired.

The Abolition Act passed in August 1833 ordered the ending of slavery as of August 1834. Agriculture workers were compelled to work for their former masters as apprentices until 1840, domestics until August 1838—but they also could buy their immediate freedom. In return for food, clothing, lodging, and medical attendance, apprentices owed 45 hours of unpaid labor per week. Special magistrates from England (rather than local justices of the peace) would judge all disputes between masters and servants. Parliament voted an outright grant of £20 million—some £25 per slave on average—to compensate owners. Since these terms appeared to be the best they could get, the colonial assemblies quickly passed the Emancipation Bill. Bermuda and Antigua freed their slaves immediately. The other colonies enacted apprenticeship.

The Anti-Slavery Society continued to fight for complete emancipation, using its customary tactics. Thousands of pamphlets described such abuses as the employment of treadmills in the workhouses and the flogging of women. In April 1838, Parliament ended apprenticeship two years early, and the colonial assemblies approved the necessary laws. At midnight on August 1, 1838, the 750,000 slaves in the British colonies became free men and women. Thousands of blacks peacefully celebrated at churches, chapels, thanksgiving parades, and public meetings throughout the islands. Their high hopes quickly evaporated, but few would have been willing to return to the hated system that had dominated the British islands since the 1640s.

The Painful Transition to Freedom in the British Colonies

The British West Indies were totally unprepared for slave emancipation. The slave society had tailored governments, taxes, and laws to its particular needs. Island governments furnished few public services, since masters provided their slaves with what passed for justice, education, and medical care. Schools, hospitals, police forces, and jails simply did not exist in 1838. Island governments had to build them for the first time, just as legislators had to rewrite the law codes. Moreover, they had to pay for services to an ever larger number of citizens. Despite several severe epidemics, the population soared after emancipation. Overall, the British colonies had almost twice as many inhabitants in 1891 (1,607,218) as in 1841 (863,971).

Unfortunately, the British colonies found themselves forced to create a new, free society while their incomes were falling rapidly. Emancipation sharply increased a planter's costs precisely as his income from the harvest was dropping. When prices fell by half—as they did between 1840 and 1848—planters had to double their output merely to stay even. But cane production fell after emancipation—by 50 percent on Jamaica—as the former slaves fled from the harsh routines of field labor. Many plantations operated at a loss, and government revenues plummeted.

Labor on a cane estate is arduous and boring. But a comparison between Jamaica and Trinidad—the two largest islands—shows that there was no substitute for a prosperous sugar industry during the 19th century. The industry collapsed on Jamaica, while indentured laborers from India sustained it on Trinidad. As a result, individuals enjoyed a higher standard of living on Trinidad. The steady growth of tax revenues allowed Trinidad—but not Jamaica—to improve its economic infrastructure and public institutions.

The Impact of Free Trade in Sugar

Sugar prices plunged as total world production increased 700 percent from the 1840s to the 1890s. Moreover, the British Caribbean now competed with regions that could produce sugar more cheaply and make a profit even as prices fell. The United States,

Table 20. **POPULATION ESTIMATES, SELECTED BRITISH COLONIES, 1773–1911**

	Total	Whites	Slaves	Free Non-Whites
Jamaica				
1834	376,200	20,000	310,000	46,200
1861	441,300	13,800	—	427,500
1881	580,800	14,400	—	566,400
1891	639,500	14,700	—	624,800
1911	831,400	15,600	—	815,800
Trinidad				
1834	44,715	3,632	22,359	18,724
1851	69,609	—	—	—
1861	84,438	—	—	—
1871	109,638	—	—	—
1901	258,000	—	—	—
Barbados				
1833–34	100,242	12,797	80,861	6,584
1851	135,939	—	—	—
1881	171,860	—	—	—
1911	172,337	—	—	—
Saint Kitts				
1861	24,440	—	—	—
1881	29,137	—	—	—
1891	30,876	2,343	—	28,533
1911	26,283	—	—	—
Nevis				
1861	9,822	260	—	9,562
1881	11,684	—	—	—
1891	13,087	182	—	12,905
1911	12,945	—	—	—
The Bahamas			(Slaves and non-whites)	
1773	4,394	2,053	2,341	
1838	21,794	—	—	—
1851	27,519	—	—	—
1881	43,521	—	—	—
1911	55,944	—	—	—

SOURCES: Patterson, *Slavery and Social Death*, 477–79 (1834); Gisela Eisner, *Jamaica 1830–1930 A Study in Economic Growth* (Manchester, England: University of Manchester Press), 153 (1861–1911); Watts, *West Indies*, 459 (Trinidad, 1851–1901); Bonham Richardson, *Caribbean Migrants: Environment and Human Survival on St Kitts and Nevis* (Knoxville: University of Tennessee Press, 1983), 93, 132; Burns, *British West Indies*, 514 (Bahamas, 1773); Aaron Segal, "Bahamas," *Population Policies in the Caribbean*, 105 (1838–1911).

Cuba, and Brazil increased production using slave labor. From the 1820s, European refiners also imported Asian sugar from the Dutch East Indies, the Spanish Philippines, and British possessions in India, Malaya, Mauritius, and (from the 1880s) Australia. Beet sugar also provided a cheap substitute for Caribbean cane. European governments heavily subsidized exports of beet sugar, and production increased tenfold between 1860 and 1895.

To offset the cost advantages of competitors producing with slave or near-slave labor, British planters had one remaining defense. Their products were protected in the British market by the Navigation Acts, which taxed imports of West Indian sugar at a lower rate than foreign sugar (see page 111). By the 1840s, however, the Industrial Revolution had made Britain temporarily the world's leading producer of industrial and consumer goods. Manufacturers, workers, and consumers united in demanding an end to all import duties so that they could obtain raw materials and food at the lowest cost. From 1846, Parliament equalized the duties on West Indian and foreign sugar—whether grown by slaves or by free workers. The planters denounced the hypocrisy of this law, which came only eight years after emancipation.

The Formation of an Independent Peasantry[7]

With emancipation, the freedmen sought to escape the drudgery of the sugar fields. For former slaves, "full free" meant ownership of at least a small plot of land. On this they might grow their own food and sell the surplus to the plantations or towns. Many also planned to work on the estates from time to time, thereby earning cash to buy land or imported products. But they were not willing to remain submissive field hands, and they left the estates when they had met their immediate goals. The freedman's natural desire for freedom only increased as plantations failed and the need for full-time employment fell on most islands.

At first most freedmen expected to remain in their cottages, which they had built with their own labor. They became outraged when owners began to demand that they pay rent in cash or in labor services for their homes. During the 1840s, freedmen moved to free villages everywhere except Barbados. But the rush from the plantations was especially striking on Trinidad and Jamaica. By 1847, only nine years after emancipation, almost half of Trinidad's laborers and fully two-thirds of Jamaica's had abandoned the plantations for free villages.

Individuals purchased land belonging to plantations or owned by the government ("Crown land"). Often entire villages moved together as missionaries bought up large estates and sold them to their congregations. Built with money borrowed from missionary societies or from sympathetic individuals, these planned villages mushroomed during the first decade after emancipation. On Jamaica, 150 to 200 free villages on 100,000 acres sprang up between 1838 and 1842. Most set aside land for a church and clergyman, and some required good behavior and forbade gambling and liquor.

The creation of planned villages slowed during the 1840s as economic conditions worsened and the British government decided to sell Crown lands only in large parcels. Individuals now squatted on Crown land or on abandoned estates—especially in the interior regions of Trinidad and Jamaica, where the government was incapable of evicting them. Their legal situation became more secure at the end of the 1860s when the governors on Trinidad and Jamaica made it easier to buy or rent Crown lands at fair prices.

THE VARYING FORTUNES OF THE SUGAR ISLANDS

Except in a few marginal areas, such as the Virgin Islands, planters tried to maintain production. Their success depended on the availability of laborers willing to work regularly for wages that permitted a profit. Overall, the ratio of population to arable land—land that can be used to grow either food or export crops—largely explains why sugar estates survived on some islands and not on others. When an island had many people and little land, planters could find laborers. Where the ratio was low—in the Windwards and especially on Jamaica—most men became independent peasants. Laborers demanded high wages or refused to work during harvest time. Unable to produce at a competitive cost, planters abandoned their estates, and production plummeted.

Antigua, Saint Kitts, and Barbados—with the highest population density in the Caribbean—continued to grow sugar into the 20th century. Indeed, Barbadian planters actually doubled their harvests between 1845 and 1865. Planters already owned most of Barbados's land in 1838. After emancipation, they converted their estates entirely to cane, and the island now imported two-thirds of its food. In order to eat, landless black laborers had to earn wages on the estates. With an abundant labor supply, Barbadian planters could ignore the worldwide trend toward large, company-owned estates. Most estates continued to use old-fashioned machinery powered by windmills. But they led all others in the use of fertilizers and manicured their fields until they resembled closely cropped gardens.

Table 21. **SUGAR PRODUCTION OF SELECTED CARIBBEAN ISLANDS,**
1820–1929 *(Annual Averages in 1,000 U.S. tons)*

	1820–1824	1850–1854	1890–1894	1925–1929
Haiti	.7	—	—	9.3
Jamaica	77.3	26.6	22.0	58.3
Antigua	8.1	9.6	14.1	16.8
Saint Kitts	5.4	5.3	16.5*	16.6
Martinique	21.3	22.4	31.0	40.7
Saint Croix	23.0	7.3	13.9*	7.8
Guadeloupe	22.3	18.1	41.7	34.8
Barbados	11.0	31.0	57.5	72.7
Grenada	11.0	5.3	—	—
Cuba	50.4	287.0	859.1	4,714.1
Trinidad	8.2	23.1	47.6	73.2
Puerto Rico	—	91.1	49.2	614.8

NOTES: Saint Kitts's production figures include Nevis after 1883. Average for two years only: Saint Croix (1890–1894), Puerto Rico (1850–1854). Average for three years only: Puerto Rico (1890–1894).

SOURCE: Averages for 1820–1929 compiled from annual data reported in Deerr, *History of Sugar,* volume I.

The Barbadian system of intensive cultivation could not succeed on Nevis or on most of Britain's Windward colonies. These islands had a good deal of empty land, both on abandoned estates and in the mountainous interiors. Many laborers took over small plots of land in the hills and grew food crops, cocoa, nutmeg, arrowroot, and bananas for export. To attract workers and preserve their estates, planters resorted to sharecropping, or *métayage*. Under this system, the sharecropper (*métayer*) grew the cane and worked in the mill in return for half his crop. Sharecropping was cumbersome, and disputes were common. It also encouraged soil erosion and prevented investment in new equipment. Thus most owners could not compete when prices fell even further at the end of the century. Production for export ceased on Grenada, Saint Vincent, Dominica, and Tobago as well as on the Leeward island of Montserrat.

Hard Times on Jamaica

Jamaican planters could not attract laborers on an island with an abundance of vacant land. Sugar production fell off sharply, with devastating effects on Jamaica's people. Exports dropped by half immediately after emancipation, and one-third of the estates were abandoned. Most planters had to use their slave compensation payments to repay estate debts. Since profits were low or nonexistent, they could not obtain loans for new technology, and large modern mills were introduced only after 1900. When sugar prices fell even further during the 1870s, many of the remaining planters also abandoned their estates. The island had exported almost 80,000 tons of sugar in the 1820s. By the 1900s, it shipped barely 13,000 tons a year. The pre-emancipation level of production was regained only in 1934.

Jamaicans found no alternative source of income as sugar exports fell. The coffee industry also collapsed as labor became scarce and foreign competition increased. Increased exports of new crops by black farmers—including logwood, pimento, ginger, and bananas—could not compensate for the loss of sugar and coffee revenues. Total exports were lower in 1890 than in 1832, while the population had doubled.

Sugar's decline brought hard times to Jamaica's black population. As the estates failed, the free peasantry could no longer earn wages or find a market for its food crops. Without income, Jamaicans could not buy imported goods, and revenues from import and property taxes also fell. Neither individuals nor the colonial government had the money to pay missionaries, teachers, or medical doctors. Schools and churches closed, and entire districts had no qualified physicians.

From the 1860s, there really were two Jamaicas. Along the coasts, the remaining white and colored planters elected the legislative assembly and maintained limited public services. In the interior, free villages originally built next to active estates now were totally isolated. The villagers struggled to survive on the produce of their tiny and often eroded plots. Hunger, disease, and theft became common. Prejudice on both sides intensified the division between the races. Black villagers had no say or interest in government and less faith in Jamaican justices of the peace, generally white and colored men of property. Racial relationships had been unusually hostile on Jamaica, where slaves rebelled more frequently than on any other island. Economic decline only increased the conflict between two incompatible cultures.

New Immigrants After Emancipation

The flight of creole laborers threatened to destroy plantations on several islands. Migrations from one island to another met only part of the need. Most migrants sought jobs in construction, while the better-educated looked for work as policemen, teachers, and nurses. Few wanted full-time work on the cane estates. Thus Caribbean planters and British officials resorted to various schemes of large-scale immigration to supply additional workers. The most successful of these brought 144,000 Indian laborers to Trinidad under five-year contracts or indentures.

While the 19th century saw vast numbers of European laborers immigrate to the United States and Canada, very few were attracted to the Caribbean. The islands were deadly for whites, who also shunned the forms of estate labor that freed blacks so obviously despised. Jamaican planters recruited some 2,500 northern Europeans, and 6,000 workers also emigrated from several islands of Portuguese Madeira. Many died of disease during their first year, and immigration from Europe practically ceased by 1860.

A small number of immigrants also arrived from Africa and China. The British government encouraged settlement by African slaves it liberated from captured Cuban and Brazilian ships. By 1865, some 23,000 Africans were placed as free wage-laborers in Jamaica, Trinidad, and the Windwards. Entitled to a free return passage after five years' work, about a third went back to Africa. The others often settled in separate villages and cultivated small farms. About 8,000 Chinese also came as indentured laborers to Jamaica and Trinidad before 1893. Most bought out the final years of their indentures, left the plantations, and set up small shops or farms. Like the Indians on Trinidad, many succeeded in retaining their ethnic identity into the 20th century.

Indentured Indian Labor
Helps Trinidad Prosper

Europe, Africa and China had added new elements to the already diverse peoples of the islands. But these small influxes did not satisfy the needs of disciplined field workers, and other sources were sought. After 1850, most immigrants were indentured laborers from India, Britain's most populous colony. Indians made ideal farm laborers, and the British government also preferred Indians since its officials could closely supervise recruitment and prevent abuses. Despite these advantages, indentured labor was costly, and island governments had to subsidize transportation to and from India. Trinidadian planters supported the scheme, but the Jamaican legislature was less enthusiastic. Altogether, between 1838 and 1917, almost 144,000 East Indian laborers came to Trinidad. Jamaica brought in 39,000, while smaller numbers reached Saint Lucia, Grenada, Saint Vincent, and Saint Kitts.

Like Jamaica, Trinidad had been hit hard by labor shortages. To attract workers, planters had to offer high pay for each task they performed, and most laborers could complete two or three tasks a day.[8] Some also forced laborers to work in return for their cottages and grounds. But neither high wages nor coercion could keep workers on the cane estates, and most estates ran at a loss in the 1840s. In 1851, the British government offered to guarantee loans made to transport immigrants, and Trinidad's planters turned to Indian labor as their only salvation.

The British and Trinidad governments subsidized the indenture system, and they also closely regulated it. An Indian laborer had to work for five years, and signed an initial three-year contract on arrival. After 10 years of residence, he received a subsidized return ticket to India. The indenture system contained a great deal of deception and injustice. Some planters skimped on housing and medical care, and planters also ignored laws guaranteeing Indians the same wages paid to creole workers. In practice, the regulations tended to favor the master. The courts fined or jailed workers found to be negligent, absent, or frequently tardy. Yet planters breaking the ordinances only paid a small fine.

Bad as some masters might be, an individual worker's term of indenture—unlike that of an African slave—ended after five years. Perhaps one-third of the workers returned to India. Many saved significant sums of money and established shops and businesses. Others bought land and sold cane to the large central mills that began to dominate Trinidad's sugar industry during the 1880s. East Indians made up almost one-third of Trinidad's population when the Indian government ended the indenture system in 1917. They formed a permanent and settled community that voluntarily segregated itself from other groups. Almost all married other Indians and continued to practice the Hindu (accepted by 85 percent) or Muslim religions. Their language, food, and culture also remained distinctly Indian, although obedience to caste rules inevitably weakened over time.

The Indians staying in Trinidad presumably felt they had profited by immigrating as indentured laborers. Their labor fostered a long period of economic growth. Many took part as small farmers or contractors during the cocoa boom that lasted from the 1870s to the World War I. However, it was the sugar industry that gained most from Indian immigration, and its prosperity after 1854 largely was due to Indian laborers. When prices fell again in the 1880s, British capitalists—confident that the industry would survive on Trinidad—financed larger and more efficient mills. By 1897, 11 central factory units produced most of Trinidad's sugar. They purchased cane from independently owned farms, thus creating something like the Cuban *central-colono* system (see page 204).

A flourishing sugar industry promoted the island's economic well-being. The influx of Indian workers allowed planters to expand cultivation, thereby increasing the demand for creole workers. Moreover, the plantations also afforded creole farmers and traders a profitable market for food and provided work to skilled artisans. With their wages, Trinidad's peoples could import needed goods. As tax revenues steadily increased, the legislature could create a rudimentary medical service and build hospitals, public baths, roads, sewer systems, and railroads.

CROWN COLONY GOVERNMENT REPLACES THE OLD REPRESENTATIVE SYSTEM

When emancipation came in 1838, British colonies were governed in two different ways. Most operated under a system of representative government that had evolved since the 1640s. Each island had a governor who appointed a council with limited powers. An elected legislature or assembly made local laws and raised taxes to pay officials. An assembly's statutes could not contradict British laws and could be vetoed by the Crown. But it had almost total control over its own taxes. On most islands, the legislative assembly levied taxes, supervised their collection, approved expenditures, supervised many legislative boards, and audited its own accounts.

The island assemblies often proved incompetent during the wars of the 18th century. Nevertheless, after some hesitation, Britain also extended representative government to the Windward islands—Grenada, Dominica, Saint Vincent, and Tobago—it occupied in 1763. However, after Britain seized Spanish Trinidad (1797) and again took Saint Lucia from France, it did not create elected assemblies for these new conquests. For a time, the British government retained the laws and courts already in force. In 1810 it decided that direct rule by the British Crown was needed to end the slave trade and to protect the free people of color.

Trinidad and Saint Lucia thus became the first Crown colonies. An appointed governor, a number of top officials, and a few local advisers formed an executive council responsible for the day-to-day running of the colony's affairs. A slightly larger body, known as the Legislative Council, advised the governor and passed local laws. In addition to the governor himself, the Legislative Council was made up of British officials and a number of "unofficial members" chosen by the governor. By 1898, Crown colony government had replaced elected legislatures everywhere except in Barbados, the Bahamas, and the Cayman Islands.[9] With some exceptions, elected representatives did not again participate in island governments until the 1920s.

The extinction of representative government in the West Indies ran counter to the general trend in Britain and in its colonies with a white majority. Throughout the 19th century, the British Parliament steadily lowered voting requirements. All men over 21 received the vote in 1918, all women in 1928. Parliament also extended representative government to Canada, Australia, New Zealand, and the Cape Colony in South Africa. By contrast, authoritarian government replaced legislatures throughout the West Indies. Here the British government suspended democracy both to rescue the white planters from their own ineptitude and to protect them against black majority rule.

Emancipation in 1838 made 750,000 former slaves free British citizens, able to vote if they passed the same tests as whites and colored freedmen. On most islands, voters had to own only a small amount of property. Over time, the rules would have allowed many blacks to vote in elections to island assemblies. To prevent this, assemblymen throughout the Caribbean revised the laws after 1838. They raised property qualifications for new voters, while allowing existing voters (usually whites) to qualify under the old rules. In practice only white or colored landowners, merchants, lawyers, and other professional men could vote in elections to the island assemblies.

As plantations were abandoned on many islands, the number of voters meeting these property tests sometimes fell to ludicrous levels. By the 1850s, Barbados registered 1,350 voters. Grenada had 191 voters, Saint Vincent had 273, and Tobago registered 135. In the 1863 election for the Jamaica assembly only 1,457 persons voted out of a population above 440,000. Not all were white. In Dominica, Montserrat, and Nevis, middle-class men of color dominated public affairs. On Jamaica from the 1850s, one-third of the representatives were men of color.

The Colonial Office did not protest the undemocratic nature of island legislatures. But it strongly objected to their financial carelessness and failure to provide needed governmental services. Many islands labored under huge debts because their assemblies did not operate under a budget, and any member could introduce bills to spend money. In 1849 and again in 1853, all government stopped on Jamaica because the assembly refused to approve taxes.

In 1853 the British government offered Jamaica a low-interest loan if the assembly would vote permanent taxes, place its finances in the hands of responsible salaried officials, and allow its accounts to be audited. The assembly gave in, setting up a three-member executive committee with responsibility for financial matters. Six islands in the Lesser Antilles also set up executive committees by 1859. However, this reform did not solve the main problem—the ease with which a small faction could prevent an assembly taking desperately needed actions. By the 1860s, the Colonial Office had lost patience with Caribbean legislatures and looked for an excuse to destroy the old representative system. Its chance came in 1865 with a tragic rebellion at Morant Bay in Jamaica.

Morant Bay: The End of an Era

Economic and racial tensions in the British colonies were aggravated by the American Civil War, which sharply increased food prices. Riots broke out on several islands, including Saint Vincent and Barbados. Because Jamaica was the largest and best-known colony, British public opinion was most strongly affected by a rebellion in 1865 at Morant Bay, east of Kingston in Saint Thomas Parish. Disturbances began at the Saturday market on October 7. The local justices found a young black man guilty of assaulting a black woman. When the court ordered the arrest of a disruptive spectator, the crowd rescued him and beat the police.

The following Tuesday, eight black policemen set off to arrest Paul Bogle (1822–65), the alleged leader of the riot. Bogle was a local property owner and a deacon and preacher in the Native Baptist Church. He also was a close associate of George Gordon (1820–65), a colored member of the Jamaica assembly who enjoyed considerable influence in the neighborhood. Several hundred armed men quickly overpowered the police. Bogle then sent them back to Morant Bay with his threat to bring his forces to the vestry meeting scheduled for the following day. The Custos,[10] the chief official in the parish, notified Governor Edward Eyre, who sent 100 men to Morant Bay on a small British warship.

On Wednesday, October 11, Bogle arrived in the town with a group of about 400 men, armed with guns, cutlasses, pikes, and bayonets. They attacked the local police station, seized the weapons kept there, and marched toward the courthouse, where the vestry was meeting. The parish Custos appeared on the stairway calling for peace, but the mob began to throw stones at perhaps two dozen volunteer militiamen stationed before the courthouse. The volunteers fired, but the crowd quickly drove everyone back inside the courthouse. The mob set the building on fire and brutally beat to death many of its occupants as they fled into the open.

In all, several dozen were murdered at Morant Bay, including the Custos, several other magistrates, the entire volunteer force, and two sons of the Anglican priest. The mob then looted the village and released the prisoners in the jail. Parties of rebels fanned out in several directions, killing four white plantation owners and several colored magistrates who attempted to reason with them. Whites and coloreds fled their homes, many escaping to Kingston on ships. There they told Governor Eyre stories of horrible atrocities at the battle of the courthouse.

Panic swept the island, as many planters feared that the Morant Bay massacre was part of a conspiracy to turn Jamaica into a second Haiti. Governor Eyre declared martial law, dispatched troops to the area, and appealed for reinforcements. He also enlisted the aid of the Maroons, whose trackers captured and executed Bogle. The government forces quickly crushed the rebels, who apparently enjoyed limited popular support. Without suffering a single casualty, soldiers marched through the parish killing any blacks they came across.[11]

White and colored planters and the Jamaican newspapers applauded Governor Eyre. However, his handling of the rebellion provoked intense controversy in England. There, influential clergymen, professors, authors, and scientists formed rival committees attacking Eyre as a murderer and defending him as a hero. For three years, the media and Parliament debated the issue, which provoked riots in the streets.

Eyre's arrest and execution of George William Gordon aroused the greatest controversy. Gordon, the son of a Scots planter and a slave, had made money as a produce broker in Kingston. Driven by religious fervor, he was a leader of the Native Baptists and had many followers among the black laborers. Hating both the Custos of Saint Thomas and Governor Eyre, he used his immunity as a member of the assembly to attack them in long, unrestrained tirades. In one speech, Gordon called on the people of Jamaica to throw out Eyre, the oppressor.

> When a Governor becomes a dictator; when he becomes despotic, it is time for the people to dethrone him. . . . I have never seen an animal more voracious for cruelty and power than the present Governor of Jamaica. . . . If we are to be governed by such a Governor much longer, the people will have to fly to arms and become self governing.[12]

Gordon had his largest following in Saint Thomas, where he worked closely with Paul Bogle, leader of the rebels. During the months before the riot, he had called on the parish's black poor to speak and act out against its vestry. Eyre and other Jamaican officials believed he had been involved in the uprising, even though he had not been in Morant Bay when it occurred. Gordon was arrested in Kingston, where martial law was not in effect. Eyre then had him taken to Morant Bay, where he was hanged on October 23 after a grossly unfair court-martial.

The British government suspended Eyre in 1866 and then dismissed him from office. Before he left Jamaica, he presided over the assembly's suicide. Under pressure from the Colonial Office, the assembly abdicated. On December 12, 1865, it asked the queen to set up whatever form of government she thought best. The following June, Britain imposed the Crown colony form of government with a nominated legislative council. The British government soon forced most other island legislatures to follow Jamaica's lead. By the end of 1875, only Barbados and the Bahamas retained their old constitutions. After a period of transition, a legislature named by the governor existed on all other British islands by 1898.

The Morant Bay rebellion uprising was confined to one small section of Jamaica, and it did not involve a large segment of the population. Indeed, few would remember Morant Bay if Governor Eyre had not so vigorously suppressed the uprising. Strictly speaking, it was not a war between the races. The rebels beat and killed black men, while black troops, Maroons, militiamen, and judges joined in suppressing the uprising. But both the Jamaican assembly and the British government viewed the riots as racially motivated. Thus the public outcry over Eyre's actions gave the Colonial Office an excuse to abolish representative government.

By 1865, the government was convinced that only direct rule from Britain could protect the black laborers, who could not yet govern themselves. The planters and merchants in the island assemblies were financially incompetent and did not represent the interests of the black majority. But the latter were equally unready for democracy. Thus only authoritarian government by British officials could protect the interests of the entire community. An official dispatch in 1868 clearly expressed the British view.

> The population at large, consisting of uneducated negroes, neither had, nor could have, any political powers; they were incapable of contributing to the formation of any intelligent public opinion; and the consequence was that the Assemblies performed their office of legislation under no real or effective responsibility. They became aware apparently that irresponsible legislation by small local bodies was not for the interest even of the members of those bodies themselves, or of the class which they represented, and still less of the inhabitants at large.[13]

The Record of Crown Colony Government

The unrepresentative governments that ruled Britain's Crown colonies until World War II generally met the relatively limited goals they set themselves. They maintained public order, provided courts, and made useful improvements in the economic infrastructure and public services. They placed less emphasis on economic growth, and many islands stagnated. No substitute product was found to replace sugar, and American companies generally preferred to invest in cane estates on Cuba and the Dominican Republic.

Crown colony government put an end to the bickering that had stalemated the former assemblies. The governor, who ruled the nominated legislatures, had both clear responsibilities and the power to achieve them. Whether or not the system worked thus depended on the energy and character of individual governors. The most successful, such as Sir John Peter Grant in Jamaica and Sir Arthur Gordon in Trinidad, came immediately after the Morant Bay riots, when the British government expected improvements. Over time, colonial government became less active, and it fell into the lazy habit of routinely following precedents.

Basic public services were provided throughout the colonies. Public works departments were created, which built roads, bridges, and railroads. By World War I, every British colony—including the smaller Leeward and Windward islands—had a police force and fire department, a government medical service, and at least one hospital. Nearly all had public libraries. Noticeable improvements were made in the towns, and especially in the capital cities. Sewage systems and public water supplies did much to cut the death rate. As one consequence, European and North American tourists began to visit some of the islands, especially the Bahamas and Jamaica.

Crown colony governments also carried out legal and social reforms, especially during the early years. They simplified the court system and modernized law codes. Because of streamlined procedures and lower costs, more peasant farmers could obtain clear titles to their lands. The Anglican Church was disestablished on Jamaica, where it primarily served the tiny white population. In Trinidad, the government began to allot funds to the Roman Catholic as well as to the Anglican Church, in proportion to the number of members each served.

One of the first aims of the Crown colony governments was to increase the number of elementary schools. The government gave grants to private and denominational schools according to the results they achieved. However, since most schools charged fees, fewer than half the black children attended, and only 52 percent of Jamaicans could read and write according to the 1921 census. A small number of secondary schools also were established. A few of the brightest students—including several future West Indian leaders—won a scholarship to a British university, where most studied law or medicine. Perhaps the greatest weakness of public education was its lack of attention to technical and scientific subjects, such as tropical agriculture.

Any argument in favor of democracy can be used with justice against the Crown colony system of government. Under the former system, with all its faults, at least some non-whites had achieved influence as judges or members of the assemblies. Now officials thousands of miles away made major decisions. Educated blacks could be teachers or lower-level civil servants, but posts as senior administrators usually went to whites, frequently sent from Great Britain. The lack of representative institutions contributed to low self-esteem among many islanders. The Crown colony system strengthened the belief that the black "natives" could not rule themselves and needed the help of white men from Great Britain.

The Leeward and Windward Federations

The British government had tried to bring the Leeward Islands under one federal government at the end of the 17th century. From 1671, one governor supervised Saint Kitts (with Anguilla), Nevis, Antigua (with Barbuda), Montserrat, and the Virgin Islands—with Dominica added from 1770 to 1940. However, each island retained its own deputy governor, council, and assembly, and thus had its own laws and treasury. Six legal systems and six civil governments served fewer than 100,000 residents.

In 1869, the Colonial Office again tried to impose federation, primarily to cut costs. However, the relatively more prosperous islands (especially Saint Kitts and Nevis) did not want to share their funds with Antigua and Montserrat, which both were bankrupt. After eighteen months of negotiations, a quasi-federal system was set up in 1871. A federal legislative council and appellate courts unified many laws. But each island maintained a separate treasury and taxes. Britain did unite Saint Kitts and Nevis in 1882, over the bitter opposition of many on the smaller island.

The British government had wanted the Leewards federation to be part of a larger union that would include Barbados and the Windward colonies. But all efforts to establish a federation of the Windwards failed. Governor John Pope Hennessy arrived in Barbados in 1876 with orders to arrange a federation between that colony and the smaller Windwards. The Barbados assembly, which did not want to support its poorer neighbors, strongly opposed a federation. Planters, both white and colored, united to form the Barbados Defense League. Pope Hennessy turned to the cane workers for support. In March 1876, political agitation culminated in a riot that killed eight persons and destroyed much property. The Colonial Office transferred the governor to another colony and dropped the scheme. Ten years later, it united Grenada, Saint Vincent, Saint Lucia, and Tobago under one governor. But each had its own legislative council, police force, judicial system, public services, and treasury. Other than the governor, the only common institution was a lunatic asylum in Grenada. In 1889, Britain removed Tobago from the Windward group and joined it with Trinidad.

CHAPTER 14

THE SPANISH ISLANDS FIGHT FOR FREEDOM

Britain, victorious in 1815, gained colonies in the West Indies. Spain—and not France—was the great loser during the Napoleonic wars. The French occupation of Spain (1808–12) allowed the creole aristocracy to seize control throughout the Americas, and the last Spanish garrison (in Peru) surrendered early in 1826. The Spanish Empire once again was confined to the Caribbean islands—almost exactly 300 years after Cortés sailed from Cuba to begin the conquest of the mainland.

For many years, Spanish officials refused to recognize they had lost the Americas. Power in Madrid alternated between supporters of absolutist monarchy and various varieties of reformers. But all Spanish governments were determined to preserve the remnants of their empire. Moreover, all sought to keep the Puerto Rican and Cuban markets as privileged preserves, reserved to Spanish merchants by discriminatory tariffs. This policy subordinated West Indian needs to Spanish commercial lobbies, reflecting the Spanish government's pressing concerns at home. Spain had remained a very poor country, while Cuban sugar planters became wealthy. Indeed, it is probable that all Cuban whites and free coloreds—perhaps even Cuban slaves—lived better than the peasants in the poorer regions of the mother country.

CUBA, THE RICHEST ISLAND

Cuba, equal in size to Pennsylvania, is by far the largest of the Caribbean islands. Ten times bigger than Jamaica and 250 times larger than Barbados, it is almost as large as all the other Caribbean islands put together. Cuba's natural riches make it an ideal producer of tropical products, such as sugar and tobacco. Cuba is the only major island not dominated by mountains. Almost three-quarters of the land forms a rolling plain at sea level, endowed with rich soil and generally adequate rainfall. In contrast to other islands, roads and railroads could be built from one end of the country to the other.

Cuba's location at the western edge of the Caribbean and an abundance of natural harbors facilitate the movement of goods and people by water. Havana is one of the finest ports in the world, while Guantánamo and Santiago de Cuba provide excellent harbors at the eastern end of the island. Its location also gives Cuba major strategic importance. The island dominates the Windward Passage separating it from Hispaniola, as well as the Yucatán and Florida Channels into the Gulf of Mexico. Cuba was, therefore, essential to the defense of the Spanish Empire, and it continues to control the sea lanes to the Panama Canal.

Only Spanish trade regulations kept Cuba from prospering before the 1760s. Under British or French rule, it would have become a major sugar producer long before. As soon as Spain opened Cuban ports to foreign ships, a great sugar boom began that lasted—almost without interruption—until the 1880s. Cuba surpassed all other Caribbean islands because of its great size and natural resources. Cuban planters also benefited from improved technologies and better types of sugarcane. They enjoyed higher yields both because their fields were virgin and not depleted and

Black workers operating a sugar mill in Cuba. Semi-mechanized mills were introduced by the middle of the 19th century. Earlier mills used smaller rollers—often vertical rather than horizontal—to crush the sugarcane.

because they used better methods than Jamaican planters.

Using Spanish and later American loans, Cuban planters introduced modern milling techniques that increased production of higher quality sugar. French refugees from Haiti introduced water mills and enclosed furnaces, and steam engines were successfully used in mills from 1817. By 1860, mills that were at least semi-mechanized produced 92 percent of Cuba's sugar. Vacuum pans—which increase the amount of sugar derived from each cane—were installed from 1841, centrifuges during the 1850s.

The expansion of the cane estates into virgin lands also spurred the expansion of transportation networks. Old roads were improved, and new ones were constructed. The first railroad opened in 1838, reducing transportation costs by 70 percent. By 1860, railroads linked the major sugar regions to seaports, and planters built private feeder tracks connecting their fields and mills to the main lines.

Cane estates continued to expand throughout the island during the 19th century. Sugar plantations replaced cattle ranches, tobacco farms, and coffee estates. For a time coffee rivaled sugar as a major export. However, a series of devastating hurricanes between 1844 and 1846 destroyed many estates and prices fell as Brazilian coffee entered world markets. Many coffee growers failed, and their plantations were replanted in cane.

The history of the older sugar islands repeated itself on a larger scale in 19th-century Cuba. Since only the mills were mechanized, sugar continued to demand vast amounts of labor. Cuban planters thus brought a truly astonishing number of slaves from Africa.[1] The island had absorbed only 60,000 slaves between 1512 to 1763. As the cane estates flourished, more than half a million slaves were imported between 1808 and the end of the trade in 1865.[2] The number of slaves increased tenfold between 1774 and 1841—almost twice as fast as the white population.

In contrast to the English and French islands, black labor did not totally replace white labor. The Spanish government encouraged emigration from the impoverished homeland, and Cuba also served as a place of refuge. French and Spanish planters fled Hispaniola during the 1790s. After the collapse of the Spanish Empire on the mainland, Spanish soldiers and colonists flooded the island, and many settled in Cuba perma-

Table 22. **CUBA POPULATION ESTIMATES, 1759–1899**

	Total	Whites	Slaves	Free Non-Whites
1759	140,000	—		
1774	171,620	96,440	38,879	36,301
1792	272,300	153,559	64,590	54,151
1827	704,486	311,051	286,942	106,492
1841	1,007,624	418,291	436,495	152,838
1861	1,396,530	793,484	370,553	232,493
1877*	1,509,291	1,032,435	211,247	265,609
1899*	1,572,797	1,067,254	—	505,543

NOTE: The category "Whites" includes persons of Chinese origin in 1877 (43,811) and 1899 (14,857).

SOURCES: Franklin Knight, *Slave Society in Cuba during the Nineteenth Century* (Madison: University of Wisconsin Press, 1970), 22 (1774, 1841); Susan Schroeder, *Cuba: A Handbook of Historical Statistics* (Boston: G. K. Hall, 1982), 40.

nently. But slaves arrived in greater numbers than white settlers. As a result, whites formed less than half the population according to the censuses of 1827 and 1841.

Slave unrest became more common with the influx of Africans. Remembering the Haitian revolt and the Jamaican uprising in 1831–32, whites lived in fear of their slaves. In 1843, Spanish authorities claimed they had discovered a far-flung plot, known as the conspiracy of La Escalera after the ladders to which jailers tied their prisoners for flogging. They pursued suspects with the same ferocity seen during slave revolts on the English and French islands. Perhaps as many as 1,000 slaves and free coloreds were executed or tortured to death.

As Cuba devoted itself almost totally to sugarcane, it came to depend on outside suppliers for food, clothing, furniture, manufactured goods, even wood for the sugar mills. Economic logic made the United States Cuba's single most important trading partner, taking the bulk of its sugar exports. By 1877, the United States took 82 percent of Cuba's total exports, Spain only 6 percent. For their livelihood, Cubans thus relied on the production of one crop for one market.

Cuban Planters Seek Freedom from Spain

By the 1860s, Cuba was devoted—like 18th-century Jamaica or Saint-Domingue—to growing sugar. At the same time, Cuba had a much larger white population, and its social order was more complex than that of the older sugar islands. The creole élite of planters and property owners was urban and involved in the world market. But they had no say in the island's government and disliked the rapacity and petty tyrannies of Spanish officials and merchants. Spain had curtailed Cuban autonomy during the 1700s, and it further increased military control as it lost the mainland colonies. A decree of 1825 gave the captain-general virtually unlimited powers, including the authority to deport, without trial, anyone he thought undesirable. Only their own inefficiency limited the oppressive power of Spanish officials.

Cubans especially resented an economic policy that enriched Spain at the expense of Cuba. By the mid-19th century, Spain's effect on the Cuban economy was wholly negative. Its taxes on imports and exports and freight charges on foreign carriers cut into the profits of producers, while sharply raising prices for all Cuban consumers.[3] Moreover, Spain's abolition of the slave trade in 1820 forced planters to use illegal slavers, greatly raising the price of new slaves.

Unlike other islands, conflict and revolution in Cuba thus pitted white creoles against white *peninsulares* (the name given to recent Spanish immigrants). At first, few creoles supported independence, partly because they feared that a white revolution against Spain might trigger a black uprising against the planters. Indeed, Spanish officials threatened to liberate the slaves if Cubans sought independence. Thus the independence struggles on the mainland inspired several conspiracies during the 1820s, but none enjoyed widespread support.

Until the 1850s, Cubans dissatisfied with colonial rule rejected independence in favor of annexation as a slave state by the United States. Many creoles sincerely admired the United States, where African slavery comfortably coexisted with democracy, economic growth, and intellectual progress among whites. Some Cubans, losing patience with diplomatic maneuvers, tried to incite annexationist rebellions. With the financial support of exiles in New York, General Narciso López led three expeditions to Cuba between 1849 and 1851. During the same years, three annexationist uprisings ɔn the island also failed. Many in the United States, especially in the southern slave states, also favored Cuba's annexation. President James Polk—who fought the Mexican War to acquire California and New Mexico—unsuccessfully offered Spain $100 million for Cuba. Six years later, in 1854, President Franklin Pierce raised the offer to $130 million, but the Spanish refused to sell.

Both in Cuba and in the United States, support for annexation peaked in the 1850s. The growth of abolitionist sentiment and the American Civil War ended the principal reason for seeking union. Planters—hit hard by the financial panic of 1857—now wanted the government to buy and free their slaves (the policy adopted by Britain in 1834). In 1865, many of the same planters that had earlier advocated annexation organized the Reformist party to seek changes in Spanish rule.

The Reformists published a lengthy petition to the Spanish parliament in May 1865. They had four basic demands: reform of the tariff system, Cuban representation in the Spanish parliament, legal equality with peninsulars, and the suppression of the slave trade. A reform government, temporarily ruling in Spain, responded favorably. Madrid authorized the election of Cuban representatives to a commission (the Junta de Información) studying changes in colonial administration. However, any hope of reform was short-lived. In 1867, a new government in Spain imposed harsh laws that almost called out for rebellion. It increased the authority of military tribunals, closed opposition newspapers, banned political meetings, and imposed higher export fees and new taxes on landowners, businessmen, and professionals.

The Ten Years' War and Slave Emancipation

Discontent rose everywhere, but it was especially high among ranchers and planters in the economically depressed eastern provinces. On October 10, 1868, the Revolt of Yara (Grito de Yara) proclaimed Cuban independence and the establishment of a provisional republic led by Carlos Manuel de Céspedes (1818–74). The war dragged on for 10 years, with neither the rebels nor the Spanish army able to win a decisive victory. The rebel leadership was divided over the issue of slavery. The military leaders, many men of color, called for immediate abolition. The creole leadership temporized, hoping to gain support from wealthy landowners in the west.

The Ten Years' War turned into a series of guerrilla campaigns that devastated the eastern provinces without seriously affecting Havana and the west. A civil war in Spain hindered efforts to crush the rebels. When it ended in 1874, the government poured more soldiers into Cuba and constructed a fortified ditch the entire width of the island. In 1877, General Arsenio Campos arrived in Cuba with even more troops and promises of compromise. Negotiations culminated in the Pact of Zanjón (February 1878), which promised a variety of constitutional and financial reforms.

During the Ten Years' War, both the insurgents and Spanish loyalists had promised to abolish slavery. In February 1880, the Spanish government issued an abolition law without compensation to owners. The freed slaves were subject to the tutelage (*patronato*) of their former masters for eight years. Like the apprenticeship system imposed by England in 1834, this system required the former slaves to work for their masters in return for monthly wages, food, and clothing. The *patronato* proved unpopular both with landowners and freedmen, and the Crown abolished it on October 7, 1886, two years before it was due to expire.

The 17 years of uneasy truce that followed the Ten Years' War began with a severe economic depression. The war had permanently ruined the coffee industry, and higher American tariffs hurt cigar exports. In Europe the production of beet sugar dramatically increased, leaving the United States as the only market with the capacity to absorb Cuban production. The Madrid government did nothing to help the Cuban economy. In fact, it worsened conditions by confiscating the estates of insurgent landowners as well as by raising tariffs and taxes, making Cuba pay the entire cost of suppressing the rebellion. Hundreds of estates went into bankruptcy and thousands of workers were unemployed.

As world prices fell, Cuban sugar plantations had to reduce their costs to remain competitive. Milling was concentrated in gigantic factories (*centrales*) equipped with advanced machinery and connected by private railways to the cane fields. The number of mills fell by 40 percent from 1877 to 1895, while output steadily rose. Production reached 1 million tons for the first time in 1895. One gigantic mill, Central Constancia, produced as much sugar as the entire island of Jamaica, burdened with 140 outmoded mills.

The vast sums of money needed to erect these immense factories generally came from the United States, usually from companies that marketed tropical products. Some Cuban planters survived as sugar farmers (*colonos*) supplying the *centrales,* others became salaried administrators for the companies owning the mills. By 1895, fewer than 20 percent of mill owners came from the old planter class. American capital and influence increasingly dominated Cuba's most important industry.

A reciprocal trade agreement between Cuba and the United States brought two years of prosperity in 1892 and 1893. However, the United States rescinded its tariff concessions in 1894, and Madrid swiftly restored a wall of protectionist duties around Cuba. An outcry of indignation and protest against Spain arose across the island. Madrid also had failed to deliver the political reforms promised in the 1870s. Creoles still had no say in government, as peninsular officials rigged elections to retain power. By 1895 the economy was in crisis, and political discontent was increasing.

After the Ten Years' War, the most dedicated separatists chose exile rather than submitting to continued Spanish rule. Most of the thousands of workers forced to seek work in other countries also were devoted to independence. A commitment to armed struggle held together the ranks of exiled separatists in the United States, Latin America, and Europe. José Martí led New York's intransigent patriotic society, the Cuban Junta. Martí was an extraordinary leader, simultaneously a skillful politician, a poet and journalist, and a philosopher with a compelling vision of *Cuba libre.* His propaganda promised a Cuban republic free of racial and social inequalities, although he never drew up specific plans to obtain these goals. It rallied both American support and the unemployed of eastern Cuba, where Martí raised the standard of revolt in 1895.

The horrors of this civil war (1895–98) far surpassed those of earlier rebellions. Martí soon died in one of the first skirmishes. Leadership of the rebel forces passed to Máximo Gómez (1835–1905) and the colored general Antonio Maceo (1845–1896), who had distinguished themselves as daring guerrilla leaders during the Ten Years' War. Poor blacks and whites swelled their forces, while boats brought arms from America. Tens of thousands of peasants provided food and supplies and spied on the Spanish army everywhere in Cuba. The war became a savage guerrilla conflict, pitting rural against urban Cuba. The insurgents sought to drive the peasants into their ranks and make Cuba valueless for Spain by burning crops and estates. General Gómez banned all sugar production, and rebel forces raided across the island with the simple torch as their most devastating weapon.

A new captain-general, Valeriano Weyler, arrived in January 1896. Weyler, a non-smoker and military technician, saw that he could not win by defending isolated plantations. To deny the insurgents recruits and supplies, Spanish and loyalist forces rounded up as many as 300,000 peasants. They forced them into hastily erected concentration camps, where thousands died of hunger, abuse, and epidemics. This policy of "reconcentration" and reinforcements from Spain allowed Weyler to regain the initiative after Maceo's death in December 1896. But the rebels denied him victory by refusing to fight major battles. Gómez retreated to the eastern provinces and continued guerrilla operations against towns and forts. When a new government in Madrid

"Starvation by Proclamation in Cuba." In 1896 and 1897, Spanish forces drove many thousands of peasant families into concentration camps. An example of illustrations and articles in American newspapers and magazines, which fostered support for war with Spain.

dismissed Weyler and gave Cuba autonomous government in January 1898, Gómez rejected any compromise short of total independence.

Many Cuban property owners called for U.S. intervention, and the war devastated American investments. In New York, the Cuban Junta waged a propaganda war to sway American public opinion. Mass newspapers (called "yellow journals" from their shoddy paper) took up the Cuban cause. Their articles graphically depicted and sometimes exaggerated Spanish cruelty and mistreatment of Cuban civilians. In 1898, the United States finally intervened in the conflict. President McKinley disliked war, as did his business friends, and he did not believe in Cuban freedom. But he could not resist public opinion.

In January 1898, Spanish army officers led riots in Havana against Madrid's new policy of autonomy. McKinley ordered the battleship *Maine* to Havana to protect American lives and property. On February 15, an explosion—which American experts attributed to a Spanish mine—tore through the hull of the *Maine*. It sank quickly, and 266 lives were lost. When Spain rejected McKinley's demands for an armistice and an end to the concentration camps, war became inevitable. Congress proclaimed Cuba independent on April 11, pledging in the Teller Amendment not to annex the island. Spain severed diplomatic relations, and Congress declared war on April 25.

The war was over in 10 weeks with little fighting in Cuba. At Manila Bay in May, Admiral George Dewey blew Spain's Pacific fleet out of the war in one hour, without a single American casualty. In July, the Atlantic squadron was as swiftly destroyed off Santiago Bay in eastern Cuba. After the two most complete naval disasters of modern times, Madrid had to surrender. By the Treaty of Paris (December 1898), Spain granted independence to Cuba, and ceded Puerto Rico and the Pacific island of Guam to the United States.

The American Congress established a military government, which at first concentrated on relieving the starving population, disarming both the insurgents and loyalists, and controlling yellow fever. Elections (under a restricted suffrage) were conducted in 1900 for town governments and an assembly to write a constitution. Most representatives supported immediate independence, and some came from radical factions.

The McKinley administration was determined to set out terms that would protect American property and the rights of minorities. Congress enacted eight provisions, which together are known as the Platt Amendment. These stipulated that Cuba would lease naval bases to the United States, make no treaties with a foreign power that might impair its independence, and acquire no debts it could not pay. On June 12, 1901, the Havana constitutional convention (by a majority of one) added the Platt proposals. The constitution, modeled on that of the United States, also provided for universal suffrage, separation of church and state, a powerful president who could serve two terms, and a relatively weak senate and chamber of deputies.

PUERTO RICO DEVELOPS A PLANTATION ECONOMY

Puerto Rico's economy and society developed in different ways, and its peoples avoided the bitter civil wars that ravaged Cuba from 1868 to 1898. Nevertheless, their common obedience to Spain linked the two islands throughout the 19th century. Spanish governments—whether constitutional or authoritarian—tended to consider the two islands together. Spanish ministers hesitated to grant reforms to Puerto Rico because they feared the Cubans would demand similar concessions.

Puerto Rico is less than one-tenth as large as Cuba. It is less generously endowed with natural assets and more closely resembles Jamaica or Haiti. Mountains and hills dominate the center of the island with plains along the coasts—about five miles wide in the northeast and rather less than that elsewhere. Only about one-third of the island is relatively level, and the soil often is poor. Since the rain-bearing winds come from the east, the southern coasts are dry, and some areas must be irrigated.

Spain saw both Cuba and Puerto Rico primarily as military bastions and did little to foster economic growth until the 1760s. During the 19th century, a sugar boom based on African slavery transformed Cuba, and it became the largest producer in the Caribbean. On Puerto Rico, however, the sugar industry flourished only after the American occupation in 1898.

Without cane estates, Puerto Rico's population remained smaller and more rural, without sharp divisions of class. Planters on Puerto Rico were not as rich as their Cuban counterparts, and they imported many fewer slaves. Whites formed a much higher portion of the population than on other major islands, and most persons of color were free. Thus a steady blending of the races, beginning early in the colonial period, continued uninterrupted through the 19th century.

Economic development became essential when the Mexican subsidies (*situado*) supporting the island's government and military ceased in 1811. By a decree of August 1815 (the Real Cédula de Gracias), the Spanish Crown, increasingly unable to keep out foreign shipping, finally opened Puerto Rico to world trade—although non-Spanish goods paid higher tariffs. It also confirmed the 1778 decree opening the island to immigration and offered free land to settlers. (Black and colored freedmen received half the grant to whites.) Settlers arrived from Haiti, Santo Domingo, Venezuela, and Spain itself.

Coffee, primarily sold in Europe, became Puerto Rico's principal commercial crop during the 19th century. Coffee plantations, initially introduced in 1736, now opened up the interior. They spread rapidly in the western mountains with their high rainfall, helping to develop the ports of Mayagüez and Ponce, which were nearest to the coffee regions. Production reached 6,000 tons in 1897 and peaked at 27,000 tons in 1920. The number of sugar estates along the coastal plains also increased, but Puer-

Table 23. **PUERTO RICO POPULATION ESTIMATES, 1820–1900**

	Total	Whites	Slaves	Free Non-Whites
1820	230,261	102,432	21,730	106,459
1836	357,086	188,869	41,818	126,399
1860	583,181	300,406	41,738	241,037
1872	618,150	—	31,635	—
1900	953,243	589,104	—	364,139

SOURCES: Arturo Morales Carrión, *Puerto Rico: A Political and Cultural History* (New York: Norton, 1983), 114, 137; Deerr, *History of Sugar*, II:281 (1836); Knight, *The Caribbean*, 238 (1860); Watts, *West Indies*, 321, 459.

to Rican sugar production always lagged far behind that of Cuba.[4] Since coffee plantations tended to be small to medium-size family holdings, a comparatively large portion of Puerto Ricans owned at least some land.

Slavery Is Abolished in Puerto Rico

A lack of slaves held back the expansion of sugar estates. In 1845, Great Britain and Spain agreed on stronger provisions to end the slave trade, nominally banned in 1820. Puerto Rican owners could not afford the higher prices of illegal imports, and the trade effectively ended after about 1850. Puerto Rico was developing into a nation—something like Haiti—of independent farmers growing food for their own needs on lands to which they had no legal title. Fully 80 percent of the population still lived in rural areas in 1899.

Seeking to make use of this large pool of peasant labor, the Spanish governor established a system of forced labor in 1849. The law set minimum landholding requirements and forbade the common practice of squatting. It required day laborers to congregate on the fringes of towns and compelled them to carry a booklet listing their employers. The law (Reglamento de Jornaleros) was difficult to enforce and was abolished in 1873.

Puerto Rico's creole élite strongly supported slave emancipation and helped to organize the Spanish Abolitionist Society in 1864. The island's mixed population encouraged egalitarian sentiment, and reformers also believed that they could not win other gains until the slaves were freed. Puerto Rican representatives to the Spanish National Assembly (Cortes)—several of them persons of color—pressed the government to end slavery.[5] After a bitter debate, a law of March 22, 1873, freed the remaining slaves with compensation to their owners.

Puerto Ricans Seek Autonomy

After its mainland colonies gained independence, Spain imposed authoritarian government on Puerto Rico, as well as on Cuba. From 1825, the governor—always a military officer—exercised unlimited powers. Municipal governments remained responsible for local administration, and judicial officials retained some autonomy. But the governor could intervene in local matters and arrest or deport individuals at will. Some members of the small educated élite sought limits on the governor and more say in local government. Only a few initially wanted complete independence, and several conspiracies in the 1820s and 1830s met with little success.

The Revolt of Lares (Grito de Lares) on September 23, 1868, was the most serious challenge to Spanish domination in Puerto Rico. Ramón Betances (1827–98), a physician trained in France, led the independence movement from Saint Thomas. It enjoyed greatest strength in the west among laborers protesting the passbook system and planters heavily indebted to Spanish merchants. On September 23, several hundred men occupied the town of Lares, near Mayagüez. The next morning they declared the independence of Puerto Rico and set up a provisional government. When the rebels tried to take San Sebastian, the next town, they met organized resistance and fled. During the following month, small guerrilla battles took place in the mountains of the region, as troops hunted down the rebels. This revolt has become a symbol to many Puerto Ricans, and September 24 is celebrated as a holiday.

Autonomist sentiment increased among the creole élite from the 1870s. After the overthrow of the Spanish republic in 1875, the governors manipulated the electoral laws in favor of *peninsulares* residing on the island. In 1887, the Liberal Party—later reorganized as the Autonomist Party—called for self-government within a federal union with Spain. Convinced that the Liberals were plotting subversion, a new governor instituted a year-long campaign of repression and torture, which ended only when he was replaced by the Spanish government.

The autonomists hoped to gain influence by an alliance with one of the Spanish political parties, but they disagreed in their choice of an ally. Luis Muñoz Rivera (1859–1916), an influential newspaper editor, strongly favored affiliation with Spain's Liberal Fusionist Party headed by Mateo Práxedes Sagasta. An alliance finally was ratified early in 1897. When a terrorist killed the Spanish prime minister in August 1897, Sagasta returned to power and kept his promises. Royal decrees in November 1898 granted autonomy to Cuba and Puerto Rico.

Puerto Rico now enjoyed political freedom—at least on paper. The decree weakened the powers of the governor appointed by the Spanish Crown. Puerto Rico's legislature had authority over local laws as well as the island's budget, tariffs, taxes, and public works. All males over 25 could vote for delegates to both houses of the Spanish Cortes. They also elected the island's legislative assembly as well as eight of the 15 members of the Administrative Council, a kind of senate.

Puerto Rico's experiment in autonomy was brief. General elections were held in March, and the legislature took office on July 17. Eight days later, the first U.S. troops landed on the southern coast. Some Puerto Ricans mourned the loss of their brief independence. However, nothing in Spain's history during the 19th century suggests that later governments would have honored its commitments to its former colony.

CHAPTER 15

HISPANIOLA AND THE LEEWARD ISLANDS

After the Revolutionary and Napoleonic wars (1791–1815), England and Spain controlled the largest and richest of the Caribbean islands. Two independent republics shared the island of Hispaniola after 1844, when Santo Domingo expelled the Haitian army of occupation. With the loss of Haiti, France now possessed only the Leeward islands of Guadeloupe and Martinique, with some 75,000 free men and 175,000 slaves. The Danes continued to occupy the Virgin Islands, and the Netherlands retained Curaçao and its three Leeward colonies.[1]

The same worldwide trends—and especially the oversupply of sugar—affected all the islands. The 19th century was an era of centralization. France, Denmark, and the Netherlands now ruled their colonies directly from Europe, and all abolished slavery—France and Denmark in 1848, the Netherlands in 1863. Like the British colonies, these islands had to look for alternative sources of income as slave emancipation hastened the decline of sugar estates. Although certainly not wealthy, the French islands were comparatively prosperous and among the least torn by social strife. Unlike Britain and Spain, France viewed these colonies as integral parts of the homeland. It allowed island delegates to sit in the French legislature, protected Caribbean sugar from foreign competition, and promoted economic development.

Haiti and Santo Domingo—the only countries without ties to a European power—virtually ceased to grow sugarcane. Both developed into nations of free peasants owning small plots of land. Political authority was unstable, as venal and opportunistic rulers took power through military coups. Particularly in Haiti, these ambitious adventurers took advantage of enduring hostility between the light-skinned élite and the darker skinned peasants.

THE FRENCH ISLANDS ABOLISH SLAVERY

Napoleon's empire had restored slavery and the slave trade in 1802. Britain forced the French government to outlaw it by 1818, although illegal imports continued until 1831. Inspired by the success of British abolitionists, Parisian intellectuals formed an abolition society in 1834. Their main spokesman was Victor Schoelcher, who poured out a torrent of books, pamphlets, and speeches during the next 15 years. Continuing slave unrest on Guadeloupe also weakened support for slavery, since French officials never forgot that Haiti had been lost through a slave revolt. A series of laws attempted to improve the treatment of slaves. In 1833, branding and mutilation of slaves was forbidden. Free coloreds—rapidly growing in numbers—became equal in law to whites.

French abolitionists gained power with a revolution in 1848. The provisional government abolished slavery and appointed Schoelcher head of a committee to enforce emancipation. He compensated the owners but did not require freedmen to serve a period of apprenticeship. The slaves, while celebrating news of their freedom, feared that the planters would refuse to accept the new law. Thousands fled the estates, and rebellious slaves on Martinique killed dozens of whites. To end the disorder, the governors of the islands declared all slaves free even before they received Schoelcher's orders. The 1848 uprising in Martinique ensured that subsequent governments could not retract the emancipation decree.

Indentured Laborers from India

As in the British colonies, many freedmen showed their contempt for field labor by moving out and squatting on vacant land. With emancipation, sugar production was halved on Guadeloupe and fell by almost one-third on Martinique. French planters, noting the apparent success of British estates using indentured labor, sought governmental help. Some imported free blacks from French colonies along Africa's western coast as well as small numbers of Chinese and Indochinese workers. Most used indentured laborers recruited in India by agreement with the British government. Between 1852 and 1887, Guadeloupe planters took in 45,000 Indians and 5,800 Africans, while Martinique received 29,400 Indians and 10,500 Africans. About three-quarters of the Indians stayed on after their indentures expired. As in Trinidad, most settled in separate communities and tried to maintain their own traditions.

Successive French governments continued to protect and support the sugar and rum industries. High tariffs kept foreign sugar out of France, and the main competition came from French beet sugar. After intense debate, a French law of 1843 taxed both products equally and gave the colonial sugar growers almost a legal right to priority in the home market. Henceforth, France effectively treated Caribbean sugar as a domestic product, and the government increased protective measures during depressions in

Table 24. **MARTINIQUE AND GUADELOUPE POPULATION ESTIMATES, 1827–1848**

	Total	Whites	Slaves	Free Non-Whites
Martinique				
1831	109,916	9,362	86,499	14,055
1848	113,357	9,490	67,447	36,420
Guadeloupe				
1827	127,574	14,958	98,368	14,978
1848	129,050	9,926	87,719	31,405

SOURCES: Patterson, *Slavery and Social Death*, 480; Leo Elisabeth, "The French Antilles," *Neither Slave nor Free*, 148–151; Lassère, *Guadeloupe*, 297.

the 1890s and 1930s. Indeed, since 1967, sugar from the French overseas departments is regulated as a European product by the European Union.

In addition to subsidizing immigration and offering a protected market, the government also encouraged investment by French banks. Modern central mills were built on both islands, and sugar production substantially exceeded pre-emancipation levels by the 1870s. Production again dropped at the end of the century with the end of Indian immigration and lower prices for French beet sugar. Only the most efficient creole planters survived, and French companies owning the central factories became large landowners.

A Creole Society with French Laws and Schools

Black and colored peasants also bought up abandoned plantations as well as public lands, growing food for local consumption on their small farms. Two separate societies evolved here as on several other islands. As large companies consolidated the plantations, the number of whites fell—especially relative to the soaring black and colored population. High French officials, white landowners, and merchants enjoyed the greatest prestige. White and colored businessmen and professionals came next, with black smallholders and farm laborers at the bottom. The various races lived in segregated communities, and racial antagonisms sometimes broke out into violent riots.

Social peace normally was maintained because French laws offered opportunities to ambitious blacks and coloreds that were lacking in Spanish Cuba or the British Crown colonies. Especially under the Third Republic after 1870, the islands were increasingly integrated with France, and French colonial officers enforced French laws. Each island sent three representatives to the National Assembly, and each also elected a General Council, created in 1854 to discuss its budget. In addition, each town had an elected mayor and a municipal council with limited powers. While elections were not always totally honest, all adult males could vote from 1849 to 1854 and again after 1871. Blacks were elected to the local councils, while men of color tended to hold the more important positions and to represent the island in the National Assembly. Although blacks and coloreds keenly appreciated their differences, they did not, as in Haiti, form opposing factions.

Elementary education was generally available after the government took over the schools in 1886. The government also opened secondary schools (*lycées*), set up a law school on Martinique in 1882, and provided a small number of scholarships to French universities. Island schools taught French courses in French under the supervision of officials from Bordeaux. Black and colored islanders who spoke French and had a French education could take posts with the government or work for the colonial administration, especially in French Africa.

THE DUTCH COLONIES SURVIVE

The Dutch West India Company had occupied several islands from the 1630s, during its failed attempt to conquer Brazil. Despite French and British efforts to destroy Dutch commerce, the company held on and kept two groups of islands as trading posts. In the Leewards it governed Sint Eustatius, Saba, and Sint Maarten, which it shared with France. Just off the coast of the mainland, it held Curaçao—with a superb harbor at Willemstad—and its two small dependencies of Aruba and Bonaire. When Napoleon occupied Holland in 1795, the British occupied all the Dutch colonies until 1815. It then restored the islands and Holland's mainland colony of Suriname.

The last remnants of its empire in the Antilles brought few profits to the Netherlands during the century after 1815. Dutch traders had prospered during the 18th century by smuggling goods and slaves into Spain's mainland colonies and the French and British islands. Britain forced the Dutch to end the slave trade in 1814, and the Spanish mainland colonies won their independence and opened their ports to European shipping. Since smuggling and the slave trade had been their most lucrative business, many Dutch traders moved to Latin America or the United States. With their small populations and arid climates, the islands had few sources of income. Thus, the Netherlands, which had to subsidize their budgets, paid little attention to its Caribbean possessions, which it treated as extensions of Suriname.

Like the Spanish, British, and French colonies, the Dutch islands now came under direct rule from Europe. The Netherlands had abolished the West India Company in 1791. It now brought its Caribbean possessions under Dutch law enforced by governors-general sent from Europe. After unsuccessfully combining all of its Caribbean possessions under one administration (1828–45), the Dutch established two governors-general. One governor enforced Dutch policies in Suriname. The other had authority over the three Leeward islands and the Curaçao group to the south. These officials were assisted by a variety of advisory councils, whose members were appointed by the governor and had no independent authority.

The Netherlands ended slavery in its Caribbean colonies on July 1, 1863, considerably later than Britain or France. Abolition enjoyed little support in Holland. Only a few academics called for emancipation, and the Reformed Church, the official state church before 1795, did not petition the government on the issue until 1858.

In spite of sporadic efforts to promote agriculture or salt mining, the islands produced few cash crops, and only 6,500 slaves remained by 1863. But the sugar planters on Suriname refused to accept emancipation without compensation. When France ended slavery on Saint-Martin in 1848, slaves in the Dutch section simply took their freedom. Thrifty planters kept records of births among the blacks they still theoretically owned, while the Dutch government carried on a leisurely debate on how much compensation owners should be paid.

Curaçao was by far the most prosperous of the Dutch Antilles during the 19th century. Trade with Venezuela now became the mainstay of Curaçao's economy. The Dutch government negotiated a commercial treaty that lifted import taxes on all merchandise imported from the Netherlands and some products from other countries. Despite tensions during Venezuela's many revolutions, Dutch merchants profited by exchanging Venezuelan products for European manufactured goods.

Curaçao's economy was wholly based on trade. Although the Dutch government heavily subsidized agriculture during the 1830s, few cash crops can live on the island's dry soils. Aruba and Bonaire grow the aloe plant, whose leaves produce a liquid used in medicines and insect repellents. Farmers on Curaçao also introduced Seville oranges. They shipped the dried bitter peels to Holland, where they are distilled into a liqueur also called Curaçao. The end of slavery had little effect on this commercial economy. Emancipation did end production at Bonaire's salt ponds, which had attracted the Dutch to the islands in the 1630s.

Holland's three tiny islands in the Leewards suffered a severe economic decline during the 19th century. Sint Eustatius's traders had prospered by smuggling goods and slaves into the neighboring French and English islands as well as to the Spanish colonies on the mainland. In February 1781, a British fleet under Admiral Rodney occupied Sint Eustatius, destroying its warehouses and plundering the ships in its harbor. Most merchants and trading companies moved to the nearby Danish island of Saint Thomas, safely neutral during European wars.

Sint Maarten was less arid and had more fertile soils. Small plantations grew sugarcane and raised cattle, and hundreds of slaves also worked at the island's huge salt ponds. When emancipation came in 1863, planters could not pay wages and make a profit. They deserted these marginal estates, which soon were overgrown by tropical brush. The freed slaves and small white populations of the three Leeward islands survived by growing their own food, making shoes, and building ships. The men migrated each year as seasonal laborers—cutting sugarcane in Cuba and Puerto Rico, mining salt on Saint Kitts, or working in the phosphate mines in French Guiana.

THE VIRGIN ISLANDS UNDER THE DANISH CROWN

The Danish Virgin Islands were under the direct rule of the king of Denmark from 1754. As in the British and Dutch islands, the royal governor had virtually unlimited powers. In 1863, two colonial councils with legislative powers were granted. Because of strict property requirements and other qualifications, only wealthy whites could vote in elections to these councils.

Prosperous conditions generally prevailed until the 1830s, when both foreign trade and the sugar industry began to decline. Unlike sailing ships, steam-driven merchant ships did not need to stop at Saint Thomas on the way to the British and French islands. Moreover, the adoption of free trade by the British Empire took away many of Saint Thomas's advantages as a free port. As the harbor at Saint Thomas declined, planters and merchants found it difficult to ship their goods.

The Danish Virgin Islands had many ties to the British colonies, and Denmark could not maintain slavery after Britain ended it in 1833. The British abolition law prompted the Danish governor-general to decree various reforms, limiting the powers of owners and preparing the slaves for freedom. An 1839 decree called for free elementary education for both free and slave residents. Schools soon opened on Saint Croix, but Saint Thomas had to wait until 1878, Saint John even longer. English was the dominant language, used in the public schools after 1850.

A slave rebellion speeded up emancipation on Saint Croix, as on other islands. In 1847, a royal decree promised slaves their freedom in 1859. The slaves on Saint Croix decided not to wait for twelve years. Led by a young man named Moses "Buddhoe" Gottlieb, blacks near Frederiksted secretly organized a revolution. In July 1848, they sacked several houses, and most whites fled to ships in the harbor. The slaves besieged the fort, demanding immediate emancipation and threatening to burn the town. When the governor finally came across the island from Christiansted, he quickly wrote out an emancipation decree that the Crown confirmed on September 22, 1848.

Sugar estates on Saint Croix became less profitable after emancipation increased expenses. Like freedmen on other islands, the former slaves refused field labor, and the cane estates faced bankruptcy. In 1849, the Danish government imposed a system of compulsory labor and internal passports that tied black laborers to the soil through yearly contracts. To cut milling expenses, it also opened a central factory in 1878, but it operated at a loss.

Full legal freedom came only after a second revolt destroyed much of Frederiksted in 1878. When they were free to leave, many black laborers emigrated to other Caribbean islands. The population of the islands continued to decline, falling by about a third between 1835 and 1911. (See Table 25.) The races remained separate, and the white minority retained economic as well as political power. Most whites sent

Table 25. **DANISH VIRGIN ISLANDS POPULATION ESTIMATES, 1835–1911**

	Total	Whites	Slaves	Free Non-Whites
Saint Thomas				
1835	14,022	3,520	5,298	5,204
1848	14,000	—	3,500	—
1880	14,389	—	—	—
1911	10,678	—	—	—
Saint Croix				
1835	26,681	1,892	19,876	4,913
1848	—	—	26,000	—
1880	18,430	—	—	—
1911	15,467	—	—	—
Saint John				
1835	2,475	344	1,929	202
1850	2,228	—	—	—
1880	944	—	—	—
1911	941	—	—	—

SOURCE: Boyers, *America's Virgin Islands*, 40, 48, 53; Patterson, *Slavery and Social Death*, 482.

their children to private schools rather than to the public schools established in 1839, and churches also were segregated by race.

The Danish government now found the colony an economic liability as revenues failed to cover its costs. Negotiations to sell the islands to the United States began in 1865, although they were not concluded until 1917. Indeed, the Danish government approved the sale of Saint Thomas and Saint John in 1867. However, the American U.S. Senate, caught up in the impeachment of President Andrew Johnson, failed to ratify the treaty.

THE FORMATION OF MODERN HAITI

Victorious over Napoleon's armies, Jean-Jacques Dessalines made himself emperor of Haiti in 1805. Dessalines and later Henry Christophe (ruling in the north until 1820) tried to keep the plantations going with forced labor. But both blacks and colored persons resisted their system, which effectively reimposed slavery under a different name. Under their successors, Haiti became a nation of two castes. In the country, black peasants produced their own food on small plots, while the colored élite in coastal towns dominated commerce and politics. Although the hated and despised white masters were gone, racial divisions continued to trouble the new nation. With some exceptions, skin color has corresponded with wealth, with lighter Haitians being richer and darker ones poorer.

Emperor Jean-Jacques Dessalines

African by birth, the new emperor had begun life as a field hand on a cane estate owned by a black freedman. Scarred for life by his master's whip, Dessalines hated both whites and people of color. Following the defeat of the French, he ordered his soldiers to kill every remaining white, and some light-colored Haitians also perished. Haiti was to be a totally black nation in which no white would ever again own any property.[2]

Dessalines wanted Haiti to be black, but he did not want a nation of free black peasants. The emperor continued Toussaint's system of state socialism and made it even more rigid. The government would become the only landlord, with his generals and high officials leasing the estates at his whim. Dessalines thus seized all estates that had been owned by white Frenchmen—as well as all lands that blacks and coloreds had acquired since October 1802. Using forgery and murder, Dessalines also took other estates that he considered valuable. By 1806, his government owned more than two-thirds of all productive plantations, and Dessalines reimposed slavery on Haiti's blacks. He decreed that all persons must labor either as soldiers or as laborers bound for life to a specific estate. The army drove the majority of men and women back to the plantations, where the overseers used physical punishments to increase production.

A system of state socialism requires an army of literate officials and managers. Although he hated them, Dessalines had to fill these important posts with people of color. Many blacks continued to flee with their families into the hills. But the most effective opposition came from the colored landowners who had held estates during the colonial period. In October 1806, an insurrection began that had the secret approval of Henry Christophe, the most senior army officer. When Dessalines moved south to crush the rebels, he was killed in a roadside ambush near Port-au-Prince on October 17, 1806.

Christophe considered himself Dessalines's successor and did not bother to attend the assembly called to name the new head of state. Alexandre Pétion's supporters packed the meeting and drew up a new constitution providing for a powerless president and a powerful head of the national assembly. They then elected Christophe president, while Pétion became leader of the assembly. When Christophe brought his army south, Pétion's troops forced him to retreat. From 1807 to 1820, Haiti was divided into two principal states. In the north, Christophe crowned himself king in 1811, while Pétion ruled a republic in the South and West Provinces.[3]

The Kingdom and the Republic

King Henry I was Haiti's most relentlessly effective and dramatic ruler.[4] He retained Dessalines's system of disguised slavery and used it to enrich his realm. The peasants remained a separate caste, bound to the soil and forbidden to marry non-workers. Christophe's largely dark-skinned followers—who now became dukes, counts, and barons—received long leases and paid one-fourth of the annual crop in taxes. As hostile as Dessalines toward the coloreds, Christophe preferred foreign whites and used them in his administration. But he entrusted his own security to the Royal Dahomets, a personal bodyguard of 4,000 warriors recruited directly from Africa and thus loyal only to the king.

Under Christophe's stern rule, sugar, indigo, and coffee once more flowed profitably from the plantations to foreign markets. Cap-Henri (the new name for Cap-Français) flourished as a commercial center, and the king issued gold and silver currency. Using the unpaid labor of his people, he built a colossal fortress (La Citadelle

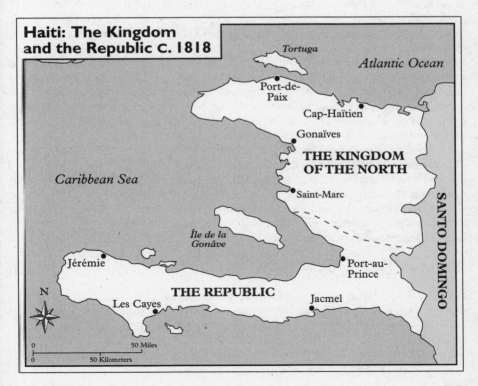

Haiti: The Kingdom and the Republic C. 1818

Tortuga

Atlantic Ocean

Port-de-Paix

Cap-Haïtien

Gonaïves

THE KINGDOM OF THE NORTH

Caribbean Sea

Saint-Marc

Île de la Gonâve

SANTO DOMINGO

Jérémie

Port-au-Prince

N

THE REPUBLIC

Les Cayes

Jacmel

0   50 Miles

0   50 Kilometers

Sans Souci Palace, near Cap-Haïtien, Haiti. With his subjects' unpaid labor, King Henry Christophe (1807–20) erected Sans Souci and a colossal fortress (La Citadelle La Ferrière) on a nearby mountain peak. Modeled after European palaces, Sans Souci was richly ornamented and furnished.

La Ferrière) on a high mountain as well as his own exquisite palace, called Sans Souci. His harsh measures finally provoked a popular uprising in 1820. Stricken by paralysis and faced with defections in his army, King Henry I shot himself at Sans Souci—according to tradition, with a silver bullet.

Pétion's republic adopted very different policies. The republic did not preserve the plantations as undivided units worked by unfree labor. From 1809, Pétion broke up many estates and divided them among the populace, while squatters settled on others. Pétion did keep some large estates and gave them to his colored generals, but their owners often could not find laborers. Thus they divided their plantations into several farms, which they leased to tenants against a share of the crop.

Most farmers in the South and West stopped growing export crops and instead planted garden crops for their own consumption. Sugar, cotton, and indigo virtually disappeared from the South. "Wild" coffee, cacao, and logwood collected in the mountains henceforth became the main export crops.[5] Both agriculture and governmental revenues steadily dwindled. But the former slaves, now secure on their own small parcels of land, loved Pétion as their *Papa bon kè* ("kind-hearted father"). Pétion's republic endured to become a reunited Haiti. The kingdom had perished with Christophe.

President Boyer

Pétion's light-skinned secretary and friend, Jean-Pierre Boyer (1776–1850), succeeded him as president for life in 1818. When Christophe died in 1820, Boyer reunited the two states under the laws of the republic. In 1822 the Haitian army easily occupied the Spanish part of the island, where Haitian officials abolished slavery. Boyer, an amiable and refined man, ruled the whole of Hispaniola until a revolution removed him from

Table 26. **HAITI POPULATION ESTIMATES, 1824–1919**

1824	590,000
1843	830,136
1863	1,100,000
1888	960,000
1900	1,270,000
1919	1,631,250

NOTE: All totals are estimates, since Haiti never has had an accurate census.

SOURCES: Watts, *West Indies,* 459 (1824–1900); Aaron Segal, "Haiti," *Population Policies in the Caribbean,* 152 (1919).

office in 1843. During these two decades, Haiti enjoyed relative peace and stability. In 1825, France accepted Haiti's independence after Boyer agreed to pay a large indemnity to compensate the planters expelled in 1804.

Boyer at first continued Pétion's policy of land distribution, but his government ran out of funds even before the imposition of the French indemnity. Boyer thus made one final attempt to conserve what was left of the plantation system. His Rural Code of May 1826 restored the disguised slavery imposed by Toussaint Louverture, Dessalines, and Christophe. The code attached workers for life to specific estates, forbade them to leave the plantations, and ordered them to work under military supervision. This time the effort failed totally, since Boyer's government lacked the officials or the military force to reimpose slavery.

Haiti now became a nation of small farmers, who grew only enough to feed their own families plus a small surplus sold at the local market. Some owned their own plots and others became sharecroppers. As the population soared many simply squatted on land in the mountains. There they cleared the forests and opened the land to massive soil erosion.

Few Haitians wanted to work on cane estates under any system. Prior to the revolution, the slaves had grown most of the island's food on their provision grounds. Now that they were free, they wanted to live as independent peasant farmers cultivating their own bit of family land. Freedom meant the right to control their own labor and keep the crops they had grown with their own hands.

Boyer's perennially bankrupt government invested nothing in the nation's infrastructure or in education. The state did not offer public education, and Roman Catholic schools did not exist until the Vatican recognized Haiti through the Concordat of 1860. In the absence of formal institutions, government was highly personalized and based on family ties and face-to-face friendships.

Haiti increasingly developed into a society of two castes. An élite group composed almost entirely of people of color controlled political power and patronage. A small number of coloreds were poor, and a small black élite group existed, especially in the North. But racial caste and economic class generally coincided. Blacks controlled the army, which was unusually large for so small a country. The colored élite dominated commerce and governmental offices and lived in the coastal cities, especially Port-au-Prince. Some collected rents from estates of varying size, but they otherwise turned their backs on and despised the black peasants.

Seventy Years of Political Instability

By 1843, Boyer had lost the confidence of the ruling élite. His ouster launched a long era of political instability. During the next 72 years, Haiti had 22 heads of state, only one of whom served out his term of office. Three died in office, one was blown up with his palace, another was hacked apart by a mob. The other 14 were overthrown by revolutions after tenures lasting from three months to 12 years. Color and the North-South split contributed to political turmoil. Politics became the game of the army and a small ruling élite. Factions within these groups made short-term alliances—sometimes crossing color lines—as they struggled to obtain and keep the spoils of office.

A series of short-lived governments ended in 1847 when the Senate elected Faustin Soulouque (1788–1873), the elderly head of the presidential guard. If the colored politicians planned to control Soulouque as a figurehead, he soon surprised them. Like Duvalier 110 years later, Soulouque purged the army and installed black-skinned administrators loyal to himself. He created a personal army and secret police. He also used priests of the Vodun religion to influence their followers among the rural population. In August 1849, Soulouque—now Emperor Faustin I—imitated Dessalines and Christophe by turning Haiti into an empire and creating a black nobility. Soulouque's costly and unsuccessful attempts to reconquer the Dominican Republic (which had become independent in 1844) weakened his government. His magic ran out in 1859, and a conspiracy led by General Fabre Nicolas Geffrard (1806–78), an élite *griffe* (born of mulatto and black parents), brought an end to the empire.

During Geffrard's eight years in power (1859–67), the colored élite now reasserted the political and social supremacy it had lost under Soulouque. Since he wanted to keep the peasants quiet, Geffrard renewed the sale of state-owned lands on easy terms and was lenient toward squatters. Exports and government revenues based on customs dues both fell to new lows. Nevertheless, Geffrard's regime did make some progress in education and religion. To weaken the Vodun, he signed a concordat with the Vatican in 1860, ending the schism dating from 1804. The Roman Catholic Church assumed an important role in education. Members of religious orders, usually Frenchmen, ran most of the principal schools, which were reserved for the French-speaking élite.

Public office now provided one of the few remaining ways for an ambitious man to become rich. Members of the colored élite and ambitious black generals competed to seize power. In addition to the army, bands of irregular soldiers, known as Cacos, also began to install presidents. Primarily owners of small farms and usually from the North, the Cacos frequently took up arms against the government until the U.S. occupation suppressed them in 1920. President Geffrard put down several rebellions, but he was overthrown in 1867 by Major Sylvain Salnave (1827–70). Salnave's term in office saw almost continuous civil war between various factions. His successor, Nissage Saget (died 1880), was among the most successful of Haiti's military dictators. He became the first Haitian president to serve out his prescribed term (1870–74) and retire to private life.

Saget's retirement led to renewed turmoil. The black and colored élites became increasingly antagonistic and formed two political groups: the Liberal Party (mainly colored) and the National Party (mainly black). During the 1870s and into the 1880s, these two parties battled to control the army and government. Louis Salomon (1815–88), leader of the Nationalists, served one seven-year term and began another (1879–88). One of the most capable presidents during this period, he founded a national bank, with financial assistance from France, distributed some state land to the peasants, and allowed foreign companies to own property in Haiti.

Political disorder, rebellion, and financial corruption now were accepted as normal. Salomon's antagonism toward the colored élite worsened racial tensions. The 11 generals gaining the presidency between 1888 and 1915 often appealed to color prejudice in attacking their opponents. However, color and political allegiance did not entirely coincide, and personal and regional loyalties also complicated the political situation.

Europeans dominated what remained of Haiti's once flourishing economy and they also openly intervened in the nation's political struggles. France bought most of Haiti's coffee and about half of her total exports, while German companies controlled wholesale and retail trade. During their brief period in office, the various presidents borrowed heavily from foreigners but spent little on useful projects. They then pawned the customs revenues to pay off the loans and granted generous concessions to unscrupulous foreign promoters. Despite their patriotic talk, many politicians depended on foreign whites to keep their opponents out of power. Foreign gunboats intervened in Haitian rebellions, and some German merchants routinely sponsored uprisings as business propositions.

SANTO DOMINGO'S VANISHED GLORY

The western third of Hispaniola, which became Haiti in 1804, was at the height of its prosperity under French rule in 1789. Santo Domingo, its larger neighbor to the east, was lightly inhabited, primarily by cattle ranchers. The first capital of the Spanish Empire in the Americas, Santo Domingo soon lost its economic and political importance. By 1789, 125,000 Dominicans faced more than 500,000 Haitians. Santo Domingo provided an obvious target to the despots ruling Haiti during the first half of the 19th century. Toussaint Louverture and Dessalines seized the neighboring Spanish colony from 1801 to 1805. And it was occupied again from 1822 to 1844 by the armies of Jean-Pierre Boyer.

Many Spaniards fled in 1801, and most of the remaining whites followed them during the second Haitian conquest in 1822. The population fell to only 63,000 in 1819, and it again reached 150,000 only in the 1860s. The Spanish estates were broken up into small farms, and Santo Domingo became a rural nation of independent peasants, most of mixed race. The nation had little commerce and no industry. A

Table 27. **DOMINICAN REPUBLIC POPULATION ESTIMATES, 1789–1897**

1789	125,000
1819	63,000
1871	150,000
1887	382,312
1897	486,000

SOURCE: H. Hoetink, *The Dominican People 1850–1950: Notes for a Historical Sociology* (Baltimore, Maryland: Johns Hopkins University Press, 1982.

few thousand persons occupied the capital city, whose old monuments recalled its former greatness.

The two periods of Haitian domination and subsequent invasions in 1849 and 1853 created an enduring hatred between the two neighboring peoples. President Boyer deliberately tried to destroy Santo Domingo's Spanish culture. He closed the universities and forbade communications between the Roman Catholic Church and Europe. The Haitians created no lasting government institutions, and illiterate soldiers ruled by brutal extortion.

Military Strongmen Rule Santo Domingo

In 1844, on Boyer's ouster, Spanish-speaking reformers proclaimed an independent republic. As in Haiti, power fell into the hands of armed bands led by rival chieftains (called *caudillos* in Spanish). The strongest of these, Pedro Santana (1801–64) and Buenaventura Báez (1810–82), generally alternated in power until 1874. Anxious to keep out the Haitians, Santana in 1861 persuaded the Spanish government to reoccupy Santo Domingo with himself as captain-general. But Spanish military rule proved unpopular here as elsewhere. In 1865, when the end of the Civil War allowed the United States to express disapproval of European intervention, Spanish armies withdrew for the last time.

After several years of chaos, Ulíses Heureaux (1845–99) seized power in 1882. Heureaux—a dark-skinned Haitian—ruled as a severe, often sadistic, and corrupt dictator until 1899. The comparative tranquility of his regime encouraged foreign investment, and American, European, and Cuban planters began to establish sugar estates. Nevertheless, the nation was bankrupt by the end of Heureaux's reign. His government borrowed heavily from Dutch and American investors to build railroads, roads, and a telegraph system. And Heureaux also spent lavishly on himself, his family, and his mistresses.

In 1895, the Santo Domingo Improvement Company, an American firm, purchased the country's foreign debt in return for the right to collect its customs revenue. Heureaux's assassination in 1899 thus left the republic without an effective government and burdened with an enormous foreign debt that could not be paid. U.S. president Theodore Roosevelt, fearing that a European power might take advantage of this vacuum to establish bases near the Panama Canal, took over the collection of customs in 1905. American supervision of Santo Domingo's finances continued to 1940, with American marines directly occupying the nation from 1916 to 1924.

PART FIVE

POVERTY AND PROGRESS IN THE CARIBBEAN SINCE 1914

CHAPTER 16

🌀

CUBA DURING THE 20TH CENTURY

From the end of the 19th century, the United States succeeded the European powers as the main economic and political force in the Caribbean. Under the centralized political systems in place until the 1950s, laws governing the Caribbean continued to be made in London, Paris, and The Hague. However, in setting policies for this area, governments in Europe now had to take American economic and political power into account.

After almost a century of economic decline, American capital provided the means to rebuild the sugar, banana, and coffee industries. American companies became the dominant growers in Puerto Rico, in Cuba (until the 1940s), and in the Dominican Republic (Santo Domingo). These companies created enormous plantations sometimes covering millions of acres and using the most modern equipment. The older and smaller plantations on Jamaica and in the eastern Caribbean could not compete with the new giants. By the 1920s, American-owned companies produced most of the world's cane sugar.

American power affected the British and French islands indirectly by setting the world market in which they competed. Between 1904 and 1934, the United

States intervened more directly in several of the independent states in the western Caribbean. During these years, the United States especially sought to protect the Panama Canal. Both Republican and Democratic administrations were highly sensitive to the canal's commercial and strategic importance. They acted to forestall two possible dangers. The first threat was direct foreign invasion. To prevent this, American military bases were constructed both in the Canal Zone and in Cuba, Puerto Rico was brought under direct American control, and the Danish Virgin Islands were purchased in 1917.

A second threat was continuing political chaos that might tempt a European power to seize an island. To preserve order and also to protect American commercial interests, the United States intervened in Haiti, the Dominican Republic, and Cuba. In Haiti and the Dominican Republic, American intervention took the form of direct military occupation by U.S. Marines.

American influence in Cuba was less heavy-handed. Small contingents of American troops were dispatched three times between 1906 and 1917, and the United States imposed governmental reforms in the early 1920s. In 1933, the American ambassador conspired with the Cuban army to force the resignation of President Gerardo Machado y Morales (1871–1939).

After the Machado incident, the U.S. government left Cuban politics alone, but America's financial strength continued to dominate the economy. The sugar industry prospered because the United States guaranteed to take its production. American corporations invested in mining and in Havana hotels as well as in sugar and tobacco plantations. Less than 100 miles from Miami, Cuba attracted an abundance of tourists. By the 1950s, Cuba was the most affluent Caribbean island. Indeed, Cuba's standard of living was higher than that of some European nations.

Despite economic prosperity, Cuba did not develop a tradition of democracy and toleration of rivals. Politicians stole openly and flamboyantly, and the more ambitious tried to rule for life. Cuban history is full of ironies. Throughout the 20th century, the prosperous and better educated were the least likely to tolerate opponents. There were no peasant uprisings, but many university students sought to seize power by force. Fulgencio Batista, who governed Cuba twice between 1933 and 1958, has been portrayed as a conservative and as a dictator. Yet Batista ruled in collaboration with the Communist Party, and he oversaw several of the most honest elections in the island's history.

Batista fled with the nation's treasury on January 1, 1959. Fidel Castro, a former student revolutionary, took control of every aspect of life on the island. Unyielding in his hostility to the United States, Castro allied with the Soviet Union during the cold war between the two superpowers. Moscow governments lavished subsidies on their Caribbean confederate. Nevertheless, despite their generous support, Castro's experiments destroyed Cuba's economy. By the end of the 1990s, Cuba was among the poorest nations in the world.

In politics, however, if not in economic matters, Castro proved more successful than Cuba's previous dictators. A powerful military and numerous secret police suppressed criticism. Indeed, insufficient enthusiasm for the regime was enough to bring down punishment. As they had during the war for independence from Spain, hundreds of thousands fled to Florida and other parts of the United States. While forcing silence or exile upon dissidents, Castro also took pains to ensure that no rival emerged from the armed forces or police.

Castro also prevailed against the United States, which had successfully ended dictatorships in 1898 and 1933. In April 1961, the United States transported more than 1,000 Cuban exiles to the beach at the Bay of Pigs—and then abandoned them to their fate. The following year, the Soviet Union removed nuclear missiles from Cuba in return for President John Kennedy's promise not to mount future attacks on the Castro regime. Kennedy's successors kept that promise, even after the Soviet Union ceased to exist.

THE CREATION OF THE CUBAN REPUBLIC

José Martí's vision of a politically mature nation failed to materialize during the years after independence. Cuba had many advantages. The largest and most populous Caribbean nation, its people occupied an entire island and had no immediate enemies. Cubans enjoyed the highest standard of living in the region, and the U.S. government agreed to purchase their exports and protect them against foreign powers.

Yet the Cuban republic never lived up to its promise. After four centuries under Spain, its citizens regarded any government as something to exploit or fight, while their leaders treated public funds as a source of personal wealth. Power remained both too concentrated and too personal after independence. While the American-style constitution of 1902 called for separation of powers and a federal system, effective rule remained with the president. Two parties emerged after independence—the Republicans or Conservatives and the Liberals. But neither stood for strong principles, and politicians easily switched allegiance. Both parties operated simply as groups of friends and relatives who banded together to win the spoils of political office. In their maneuvers, both combined the worst aspects of the Spanish and American systems.[1]

The first president, Tomás Estrada Palma (1835–1907), accomplished a great deal. Despite the opposition of American sugar growers, he pressed the United States to sign a reciprocity treaty cutting tariffs on imports from Cuba. In another treaty, the U.S. gave up its claim to the Isle of Pines. Unlike his successors, President Estrada did not personally loot the treasury, and it contained a surplus. Estrada believed he deserved another term, and won reelection in 1905 after fraud on both sides.

In August 1906, Estrada's Liberal opponent, José Miguel Gómez (1858–1912), led an insurrection that quickly spread over the island. Estrada, who had only a tiny army, appealed for help to President Theodore Roosevelt. Roosevelt, refusing to intervene, instead sent William Howard Taft, the secretary of war, to negotiate a compro-

Table 28. **CUBA POPULATION ESTIMATES, 1919–1990**

1919	2,889,004
1943	4,778,583
1970	8,495,404
1990	10,609,000

SOURCE: Schroeder, *Cuba: A Handbook of Historical Statistics*, 40.

mise. Standing on principle, Estrada and his vice president resigned in September 1906, leaving the country without a government.

Roosevelt now had no alternative and named Charles E. Magoon, the former head of the Panama Canal Zone, to supervise governmental operations. Magoon stayed until the Cuban political parties were ready to hold elections in December 1908. Assisted by Enoch Crowder, Magoon imposed a number of needed laws, including one giving the vote to all males. Some Cubans later accused Magoon of condoning graft and theft of government funds. But the evidence shows that Magoon was personally honest.

Economic Boom and Gaudy Politics

Gómez again ran as the Liberal candidate, and his inauguration in January 1909 ended the second U.S. occupation. President Gómez, ruling during a period of general prosperity, became a millionaire and also allowed his subordinates to plunder state funds. Although Gómez—a major general during the independence struggle—was generally popular, Alfredo Zayas (1861–1934) disputed his control of the Liberal Party. Their personal feud allowed the Conservative candidate, Mario García Menocal (1866–1941), to win the presidency in 1913. Another hero of the wars of independence, Menocal began his rule with major initiatives in education, public health, and government finance. However, as sugar profits soared during the First World War, Menocal's administration became even more corrupt and ineffective than that of Gómez, and Menocal increased his own fortune to $40 million.

Despite his promise not to stand for reelection, Menocal ran again in November 1916, opposed by the Liberal Party's Alfredo Zayas. Both sides padded the vote in the localities they controlled. Altogether, 800,000 votes were cast by fewer than 500,000 eligible voters. When it seemed likely that Zayas had won, the minister of the interior lost the ballots from the eastern provinces and declared Menocal elected.

The Liberals put off their plans for a revolution when the United States announced that it would support only governments that took power constitutionally. President Wilson, who was about to enter World War I, wanted a quiet Cuba. After some disorder, Menocal took office on May 1917, while the United States sent 2,600 troops—who remained until 1923—to the eastern provinces. Until 1921, Menocal reigned more or less as a dictator, governing largely by decree. He made huge profits from the sugar boom, while all Cuba embarked on a drive for unprecedented wealth.

The November 1920 presidential election was held during a period of acute economic depression following the collapse of the wartime sugar boom. Alfredo Zayas now left the Liberals and enjoyed President Menocal's support against ex-president Gómez. As in 1916, the election was marked by fraud and violence, and Menocal's government declared Zayas the winner. The 1920 election triggered another American intervention in Cuba. The collapse of sugar prices in June 1920 threatened to bring down the banks, and Cuba desperately needed an American loan. In January 1921, President Wilson sent General Crowder to Havana on the battleship *Minnesota*. The Republicans under Warren G. Harding kept Crowder in Cuba, where he briefly became the real power.

When Zayas finally took office in May 1921, the Cuban economy was prostrate. Large stocks of unsold sugar filled the warehouses, and all Cuban-owned banks had failed. Crowder used the urgent Cuban need for a North American loan to force reform on Zayas. Pressed by Crowder, Zayas appointed the so-called Honest Cabinet.

The government cut the budget in half, dismissed unneeded employees, levied a sales tax, and renegotiated corrupt contracts. In return, the U.S. government sponsored a long-term loan of $50 million in January 1923.

Almost as soon as the loan was final, President Zayas declared that Crowder's reforms offended Cuban sovereignty. He dismissed the Honest Cabinet, and his government soon degenerated into a carnival of nepotism and graft. Large sugar harvests and higher prices from 1922 to 1925 restored a surface prosperity. But many Cubans, and especially many intellectuals, lost all respect for the republic and abandoned hope of achieving progress through it.

Zayas's last years as president saw the beginning of large demonstrations by students and veterans protesting Cuba's dishonest and incapable political system. Rejected as a candidate by the Conservatives, President Zayas returned to the Liberal Party and endorsed General Machado y Morales. Although Zayas used force on his behalf, Machado probably would have won a majority in any case.

The Machado Dictatorship

Despite episodes of American intervention, Cuba remained Spanish in population and culture. The Treaty of Paris had guaranteed the private property of Spaniards, and more than 400,000 new immigrants arrived between 1902 and 1916. Many came as penniless workers. But Cuba's prosperity (when sugar prices were high) also attracted businessmen and professionals, who were influenced by political and intellectual trends in Europe. Thus Machado's dictatorship was inspired by and may be compared to the authoritarian governments that took power everywhere in Europe during the 1920s.

Like Mussolini in Italy, Machado tried to create a strong one-party state under his personal control. He controlled the army (some 12,000 strong), the congress, and the courts through threats and bribery. In 1926, as sugar prices again began to fall, he imposed production quotas to cut output, thus beginning the state intervention that culminated in Castro's government takeover. Like Mussolini, Machado sought to promote prosperity by a vast program of public works. His pride was the great central highway that ran for 750 miles from the western to the eastern tip of the island.

Machado did not tolerate opposition. He took over the Conservative Party and combined it with his own Liberals and other smaller parties, thus running as the only candidate in November 1928. He attacked the Cuban Communist Party, founded in 1925, and crushed strikes by labor unions associated with the European anarchist movement. American officials remained silent about Machado's crimes and illegal changes in the 1901 constitution. After the failure of the 1923 intervention, the U.S. government had decided to refrain from political meddling.

Machado's dreams of imitating Mussolini or Salazar in Portugal ended with the Wall Street crash of October 1929. The worldwide depression crushed the already weak Cuban economy, and new U.S. tariffs made matters worse. In mid-1930, the Hawley-Smoot Tariff Act increased the import tax on Cuban sugar to protect producers in the United States, the Philippines, Hawaii, and Puerto Rico. Cuba's share of the U.S. market was cut in half between 1930 and 1933. As both sugar prices and output collapsed, foreign trade dropped to one-tenth of the 1929 level. Government revenues also fell and American banks—many themselves failing—had no money to lend Cuba. Unemployment, wage cuts, and bankruptcies brought widespread misery.

Since Machado had absorbed both the Liberal and Conservative machines, his opponents formed extra-legal organizations. Moderate politicians led an armed uprising in August 1931 that failed ingloriously, and more radical groups took over. By far his loudest and most dangerous enemies were the university students, often led by professors and men who had already graduated. In September 1930, Machado closed the university and many high schools. Students, intellectuals, and young professionals formed the ABC, a terrorist group organized in secret cells. Machado's gunmen retaliated, paying murder for murder. The countryside became as lawless as it had been during the final days of Spanish rule.

The new administration of Franklin Roosevelt wanted to find a peaceful solution before civil war made armed intervention necessary. The president named Sumner Welles (1892–1961), a State Department expert on the Caribbean, as ambassador extraordinary to Cuba. Welles arrived in Havana on May 8 and began to press for Machado's resignation. President Machado at first defied the United States to intervene. But he lost the support of many officers, and a general strike paralyzed Havana. Machado fled to the Bahamas on August 12, 1933, narrowly escaping fire from ABC terrorists as his plane left the runway.

Batista's First Dictatorship

Ambassador Welles installed Carlos Manuel de Céspedes (1871–1939) as provisional president. A son of the man leading the 1868 rebellion, Céspedes had a famous name but little support from any faction. His government could not control growing violence as the economy continued to collapse. Looting and riots ravaged Havana, while armed gangs took over sugar mills in the country.

After only a few days, student radicals temporarily allied with soldiers led by Fulgencio Batista y Zaldívar (1901–73), a 32-year-old sergeant. On September 4, 1933, Batista walked into the office of the chief of staff and arrested him at gunpoint. Declaring himself a colonel and the new military head, he fired 500 officers and replaced them with common soldiers loyal to himself. With the support of the Directorio Estudiantil Universitario, the main student group, Batista took possession of Havana. Despite several pleas by Welles, President Roosevelt refused to intervene under the Platt Amendment.

The revolution in September 1933 gave power to two armed political forces, the army and university students. It at first became more radical under Dr. Ramón Grau San Martín (1887–1969), a fashionable physician and professor who became provisional president on September 10. Grau abrogated the 1901 constitution and proclaimed a socialist revolution that both alienated many groups in Cuba and also aroused American hostility. U.S. refusal to recognize Grau encouraged opposition by the Communists, displaced army officers, and ABC terrorists. While Grau's power melted away, Batista solidified his hold on the army. On January 14, 1934, Batista forced President Grau to resign, naming Carlos Mendieta (1873–1960) as provisional president two days later. The United States, which saw Batista as the one leader capable of maintaining order, soon recognized Mendieta's government.

After crushing student unrest and a general strike in March 1935, Batista maintained tight political control through a series of puppet presidents. President Roosevelt's "good neighbor" policy strengthened his regime. In May 1934, the United States signed a treaty that annulled the hated Platt Amendment, while retaining the naval base at Guantánamo. In August, the two nations agreed to a new reciprocity treaty that repealed the Hawley-Smoot tariffs. The American import tax on sugar was reduced, while Cuba allowed most American goods to enter with little or no duty. For the next 25 years, Cuba received a fixed quota of the American market that rose to 49 percent by 1949.

Batista was in no sense a conservative. In the Latin American context, he can be compared to other left-wing soldier-presidents, including Juan Perón of Argentina and Lázaro Cárdenas of Mexico. His policies during the 1930s installed a form of state socialism popular with the Cuban masses. Laws providing pensions, insurance, and limiting working hours largely satisfied the demands of the urban workers. At this time, Cuban Communists under Russian direction worked closely with Batista. Communists directed a labor confederation created in 1939, which bargained directly with the government rather than employers.

The government extended these social security benefits to farm workers in 1941, gave out state lands to small growers, and built many rural schools. A more radical step was a law of September 1937 that brought the sugar and tobacco industries under close state direction. The law organized small farmers in cooperatives and agricultural workers in unions. Above all, it guaranteed the jobs of the *colonos*, the small farmers that supplied sugarcane to the mills. Mills could not lay off a cane farmer, and they could never cancel a farmer's lease, as long as he worked the land.

Democracy Is Restored

His control of the army and alliance with the Communists gave Batista a strong political position by 1939. In November, he held honest elections that gave the opposition a majority in an assembly to write a new constitution. Although it was ignored in later years, the 1940 constitution created a democratic and mildly socialist state—at least on paper. Under its provisions, the president served only one four-year term, women received the vote, and many social welfare benefits were guaranteed. With the constitution accepted, Batista resigned as chief of the army to run against Dr. Grau in the July 1940 presidential election—the first reasonably honest presidential election since 1912. Although the Communists proved his strongest allies, Batista enjoyed wide support and won almost 60 percent of the vote.

Batista was fortunate to hold office as elected president during World War II. As it had during World War I, Cuba concentrated on producing sugar. From 1942 through 1947, production surged as the United States bought Cuba's entire crop at a guaranteed price, and the war also benefited steel and manganese mines in eastern Cuba. Given this economic boom, Batista was confident that Cubans with property backed him. Thus he continued to court the labor unions, established diplomatic relations with the Soviet Union, and gave the Communists two seats in his cabinet.

Batista assumed his prime minister would win the 1944 presidential election, and he thus permitted an honest count. Despite vigorous Communist support for Batista's candidate, his old opponent Dr. Ramón Grau won. Batista had not stopped the theft of government funds, but Grau used the continuing sugar boom to set a new record in corruption. Although he was already a rich man, Grau turned his presidency into an orgy of theft behind a mask of emotional nationalist speeches. He also tolerated the growth of private armies, in many cases placing their leaders on government payrolls. Armed gangs took over the University of Havana, which now became totally corrupt.

231

As the cold war between Russia and the United States worsened, Grau broke with the Communists and created a rival labor confederation. Overall, Ambassador Summer Welles apparently was correct in refusing to accept a Grau presidency in 1933.

The election of 1948—the last free election to date—brought in Dr. Carlos Prío Socarrás (1903–77). Prío promised to restore an effective administration, end violence, and remove Communists from powerful positions. He failed in all of these goals, while personally stealing millions. Labor racketeering discouraged honest businessmen, and violence by armed gangs increased. In 1951, Prío's government finally indicted ex-president Grau for stealing $40 million. But the courts never convicted Grau, whose trial was constantly delayed by frivolous appeals and open violence.

Batista's Second Dictatorship

In March 1951, Batista returned to Cuba from Florida and announced his candidacy for president in the 1952 elections.[2] Fearing that he might not win, Batista overthrew Prío's regime on March 10 in a bloodless coup. Within two hours, his men were in charge of the army and police, and President Prío sought asylum in the Mexican embassy.

The Cuban economy prospered during Batista's second regime. A sugar stabilization fund helped hold up prices when overproduction weakened the world market. Partly because of the rigid labor laws imposed during the 1930s, few foreigners now wanted to invest in sugar mills, which were mainly Cuban-owned. However, Batista's return to power did encourage foreign investment in mining, cattle raising, and tourism. The government financed low-cost housing as well as completing a new water system for Havana and other public works Grau and Prío had neglected, albeit with the usual graft. As in the 1930s, Batista won over the major labor leaders as well as most union members. However, the Communists now refused to cooperate with the president because of his close ties to the United States.

On July 26, 1953, a delayed revolt against Batista finally broke out. Probably sponsored by deposed president Prío Socarrás, some 130 young men attacked the Mocada army barracks near Santiago. Their leader was Fidel Castro Ruz (1927–), a 26-year-old lawyer from a wealthy family and long involved in university intrigue and terrorism. The effort failed miserably. Some of the attackers were massacred, and another 68 died in prison. Castro himself escaped to the mountains but was captured and sentenced to 15 years in prison.

In the Sierra Maestra

Pardoned by Batista, Castro fled to Mexico and recruited new supporters, among them Ernesto "Che" Guevara, a young Argentine socialist. In December 1956, Castro took about 80 men to southern Oriente Province. Alerted to their arrival, government forces ambushed the landing party, killing all but a dozen and a half. The survivors, without ammunition or supplies, retreated into the wilderness of the Sierra Maestra.

Oriente Province had been a center of rebellion against Spain during the 19th century. It remained a rough and isolated region, inhabited mainly by squatters eking out a precarious living on small plots. Che Guevara later created an influential mythology in which virtuous rural rebels purified Cuba's corrupt cities. But Castro's

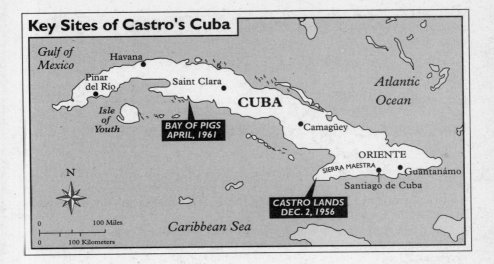

revolution was not a peasant uprising. Castro and Guevara were not peasants, they never intended to wage war from a rural base, and most members of their July 26 movement came from Cuba's cities.

Barely 10 weeks after landing in Cuba, Castro staged a brilliant publicity stunt by smuggling Herbert Matthews, a *New York Times* journalist, into the mountains. Raúl Castro, Fidel's brother, kept marching the same men back and forth in front of Matthews, who wrote that Castro commanded a large army. Matthews described Fidel in glowing and idealistic terms, making him an instant romantic hero to thousands of Americans.

A general strike in April 1958 found limited support. Ironically, its failure actually strengthened Castro's leadership of the July 26 movement. With little support in the cities of western Cuba, the movement was totally dependent on the rebel army. Castro also drew closer to Cuba's Communist Party, the Partido Socialist Popular (PSP), which enjoyed some support among urban workers.

Making effective use of a radio station, installed early in 1958, Castro presented himself as a moderate and democrat. He promised to restore constitutional government, end the stealing of governmental funds, and develop the domestic economy. The Roman Catholic hierarchy called on Batista to resign, and the United States halted arms shipments to Cuba in March 1958.

The Cuban army carried out its only major campaign against the rebels during the summer of 1958. Twelve thousand troops, backed by tanks and small airplanes, failed to dislodge Castro's forces. Late in the summer, Castro, Guevara, and Camilo Cienfuegos began to march east.

The U.S. government and Cuban religious, professional, and business groups continued to press for Batista's resignation. Few voters participated in the rigged elections of November 1958, and half a dozen conspiracies were brewing among military leaders. Batista said good-bye to 1958 with shouts of "Viva!" and champagne toasts. Early the next morning, on January 1, 1959, the president suddenly flew off to the Dominican Republic, taking along his family, his closest associates, and a substantial part of the Cuban treasury.

President Batista fled because he had lost popular support. Spurned by the Cuban people and betrayed by the army and the Americans, Batista escaped at dawn. Perhaps he remembered that President Machado in 1933 had been undone by an alliance between the army and the U.S. embassy.

CASTRO IMPOSES A TOTALITARIAN DICTATORSHIP

Che Guevara's forces moved into Havana on the night of January 1. But Fidel Castro deliberately held off and entered the city a week later, theatrically riding on a tank. In marathon speeches to a crowd of more than a million, Castro chastised the people of Havana for not having joined his revolution earlier.

When Castro arrived in Havana, the Cuban living standard was equal to that in many European nations. Within Latin America, Cubans ranked second in per capita income and third in food consumption. At least 80 percent were literate, and a relatively high number owned radios and television sets. In proportion to its population, the island had more doctors and dentists than France, the Netherlands, and Great Britain. The one thing Cuba lacked was a functioning government. The army had collapsed, and the police had disappeared. The old political leaders were held in contempt, while the labor unions had been discredited by their alliances with a series of corrupt governments.

During 1959 and the first months of 1960, Castro gradually consolidated his rule. Although he initially named a civilian president, he kept all real power even before he appointed himself prime minister in March 1959. Castro had no intention of returning to the democratic constitution of 1940. His goal was a totalitarian government that would control every aspect of Cuban society and life. To that end, Castro either abolished the nation's institutions or brought them under his control. The university students' Revolutionary Directorate, which had conducted an independent battle against Batista, was merged into the revolutionary army. Except for Cuba's relatively small Communist Party, the government abolished the existing political parties. And Castro, in any case, put off elections indefinitely.

The military remained Castro's first source of power. The Cuban leader began to build a much larger army, supplemented by a militia that reached 100,000 by 1960. Both were controlled by Raúl Castro. Another power base was the communist Partido Socialist Popular, which had accepted Castro's leadership. From the fall of 1959, party members moved into top positions in the government, labor and trade unions, and the army.

During 1959, Cuba's government began the process of taking over the nation's farms, factories, and retail stores. The regime seized without compensation all property owned by past civilian and military officials. It arbitrarily increased wages, and it reduced rents by 20 to 50 percent. In May 1959, the government issued the first Agrarian Reform Act. This decreed limits on land holdings and seized all estates above these limits, whether they were owned by Cubans or by foreigners. Altogether, 2.5 million acres of American sugar and cattle land were seized. When the U.S. government protested, Castro promised to pay the owners with 20-year bonds.

The confiscated land was carved up into state-owned collective farms worked by peasant employees, who received salaries like factory workers. The law also established ε National Institute for Agrarian Reform (INRA), which rapidly took charge of most programs in rural Cuba, including road construction, health, education, and housing.

The Maximum Leader Seizes Center Stage

From the very beginning, however, it was Castro himself who ruled directly and personally through a kind of perpetual dialogue with his followers. For four decades, the regime relied on Castro's ability to maintain order through direct popular appeals, massive "mobilizations" (such as the 1961 literacy campaign), and appeals against external and internal "enemies."

Already in the Sierra Maestra, Castro had sought to build up his personality cult through radio broadcasts and newspapers interviews. From January 1959, the full power of Cuba's government was thrown behind this effort. Photographs of the "maximum leader" appeared everywhere, while radio and television constantly repeated his name. Slogans, music, songs, and announcements encouraged Fidel worship. Above all, Castro relied on his extraordinary gift of oratory. On average, between 1959 and 1989, he made a speech every four days, varying in length from about one hour to half a day.

During four decades, although Cuba's policies and personnel frequently changed, Castro always remained the embodiment of the unending revolution. Standing before the vast crowds in the Plaza of the Revolution, he endlessly aroused and hectored them, always demanding more from his beloved "masses."

Castro's revolutionary nickname was "Horse." The reference to sexual virility is obvious, but the name also carried another meaning. In Santería cults, the priest is known as the "horse" of the saint. During ceremonies, the saint takes possession of the initiate and spiritually "mounts" him, as a rider mounts a horse. The term accurately describes how Fidel Castro took possession of the Cuban people.

🌣 THE PLAZA DE LA REVOLUCIÓN

Throughout his long reign, the Plaza of the Revolution provided Fidel Castro with a grand stage for media events and endless harangues. Surrounded by impressive government edifices and decorated with monuments to José Martí, this vast public area came to symbolize Castro's Cuba. Particularly when flooded with hundreds of thousands of Castro's chanting followers, the plaza itself seemed to represent "power to the people."

Both Cubans and non-Cuban observers would be surprised to learn that the square with all its buildings and monuments was erected during the second presidency of Fulgencio Batista. Batista inherited the plans for a unified compound of government buildings. However, he deserves the credit for pushing through to completion what was, at that time, a model of urban planning on the outskirts of Havana. Batista got the project done—although the cost was inflated by official corruption. Castro simply renamed the square and buildings and turned them into a setting for his galas.

In his personal ambitions, Castro resembles Papa Doc Duvalier in Haiti, who had seized power 18 months earlier in 1957. Since Cuba was a wealthier and more literate society than Haiti, Castro and Duvalier used different methods. In both cases, however, the nation's ruler concentrated power in his own hands while subordinating or destroying any individual who might prove a possible rival. To prevent U.S. interference with his plans, Cuba's leader chose to ally with the Soviet Union. But Castro remained in control and never became a mere puppet of the Soviets.

The Revolution Devours Its Children

From the beginning, Castro chose to imprison and execute his opponents. Since they often were condemned in secret trials, the exact number of victims is not known. In 1965 Castro acknowledged that his government held some 20,000 political prisoners. Perhaps 2,000 had been executed by early 1961.

The first victims of these "revolutionary trials" were former Batista officials. Brought to the Sports Palace, they quickly were condemned by the frenzied mob, shrieking *Parédon!*, "To the Wall!" Castro showed particular brutality toward 43 air force pilots. Since there was no evidence that they had committed crimes, a military court acquitted the pilots. Castro forced a new trial that sentenced the men to 30 years in prison.

Revolutionary terror also was turned against Castro's former companions in the Sierra Maestra. Disturbed by Castro's personal ambitions and the Communists' growing influence, Major Huber Matos resigned in October. Castro personally commanded a political trial that handed Matos a 20-year sentence. Camilo Cienfuegos, another military commander during the revolution, protested this judicial lynching. His small plane mysteriously vanished on a brilliantly clear day.

Matos and Cienfuegos were typical of many democrats and nationalists within the July 26 movement, who formed groups opposed to Castro's dictatorship. Some engaged in clandestine attacks on government installations. The army did not crush one group in the Sierra Escambray in central Cuba until 1964.

Cuba Allies with the Soviet Empire

American leaders cordially welcomed Castro's rise to power. In April 1959, Castro visited New York and Washington at the invitation of the American Society of Newspaper Editors. He was feted, admired, and celebrated everywhere he went. He addressed the Senate Foreign Relations Committee and received an adoring welcome at Princeton and Harvard. However, Castro turned down the U.S. government's offers of financial assistance.

Relations began to cool when Castro refused to discuss compensation for lands and businesses seized from U.S. citizens. Castro's attempts to spread his revolution to other Caribbean nations also caused concern. During the first months after taking power, Castro sponsored expeditions against Panama, the Dominican Republic, and Haiti. Although these failed, money and men continued to flow from Havana to anti-American conspirators throughout the region.

Meanwhile Castro's government drew closer to the Soviet Union. In February 1960, Soviet Foreign Minister Anastas Mikoyan headed a trade delegation that promised financial aid and also agreed to purchase more than 4 million tons of sugar through 1964. Copying Eastern European systems, Castro created a Central Planning

Board to direct Cuba's economic development. Che Guevara was put in charge of a Ministry of Industry to run major industrial installations.

Events moved rapidly. On March 28, 1960, Castro publicly repudiated Cuba's obligations under the 1947 Rio pact, demonstrating his break with the Inter-American system. In April, the Soviets agreed to sell Cuba crude oil at low prices. The following month, Texaco and Shell refused to modify their refineries to process the Soviet petroleum. Castro seized the companies. In return, President Eisenhower reduced the Cuban sugar quota to zero.

Castro now launched an all-out war on American businesses. By the end of 1960, his government had taken over all U.S. and most other foreign businesses, confiscating more than $1 billion of American property without compensation. In October, President Eisenhower retaliated by ordering a partial trade embargo (except for medicine and food). In January 1961, when Castro ordered the United States to drastically reduce its embassy staff, Eisenhower broke diplomatic relations.

Castro and the Soviets publicly celebrated their new alliance. In July 1960, three days after Eisenhower's sugar quota announcement, Khrushchev proclaimed the death of the Monroe Doctrine and promised to send Soviet troops to Cuba. From the island, Khrushchev boasted, they easily could hit the U.S. with accurate rocket fire. Before the U.N. General Assembly in September, Castro delivered a five-hour tirade against the United States. Giving his ally a bear hug, Khrushchev let him use his personal airplane to fly back to Cuba.

Cuba's business and professional leaders sought refuge in the United States. Travel between the two countries was not restricted until January 1961, when Cuba and the United States broke diplomatic relations. Altogether, as many as 250,000 Cubans fled between January 1959 and the end of 1962. Among the refugees were highly skilled technicians, engineers, physicians, and experts in the sugar industry—often in their 30s and 40s and at the peak of their careers.

Cubans who opposed Castro's growing dictatorship lost their property and their jobs. Nationalization made the government their landlord and employer, and those with insufficient ardor for the revolution were fired and replaced with Castro enthusiasts. Most believed their absence would be brief. They were convinced that the United States would intervene as it had in 1898 and 1933.

The emigration of skilled professionals crippled the Cuban economic system. But it also exported opposition to Castro and ended the possibility of an internal challenge to his regime. Opposition groups increasingly became dependent on exiles in the United States or, in some cases, on the Central Intelligence Agency.

The Bay of Pigs Expedition

In March 1960, President Eisenhower approved possible guerrilla action by a paramilitary force trained outside of Cuba. The CIA initially envisioned sending a small guerrilla band into the mountains. However, the scope of operations expanded after John F. Kennedy became president. The final plan assumed that, as soon as a beachhead was secured, the Cuban government in exile would be flown in, declare the formation of a free Cuba, and call for international assistance. The Cuban exiles believed that the United States would provide assistance. However, President Kennedy approved the plan with the reservation that U.S. forces would not be directly involved.

On April 1, 1961, Kennedy changed the invasion site. The landings took place on two beaches, the most important called Playa Girón, situated in the Bay of Pigs in a remote region of Matanzas Province. The sparsely populated site was surrounded by swamps and offered little access to the mountains. In any case, the CIA did not trust the opposition within Cuba. The agency deliberately excluded the guerrillas in the Escambray, and it did not tell the urban underground about the landing until the day it occurred.

On April 15, exile pilots flying B-26 bombers attacked Cuban airbases to knock out Castro's small air force. Confused by the international uproar, President Kennedy cancelled the second wave of air attacks at the last minute. The exile infantry force landed on the beach on April 17. Castro's air force soon sank two of the brigade's transports with most of the ammunition and radio equipment. When bombs hit the CIA command ship, the rest of the fleet fled, leaving almost 1,500 men stranded. After two days of fighting, Castro's army took 1,189 prisoners. After exploiting and humiliating them in mass trials, Castro sold his prisoners to the United States for $53 million in ransom.

On May 1, before a mass meeting of 2 million, Castro boasted of having defeated a Yankee-sponsored invasion. The Bay of Pigs fiasco disillusioned anti-Castro forces both inside Cuba and in the United States. Moreover, the invasion gave Castro an excuse to move against his foes. More than 100,000 persons were imprisoned, and no one opposing the government remained free after this time. The resistance in Cuba never recovered, and opposition to Castro was now centered in Washington, D.C.

CIA officials began making plans to assassinate Castro in 1960, when they recruited Mafia chiefs who had lost their casinos in Cuba. Following the failure of the Bay of Pigs invasion, President John F. Kennedy was determined to bring down the Castro regime. He devoted more than $100 million to Operation Mongoose, headed by his brother Robert Kennedy. The agency sought to murder Castro and also to destroy the Cuban economy. CIA operatives conspired to flood the island with counterfeit currency. They attacked sugar mills and factories in Cuba, and they sabotaged cargoes going to the island from Europe. Corrosive chemicals were added to lubricating fluids, and defective wheel gears and off-center ball bearings were manufactured.

🖾 OPERATION MONGOOSE

President John F. Kennedy ordered the Central Intelligence Agency to spend whatever was needed to assassinate Fidel Castro. Since the Cuban leader took great care over his personal security, CIA scientists developed an array of wonderfully wacky weapons. Agency operatives unsuccessfully tried to do in Castro with, among other devices, cigars with deadly botulism, a poisoned milkshake, and an exploding sea shell.

CIA chiefs believed that Castro's "macho" or manly reputation contributed to his personal charisma. If they could not kill him, they were determined to at least ruin his image. An attempt was made to get Castro into a poisoned wet suit that caused a chronic skin disease. CIA laboratories worked to develop a chemical that would dissolve Castro's beard. To discredit Castro, one agent suggested staging the Second Coming of Christ, but this project was rejected as too expensive.

CREATING COMMUNISM'S "NEW MAN"

Emboldened by America's defeat at the Bay of Pigs, Castro's 1961 May Day speech rejected any thought of elections and reiterated that his was a "socialist regime." In December 1961, Castro explicitly proclaimed on television, "I am a Marxist-Leninist and shall remain a Marxist-Leninist until the day I die." However, there always was a considerable degree of ambiguity—or even duplicity—in Castro's use of socialist dogmas.

Militant communists in Cuba's PSP continued to increase their influence, particularly in training the many new government officials needed to run a socialist state. However, the PSP itself quietly was dissolved. In July 1961, Castro announced the formation of a new ruling party, the Integrated Revolutionary Organizations (ORI). Castro kept party leaders under tight control, and there was no "communist takeover." In March 1962, during a major television broadcast, Castro publicly expelled the PSP's former leader from the ORI. Other veteran communists were purged in 1964 and 1968.

In communist Cuba, no one was allowed to be neutral. "In a revolutionary process," Fidel Castro announced, "there are no neutrals, there are only partisans of the revolution or enemies of it." Through rationing, residence permits, and worker identity cards, the government controlled where and how every Cuban lived. The Committee for the Defense of the Revolution (CDR), created in September 1960, ensured that no Cuban could escape Castro's revolution. Organized block by block and in every factory, the CDRs reported on the political and ideological beliefs of every resident and worker. CDR members were empowered to stop, forcibly if necessary, any activity or behavior they considered suspect.

But Cuba's government demanded much more than mere subservience. The regime was determined to create a "new man" possessing a "revolutionary conscience." In addition to behaving correctly, this new man also would be filled with revolutionary fervor expressed through selflessness, sacrifice, and unswerving loyalty to the government.

To mold the minds of Cuba's inhabitants, it was essential to control all means of communication and popular culture. During the first half of 1960, the government took over or shut down all newspapers and radio and television stations. Castro personally supervised and dictated copy. With the exception of some Soviet publications, foreign newspapers and journals were outlawed.

Fidel Castro had no artistic interests, and he disliked intellectuals. He thus turned cultural endeavors over to veteran communists. Communist bureaucrats directed state-run organizations, including a film institute, writers' union, and the National Council of Culture. Since the government controlled all funding, only those expressing the proper sentiments could work in the arts. Cuban publishing houses produced only blatantly pro-Castro works. Books or magazines criticizing the government could not be sold in Cuba even if their authors published them abroad and at their own expense.

The regime early on ended the autonomy of the University of Havana. Faculty members and students were expelled and replaced with those demonstrating revolutionary enthusiasm. Following the Bay of Pigs invasion, the regime took over all levels of education. Religious and other private schools were closed. Courses in marxism were obligatory at public schools.

Spending on education skyrocketed, with special emphasis on primary schools and technical and vocational training. A massive literacy campaign took place in 1961. Hundreds of thousands were mobilized and sent into the countryside to teach basic skills. The government claimed that illiteracy was reduced from about 20 percent to less than 4 percent.

At all levels, discipline, obedience, and subordination were stressed. Fostering politically correct attitudes was considered more important than transmitting knowledge. The ideological heavy-handedness of poorly trained teachers often led to high dropout rates.

Pre-Castro Cuba was only nominally a Roman Catholic country. In 1953, there were fewer than 800 parish priests in a nation of some 6 million. About two-thirds were Spaniards, many of whom were deported after the Bay of Pigs invasion. Their expulsion and the suppression of religious schools and publications eroded the church's influence. While the regime did not actively persecute Catholics, they could not join the Communist Party, attend university, or be employed in influential positions.

Castro's speeches stressed the need for austerity. To accumulate funds for industrial development, private consumption had to be sacrificed. Moreover, in addition to costing money, vice viscerally offended Castro and other government leaders, who were personally moralistic. The government closed down Havana's gambling casinos. It outlawed even such traditional and popular Cuban institutions as the lottery and cockfighting. Repressive sexual regulations also were imposed. Brothels were closed, adultery was harshly treated, and local authorities harassed homosexuals. Contraception and abortion were permitted—but only to those living in monogamous heterosexual marriages.

The 1962 Missile Crisis

The Bay of Pigs fiasco accelerated Soviet involvement in Cuba. Nikita Khrushchev had concluded that Kennedy was an inexperienced young leader who could be intimidated and blackmailed. His Soviet allies disliked Castro's purge of the PCP and his military adventures in Latin America. But aiding Cuba provided an easy and relatively inexpensive way of exerting pressure on the United States.

The Soviets moved swiftly. Increased economic and technical aid were sent to Cuba along with 42,000 Soviet combat troops. For the first time since Napoleon III's Mexican adventure in the 1860s, a non-American nation established military bases in the Americas. In mid-1962, the Soviets began secretly delivering bombers and ballistic missiles capable of carrying nuclear warheads deep into the United States. By September, at least 42 missiles and dozens of nuclear warheads were in place. Although Russian leaders denied everything, U-2 spy planes provided photographic evidence of the missile emplacements.

On October 22, President Kennedy asked Khrushchev to withdraw the bombers and missiles already in Cuba. He also imposed a naval blockade along a line 500 miles from the island. United States naval forces were ordered to stop, inspect, and disable (but not sink) Russian vessels carrying offensive weapons. Confrontation between the two superpowers seemed inevitable. U.S. military forces and the Strategic Air Command were placed on full combat alert. Soviets ships continued toward Cuba, and work on the missile sites was speeded up. The world seemed to be on the brink of World War III.

Then on October 27, Premier Khrushchev wrote the president that he would pull out the nuclear missiles if the United States would agree not to attack Cuba. Khrushchev did not consult Castro, who learned of the U.S.-Soviet compromise while talking with Che Guevara. In his rage, Castro kicked the wall, breaking a mirror. Hoping to launch nuclear warheads against Washington and New York, the Cuban leader sent troops to seize the missile sites. Despite casualties, the Russians successfully defended the sites and later took the missiles and bombers back to the Soviet Union. While there was no formal announcement of the U.S.-Soviet agreement, all succeeding presidents acted as if Kennedy had firmly pledged that the United States would never invade Cuba.

Soviet-Style and Chinese-Style Communism

In 1960, Castro had seized the largest Cuban-owned industries as well as those owned by Americans. Confiscations continued during 1961. By the end of the year, the state controlled some nine-tenths of Cuba's industry. Only some small farmers (mainly those growing tobacco) and retailers remained nominally independent under strict government supervision.

Following Soviet models, a state-controlled bureaucracy centered in Che Guevara's Ministry of Industry ran Cuba's entire economy. Under Guevara's direction, ambitious plans were drawn up to produce industrial goods, including chemicals, heavy machinery, and transportation equipment. Non-sugar exports were to be rapidly increased, while sugar production would be maintained to pay for industrialization.

This strategy failed absolutely. Decisions were imposed from the top down almost at whim, without attention to cost-effectiveness or the availability of necessary technology and skilled labor. Industrial production suffered a severe decline. Agriculture fared even worse. In two years, sugar production fell almost by half, from 7.4 million tons in 1961 to 4.2 million tons in 1963. The Cuban economy's collapse led to huge increases in debt to foreigners, particularly to the Soviet Union and other Eastern European countries.

Production of food products fell to the lowest level since the 1940s. Rationing, imposed in March 1962, became a permanent feature of Cuban life. Adults were entitled to two pounds of fat, six pounds of rice, and one and a half pounds of beans a month. They also were promised five pounds of meat or fish, a quarter pound of butter, and five eggs each month. But even these limited supplies often failed to arrive. Retail stores were empty and lacked even the most ordinary goods, such as toothpaste and toilet paper. Without repairs, homes and apartments began to decay, particularly in Havana.

Beginning in 1963, Castro reversed his economic policy. The emphasis on rapid industrialization was dropped. In a speech in June, Cuba's leader called for a return to the traditional reliance on sugar and tobacco. Self-sufficiency in food became a national goal—albeit a goal that never was achieved.

Castro let Che Guevara take the blame for economic failure. Che resigned his government positions in 1965 and went to Africa to assist rebels in the Congo. The next year, he set up a guerrilla base in Bolivia, where he was killed by the army in 1967. After ignoring him for many years, Cuban propaganda began to extol Guevara as a revolutionary saint. His body was brought back to Cuba in 1997 and reburied with great ceremony.

To make it clear that he remained in control, Castro in 1964 orchestrated the public trial and execution of a prominent communist leader. In 1965, assured of the party's subservience, Castro felt safe in creating a new Communist Party to replace the ORI. Castro became the party's first secretary and head of its collective executive, the Politburo (political bureau). In 1965, Castro also took control of the economy, as president of INRA. He already was prime minister and commander in chief of the military. From 1965, Fidel Castro thus held the top positions in the party, the economy, the government, and the military. In each case, his brother, Raúl Castro, held the second position.

The new economic policies led to an interest in Chinese experiments, which seemed to apply marxism to a rural society. Cuban officials favored the countryside at the expense of cities, and bureaucratic structures were dismantled. Overtime pay and other material incentives were abolished and replaced with moral incentives. Workers were exhorted to greater efforts as part of a new communist morality. Production achievements were acknowledged with badges, titles (such as Vanguard Worker), and mass rallies.

At the same time, Castro intensified attacks on nonconformists. Artists and writers came under increasing pressure. In 1965, a nationwide campaign was launched to eradicate homosexuality. Thousands of men and a few women suspected of sexual deviancy (often inaccurately) were arrested. Herded into military labor camps, they were treated with great harshness, given little food and medical care, and subjected to frequent beatings. These camps eventually were closed. However, as were Roman Catholics, homosexuals continued to be excluded from higher education, the Communist Party, and employment in government, education, or commerce.

In 1968, the government ended the last remaining vestiges of private ownership. Retail shops, repair centers, and cafes were seized; all bars selling alcohol were closed. Only a few small farms for producing tobacco survived. Cuba became the most "socialist" society in the world. Many goods and services were provided without charge, and Cuban officials advocated the abolition of money altogether.

To obtain hard currencies, the entire nation was mobilized along military lines to produce as much sugar as possible. The effort culminated in 1970 with a massive national campaign to produce 10 million metric tons of raw sugar. More than 1.6 million men, women, and children were sent into the fields to harvest sugarcane. In the end, the harvest produced 8.5 million metric tons, a record crop but short of Castro's goal.

Once again an attempt to force economic progress had ended in abysmal failure. The production of consumer products and other foodstuffs had been sacrificed to the 10-million-ton campaign. Meat virtually disappeared, while milk, vegetables, and fruits were in short supply. Overall economic production during 1970 showed little increase from the severely depressed levels of 1965.

The regime supplied free public services, but these were of poor quality and failed to make up for the lack of consumer goods. Although doctors and dentists no longer charged, their services were far inferior to those prior to the revolution. More than half of all physicians and dentists had fled the country. To replace them, the government drastically lowered educational standards. Infectious diseases increased, general death rates rose, and infant mortality sharply increased.

With the economy in collapse, many ordinary Cubans fled into exile. In September 1965, Castro publicly announced that all Cubans were free to leave. (However, he later barred the exit of young men and skilled technicians.) Through the Swiss embassy, President Lyndon Johnson arranged for an airlift from Havana to Miami.

Before Castro ended the flights in April 1973, nearly 300,000 persons left the island. Many, as during the exodus in the early 1960s, had been managers and professionals. But, workers, farmers, and fishermen also began to leave. Those that remained in Cuba worked as little as possible. In 1970, more than 20 percent of workers were absent on any given day.

CUBA BECOMES A SOVIET SATELLITE

As the 1960s ended, Castro's revolution was in desperate shape. The economy was in ruins, and many Cubans had turned against the regime. Moreover, the nation was isolated internationally and without allies. Relations between Cuba and the Soviet Union were strained after the 1962 missile crisis. Cuba extended moral and material support to guerrilla movements across Latin America. As symbolized by Che Guevara's execution in Bolivia, these military adventures failed dismally. They also were in sharp conflict with Soviet efforts in Latin America, where communist parties were trying to gain power through peaceful means.

Fidel Castro responded to this crisis with remarkable pragmatism. Reversing his policies yet again, he suspended guerrilla activities in Latin America and made peace with the Soviets. In a September 1968 speech, Castro endorsed the Soviet invasion of Czechoslovakia. In 1969, Cuba strongly supported the Soviet Union in its quarrel with the Chinese leadership.

Following the abortive sugar harvest campaign of 1969–70, Castro dropped efforts to impose total communism. With the help of numerous Soviet advisers, Cuba's economic institutions were brought into line with those of the Soviet Union. In 1972, Cuba became the first nation outside of eastern Europe to join the Soviet bloc's common market.

Government agencies were restructured to bring more continuity and rationality into economic decisions. To increase productivity, the regime stopped solely relying on exhortation. "Moral incentives" were replaced with material rewards and punishments. Fees were reintroduced for many services previously offered for free. Managers cut the wages of workers failing to produce a set quota, while those exceeding quotas were given access to scarce consumer goods. Labor unions were set up to enforce discipline. Under a 1971 "anti-loafing" law, every man between 16 and 60 was required to work.

Immediately after the reforms of the 1970s, the economy rebounded from the low point reached during the previous decade. The Soviet Union sent generous financial aid, and world sugar prices reached an all-time high in 1974. There was a modest improvement in food rations, and some consumer goods became available. School enrollment expanded, as did the availability of medical services. However, as the population increased, housing conditions continued to deteriorate. The situation in Havana approached calamity as more and more dwellings became structurally unsound and had to be abandoned.

During the 1970s Castro also imposed new political as well as economic institutions. A new constitution, effective in 1976, established three pyramids of power in imitation of Soviet models. A Council of Ministers governs the nation. The Communist Party, dominated by the politburo, is recognized as "the highest leading force in state and society." Finally, an elaborate series of indirect elections chooses advisory assemblies (the so-called Organs of Popular Power). The 1976 constitution divided Cuba's six historic provinces into 14, which in turn were subdivided into 169 municipalities. Citizens in each municipality elect an assembly, which sends delegates to provincial assemblies and to the National Assembly. The latter appoints the Council of State, supposedly the nation's highest political authority.

Throughout Cuba, the Communist Party serves as a parallel government that supervises the economic and political bureaucracies. Party officials manage government departments and industrial and agricultural enterprises. Party organizations also monitor and oversee all aspects of Cuban society. For example, the party's department of religious affairs regulates the activities of clergy and believers.

To meet its increased responsibilities, the Communist Party was expanded and strengthened. Membership rose sharply from only 55,000 in 1969 to 400,000 in 1980. A Party Congress finally met in 1975 and rehabilitated veteran communists dismissed during the 1960s.

Only the armed forces are more powerful than the Communist Party. Every Cuban man and woman serves in the military. At any time, as many as 250,000 are on active duty supported by more than 500,000 in the militia. Despite economic difficulties, the military has been lavishly supplied and has absorbed a high percentage of Cuba's output each year. As the best trained group in the nation, military officers are directly involved in running the country. The top ranks of the military are members of the Communist Party, and they also manage many industrial enterprises. It is their loyalty that has kept Fidel Castro's regime in power for four decades.

The 1976 constitution consolidated and even increased Castro's total control of Cuba's government and society. The constitution recognizes Castro as president and head of state. He appoints and presides over the Council of Ministers and heads the Council of State. He also is first secretary of the Communist Party and head of its politburo.

Protecting Marxist Revolutions Throughout the World

Henry Kissinger, U.S. secretary of state from 1974, adopted a conciliatory approach toward Cuba's government. In 1975, with U.S. approval, the Organization of American States dropped sanctions against countries establishing diplomatic relations with Cuba. Foreign branches of U.S. firms could sell to Cuba, and foreign ships that transported goods to Cuba were allowed to use U.S. ports. The United States dropped its ban on foreign aid to countries trading with Cuba.

The U.S. government's prestige plummeted during the 1970s. The Watergate scandal erupted in early 1973, and President Richard Nixon resigned in August 1974. The following April, the United States allowed the North Vietnamese army to overrun South Vietnam. Meanwhile, Congress drastically slashed the size and readiness of the U.S. military.

Convinced that America's power was rapidly declining, Soviet rulers dropped their opposition toward Castro's foreign adventures. Taking advantage of Cuba's large black population, Moscow encouraged military intervention in Africa. In August 1975, Cuba sent 20,000 troops to Angola to support Agostinho Neto's marxist regime. Two years later, another 15,000 Cuban soldiers were sent to Ethiopia to help defeat Somalia.

Despite Cuba's African expeditions, U.S. president Jimmy Carter, who took office in January 1977, worked hard to improve relations. The Carter administration approved of some marxist regimes in "Third World" countries and supported some groups claiming to be revolutionary. Andrew Young, U.S. ambassador to the U.N., praised Cuban intervention in Angola. George McGovern and Frank Church, influential Democrat senators, traveled to Cuba and extolled Castro's regime.

Ignoring Carter's friendly overtures, Castro renewed support for revolutionary groups in Central America and the Caribbean. In Nicaragua, President Anastasio Somoza's government came under attack from the Sandinista National Liberation Front, led by Tomás Borge, Castro's long-time friend. Cuba sent weapons, military advisers, and even soldiers. The Sandinistas took over Nicaragua in July 1979. A few months earlier, in March 1979, Maurice Bishop had seized power in Grenada.

The victories in Nicaragua and Grenada vindicated Castro's belief that violence would bring marxist victory. Working through the Sandinista regime, Cuba increased its aid to insurgent groups in El Salvador, Guatemala, and Colombia. In Jamaica, Prime Minister Michael Manley sought to create a socialist economy with Cuban assistance.

The Mariel Boatlift

Castro's foreign victories could not conceal Cuba's continuing economic depression. World sugar prices fell, while industrial production remained dismal. (In all of 1980, Cuba produced only 25,000 refrigerators for its 10 million inhabitants.) When it arrived, the monthly food ration provided only five pounds of rice, 3.5 pounds of meat, and four ounces of coffee. Men received two pairs of trousers, one shirt, and one pair of shoes each year—all of abysmal quality. To maintain order, Castro intensified political and religious repression during the 1970s. Amnesty International counted at least 20,000 political prisoners held in extraordinarily harsh conditions.

After the Havana-Miami airlift had ended in 1973, it became a crime to leave Cuba. In March 1980, six men crashed a stolen bus through the gates of the Peruvian embassy. Castro suddenly pulled all guards from around the embassy compound. Before Cuban police returned 48 hours later, almost 11,000 men, women, and children had taken refuge inside the embassy grounds. They remained there for more than a month under appalling conditions, without food, water, or toilets. Exile leaders in Miami pressured the United States to act.

On April 20, Castro announced that any Cuban could leave by boat from the port of Mariel, some 20 miles west of Havana. Within a week, exiles in the United States had sailed some 500 boats to Mariel, and hundreds more soon followed. On May 14, President Carter ordered the U.S. Coast Guard to stop the boat flotilla. The U.S. naval blockade failed, and approximately 125,000 refugees reached Key West before Castro stopped emigration in September.

Castro used the Mariel boatlift to get rid of physically and mentally disabled persons. However, American news media exaggerated the number of criminals among the Mariel refugees. Thousands of refugees had been jailed in Cuba. But their crimes included homosexuality and membership in religious groups such as the Jehovah's Witnesses and Seventh-day Adventists. Some had been political prisoners, such as the poets Reinaldo Arenas and Roberto Valero. Fewer than 350 of the 125,000 refugees had committed serious crimes under U.S. laws.

Continuing Economic Frustrations

According to official statistics, Cuba's economy grew rapidly during the 1980s. In fact, there was little or no increase in production, and the island imported most manufactured goods. Since sugar sales consistently brought in less than the cost of these foreign goods, Cuba thus ran a foreign trade deficit almost every year after 1959.

Enormous subsidies from the Soviet bloc kept the economy afloat. In addition to providing billions of dollars in free military equipment, the Soviet paid inflated prices for Cuban sugar and supplied oil at bargain rates. The Kremlin also financed Cuba's trade deficits and postponed payment of Cuba's debts. During the 1980s alone, the island received some $40 billion in Soviet loans and subsidies. Soviet aid provided at least 20 percent of Cuba's annual production of goods and services.

The Cuban regime also ran up huge debts with noncommunist nations. Soviet goods were of poor quality, and eastern Europe could not supply advanced technology. When Western nations renewed relations in the early 1970s. Cuba's government financed trade with loans from commercial banks. As sugar prices fell after 1975, Cuba continued to roll over short-term loans at high rates. Debt to Western banks reached 8 billion to 10 billion dollars by 1986, when Cuba's government stopped payment of principal or interest.

This borrowed money helped to pay for Castro's social welfare programs. Special efforts were made to slow the rate of urban growth and to improve the quality of rural life. Spending on housing and social benefits deliberately favored rural towns, which received running water, electricity, clinics, and schools.

Medical care had plummeted after the revolution. However, as the government poured money into hospitals and medical training, Cuba's health care system significantly improved during the 1980s. By 1989, the nation had one doctor for every 300 Cubans, compared to one for every 1,000 in the 1950s. Infant mortality fell sharply, while average life expectancy soared.

Substantial sums also were devoted to education. Almost all children attended primary school, and three out of four went on to secondary schools. By 1990, classrooms had one teacher for every 11 or 12 children, and the government also provided free day care centers and boarding schools.

The Castro regime could compel individuals to work in medicine and education.

Table 29. **SOVIET ECONOMIC AID TO CUBA, 1960–1990** *In Billions of U.S. dollars*

| | Repayable Loans (debt) | | | |
Period	Trade Deficit	Development	Nonrepayable Price Subsidies	Total
1960–70	2.08	.34	1.13	3.56
1971–75	1.65	.75	2.40	3.54
1976–80	1.12	1.87	11.23	14.22
1981–85	4.05	2.27	15.76	22.07
1986–90	8.21	3.40	10.13	21.73
Total	*17.10*	*8.63*	*25.73*	*65.12*

SOURCE: Carmelo Mesa-Lago, *Cuba after the Cold War,* page 148.

However, Cuba's socialist economy proved unable to produce and distribute even basic products. After 1968, the government owned retail stores and fixed prices by fiat. Cubans had to stand in long lines at several stores to obtain supplies, when these were available. Food rations were barely sufficient to sustain life; the amount of protein and vitamins often was inadequate for good health.

To give Cubans economic incentives to work harder, the government relaxed its control over a few sectors of the economy. A system of "parallel markets" was created in 1973. In this second layer of state-owned retail stores, Cubans could buy additional amounts above their rations. In 1980, municipalities were authorized to set up "free farmer's markets" in which producers could sell whatever they had left after meeting government quotas.

Beginning in 1976, because of the extreme shortage of housing, a few self-employed workers were allowed to offer services such as carpentry and auto and appliance repair. In 1984, the regime permitted limited short-term private rentals and encouraged individuals and cooperatives to build housing for their own use.

All these reforms suddenly ended in the mid-1980s. Many Cubans had become fed up with shortages of rationed goods, the poor quality of services such as public transportation, and the high price of food sold on the parallel market. However, few dared to attack Cuba's marxist system. Critics instead blamed individual speculators as well as officials who exploited the socialist system.

Just as in the Soviet Union, high-ranking officials—in the government, military, and Communist Party—award themselves special privileges that ordinary citizens cannot obtain at any price. These perquisites include decent housing, vacation homes, and the use of government vehicles. Fidel Castro himself enjoys opulent comfort in several mansions and vast country estates.

Members of the ruling élite have access to well-stocked retail stores and restaurants not open to other Cubans. Their children attend separate schools, and their illnesses are treated at special hospitals with superior facilities and physicians. Party bosses use government property as if it were their own. They routinely take bribes, pad expense accounts, and trade government property for favors.

Cuba's ruling élite lived most lavishly during the mid-1960s, when many indulged in heavy drinking, drugs, and sexual excesses. Their abuses became less flagrant when Cuba was integrated into the Soviet system. Nevertheless, ordinary folk still resented the élite's many privileges.

With his habitual pragmatism, Castro took up the citizenry's complaints in 1986. The regime launched a so-called Rectification Process, which represented a return to the pure communism of the late 1960s. The government restored centralized controls. It suppressed all the free-market reforms since the 1970s, including the free farmer's markets, street vending, and construction of homes for personal use. With the possible exception of North Korea, Cuba was once again the most socialist country in the world.

With the Rectification Process, Castro once again asked Cubans to work harder and consume less. Work quotas were increased without raising wages, and citizens contributed many hours of "voluntary" labor to special projects. As in the 1960s, the regime appealed to the "communist work spirit" and the "revolutionary conscience."

The Soviet Union also faced economic collapse during the 1980s. Premier Mikhail Gorbachev tried to improve conditions through economic reforms, including some free-market mechanisms and the restoration of private property. Gorbachev's reforms and Castro's Rectification Process thus went in precisely opposite directions.

Table 30. **MONTHLY RATIONS FOR EACH ADULT IN CUBA, 1958–1989**

	1958 (Average Consumption)	1962	1969	1983	1989
Rice (lbs)	10.2	6.0	4.0	5.0	5.0
Beans (lbs)	2.1	1.5	1.5	1.25	0.62
Fats (lbs)	3.0	2.0	2.0	0.5	—
Beef (lbs)	9.0	3.0	3.0	1.25	0.75
Chicken (lbs)	3.2	2.0	1.0	—	—
Fish (lbs)	2.2	1.0	2.0	1.625	—
Eggs	7.0	5.0	15.0	NR	NR
Coffee (lbs)	1.3	NR	0.375	0.25	0.25
Sugar (lbs)	—	NR	6.0–4.0	4.0	—

NOTE: NR indicates "Not Rationed." The 1958 data do not refer to rations; they represent average monthly consumption during that year. There was no rationing under the Batista government.

SOURCE: Jorge Pérez-López, *Cuba's Second Economy*, page 45.

The Soviet Foreign Legion

During the 1980s, the Soviet Union was especially generous in supporting Castro's ambitious foreign adventures. Havana and Moscow worked together to impose pro-Soviet regimes in many parts of the world. Some 8,000 Soviet military personnel were stationed in Cuba, and Moscow shipped billions of dollars of arms to the island. Cuba provided men to pro-Soviet governments throughout the world. Thousands of Cuban troops arrived in North Korea, South Yemen, and Libya. Havana remained a major center for training guerrilla forces around the world.

Castro's greatest commitment was to Africa. Throughout the 1980s, some 57,000 Cuban troops defended Agostinho Neto's communist government in Angola. Thousands more remained in Ethiopia until 1991 and also protected dictators in a host of other African countries. By the decade's end, half a million Cubans had served in Africa. Casualties were high, and these African expeditions brought no lasting benefits to Cuba. In 1988, massive Cuban aid helped win military victory for Angola's communists, and Cuba withdrew its military forces in 1991. Showing little gratitude, the Angolan government turned away from Cuba after the Soviet Union collapsed.

Cuba provided civilian as well as military assistance to foreign countries. An estimated 20,000 construction workers, physicians, engineers, agronomists, and teachers served in nearly 40 countries. In addition, thousands of Latin American and African students received full boarding scholarships to Cuban schools.

Castro continued to try to export his regime to nearby nations in the Caribbean and Latin America. Cuba sent 2,000 military advisers to Nicaragua and 800 to Grenada. Supplies and arms also flowed to guerrillas in El Salvador, Guatemala, and Colombia. In Colombia, Cuban spies dealt with drug dealers, and Castro in 1989 accused top officials of running millions of dollars of cocaine into the United States. They were tried and executed along with General Arnaldo Ochoa Sánchez, hero of the Angolan campaign.

Castro denied that he was personally involved in drug deals. However, the Cuban leader maintained close ties with General Manuel Noriega, Panama's dictator, who was later convicted of drug trafficking. Beginning in 1988, Castro sent military instructors to Panama, where they trained "Dignity Battalions" made up of violent criminals.

Except for the Grenada invasion in 1983, U.S. president Ronald Reagan acted cautiously in the Caribbean. Moreover, from 1984 to 1986, the U.S. Congress prohibited assistance to opponents of the Sandinista regime in Nicaragua. The tide began to turn under President George Bush. In December 1989, the United States invaded Panama. Although the Cuban-trained "Dignity Battalions" resisted for several days, U.S. troops succeeded in arresting General Noriega. Meanwhile, the Soviet Union cut economic and military aid to its Caribbean allies. In 1990, the Sandinista regime permitted free elections and lost control of Nicaragua. A peace agreement was reached in El Salvador in January 1992.

AFTER THE SOVIET UNION'S COLLAPSE

Throughout the 1980s, Cuba remained absolutely dependent on aid from the Soviet Union. Cuba traded almost solely with Soviet bloc countries. The Soviets bought Cuban sugar at guaranteed prices, sold Cuba cheap oil, and provided credits to cover Cuba's trade deficit.

Suddenly the Soviet empire was gone, with dramatic consequences. Cuba was almost destroyed as Communist regimes in eastern Europe collapsed and the Soviet Union itself vanished at the end of 1991. Trade with the former Soviet bloc fell from $9 billion in 1991 to $750 million in 1993. Oil shipments went from 13 million tons to 1.8 million. Eastern European nations stopped supplying raw materials, spare parts, fertilizer, and animal feed. Without fuel and parts for farm equipment, the sugar harvest plummeted. Without raw materials, three-quarters of factories halted or reduced production. Without oil, transportation virtually came to a halt.

Throughout the 1990s, Cubans faced a grim struggle to survive. Spending on medicine and education plummeted, reversing the improvements of the 1980s. Clothing and soap disappeared, while food shortages threatened starvation. In 1993, more than 50,000 persons suffered eye damage due to a lack of vitamin B.

Faced with total economic collapse, Cuba's leaders responded with temporary piecemeal measures. In early 1990, Castro announced a Special Period in Peacetime: Fuel and electricity were cut, and farmers were encouraged to use oxen. Hundreds of thousands of students and other city dwellers were sent into the fields. The government distributed a million bicycles, which formed the main means of transportation, even for the military.

As the crisis deepened, some economic reforms occurred. In July 1993, Castro legalized the use of U.S. dollars within Cuba. Early the following year, the government eliminated subsidies on many goods and services, introduced progressive taxation, and restored the free farmers' markets that had been suppressed in 1986.

With the Soviets gone, the regime had to find new outlets for Cuba's sugar, nickel, citrus fruits, and tobacco. To attract capital and know-how, Castro solicited joint ventures with foreign firms. Cubans provided the labor force, and foreigners supplied the market and needed technology.

The most successful joint ventures took place in tourism, with Spanish, French, Canadian, and Mexican firms predominating. New hotels, restaurants, nightclubs, and cabarets arose along the beaches, especially near Havana. The number of tourists soared from 350,000 in 1990 to about 1.3 million in 1997. Most opted for low-cost prepaid packages that placed them in shabby older hotels with limited food. Nevertheless, tourists spent $1.6 million in 1997, about one-fourth of the island's total export earnings.

To attract foreign visitors, Cuba's government tolerated and even encouraged prostitution. In the early 1960s, Castro had imposed rigid sexual morality and prohibited trading sex for money. By the late 1990s, prostitutes were more numerous than before Castro's takeover.

Several distinct and mutually exclusive economies existed on the island. Joint-venture factories produced goods solely for export. Socialist Cuba was characterized by unpaid labor and severe rationing, while a thriving black market provided the population's basic food supplies. Cubans with dollars could purchase goods in special stores and markets that accepted only that currency. Foreign companies could not hire Cuban workers directly and paid their wages to the government; however, Cubans received dollars as tips and through prostitution and illegal private businesses.

By not enforcing laws against nonpolitical crimes such as prostitution and money-laundering, Castro's government managed to hang on. As the island approached the celebrated the 40th anniversary, life remained bleak. On average, Cubans consumed fewer than 1,900 calories a day, below the minimum necessary for good health. Unless one had dollars, meat was rare, while toilet paper, soap, and other basic necessities were nonexistent. The cheaply built apartments crumbled away, while water and electricity were provided only every other day. Medical care and other public services—once the pride of Castro's revolution—barely functioned. Hospitals were crowded and filthy. Patients waiting for surgery had to bring their own sheets and buy sutures, painkillers, and medicine on the black market.

African-Cubans and Women in Castro's Revolution

From the beginning, Castro sought to incorporate blacks and women into his revolution. In March 1959, the government outlawed segregation by race, opening hotels, beaches, nightclubs, resorts, and restaurants to blacks. The forces sent to Africa were black and mulatto, and Castro portrayed his involvement as repayment of the island's debt to its African-American heritage. In 1960, Vilma Espín, Raúl Castro's wife, founded the Federation of Cuban Women (FMC), which had enrolled more than 80 percent of women by 1985. At all times, however, women and blacks rarely held high-ranking administrative and government posts. As late as 1991, only 20 percent of the Communist Party's Central Committee were women.

Particularly during the 1960s, the government attempted to bring women into the workforce and to change traditional gender roles. However, officials sought to improve overall economic productivity; they were not interested in increasing opportunities for individual women. The socialist "new man" (and "new woman") was expected to work solely for Cuba without even trying to obtain individual fulfillment. In contrast to the United States and Europe, Cuba did not tolerate any independent feminist movement. The FMC described itself as a "feminine" and not as a "feminist" organization. Vilma Espín and other FMC leaders consistently attacked U.S. feminists for pitting women against men.

During the push for the 10-million-ton harvest in 1969–70, 200,000 female workers were brought into agricultural cooperatives. Women also became teachers and worked in service and retail enterprises. To facilitate incorporating these women into the workforce, the government built day care centers. It also expanded free lunches and child care after school. In 1974, a new Family Code sought to equalize sex roles in family and marriage. It gave both partners the right to pursue careers, and it also ordered both to share housework.

However, as the economy fell apart from the late 1970s, Cuba had too many workers, not too few. The government no longer wanted more women to work. Thus it ceased to expand day care centers and other social services for working women. All efforts to achieve gender parity ended during the severe depression of the 1990s, when officials stressed traditional female roles. Thus they exhorted women (but not men) to make their own clothes, their own soap, and their own candles for lighting.

Socialism or Death

While trying to reintegrate Cuba into the world market, Castro hardened totalitarian control at home. Throughout the 1990s, Cuba's leader defiantly reaffirmed his commitment to Lenin's principles. "Socialism or death" became the rallying cry to all his speeches. During a six-hour speech before the Fifth Communist Party Congress in October 1997, Castro reaffirmed his commitment to one-party dictatorship. Despite its collapse everywhere else, Castro pledged that Cuba would never renounce communism. "Anything but retreat; anything but surrender," vowed Cuba's leader.

Castro intended to remain in power indefinitely. Elections continued under the 1976 system that permits only one party and one candidate for each office. As he had in the 1960s, Castro personally controlled the economy, relying heavily on Cuba's military. Army officers took control of the sugar industry and other businesses and construction brigades. The secret service continued to arrest and imprison critics of the regime.

However, the economic crisis ended Castro's adventures outside Cuba. All military aid ceased when the Soviet Union disappeared, and the last Russian troops left in 1993, having garrisoned the island for 31 years. In 1992, Castro announced that his regime no longer could provide military help to insurgent groups or governments abroad. Thousands of civilian workers who had been sent to foreign countries were brought home.

Although Cuba no longer threatened its Caribbean neighbors, the United States maintained and even strengthened its economic embargo. Just before the 1992 U.S. presidential election, President George Bush signed the Torricelli Act, forbidding trade with Cuba by subsidiaries of U.S. companies based in third countries. The act also prohibited ships from visiting U.S. ports for six months after landing in Cuba.

As president, Bill Clinton took a softer line. However, relations soured in 1994 as many Cubans again sought refuge in the United States. Some fled in small boats and even on rafts. In August, Castro announced that his government would no longer prevent Cubans from leaving for the United States. To avert mass migration on the scale of the 1980 Mariel exodus, U.S. naval vessels seized Cuban rafters and transferred them to the Guantánamo Naval Station. More than 21,000 Cubans were interned by September 1994, when the U.S. and Cuba negotiated a pact allowing additional Cubans to migrate to America.

The U.S. Congress tightened sanctions with enactment of the 1996 Helms-Burton Act, which deterred investments in Cuba by non-U.S. firms. The law was passed following public outrage when Cuban fighter jets shot down two small and unarmed civilian aircraft flying over international waters, where they had been searching for refugees fleeing Cuba on rafts. The act denied U.S. entry visas to foreigners dealing in expropriated American property. The Helms-Burton Act also allowed U.S. citizens to use U.S. courts to sue foreigners that traffic in properties seized by Castro's regime.

Despite the Congress's intentions, President Clinton did not enact these severe restrictions. The Helms-Burton act was never fully put into effect, as Clinton imposed a series of waivers suspending the law's enforcement. Moreover, following the papal tour of Cuba in January 1998, Clinton acted to facilitate humanitarian aid. He also allowed direct flights to Cuba and made it easier for Cuban-Americans to visit and transfer money to relatives on the island.

Diplomatic Efforts to End the U.S. Trade Embargo

To keep Cuba's economy afloat, Castro had to reestablish relations with noncommunist nations. Above all, he sought the removal of the U.S. trade embargo established in 1962, and he launched a diplomatic and public relations drive to achieve this goal. As part of this campaign, Castro invited Pope John Paul II to Cuba when the two men met at the Vatican in 1996. Eager to travel to one of the few countries he had not already visited, the pontiff toured Cuba for five days in January 1998.

Cuba's government granted temporary visas to a large number of foreign journalists, and Castro used the occasion to parade his regime's toleration of religion. While all newspapers and magazines are controlled by the government and heavily censored, Castro, (after some hesitation) permitted live nationwide telecasts of the pontiff's outdoor masses. The pope thus was able to get his message across to the Cuban people.

At five crowded masses and other gatherings, the pope's homilies largely addressed spiritual issues. But John Paul also bluntly criticized Cuba's one-party government and continuing suppression of religious and personal liberties. He urged the release of political prisoners and called for a larger role for the church in the educational system. U.S. economic sanctions also came under criticism. The pontiff urged the United States to restore ties with Cuba, and he specifically attacked the trade embargo.

More than 250,000 persons, including Castro and senior government officials, attended the pope's final mass at the Plaza of the Revolution in Havana. Security was extremely tight, and police dragged off those shouting anti-Castro slogans or criticizing the government before TV cameras. Nevertheless, repeated chants of "Freedom! Freedom" broke out in an open display of discontent with the government.

After he returned to Rome, John Paul II expressed his hope that his visit would encourage reforms similar to those in Poland following papal visits to that country. But Castro permitted no changes in Cuba's oppressive political system. Concessions to religion disappeared as soon as the pope left. Any mention of religious matters again was banished from the state-run radio and television. Catholics still were not permitted to teach schoolchildren. The only American priest working in Cuba was expelled for working with dissidents. The Cuban government did accept millions of dollars in aid from U.S. Roman Catholics. Catholic charitable organizations sent medicine and medical equipment, and the church also sponsored care for infants and persons with mental illnesses and AIDS.

In response to a papal request, Cuban prisons released nearly 300 persons, but most were common criminals. Only 60 were political prisoners, all of whom had served lengthy sentences and were long overdue for parole. Cuban prisons continued to be filled far beyond capacity with prisoners of conscience. Any expression of politically incorrect views was harshly punished. CDR officials went on repressing anti-Castro speech, and it remained a crime to write anything considered hostile to the government. Dissenters had no access to the airwaves or the press, and they were not allowed to hold public meetings. Many received long prison sentences simply for speaking with foreign journalists. Confined in dim cells, which they did not leave for months on end, political prisoners were hardly fed at all and died of starvation.

Although it led to no real changes within Cuba, the papal visit succeeded in importing Castro's image internationally. European nations that had cut off diplomatic relations with Cuba reestablished those ties. Relations became even closer with friendly governments in countries such as Canada and Spain.

Castro especially cultivated ties with other Caribbean nations. There was a significant increase in financial and technical assistance, especially to the smaller, poorer islands, such as Grenada and Dominica. Although aid remained far below its peak years in the 1980s, Cuban engineers, technicians, and physicians were sent to these nations, while Caribbean students once again were recruited for free training there in agricultural science, medicine, and education.

Caribbean leaders were invited to Havana, and Castro traveled throughout the region. In July and August 1998, he toured Jamaica, Barbados, and Grenada and then attended a meeting in the Dominican Republic of Caribbean heads of state. Castro's grand tour was characterized by heavy-handed symbolism. Throughout Castro wore his signature olive drab fatigues and bill cap. In Jamaica and Grenada, he paid homage at the tombs of Michael Manley and Maurice Bishop, his friends and disciples. In Grenada, he also called on Bishop's aged mother.

Despite the continuation of Castro's totalitarian regime, Jamaica, Grenada, the Dominican Republic, and other Caribbean nations restored diplomatic relations with Cuba. Caribbean leaders believed that Castro's army no longer posed a military threat. Many also acted to annoy the United States, which seemed to have lost interest in the region following the end of the cold war.

Caribbean political leaders were willing to accept Cuban foreign aid. They followed the example of Pope John Paul in criticizing the U.S. trade embargo. However, their cordial reception of Castro did little to help Cuba's ailing economy. It is notable that Caribbean governments did not grant Cuba membership in CARICOM, and they specifically opposed any extension of European trade preferences to benefit the Caribbean's largest nation.

CHAPTER 17

THE DOMINICAN REPUBLIC AND HAITI

The Dominican Republic and Haiti share the
island of Hispaniola. Like members of one family, their histories are similar and closely linked,
but also marked by ambivalence and hostility.
Nineteenth-century Haiti occupied its much
less populous neighbor. Even today, Dominican
Independence Day celebrates the anniversary of
liberation from Haiti in 1844.

The relationship was reversed during the 20th century. Haiti's economy continued
to stagnate. The Dominican Republic flourished as a producer of tropical products,
especially during the dictatorship of Rafael Trujillo (from 1931 to 1961). Thousands of
Haitians moved east to cut cane and work in grinderies. By the end of the century,
600,000 Haitians comprised almost 10 percent of the Dominican population.

Dominicans express both contempt for and fear of their many Haitian guests.
Although three out of four Dominicans are of mixed racial origin, they prefer to think
of themselves as wholly white. They are afraid that a flood of darker-skinned
"Africans" will make their country as poor as Haiti. Never far below the surface, these
racial animosities significantly influenced presidential elections in 1994 and 1996.

Democracy never has flourished on Hispaniola. At the end of the 19th century, savage civil wars afflicted both Haiti and the Dominican Republic. Brutal men seized power, plundered the national treasury, and borrowed heavily from foreign bankers. There was a real possibility that Germany or another European power would take over one or both countries to collect on their debts.

To restore order and prevent European occupation, President Woodrow Wilson sent in the U.S. Marines. American troops stayed in the Dominican Republic from 1916 to 1924, and they remained in Haiti from 1915 until 1934. American administrators reorganized the national finances, created schools, and introduced public health systems. They made many physical improvements, building roads and sewage systems and securing safe water supplies. In both countries, the United States trained a well-armed local police force that seized power once the Americans left.

In the Dominican Republic, General Rafael Trujillo (1891–1961) took control in 1930, installing an autocratic but efficient regime that copied European fascism. Trujillo's assassination in 1961 precipitated a political struggle that ultimately led to civil war. U.S. troops invaded again in 1965—this time staying only for one year.

The last honest election for several decades made Joaquín Balaguer (1906–) president in 1966. Balaguer won reelection in 1970 and 1974 partly by terrorizing his opponents. Helped by their political ineptitude, he returned for three more terms as president from 1986 to 1996. Balaguer used the nation's economy as a source of patronage. His legacy included a bloated and incompetent bureaucracy and government companies that could not meet the nation's needs for electricity and other basic services.

In Haiti, no one initially succeeded in taming the army, as Trujillo had done in the Dominican Republic. After the United States withdrew in 1933, several dishonest and opportunistic presidents looted the country until they were overthrown in palace revolutions. François "Papa Doc" Duvalier (1907–71) won the presidency in an election in 1957 but then installed a strong dictatorship. Duvalier managed to hold on to power until his death in 1971. He was succeeded by his son, the 19-year-old Jean-Claude (1951–), nicknamed "Baby Doc."

After Jean-Claude Duvalier went into exile in 1986, a series of short-lived governments, usually military, ruled Haiti until U.S. pressure forced elections in late 1990. The surprise winner as president was Jean-Bertrand Aristide, (1953–), a defrocked priest. Aristide's fiery rhetoric inflamed his followers, who took to the streets in mass outbreaks of violence. Relying on his personal charisma, Aristide failed to build a political organization. As president, he threatened Haiti's military and business leaders before he could oust them. In September 1991, his opponents took over Port-au-Prince. Aristide fled to Venezuela and then to Washington, D.C.

Aristide scorned Americans and despised their free-market economic system. (The United States is always "the cold country to the north" in his writings.) However, he was determined to regain the presidency by promoting a second U.S. invasion of his country. Aristide skillfully manipulated American public opinion, helped by the well-publicized brutality of the military regime ruling in Haiti. American troops landed in September 1994, and Aristide returned the next month.

United Nations and U.S. forces stayed on in number for three years, until the end of 1997. When his five-year term expired in February 1996, Aristide arranged for the election of René Préval, a close friend and longtime follower. But Aristide soon turned against his successor, using his influence to prevent reform of corrupt and inefficient government companies.

THE U.S. INTERVENES IN THE DOMINICAN REPUBLIC

Following the murder of President Ulíses Heureaux in 1899, several governments under self-proclaimed generals ruled the Dominican Republic. The nation was bankrupt, and the European states holding its debt threatened to take over to recover their investments. President Theodore Roosevelt thus forced the Dominicans to place their customs—the major source of revenues—under U.S. supervision. As president, Ramón Cáceres (1868–1911) gave the nation five years of firm and quiet government from 1906 to 1911. But Cáceres's assassination plunged the republic once more into chaos. A series of short-lived presidents gutted the national treasury to pay bribes and purchase loyalty.

U.S. president Woodrow Wilson believed in America's responsibility to foster democracy around the world. He found the Dominican Republic in turmoil and increased U.S. efforts to avert total financial collapse and political anarchy. In November 1915, he demanded that the Dominican government allow U.S. officials to control government finances and train a new police force, replacing the existing army and militia. The Dominican Chamber of Deputies refused to accept Wilson's proposal, and anti-American feeling became intense. In May 1916, American marines landed in Santo Domingo, beginning an eight-year U.S. occupation.

American commanders, who could not find a compliant Dominican politician to act as president, ruled the country under martial law. The American occupation forces reformed the nation's courts and finances. In order to improve life in the rural areas, they built roads, created public schools, and improved public sanitation. Due to better medical care, the population rose sharply.

Armed bandit gangs formed the most serious problem in the countryside. The United States therefore replaced the old army with a new National Guard trained by American soldiers. Criticism by the Republicans during the 1920 presidential campaign hastened the end of U.S. rule. American forces left in 1924, after the U.S. and Dominican politicians negotiated an agreement that retained American supervision of the customs. U.S. supervision ended in 1940.

Table 31. **DOMINICAN REPUBLIC POPULATION ESTIMATES, 1897–1993**

1897	486,000
1920	1,140,000
1940	1,759,000
1960	3,030,000
1981	5,546,000
1993	7,089,000

SOURCE: Hoetink, *Dominican People* 19 (1897); Carmen A. Miró, *La población de America Latina en el Siglo XX* (Santiago de Chile: Centro Latinoamericano de Demografía, 1970), page 2 (1920–1960); census results (1981, 1993).

Trujillo's Long Dictatorship

The Dominican National Guard was the most lasting legacy of American occupation. The United States wanted it to keep order and to stay out of politics. In 1927, Rafael Leónidas Trujillo Molina received command of the guard, which turned itself into the Dominican army the following year. By 1930, the army had regained control of Dominican politics, and General Trujillo gained the presidency.

Trujillo took power during a time of crisis. A hurricane in September 1930 killed thousands and almost totally destroyed Santo Domingo City. The worldwide economic depression increased unemployment and made reconstruction more difficult. Trujillo gained extraordinary powers to deal with the emergency, retaining them until his death in 1961. The president soon eliminated his enemies and erected an autocratic but effective regime. He insisted on being treated with something approaching worship and changed the name of the rebuilt capital to Trujillo City (Ciudad Trujillo).

Under Trujillo, exports of sugar, tobacco, and cacao boomed, especially during the Second World War. The quality of life improved for the average Dominican. Poverty persisted, but the economy grew overall, foreign debts disappeared, the currency remained stable, and the middle class expanded. The government built new roads, railways, public buildings, hotels, and airports, and encouraged tourism. The public education system grew and illiteracy declined.

Since Dominicans had never known a responsible democratic government, the results under Trujillo were impressive. Up until the final years of his long reign, he might have won a free election. However, Trujillo chose to run the country as a dictator, using torture and murder to suppress possible rivals. He enriched his family, which built up a fortune of more than $500 million and owned companies controlling 60 percent of the nation's assets and workers.

Trujillo's empire began to crumble in the late 1950s. Sugar provided most foreign revenues, and prices plummeted. In 1960, Trujillo tried to assassinate the president of Venezuela. The Organization of American States banned weapons sales to the country, the U.S. Congress cut price supports for Dominican sugar, and rumors of unrest kept away tourists. Despite Trujillo's usual elaborate precautions, a seven-man team killed him on May 30, 1961. The assassins were Dominican army officers who wanted Trujillo dead for personal reasons. While the U.S. Central Intelligence Agency was not directly involved in Trujillo's murder, it helped to plan it and supplied some of the weapons used.

Joaquín Balaguer was the figurehead president when Trujillo died. Ramfis, Trujillo's eldest son, took command of the army. However, the U.S. government would not allow the Trujillo family to retain power. Some of the family temporarily seized control, but they fled when the United States sent warships to Trujillo City. In December 1962, Juan Bosch (1909–   ) became president after the first democratic election since 1930.

During his tenure (February–Septumber 1963), Bosch tried to impose major economic and social changes with substantial financial aid from the United States. The government confiscated more than 7 million acres of Trujillo-owned land and gave it out to 70,000 landless peasants. A new constitution weakened the Roman Catholic hierarchy, and Bosch threatened to reduce the power of the army. His toleration of the Communist Party—not long after Castro seized Cuba—angered the more conservative army officers. On September 25, 1963, the military arrested Bosch and exiled him to Puerto Rico.

The Second U.S. Occupation

The new military government promised to hold free elections, but various factions plotted to seize power. Bosch's party allied with the communists, and the former president published a book attacking the ruling groups and calling for sweeping changes. On April 24, 1965, young army officers supporting Bosch seized sections of the capital and seemed on the verge of defeating the loyalist forces. Although he wanted to stay out of this civil war, U.S. president Lyndon Johnson felt he could not be reelected if he permitted a "second Cuba" under communist rule. On April 28, U.S. military forces flew into the capital city to halt the rebel advance. In a repeat of the 1916–24 occupation, 23,000 American troops ultimately occupied the country.

The Americans—augmented by small numbers of Brazilian, Honduran, and Costa Rican troops—remained in Santo Domingo for a year. A political solution eventually emerged after four months of military stalemate in which some 2,000 Dominicans were killed. In June 1966, Joaquín Balaguer won the presidency with 57 percent of the vote in a relatively honest election, and his Reformist Party also captured majorities in the assembly and senate. Juan Bosch went into exile in Europe.

An Authoritarian System of Government

After gaining independence in 1844, the Dominican Republic adopted the Napoleonic French tradition of strong central authority and rule from the top down. The president traditionally dominated both the legislature and the judiciary. Under some of the nation's dictators, the congress did not bother to meet.

The 1966 constitution preserved both an all-powerful central government and presidential control. There are no local laws or police. All laws are national laws, and there is only a single national police force. Neither provinces nor municipalities can levy taxes. Education, social services, roads, electricity, public works—all are funded and administered at the national level.

The constitution grants the president control over the national administration, the armed forces, and all public affairs. He directly controls the majority of the national budget. In times of emergency he may suspend basic rights and rule by decree. The president also commands the many government companies that dominate the nation's economy. During the political crisis that followed Trujillo's death, his personal property was transferred to the government. Worth $800 million at the time, Trujillo's assets included factories, commercial and service companies, urban real estate, and extensive rural land holdings.

The president appoints and can fire at will virtually all public officials, from the lowest ranks to cabinet ministers, the governors of provinces, and the head of the central bank. No law effectively protects the jobs of government employees, who are expected to show loyalty to their patrons. Merit and competence are seldom the main criteria guiding appointments. Theft of government resources, bribery, special exemptions from the laws for favored persons—all these forms of corruption have flourished.

Dominican presidents use the government's resources to build their own personal following. As on many other Caribbean islands, political ideologies and party and bureaucratic organizations have relatively limited influence on voting habits. The Dominican Republic is a small country, with only one main city. Informal networks based on patronage, friendships, family ties, and ethnic connections strongly influence political allegiances. Under this "clientalist" political structure, a politician's supporters expect to be rewarded with government jobs and favors.

Joaquín Balaguer's First Reign

A poet and historian, Joaquín Balaguer Ricardo served as a diplomat in Spain and Colombia, joined Rafael Trujillo's government in 1950, and was appointed nominal president in 1960. A relative nonentity under Trujillo, Balaguer demonstrated as president the astuteness with which he had studied the late dictator's techniques. Following his election in 1966, he headed off opposition from the armed forces by rewarding officers loyal to him, purging those he suspected of opposing him, and rotating every officer's assignment on a regular and frequent basis.

Civil violence continued during Balaguer's first term in office. Leftist guerrilla groups robbed banks and stores and attacked policemen. Anticommunist military patrols and paramilitary bands terrorized those who had participated in the revolution, targeting organized labor, student groups, and leftist political leaders. More than 3,000 were murdered between 1966 and 1974, and thousands more were jailed. President Balaguer won reelection in 1970 and 1974 virtually without opposition. Bosch's People's Revolutionary Party (PRD), the only broad-based opposition party, boycotted both elections to safeguard the lives of those who would have been its candidates.

The PRD also was weakened by internal dissent. Juan Bosch had returned from exile in 1970. Deeply embittered by the U.S. intervention in 1965, Bosch contacted the Chinese and North Vietnamese governments, become an overt Leninist, and renounced his faith in democracy. Unable to impose his new beliefs on the PRD, Bosch resigned from the party in 1973 and founded the Dominican Liberation Party (PLD). José Peña Gómez (1937–98), a more moderate socialist, emerged as the PRD's new leader.

Up to the mid-1970s, the Dominican Republic relied on exports of sugar, coffee, cacao, and tobacco. As in other Caribbean nations, the government sought to foster economic growth and created corporations to manage Trujillo's properties and promote industries other than sugar production. The Balaguer administration erected tariffs to spur domestic industries and promoted mining, assembly manufacturing, construction and tourism. Helped by substantial U.S. aid, higher sugar prices, and growing foreign investment, the Dominican economy expanded at a record rate of almost 10 percent each year.

Balaguer was especially careful to court the support of the peasantry, still one-half of the population. In the early 1970s, an agrarian reform program gave peasants title to farmland, and the government built roads, hydroelectric projects, irrigation works, schools, and churches in the countryside. Into the 1990s, Balaguer toured the most remote areas of the country by helicopter. Dominican peasants responded by giving him their votes throughout his years in office.

A Nation Again in Crisis

Economic expansion slowed during the later 1970s. Inflation and unemployment soared as petroleum prices exploded, while sugar prices plummeted. Seeing an opportunity to win power, Bosch's former party, the PRD, revived its grass-roots organization. Its candidate in 1978, Antonio Guzmán (1911–82), was a millionaire landowner and businessman who had supported Bosch during the 1965 civil war. When the vote count showed Guzmán with a strong early lead, military officers seized the ballot boxes and tried to annul the election. Under considerable pressure from U.S. president Jimmy Carter and threatened by a massive general strike, Balaguer agreed to step down. In August 1978, Balaguer passed the presidential office to Guzmán, arguably the first peaceful transfer of power after almost two centuries of political disorder.

Guzmán took office enjoying widespread public support, which he used to weaken the military oligarchy. He removed officers of questionable professionalism and required formal training courses. He also freed political prisoners and allowed exiles to return home. However, it soon became apparent that President Guzmán had fired Balaguer's cronies solely to replace them with his friends and family members, many of doubtful honesty.

Guzmán increased the vast army of government employees by 60 percent in four years. Rather than firing Balaguer's appointees, Guzmán simply added another layer loyal to himself. Many PRD appointees were poor men in a hurry to get rich. Bribery and theft of government property expanded as rapidly as the bureaucracy. The government's payroll swallowed up 85 percent of the nation's revenues, leaving little for investment. In 1979, two devastating hurricanes ravaged the republic, killing more than 1,000 persons and leaving another 400,000 homeless. Foreign hurricane relief funds were grossly misappropriated, and President Guzmán was blamed.

In a rare move, the PRD withdrew all support from the party's sitting president and nominated Salvador Jorge Blanco (1926–   ) for the 1982 election. With a campaign that adopted many American marketing techniques, Jorge Blanco easily defeated the perennial candidates, Joaquín Balaguer and Juan Bosch. As accusations of corruption mounted, President Guzmán killed himself six weeks before Jorge Blanco's inauguration.

Jorge Blanco represented the PRD's socialist wing and promised to install "economic democracy." But 1982 was the year the bottom dropped out of the Dominican economy. The country felt the full impact of rising oil prices and a recession in the United States. Moreover, in response to lobbying by domestic producers, the United States cut Dominican sugar quotas by 70 percent between 1981 and 1987. With falling income from sugar exports and tourism, the Dominican Republic could no longer pay for needed imports.

In return for aid from the International Monetary Fund (IMF), austerity measures were imposed that froze wages, cut government budgets, and restricted credit. In April 1984, the government removed price controls on imported goods and many basic foodstuffs. In response, rioters in Santo Domingo looted and burned stores. During the next three days, violence spread to more than 20 other cities and towns. More than 100 rioters were killed before order was restored.

The rioting split the PRD further as a moderate wing led by Senator Jacobo Majluta Azar (1934–96) openly feuded with radicals supporting the party leader, José Peña Gómez. At the PRD's November 1985 convention, armed men invaded the party headquarters to halt the counting of votes and prevent Majluta's nomination.

Balaguer Returns

With the PRD badly divided, Jorge Balaguer returned to the presidency for the fifth time in 25 years. Before the 1986 campaign began, Balaguer merged his party with the Christian Democrats to form the Social Christian Reform Party (PRSC). Although nearing 80 and legally blind, Balaguer still enjoyed widespread popularity and was associated with the 1970s economic boom.

Balaguer began his fifth term by ordering an investigation into corrupt practices by the outgoing administration. Jorge Blanco, the former president, fled to the United States after Venezuela denied him political asylum. Returning to the Dominican Republic, Blanco was sentenced to 20 years' imprisonment in 1991 but granted amnesty in 1994.

Back in power, Balaguer and his advisers reversed Jorge Blanco's austerity policies, which they blamed for slow economic growth. Rejecting all conservative and free-market principles, Balaguer's government pumped out vast amounts of paper money to pay for public housing projects, roads, and hydroelectric plants. By 1988, inflation reached 60 percent a year.

High inflation and persistent deficits masked several positive trends during the 1980s. The Dominican Republic had some success in finding other sources of foreign exchange as sugar became less important. New jobs in assembly manufacturing and tourism offset many of the lost jobs in the cane fields.

Factories assembling goods for reexport mainly have been established in so-called free zones. Under a 1983 law, industries erecting factories in these zones were exempted from import duties and taxes for up to 20 years. Many companies also took advantage of the Caribbean Basin Initiative as well as the U.S. tax exemptions granted to goods partly finished in Puerto Rico. These companies thus paid no taxes either to the Dominican Republic or to the United States. The number of companies operating in free zones went up 50 percent between 1985 and 1989, while employment jumped from 36,000 to 100,000.

The Dominican tourist industry also grew tremendously during the later 1980s. More than 1 million tourists visited the island in 1987, compared with 278,000 in 1975. The falling value of the peso made the country the least expensive Caribbean resort. By 1989 the nation had more hotel rooms than any other Caribbean location. In some cases, however, these new hotels lacked skilled workers as well as adequate supplies of clean water and electricity. Tellingly, a relatively low number of tourists, by Caribbean standards, returned for a second visit.

The nation's economy again went into crisis in 1989. The bloated bureaucracy did a wretched job of delivering such basic services as water, electricity, and garbage collection. Meanwhile, having run out of foreign reserves, Balaguer's government ceased payment on its debts in August 1989. Foreign suppliers canceled deliveries of food, medicines, and raw materials. When Venezuela stopped delivering oil, electricity was cut to three hours a day.

Strikes and riots became a daily occurrence, as the government's many employees demanded higher wages. In June 1989 a nationwide walkout paralyzed the country for 48 hours. Four persons were killed, and 3,000 were arrested.

Because of widespread poverty, illegal emigration soared during the 1980s. Many took the risks involved in crossing the Mona Channel to Puerto Rico, then went on to the mainland. (No visas or immigration papers are needed to go from Puerto Rico to the United States). By 1990, New York was the illegal home of a million Dominicans, one-twelfth of the nation's entire population.

And Yet Again Balaguer

The PRD remained enmeshed in factional disputes during the 1990 elections. The main candidates were the nation's aging *caudillos,* Joaquín Balaguer and Juan Bosch. After 30 years of enmity, however, these two octogenarians had switched ideologies. Bosch, an avowed marxist during the 1970s, now promised industrial development and privatization of government-owned businesses.

Despite the desperate economic situation, Balaguer won a sixth term as president. Bosch showed his age in dull and hesitant speeches. He also erupted in emotional verbal abuse of those he considered opponents, including the Roman Catholic archbishop. With many boycotting the election, Balaguer took 35 percent of the vote to Bosch's 34 percent. Former U.S. president Jimmy Carter, who led a team of OAS observers, declared the election "adequate and honest."

Balaguer's opponents continued to stage strikes and protests. Meanwhile, oil deliveries were suspended after the government again failed to pay suppliers. From September through November 1990, the nation was crippled and without fuel, electricity, running water, gasoline, or basic foodstuffs.

Abruptly reversing his policies, President Balaguer negotiated an agreement with the IMF and brought government accounts into balance, slowing the pace of inflation. The economy improved in 1992, thanks partly to new public edifices associated with the 500th anniversary of Christopher Columbus's discoveries. In addition to extensive improvements in Santo Domingo, these included the world's largest lighthouse (*El Faro a Colón*), to which the explorer's remains were transferred. Shaped like a gigantic cross, this impressive structure projects a powerful beacon of light for many miles out to sea. Given the continuation of severe electricity shortages, its erection contained an element of irony.

Balaguer sought a seventh term as president in May 1994. This time Peña Gómez, the PRD candidate, was his strongest opponent. The PLD once again nominated Juan Bosch. Racial issues and the Dominican Republic's relationship with neighboring Haiti affected the outcome of the 1994 election. Peña Gómez is a dark-skinned black; by reiterating allegations of his Haitian birth, his opponents reminded voters of Peña Gómez's race.

Despite charges of widespread fraud, Balaguer ultimately was proclaimed the winner. He promised a new election in two years, and he agreed to pass a law prohibiting a president from serving two consecutive terms. Since it was gearing up for the invasion of Haiti on September 18, 1994, the U.S. government pressured President Balaguer to accept this compromise. In return for U.S. support, Balaguer also began to enforce the embargo of Haiti, which he previously had ignored.

A New Era?

The August 1996 election was conducted under a new system. If no candidate secured a majority, a runoff election would be conducted between the two leading candidates. For the first time in more than 30 years, neither Balaguer nor Juan Bosch was a candidate. The PRSC named Jacinto Peynado. As he had in the previous two elections, Peña Gómez again represented the PRD. Bosch's PLD nominated Leonel Fernández Reyna (1954–   ). A young lawyer who had not previously held political office, Fernández had lived with his mother on Manhattan's Upper West Side from 1962 to 1971 before returning to Santo Domingo.

Racial attacks on Peña Gómez again played a major role in the campaign. Ultimately, however, it was the 89-year-old President Balaguer who chose his successor. Balaguer considered Peña Gómez the greater enemy. Convinced that his own PRSC had no chance of winning, the president gave his support—and large amounts of government money—to the PLD candidate, Fernández.

During the runoff election in June 1996, Fernández defeated Peña Gómez by a small margin. His victory was assured when Balaguer and Bosch met to form an alliance against their mutual foe. With a ceremonial embrace, they ended decades of rivalry. In one sense, their alliance ended an era. Yet their cynical appeal to clientalism and personality cults was itself characteristic of Dominican politics during the Balaguer-Bosch decades.

During the 1990s, most investment, both domestic and foreign, continued to go into the industrial free zones and the tourist industry. By 1997, more than 2 million visitors a year filled more than 30,000 hotel rooms, the largest number in the Caribbean. More than half of all visitors came from Europe, partly attracted by historical or family connections.

The industrial free zones also continued to grow rapidly. A 1995 law allows companies, which pay no taxes, to repatriate all their capital and profits. Dozens of such industrial areas have sprung up, primarily in the south and southeast, and others are being built. With rare exceptions, the companies are owned by foreign investors, mainly U.S. and Canadian. As cigars became popular in the mid-1990s, foreign companies also invested in tobacco.

Free-zone assembly plants and tourist hotels brought in needed export revenues and provided a limited number of semi-skilled jobs. But they did little to improve the infrastructure or worker competence. An estimated 25 percent of the labor force was unemployed and a further 30 percent underemployed at the end of the 1990s.

Beginning in 1995, the economy again was severely affected by frequent electricity shortages lasting up to 20 hours a day. However, political quarrels blocked efforts to privatize the government electricity company and the ailing government sugar company. During his first two years in office, Fernández could not make fundamental changes without support from his political opponents. The two opposition parties controlled the legislature, where Fernández's PLD had only one of 30 senators and 12 of 120 representatives. As electricity shortages continued and food prices escalated, strikes were widespread throughout 1997. More than 500 persons were arrested during a nationwide general strike in November.

THE U.S. MARINES OCCUPY HAITI

The United States failed to create stable, democratic governments in Cuba and the Dominican Republic. But the occupation of Haiti (1915–1934) undoubtedly represents

America's least successful intervention in the Caribbean. President Woodrow Wilson occupied Haiti in 1915 to prevent Germany from taking over the country. He also wished to create an honest and effective government that would foster economic development. Instead, after the United States withdrew, a series of dishonest presidents was followed by François Duvalier and his son, Jean-Claude. Under the two Duvaliers—"Papa Doc" and "Baby Doc"—the Haitian people endured 30 years (1957–86) of cruel and greedy tyranny.

Like the Dominican Republic, Haiti's government was deeply in debt to foreign companies by the early 1900s, and German merchants and companies were dominant. German nationals controlled nearly 80 percent of Haiti's foreign trade, owned major public utilities, and frequently sponsored revolutions to install client governments. Some American companies also had interests in Haiti, but direct American investment in Haiti was tiny. In 1913, U.S. ventures amounted to no more than $4 million. (In contrast, American companies had invested some $200 million in Cuba.)

President Wilson feared that France or especially Germany—now enemies in World War I—might occupy Haiti. The government's bankruptcy and continuing political chaos offered foreign powers both an opportunity and an excuse. Between 1908 and 1915, there were seven presidents and about 20 uprisings and attempted insurrections. Although poor, Haiti had great strategic and military importance since it controlled the Windward Passage—the most direct route to the Panama Canal. Wilson's government thus drafted the necessary plans for an occupation as early as July 1914.

A particularly gruesome violation of diplomatic immunity gave Wilson a reason to intervene in 1915. President Vilbrun Guillaume Sam (d. 1915) seized power in February 1915 but was himself suddenly overthrown late in July. As rival forces took Port-au-Prince, Sam ordered the massacre of 167 political prisoners, many of them members of prominent families. Sam took refuge in the French legation, while the chief executioner, General Oscar Etienne, fled to the Dominican legation. Enraged mobs invaded both sanctuaries, killed Etienne, and literally tore President Sam limb from limb. They paraded portions of his body around the streets of the capital.

American sailors and marines took Port-au-Prince on July 18, 1915. Within six weeks, some 2,000 marines occupied the country's customs houses and other governmental offices. Wilson needed a compliant Haitian government to legitimize American rule. Protected by American soldiers, the Haitian congress elected Sudre Dartiguenave as president on August 12. Dartiguenave, the first colored southerner to hold the office in a generation, believed that cooperating with the United States would benefit Haiti. However, hostility toward American troops increased, and the American commander declared martial law, allowing American military courts to try Haitian political offenders.

On November 11, the United States also forced a reluctant Haitian senate to sign a treaty that legalized the American occupation. This act placed Haitian finances and government under American control, abolished the existing army, and created a single police force (the Gendarmerie d'Haiti) under American officers. A new legislature, elected early in 1917, rejected a constitution written by the Americans. The American authorities quickly dismissed the assembly and submitted the constitution to a popular referendum. It was approved overwhelmingly, but fewer than 5 percent of Haitians voted. The 1917 constitution allowed white foreigners to own property in Haiti for the first time since 1805. It also made the American-led Gendarmerie the only legal armed force.

The Péralte Rebellion, 1918–1919

American troops found it difficult to move between towns because the roads—most built before 1789—had fallen into ruin. Since the Haitian government had no money, the Americans revived an 1864 law requiring peasants to work on local roads for three days a year. Although conscripted Haitians built a large network of roads, some American officers abused this system of forced labor, known as the *corvée*. Gendarmerie guards brutally abused Haitian laborers, forced them to march tied together by ropes, and made them work outside their own districts for weeks or even months. Haitians resented these practices, which recalled French slavery. Aware of increasing hostility, the marine commandant abolished the *corvée* in August 1918. However, the officer in charge of the northern and central regions illegally continued it into 1919.

The American invasion of July 1915 had met little resistance. During the first year of occupation, American forces quickly crushed the Cacos, armed peasant irregulars supporting President Sam's onetime interior minister. Late in 1918, Charlemagne Péralte and Benoit Batraville led a more serious rebellion protesting the *corvée*. The rebels—variously estimated at 2,000 to 40,000— easily defeated the local *gendarmerie*, took over much of the northern mountain country, and twice threatened Port-au-Prince. From March 1919 to November 1920, the marines systematically destroyed the rebels, using, for the first time ever, airplanes to support combat troops. According to official records, the marines lost 13 of their number while killing 3,071 Haitians.

The Record of the U.S. Occupation

The new constitution went into effect in 1918, and legislative elections were held the following year. President Dartiguenave and an appointed Council of State served as figureheads for American officers and officials. However, Dartiguenave refused to sign an agreement repaying existing debts with a new loan from the National City Bank (now Citibank). In 1922, the American officers simply replaced Dartiguenave with the more compliant Louis Borno (1865–1942), another member of the colored élite. The Wilson administration, fully occupied with the First World War, paid little attention to Haiti after the 1915 invasion. In 1922, the new Republican administration appointed General John H. Russell as high commissioner. Russell coordinated all American activities in Haiti until 1930 through a joint dictatorship with President Borno, an avowed admirer of Mussolini.

Under the Russell-Borno dictatorship, Haiti was comparatively tranquil and prosperous, thanks to good coffee crops during years of high prices. Long-term economic progress was limited because the American administration used most tax revenues to pay off old debts, and few American companies invested in Haiti. However, Russell's administration did build needed public works. New roads and bridges made it possible for peasants to market their crops in the cities. American engineers also installed telephones, built wharves, lighthouses, barracks, schools, a courthouse, and a college. Temporary progress was made in public health, sanitation, and rural education. Until it was abandoned, an agricultural service (the Service Technique) gave a vocational education to several thousand students.

Despite these improvements, racial and cultural tensions remained high. The marines, who were white and mainly from the Deep South, imposed a rigid system of segregation that excluded both black and colored Haitians. Commissioner Russell and his wife—one of the few Americans who spoke good French—were scrupulously polite in their relations with the Haitian élite. However, not even President Borno could enter the American Club, the social center for U.S. residents. While some American officers and officials were personally kind, almost all held the Haitians in contempt. The colored élite responded in kind, pretending a French disdain for American crudeness. For the rural peasants, the Americans were merely oppressors from the dreaded white race.

Instead of seeking to win popular support, Commissioner Russell strengthened American authority. In 1928, the joint dictators imposed constitutional amendments increasing presidential power and extending Borno's term from four to six years. From October 1929, students throughout Haiti went on strike. Riots spread to the towns, and Russell declared martial law. Tensions reached a high point at Les Cayes on December 6. Fifteen hundred angry peasants, armed with stones, machetes, and clubs, surrounded a detachment of 20 inexperienced marines. When they were attacked, the marines fired into the crowd, killing 24 and wounding scores.

The 1929 uprisings attracted worldwide attention. U.S. president Herbert Hoover, who had introduced a "good neighbor" policy, was especially concerned about adverse reaction in Latin America. Hoover wanted out of Haiti and sent two special commissions to ease tensions. Borno was ousted, and an unusually fair election selected a new legislature in October 1930. As president, the National Assembly elected Sténio Vincent (1874–1959), a member of the colored élite and an articulate nationalist.

Vincent pressed for immediate departure, and the American withdrawal was carried out in haste. Haitians quickly replaced Americans throughout the government, and the Gendarmerie became the Garde d'Haiti under Haitian officers. In August 1933, Vincent and U.S. president Franklin D. Roosevelt signed an executive agreement under which all American troops left in August 1934. The National City Bank sold the Banque Nationale to Haiti for $1 million, although Americans continued to supervise government finances until Haiti paid off the 1922 loan in 1947.

The occupations's influence sometimes is exaggerated. The new roads and telephones soon ceased to function. The occupation briefly reduced government corruption and reduced the foreign debt, but it also centralized economic and political power in Port-au-Prince. In contrast to the Dominican Republic, American occupation did not make the army all-powerful. Although the Haitian Garde or army quickly grew in size, its commander led a failed revolution in 1938 and was forced into exile.

Perhaps the fairest judgment is that the American occupation worsened unfortunate tendencies in Haitian political and cultural life. For example, the occupation aggravated the hatred between black and colored Haitians that had existed since the revolution of 1791. American administrators installed three puppet presidents from the colored élite, and they generally appointed only light-skinned officials. At the same time, by constantly showing their contempt for these colored men, the Americans led black intellectuals to reaffirm their African roots. François Duvalier later came to power as a representative of this "black power" movement.

Haiti's Enduring Social and Economic System

Since 1933, Haiti has suffered from frequent political rebellions and military coups. However, under this surface froth of political violence, the nation's fundamental

Table 32. **HAITI POPULATION ESTIMATES, 1919–1990**

1919	1,631,250
1930	2,652,290
1950	3,379,813
1960	4,155,597
1970	5,269,392
1990	6,486,000

SOURCES: Leyburn, *Haitian People*, 128 (1930); Segal, "Haiti," 182.

power structure has changed little since the 1840s. Haiti's rulers traditionally treat the citizenry the way lions treat gazelles. Their objective is simply to plunder the nation without any regard for the welfare of its citizenry. A small élite—perhaps 2,000 persons, mainly but not exclusively colored—has continued to dominate commerce and the professions. Capitalism and the free market never have existed in Haiti. The commercial élite has forestalled market competition by buying licenses giving them the exclusive right to export, import, or sell certain goods. Through these licenses, a few mulatto families have both controlled the economy and kicked back part of their immense profits to the black middle class controlling the government.

Much as economic institutions have been perverted to benefit the commercial caste, the government has served solely to provide a living for those in office. Haitian officials have lived off politics by soliciting bribes and by stealing public revenues. Haitian governments do not provide public services in areas such as education, health, employment, or finance. Taxes enrich politicians; they are not spent to build roads or to make other needed infrastructure improvements.

Given Haiti's mountainous terrain, population density effectively approached 1,000 per square mile by the 1930s, and it has continued to soar. The overwhelming majority of Haitians have provided for themselves through subsistence farming, cultivating tiny plots with primitive tools. The Haitian government never has registered land ownership. Most peasants with farms have no legal titles for them and little incentive to conserve the soil. Moreover, charcoal has remained the main source of energy in Haitian homes. Overcultivation and the burning of trees for charcoal have stripped the soil from half of the land area, turning the countryside into a rocky desert and creating in irreversible ecological disaster.

From Vincent to Duvalier

Vincent was reelected president in 1935 for a term extended to 1941 by a fraudulent referendum. The worldwide depression further reduced the peasantry's modest income from coffee sales during the 1930s. Vincent ruled as a dictator, using threats and bribes to gain the loyalty of a small clique of merchants and army officers. Those objecting to his rule were jailed or exiled.

President Vincent maintained close ties with the United States, which became Haiti's main source of income. However, in October 1937 hostile relations with the Dominican Republic became worse. The Dominican army, acting under orders from

President Trujillo, massacred perhaps as many as 50,000 Haitian laborers. Street riots and pressure from the United States forced Vincent to retire in 1941, and the assembly elected Élie Lescot (1888–1974) to a five-year term (1941–1946). Vincent thus became the first president of Haiti since 1874 to peacefully hand over his office and remain in the country.

During Lescot's reign, coffee sales boomed, and the United States also imported large amounts of Haitian sisal, a strong fiber made from the leaves of the agave plant. However, Lescot was less politically skilled than Vincent. Corruption and nepotism became even more blatant, and Lescot lost the support of the black élite. Light-skinned men dominated Lescot's administration, his attacks on Vodun alienated black intellectuals, and his unsophisticated views offended the more radical. In January 1946, using student riots as a pretext, three army officers—including Paul Magloire (1907–   ), the head of the palace guard—removed Lescot and dissolved the assembly.

As angry mobs continued to riot, the military staged relatively clean elections for the legislature in May 1946. The National Assembly elected Dumarsais Estimé (1900–53), the first black president since 1915. Yet another constitution restored the ban on foreign property ownership, gave labor the right to organize, and imposed an income tax. High coffee prices after World War II permitted some economic improvements, but Estimé and his followers continued to loot millions in government funds.

Estimé's greatest mistake was to decide, like so many Haitian presidents, that he should rule for life. After a rigged election, he sent a mob to pillage the Senate and threaten his opponents. Two days later, on May 10, 1950, the three army officers who had thrown out Lescot in 1946 also deposed Estimé. Their leader, Paul Magloire, had himself elected president through a popular election. (Under previous constitutions, the National Assembly had elected the president.)

Continuing high prices for Haiti's exports raised tax revenues, and Magloire's government made some improvements in urban areas. However, arbitrary arrests continued, and corruption remained obvious as Magloire and his police chief lived in ostentatious splendor. Once again, Haiti's president seemed unlikely to retire when his term ended. A general strike paralyzed Port-au-Prince in December 1956. On December 10, told that many young army officers opposed him, Magloire left the country with $12 million to $18 million in stolen government funds. His fall showed that the military could no longer ensure order. In a larger sense, it indicated a loss of power by the small élite that had controlled Haitian politics for more than a century.

Papa Doc Takes Power

Eight months of chaos followed Magloire's fall. By September 1956, François Duvalier had captured the allegiance of the army, and he also enjoyed significant popular support. Duvalier at this time had a reputation for relative honesty. He was a writer in the black power (noiriste) tradition who had wooed the more important Vodun priests and peasant leaders. Young members of the black middle class followed him because he had helped to write major social legislation under President Estimé. With the help of the army, Duvalier won an overwhelming majority in the September 1957 presidential election.

François Duvalier surprised both his supporters and his opponents by creating a totalitarian dictatorship. Duvalier's single purpose was to remain in power. A true master of political tactics, he took over or destroyed all possible sources of power that a rival might use against him. Duvalier perfected terror and bribery, the traditional means of control in Haiti, and brought them under his personal control. Soon after the 1957 election, Duvalier got rid of the chief of staff and seized direct command of the army. He then closed the military academy and created several competing military bodies, headed by his own men. The Tontons Makoutes (a secret police directly under Duvalier) spied on and terrorized the cities. A civil militia (the VSN) recruited major Vodun priests and prosperous peasants in the countryside. In 1964, sure of his power, François Duvalier declared himself "President for Life."

President Duvalier subverted or closed down civilian institutions that threatened his power. He personally chose the members of the National Assembly, corrupted business associations, and gave good-paying government jobs to middle-class intellectuals. Duvalier closed the unions, the press, even the boy scouts. He weakened the Roman Catholic Church by expelling its priests (mostly whites), closing its seminary, and compelling the Vatican to name five Haitian bishops of his choice.

Haiti was left without functioning national organizations. In the countryside, Haitians gravitated—for assistance and protection—toward whomever was seen to be the *"gwo neg"* ("big man"). Under the Duvaliers, the *gwo neg* usually was the local section chief or sheriff, who acted as policeman, judge, tax collector, torturer, and executioner.

However, the Duvalier regime did not rely solely on brute force to stay in power. François Duvalier—and later Jean-Claude Duvalier—bought support by giving out government jobs and economic monopolies. As government bureaucracies swelled, those with the top jobs gained the most. But the bureaucracy also was padded with thousands of lower-paid "zombies," employees who turned up just to collect their checks.

Presidential Palace, Port-au-Prince, Haiti. Begun after rebels blew up the previous palace in 1912, this building was completed during the American occupation. Under "Papa Doc" Duvalier and his successors, it also housed several élite army units and the national armory.

The Duvaliers also expanded the system of monopoly licenses and increased the number of state-owned companies. As well as controlling water, electricity, telecommunications, radio and television, insurance, banking, and the lottery, public companies dealt in products such as sugar, cooking oil, cement, flour, milk, herring, and codfish. These public monopolies used wasteful technologies to produce shoddy goods. Created to enrich the Duvaliers and their cronies through kickbacks, the monopolies also provided thousands of jobs for Duvalier supporters. Moreover, they strengthened the regime's alliance with Haiti's commercial élite. Just as they dominated exports and imports, the wealthiest families also bought licenses to distribute the goods produced or imported by the state companies.

Under Duvalier's oppressive rule, the small ruling group pillaged the nation. The black peasants became even poorer and more desperate, while many members of the colored middle class fled to other countries. Although he posed no threat outside of Haiti, Duvalier and his son were a continuing embarrassment to a series of American presidents. All faced the same problem. Given Duvalier's destruction of civilian and military institutions, American intervention might well install an equally repulsive regime.

The Overthrow of Baby Doc

François Duvalier died in April 1971, after naming his 19-year-old son, Jean-Claude, his successor as president for life. The uneasy balance of power between the various military forces enabled the dynasty to survive the change in leadership. At first many Haitians considered the young Duvalier an indolent playboy under the influence of his mother and sister. From 1975 to 1980, the Haitian government, prodded by the Carter administration, proclaimed some superficial freedoms. Some 60,000 Haitians, many of them women, found employment in the so-called "assembly industries." These factories, mostly owned by American companies, imported materials and parts and assembled them into finished products for export back to the United States.

A new wave of repression followed the second Duvalier's marriage to Michele Bennett in 1980. Jean-Claude now began to replace his father's appointees with his own men. By marrying the light-skinned daughter of an importer, Jean-Claude had made a lie of his father's *noiriste* (black power) rhetoric. Moreover, his wife's arrogance and wanton greed became a symbol of his presidency. In 1985, during a severe food shortage, Madame Duvalier reportedly spent $1.7 million on one shopping spree in Paris. Altogether, Jean-Claude Duvalier, his wife, and their closest collaborators are said to have siphoned more than $505 million from the public treasury. Defiance in the provincial towns received the support of many Roman Catholic priests. Thanks to the first Duvalier's expulsion of foreigners, most priests now were Haitian and from modest backgrounds. Younger army officers also began to lose their enthusiasm for the regime. As demonstrations grew in size and intensity, so did the U.S. government's disapproval of Jean-Claude's regime.

Pressured by allies and foes alike, Duvalier wavered between brutal repression and reform. The army shot at demonstrators, but Duvalier also announced price cuts and dissolved part of the hated Tonton Makoute network. Encouraged by the false news that the government had collapsed on January 30, mass protests spread to Port-au-Prince. On February 7, 1986, Jean-Claude Duvalier and his wife fled to France with their immediate family and a small group of followers.

Haiti After the Duvaliers

Following Jean-Claude's exile, Haiti suffered through an era of political instability resembling the half-century ending in 1914. Brief-lived governments took power in rapid succession, with no president completing his term in office. Industrial production collapsed as fearful foreign investors withdrew their investments. Most Haitians were still peasants, trying to survive on the food from their own small plots. However, as the population soared and farmland was destroyed by erosion, hundreds of thousands fled to the slums of Port-au-Prince. Without regular jobs, most were forced into the so-called "informal sector," where they survived by selling whatever they could get their hands on or by frying food for sale along the roadside.

The nation needed patience, strong leadership, and some measurable economic progress. But three decades of Duvalier rule had destroyed or thoroughly discredited its political and military institutions. Ordinary Haitians—including many soldiers—distrusted the light-skinned political, business, and professional leaders associated with Jean-Claude's régime. Alternative governments sprang up as the peasants and urban poor formed local associations and communes, often affiliated with religious factions.

With no effective police force, the country remained prey to violence by rival private armies. The government officially disbanded the Tontons Makoutes, but former Tontons joined together in various gangs, committing crimes for whoever paid them. Some antigovernment groups created their own quasi-military forces, which killed thousands suspected of being Tontons or former Duvalierists.

After Jean-Claude Duvalier went into exile, Henri Namphy (1930–   ), commander of the army, seized power in Port-au-Prince. Demonstrations continued, as did mob executions of lower-rank Duvalierists. Most Haitians boycotted the October 1986 elections that chose an assembly to draft a new constitution—the nation's 22nd. Despite this initial setback, the assembly came up with a thoroughly democratic document, overwhelmingly approved in a March 1987 referendum.

The complex and immensely detailed 1987 constitution deliberately divides power among various officials and levels of government. Laws must be approved by an elected Senate and National Assembly. The president, the only official elected nationwide, serves for five years and cannot be reelected while in office. As head of state, the president designates judges from a list submitted by the Senate.

The president nominates the prime minister. Together the president and prime minister jointly nominate other government ministers. Their appointment must be approved by the Senate and the National Assembly, which can dismiss the government at any time by a "no confidence" vote. These provisions were meant to safeguard against the rise of another Duvalier. In fact, they have locked the president, the prime minister, and the legislature into adversary positions and have guaranteed political deadlocks.

Under the 1987 constitution, elected councils govern in the countryside. Other clauses separated the police from the armed forces and set up an independent electoral council to supervise elections. The constitution recognized Creole as Haiti's national language, and it decriminalized Vodun practices. Article 291 specifically prohibited "notorious" and "zealous" Duvalierists from participating in elections for 10 years.

A wave of violence made it impossible to conduct elections under the new constitution in November 1987. More killings and a low turnout marked the army-run election of Leslie François Manigat (1930–   ) as president in January 1988. Manigat, an honest man and a distinguished economist, apparently thought he could outsmart the conniving generals. He lasted barely six months, as General Namphy seized the presidency in June 1988.

Namphy was brought down the following September by a mutiny among non-commissioned officers and enlisted men. Lieutenant General Prosper Avril (1937–   ), a former adviser to both Duvaliers, emerged as president and managed to cling to power for 18 months. Avril was the commander of the 1,200-man Presidential Guard, an élite battalion housed in the presidential palace. But he never controlled the entire army and had to suppress several mutinies.

Although he initially tolerated his critics, Avril declared a state of siege in January 1990 and exiled several opposition leaders. Violent demonstrations against his rule increased, as did robberies and killings blamed on Tontons and members of the Presidential Guard. In March 1990, troops breaking up an antigovernment demonstration accidentally killed a young girl, triggering widespread protests and strikes. As rioting spread, mobs burned cars and set up flaming barricades.

Under intense pressure from the American ambassador, Avril resigned and fled to Florida. Supreme Court justice Ertha Pascal-Trouillot (1944–   ) served as interim president until elections—delayed by a lack of money—could be held. The December 1990 elections were unquestionably the most honest Haiti has known. The provisional government had disbanded the Presidential Guard, and the regular army behaved impeccably. Led by General Raoul Cédras (1950?–   ), the soldiers maintained order during the elections. Three weeks later, they crushed an attempted revolution by Roger Lafontant, former head of the Tontons Makoutes.

The Aristide Era

Jean-Bertrand Aristide (1952–   ) won the presidency in 1990 with more than two-thirds of the vote in a heavy turnout. Trained as a Roman Catholic priest—although suspended by his church, he was not formally laicized until 1995—Aristide is a fiery orator and proponent of "liberation theology." This ideology, which mingles religious fervor with marxist theories, holds that the clergy must help the poor improve their lot through radical political actions. While liberation theology was most popular in Latin America, it fits well with Haiti's Jacobin tradition of violent revolution (See pages 166–170.) Like "Papa Doc" Duvalier, as well as such figures as Eric Gairy of Grenada and Rafael Trujillo of the Dominican Republic, Aristide began his career as an apostle of black pride among the Haitian poor. Aristide is a master at inflaming the passions of his supporters while weaving a web of mystery and charisma around his own person.

Aristide grew up in a poor section of Port-au-Prince. He was educated by and ordained as a member of the Salesian order of missionaries. In 1985, he returned to the slums as a priest, preaching passionately against Jean-Claude Duvalier and his successors. The Salesians expelled him in 1988 for "exalting violence and class struggle." However, Aristide continued to preach and even perform the sacraments, contrary to Roman Catholic rules. He gained national fame in September 1989 when a band of thugs (possibly sent by the Namphy government) attacked his congregation during services, killing 13 persons.

Aristide's passionate speeches and radio broadcasts won him the support of rural communes as well as the poor of Port-au-Prince.[1] Appealing to the nation's pent-up rage, his electoral slogan Opération Lavalas ("Operation Avalanche") referred in Creole to the torrential flood that follows a tropical rainstorm. His followers practiced a grotesque form of murder—known as "necklacing" elsewhere but called Pé Lebrun in Haiti, after the name of a large tire store. Enclosed in a burning rubber tire, its victims suffer horribly before they die. When the Roman Catholic archbishop of Haiti attacked liberation theology in January 1991, Aristide's supporters burned down several buildings owned by the church. At least 50 people suspected of being Tontons died after meeting Pé Lebrun.

Inaugurated as president on February 7, 1991, Aristide retained power for less than eight months. Lavalas was not an organized political party, possessing a democratic structure and accountable to a well-defined constituency. Relying on Aristide's personal charisma, the president and a small coterie of his disciples commanded a shifting coalition of organizations and political groupings.

Despite his personal popularity, Aristide's followers did not win a majority in the National Assembly. Refusing to compromise with other factions, Aristide chose a cabinet from among close friends with little government experience. As prime minister, he named René Préval (1943–   ), a professional agronomist who had worked with Aristide's projects since 1986. The economy moved perilously close to total collapse. The government imposed high tariffs on imported food (including Dominican sugar and American rice), and it frightened the business sector by proposing to set up collective farms and seize funds that had been sent abroad.

President Aristide's mass following allowed him to circumvent his political critics. Defying the 1987 constitution, he refused to send judicial and military appointments to the National Assembly for approval. In August 1991, his followers surrounded the Legislative Palace, beating several legislators and forcing the Senate to suspend a vote of no confidence. But the president lost the backing of the army. Aristide named General Cédras as acting head of the military. However, he failed to make Cédras's appointment permanent and stopped him from punishing the torture and death of five teenage boys. Raising fears of a new Tontons Makoutes, Aristide also created a special 300-member security force, apart from the armed services and trained by Swiss advisers.

Few Haitian presidents take the risk of leaving the country before they have been deposed. In September, while the president was in New York speaking to the United Nations, the army disarmed Aristide's private security force. On his return, Aristide called for a popular uprising and endorsed the use of Pé Lebrun. A mutiny among enlisted men was joined by General Cédras and other officers. On September 30, 1991, Aristide fled to Venezuela, following so many of his predecessors into exile. Early in 1992, he moved to Washington, D.C., his headquarters until he returned to Haiti in October 1994.

In Haiti, a provisional president and prime minister were named to replace Aristide and Préval. Soldiers arrested Aristide officials and terrorized his followers in the Port-au-Prince slums. As the months passed, the military regime sought to shut down the mass organizations comprising the Lavalas coalition. Particularly in rural areas, beatings and intimidation were used to keep these groups from meeting. In addition to the 7,000 men and officers in Haiti's military, the regime also recruited thousands of civilian ruffians, known as attachés.

U.S. president George Bush blamed the coup in part on Aristide's encouragement of mob violence. Nevertheless, the United States took quick action against the military regime. President Bush ordered an embargo banning all commercial trade with Haiti, and he also seized the Haitian government's accounts in American banks. U S. officials also persuaded other members of the OAS (and later the United Nations) into imposing their own embargoes.

The United States did not, however, erect a naval blockade to enforce the embargo. Fuel, arms, and other merchandise reached Haiti from Europe and the Dominican Republic. Nevertheless, the embargo helped to destroy the Haitian economy. The poor suffered the greatest harm as both unemployment and prices soared. In theory, humanitarian aid could still be sent into Haiti, but the embargo on oil made it difficult to distribute food and medicine.

To escape economic hardship and political violence, more than 35,000 Haitians fled by boat during the six months following the coup. Sensitive to the electoral damage the 1980 Mariel boatlift had caused the Carter administration (see page 245), President Bush sought to prevent a new flood of illegal immigrants. Under a 1981 agreement, the United States could seize Haitians found in international waters. These refugees were returned to Haiti unless they could prove political persecution.

Haitians detained at sea soon filled up the facilities at Guantánamo, Cuba. In May 1992, President Bush ordered the Coast Guard to return new refugees to Haiti. Those seeking political asylum might apply at the U.S. embassy in Port-au-Prince. As a candidate during the 1992 presidential campaign, Bill Clinton denounced Bush's orders. However, when he took office in January 1993, Clinton maintained Bush's policy of interdiction.[2]

Aristide's supporters never tried to restore the former president through an armed uprising. Haiti's fortunes were determined in Washington. Aristide, famed as a master of charismatic speechmaking, proved to be just as adroit in manipulating American public opinion. Haitians living in America and Canada formed his initial base of support, while the American government provided generous amounts of money. President Bush allowed Aristide to draw upon Haitian government bank accounts seized by the United States. During the next three years, these accounts supplied the exiled president with as much as $50 million.

Aristide, Préval, and other exile leaders lived well in comfortable Washington apartments. But most of the money went to hire attorneys, public relations experts, and former U.S. government officials with influential connections. The military regime and its wealthy supporters also procured American lawyers and lobbyists. But Aristide's team proved far more adept at influencing U.S. government decisions.

Whatever their private reservations about Aristide, American officials gave unwavering public support to the exiled president. From the beginning, U.S. leaders not only called for a restoration of democracy, but they also insisted that Aristide himself must be returned to power. However, the embargo proved ineffective, and the American public opposed a military invasion of Haiti. The U.S. government thus tried to broker a negotiated agreement between Aristide and the Haitian parliament and military leaders. Aristide soon dropped Préval and agreed to a series of compromise prime ministers. However, he refused either to put off his own return or to guarantee an unconditional amnesty for the military leaders.

In June 1993, the Clinton administration racheted up the economic pressure on Haiti. It froze the assets of state-owned businesses and of Haitians supporting the coup. Prodded by the United States, the UN Security Council banned the sale to

Haiti of petroleum products, arms, ammunition, and military vehicles and equipment. Heretofore, the United Nations had only imposed such severe sanctions during a civil war or to end a threat to peace. The use of sanctions merely to restore a deposed political leader was without precedent.

At the end of June, General Cédras and President Aristide met at Governor's Island in New York City. There they negotiated an agreement calling for a general amnesty and a multinational military and police training mission in Haiti. The military leaders promised to resign, allowing Aristide to return to Haiti by October 30. With the Governor's Island Accord in place, the United Nations and United States suspended their embargoes at the end of August.

The military regime now launched a terror campaign. Attachés killed more than 100 pro-Aristide leaders during the next few months. In September 1993, attaché bands and former Duvalierists formed the militant organization known as FRAPH (Front for the Advancement and Progress of Haiti).

On October 11, the U.S.S. *Harlan County* arrived at Port-au-Prince, carrying 200 U.S. and Canadian soldiers, who had been sent to train the Haitian army and oversee Aristide's return. The ship turned back when FRAPH attachés threatened the foreign diplomats who were waiting to welcome the troops. Soon after, attachés murdered Guy Malary, the minister of justice newly appointed to reform the police. The United States reimposed the trade embargo on October 15 and sent warships to enforce it. Meanwhile, violence continued to increase. In December 1993, more than 1,000 homes in the Cité Soleil slums of Port-au-Prince were burned to the ground to avenge the necklacing of a FRAPH treasurer.

Determined to force a U.S. invasion of Haiti, President Aristide launched an impressive public relations campaign. In January 1994, Aristide convened a conference in Miami, Florida, attended by Jesse Jackson, other Haitian and Afro-American activists, and members of the Black Caucus of the U.S. House of Representatives. Those present harshly criticized Clinton's refugee policy as racist and demanded U.S. military intervention.

Acting as Haiti's president, Aristide announced that he was rescinding the agreement allowing the United States to intercept Haitians at sea. Powerful Democrat senators loudly blasted Clinton's refugee policy. Letters denouncing President Clinton were signed by labor and religious leaders as well as by 150 Hollywood celebrities, organized as Artists for Aristide. Members of Congress chained themselves to the White House fence. Randal Robinson, director of a radical lobbying organization known as TransAfrica, declared that he would starve himself to death unless Clinton changed his Haiti policies.

On May 8, 1994, President Clinton announced that all refugees could seek political asylum at hearings aboard U.S. ships or in third countries. Haitians once again fled in great numbers. In just a few weeks, 20,000 refugees were picked up at sea and taken to Guantánamo Bay.

Meanwhile, the UN Security Council on May 6 had imposed a total trade embargo against Haiti, enforced by U.S. naval vessels. On June 10, President Clinton halted all air flights to Haiti and banned any Haitians from entering the United States. He also prohibited financial transfers to Haiti and seized U.S. bank accounts and properties owned by Haitians. The impact on Haiti was devastating. All businesses closed. Without electricity, medicine and food could not be refrigerated. Malnutrition, famine, and disease killed thousands.

Despite these harsh actions, the military regime refused to surrender, and the Clinton administration decided to expel the generals by force. On July 31, the United Nations authorized an invasion by U.S. troops. Once Aristide was restored, the U.S. soldiers would be replaced by a multinational UN peacekeeping force.

At the very last minute, former president Jimmy Carter led a final effort to avoid bloodshed. During negotiations on September 17 and 18, General Cédras and other top military leaders agreed to leave Haiti, allowing U.S. forces to land without opposition on September 19. On October 15, 1994, Aristide arrived in Port-au-Prince, accompanied by three planeloads of loyal fans and friends. With his return, the United States and United Nation lifted all sanctions.

The Second American Occupation

Jean Bertrand Aristide returned to a country even poorer and more destitute than the one he had left in September 1991. The military occupation and the American embargo had severely exacerbated Haiti's underlying economic and social problems. Overall, the economy had shrunk by a third or more since 1990, while prices had soared. By 1995, average income had fallen to roughly $220 per person, and food production per capita was cut in half. The embargo closed down the factories assembling goods for export. Roads no longer were passable; telephones, electricity, and waterworks had ceased to function.

Haiti's political and economic difficulties are closely connected. Both Haitians and foreigners have been reluctant to invest in a nation plagued by brutal and dishonest governments. Since the 1980s, money instead has flowed out of the country, as Haitians have sent their funds to safer havens.

When they invaded Haiti, the United States and United Nation were determined to create the conditions for economic growth. In addition to hundreds of millions of dollars in humanitarian aid, Haiti was promised more than $2 billion to foster economic development. In return, Aristide committed himself in writing to uphold the Haitian constitution and to leave office when his term expired in February 1996. At the time of the U.S. invasion, Aristide also expressed support for free-market economic reforms, including privatization of state-owned industries, tariff cuts, the elimination of import quotas and licenses, and a halving of personnel in the civil bureaucracy.

In March 1995, U.S. officers transferred responsibility for maintaining order to 6,000 UN peacekeepers from several nations. The main U.S. contingent left early in 1997, and forces from other countries moved out the following December. About 500 American soldiers stayed behind to help construct public works.

The UN troops were ordered to create a less brutal and more effective police force. In February 1995, President Aristide cut back the Haitian army to 1,500 men and forcibly retired the senior officers. The new national police were deployed in June 1995 after only four months of instruction.[3] Later on, recruits were offered more extensive training by foreign law officers, including Haitian-American cops. Despite these efforts, ordinary criminals and organized gangs ran rampant. When the police did catch offenders, they were often set free by the poorly educated and corrupt judiciary. Perhaps in frustration, some police officers continued to torture prisoners.

Political murders also persisted. After Aristide returned, several dozen conservative leaders and supporters of the military regime were murdered. Called in to investigate, the American FBI linked several killings to Aristide's interior minister as well as to the Presidential Security Unit. Perhaps in retaliation, a Lavalas legislator was murdered in November 1995. Aristide's fiery speech at the funeral sparked widespread attacks on supporters of the military regime, and more than 10 persons died during the riots.

Aristide initially retained his popularity with Haiti's masses. In a series of elections from June through September 1995, the Lavalas coalition won overwhelming control of Haiti's National Assembly and Senate. Under intense U.S. pressure, Aristide ultimately did keep his promise to leave office at the end of his five-year term. René Préval, Aristide's personal choice as the Lavalas candidate, was elected president in December 1995.

The Vatican had restored Aristide to lay status, and the former priest married Mildred Trouillot, a Haitian-American lawyer, in January 1996. They moved to a luxurious 11-acre walled estate on the outskirts of Port-au-Prince, guarded by former soldiers from the defunct Haitian army. An excellent road, constructed with funds donated for use in the city's slums, connected their home to the city.

President Préval, who took office in February 1996, was Aristide's longtime supporter and served as his prime minister in 1991. The two friends were so close that Haitians referred to Préval as Aristide's twin. Nevertheless, Aristide soon sought to discredit Préval and frustrate his policies. The Lavalas coalition split into two political parties, the Lavalas Political Organization and Aristide's personal following, called the Lavalas Family.

The two men ostensibly split over economic reforms, including the privatization of Haiti's state-owned companies. Inefficient legacies of the Duvalier era, the public monopolies used outmoded and wasteful technologies to produce shoddy goods at high cost. U.S. and international bodies had suspended aid late in 1995, when Aristide broke his promise to support privatization and civil service reform. President Préval supported privatization but turned it into a scheme of joint ventures and long-term leases. The state would continue to own the underlying asset, such as an airport or electric utility.

Préval's concessions failed to mollify Aristide. Parliamentary elections in April 1997 were marked by low turnout and fraud. As Lavalas Family legislators blocked Préval's proposals and rejected his nominations for prime minister, U.S. and international financial assistance remained on hold—as did efforts to jump-start Haiti's economy. International agencies fed about 1.1 million Haitians daily. The nation survived without a government thanks to international aid, drug smuggling, and an estimated $400 million to $500 million a year in remittances from Haitians living abroad.

The impasse went on for months. Because parliament could not pass a budget, hundreds of thousands of Haitians failed to receive a raise or even worked without pay. In January 1999, when the parliament's term expired, President Préval unilaterally appointed a prime minister and cabinet. But Haitian politicians considered Préval a weak leader and turned their attention to the presidential election set for 2000. Aristide's supporters pressed for his reelection, and partisan infighting turned nasty, with as many as a dozen assassinations of political leaders.

CHAPTER 18

COLONIALISM'S
MIXED BLESSINGS

The Caribbean islands differ in languages, political systems, and cultural traditions. But all have had to find new sources of income as demand has fallen for their sugar, coffee, and bananas. Under the colonial system, the islands purchased manufactured goods from the "metropolitan" power, which in turn guaranteed markets for agricultural exports. Because they benefited from American quotas, sugar plantations remained profitable in Cuba, Puerto Rico, and the Dominican Republic for several decades after they had disappeared from much of the eastern Caribbean. However, by the late 1970s, all the islands had to search for new ways to pay for the imports they needed. By then, it was difficult to create manufacturing industries that could compete with those in the United States, Europe, and Asia.

Whatever their political status, most islands came to depend on a mix of tourism, "offshore" banking, and "assembly" factories that put together and reexport imported goods. These three industries do not furnish dependable sources of export revenue. Like sugar, bananas, and other primary products, they remain subject to fluctuations that island governments cannot influence. Tourist revenues vary with the whims of travelers, and they rise and fall with economic conditions in the Americas and Europe.

Assembly industries do not make major investments in their facilities. They remain free to leave whenever another host nation offers lower wages or greater tax concessions.

The offshore banking industry began in the 1920s in the Bahamas and had reached the Netherlands Antilles by the 1940s. During the 1980s, the Cayman Islands attracted thousands of banks and insurance companies. Offshore financial institutions also have been pursued by Antigua, Barbados, Anguilla, the British Virgin Islands, Montserrat, and the Turks and Caicos.

Because they compete with each other to attract branches of foreign banks and insurance companies, island governments have had to strike a delicate balance in financial regulations. To recruit foreign companies, they have limited taxes, guaranteed confidentiality, and granted virtually unlimited freedom of operation. In some cases, government officials have failed to impose the necessary minimum level of regulation. Legitimate businesses have been quick to move on whenever a financial haven has gained a reputation for fraud and "laundering" of profits from crimes.

THE FRENCH, DUTCH, AND U.S. CARIBBEAN

The two decades following World War II saw the abandonment of old-fashioned colonialism, under which governors were sent from Europe or the United States to rule foreign lands. France, the Netherlands, and the United States retained their island possessions but did grant the islanders some say in local affairs. The United Kingdom recognized the independence of virtually all its Caribbean colonies. Britain retained only five tiny territories, which were awarded a large measure of self-government.

Martinique and Guadeloupe (along with Saint-Martin and Saint-Barthélemy) became integral parts of France. Those born on these islands are as much French citizens as are inhabitants of Paris and Marseilles. They vote in French elections and are governed by French laws.

The Dutch colonies—Aruba, Bonaire, Curaçao, Sint Maarten, Sint Eustatius, and Saba—entered into a unique constitutional arrangement with the Netherlands. The Dutch monarch rules over one Realm consisting of the three kingdoms of the Netherlands, the Netherlands Antilles, and Aruba. Dutch Antilleans are citizens of the common Realm, but they elect governments that are autonomous in local matters.

Puerto Ricans and U.S. Virgin Islanders adopted yet a third type of arrangement. They are American citizens, but they cannot vote in mainland elections. They elect a governor and legislature, but the U.S. Congress can overrule local laws. Puerto Rico and the Virgin Islands thus enjoy more autonomy than the French Antilles but less than the Netherlands Antilles.

Despite differing constitutional arrangements, inhabitants of these islands are tied to the metropolitan country by golden chains. French Antilleans enjoy every service provided by France's comprehensive welfare system. The U.S. Congress has granted Puerto Ricans many benefits enjoyed by mainland Americans, and the Netherlands also provides generous financial assistance. At the end of the 1990s, French subsidies made up three-fourths of disposable income in Martinique and Guadeloupe. U.S. transfer payments contributed to one-third of Puerto Rico's income. Aid to the Netherlands Antilles was among the highest per person in the world.

War memorial, Place de la Victoire, Pointe-à-Pitre, Guadeloupe.

Thanks to these grants, incomes are much higher in the French, Dutch, and U.S. Antilles than on other Caribbean islands. (See Table 37 on page 327.) But continuing subsidies have discouraged entrepreneurs and failed to promote local industries. Ambitious islanders migrate to the "metropolitan" country. One in three Puerto Ricans resides on the mainland. One-third of Dutch Antilleans have moved to the Netherlands, while half of all Guadeloupeans live in France. Their places are taken by migrants from independent but impoverished islands. Thousands of undocumented Dominicans come to Spanish-speaking Puerto Rico each year. Eastern Caribbean peoples travel to Guadeloupe and Martinique. English-speaking islanders find work in the U.S. (and British) Virgin Islands.

By fostering dependency and emigration, continued attachment to the metropolitan center has proved to be a mixed blessing for the French, Dutch, and U.S. Caribbean. Nevertheless, islanders consistently have endorsed the economic security and the right to emigrate afforded by a modified form of colonialism. In 1993 and 1994, Dutch Antilleans rejected independence by wide margins. Most Puerto Ricans have similarly favored commonwealth status over either independence or statehood.

GREAT BRITAIN'S LAST CARIBBEAN TERRITORIES

After granting independence to most of its colonies, Great Britain retained five small and lightly inhabited Dependent Territories (renamed Overseas Territories in 1998)—the Cayman Islands, the Turks and Caicos, the British Virgin Islands, Anguilla, and Montserrat. Each of these islands or island groups has a separate constitution. A governor, appointed by the British government, is responsible for defense, external affairs (including international finance), and internal security. Local laws, taxes, and economic development are the responsibility of the executive and legislative councils, each with a majority of elected members. Residents born on the islands do not enjoy British citizenship and do not have an automatic right to live in Great Britain.

All five have flourished as tourist centers, havens for tax-free offshore banking, and (from time to time) as drug transhipment points. Montserrat prospered until 1995, when it was devastated by volcanic eruptions (see page 308). The Caribbean territories have been a very minimal economic burden to Great Britain. While several continued to receive assistance for major development projects, their citizens do not receive British welfare payments.

As is the case in the French, Dutch, and U.S. territories, most residents of the British islands wish to remain associated with the colonial power. Public opposition to independence increased rather than declined during the 1980s and 1990s, partly because of events in newly independent neighboring islands. Island leaders are convinced that association with Britain contributes to political, economic, and social stability. A reputation for order and financial integrity is crucial to the success of these tourist and banking centers. Britain also is valued as a source of assistance in the event of a natural disaster, such as that on Montserrat.

TRAFFICKING IN ILLEGAL DRUGS

Because of their location, the Caribbean islands have been at the center of the illegal drug trade. The islands are a land bridge that links South America (the world's largest drug supplier) to the United States (the world's largest drug consumer). Venezuela lies within seven miles of Trinidad, while Bimini in the Bahamas is only 40 miles from Florida. Given their continuing political and economic ties to Great Britain, France, and the Netherlands, the islands also provide comparatively easy access to drug consumers in Europe. From the late 1960s, islanders passed along shipments traveling north from South America. Money laundering—the process of attributing a legal provenance to drug profits—helped to build major offshore banking centers. During the 1990s, marijuana cultivation became widespread, replacing sugar and bananas as the largest cash crop on many islands.

Cocaine grown in Colombia was introduced to the United States by Cubans fleeing Castro's revolution. From the late 1960s, Colombian dealers established independent trafficking networks. Thanks to their strategic location in the flight path between Colombia and south Florida, the Bahamas were the main transit point for cocaine, hashish, and marijuana during the 1980s. During the latter part of the decade, anti-drug operations in south Florida forced dealers to develop new routes passing through the eastern Caribbean.

During the 1990s, marijuana continued to flow through the Bahamas and Jamaica, while cocaine took the easterly route through the Dominican Republic, Puerto Rico, and the U.S. Virgin Islands. Aruba and the Netherlands Antilles also emerged as centers for major drug networks. On Aruba, a family linked to organized crime bought up casinos, hotels, and banks as well as police and customs officials and the ruling and opposition parties. The island became, in the words of Claire Sterling, "the world's first independent mafia state."[1]

Marijuana cultivation became more widespread during the 1990s. Until the mid-1980s, only Jamaica produced significant amounts of the crop. During that decade, "ganja" is said to have brought in between 1 billion and 2 billion dollars in foreign currency, surpassing both tourism and all other exports. Beginning in 1985, joint U.S.-Jamaican eradication programs cut production and forced growers to relocate in remote highland regions, such as the Blue Mountains. As Jamaican exports fell, other Caribbean countries began growing marijuana. Ganja overtook bananas as the most lucrative export crop on the eastern Caribbean islands of Saint Lucia, Dominica, Grenada, Saint Kitts, and Montserrat (until the 1995 volcanic eruption). By the mid-1990s, tiny Saint Vincent was second only to Jamaica in marijuana cultivation. (A single operation there in 1996 found and destroyed 1.2 million mature cannabis plants and 7 million seedlings.) Marijuana production also soared in Trinidad, Puerto Rico, Haiti, and the Dominican Republic as well as throughout the Bahamas chain.

The offshore banking industry has become an important source of income, especially for small islands without the natural resources to support farming and manufacturing. Judging by the success of police sting operations, large sums have been laundered through financial centers in the Bahamas, the Netherlands Antilles, and the Cayman Islands. In 1992, British inspectors closed down most offshore banks on Montserrat. On Anguilla, a sting operation in 1994 led to 116 arrests.

Drug trafficking has brought additional income to Caribbean nations suffering from slow economic growth, dependency on foreign imports, high unemployment, and huge public debts. Thousands of islanders grow marijuana. Others work as drivers, pilots, and guards, while laundering the receipts gives work to accountants, bankers, and lawyers. All those involved purchase goods and services, supplying jobs for many others. As part of the money-laundering process, drug money turns into capital for investment and provides importers with foreign currency. After they enter the legal economy, drug profits are subject to taxes on property, sales, and income.

But the illegal drug trade also has damaged Caribbean nations. Murder, assault, and theft have skyrocketed on precisely those islands that are the main centers of the drug trade. Caribbean drug dealers also traffic in weapons, and they are heavily armed. Organized gangs, such as the Jamaican posses, have branched out to kidnapping, robbery, prostitution, and murder.

Revenue from drugs has been offset by the increased costs of larger police and defense forces, which have ballooned along with the trade. Many countries have passed strict anti-drug laws, which often infringe on the civil rights of citizens; in Jamaica and Trinidad, these laws have contributed to violence and murder by the police forces. Drug convictions have crowded prisons far beyond their capacities. A Trinidad prison, built in 1812 to house 250 convicts, held a daily average population of 1,100 during 1994.

Drug trafficking also inflicts damage indirectly. Publicity about drug abuse and crime has adversely affected tourism, and charges of money laundering have frightened legal clients away from offshore banking centers. The most damaging indirect cost has been the corruption of officials, who use government institutions to shield their drug dealings. High-ranking members of the government have been implicated in drug trafficking in the Bahamas, Jamaica, Trinidad, Saint Lucia, and the Turks and Caicos. On Antigua, the head of the army and a son of the prime minister were dismissed in 1989 after they supplied weapons to a Columbian drug cartel. On Saint Kits, the leaders of both political parties have been linked to the drug trade.

The corruption of high public officials has weakened the government's authority and undermined the sovereignty Caribbean nations have gained since World War II. In parts of Haiti, Jamaica, and Trinidad, private militias or vigilantes have taken over the police function. Agencies of the United States government pursue drug dealers without regard to territorial waters, and American officials have acted against offshore banks without the permission of island authorities. At the end of the 20th century, their inability to curb drug trafficking threatened the independence and prosperity of the Caribbean nations.

Table 33. **CARIBBEAN DRUG SEIZURES, 1991–1995 (IN KILOS)**

C = Cocaine.   M = Marijuana

Country		1991	1992	1993	1994	1995
Antigua-Barbuda	C	NA	500	NA	130	110
	M	NA	NA	10,095	3,380	217
Bahamas	C	5,260	4,800	1,800	490	390
	M	1,180	1,000	650	1,420	3,530
British Virgin Islands	C	15	24	709	450	1,194
	M	NA	NA	NA	1,000	235
Dominican Republic	C	1,810	2,360	1,070	2,800	3,600
	M	400	6,450	310	6,800	NA
Haiti	C	188	56	157	716	550
	M	330	NA	2,520	500	NA
Jamaica	C	60	490	160	180	570
	M	4,300	3,500	7,500	4,600	3,720
Trinidad & Tobago	C	NA	NA	NA	311	110
	M	NA	NA	NA	3,977	1,634

SOURCE: U.S. Department of State, *International Narcotics Control Strategy Report* (various years).

PUERTO RICO: FROM COLONY TO COMMONWEALTH

Under Spanish rule, Puerto Rico's fate was linked to that of the larger and richer colony of Cuba. The United States went to war in 1898 primarily to expel the Spanish from Cuba and the Philippines. As American forces advanced, the United States decided to end the Spanish Empire and sent a small army to take Puerto Rico. After some debate, Congress voted to keep the island, at least for a time. Puerto Rico seemed too small and too poor to be given independence. But American leaders did not want to grant the island statehood because of its Spanish culture and the large number of people of color—40 percent of the population, according to an 1899 census.

By the Foraker Act of 1900, Congress imposed a system of government copied from the British Crown colonies. The U.S. president appointed the Supreme Court and the governor. The governor in turn named an 11-member Executive Council, while a 35-member House of Delegates was elected by popular vote. The governor and the nominated Executive Council had to approve island laws, and the U.S. Congress also retained a veto. The Foraker Act abolished tariffs between the United States and the island from 1902, but the island's peoples became citizens of Puerto Rico and not of the United States.

Influential Americans criticized the Foraker Act as undemocratic. In Puerto Rico, the broadly based Union Party denounced it as granting neither statehood, independence, nor even home rule. Reform finally came in 1917 under Woodrow Wilson. President Wilson believed in the military importance of the Caribbean, where Puerto Rico formed a strategic triangle with American bases at Guantánamo and the Canal Zone. To keep Germany out of the region, Wilson intervened in Haiti in 1915 and purchased the Virgin Islands in 1917. From the same defensive motives, he wanted to bring Puerto Rico under the American flag, binding its people to the United States "by ties of justice and interest and affection."[2] On March 2, 1917 Wilson signed the Jones Act, which defined Puerto Rico's legal status until 1948.

Under the Jones Act, Puerto Ricans became American citizens, protected by several of the guarantees in the U.S. Constitution. They were free to travel to the mainland and subject to the draft. However, they did not pay federal taxes or vote in federal elections. The Jones Act also gave Puerto Rico more power over local laws. From now on, the Puerto Rican Senate as well as the House were elected by universal male suffrage, with women receiving the vote in 1929. Both houses enjoyed somewhat greater powers, but Puerto Rico did not enjoy all the powers of an American state. The president continued to appoint its governor and other top officials as well as its supreme court judges.

In 1947, Congress amended the Jones law and granted Puerto Ricans the right to elect their own governor. Yet this still made the U.S. Congress the source of Puerto Rican rights. In campaigning to become the first elected governor in 1948, Luis Muñoz Marín (1898–1980) proposed that Puerto Rico become a commonwealth, a free associated state (*estado libre asocado*). When Muñoz won 61 percent of the vote, the U.S. Congress moved with unusual speed. In July 1950, President Truman signed Public Law 600, which invited the Puerto Rican people to draft their own constitution.

As a commonwealth (since July 25, 1952), Puerto Rico enjoys a unique legal status. The island is self-governing in local matters, and Puerto Ricans do not pay

Table 34. **POLITICAL STATUS OF THE CARIBBEAN ISLANDS, 1992**
(Reading from Northwest to Southeast)

GREATER ANTILLES

Cuba	Independent (1902)
Jamaica	Independent (1962)
Haiti	Independent (1804)
Dominican Republic	Independent (1844)
Puerto Rico	Commonwealth associated with the United States (1952)
Cayman Islands	British Associated Territory (1972)
Bahamas	Independent (1973)
Turks and Caicos	British Associated Territory (1976)

LESSER ANTILLES

U.S. Virgin Islands	U.S. territory with local self-government (1968)
British Virgin Islands	British Associated Territory (1967)
Anguilla	British Associated Territory (1982)
Saint-Martin	Administrative district of Guadeloupe (1946)
Sint Maarten	Member of the Netherlands Antilles (1954)
Saint-Barthélemy	Administrative district of Guadeloupe (1946)
Sint Eustatius	Member of the Netherlands Antilles (1954)
Saba	Member of the Netherlands Antilles (1954)
Saint Kitts and Nevis	Independent (1983)
Antigua and Barbuda	Independent (1981)
Montserrat	British Associated Territory (1966)
Guadeloupe	Overseas *département* of France (1946)
Martinique	Overseas *département* of France (1946)
Dominica	Independent (1978)
Saint Lucia	Independent (1977)
Barbados	Independent (1966)
Saint Vincent and the Grenadines	Independent (1979)
Grenada	Independent (1974)
Trinidad and Tobago	Independent (1962)
Aruba	Member of the Kingdom of the Netherlands (1986)
Bonaire	Member of the Netherlands Antilles (1954)
Curaçao	Member of the Netherlands Antilles (1954)

NOTE: For independent states, the date in parentheses represents the year in which sovereignty was achieved. For colonies, it represents the year when the political status noted was established. Aruba and the members of the Netherlands Antilles enjoy local self-government within the Kingdom of the Netherlands.

federal taxes. Yet the island is not fully independent. The United States handles defense and foreign relations, and the federal government operates alongside the island government, as it does in mainland states. Puerto Ricans receive federal transfer payments, such as food stamps. Within the Caribbean context, Puerto Rico thus enjoys less autonomy than the remaining British and Dutch colonies. Even though Puerto Ricans do not send voting representatives to Congress, United States treaties and laws apply to the island. U.S. laws can even override provisions of the commonwealth constitution.

Commonwealth status has had distinct economic advantages, but it also denies Puerto Ricans a vote for the American president and other officials whose actions affect their lives. Nevertheless, in a 1967 plebiscite, 61 percent favored retaining commonwealth status, 39 percent voted for statehood, and less than 1 percent called for independence. In 1993 and 1998 plebiscites, Puerto Ricans were more evenly divided, with commonwealth status and statehood each receiving about half the votes; hardly anyone voted for independence.

The Sugar Industry Dominates the Island

Before 1898, the sugar industry had been of minor importance. Between the U.S. occupation and the World War II, it dominated the entire island. Sugar imports from Puerto Rico were free of American tariffs and protected by government quotas. American corporations bought up much of the island's farmlands and constructed large modern sugar mills (*centrales*). The Foraker Act of 1900 limited a corporation's land holdings to 500 acres. However, it was difficult to enforce and had little effect before the 1940s.

Sugar now became the island's main product. During the generally prosperous years before 1925, sugar exports rose tenfold.[3] During the same years, coffee—produced on smaller farms—became less important. World prices fell, and hurricanes in 1899 and 1928 damaged much of the crop. The United States did not replace Europe as a consumer because Americans preferred South American coffee. Most workers now became landless laborers on large sugar estates, receiving low wages and suffering long periods of unemployment. The Free Federation of Workers (FFW), was founded in 1899 with the support of American labor leader Samuel Gompers. But only a small number of workers belonged to the FFW, which was allied to the Socialist Party instead of one of the two major parties.

The island's income did not keep pace as the population rapidly increased. Thanks to American success in checking diseases and a lower infant mortality rate, the number of islanders roughly doubled between 1899 and 1940, and the population density was one of the highest in the world. (See Table 35.) The island's dependence on one crop became especially harmful when sugar prices fell after 1925. In 1929, Puerto Ricans had on average an income of $122 per year, about one-fifth of the level on the mainland. By 1933, during the Great Depression, the average yearly income fell to $84.

Table 35. **PUERTO RICO POPULATION ESTIMATES, 1920–1990**

1920	1,312,000
1940	1,800,000
1960	2,361,000
1990	3,522,000

SOURCE: Miró, *La poblacion de America Latina*, 2 (1920–60).

Three Decades of Rapid Growth

Efforts to improve Puerto Rico's economy began with President Franklin Roosevelt's New Deal. Federal agencies poured hundreds of millions in transfer payments into the island but achieved little. Real progress became possible in 1940 when Luis Muñoz Marín's Popular Democratic Party (Partido Popular Democrático, or PPD) won control of the legislature. The son of independence leader Luis Muñoz Rivera and a charismatic politician, Muñoz Marín held power for 24 years as Senate leader and then as governor (1948–65). Under his rule, Puerto Rico underwent a profound social and economic transformation. Sugar collapsed and was replaced by manufacturing and tourism. Although the population continued to grow, the economy grew faster. Between 1940 and 1987, the per capita gross national product skyrocketed from only $154 to $4,850.

As a pragmatic reformer, Muñoz Marín was able to work with both Roosevelt's New Dealers and Eisenhower's more conservative Washington. In 1941, President Roosevelt named Rexford Tugwell, a fervent radical, as governor. His administration, ending in 1946, devised the governmental machinery and corps of officials needed to carry out economic planning. In 1942 the government organized a central planning board, a government development bank, and the Puerto Rico Industrial Development Company, known as Fomento. The return of federal taxes on Puerto Rican rum sold in the United States provided the initial funds for development.

Muñoz Marín's reform program began with the enforcement of the 500–acre limitation on land ownership. The government purchased land from the large sugar companies. Some was held by state farms, with a worker's wages including a share of the profits. Other land was sold in small plots, or given to landless farm workers. The companies continued to run the *centrales,* but government farms and *colonos* (family-run sugar farms) supplied most of the cane.

Economic growth was relatively slow in the 1940s as the government attempted to build its own factories, all of which lost money. Real progress began when the legislature passed the Industrial Incentive Act of 1947. This granted new industries direct and indirect subsidies as well as exemption from corporate, personal, and property taxes for periods ranging from 10 to 30 years. Investment was especially rapid during the 1960s, when Puerto Rico enjoyed one of the highest sustained growth rates in the world.

Most companies moving to Puerto Rico were subsidiaries of corporations headquartered in the United States. The local unit served as an assembly plant that imported raw or semifinished materials and reexported the finished output back to the United States. Islanders benefited from the wages paid by U.S. subsidiaries. However, the firms already were integrated into supply and distribution networks in the United States. Their presence on the island did little to nurture Puerto Rican entrepreneurs and island industries.

By the end of the 1960s, Fomento staff noticed that U.S. corporations no longer were as willing to operate assembly plants using unskilled labor. Tax exemptions could not offset rising Puerto Rican wage levels, now higher than those in Asia and in some other Caribbean countries. Fomento thus began to promote Puerto Rico to capital-intensive firms requiring semiskilled and skilled workers. During the 1970s and early 1980s, the island attracted substantial investment in oil-refining, petrochemical, machinery, metals, drug and pharmaceutical plants.

Heavy manufacturing factories offered islanders better paid but fewer jobs. Like assembly plants, they used mainland supply and distribution networks; thus they also failed to encourage local development. Because petroleum refining and petrochemicals had become major industries, the island was hard hit by the OPEC oil boycott of 1973 and the subsequent quadrupling of oil prices. Many factories closed their operations in Puerto Rico and moved to countries with lower wages.

Exemption from Federal Taxes Spurs Investment

In response to these dire economic conditions, the commonwealth government, supported by U.S. corporations operating in Puerto Rico, petitioned Congress for tax relief. In 1976, Congress placed U.S. firms with branches in Puerto Rico into Section 936 of the U.S. tax code, allowing them to escape taxes on the profits they sent back to the United States.[4] When combined with existing incentives, tax exemptions, and lower wages than on the mainland, Section 936 made operating in Puerto Rico extremely profitable.

The commonwealth's economic progress after 1976 thus become even more dependent on tax exemptions. The impact of 936 benefits was dramatic. Multinational firms making pharmaceuticals, electronic equipment, and precision instruments moved their operations to Puerto Rico.

These corporations also transformed the financial sector. The interest on profits left on the island also received tax exemption. This encouraged 936 corporations to deposit their earnings in Puerto Rican banks. Over time, Puerto Rico increasingly became a regional center for financial services. However, unlike several other islands, Puerto Rico is not attractive to "offshore" banks. Most federal financial regulations and corporate laws apply to Puerto Rico, making it difficult to engage in marginally legal transactions.

After manufacturing, tourism became Puerto Rico's second source of wealth. In 1940, the entire island had only 600 guest rooms. As part of its economic development plan, the government built several large hotels, whose success stimulated private investment. Aided by inexpensive airfares from U.S. cities, Puerto Rico captured much of Cuba's tourist business following Castro's 1959 revolution.

While industry and tourism thrived, farm production sharply declined. As workers found better-paying jobs, sugar production fell drastically—from a peak of 1.3 million tons in 1952 to 249,000 in 1973 and only 34,000 in 1996. Coffee production also has fallen, and almost no tobacco is grown. Indeed, Puerto Rico now imports nearly all its sugar, tobacco, and coffee, the crops that dominated its lists of exports for centuries.

Unemployment, Welfare, and Emigration

Heavy manufacturing, tourism, and banking have generated relatively few jobs. Since Puerto Rico's population has continued to increase, long-term unemployment also has risen. Moreover, the health of manufacturing and tourism depends on the state of the mainland economy. When the United States goes into recession, Puerto Rico's economy plummets.

To keep up employment, the commonwealth and municipal governments have used federal funds to create employment. An astounding seven out of 10 new jobs from 1960 to 1970 were created by government. Many other Puerto Ricans survived on federal transfer payments, which also were expanded during the 1970s. At the end of the 1990s, the government employed 60 percent of the labor force. Two-thirds of the population received some kind of direct assistance from the U.S. federal government, primarily social security benefits and food stamps.[5] Altogether, U.S. grants and transfer payments provided about one-third of Puerto Rico's total income.

When U.S. aid is taken into account, Puerto Rico is prosperous compared with most other Caribbean and South American nations. But Puerto Ricans compare themselves to mainlanders and not to other residents of the Caribbean. There are no legal impediments to emigration, and transportation is inexpensive. During hard times, Puerto Ricans leave to find work on the mainland United States.

Mass emigration began in 1946. By 1960s, the census reported that 900,000 persons born in Puerto Rico were resident in the U.S. The most dramatic exodus took place during the 1950s, when 470,000 left, mainly for New York City. Fewer moved out during the 1970s, but emigration increased as the economy stagnated during the 1980s and early 1990s. The 1990 census counted about 1 million Puerto Ricans on the mainland. If one adds in children born on the mainland with at least one Puerto Rican parent, up to 3 million persons in the U.S. had some tie to the island.

The number of Puerto Ricans on the mainland has not significantly increased since 1960. But this apparent stability conceals a great deal of movement back and forth. During the 1980s, for example, 433,000 persons left, while 316,000 moved to the island. Many of the latter were former emigrants returning home. The returning flow also included children of islanders born and brought up in the United States.

🌀 PUERTO RICANS ON THE MAINLAND

In 1961, when *West Side Story* portrayed Puerto Rican street gangs, islanders primarily lived in East Harlem and the Lower East Side of Manhattan as well as in the South Bronx. Over the years, the Puerto Rican population has become more dispersed. Two out of three Puerto Ricans settled in New York City in 1960. By 1990, only one-third lived there. Puerto Ricans were scattered from California to Connecticut, from Florida to Massachusetts. No longer concentrated in homogeneous ghettos, many have assimilated into their local communities and have been elected to local and state office.

Despite emigration, Puerto Rico's population has risen rapidly, from about 1 million in 1900 to an estimated 4 million by 2000. Only 100 miles long by 34 miles wide, the island is extraordinarily congested, with more than 1,000 persons per square mile. No state has a higher population density, and only the largest U.S. cities are as crowded.

The End of Consensus

As economic growth stalled, the remarkable political unity of the 1940s and 1950s came to an end. In 1964, Muñoz Marín decided not to run for a fifth term as governor. No subsequent leader has enjoyed his widespread popularity. Muñoz Marín's Popular Democratic Party (PPD), which favors a continuation of commonwealth status, has been locked in close elections with the pro-statehood New Progressive Party (PNP).

The two main parties are divided over the island's future political status. More-

Isla Verde Beach, San Juan, Puerto Rico. Since the 1960s, international corporations have erected high-rise hotels in this area, just east of the colonial city now known as Old San Juan.

over, the PPD maintains an association with the U.S. Democratic Party, while the PNP is aligned with the Republicans. Nevertheless, the PPD and PNP generally have adopted similar policies on key economic issues. When they are in power, PNP governors have supported incentives and tax exemptions for U.S. companies just as strongly as their PPD opponents.

Roberto Sánchez Vilella (1913–), Muñoz Marín's top assistant for many years, won the governorship in 1964. Four years later, however, internal quarrels ended 23 years of uninterrupted PPD rule. The party did not renominate Sánchez Vilella, who founded his own political organization. The weakened PPD lost to the newly founded New Progressive Party. Luis A. Ferré (1904–), a millionaire industrialist and patron of the arts, won the governorship, and the PNP also took the House of Representatives.

The PPD returned to power from 1972 to 1976 with Rafael Hernández Colón (1936–), a young senator and former attorney general. Hernández Colón had the misfortune to take office just as the economy went into recession. As unemployment rose to 20 percent in 1976, the Hernández Colón administration increased the number of government jobs by buying the telephone company and several shipping lines. It also worked with U.S. companies to win Section 936 tax exceptions. Nevertheless, the economy continued to stagnate.

Carlos Romero Barceló (1932–), the former mayor of San Juan, became governor in 1976, and the PNP also recaptured the legislature. Governor Barceló won reelection in 1980 by a tiny margin and was accused of rigging the vote. The island continued to suffer from the worst economic crisis since the 1930s, with more than one out of four unemployed. Hernández Colón and the PPD returned to power in 1984 on the strength of a pledge to make job creation the main priority.

Once in office, Hernández Colón embarked on a "twin-plants" program, which used the recently passed Caribbean Basin Initiative (CBI) to promote industrial development. Under the CBI, goods from designated countries in the Caribbean and Central America did not have to pay U.S. tariffs. To avoid these import taxes, at least 35 percent of the product's production value (or cost) had to have been added in the beneficiary countries. However, labor or materials added in Puerto Rico could also be counted as part of the necessary 35 percent.

Under Hernández Colón's twin-plants proposal, the first and labor-intensive stages of assembly would took place in low-wage Caribbean countries. The more sophisticated steps and final packaging would be done in Puerto Rico. Hernández Colón also promised that the huge pool of Section 936 funds deposited in Puerto Rican banks would be used to finance investment in the Caribbean. In fact, few twin-plants projects were implemented. However, by rhetorically supporting the politically popular Caribbean Basin Initiative, Hernández Colón thwarted the Congressional budget cutters who wished to eliminate the Section 936 tax exemption.

Hernández Colón's second term as governor coincide with economic revival on the mainland and falling world oil prices. Puerto Rico's economy began to grow again. Unemployment fell to 17 percent overall in 1990, although it remained as high as 40 percent in some rural areas.

Life without Section 936

Hernández Colón did not run for a fourth term in 1992. Pedro Rosselló (1944–), a distinguished physician, defeated Muñoz Marín's daughter, Victoria Muñoz Mendoza in the governor's race; the PNP also won the legislature. Rosselló advocated the development of a free-market economic structure. His administration promised that private companies and not the commonwealth government would become the island's main employer. Plans were made to sell government companies, including the sugar corporation, the telephone company, and the maritime shipping company. The government reduced and streamlined regulations to encourage investment by Puerto Rican as well as by U.S. businesses.

For 50 years, Puerto Rico's governments sought to attract mainland companies by offering tax exemption. U.S. firms also enjoyed exemption from U.S. taxes beginning in 1976. But Puerto Rico's economic circumstances drastically changed in August 1996, when Congress ended Section 936 exemptions for future investments in Puerto Rico. (Companies already operating on the island could take the tax exemption until 2005.)

Governor Rosselló, who was reelected to a second term in 1996, continued the PNP's emphasis on fostering private investment. The state-owned telephone company lost its monopoly, and factories were allowed to start producing their own electricity. Government-owned health facilities were privatized by the end of 1998. As islanders searched for new strategies to encourage economic development, they were fortunate that the economy was relatively prosperous when Section 936 tax exemptions were abolished. During the 1995 to 1996 tourist season, more than 4 million tourists visited the island, setting a record and spending nearly $2 billion.

Puerto Rico and the United States

Debating the island's constitutional future is among Puerto Ricans' favorite pastimes. Other issues influence elections; a vote for the PNP candidate, for example, does not necessarily indicate support for statehood. However, the status debate dominates political rhetoric.

Ever since the 1952 constitution was adopted, both major political parties have tried to gain more powers for the commonwealth government. President George Bush was zealously pro-statehood, but the U.S. Senate failed to pass plebiscite legislation. In December 1991, Governor Hernández Colón held his own referendum on a "charter of democratic rights," including guarantees of U.S. citizenship and retention of Spanish as the official language. Only 46 percent voted for the proposed charter; its defeat was widely considered a vote for the existing commonwealth status.

Rosselló, who became governor in January 1993, held another plebiscite in November of that year. Although the plebiscite had no legal effect, it was intensely contested. In television advertisements, former U.S. presidents Gerald Ford, Ronald Reagan, and George Bush called for statehood. Puerto Ricans supported commonwealth status in 1993, although by a smaller margin than in 1969. With three out of four voters taking part, 49 percent voted for the commonwealth option, while 46 percent supported statehood; 4 percent chose independence. Governor Rosselló, reelected in November 1996, pressed the U.S. Congress to authorize yet another plebiscite. When Congress failed to do so, Rosselló forced a referendum through the island's legislature. In December 1998, again with a heavy turnout, voters split almost evenly. Some 47 percent wanted statehood, but 50 percent checked "none of the above," the option backed by commonwealth supporters.

Public debates over the island's status often have focused on financial matters. If Puerto Rico were a state, individuals and corporations would have to pay federal income tax. But statehood also would eliminate current caps on welfare imposed by Congress, thus making islanders eligible for additional public assistance. Friends and foes of statehood add up the numbers differently. Moreover, these financial arguments are based on existing laws, which future Congresses can change at will.

For many voters, cultural issues undoubtedly are as important as financial calculations. Because the island was a Spanish colony, Puerto Ricans believe they enjoy a unique cultural identity. Despite Spain's brutal oppression of the island during the 19th century, they treasure this "Hispanic" heritage, and they are afraid it would be lost with statehood. Their Spanish language is particularly crucial to many voters. Spanish is the language of instruction in school. Eight out of 10 Puerto Ricans do not understand English, and they do not want to learn the language. The small bilingual minority also prefers Spanish.[6]

Since World War II, Puerto Rico has ceased to be part of the Caribbean except in a geographical sense. The island is an extension of the U.S. into the Caribbean, not a Caribbean nation. One out of four Puerto Ricans resides in the United States. The economy depends on federal assistance and federal laws encouraging investment by American corporations.

Puerto Rican politicians thus spend much of their time lobbying the U.S. Congress. They have ignored their Caribbean neighbors and failed to join Caribbean organizations, such as the Caribbean Development Bank and the Association of Caribbean States. Pro-statehood PNP officials fear that regional affiliations might interfere with Puerto Rico's full integration into the U.S. But most PPD governors also have shunned ties with the Caribbean and Latin American nations. At least in part, racial biases lie behind Puerto Rico's isolation, and they also provoke the emotions surrounding the political status debate. Repudiating the island's African heritage, Puerto

Table 36. **TOURIST ARRIVALS IN THE CARIBBEAN, 1988 AND 1995**
(*Thousands of Arrivals*)

	Total		Overnight	
	1995	1988	1995	1988
Puerto Rico	4,086	2,801	3,131	2,077
Bahamas	3,239	3,158	1,598	1,479
Dominican Republic	1,932	1,216	1,902	1,116
U.S. Virgin Islands	1,733	2,032	454	599
Jamaica	1,624	1,020	1,019	649
Cayman Islands	1,043	535	361	219
Barbados	927	742	449	451
Aruba	912	359	619	278
Cuba	—	742	—	738
Bermuda	588	585	388	427
Sint Maarten/Saint-Martin	—	496	445	480
Antigua and Barbuda	479	416	212	187
Saint Lucia	436	—	232	—
British Virgin Islands	420	—	253	—
Curaçao	402	—	232	—
Grenada	369	—	108	—
Saint Vincent and the Grenadines	218	—	60	—
Saint Kitts and Nevis	203	—	79	—

NOTES: "Total" refers to the number of international visitors arriving for pleasure at each destination and not to the number of individuals; if the same person makes several pleasure trips to the same country, she or he is counted each time as a new arrival. "Overnight" refers to visitors staying in the country one or more nights; it primarily excludes tourists arriving on cruise ships.

SOURCE: World Tourism Organization, March 1980 and March 1997.

Rican nationalists insist their traditions are wholly Spanish. They are adamant that the island has nothing in common with the "black republics" of the Caribbean,[7] yet they also reject the culture of the English-speaking mainland. Hence the islanders' continuing ambivalence over ties to the United States.

THE U.S. VIRGIN ISLANDS

In 1917, the United States bought the three Danish Virgin Islands for $25 million to keep them from falling under German control. After the war, the threat to the Canal Zone diminished, and the United States almost forgot about the Virgins. At first the U.S. Navy administered the islands, and they were placed under the Department of the Interior in 1931. The inhabitants received American citizenship in 1927, but not the right to vote in federal elections for president or the Congress.

The United States initially retained the Danish system that gave full powers to an appointed governor, but the political system has become more democratic since the

1930s. The Organic Act of 1936 gave the local government control over all federal taxes collected in the islands, and it guaranteed inhabitants the freedoms included in the U.S. Constitution. The act removed the highly restrictive qualifications for voting enacted in 1863. It gave the vote to all adult residents who were citizens of the United States and able to read English.

The islands gained limited self-government in 1968 with a bill abolishing the presidential veto of island laws and allowing islanders to elect their own governor beginning in 1971. One 15-member senate is elected every two years; it replaced the two separate councils at Saint Croix and Saint Thomas in 1957. Residents cannot vote in presidential elections. They elect a delegate to the U.S. House of Representatives, who normally votes only in committees.

Since 1954 there have been five attempts to give the islands increased control over local affairs. Each time, a popular referendum has rejected the changes, mainly because Virgin Islanders believe greater autonomy would bring higher taxation. At an October 1993 referendum, 80 percent voted to keep the island's present status.

Sugar from Saint Croix remained the main export, and the Virgins saw little economic development until the rise of mass tourism after World War II. Tourism began to boom during the 1950s as jet airplanes made the islands an inexpensive destination for increasingly affluent Americans. Many tourists were also attracted by Saint Thomas's status as a free port. The United States did not impose American tariffs, and foreign products were sold there at bargain prices. In 1995, more than 2 million tourists and cruise ship travelers visited the islands—compared with fewer than 50,000 visitors yearly in the early 1950s.

The Virgin Islands, once among the poorest islands, are now among the wealthiest. Thanks to tourism, per capita income rose dramatically—from about $400 a

Concordia campground on Saint John, United States Virgin Islands. To protect the foliage, "tent cottages" are connected by a raised boardwalk.

year in 1950 to almost $9,000 in 1987. Prosperity brought about an equally sharp increase in population. The inflow has included workers from neighboring Caribbean countries as well as wealthy white settlers from the U.S. mainland, attracted by the climate and low taxes. At the 1990 census, about a third of the population had moved in from other Caribbean islands, while 13 percent came from the mainland United States.

After Hurricane Hugo struck the islands in September 1989, the U.S. government spent almost $600 million on recovery measures. Widespread looting broke out on Saint Croix following the storm, until 1,200 U.S. troops arrived to restore order. Hurricane Marilyn in September 1995 and Hurricane Bertha in July 1996 also caused severe damage, particularly on Saint Thomas.

Much of the tourist industry is concentrated on Saint Thomas. The Virgin Islands government has copied Puerto Rico in using tax incentives to encourage manufacturing on Saint Croix. One of the world's largest refineries processes imported oil there, and smaller factories make clocks, textiles, rum, and pharmaceutical products. In 1995, the Alcoa company acquired and restored to operation an aluminum processing plant that had been closed in 1985. In contrast, Saint John is almost entirely a park and has only one small village. The Virgin Islands National Park, originally established in 1956 through gifts from Laurance Rockefeller, now includes almost 80 percent of the island.

PROBLEMS OF ECONOMIC DEVELOPMENT IN THE EUROPEAN COLONIES

The European colonies generally faced hard times between the two world wars, and the Great Depression of the 1930s was unusually severe on many islands. Sugar plantations no longer flourished on many islands, and alternative sources of livelihood were slow to develop. Island governments tried to build up industries producing consumer products for local consumption, but most continued to import even everyday products from Europe and the United States.

On some islands, the oil industry provided employment. In Trinidad, oil production began in 1911. Trinidad also profited from its remarkable pitch lake, which provided asphalt for roads throughout the world. Oil also benefited other islands that became home to large refineries. In 1916, a subsidiary of the Royal Dutch/Shell Group built an enormous refinery on Curaçao that processed oil from Venezuela and later from Colombia. Standard Oil of New Jersey (Exxon) built a second large refinery on Aruba in 1929.

The worldwide economic depression of the 1930s was especially hard on the fragile island economies. Because of the oil industry, the Dutch colonies of Aruba and Curaçao were spared the worst effects of the depression. In the French colonies, the government both protected the markets for island products and provided some of the social welfare programs offered in France. Moreover, political participation headed off discontent. Every adult male could vote for representatives to the National Assembly in Paris as well as for mayors and other local officials. There were fewer large disturbances than in the British colonies, and the Caribbean territories remained loyal to France when it was occupied during World War II.

THE NETHERLANDS ANTILLES

The six islands in the Netherlands Antilles enjoyed varying economic fortunes during the first half of the 20th century. Bonaire and the three Leeward Islands of Sint Maarten, Sint Eustatius ("Statia"), and Saba underwent little economic development. Many of their inhabitants migrated to other islands, and they now have less than 5 percent of the population of the entire group. In contrast, their large oil refineries gave Curaçao and Aruba one of the highest standards of living in the Caribbean and indirectly provided income and social services for the four smaller islands.

🖾 THE ENGLISH- AND SPANISH-SPEAKING NETHERLANDS ANTILLES

Because of their poor soils and inadequate water supplies, sugar plantations did not flourish on the six islands of the Netherlands Antilles. The Dutch West India Company initially occupied the islands as bases for piracy; they later became posts for trading and smuggling with Latin America. Few Dutch setters arrived in the Caribbean.

On islands colonized by Spain, France, and Great Britain, the residents still speak creole versions of their former rulers' language. In the Netherlands Antilles, Dutch is used solely for administrative purposes. The inhabitants of Sint Maarten, Saba, and Sint Eustatius mainly speak English. On Aruba, Bonaire, and Curaçao, the dominant language is Papiamento—a mixture of Dutch, Spanish, English, Arawak, and several West African dialects. Because of their proximity to Venezuela on the mainland, Spanish also is widely spoken on these islands.

Following World War II, the Netherlands Antilles was granted universal adult suffrage (in 1948) and internal self-government (in 1950). After considerable discussion, the Dutch government and its American colonies adopted an unusual constitutional experiment, the Statute of the Realm, which became effective in December 1954. Under the Statute, the Dutch monarch reigned over a composite kingdom made up (in 1954) of the three kingdoms of the Netherlands, Suriname, and the Netherlands Antilles.[8]

The statute grants the Dutch islands considerable autonomy. The Realm has jurisdiction over defense, foreign affairs, the shared citizenship, and certain other specific matters. All other governmental powers are reserved to the former colonies. Even in foreign affairs, the Netherlands Antilles can join international bodies, and the Realm may not make or break treaties affecting its Caribbean members without their consent.

In practice, however, the islands are not totally autonomous. Under the statute, the Netherlands is obligated to preserve order and stability in each territory. In 1969, Dutch marines were sent to Curaçao, where high unemployment had helped to pro-

Royal Dutch/Shell Refineries light up the sky, Curaçao. Built from 1916 to process Venezuelan oil, these refineries remained profitable until the late 1970s, giving Curaçao one of the highest standards of living in the Caribbean.

voke serious riots. To prevent social unrest, the Netherlands underwrites a generous level of government services. Aruba, Curaçao, and Sint Maarten need help in funding major projects. Bonaire, Sint Eustatius, and Saba cannot support their inhabitants. In 1995, the Dutch government granted the islands (with about 175,000 residents) almost $150 million in assistance. In addition, no payments were made on more than $500 million in debt owed to the Netherlands. In return for aid, island administrations permit Dutch supervision of their expenditures.

Dutch governors ruled from Curaçao for centuries and dispatched natives of Curaçao to administer the smaller territories. Leaders on the other islands remain convinced that Curaçao treats them unfairly and takes too much of their money. In order to retain economic assistance and the right to migrate to Europe, islanders vigorously oppose independence from the Netherlands. But they would prefer to deal directly with the colonial power rather than operate through the Antilles federation. For its part, the Dutch government knows that six separate island administrations would cost it even more than the current anomalous situation. The Netherlands maintains that any island leaving the federation must become an independent nation.

In January 1986, when Aruba was permitted to secede from the Antilles federation, Dutch officials thus demanded that the island accept independence 10 years later. Eventually, however, they bowed to Aruban public opinion. In March 1994, it was agreed that its status as a sole constituent of the Realm could be continued indefinitely. (Suriname had gained independence in 1976. Hence, since 1986, the Netherlands, Aruba, and the "Antilles of the Five" have been the three constituent members of the Realm.)

The Statute of the Realm created an elected federal assembly of 22 members. Each island also has an elected assembly to handle local affairs. When Aruba left the federation, a new parliament was organized for the Antilles of the Five. Curaçao has 14 seats, and Bonaire and Sint Maarten each has three, with one each for Sint Eustatius and Saba.

While islanders continue to grouse about the existing political structure, there is little support for radical change. Following Aruba's secession in 1986, its government had to make large cuts in spending. At plebiscites in 1993 and 1994, citizens on the other five islands apparently placed economic security above other considerations. By large margins—ranging from 60 percent on Sint Maarten to 91 percent on Statia—voters supported continued membership in the existing Netherlands Antilles federation.

Each island has its own political parties and leaders, who join together to form coalitions in the federal parliament. There are no ideological differences between the many parties that have presented candidates for office. Elections are decided by "machine" politics based on patronage. The island governments provide generous welfare benefits and free medical care. In addition, government is the largest source of jobs. The local and federal administrations have numerous employees on each island, and they also own or are involved in many business enterprises. On Bonaire, for example, nine out of 10 voters work for the government in one way or another.

In dividing up the spoils—government jobs, schools, health clinics, even public telephones—politicians attempt to give something to every sector of the island they represent. Because of the islands' small populations, political alliances are based on contact and are intensely personal. Leaders who are perceived as meeting client needs may retain power for long periods of time. Dr. Claude Wathey (1926–   ) was Sint Maarten's political boss, for example, for more than 35 years.

Oil Refineries, Tourism, and Offshore Banking

All six Dutch islands must acquire foreign currency to purchase imported food and goods. Aruba and Curaçao traditionally have depended on the oil industry, tourism, and offshore banking. With more than 1 million day-trip and overnight visitors each year, tourism has been the main source of income on Sint Maarten. Bonaire, Sint Eustatius, and Saba attract smaller numbers of annual visitors—fewer than 50,000 each in the 1990s—who mainly come to enjoy water sports, especially scuba diving. Particularly on Aruba and Sint Maarten, drug trafficking and money laundering were other sources of revenue during the 1990s.

Their long dependence on the oil industry brought difficult times to Aruba and Curaçao during the 1980s, as changing economic conditions threatened the refineries on both islands. When Exxon closed its plant in March 1985, Aruba suddenly lost more than half its income. The plant partially reopened in late 1990 with a smaller production. Curaçao never entirely lost its Shell refinery. The Antilles government purchased the refinery and leased it to the Venezuelan state oil company until 1994; the lease subsequently was renewed for another 20 years. However, both production and employment fell from earlier levels.

Tourism rescued Aruba after the Exxon refinery's closing. Aruba's government guaranteed debts incurred in hotel building. From only 2,300 in 1986, the number of rooms soared to more than 10,000 in 1994. Aruba's government also created a new national airline and aggressively marketed the island's beaches, reefs, and free-wheeling

Undersea scuba diving on the lush reefs just offshore provides the main attraction for tourists to Bonaire, Netherlands Antilles.

casinos. In addition to 260,000 cruise ship passengers, more than 600,000 tourists stayed overnight in 1995—compared with only 181,000 in 1986.

Curaçao experienced greater difficulties in adapting to altered economic fortunes from the mid-1980s. The government lured manufacturing by creating tax-free zones, but wages were unusually high, a heritage of the oil-refining era. Unable to offer sand beaches, the island promoted tax-free retail stores in Willemstad. In addition to 200,000 cruise passengers, 250,000 visitors stayed overnight in 1995, many from nearby Venezuela.

The governments of Curaçao and Aruba have encouraged "offshore" banking to supplement tourism revenues. Curaçao was an early offshore center thanks to a 1963 tax treaty with the United States. Funds deposited in Curaçao banks not only escaped local taxes; they also could be withdrawn and spent in the United States without paying American taxes. The financial industry stagnated after the United States abrogated this tax treaty in 1988. It recovered somewhat at the end of the 1990s with an emphasis on private companies operating in tax-free zones.

When it gained independence in 1986, Aruba developed offshore facilities and regulations aimed particularly at the Latin American market. During the 1990s, the island's financial institutions benefited from an inflow of drug money. Smuggled in from Colombia and Venezuela—only 20 miles away—cocaine and heroin were repackaged and shipped out again to Puerto Rico, the U.S. Virgin Islands, the Netherlands, and Italy. The profits from drug transactions were "laundered" through the island's banks, casinos, hotels, and tax-free import-export zone. In November 1996, the U.S. government listed Aruba among the chief drug transit countries. From 1993 through 1996, the island's 83,000 inhabitants reported legal transfers of $1.4 billion to the U.S. Overall, the profits from laundering drug money were said to exceed those from tourism.

The Mikvé Israel–Emanuel synagogue in Curaçao, the oldest synagogue in continuous use in the Western Hemisphere. Built in 1732, the interior preserves furnishings in the Dutch manner, with silver and brass ornaments and richly carved mahogany woodwork.

Sint Maarten pinned all its hopes on tourism. Determined local leadership working with foreign investors (mainly from the U.S.) transformed the island. The traditional formula of sun, sand, gambling, and duty-free shopping paid off handsomely. The first hotel for tourists opened in 1955 with 20 rooms. In addition to 700,000 cruise ship passengers, more than 600,000 tourists stayed overnight on Dutch half of the island in 1994. Revenues temporarily plunged after Hurricanes Luis and Marilyn devastated Sint Maarten in September 1995, destroying more than 80 percent of the hotels and infrastructure.

In contrast to Aruba, Curaçao, and Bonaire, none of Sint Maarten's hotels were developed by the island's government. The island stopped soliciting operating subsidies from the federal government in 1984. Nevertheless, in July 1992, Dutch officials placed Sint Maarten under "higher supervision," limited the local administration's financial authority and arrested prominent politicians and businessmen. In 1994, several were convicted and imprisoned for chicanery during expansion projects, including Claude Wathey, the island's longtime political boss.

THE FRENCH ANTILLES

The inhabitants of Martinique and Guadeloupe voted for political union with France in 1945.[9] The following year, these former colonies became *départements* (administratve districts) of France—much as Hawaii is geographically separated from but politically incorporated into the United States. (For administrative purposes, the *département* of Guadeloupe includes the smaller islands of Saint Barthélemy and Saint-Martin.) Since the 1980s, islanders have regained some autonomy in local affairs. However, they remain totally dependent on France for economic survival.

Political parties in the islands have continued to debate the relationship with France. Prior to World War II, local white landowners dominated conservative groups, which generally endorsed maximum autonomy. Parties on the left, which had significant numbers of black and colored members, wanted to gain economic and political equality through union with France. Once the islands were integrated into France in 1946, this division of sentiments was exactly reversed. Since then, conservative parties generally support a continuation of the present situation. Only the relatively small socialist and communist parties have called for independence or increased local autonomy.

Guadeloupe and Martinique are each governed by a prefect (governor) sent from Paris. As in France, the prefect carries out the directives of the central government and controls local public services. Because of the distance from Paris, the prefect also controls the armed forces and can declare martial law. Local councils continued to be elected following union with France; initially, however, they simply advised the prefect. In 1960, following a riot in Martinique, the island council was granted a larger say over local laws and greater powers over public funds.

With the intention of decentralizing political authority throughout the whole of France, the government significantly modified the administrative system in 1982 and 1983. These reforms have given the island increased autonomy by taking authority from the prefects and transferring it to local councils and their leaders. Because of the way the reforms were applied overseas, voters on each island elect two separate councils. A General Council manages everyday matters on each island, while a Regional Council

The opera house's grand staircase is among the few remains of Saint-Pierre. Martinique's largest city was buried by a sudden volcanic eruption in 1902.

promotes economic growth. The regional councils also encourage the use of the Creole language in education and the media and fund local artistic and cultural groups.

These reforms eroded support for independence. Out of frustration, some pro-independence groups set off bombs in the islands as well as in Paris in the early and mid-1980s. However, most politically active islanders continue to support the existing constitutional status. They depend on French economic assistance, and they want to retain the right to migrate to Europe.

Following integration with France in 1946, agriculture became less important. High production costs make it difficult for the Antilles to compete on the international market. Some sugar still is produced (especially in Guadeloupe), and some land is devoted to bananas and pineapples (especially in Martinique). However, tourism and other service industries now are most important in the island economies. In addition to cruise ship arrivals, almost half a million visitors stayed overnight in Martinique in 1995, while 640,000 visited Guadeloupe. Eight out of 10 tourists came from France or its dependent territories.

The collapse of traditional agriculture has led to high and continuing unemployment. Since they are treated as integral parts of the French nation, the islands are provided with all the economic, educational, and welfare services available in France itself. Assistance from France contributed three-fourths of the income of the islands at the end of the 1990s. Only one-fourth came from the export of goods and services. More than one-half of all salaries and wages were paid out by the French government.

Thanks to French generosity, living standards are considerably higher than on many neighboring islands. Ambitious islanders readily move to France to better their circumstances. The 1990 census reported more than 100,000 emigrants from Guadeloupe and Martinique living in France. At the same time, thousands come to the islands each year—most illegally—from the impoverished neighboring islands of the eastern Caribbean.

THE BRITISH OVERSEAS TERRITORIES

The five British territories thrived in the 1980s and 1990s by encouraging tourism and offshore banking. The Cayman Islands and the British Virgin Islands have been particularly successful; the average income is higher there than in Great Britain. The economy grew somewhat more slowly on Anguilla and the Turks and Caicos Islands, which were plagued by scandals related to drug trafficking and money laundering. Despite its own financial scandals, Montserrat attracted significant numbers of tourists and foreign residents. However, beginning in 1995, repeated volcanic eruptions devastated Montserrat. The southern half of the island was abandoned, and most inhabitants sought refuge on other islands or in Great Britain.

The Cayman Islands and the Turks and Caicos

Like the Bahamas, the small and lightly inhabited Cayman Islands and the Turks and Caicos group have thrived by encouraging tourism and offshore banking. The three Cayman Islands are located just south of Cuba in the western Caribbean. The Turks and Caicos, a group of eight inhabited islands and some 40 small islets and cays, form the southeastern end of the Bahamas archipelago. Both groups are low-lying and arid, and their small populations lived, until recently, by fishing and (in the Turks) salt gathering. The British placed them under the governor of Jamaica during the 19th century, and both became separate Crown colonies when Jamaica became independent in 1962.

The 20,000 Caymanians enjoy one of the highest living standards in the Caribbean. Caymanian politics are stable, and islanders strongly favor continued ties to Britain. A British-appointed governor controls external affairs and defense. Local affairs are managed by a legislative council with a majority of elected members. There are no political parties, and candidates run as independents or as members of informal teams. In August 1991, the territory's first formal political organization since the 1960s was formed, the Progressive Democratic Party. Renamed the National Team, it won legislative elections in 1992 and 1996.

Tourism and offshore banking provide the main sources of income and employment in the Caymans. The three islands, which rise abruptly from the ocean floor, have a special appeal for scuba divers. Many hotels and condominiums have been built, especially on Grand Cayman. More than 1 million travelers visited the islands in 1995, including 682,000 on cruise ships.

Laws protecting the secrecy of bank accounts and other professional information were introduced in the late 1960s. By the late 1980s, Grand Cayman was second only to the Bahamas as an offshore financial center. At the end of 1994, 389 insurance companies and 561 banks (including 47 of the world's largest 50) were registered in the Caymans, where individuals and corporations pay no income, property, or inheritance taxes. A stock exchange began operations in July 1997.

Immigrant labor and illegal drugs provided the main political issues. More than three-fourths of all thefts and burglaries during the 1990s were attributed to the drug trade. A mutual assistance treaty with the United States came into effect in 1990. This allows U.S. law enforcement agencies to inspect bank records when there is evidence funds were gained through drug trafficking or other serious criminal activity.

The Turks and Caicos (current population about 13,000) were accorded their own resident governor in 1972. Since the first elections in 1976, the People's Democratic Movement and the Progressive National Party have alternated in power. Both have sought, with some success, to emulate the Caymans as a diving, tourist, and banking center. The production of salt through evaporation, the islands' traditional economic activity, ceased in 1964. However, the islands continued to export spiny lobsters and conch.

In May 1985, officials in Miami arrested the chief miniser, Norman Saunders (1943–   ), and two other members of the Legislative Council. U.S. courts convicted them of conspiring to protect drug shipments passing through the islands. Saunders, who received an eight-year sentence, resigned from office and was replaced by Nathaniel Francis (1912–   ).

A commission of inquiry was appointed after fire destroyed a government building. In July 1986, the commission reported that Francis and two other ministers were unfit for office. All three subsequently resigned, and constitutional amendments increased the governor's powers.

The PDM won a majority at the 1995 elections. (Saunders, now out of jail, was elected as an independent.) Derek Taylor became chief minister and soon was at odds with Governor Martin Bourke. Taylor was especially outraged when Bourke, interviewed by a financial magazine, portrayed the islands as pervaded by drug-related crime and corruption. The members of Legislative Council petitioned for Bourke's removal. However, the British government rejected their demand, stationed a frigate in the island's waters, and prepared to send in 100 police officers if riots broke out.

The Virgin Islands, Anguilla, and Montserrat

These three Leeward Islands are among the oldest British colonies.[10] Despite all efforts, however, they did not flourish as plantation islands. Montserrat is mountainous with little level land. Anguilla and the Virgins are too arid to support extensive cultivation. Sugar production ended on the Virgins and Anguilla in the 1830s and it died out on Montserrat by the 1920s. As the economy declined, most of the white planters moved out, and the freed slaves made their living by fishing and growing food crops. During recent years, the three islands have become increasingly dependent on tourism. The British Virgins are especially popular with sailors, while Anguilla emphasizes scuba diving. Until 1995, Montserrat's lush beauty and tranquility attracted a growing number of tourists, and the island also became a retirement haven for several hundred Europeans and Americans.

The three islands lost their local legislatures during the 19th century and were merged into the Leeward Islands Federation until it was dissolved in 1956. All subsequently have become individual dependent territories. The Virgin Islands chose not to join the 1958 West Indies Federation, and Montserrat reverted to Crown colony status when the Federation collapsed in 1962. Anguilla seceded from Saint Kitts and Nevis in 1969 and received its own constitution in 1982.

Workers harvesting sugarcane, Saint Kitts. Cane estates survived into the 1980s thanks to centralized milling. Since 1910, the entire cane harvest has been processed by only one sugar factory, linked to each estate by a road and narrow-gauge railway circling the island.

Local laws, taxes, and economic development are the responsibility of the Legislative Council, whose elected members choose the chief minister. Citizens on the three islands favor continued affiliation with Great Britain. Each has a stable political system with competing political parties. The major parties support similar polices to achieve economic growth, and their leaders' personalities are the main factor deciding elections.

The British Virgin Islands enjoys the highest per capita income in the Caribbean. With prosperity has come a significant increase in population, from 11,000 in 1980 to about 19,000 in 1995. A significant number of white immigrants has joined the resident population, while many of the original inhabitants work away from home, especially in the U.S. Virgin Islands.

The British Virgin Islands were among the first to develop a major tourist industry. By the mid-1970s, 70,000 tourists visited the islands each year. Their number soared to more than 250,000 a year by the mid-1990s, with the industry contributing over half of national income and providing the majority of all employment. The islands are the largest center for boat chartering in the Caribbean; some two-thirds of all visitors stay aboard yachts.

The financial services and insurance industries have flourished since the passage of favorable laws in 1984. Growth has been phenomenal, partly because of scandals in the Bahamas, political disturbances in Panama, and uncertainty over Hong Kong's future under Chinese rule. Compared with only 12,000 six years earlier, 170,000 companies were registered in the British Virgins by 1995. The government has made efforts to limit the laundering of illegal profits from criminal acts and drug trafficking.

The Virgin Islands enjoy a relatively stable two-party political system. Most citizens prefer continued affiliation with Britain, and both parties have followed a fiscally conservative course in building up the nation's economy. Under the leadership of Lavity Stoutt (1929–1995), a building contractor, the Virgin Islands Party usually won the largest number of seats in the Legislative Council. The islands' first chief minister from

Sailing yachts anchored near Jost Van Dyke in the British Virgin Islands

1967 to 1971, Stoutt was reelected for a 1979–83 term and again served from 1986 to his death in 1995. (Ralph T. O'Neal was appointed chief minister, May 15, 1995.)

Anguilla has tried to follow the path to economic prosperity blazed by the Bahamas, the Cayman Islands, and the British Virgins. Trading on its perceived stability as a British possession, Anguilla has sought to attract tourists and offshore banks. The territory's main political leaders have had no real policy differences. All have supported continuing affiliation with Britain, and all have frequently expressed dissatisfaction with the British government's level of investment in development projects.

In 1978, only 5,000 visitors, many travelling on business, arrived on Anguilla. Including day trips from neighboring Sint Maarten/Saint Martin, more than 107,000 persons visited in 1995. Tourism had become the primary industry, and Anguilla's government imposed height and size regulations on resorts to preserve its sandy beaches and coral reefs.

Bank secrecy laws lured 45 offshore banks to Anguilla by the end of the 1980s. In 1990, however, following an investigation of the industry, the government withdrew the licenses of 30 banks and imposed more stringent financial regulations. Hoping to discourage money laundering by drug traffickers, several police organizations conducted an international sting operation that included the creation of a fake bank on Anguilla. The operation led to the seizure of $40 million and the arrest of more than 90 persons in 1994.

Even before volcanic eruptions began in 1995, barely one-fifth of Montserrat's total area was suitable for crops and pasture. Soils were poor, and scant rainfall and periodic droughts frequently limited yields. To make the island more attractive to visitors, Great Britain funded improvements in roads and other infrastructure during the 1980s. Despite the lack of a modern harbor and airport, Montserrat succeeded in attracting tourists and foreign residents. From 1985 through 1994, the economy grew

Salt pond near Sandy Ground, Anguilla. Before the development of mass tourism, salt was among the few sources of income on flat, arid islands such as Anguilla and the Turks and Caicos.

more than 10 percent a year on average. Per capita income reached almost $5,000 a year by 1994, higher than many other islands in the region.

The installation of modern telecommunications enabled Montserrat to become a center for data processing and financial services. By the end of the 1980s, Montserrat had licensed more than 300 branches of foreign or "offshore" banks. Beginning in early 1989, the British police investigated charges that some of these banks laundered illegal funds from a variety of criminal activities. Most banking licenses were revoked, and British officials took responsibility for bank regulation away from the Montserrat government. In December 1991, Montserrat agreed to impose stricter controls. However, more than 90 percent of the island's 343 banks were closed down in 1992 following further investigations by British inspectors.

Hurricane Hugo devastated the island in September 1989. With British assistance, an extensive recovery program restored much of the island's housing and infrastructure. But, in July 1995, after lying dormant for more than a century, Chances Peak volcano suddenly erupted. Life on Montserrat came to a sudden halt as two–thirds of the island was abandoned to fiery lava and volcanic ash.

The volcano is located in the Soufrière Hills at the southern end of the pear-shaped island. Geologists at first believed that the island's northern third was unlikely to be affected. Thus, the government temporarily evacuated the population to the north following further eruptions in August and December 1995. Some 5,000 persons were housed in churches and schools as well as in tents provided by the British army. Evacuation became permanent in April 1996, when the capital city of Plymouth and the entire south of the island were abandoned.

The volcano erupted once more in June 1997, killing 19 persons who had disregarded the evacuation order. In August, British officials offered to assist islanders that moved either to Britain or to other Caribbean islands. By the end of 1997, all but about 3,200 of Montserrat's 11,000 residents had left. Most of those remaining on the island lived in temporary shelters and existed on government food vouchers. The British government promised to pay for new housing for those choosing to remain, but these plans were put on hold while the volcano remained active.

CHAPTER 19

THE BRITISH COLONIES GAIN INDEPENDENCE

Following victory in the Napoleonic wars, the British Empire included the Bahamas, Jamaica, and most islands in the Leewards and Windwards, from the Virgin Islands in the north down to Trinidad and Tobago in the south. The British people and politicians were proud to be imperialists, and public opinion remained in favor of keeping Britain's oldest possessions, going back to 1625. But by the 19th century the Caribbean islands no longer were profitable possessions compared with newer colonies in Asia and Africa. Dukes and earls went to India, while ordinary civil servants took their place in the Caribbean. British companies also found more lucrative and glamorous investments in the East. Britain's Caribbean colonies tended to stagnate. Although legally free, the black majority was poor, uneducated, and alienated from the political system.

Conditions deteriorated even further following World War I. Sugar producers found it difficult to compete with American companies that had invested in modern plantations and refineries in Cuba, Puerto Rico, and the Dominican Republic. Because they depended on one or two major export products, the islands were hard hit by the worldwide depression of the 1930s. Prices and sales plummeted, government revenues dropped with the fall in income from export duties, and many colonies had to suspend the public works programs that previously had given employment to part-time laborers. At the same time, several countries in the region forcibly expelled foreign laborers and closed their doors to further immigration. Unemployment, hunger, and desperation contributed to strikes, demonstrations, and violent riots on many islands during the 1930s.

Island leaders believed that economic problems were exacerbated by the absence of self-government. Color prejudice unquestionably played a role in the denial of political rights. But the British refused to share power even with the white population, who had enjoyed local autonomy prior to the 1860s. From the 1920s, those of both races meeting strict property qualifications could vote for some members of the governor's advisory councils. But these "unofficial" members were expected to support the laws sought by the governor. Not until the late 1940s and early 1950s were universal suffrage and greater autonomy granted to the British islands.

From the 1890s, professionals and planters formed associations to protect their economic interests and lobby the colonial government. But it was the disturbances and riots of the 1930s that gave rise to the first strong labor movements among workers and farm laborers. On some islands, most of the population joined unions that led successful strikes, provided economic help, and developed into political parties. The leaders of these unions dominated their islands' politics for several decades.

After World War II, as the British were expelled or withdrew from Asia and Africa, the Caribbean colonies became an anachronism. However, British officials considered it impossible for "the present separate communities, small and isolated as most of them are, to achieve full self-government on their own."[1] Although London governments never made their intentions clear, they probably would have preferred an arrangement something like that in the Netherlands Antilles—one federated state in some sort of loose association with the United Kingdom.

The West Indies Federation, with a relatively weak central government, did come into existence in 1958. It lasted barely three years. Most inhabitants have too intense a loyalty to their own island, and only a small group of intellectuals expressed enthusiasm for federal government. Moreover, by the time the federation finally arrived, the British government no longer felt compelled to force union on its Caribbean possessions. Granted increased powers of self-government, the individual territories had demonstrated their ability to rule themselves. In addition, several islands, notably Jamaica and Trinidad, had experienced several years of economic growth.

In 1962, irreconcilable differences between Jamaica and Trinidad broke up the federation, and both these islands became independent. Once it began, the process of breakup accelerated, and attempts to create smaller federations also failed. In 1966, Barbados received independence. The smaller islands were grated the status of associated statehood, giving them internal self-government but leaving matters of defense and foreign relations to Britain.

During the 1970s, London officials decided to desert the region. They granted independence to any government that asked for it, without requiring a referendum or other evidence of popular support. A general strike and violent disturbances showed that many Grenadians opposed Eric Gairy (1922–97) and his government. Nevertheless, Grenada was granted independence in 1974. Antigua similarly received independence in 1981, even though the government of V. C. Bird (1909–   ) used the army to crush opponents. By the mid-1980s, Britain's Caribbean empire was reduced to five tiny dependencies sustaining fewer than 65,000 people—Montserrat, Anguilla, the British Virgin Islands, the Cayman Islands, and the Turks and Caicos. British officials hoped that these territories also would depart, but they were forced to continue the colonial administration because island leaders stubbornly refused to become independent.

CROWN COLONY GOVERNMENT

Beginning with Jamaica in 1866, the British government had suppressed island legislatures. Except in Barbados and the Bahamas, it ruled its West Indian possessions directly from London. Under this system of Crown colony government, the British Parliament passed laws regulating their constitutions and overall legal structure. The governor and other chief officials appointed by the Colonial Office formed an Executive Council in charge of governmental operations. A Legislative Council—with from nine to 22 members—advised the governor and made local laws and regulations. It generally contained an equal number of officials and "unofficial" members named by the governor from among the colony's most prominent men. Until the 1920s, all the British colonies, except Jamaica and Barbados, had wholly appointed legislatures. Elected town councils or public health boards did survive in most colonies, but these had only those powers granted them by the governor and the appointed legislative council.

The legislature in a Crown colony government did not represent the island's inhabitants. Officials were named by and responsible to the Crown and not to the island legislature. The governor controlled the vote of official members. Moreover, the British government expected even the appointed members "to give a general and effective support to the Governor's measures in the Legislature" and might force them to resign if they failed to do so. Finally, the governors always retained certain "reserve powers" that gave them the final say over the police, the law courts, and appointment of senior officials.

The First Steps toward Self-Government

In the absence of elected local officials and political parties, individuals formed associations based on specific economic interests. Between 1880 and 1920, many commercial and professional organizations sprang up. Some represented middle-class professionals such as teachers, lawyers, and retailers. Others helped producers of primary agricultural products—bananas, cocoa, cotton, rice, coconut, arrowroot, and citrus products—negotiate with the large corporations buying their products.

Less affluent black workers also began to form labor unions during the 1890s, some derived from the mutual aid and benevolent societies of the slavery era. But these found it difficult to organize seasonal plantation workers or the many laborers emigrating for a time to other parts of the region. And laws restricting picketing and permitting suits for damages or losses caused by strikes also weakened unions.

While these local self-help organizations often tried to influence the government in their own interest, other groups directly attacked the Crown colony system itself. Popular resentment against Crown colony government increased after 1900, both on

Jamaica and Trinidad and on the smaller islands. Its first critics included white and colored professionals—lawyers, merchants, doctors, journalists, and civil servants—in the larger towns. All had attended secondary schools, and some had gone to British universities. They considered themselves more qualified to lead local government than transient British officials.

The self-government movement became more vocal during the 1920s, often led by men who had served in the British West India Regiment during World War I. One of its most distinguished early leaders was T. Albert Marryshow (1887–1958) of Grenada. Strongly critical of Crown colony rule and an advocate of federation, he gathered a group of middle-class colored Grenadians who formed the Representative Government Association in 1914. Professional men founded similar associations on most of the smaller islands. All demanded the election of at least some members of the colonial legislative councils and a role in local government for the elected members. Some also supported a political federation of the West Indies colonies.

Labor unions also gained members and won increased recognition during the 1920s and 1930s. New unions emerged throughout the Caribbean in response to collapsing sugar prices and economic depression. In the British colonies, they had the support of the British Labour Party, and especially its Fabian or socialist wing. British labor unions helped to create West Indian affiliates, and they encouraged the island unions to adopt relatively moderate policies. In this way, the Fabians hoped to prevent Russian-dominated communists from taking control, as they had in Cuba and some other parts of the British Empire.

On the British islands, middle-class professionals and rural laborers could work together because Crown-colony government provided them with a common foe. As a result of these increasingly vocal protests, a commission headed by the colonial undersecretary, E. F. L. Wood (later Lord Halifax), visited most of the islands as well as British Guiana from December 1921 to February 1922. Following Wood's cautious recommendations, elected members were added to the legislative councils. In all cases, voters had to meet high property qualifications. In 1939, the small number of islanders entitled to vote ranged from only 2 percent in Saint Lucia to 7 percent in Trinidad.

On Trinidad, Arthur Cipriani (1875–1945) took advantage of these modest reforms to forge the first successful alliance between a political organization and a mass union. Cipriani, a member of a creole family of Corsican descent, rose to the rank of captain in the BWI Regiment during World War I. He joined the Trinidad Workingmen's Association (TWA) in 1919 and became its president in 1923. Cipriani was an outstanding orator with great personal magnetism. Under his leadership, the TWA rapidly increased its membership, and it actively sought to recruit Indian as well as black workers.

Captain Cipriani won a seat on the Legislative Council in the elections of 1925—the first since the British occupied Trinidad in 1797. He was reelected until his death in 1945 and also won election to the Port of Spain city council. Cipriani formed a one-man opposition to the government. One of the first West Indian leaders to consider himself a socialist, Cipriani forged close links to the British Labour Party. The avowed "champion of the barefoot man," he campaigned—without immediate success—for a minimum wage, workers' compensation, an eight-hour day, and the prohibition of child labor.

The Turbulent 1930s and the Moyne Report

Acute economic distress during the 1930s created bitter resentment, which eventually erupted into strikes and violence throughout the British Caribbean. New leaders emerged who organized effective unions and mass parties, which demanded first self-government and then independence. The political alliances created during these years endured for more than 40 years, until the 1970s. Throughout the British Caribbean, labor unions and political parties became fused or merged under one strong leader—usually a persuasive orator with a magnetic and charismatic personality. The leaders of these unions became dominant political figures, often serving as the first heads of government when their islands gained independence.

Since most islands depended on one or two major export crops, the Great Depression was unusually severe. By 1933, prices for the islands' principal exports had been almost halved. Wages fell, taxes rose, and unemployment increased. Funds from laborers employed in other countries also fell drastically. The United States restricted immigration; Cuba, the Dominican Republic, and the Central American states rounded up and deported laborers from the British colonies. Many workers lacked adequate food, housing, and medical care, and the islands provided only limited welfare programs.

Demonstrations, strikes, and riots were frequent throughout the British Caribbean between 1935 and 1938. In 1933, the oilfield workers in Trinidad organized a hunger march to publicize their difficulties, and there were strikes and riots in the island's sugar belt in 1934. The following year saw violent demonstrations among sugar workers on Saint Kitts and Saint Vincent. The governors of these islands restored order with the help of British warships, and 1935 generally was quiet. But

Interisland launch leaving Nevis. While tourists travel on luxurious cruise ships or crowded jet planes, small motor vessels provide inexpensive if slow transportation between the islands for both freight and passengers.

new and more violent outbursts occurred in the larger colonies of Trinidad, Barbados, and Jamaica in 1937 and 1938.

On Trinidad, Cipriani had refused to support strikes and marches because he preferred legal methods. Tubal ("Buzz") Uriah Butler (1897–1977), a Grenadian laborer, emerged as the new leader of the predominantly black oilfield workers. Butler's racially based party won wide support because of his strong personality and his forceful way of speaking at meetings that resembled religious crusades. Butler was firmly convinced that God was on his side. As "God's Appointed" and "Chief Servant of the Lord," he saw himself as a new Moses sent to lead the suffering black workers from the "wilderness of colonialism."

In June 1937, Butler called a general strike of oil workers that was joined by the cane workers and laborers in Port of Spain. An attempt to arrest Butler triggered widespread riots in which two policemen and 12 civilians were killed. In July, Clement Payne, one of Butler's associates, tried to take his crusade to Barbados. Payne called on black Bridgetown laborers to unite and force employers to raise wages. When the police attempted to deport Payne, a mob looted Bridgetown, and rioting occurred in the countryside. At least 13 persons were killed, 47 wounded, and more than 500 imprisoned. In 1938, violence spread to Jamaica. A series of strikes and riots among sugar workers and Kingston laborers claimed 46 lives.

Other islands also suffered violence and political oppression during the Great Depression. Rafael Trujillo imposed a police state on the Dominican Republic, while a civil war ended Gerardo Machado's attempt to establish one-man rule in Cuba. Nevertheless, violence in its West Indian colonies alarmed the British government, which sent a series of commissions to inquire into their causes. The most influential, chaired by Lord Moyne, was dominated by Fabian socialists, including the secretary of the British Trades Union Congress. The Moyne Report placed much of the blame for the disturbances on the Crown colony form of government. It called for stronger labor unions, more elected members of the Legislative Councils, and the eventual extension of the vote to all islanders.

Great Britain was already at war when the Moyne Commission issued its report in November 1939. The government temporarily put aside its recommendations for more self-government, but it did take steps to improve economic conditions and to strengthen labor unions. Britain in 1940 created a government office to fund public works and economic development projects in the islands. To qualify for grants, colonial governments had to recognize trade unions. They also were required to create labor departments and pass laws regulating working conditions and providing workers' compensation and unemployment insurance.

Governments, Unions, and Parties

Throughout the British colonies, the hardships and disturbances of the 1930s gave rise to strong labor unions headed by emotional and charismatic leaders. Earlier labor organizations often had organized only skilled workers in a specific craft. (Captain Cipriani's broad-based TWA was an exception.) The new movements were island-wide and sought to enroll both skilled and unskilled workers in a wide variety of occupations into one large, comprehensive union. Especially in the larger territories, they attracted support from lawyers, doctors, teachers, and journalists as well as from unskilled farm workers.

The leaders of these unions believed that they could obtain their goals only by taking control of the government. They accordingly formed mass-based political parties that sought autonomy from Britain. Although parties and unions legally may be separate bodies, they are closely integrated in practice. Most political parties depend on trade unions both to provide funds and to get out the vote. One leader heads the union and the party, and the same individuals hold high offices in both bodies, which thus share a common leadership. While this fusion of unions and parties is not unique, they are more closely integrated in the British West Indies than in most other regions. Many West Indian party leaders in fact come from middle-class backgrounds. But they rise to power through careers in the trade union movement rather than (as in the United States) as lawyers.

Most West Indian parties have used the word *labour* in their name and describe themselves as socialist. In fact, their policies have been relatively moderate, and private ownership of industry has survived on most islands. The close ties between unions and governments is understandable given the region's history. When the parties were formed, most industries were owned by foreign companies or by a small racial minority. As the majority of people were poor agricultural workers, every party had to claim to represent this group. Most West Indians are socially conservative, embrace their island's traditions, and oppose radical experiments. But any party that called itself "conservative" or that advocated "capitalism" would commit suicide.

No matter what their platforms said, Caribbean political parties united around a forceful leader rather than "issues" or cohesive political principles. And the personalities of leaders continue to be the most important factor deciding elections. There are few sharp differences between Caribbean parties. All initially were concerned with achieving independence, and all subsequently promised better education, more social welfare, and improved economic conditions.

Labour Parties in Jamaica, Barbados, and Trinidad

On the larger islands—Jamaica, Barbados, and Trinidad—the leaders of the unions and parties founded during the 1930s often were light-skinned members of the small élite educated in Britain. Most called themselves socialists or social democrats and tended to borrow the traditions and slogans of the British Labour Party. Their party platforms often favored governmental management of the economy, land reform, and the redistribution of incomes through high taxation and welfare payments. These socialist parties include the People's National Party in Jamaica, the Democratic Labour Party and the Barbados Labour Party in Barbados, and the People's National Movement in Trinidad and Tobago.

Jamaica In Jamaica, two strong parties were founded by distant cousins—Alexander Bustamante (1884–1977) and Norman Manley (1893–1969). Although they initially worked together before becoming political rivals, Bustamante and Manley had very different personalities. Bustamante, the son of an Irish planter father and a Jamaican mother, practiced several different trades in North, South, and Central America. He returned in 1934, using his sizable fortune to set up a real estate and money-lending business in Kingston. Where Bustamante had an unfailing gift for the common touch, Norman Manley was a cultivated, aloof lawyer who was most at ease with other middle-class professionals. Of Irish and black descent, he won a Rhodes Scholarship to Oxford and became a prominent lawyer who represented many of the island's largest corporations throughout his life.

Both men became deeply involved in the political unrest that erupted in 1937. A picturesque man of the people with a striking presence, Bustamante helped to organize a series of mass meetings on behalf of the strikers. His following increased when the British imprisoned him in 1938 for sedition and incitement to riot. Manley successfully defended Bustamante in court. On his release, he founded and became president for life of the Bustamante Industrial Trade Union (BITU), a general union of skilled and unskilled workers.

In September 1938, Manley and Bustamante cooperated in forming the People's National Party (PNP), which at first served as the political wing of the BITU. Under Manley's guidance, the PNP formally adopted a socialist platform in 1940, and it later joined the Socialist International. The PNP now favored large cooperative farms and called for the nationalization of major industries and utilities, state management of the economy, and increased welfare payments.

Jamaica gained a second mass party, the Jamaica Labour Party (JLP), in 1942. When he threatened a dock workers' strike in September 1940, the British had imprisoned Bustamante without trial for 17 months, further increasing his reputation as a martyr and hero. After he was freed, Bustamante split with Manley and the PNP. Accusing them of betraying his trust, he founded the Jamaica Labour Party to contest the elections of 1944, the first under universal adult suffrage. Finding himself without the necessary union support, Manley formed the Trade Union Congress and later turned it into one general union supporting his party.

Jamaica thus found itself with two union-based parties, each under one strong leader. Manley and Bustamante alternated in power for the next 30 years, and the parties they founded continue to dominate Jamaican politics. While both had broad appeal, Manley's PNP enjoyed its greatest strength among middle-class professionals and urban workers. Bustamante's JLP was strongest in rural areas and also had substantial backing from white businessmen.

The JLP gained the majority of seats in the lower house in the elections of 1944 and 1949, and Bustamante thus became Jamaica's first elected chief minister when the island was granted full internal autonomy in 1953. Bustamante won by attacking PNP leaders as communists and atheists. Socialism and the creation of cooperative farms did not appeal to small farmers owning their own land. In 1949, Norman Manley thus had to reassure the voters in his own district that the PNP planned to nationalize only the largest manufacturing industries.

Two successive electoral defeats convinced Manley to dilute the PNP's socialist rhetoric. In 1952 a PNP conference expelled as communists four prominent members who had controlled its Trade Union Congress. The PNP then formed the more conservative National Workers Union. The economic policies of the PNP and JLP became increasingly similar during the 1950s. Until 1974—when the party's radical tradition was revived (see page 330)—the PNP accepted private property and foreign investment. With these more moderate policies, Manley came to power in 1955 and remained in office until 1962.

Barbados Grantley Adams (1898–1971), who dominated the politics of Barbados from 1937 to 1961, combined Manley's parliamentary skills with some of Bustamante's personal charm. Adams, a colored lawyer who had won an island scholarship to Oxford, was an avowed socialist with close ties to the radical wing of the British Labour Party. He founded the Barbados Labour Party (1938) and the Barbados Workers' Union (1941), building up a wide mass following through his speeches and his powerful charismatic appeal.

In a development reminiscent of the earlier split between Bustamante and Manley, Barbados acquired a second labor party in 1955, when Errol Barrow (1920–1987) left Adams's BLP and founded the Democratic Labour Party (DLP). Like Adams, Barrow had studied law in London, and he became Adams's protégé in the early 1950s. Barrow now claimed that Adams had become too closely linked to the British governor and had lost contact with union members. His DLP gained popularity by winning benefits for Barbados's sugar workers while Adams was away from the island as the first (and only) prime minister of the West Indies Federation. The DLP won the elections of 1961 and 1966, and Barrow became the first leader of an independent Barbados in the latter year.

Trinidad and Tobago   Eric Williams (1911–1981), who headed the government of Trinidad and Tobago from 1956 to 1981, was the only West Indian leader to take power without the backing of a major labor union. His People's National Movement (PNM), established in 1956, succeeded only because the unions were themselves sharply divided. In contrast with other British islands, where one or two mass parties captured wide support, political loyalties on Trinidad are highly fragmented. When universal suffrage came in 1945, many small parties and organizations appealed to different and competing racial and economic interests.

The fragmentation of political parties reflects the deep divisions in Trinidad's society. Most islands are racially homogeneous, and the colored middle class joined the black majority in the struggle for self-government. Trinidad is a divided or segmented society in which a large number of groups think of themselves as separate and distinct. Before the island gained independence, the small white élite was divided between British officials and Roman Catholic creoles born on the island. The opinions and interests of the colored and black middle class—distinguished by education and white-collar jobs—often differed from those of black oilfield and farm workers. Blacks considered themselves totally distinct from the East Indian population (about 40 percent of the total), which was in turn divided between Muslims and Hindus. As Bridget Brereton concludes, "Class, colour, caste and race combined to create an immensely complex pattern of human relationships."[2]

During the 1920s and 1930s, Captain Arthur Cipriani's union actively sought to recruit East Indian members. However, Buzz Butler brought race back into Trinidadian politics by presenting himself as a black leader for black workers. The emergence of black nationalism increased race consciousness among all groups, and the nationalist movement in the Indian homeland also encouraged a sense of racial identity among East Indians. During the first elections under universal suffrage in 1946 and 1950, the labor vote fragmented. Blacks and East Indians clashed, and racial slurs became a common part of campaign rhetoric.

The election of September 1956 set the course of Trinidad and Tobago for the next 30 years. Few expected victory for the PNM, launched the preceding January by Williams. But the PNM took 39 percent of the vote and won 14 of the 24 seats on the Legislative Council. Under Williams's strong-willed leadership, the PNM brought Trinidad to independence in 1962 and retained power until 1986.

Williams was a skilled politician who made the PNM into an effective political

"An Indian family, Trinidad, B.W.I.," early 20th century. Almost 144,000 Indians came to Trinidad as indentured or contract laborers before 1917. About two-thirds chose to remain, forming separate and distinctive communities of farmers and small businessmen.

machine. He owed his initial success to his own personal magnetism, his speaking ability, and his deep identification with the needs of lower-class blacks. A dark-skinned creole, Williams had spent almost 10 years in Britain and the United States. Although his family was poor, he was a superb student and won an all-island scholarship to Oxford. There he earned both a first-class degree and a doctorate in history. He taught at Howard University and worked for the Anglo-American Caribbean Commission from 1948 to 1955.

Despite these successes, Williams always believed that he had been discriminated against because of his skin color. He developed a strong sense of West Indian nationalism, which emphasized the contribution of black workers. During 1955, Williams hammered home these views to crowds of thousands in Woodford Square—a public park in front of the colony's legislative building. His interpretation of Caribbean history aroused tremendous pride among his listeners—as well as adulation of Williams himself. Unlike other parties, the PNM claimed to be a multiracial organization. At this time, the PNM also welcomed investment by foreign companies. With the slogan "nationalism and democracy," it called for "a rally, a convention of all and for all, a mobilisation of all the forces in the community, cutting across race and religion, class and colour."

The Lesser Antilles

In the smaller and less-developed islands, unions and parties also were fused under one charismatic leader who took the island to independence and then ruled for several decades. Here, however, political leaders usually came from working-class backgrounds rather than from the British-educated élite. Self-made men who emerged through the labor movement, they had fewer ties to British and European socialism. Their party platforms instead stressed greater opportunities for small businesses as well as for farmers and rural laborers. These populist parties, which held power at least until the 1970s, include Saint Lucia's United Workers' Party, the Grenada United Labour Party, and the labor parties of Saint Kitts, Antigua, and Dominica.

On Saint Kitts, Robert Bradshaw (1916–1978), a worker in a sugar factory, became vice president of an organization representing black sugar workers in 1932. From 1940, he combined the presidency of an island-wide union with that of the Saint Kitts-Nevis–Anguilla Labour Party, which won every election from 1946 until 1980. A former Salvation Army captain, Vere Conwall Bird won the presidency of the Antigua Trade and Labor Union in 1943. The allied Antigua Labor Party has controlled the assembly almost continuously, and Bird became the first (and only) prime minister with the island's independence in 1983. On Dominica, Edward Oliver Leblanc (1923–   ), a small farmer, similarly lead the Dominica Labour Party from 1960 to 1974.

Eric Matthew Gairy of Grenada was the most controversial of the union leaders in the Lesser Antilles. An elementary school teacher and later a union organizer on Aruba, his union and Grenada United Labour Party (GULP) were especially popular among rural peasants. In 1951, Gairy forced the British governor to negotiate by calling a strike that turned into a violent insurrection. He lost the 1962 election to the Grenada National Party led by Herbert Blaize (1918–   ), who promised to unite with neighboring Trinidad and Tobago. When Prime Minister Williams of Trinidad totally rejected any union, Gairy returned to power in 1967. His corrupt and despotic government became unpopular, preparing the way for a marxist revolution in 1979 (see page 359).

THE COMING OF INDEPENDENCE

The Moyne Commission had agreed in its 1940 report that the ultimate goal of Britain's Caribbean colonies should be self-government based on universal suffrage. World War II increased pressure on the British and other European empires throughout the world. Beginning in 1947, Britain began to free its colonies in Asia, Africa, and the Middle East. Influential Britons began to think of their future as linked to Europe, and they increasingly viewed the poor West Indian possessions as a costly anachronism.

After World War II, successive British governments reaffirmed Britain's commitment to replacing Crown colony governments with self-government by elected officials. But self-government did not, in the British view, require immediate independence. Most British officials, of all political parties, believed that the island peoples still needed guidance by Europeans. They also were convinced that the smaller colonies were too poor to survive as viable states. Thus British officials wanted to unite the West Indian colonies in some sort of federation and tied independence to union.

The British government never drew up an overall plan for its West Indian colonies. Instead it tended to react to events in each colony, and the speed of progress toward self-government depended on the strength of local political leaders. British officials wanted to turn over political responsibility to men who enjoyed popular support but who also supported relatively moderate policies. For this reason, although the British colonies went through the same constitutional stages in gaining autonomy, the timing of independence varied greatly.

The Westminster Model

Most of the former British colonies have had several constitutions since the 1940s. However, all have adopted and continue to use the British system of government. Unlike the United States, all are unitary states in which legislative power is vested in an elected representative assembly. (Most also have a second or upper house, partly or wholly appointed, with only limited powers.) The assembly may delegate certain responsibilities to towns or local commissions, but these have no independent authority.

As in Great Britain, there is no separation between the executive and the legislative branches of government. West Indian constitutions usually provide for a figurehead governor-general (or for a president in the case of Trinidad) representing the queen. However, the real leader of the government is the prime minister (or premier), who is elected by the party gaining the most seats in the lower house of parliament. The prime minister forms a cabinet that includes the ministers or heads of various government ministries (departments). Each electoral district sends only one representative to the lower house. Victory goes to the man or woman receiving the most votes, even if the candidate does not receive a majority. As in Great Britain and the United States, this "winner take all" system makes it very difficult to establish a third party.

The legal and judicial systems also are based on British precedents, and island constitutions separate the courts from the legislature. Judges are appointed for set periods, and their decisions can be appealed to local or regional appellate courts. In some cases, appeals still can be carried to the Judicial committee of the Privy Council in Great Britain.

Under this system of parliamentary democracy, the British territories evolved from Crown colony government to self-rule in a series of steps or stages. The first stage involved the granting of universal adult suffrage. This allowed every adult man and woman to vote for members of the governor's Legislative Council—which ultimately became the lower house in the island parliament or assembly. The British introduced adult suffrage first in the larger islands of Jamaica (1944) and Trinidad (1946). New constitutions established adult suffrage in the smaller Leeward and Windward colonies between 1951 and 1953.

Britain took a second step toward self-government when it allowed members of the assembly to take part in the government. Usually they first were chosen to sit on the governor's Executive Council but without any major responsibilities. Then elected members were given charge of a governmental department or ministry. At some stage the Executive Council became a governing cabinet when the majority of ministers were members of the elected assembly. This step—ministerial governments responsible to Parliament—was taken in all the islands by 1956.

Full internal self-government came when the leader of the largest party took over from the governor as chairman of the cabinet and became the territory's chief minister. This stage was reached in Jamaica in 1953 and in Trinidad in 1959. A territory that achieved internal self-government—thus becoming an "associated state" in the British Commonwealth—was not fully independent. The British Colonial Office remained responsible for the colony's foreign policy and its defense forces.

The West Indies Federation, 1958–1962

By the late 1950s, all British territories had taken significant steps toward self-government. But they remained colonies in which British governors retained important powers. Before granting full independence, Britain first tried, between 1958 and 1961, to create a West Indies Federation. The British islands became sovereign states or received full internal self-government only after the federation failed.

For several centuries, the British Colonial Office had tried to unite several islands under one federal government. In this way, it hoped to increase governmental efficiency and thus cut expenditures. But the island assemblies—dominated by a few white planters—strongly resisted federation. Attempts to unite Barbados and the Windwards failed during both the 17th and the 19th centuries. The British created loose confederations for the Leewards (1871) and Windwards (1885), but these were generally unpopular and had few powers.

During the economic troubles of the 1930s, many island leaders accepted the British view that the Caribbean territories were too poor to survive without some form of union. Successive British governments favored federation, and it was approved again and again by the West Indian legislatures. Leaders of the parties linked to unions believed that a West Indian federation would speed up the transition from Crown colony government to self-rule. Political union also might help increase economic growth, and it would make it easier for West Indians to bargain with a foreign company operating on several islands.

The British government encouraged federation, but it did not force it upon its colonies. In 1947, it called a conference at Montego Bay, Jamaica, that included representatives of all its territories. The leaders of the labor parties strongly endorsed a federation, and almost all nongovernmental organizations also supported it. Several regional bodies, including the University of the West Indies, were added to those already in existence. A permanent committee was set up to plan the new federation, and several more regional meetings were held. On January 3, 1958, a West Indies Federation finally came into existence. It included 10 island territories—Jamaica, Trinidad and Tobago, Barbados, Grenada, Saint Kitts-Nevis–Anguilla, Antigua and Barbuda, Saint Lucia, Saint Vincent and the Grenadines, Dominica, and Montserrat. Only the northern territories of the Bahamas and the British Virgin Islands remained outside.

The federation's constitution did not provide full internal self-government. Executive power was vested in a British governor-general, who could veto bills and appointed the Council of State, the federal cabinet. A federal House of Representatives was elected by universal suffrage, and it in turn chose the federal prime minister. Both the national and island legislatures were empowered to make laws, with federal legislation prevailing in case of conflict.

The West Indies Federation began without agreement on three fundamental concerns—interisland immigration, federal taxation, and common import taxes. To bring the federation into existence, the territories had agreed that it could not make any laws for five years concerning these three issues. Its first prime minister, Sir Grantley Adams of Barbados, sought to keep the new nation alive for those five years while building up a sense of nationhood among the peoples of the 10 territories. Unfortunately, the leading politicians in both Jamaica (Prime Minister Norman Manley and Alexander Bustamante) and Trinidad (Eric Williams) did not take part in the 1958 federal elections, which thus aroused little popular interest.

A cricketer rests between innings. By the early 20th century, cricket was the favorite athletic contest among islanders of all races. Recognition of black and colored players on national teams during the 1940s and 1950s preceded and foreshadowed racial integration of island societies.

The federation might have succeeded had it been given time to gain popular support. It died after only three years because of major differences between Jamaica and Trinidad, its largest units. During the 1950s, both islands saw substantial economic growth thanks to bauxite mining on Jamaica and increased oil exports from Trinidad. Jamaica became the world's leading exporter of bauxite, the ore from which aluminum is derived. Trinidad and Tobago benefited from higher oil prices and increased exports, with oil production rising by one-third during the 1950s. Jamaica and especially Trinidad also had begun to develop significant manufacturing industries, helped in part by government efforts to lure foreign investment.

Because of their relative prosperity, the economic benefits of federation seemed less important to them. Many political leaders on both islands feared that their economies would be drained by the poorer islands of the eastern Caribbean. Trinidad's representatives vehemently opposed unlimited immigration from the smaller islands. Alexander Bustamante, at that time leader of the Jamaican opposition, would not accept a binding customs union. He charged that with free trade, Trinidadian factories would sell their products below cost to prevent the growth of manufacturing in Jamaica.

The West Indies Federation came to an early end when Jamaica withdrew in 1961. Bustamante's JLP, which originally had supported the federation, denounced it during the 1959 election campaign. Manley's PNP won, but membership remained an issue. Both Bustamante, now 76 years old, and Norman Manley, 10 years younger, were struggling to maintain control over their parties. In May 1960, Bustamante suddenly demanded a national plebiscite to determine whether the island would remain in the federation. The following day and without consulting his own party, Manley promptly accepted his cousin's challenge. In September 1961, by a small majority, Jamaicans voted to withdraw from the West Indies Federation. The British government accepted the result of the Jamaican plebiscite and introduced legislation granting Jamaica independence. Eric Williams, premier of Trinidad and Tobago, then announced that Jamaica's withdrawal made a strong and unified federation impossible. Britain dissolved the federation, and both Jamaica and Trinidad became fully independent members of the British Commonwealth in August 1962.

Grantley Adams tried hard to hold together a smaller federation of Barbados and the other colonies in the eastern Caribbean. But the smaller islands feared domination by Barbados, while Barbadians did not want to assume financial responsibility for their poorer neighbors. In November 1966, Barbados became independent, and Britain granted new constitutions to its remaining colonies. Most became associated states with internal self-rule and subsequently were granted full independence. The Bahamas broke away in 1973, and they were soon followed by Grenada (1974), Dominica (1978), and Saint Lucia (1979). By the mid-1980s, even the smaller islands of Saint Vincent (1979), Antigua (1982), and Saint Kitts-Nevis (1983) had gained full independence.

Britain retained only a few thinly populated colonies, whose inhabitants feared assimilation with their larger neighbors. In 1966, Montserrat again became a direct dependency of the British Crown—as did several groups of tiny islands that had never joined the original federation, including the British Virgin Islands, the Cayman Islands, and the Turks and Caicos. Each territory made a separate agreement, which usually granted some self-government through an elected assembly and appointments to the governor's council. The appointed governor kept responsibility for defense, foreign affairs, and internal security.

Anguilla's situation was somewhat more complicated. In 1967, when Saint Kitts-Nevis–Anguilla became an associated state with internal self-government, the Anguillans almost immediately evicted the Saint Kitts police force and began to rule themselves through a local council. In 1969, the British government sent army engineers and London policemen to the island, installed a British commissioner, and reluctantly accepted Anguilla's request for a return to colonial status. In 1982, a new constitution granted the island the status of an associated state with internal self-government.

CHAPTER 20

JAMAICA, TRINIDAD, BARBADOS, AND THE BAHAMAS SINCE INDEPENDENCE

Britain's 10 former colonies have retained its parliamentary style of democracy. While newly sovereign nations in other parts of the world have been plagued by violence and tyrannies, the English-speaking Caribbean nations have remained faithful to democratic political systems. Since they gained independence, nine of the 10 nations (Grenada excepted) consistently have held open elections, and they also have been free from unconstitutional seizures of power. Following at least one election in every country, the political party peacefully turned over power to the opposition party. The record of the Anglophone Caribbean nations is superior to that of Latin America. And they also have maintained a tradition of civilian rule with greater success than the former British colonies in West Africa—from which the ancestors of Caribbean leaders arrived as slaves.

The islands of the Commonwealth Caribbean are not perfect democracies. Political parties are often dominated by a small group of leaders who personally select candidates for office. Especially in the smaller states, the party in power monopolizes the government-owned media, which often are the only source of information on the island. On Antigua, while retaining the formal constitutional mechanisms, the Bird family has constructed a system of monarchical rule. In addition to the successful coup in Grenada in 1979, there have been other attempts at military takeovers—most notably in Trinidad in 1970 and 1990 and in Dominica in 1981. Nevertheless, a democratic tradition has been established, with continuing peaceful transitions of power both between and within political parties.

Trading Benefits for Votes

Except in Trinidad, trade union bosses became the first political leaders after independence. In addition to parliamentary democracy, the independent states of the Caribbean also inherited the welfare state politics of the British Labour Party. Island leaders believed that governments had a moral obligation to increase the economic well-being of poorer citizens. During their first decades in power, they created elaborate systems to distribute housing, education, and health care. In the process they also provided thousands of jobs in government departments, welfare offices, and state-owned corporations. Through these subsidies and government jobs, income and employment were distributed broadly through society.

The first generation of Caribbean politicians also believed that governments should actively manage the economy. In practice, this meant protecting local companies as well as local workers. To provide substitutes for imported goods, island governments encouraged investment in manufacturing, and they permitted local businessmen to form monopolies and cartels. They directly subsidized the operations of inefficient companies, and they erected high tariffs to protect them from international competition. These programs rarely achieved their goals. The domestic products were more expensive than foreign ones, and the factories producing them provided relatively few jobs for the amount invested.

This "clientalist" system, which trades benefits for votes, became characteristic of the English-speaking Caribbean. Voters expected to receive tangible advantages in exchange for support on election day. The poor wanted jobs, housing, food, bureaucratic favors, and visas to Canada or the United States. Entrepreneurs needed licenses and bank loans on easy terms. Like 19th-century pork-barrel or "machine" politics in the United States, this system can create strong ties between political parties and citizens. However, when political leaders fail to deliver on their promises, some voters strike a new bargain with the party in opposition. Perhaps 10 or 15 percent of the electorate will switch allegiances—enough to ensure a swing from one party to another every two or three elections.

The rapid expansion of island welfare systems was possible thanks to comparatively rapid economic growth during the 1950s and 1960s, the decades when the largest British colonies gained independence. Fast jet aircraft were put into service, bringing mass tourism to the Bahamas, Barbados, and Jamaica. The islands enjoyed high prices for exports of basic materials such as sugar and bauxite. But prosperity based on primary products and tourism could not create sufficient jobs, and the islands suffered from pockets of unemployment and poverty. For a time, however, governments could afford to patch over these problems by providing welfare and jobs.

Two Decades of Economic Hardship

Unfortunately for the largest English-speaking states—Jamaica, Barbados, Trinidad and Tobago, and Barbados—the good times soon were over. During the 1980s and 1990s, these nations were forced to restructure their economies to cope with severe economic downturns. Economic growth also stalled in the Bahamas, but the government managed to avoid incurring a crippling burden of debt. Taken together, Trinidad, Jamaica, and Barbados are home to more than 4 million persons, and the Bahamas add another 275,000. Most of the Caribbean's English-speaking population suffered through almost two decades during which the economy deteriorated or at best stagnated.

World oil prices rose sharply from 1971 to 1973 and again in 1979 with differing effects on the island nations. Trinidad, which exports significant amounts of petroleum, enjoyed a decade of prosperity as per capita income increased by 55 percent between 1970 and 1980. Trinidad's boom times abruptly ended in 1982, when world oil prices fell sharply while oil reserves began to run out. Unemployment soared, and per capita income was cut in half.

Hard times began earliest and have been most severe in Jamaica. While Trinidad flourished during the 1970s, average income dropped by a third in Jamaica, and it continued to stagnate during the next two decades. Adjusted for population growth, Jamaica's gross domestic product was lower at the end of the 1990s than in 1965.

For more than two decades after it achieved independence, Barbados enjoyed economic prosperity as well as political stability. As national spending ran ahead of income, the government incurred massive debts to finance the expansion of tourism and manufacturing. Toward the end of the 1980s, economic stagnation set in as interest expenses mounted while foreign sources refused to make new loans. In 1991, national income fell for the first time in 50 years.

With little agriculture or manufacturing, the Bahamas are wholly dependent on tourism, banking, and other service industries. During the 1980s and 1990s, the economy faithfully mirrored North American tourism trends. Depressed during the recession of the early 1980s, Bahamas tourism prospered during the rest of the decade but lost market share to other Caribbean destinations during the 1990s. Overall, while growth has slowed there has been no major depression.

Given their "clientalist" tradition of benefits for votes, island leaders tried to cushion hard times by increasing both welfare assistance and subsidies to failing industries. In the 1970s and 1980s as economies stagnated, tax revenues also fell. Rather than cut spending, island governments chose to borrow. The importance of the state to the economy tended to move all decisions into the political arena, where increased subsidies were the easiest solution to every problem. Similar political pressures also led to a persistent overvaluation of the exchange rate, encouraging consumption and imports at the expense of exports.

Meanwhile, private foreign investment fell from the end of the 1980s. The U.S. and other governments also cut back aid as the cold war ended; despite their economic problems, many Caribbean nations were better off than the former communist countries in eastern Europe. Public debt continued to swell while foreign investment and assistance plummeted. Ultimately island governments did not have enough both to finance imports and to make the payments due on their accumulated debt.

To remain solvent, the four largest Anglophone nations borrowed from the International Monetary Fund and the World Bank. These multinational organizations attached stringent conditions to their loans. To obtain aid, island leaders agreed to reduce government spending by cutting welfare, employing fewer persons, and paying lower wages. They pledged to abolish government trading monopolies and to sell government-owned companies. Island governments also promised to stop protecting

Table 37 **ECONOMIC DEVELOPMENT IN THE CARIBBEAN, 1980–1995**

	Gross Domestic Product per Capita in 1980 (in 1980 Prices)	Gross Domestic Product per Capita in 1995 (in 1995 Prices)	Average Annual Inflation Rate 1985–1995
CARIBBEAN COMMUNITY (CARICOM)			
Bahamas	3,450	11,940	3.2%
Barbados	3,270	6,560	2.5
Haiti	280	250	14.7
Jamaica	1,090	1,510	28.3
Trinidad & Tobago	5,010	4,851	19.6
CARICOM MEMBERS ALSO BELONGING TO THE ORGANIZATION OF EASTERN CARIBBEAN STATES (OECS)			
Antigua and Barbuda	1,380	7,690	4.4
Dominica	640	2,990	4.4
Grenada	780	2,980	5.3
Saint Kitts and Nevis	960	5,170	5.5
St Lucia	890	3,370	3.2
St Vincent and the Grenadines	540	2,280	3.6
OTHER INDEPENDENT NATIONS			
Cuba	—	—	—
Dominican Republic	1,190	1,460	26.3
ASSOCIATED WITH THE U.S.			
Puerto Rico	—	12,189	—
U. S. Virgin Islands	—	—	—

ASSOCIATED WITH BRITAIN			Annual Inflation Rate in 1995
Anguilla	—	5,762	1.6%
Cayman Islands	—	—	2.3
Montserrat	2,117	2,721	2.3
Turks & Caicos Islands	—	6,923	—
British Virgin Islands	—	18,497	—
ASSOCIATED WITH THE NETHERLANDS			
Aruba	—	10,714	—
Netherlands Antilles	—	8,800	—

SOURCES: Caribbean Development Bank, *1996 Annual Report;* World Bank, *1997 Atlas.* 1994 data for Aruba and the Netherlands Antilles.

Table 38. **DEBT OWED TO FOREIGN LENDERS BY CARIBBEAN NATIONS, 1991**

	External/Foreign Debt as a Percentage of Gross Domestic Product	Yearly Payments on Debt as a Percentage of Government's Yearly Revenues
Jamaica	110.7%	51.1
Dominican Republic	62.4	28.0
Antigua	61.6	8.1
Dominica	47.8	7.8
Trinidad & Tobago	41.6	28.6
Grenada	40.9	6.2
Haiti	35.2	15.8
St. Vincent	26.2	7.1
Barbados	25.9	24.7
St. Kitts–Nevis	21.5	7.8
St Lucia	16.7	5.8
Bahamas	11.3	9.0

SOURCE: Inter-American Development Bank, *Economic and Social Progress in Latin America.* Caribbean Development Bank.

local industries; thus they agreed both to lower tariffs on imports and to lower the value of their currencies in relation to the U.S. dollar.

These reforms were intended to make both governments and private companies more efficient. After they sold state-owned corporations to private owners, governments could devote themselves to public activities, such as education and road maintenance. Cutting taxes would make more resources available for local business. Lower tariffs would subject them to international competition, while devaluing the currency would increase exports.

Austerity policies imposed burdens on less affluent islanders. Government welfare programs were cut, unemployment increased, and currency devaluations led to higher prices for consumer goods. Jamaica, Trinidad, Barbados, and the Bahamas all suffered from flat economies throughout the 1990s. Because of slow growth, governments kept taxes high to make interest payments on their accumulated debts.

THE CARIBBEAN COMMUNITY AND THE ASSOCIATION OF CARIBBEAN STATES

Great Britain failed to bring its former colonies together in the West Indies Federation, which was disbanded in 1962. Public opinion and the ambitions of charismatic politicians demanded that each island become a separate and sovereign nation. Nevertheless, island leaders realized the real advantages of integration in many economic and technical areas. In 1968, several of the new nations formed the Caribbean Free Trade Association, which was transformed into the Caribbean Community (CARICOM) in 1973. By the end of the 1990s, the member nations included all the inde-

Table 39. **POPULATION ESTIMATES, FORMER BRITISH COLONIES, 1921–1970**

	Jamaica	Barbados	Saint Kitts and Nevis		Bahamas
1921	858,100	156,774	33,984		53,031
1943	1,246,200	—	—	—	68,846
1946	—	193,680	41,206	—	—
1960	1,605,546	232,820	—	—	
1963	—	—	—	—	130,220
1970	1,848,512	236,891	44,844	—	168,812
1990	—	278,000	—	—	278,000
1991	2,366,067	—	40,618		—

SOURCES: Eisner, *Jamaica 1830–1930*, 153; *Population Policies in the Caribbean*, 26, 50, 105; Richardson, *Caribbean Migrants*, 146. Official census results.

pendent English-speaking nations as well as the British Virgin Islands and the Turks and Caicos. Suriname was admitted in 1995; Haiti joined in 1997. (See Table 37 on page 327.) Ten other countries and colonies had various forms of "observer" status. With the exception of Cuba, the French Antilles, and the U.S. Virgin Islands most of the Caribbean is represented.[1]

The Caribbean Community was founded to foster economic integration, but it has been slow to achieve this goal. The CARICOM nations consult each other and sometimes coordinate their diplomatic efforts in Europe, North America, and the United Nations. Overall, however, CARICOM governments pursue their perceived national interests through individual actions. Member states vary greatly in size and economic development, and economic difficulties aggravate these disparities. During the 1980s, for example, Jamaica and Trinidad suffered from severe shortages of foreign currency. These larger states imposed various barriers to foreign imports, including imports from other Caribbean nations.

Tariffs on goods shipped between member nations were removed by the early 1990s. However, various forms of non-tariff barriers to intra-CARICOM trade remained, and individuals could not move freely between member countries. Uniform taxes on imports from outside the region were even slower to materialize; the Common External Tariff gradually came into effect during the 1990s.

Greater regional cohesion has been achieved by institutions acting in specific areas, such as health, education, air transportation, and meteorology. The University of the West Indies shares campuses in Jamaica, Barbados, and Trinidad, while the Caribbean Tourist Organization coordinates marketing activities. CARICOM's Legal Affairs Council facilitates compatibility of laws and coordinates a regional program to protect witnesses in drug cases. A Caribbean appellate court has been proposed to replace London's Privy Council as the final court of appeal. To foster judicial independence, a regional commission and not island governments would appoint the judges.

All the English-speaking nations and territories belong to the Caribbean Development Bank, which came into existence in 1970. Using financial resources largely procured outside the region, the CDB has trained regional financial specialists and promoted economic development. In the six small countries of the Organization of Eastern Caribbean States, the bank provided the bulk of financing to build roads, ports, and other infrastructure and public sector projects. During the 1990s, the CDB placed greater emphasis on loans to small and medium-sized private sector enterprises.

Because of economic and mental habits inherited from colonial times, most CARICOM members have had little interest in Latin America. In July 1994, the CARICOM countries and 12 Spanish-speaking Central and South American nations established the Association of Caribbean States (ACS) to promote increased economic integration. ACS members pledged to work toward a free-trade bloc with more than 200 million in population. Breaking out of its diplomatic insolation, Cuba was among the founders of the ACS, along with the Dominican Republic, Mexico, Colombia, and Venezuela.

NEW LEADERS FOR JAMAICA

Jamaica's two founding fathers, Norman Manley and Alexander Bustamante, dominated the nation's politics until the late 1960s. Under their leadership, Bustamante's Jamaican Labour Party (JLP) and Manley's People's National Party (PNP) adopted similar and generally moderate views, and they alternated in office about every 10 years. The JLP won the 1962 elections, but illness forced Bustamante into semiretirement in 1965. After another but narrow JLP victory in 1967, Hugh Shearer, president of the party's union, served as prime minister until 1972. Despite the world economic boom of the 1960s, unemployment and inflation both increased. Moreover, the Shearer government gained a reputation for weak management, party infighting, and corruption.

The two parties began to follow widely different courses when a new generation came to power at the end of the 1960s. Norman Manley died in 1969, and his son Michael assumed leadership of the PNP. Under Michael Manley (1924–1997) the PNP revived the socialist heritage it had dropped in 1952. Tall, eloquent, and charismatic, Michael Manley took control of the PNP in 1969 because of his own personal dynamism as well as his father's reputation.

Manley, himself almost entirely white, worked hard to gain the support of the black power movement that had grown up during the 1960s. PNP leaders adopted the clothing and manners associated with the black lower classes, and Manley made a special effort to gain support from the Rastafarians.[2] With the slogan, "the politics of participation," the PNP decisively defeated the JLP in the 1972 elections. It gained votes among the Rastafarians and also from Jamaican businessmen and professionals disenchanted with the Shearer government.

Michael Manley and Democratic Socialism

During his first two years in office, Manley increased welfare benefits and cultivated friendships with Fidel Castro and African members of the Nonaligned movement.[3] In September 1974, the PNP government startled the people of Jamaica by suddenly announcing its conversion to socialism. Prime Minister Manley declared his intention of seizing or nationalizing Jamaica's largest businesses.

Although private companies survived, Manley's government took control of large segments of the economy between 1974 and 1978. It set up agricultural cooperatives, and it nationalized (with artificially low compensation) the island's electricity, telephone, and transportation companies as well as sugar factories, hotels, and a major bank. It also purchased 51 percent of the bauxite mines from foreign-owned aluminum companies. To help pay for these acquisitions, Jamaica in 1974 suddenly broke its existing contracts with the mining companies and sharply increased the levy (tax) on all bauxite production. As a way of emphasizing his socialist goals, Manley traveled to Cuba in 1975. There he and Fidel Castro embraced and expressed enthusiasm for each other's policies. Hundreds of Cubans came to Jamaica, while thousands of Jamaicans went to Cuba for training.

During Manley's first term, Edward Seaga (1930–   ) succeeded Shearer as leader of the JLP. Seaga and Manley continued the personal rivalry that earlier pitted Alexander Bustamante's JLP against Norman Manley's PNP. However, in an ironic reversal of roles, Michael Manley adopted Bustamante's angry and emotional style, while Seaga preferred the more formal and remote manners associated with Norman Manley. While he lacked Michael Manley's fiery rhetorical style, Seaga was perceived as disciplined, hard-working, and intelligent. Despite being wealthy, he won election to parliament from one of the poorest districts in West Kingston. His talents soon brought him high office as minister of development (1962–67) and minister of finance and planning (1967–1972).

During the December 1976 elections, Manley and Seaga supported totally different policies. The JLP charged that the PNP's socialism inevitably led to godless communism, and it also attacked the PNP's close relations with Cuba. Although the PNP won a sweeping victory in 1976, it no longer represented all Jamaicans. For the first time, different economic groups tended to support one or the other of the two parties—both originally based on nationwide unions. The PNP won the votes of unskilled workers and the unemployed, while professionals and white-collar workers swung to the JLP.

Manley began his second term by turning to the radical wing of the PNP, which had close ties to Jamaica's Communist Party. The government took over more companies, and it created a Ministry of Mobilization to educate the population in socialist beliefs. By the fall of 1977, however, a severe economic crisis forced the government to ask for international help, and the prime minister began to support more moderate elements within the party.

The Jamaican economy had fallen into deep depression partly because of the sharp increase in world oil prices in 1973. But the government's policies clearly made matters worse. The new tax on bauxite agreements frightened off foreign investment, and it encouraged the mining companies to develop new sources of supply in other countries. The government ran up large foreign debts both to pay for higher welfare benefits and also to cover loses by state-owned companies. Manley's friendship with Castro dismayed foreign investors, while bankrupt Cuba had little money for aid to Jamaica.

By 1977, Jamaica had run out of foreign currency to purchase needed imports, and Manley's government was forced to ask the International Monetary Fund for help. In return for its loans, the IMF insisted that the government reduce its huge deficit by cutting spending and raising taxes. Although they may have been needed, these reforms further reduced wages in the short run. Overall, six years of socialist government led to a severe decline in living standards. By 1980, production had fallen by 16 percent, prices had tripled, and a third of Jamaican workers were unemployed.

Ordinary Jamaicans had had enough of socialism by the elections of October 1980. Seaga's JLP won a massive victory as one-third of those voting for the PNP in

1976 switched to the JLP in 1980. The 1980 election was a personal victory for Edward Seaga, who became both prime minister and minister of finance. Seaga imposed the second major shift in economic policy since independence. The Seaga government supported private enterprise and tried to increase exports.

Michael Manley Returns to Power

Helped by a fall in oil prices in early 1986, the Jamaican economy improved and grew significantly in 1987 and 1988. Nevertheless, a majority of Jamaicans turned against the JLP, which had reduced government spending on education, health, and housing. Voters also feared increasing violence and drug-related crime, and many Jamaicans simply preferred Michael Manley's more charismatic style. During the election campaign, Manley presented himself as a moderate leader who had learned from his mistakes during the 1970s. Manley pledged to increase spending on education and welfare benefits, and he promised to reverse Seaga's policy of returning companies to private ownership. But he also stressed the importance of American trade and assistance and promised to cooperate with the Jamaican business community and foreign investors.

The PNP won a landslide victory in February 1989, giving Manley an unprecedented third term as prime minister. Following the election, he appointed a cabinet from the moderate wing of the party. The new Manley cultivated good relations with the United States and western Europe. While restoring diplomatic recognition of Cuba, he was careful not to revive his close friendship with Fidel Castro.

Despite its promises during the election, the PNP government continued Seaga's efforts to sell government-owned hotels and businesses to private companies. Prime Minister Manley acknowledged that Jamaica is too dependent on for-

Former sugar plantation "big house" restored by Jamaica's government

eign investment to create a socialist state. After decades of independence, the nation continues to rely on imports, both of consumer goods and of materials used in the island's factories. Without foreign currency to purchase fuel, food, and industrial goods, Jamaica's economy would collapse.

Because of health problems, Michael Manley retired in March 1992. He was succeeded by P. J. Patterson (1935–   ), who had been deputy prime minister since 1989. After studying law in Britain in the early 1960s, Patterson went to work for the PNP and quickly won high party office. A low-key technician with a nonconfrontational style, Patterson ably backed up the more flamboyant Manley during the 1970s. When the PNP returned to power in 1989, he helped manage the transition from socialism to a free market.

Taking advantage of an economic upswing, Patterson called an early election in March 1993. Under his leadership, the PNP overwhelmingly defeated the JLP, still led by Edward Seaga. Patterson and Seaga each presented himself as the candidate best able to manage the country's free-market economic policies. In addition, Patterson overtly appealed to racist sentiment by reminding voters that no dark-skinned prime minister had previously won a general election. His slogan, "Black man's time has come," was a direct reference to his own racial origins—and an indirect reference to Seaga's Lebanese heritage.

During his first full term as prime minister, Patterson continued to deregulate business, and he privatized state-run sugar factories and Air Jamaica, the national airline. Yet economic growth continued to be anemic, with continuing high inflation and unemployment. Moreover, Jamaica had become a major transfer point for drug trafficking between South America and the United States during the 1980s. The government seemed unable or unwilling to fight dealers, who provided both jobs and foreign currency. Violence increased, and a nation of 2.34 million suffered 11,000 murders in 1997. The Jamaican police force often responded with haphazard brutality; in some years, police officers accounted for more than one-third of the murders committed on the island.

Ignoring these difficulties, Jamaica's voters in December 1997 gave Patterson's PNP a third term in office with 50 seats in Parliament to 10 for Seaga's JLP. The two parties espoused similar policies. But his years in politics had made Prime Minister Patterson a master of Jamaica's patronage system, able to convince both the unemployed and prosperous investors that the PNP cared about their needs. "A reticent man in a loud mouth country," according to the *Economist* magazine, Patterson was "trusted by Jamaica's rich white and brown businessmen and supported by the rising black entrepreneurs who have long seen him as their man."[4]

TRINIDAD'S UNIQUE OIL WEALTH

Differences in climate and in the history of settlement and development have given each of the Caribbean islands its own individual character. None is more distinctive than Trinidad—the only Caribbean island to possess oil and natural gas. Although they form only a small fraction of total world production, oil exports provide Trinidad's 1.3 million inhabitants with their main source of income. The highly mechanized oil industry directly employs only about 10 percent of the nation's workers, but it subsidizes the rest of the economy. Trinidad resembles the oil-rich nations in the Middle East rather than the other Caribbean states. Indeed, since Trinidad exports oil, which all other islands must import, its economic fortunes are almost the exact reverse of other nations'. A rise in oil prices, which harms the economies of the other islands, is good for Trinidad. Falling oil prices benefit the other islands but are disastrous for the Trinidadian economy.

Trinidad also differs from the other islands in its striking ethnic diversity. Africans and East Indians both make up about 40 percent of the entire population; the rest identify themselves as Europeans, Chinese, Syrians, or as of mixed heritage. Until recently, blacks formed the majority of oil workers and preferred to live in the cities, while East Indians lived in the country and worked on the sugar estates. Because of these ethnic divisions, Trinidad's labor leaders have not succeeded in creating the large nationwide unions found throughout the rest of the West Indies.

For 30 years beginning in 1956, Trinidad's politics were controlled by Eric Williams and the party he founded, the People's National Movement. Even after his death in 1981, Williams's legend helped win another five-year term for the PNM, and other parties came to power only in 1986. Labor leaders often opposed the Williams government. There were many strikes, and various unions formed parties and alliances against the PNM. But none of these labor parties could win enough votes to gain control of the government.

Despite Williams's compelling personality, the PNM did not retain power without opposition. The Democratic Labour Party (DLP), founded in 1958, attracted East Indians and others who felt left out of the PNM. It remained the main opposition party until 1972, although it never won a majority in parliament. Low oil and sugar prices weakened Trinidad's economy between 1962 and 1973, and unemployment rose. Nevertheless, the PNM decisively won the 1966 and 1971 elections. Black workers remained loyal to the PNM, while the DLP and other opposition parties were torn by internal struggles for power. The opposition's weakness allowed the PNM to control the parliament, but it won a smaller number of votes in each election. The government became increasingly authoritarian. Williams and a few advisers made most decisions without explaining their actions to the party or to the news media.

The Black Power Revolt

The PNM sought to build up the economy by attracting foreign investment, and multinational corporations dominated the oil, sugar, and banking industries. In 1969 and 1970, Williams's acceptance of foreign (and thus white) ownership came under attack from black power militants and labor leaders, who tried to take over the government by force. However, partly because they failed to gain support from the East Indian community, Williams was able to crush the rebels.

Intellectuals with ties to American black militants created a black power movement in Trinidad during the late 1960s. The most radical group was the National Joint Action Congress (NJAC) at the University of the West Indies. Under the Williams government, the NJAC charged, white and colored businessmen—both Trinidadian and foreign—still owned the nation's industries. NJAC leaders wanted to install a government that would totally control the economy and own all land as well as the entire sugar industry. They rejected parliamentary democracy and were willing to use force to take power. A party publication, *Slavery to Slavery,* insisted that "We need to destroy . . . the system from its very foundations . . . to get out of our economic mess (and) build a new society."[5]

A major political crisis began at the end of February 1970. Several black power marches attracted thousands of demonstrators, and individuals linked to the NJAC bombed banks, stores, and government offices. Just as these marches and strikes reached their peak in mid-April, the deputy prime minister, A. N. R. Robinson (1926–) resigned from the cabinet—suggesting that the PNM was breaking up. Black power leaders and several unions scheduled a general strike and march on the capital, Port of Spain, for April 21. Prime Minister Williams decided to attack first, declared a state of emergency, and arrested the movement's leaders.

Despite riots and arson, the police maintained control of Port of Spain. But the government was further threatened when the junior officers and some men of Trinidad's small army (800-strong) mutinied. They apparently sympathized with the black power movement and intended to take power after assassinating members of the government. The coast guard remained loyal and stopped the revolt by shelling the only road to the army base, located on the Chaguaramas Peninsula north of the capital.

Following the 1971 rebellion, Prime Minister Williams moved to strengthen governmental powers. One proposed law required police permission to hold public meetings and forbade statements inciting racial hated or violence. Although Williams withdrew this law when it aroused intense opposition, the parliament passed several other laws that introduced licenses for guns and gave the police the power to search for unauthorized weapons. Many Trinidadians were unhappy with the Williams government by the May 1971 elections, but the various factions once more failed to come together. With the opposition parties—and most voters—boycotting the election, the PNM captured all 36 seats in the parliament.

The PNM Creates a Socialist Economy

The Arab oil embargo in November 1973 rescued the Williams government by quadrupling the world price of oil. While most Caribbean countries entered a deep recession, Trinidad enjoyed 10 years of economic boom. The Williams government used taxes on oil exports to take control of the economy. It purchased foreign corporations, built ambitious public works, subsidized consumer goods, and created new manufacturing companies.

The government began to buy up key industries before 1973 in response to criticism of foreign ownership by union and black power leaders. Its ownership accelerated as oil revenues grew. The government purchased several oil companies in 1969, and it nationalized the remaining oil firms and all gas stations in 1975. State-owned companies also took control of other major industries—including sugar producers, electricity and water utilities, airlines, banks, and insurance companies.

Throughout the 1970s, oil revenues fueled a continuing boom. As funds poured in, Prime Minister Williams remarked that "Money is no problem."[6] His government used oil revenues to maintain artificially low prices for consumer goods, such as gasoline. And it spent lavishly on education, public works, and welfare programs from food stamps to old-age pensions. As in other Caribbean nations, the government gave out economic benefits in return for votes. The National Housing Authority, for example, was used to channel patronage to black contractors and construction workers. Once the housing was built, black voters with low incomes received either mortgages with reduced interest rates or very low rents, in some cases paying $100 a year for new apartments that had each cost $200,000 to build.

The government also attempted to create heavy industries that could compete on the world market. (Earlier programs during the 1950s and 1960s had emphasized the manufacture of consumer goods for local use.) State funds were poured into projects such as a multibillion-dollar industrial park at Point Liasas, on the coast about 10 miles north of San Fernando. At enormous cost, factories were built to produce petrochemicals, fertilizers, cement, iron, steel and automobiles.

By the early 1980s, the government employed two-thirds of all workers, and it had more control over the economy than in any other Caribbean country except Cuba. Although Trinidad had taken socialism much further than the Manley government in Jamaica had, Williams escaped criticism. Because of its great oil wealth, Trinidad could afford to pay full market price for foreign companies, which also were invited to participate in joint ventures under government supervision.

As the Williams government increased its control over Trinidad's economy during the 1970s, the prime minister became even more autocratic and aloof. Commissions under his control supervised the government and state companies. From 1976, one National Advisory Council controlled all economic planning. Since government officials did not have to account for their actions to the parliament, bribery and corruption became common. In 1980, high officials were charged with taking bribes from U.S. companies to influence their choice of airplanes for the military and the state airline.

Because of the economic boom and continuing ethnic divisions within the opposition, Williams easily won the 1976 elections. However, Tobago elected representatives from a new party, the Democratic Action Congress (DAC). Founded by A. N. R. Robinson, the PNM minister who had resigned during the 1970 black power riots, the DAC sought greater autonomy for Tobago. Although the British had united the two islands in 1888, they have little in common. In its history and economic development, Tobago resembles the other small islands of the Lesser Antilles rather than oil-rich Trinidad. After the sugar plantations collapsed during the 1870s, the island's primarily black inhabitants (now about 50,000) became independent farmers producing crops such as cocoa and coconuts. Most long have wanted to be independent of their larger neighbor. In 1980, Trinidad's parliament set up a 15-member elected assembly on Tobago and gave it responsibility for local finance and economic planning.

The Economic Depression of the 1980s

When Eric Williams died in March 1981, the PNM named George Chambers (1930–1997) as party leader and prime minister. Chambers easily won the 1981 election, but his government soon became unpopular. Falling oil prices beginning in 1982 plunged Trinidad into deep economic depression. From $26 a barrel, oil prices plunged to $9 a barrel in 1986. Unemployment soared, while per capita income was cut by more than half—from $6,800 in 1982 (among the highest in the region) to $3,000 in 1989. The economic downturn was especially devastating because Trinidadians had become dependent on imported consumer goods during the 1970s boom. Farm production had declined sharply, and Trinidad was importing three-fourths of

Waterwheel at Speyside, Tobago. Tobago's tranquility provides a distinct contrast to the industrialized activity of neighboring Trinidad. Sugar exports ended about 1900, idling the waterwheels on cane estates.

its food. With falling oil revenues, the island ran up large trade deficits to buy needed foreign goods.

Crippled by debt, the Chambers government raised taxes while cutting spending. To reduce consumption, it devalued the currency by one-third and also lowered subsidies on imported goods. In December 1986, the PNM lost power for the first time since independence. A coalition of four political parties formed the National Alliance for Reconstruction (NAR), headed by A. N. R. Robinson. Campaigning under the slogan "one love," the NAR appealed to all ethnic groups and promised to increase employment and end governmental corruption. It annihilated the PNM at the polls, taking 33 out of 36 seats in the House of Representatives.

For the first and only time, a political party won the support of a majority among every ethnic group. Indians overwhelmingly favored the NAR, but almost half of the black electorate also supported the new alliance. Because dissident members of the PNM had helped create the NAR, black voters perceived the party as not merely an Indian organization. In general, however, only more prosperous blacks switched allegiance to the NAR, while poorer blacks stayed with the PNM. In effect, middle- and upper-class blacks had jettisoned their alliance with the urban poor and replaced it with an alliance with rural Hindus.

Once in office, the NAR imposed economic austerity programs more stringent than those of previous PNM governments. Prime Minister Robinson increased taxes, further devalued the currency, and continued to cut back on subsidies and patronage. In 1989, the pay of government employees was cut by 10 percent. Real incomes plummeted, while unemployment exceeded 18 percent every year from 1986 through 1994.

The Robinson government also began reducing government ownership in the manufacturing, retail, and service sectors. It closed down unproductive companies and privatized other firms, including the telephone company and several financial enterprises. The NAR also tried to reform the national sugar company, where the cost of producing a ton of sugar was twice the selling price. The government intended to distribute land to peasants for use in growing other crops. However, this plan could not be carried out because sugar plantations were closely identified with Hindu culture.

Between 1988 and 1990, Trinidad negotiated with the International Monetary Fund (IMF) to put off debt payments. However, Prime Minister Robinson maintained that the IMF had not forced cutbacks upon his government. Austerity was needed to restructure Trinidad's economy away from socialism and dependency on oil, he said. The government, Robinson argued, could no longer be "a tireless mother, forever providing, a guarantor of welfare, and a haven of security."[7]

The NAR's multiracial coalition soon broke up. The 1986 election results encouraged an outburst of Hindu assertiveness. Fundamentalists sought to preserve traditional habits, fast disappearing as Hindus assimilated into Trinidad's overall culture. They demanded that Hindi be taught in the public schools and objected to conversions to Christianity. They also wanted the NAR to accept the Indian government's offer to build a Hindu cultural center.

NAR leaders did not accommodate Hindu politicians on these cultural issues, and the government had no money to spend on the rural Hindu population. In late 1987 and early 1988, the NAR government dismissed Basdeo Panday (1932–   ), and three other cabinet ministers. In April 1989, Panday and other dissidents announced the formation of the United National Congress (UNC), which replaced the PNM as the main opposition party.

The Abu Bakr Coup

By July 1990, the government was widely unpopular. Led by Yasin Abu Bakr (1942–   ), a former policeman born Lennox Phillip, several hundred Afro-Muslims exploded a bomb in the national police headquarters and occupied the parliament building and state television station. There they seized 54 hostages, including Prime Minister Robinson and seven cabinet ministers, and held them captive for five days.

Known as the Jamaat Al Muslimeen (Grouping of Muslims), the rebels had received money and weapons from Libya's ruler, Colonel Muammar Gadafi. The Jamaat issued a statement condemning drugs, corruption, and poverty. They insisted that Prime Minister Robinson resign immediately and hold new elections within 90 days. They also demanded a pardon before they would lift the siege. Robinson was shot in the leg after refusing to sign a letter of resignation. Later, he appeared to have agreed to the rebels' demands, and Trinidad's acting president granted them amnesty.

Residents of the capital did not join Abu Bakr's rebels, who surrendered when they ran out of food. But large numbers did take to the streets, looting many stores and burning others. Before the army restored order, more than 30 persons died and 500 were wounded during the worst violence since the black power riots in 1970.

After the rebels surrendered, the government insisted that agreements made under duress were invalid. Abu Bakr and 113 other Jamaat members were charged with treason and murder. In November 1991, Great Britain's Privy Council (still the final court of appeal) declared that the amnesty's validity had to be considered before the rebels were tried. Trinidad's courts ruled that the pardon was valid, released all 114 of the accused, and ordered that they receive paid compensation for wrongful imprisonment. The government appealed these decisions back to the Privy Council, which in October 1994 ordered the case closed. Although the pardon was not legitimate after all, the government could not rearrest the 114 Jamaat rebels.

The Return of Ethnic-Based Governments

Ethnic-bloc voting reemerged at the general elections in December 1991. The black-oriented PNM took 21 seats while the Indian-dominated UNC won 13. The NAR won only the two Tobago seats. Now led by Patrick Manning (1946–), the PNM continued to restructure Trinidad's economy. Manning's government sold inefficient state-owned companies and reduced subsidies on consumer goods. It reformed trade regulations and made the Trinidad dollar freely convertible into other currencies. These reforms were not popular. Strikes were widespread and often violent throughout the 1990s, and government employees also protested the salary cuts imposed by the NAR.

Drug trafficking increased during the 1980s and 1990s. Located seven miles off South America's northeast coast, Trinidad is a convenient stop for drug smugglers moving their product to American and European markets. In mid-1992, the government hired British police detectives to look into organized drug rings within the national police. The investigators reported widespread drug sales and other forms of corruption, and the government sought to reform the police.

In the November 1995 election, the PNM and the UNC each secured 17 seats, while the NAR retained two seats. A. N. R. Robinson, the NAR leader, formed a coalition government with the UNC. Basdeo Panday became the first Indian to hold the office of prime minister.

Panday was fortunate in taking power just when economic restructuring by previous governments began to produce results. Trinidad's economic output had fallen virtually every year from 1980 through 1993. Recovery began in 1994. Government incentives encouraged petroleum exploration, and new reserves of oil and especially of natural gas were discovered. Despite these recent discoveries, oil production fell by half from the 1970s to the 1990s. Natural gas is another story, with new finds being reported regularly. Known reserves will last well into the 21st century.

The enormous investment in the Port Liasas industrial park also paid dividends in the late 1990s. In 1993 and 1994, the government wholly or partially sold off its petrochemical companies to foreign enterprises. Under private ownership, output increased by over 500 percent in one year. Huge petrochemical facilities and pipelines were erected to turn natural gas feedstock into ammonia, methanol, and urea, potentially making Trinidad the world's largest exporter of these products.

Despite the boom at Port Liasas, unemployment remained at 14 percent in 1997—still far above the level in 1982, before the nation's 12-year recession began. Foreign companies also invested in Tobago's tourist industry, and there was some increase in exports to South America of nonpetroleum products. However, after all the efforts to restructure Trinidad's economy, the nation remained dependent on petroleum and thus vulnerable to fluctuations in world oil prices.

BARBADOS'S STURDY DEMOCRACY

Barbados has enjoyed remarkable political stability. Most British colonies lost their representative assemblies at the end of the 19th century. Barbados (along with the Bahamas) retained its assembly—which first met in 1639—until it was replaced by the 1966 constitution granting independence.

The Democratic Labour Party (DLP) and the Barbados Labour Party (BLP) have alternated in power since the 1950s. The DLP's rhetoric has been somewhat to the left of the BLP. In practice, the two parties have followed similar policies, and they have been distinguished mainly by the personalities of their leaders. Both began as socialist parties tied to labor unions. Since independence, however, they have supported private ownership of industry, while simultaneously increasing welfare benefits and public employment.

The BLP and the DLP both draw support from diverse social, racial, and ethnic groups in what is a strongly homogeneous society. Although they form less than 3 percent of the population, white families continue to own most of the nation's land and corporations as well as large segments of the marketing and services sectors. Both parties thus have sought a conciliatory arrangement between white corporate power and black political power.

The two parties competed in building a generous welfare system that included free education through the university, free medical care, and free medicines. Subsidized public housing was provided. Electricity, drinkable water, and sewer systems were extended to most of the island. To finance these benefits, government spending consistently ran ahead of revenues. With independence, however, the government gained control of the currency and national bank. Until 1981, Barbados succeeded in financing its growing debt from local sources.

The island's economy expanded rapidly until the early 1980s. Oil was discovered in sufficient quantities to meet part of the island's own needs, and the government borrowed to encourage growth. Moreover, foreign companies were eager to invest in a nation that enjoyed a reputation for social peace and the best-educated population in the Caribbean.

Tourism and manufacturing replaced sugar plantations as Barbadians made the transition to more skilled and lucrative occupations. Barbadian planters continued to grow sugarcane after it had disappeared from other islands. As late as the 1960s, they regularly produced between 175,000 and 220,000 tons each year. By 1995, however, production had fallen to 42,000 tons.

Tourism grew rapidly, and the government also succeeded in attracting light-manufacturing plants, especially those assembling clothing and electronic goods for reexport. Employment in assembly plants peaked at the end of the 1980s. In its place, Barbados companies began to process computer data sent—by courier or over the telephone—by North American businesses, particularly insurance companies. From simple keyboarding, Barbadians graduated in the 1990s to processing health claims and adapting software.

Led by the popular Errol Barrow (1920–87), the DLP brought Barbados to independence in 1966. Taking credit for the island's prosperity, the party won elections in 1966 and 1971. After 15 years in opposition, the BLP returned to power in 1976 under J. M. G. M. "Tom" Adams (1931–85), who campaigned against government

Table 40. **LEVELS OF LITERACY AND EDUCATION IN THE CARIBBEAN ISLANDS**

	Literacy Rates Among Those Aged 15+. Latest Available Estimates.		Those Aged 25+ Who Have Completed the First Level of Schooling. Latest Available Estimates.	
CARIBBEAN COMMUNITY (CARICOM)				
Bahamas	98%	(1995)	71%	(1990)
Barbados	97	(1995)	36	(1980)
Haiti	44	(1995)	10	(1986)
Jamaica	85	(1995)	17	(1982)
Trinidad & Tobago	97		69	(1980)
CARICOM MEMBERS ALSO BELONGING TO THE ORGANIZATION OF EASTERN CARIBBEAN STATES (OECS)				
Antigua & Barbuda	—		—	
Dominica	—		13	(1981)
Grenada	—		10	(1981)
Saint Kitts & Nevis	97	(1980)	70	(1980)
St Lucia	—		8	(1980)
St Vincent & the Grenadines	—		10	
OTHER INDEPENDENT NATIONS				
Cuba	—		74	(1981)
Dominican Republic	82	(1995)	—	
ASSOCIATED WITH THE U.S.				
Puerto Rico	88	(1980)	74	(1980)
U. S. Virgin Islands	—		72	(1980)
ASSOCIATED WITH BRITAIN				
Anguilla	—			
Cayman Islands	—		—	
Montserrat	—		14	(1980)
Turks & Caicos Islands	—		25	(1980)
British Virgin Islands	98	(1995)	56	(1991)
ASSOCIATED WITH THE NETHERLANDS				
Aruba	—		48	(1991)
Netherlands Antilles	95	(1992)	64	(1992)
ASSOCIATED WITH FRANCE				
Guadeloupe	90	(1982)	44	(1982)
Martinique	93	(1982)	26	(1982)

NOTE: In the United States, the "first level of schooling" more commonly is called "grade school."

SOURCE: UNESCO *1997: Statistical Yearbook.*

corruption. Like his famous father, Sir Grantley Adams (and Errol Barrow as well), Tom Adams had won the Barbados Island Scholarship for study in Great Britain.

The BLP won reelection in 1981. But Tom Adams's second term was marked by an economic recession, with falling revenues from sugar, tourism, and manufacturing. Using money borrowed from the United States and the International Monetary Fund, the government began a program of extensive public works. Adams died suddenly in 1985 and was succeeded by his deputy, Bernard St John (1931–   ).

In 1986, Barrow and the DLP returned to power with a stunning victory, taking 24 Assembly seats to three won by the BLP. Nationalists were offended by the BLP's support for the U.S. invasion of Grenada. For some voters, the BLP was too closely identified with the light-skinned business élite, from which it received substantial funds. But Barrow primarily won over Barbadians—including members of the black middle class and white community—by promising very sharp cuts in personal taxes.

In June 1987, Errol Barrow died suddenly at the age of 65. With an unprecedented display of sorrow, Barbadians mourned the death of the nation's founding father and most popular nationalist leader. Barrow was succeeded by L. Erskine Sandiford (1937–   ), who took direct control over the economy. To avoid cutting spending, Sandiford borrowed heavily; in place of the promised tax cuts, his government actually increased taxes. Thanks to a revival in tourism, however, the economic outlook seemed to have improved. Although by a smaller margin than in 1986, Sandiford and the DLP won the 1991 election.

The true extent of the economic crisis became apparent in 1991. Sugar production plummeted. Because of the Gulf War as well as Barbados's reputation for high prices, tourist arrivals fell sharply. Like other Caribbean nations, Barbados imports most consumer products. Sandiford's government was forced to borrow to cover the nation's trade deficit. As a condition of aid, the IMF insisted on tax increases as well as reduced staffing and pay cuts for government employees. Barbados's telephone company was sold, and other state companies were slated for privatization. Due to these austerity measures, unemployment soared to more than 25 percent of the workforce. Increasingly unpopular even within his own party, Sandiford was forced to call an early election in September 1994.

With Owen Arthur (1949–   ) as leader, a revived BLP won 19 of 28 assembly seats in 1994. Arthur, a professional economist, tried both to increase international competitiveness and to encourage economic recovery. In January 1997, his government imposed a "value added tax" (a concealed sales tax) in order to increase revenues and reduce the government's recurring deficit. Arthur also continued to sell government companies to private investors. Despite reductions, the government in 1996 still employed almost one-fourth of the entire workforce.

While continuing the austerity program, the Arthur government gave wage increases to the poorest workers, and it passed a constitutional amendment forbidding future reductions in the wages of public employees. To promote social harmony, Arthur's administration even included a white businessman, the first white person to hold public office in almost 50 years. Thanks to a legacy of debt, there are no easy options for any Barbados government. By the late 1990s, production had fallen back to the level of 1980, leaving the growing population with an unemployment rate above 20 percent. Nevertheless, in January 1999, Prime Minister Arthur and the BLP regained power for a second consecutive term, whipping the opposition DLP by 26 seats to two.

THE BAHAMAS

Unlike Jamaica and Trinidad, the many small islands and cays forming the Bahamas archipelago have few natural resources. Because of their poor soil and dry climate, sugar estates did not develop, and farming remains of little importance. Bahamians traditionally have made their living from the sea, and they also have profited from their close location to the United States. During the 17th and 18th centuries, the Bahamas provided an ideal base for pirates. They welcomed Confederate blockade runners during the American Civil War and alcohol smugglers during the Prohibition era. They owe their current prosperity primarily to the tourist and banking industries.

Because the islands lie just off the east coast of the United States and enjoy a moderate climate, tourism flourishes year-round and provides three-fourths of the nation's income. The Bahamas also leads in "offshore banking"—the provision of services by branches of foreign banks. Personal and corporate accounts in these branches escape the taxes and regulations imposed on such accounts in the United States. The Bahamian shipping register, founded in 1976, also has prospered. By 1996, more than 1,500 ships sailed under the Bahamian flag.

Given their limited natural resources, the Bahamas were among the first to tie their fortunes to these service industries. Offshore banking began in the 1920s. Growth in tourism was dramatic after World War II. From 32,000 in 1949, the number of visitors increased by an annual average of 12.5 percent, reaching 1.1 million in 1979 and 3.7 million in 1991. Nine out of 10 tourists come from North America.

As the sugar industry died out on other Caribbean islands, the Bahamas began to face fierce competition for tourist dollars, while rival offshore financial centers

Stone church on Eleuthera Island, the first permanent settlement in the Bahamas

sprang up in the Cayman Islands, the British Virgin Islands, and the Netherlands Antilles. The Bahamas are, in a sense, a model other Caribbean islands are striving to emulate and surpass. However, the country continues to be the most popular travel destination in the Caribbean, and it also remains competitive in financial services.

Bahamians have elected a representative assembly since 1729, but universal adult suffrage was not granted until 1962. Led by Lynden Oscar Pindling (1930–   ), the Progressive Liberal Party (PLP) won every election from 1968 to 1992, and Pindling served five terms as prime minister after independence was gained in 1973. The PLP, founded in 1953, initially faced strong opposition from the United Bahamian Party (UBP), which represented white business interests on Nassau. When the UBP won several elections during the 1960s, the PLP attributed its losses to unfair electoral boundaries. Pindling, as official leader of the opposition, dramatically protested in 1965 by throwing the speaker's ceremonial mace through a window while the assembly was in session. The PLP came to power in 1968 by appealing to black pride and the interests of workers.

Unlike many other Caribbean political parties, the PLP was not closely tied to a labor union. It carried out major public works, favored free enterprise, and held taxation to the lowest level in the Commonwealth Caribbean. The party owed its continued popularity to Pindling's charismatic leadership during 25 years of economic prosperity and improved material conditions for most Bahamians. By the end of the 1980s, per capita income was the highest in the Caribbean. Bahamians also gained significant—but unmeasurable—income by smuggling cocaine, marijuana, and other illegal drugs to the United States. According to the U.S. Drug Enforcement Administration, three-fourths of the cocaine and half the marijuana entering the United States between the early 1970s and early 1990s passed though the Bahamas.

Prime Minister Pindling's government was hit by a major drug scandal soon after he won his third term as prime minister. A 1983 report on U.S. television alleged that Pindling and other government members were involved in the illegal drug trade. Pindling responded by creating an independent commission of investigation. In its December 1984 report, the commission implicated several ministers and senior government officials. The report found no evidence of direct involvement by Pindling, but it did note that the prime minister had spent eight times his reported income during the previous seven years.

Despite the evidence of corruption, Pindling fired only a few officials. Hubert Ingraham (1947–   ) was forced out of office for demanding additional resignations and subsequently became leader of the main opposition party, the Free National Movement (FNM). Prime Minister Pindling overcame the scandal and won reelection in 1987 by skillfully appealing to Bahamian nationalism. In fiery speeches, he accused the United States of blaming the Bahamas rather than admitting its own inability to control illegal drugs.

While publicly criticizing the U.S. government, Pindling simultaneously began to cooperate with American authorities. The Bahamas increased spending on the police and coast guard. A joint drugs-interdiction force was formed, and the Bahamian police collaborated with the U.S. Drug Enforcement Administration and Coast Guard in searching for drugs. The two countries also signed a treaty in 1989 making it easier to investigate money laundering by drug traffickers. By 1992, U.S. authorities judged that Bahamian drug trafficking had fallen to an irreducible minimum.

After two decades of growth, the Bahamas moved into recession in 1988, and the economy shrank from 1991 through 1993. A slowdown in the United States severely affected the tourist industry, which had overexpanded. Prime Minister Pindling was forced to cut spending, raise taxes, and put restraints on borrowing. His government also was tarnished by revelations of corrupt practices in government-owned companies.

In August 1992, the PLP lost power for the first time since 1967. The opposition FNM took two-thirds of the seats in parliament, and Hubert Ingraham replaced Sir Lynden Pindling as prime minister. Ingraham capitalized on his relative youth and reputation for honesty. Having grown up in a poor black family on Abaco Island, he was perceived as understanding popular needs. Older Bahamians still associated the FNM with the former white-dominated UBP. In this case, because of Ingraham's nationalist credentials, Pindling could not appeal to racial identification.

Following the 1992 election, a commission of inquiry investigated the national airline, telephone company, and hotel corporation. Its report revealed extensive nepotism, managerial incompetence, and theft by government officials and employees. Canadian authorities investigated allegations that an aircraft manufacturer paid $800,000 in bribes to Bahamas officials. Pindling himself had accepted $375,000 from two contractors while he was chairman of the hotel corporation.

Prime Minister Ingraham's administration cut government regulations and began to return state-owned companies to private ownership. By 1996, almost all state-owned hotels had been privatized, and the government announced its intention of selling the electricity and telecommunications companies. Privatization temporarily

The cloister at the Ocean Club on Paradise Island, just offshore from New Providence Island in the Bahamas. Huntington Hartford, the A & P grocery-chain heir, developed this luxury resort during the 1960s. Hartford purchased the monastic cloister, erected in France during the 12th century, from William Randolph Hearst's ranch at San Simeon, California.

increased unemployment, and the problem was exacerbated by the arrival of thousands of illegal immigrants from Haiti and Cuba.

The economy began to grow again in 1994. With the end of government controls, the tourist industry attracted foreign investment in luxury properties appealing to high-spending customers. One South African company, Sun International, invested $250 million in renovating hotels on Paradise Island off Nassau. Investment in industry also increased. In 1995, a Hong Kong–based company took over Freeport harbor on Grand Bahama Island and built a $78 million deep-water terminal capable of handling the largest container ships.

The Ingraham administration also took action to restore the financial services industry. Frightened by the country's reputation for corruption, many institutions had moved to other offshore financial centers. Altogether the Bahamas had fallen from third to 12th place among banking havens during the 1980s. The industry recovered as the government moved to eliminate illegal transactions while simplifying procedures and granting added tax concessions.

The FNM won a large majority in the March 1997 election, and Ingraham returned as prime minister. Although he retained his own seat in the assembly, Sir Lynden Pindling resigned as head of the PLP. The "father of the country" became a millionaire while in office, but—unlike some other Caribbean leaders—he at least rejected the temptation to authoritarian rule.

CHAPTER 21

THE ENGLISH-SPEAKING EASTERN CARIBBEAN STATES

*S*even small English-speaking islands in the Eastern Caribbean—all of which also belong to CARICOM—form the Organization of Eastern Caribbean States (OECS). Members include Montserrat as well as the nations of Antigua and Barbuda, Dominica, Grenada, Saint Kitts and Nevis, Saint Lucia, and Saint Vincent and the Grenadines. These countries became sovereign nations between 1974 and 1983. During these years, the economic and political climate was remarkably different from that of the 1960s, when Jamaica, Trinidad, Barbados, and the Bahamas were born.

Economic circumstances throughout the 1970s and 1980s were unstable and generally unfavorable. Britain's entry into the European Common Market led to modifications in the old "preferential" system, which favored imports from the Commonwealth. Demand for the islands' main sources of income—bananas and tourism—fluctuated widely. The political situation also was hazardous. The Soviet Union entered the Caribbean in force, and communist Cuba poured troops and money into revolutionary movements throughout the region. The Manley government in Jamaica adopted a socialist economic system. A radical marxist government seized control of

Grenada in 1979, and there were other attempts to destroy democracy in the eastern Caribbean nations.

Political leaders on these tiny islands were aware that independence did not provide an optimal basis for development. The economic and political climate of the 1980s and early 1990s fostered integration and even encouraged calls for future political unity. In June 1981, the seven nations created the OECS. The heads of government form a governing body that has authority over foreign affairs, defense, security, and economic affairs. The organization maintains offices in Saint Lucia and Antigua, while judicial activities are coordinated through a joint Supreme Court.

The OECS nations are most closely integrated in economic matters. The East Caribbean Central Bank issues one common currency for member states. Member states have created an exclusive fishing zone, and they have abolished tariffs on most goods within the Eastern Caribbean Common Market. Through the OECS, governments jointly promote tourism, coordinate civil aviation activities, and send out overseas missions.

By the end of the 1980s, increased tourism and greater agricultural diversity seemed the most likely sources of economic growth. As in the larger islands, governments have had to shift resources to the private sector while improving the physical infrastructure to attract foreign investment. These were problems that could not be solved at the local level. From the end of the 1980s, OECS governments created new regional institutions to promote investment, develop exports, and facilitate agricultural diversification.

The creation of a joint military force accompanied economic integration. After gaining independence, only Jamaica and Trinidad created armies. The revolution in Grenada and attempted military coups on other islands demonstrated the inadequacy of the police forces and volunteer militias inherited from the colonial era. In October 1982, the Eastern Caribbean Regional Security System (RSS) was formed by Antigua, Barbados, Dominica, Saint Lucia, and Saint Vincent. Saint Kitts and Nevis joined in 1983, Grenada in 1985. RSS troops did not take part in the 1983 Grenada invasion (see p. 363–365), but they did help to restore order afterwards. The American, British, and Canadian military have provided training as well as new equipment; Jamaica and Trinidad have participated in the force's annual war games. Nevertheless, the RSS lacks the manpower and weaponry to police the region's sea lanes and combat drug traffickers.

John Compton (1926–   ), prime minister of Saint Lucia from 1982 to 1997, strongly supported advancing from economic and military cooperation to the creation of one Eastern Caribbean nation. However, the government of V. C. Bird on Antigua fought closer affiliation within either CARICOM or the OECS. Leaders of the English-speaking Windward Islands thus have called for closer union between their four countries. The Windward Islands Regional Constituent Assembly held meetings in the early 1990s. The assembly reported that the four nations backed a federal system of political union, and they have continued to move slowly toward integration.

Tourists and Bananas

In contrast to the situation in larger CARICOM nations, the OECS countries enjoyed economic expansion into the 1980s and 1990s. Antigua entered a phase of rapid expansion as a maturing tourist resort. Saint Lucia, Saint Vincent, and Saint Kitts benefited from the development of hitherto unexploited beaches and other national attractions. Even Dominica, a mountainous island without beaches, saw an upsurge in tourism. Foreign investors were slow to return to Grenada after the U.S. invasion in 1983 evicted the People's Revolutionary Government. By the late 1990s, however, luxury hotels and resorts had also sprung up on that ill-starred island.

Although the OECS nations tied their future to tourism, they still depended on primary agricultural products. Saint Kitts produced sugar, while Dominica, Saint Lucia, and Saint Vincent depended on bananas. These exports brought in foreign currency and they also supplied a livelihood for large numbers of politically active farmers. On several islands, a government marketing board purchased the crop. In December 1995, island governments purchased a stake in the shipping and British distribution of bananas in a joint venture with an Irish company.

Because of the relatively high costs of production, Caribbean bananas and sugar could not compete on the world markets. These industries survived because of arrangements under which the European nations guaranteed the islands a share of their market. Bananas, sugar, and rum were governed by the Lomé Convention, which benefited Haiti and the Dominican Republic as well as the CARICOM nations. The United States disputed the Lomé agreements, arguing that they restricted banana sales by American and Latin American producers. In September 1997, the World Trade Organization ruled in favor of the United States. Nevertheless, despite repeated U.S. propests, the European Union refused to end preferences benefiting Caribbean bananas.

ANTIGUA AND BARBUDA

Antigua's national life has been dominated by Vere Cornwall (V.C.) Bird and his sons. Beginning in the 1940s, the Birds have constructed a political machine that controls the government and the economy. Personal rule by charismatic leaders has been characteristic of the Commonwealth Caribbean. In most cases, however, two or more political parties alternate in power. Even though the outward forms of parliamentary democracy have been preserved, Antigua is a one-party state.

Under the Bird family's rule, the distinction between public and private has been obliterated. The political patronage and "clientalism" found on Jamaica, Barbados, Trinidad, and many other island states has been carried to extremes. Public offices and public companies are used to channel jobs, services, access to land, and union rights to supporters. In the process, the Birds have become enormously wealthy.

More than on most other English-speaking islands, moreover, the Bird machine has used the powers of government to harass opponents. The family has manipulated the police, judiciary, and civil service to deny civil rights, curtail public criticism, and eliminate opposing parties and unions. In some cases, Antigua's high court and the OECS Court of Appeal have reversed government decisions and criticized officials. But the Birds' victims often cannot afford to carry on lengthy court cases, and Antigua's government refuses to enforce judicial rulings.

In her autobiographical *A Small Place,* the Antiguan author Jamaica Kincaid (1949–   ) has compared the Bird family to the Duvaliers of Haiti. While the comparison is accurate in some regards, the Bird regime has been less openly brutal than that of Papa and Baby Doc. Perhaps it simply is easier for a single family to control an island 12 miles long and 9 miles wide, with 50,000 inhabitants.

V. C. Bird, a former Salvation Army captain, helped form the Antigua Trades and Labour Union in 1939 and became its president in 1943. As the British government moved toward independence, Bird created the Antigua Labour Party (ALP) in 1951. The ALP won every elective seat on the legislative council in that year and again in 1956, and Bird became chief minister in 1960. After winning reelection in 1961, his government began turning the island away from sugar toward large-scale, foreign-backed tourist development.

In 1967, aided by a loan from Great Britain, Antigua's government took over 13,000 acres of sugar lands. Bird now controlled most of the island's farmland, a powerful trade union, and the entire apparatus of government. (Only Barbuda enjoys any form of local government; a cabinet minister administers Antigua's towns.) In 1970, Bird opened ZDK, a family-owned radio station that provides the only alternative to the government station. Later the family installed the island's only cable television system.

Bird ruled his union with an iron fist, regularly purging anyone who challenged his leadership. In 1967 he expelled George Walter, who formed a rival union and political party, the Progressive Labour Movement (PLM). Walter insisted that workers be allowed to choose between Bird's union and his own. When Bird's government fought this attempt, Walter called a general strike. Violence erupted both before and after Bird declared a state of emergency and called out the army against the strikers.

The PLM carried the 1971 election, and Walter became premier. A recession in the early 1970s brought hard times and high unemployment. The last vestiges of the sugar industry shut down, Antigua's oil refinery closed, and tourism fell sharply. Meanwhile, bombs were set off around the island. Premier Walter issued orders restricting the press and requiring police approval for public meetings.

The ALP easily won the elections of 1976 and 1980. V. C. Bird returned as head of government and became prime minister when Antigua gained independence in 1981. After five years out of office, Bird apparently resolved never to lose power again. Following the 1976 election, he charged Walter with profiteering while in office. Because of evidence that Bird had tampered with the jury, Walter's conviction was overturned on appeal. But he was in jail long enough to be barred from the 1980 election.

Vere Bird Junior (1936–   ) and Lester Bird (1938–   ), two of the prime minister's sons, were also elected to parliament and became part of Bird's government. From about 1980, because of V. C. Bird's advanced age, routine business was conducted through his son Lester, putative heir to the throne as well as deputy prime minister, minister of foreign affairs, and minister of economic development. As minister of public works, aviation, and communications, Vere Junior took charge of distributing patronage. A third brother, Ivor, ran the family radio station.

The Bird family has frequently sold sanctuary to fugitives from other jurisdictions. In 1978, an American court convicted Gerald Bull (who later attempted to build a super-gun for Sadam Hussein of Iraq) of selling howitzers, shells, and radar tracking systems to South Africa despite an international embargo. Bull had set up a partnership with the Birds and shipped the weapons through Antigua. Robert Vesco, an American wanted for financial fraud, hid out in Antigua during the early 1980s after he was expelled from the Bahamas.

The tourist industry slumped again between 1980 and 1982 but recovered before the 1984 elections. Helped by divisions within the opposition, Bird's ALP won every seat in parliament except those reserved for Barbuda. Throughout the 1980s, the government fostered foreign investment in large resort complexes, and it borrowed heavily to build the infrastructure for tourism. By the 1990s, this sector provided approximately 35 percent of employment and accounted directly and indirectly for some 80 percent of GDP.

Most profits from tourism are expatriated, and foreign nationals hold the top positions in the industry. Tourism is also subject to severe recessions, as in 1995 when the island was severely damaged by Hurricane Luis. However, tourist revenues have allowed the government to purchase a wide range of industries, including ports, airports, water supply, electricity, telecommunications, hotels, banks, an insurance company, and most of the prime agricultural land. Government companies rarely make a profit, but they offer ample opportunity for political patronage as well as financial kickbacks to the Bird family. The government also provides a variety of pension benefits and subsidized health care.

The Bird Family's Second Generation in Power

In 1986, Vere Bird Junior was accused of fraud in negotiating and misusing a French loan of $11 million to repave the runways at the V. C. Bird International Airport. An official inquiry concluded that the prime minister's eldest son had acted "in a manner unbecoming a minister of government." Some in government, including Lester Bird, demanded that Vere Junior resign, but Prime Minister V.C. Bird refused to dismiss him. Despite these rifts within the family and the ALP, the party again won a large majority at the 1989 elections.

HEDONISM IN PARADISE

Caribbean governments increasingly look to tourists to provide the hard currencies to pay for needed imports. Without even counting cruise ship passengers, 14 million visitors descended on the Caribbean islands in 1995. Over the course of a year, they vastly outnumber the native inhabitants. Some 600,000 came to Sint Maarten, 13 square miles with a population of 32,000; 400,000 went to the Cayman Islands, home to 36,000.

The beaches are saved from overcrowding because most tourists stay only for a week or two. Before long-haul jets were introduced in the 1960s, most visitors were wealthy escapees from the long northern winters. Now Jamaica is only four hours from New York, and Germans can reach the Dominican Republic in nine hours. Tourists arrive year-round, as all-inclusive packages appeal to those with short holidays and average incomes.

Most islands try to attract every sector of the tourist market—offering accommodations from below $60 a day to more than $6,000. Very expensive

---

hotels in guarded beach-side enclaves offer "luxury" in bucketfuls to the wealthy and fashionable. Down the road or across the island, modest hotels and condos (often not directly on the beach) cater to those on cheaper package tours. There always are more of the latter, as the poor outnumber the rich.

Whatever they spend, all tourists are expected to be searching for the same thing—a tropical paradise for sun-soaked fun and carefree hedonism. Brochures and advertisements targeting Caribbean tourists are very different from those selling, for example, archaeological and historical tours in North Africa. Tourists to the Caribbean, advertisers and travel writers assume, are not well-educated, and they definitely do not want "adventures." They want safety and security in the sun.

The Caribbean islands sold to tourists are untouched natural paradises, far from machinery and pollution. Their inhabitants are colorful, carefree men and women; innocent and childlike, they give themselves to the simple pleasures of music, dance, and sex. Tourists are encouraged to "go native" and also live like children, far from their business suits and jobs.

In virtually every brochure, visions of sex and romance complete the picture of an enticing natural paradise. Couples embrace as the sun sets, or they walk barefoot and hand-in-hand down a pristine beach. Marketed to couples only, "all-inclusive" retreats promise them pleasure, play, and love. Yet the advertising also insinuates that the unattached may well find partners for their fun in the sun.

It seems a truism that these fantasies are far from the reality of life for islanders, who are not as mindlessly carefree as the brochures suggest. Yet island leaders have chosen to pin their economic plans on tourism, and these images succeed in bringing in more and more tourists. Millions arrive and act out their fantasies, turning them at least temporarily into realities. As they live their dreams of sun-soaked escapism, tourists overlook other realities. While walking down a sandy beach hand-in-hand, for example (as Jamaica Kincaid comments), visitors seldom pause to question the destination of wastes from their resort.

In April 1990, Colombia's government complained that Antigua was arming the Medellín drug cartel. Ten tons of weapons bought in Israel for the Antigua Defense Force (which consisted of fewer than 100 men, already armed by the United States) had ended up on the farm of Medellín henchman José Rodriguez Gacha. Some of the guns were used during the assassination of Colombian presidential candidate Luis Carlos Galán. An inquiry established that British and Israeli mercenaries, hired by Colombian drug cartels, had shifted operations to Antigua because of pressure from the Colombian government. Vere Bird Junior was implicated once again. This time he was dismissed and supposedly banned for life from holding public office.

Lester Bird succeeded his father as leader of the ALP in 1993, and he took over as prime minister following the 1994 elections. Barred from public office in 1990, Vere Bird Junior nevertheless was elected to parliament. Although the opposition was not permitted access to government-owned media, the election generally was considered honest.

In February 1995, an ALP activist was arrested and charged with threatening to murder Tim Hector (1942–   ), editor of an opposition newspaper. Prime Minister Lester Bird intervened and released the accused without trial. In May, Ivor Bird was arrested at the airport after he collected luggage containing 12 kilograms of cocaine. Lester Bird ordered his brother released after he paid a fine equivalent to $74,000.

Charges of fraud and bribery continued in 1996 and 1997. In May 1996, Vere Bird Junior was appointed special adviser to the prime minister, despite the 1990 ruling declaring him unfit for office. In September, the minister of finance resigned amid accusations that he had avoided paying customs duty for a vintage automobile. Ten thousand Antiguans demonstrated to demand a full inquiry into the affair. A Russian-owned bank failed in August 1997 amid allegations of fraud. The bank's marketing had touted Antigua's low level of regulation. The U.S. State Department described Antigua's 50 offshore banks as havens for questionable and illegal practices.

Barbuda, a smaller island with a population of 1,200, receives too little rainfall to supply adequate amounts of drinking water. Most of the island's income comes from sand mining and remittances from family members living abroad. Barbuda has always opposed its association with Antigua. Despite a strong campaign for separate independence by Barbudans, Britain granted the two islands independence as a unitary state.

Up to independence in 1981, a century-old Crown ordinance reserved the island's land for Barbudans, who owned the island collectively rather than as individuals. A Barbuda Council was established in 1976 to provide local government. However, successive Bird governments have ignored the council and repealed laws protecting Barbuda's resources. Companies owned by the Bird family or by its cronies have grabbed control of much of the island.

SAINT KITTS AND NEVIS

Until he died in 1978, Robert Bradshaw led both the Saint Kitts Trades and Labor Union and the Saint Kitts Labour Party, which won every election from 1946 until 1980. During Bradshaw's long tenure, Labour increasingly intervened to prop up the failing sugar industry. In 1975 the government took control of all sugarcane fields, and it acquired the island's one central sugar factory in 1976. From the late 1960s, Bradshaw's opponents accused the Labour government of using illegal means to suppress political opposition. Anguilla seceded from the union with Saint Kitts when Bradshaw became premier in 1967 with the granting of associated statehood. The inhabitants of Nevis also believed that their needs were ignored by the Labour Party, based on Saint Kitts.

In 1980, after 30 years in power, the Labour Party was ousted by a coalition of the People's Action Movement (PAM) and the Nevis Reformation Party (NRP). Led by Kennedy Simmonds (1936–   ), a physician, the PAM called for greater emphasis on tourism and increased autonomy for Nevis. The 1983 independence constitution created a federal government for the two islands. A separate Nevis Island Assembly enjoys autonomy in local matters and is subject to the National Assembly only with regard to foreign affairs and defense. This constitutional change temporarily ended Nevisian threats of secession, and Britain granted the two-nation state independence in September 1983.

At elections in 1984 and 1989, Simmonds's PAM/NRP coalition retained power in an enlarged National Assembly, with eight representatives from Saint Kitts and three from Nevis. Dr. Simmonds's electoral success reflected continuing economic development. To maintain employment, Saint Kitts continued to grow sugarcane, sometimes selling the crop at prices below production costs. A light manufacturing industry assembled electronic components and textiles for reexport. But the tourist industry provided the main source of economic growth. By the mid-1990s, revenues from tourism contributed at least one-fourth of the nation's gross domestic product. Pleased with their relative prosperity, voters ignored persistent rumors of official connivance in drug-trafficking activities.

Denzil L. Douglas (1953–   )—like Simmonds, a physician—became the head of the Labour Party in 1984 and broadened the party's appeal beyond its working-class base. In November 1993, Simmonds's PAM and Douglas's Labour Party each elected four representatives to the assembly. On Nevis, the NRP won only one seat; the other two representatives were elected by the independence-minded Concerned Citizens Movement, headed by Vance Amory. When the PAM and the NRP formed a minority government, Labour Party supporters protested in the streets, sometimes violently. In December 1993 the Governor-General declared a 21-day state of emergency. A contingent of the Regional Security System, dispatched from Barbados, helped to restore peace.

A rise in violent crime in late 1994 prompted renewed concern over the drug trade. During the 1980s, the nation's ambassador to the United Nations had been implicated in money laundering and drug trafficking. In July 1994, the ambassador and his family disappeared mysteriously at sea amid suspicion of foul play related to drugs. In October, a son of Sidney Morris, the deputy prime minister, was found murdered together with his fiancée. Soon after, the head of the police investigations unit was killed on his way to work. The following month, two other sons of Deputy Prime Minister Morris were arrested for trafficking 121 pounds of cocaine and for possessing illegal weapons. They also were implicated in the murders. When the two younger Morrises were granted bail, public protests and a prison riot forced Sidney Morris to resign. The prisoners totally destroyed the central prison and many escaped, but most were recaptured with the help of the Regional Security System.

Fierce electoral campaigning led to renewed violent clashes between PAM and Labour Party supporters prior to elections in July 1995. After 15 years in opposition, Labour won an overwhelming victory. Douglas replaced Simmonds as prime minister. Following Labour's victory, Douglas clashed with the Nevis administration led by Amory as the National Assembly passed bills transferring authority away from Nevis.

In June 1996, the Nevis Island Assembly announced its intention to break away from the federation with Saint Kitts. Lawmakers unanimously voted for independence in October 1997, but the move needed approval by two-thirds of Nevis's 5,000 voters. In August 1998, the number of those supporting secession fell just a few votes short of the two-thirds majority needed under the constitution. Some voters said they voted "no" in the hastily called referendum because they were unsure how independence would be implemented. They complained that Vance Amory, the main force behind the secession drive, did not explain whether Nevisians would still be able to visit Saint Kitts, only two miles away by ferry.

DOMINICA

Because of its rugged terrain and the frequency of heavy rains and hurricanes, Dominica is not well-suited for large-scale agriculture. One of the last islands to be colonized, Dominica had few sugar plantations and only a small slave population. Over the years, the best land has been planted with a succession of export crops, including cocoa, coffee, limes, and coconuts. Bananas were introduced during the 1930s and have become the main crop, providing almost half of export revenues in the 1990s.

For several decades after slave emancipation (1834–38), Dominica's legislature had a colored majority. The island came under direct British rule as a Crown colony in 1898. With the restoration of elections in the 1950s, a labor party and trade union representing workers and small farmers came to power on Dominica, as on other British Caribbean islands. Edward Oliver Leblanc, a farmer and agriculture instructor, led the majority Dominica Labour Party from 1960 until 1974, winning self-government from Britain in 1967. At the end of the 1960s, a radical political organization patterned after the Rastafarians in Jamaica (called "Dreads" on Dominica) emerged among the black lower classes. As unrest grew, the DLP passed a law curbing press criticism of government. Mary Eugenia Charles (1919–   ), a lawyer and member of a prominent family in the capital of Roseau, founded the Dominica Freedom Party (DFP) to protest this legislation.

Leblanc remained popular among rural Dominicans, and the DLP easily defeated the DFP in the 1970 election. In the midst of growing turmoil, Leblanc resigned in 1974 and was replaced by Patrick John (1937–   ). To control the Dreads' criminal activities, John's government passed repressive laws, including an act allowing any private citizen to kill members of illegal societies. John won the 1975 election and gained Dominica's independence in 1978. His government increasingly used the army against opponents and proposed new laws outlawing strikes and limiting freedom of the press. The political crisis reached a peak in May 1979. More than 10,000 demonstrators rallied in front of the assembly to protest the new laws. When the Dominican army fired on the crowd and killed several persons, a general strike shut down the country and forced John to resign.

After a bitter campaign, the Dominica Freedom Party gained a landslide victory in 1980. Eugenia Charles became the Caribbean's first female prime minister and won reelection in 1985 and 1990. Under her leadership, Dominica strongly supported United States policies in the Caribbean. As head of the Organization of Eastern Caribbean States, Prime Minister Charles invited American intervention in October 1983, following the murder of Maurice Bishop in Grenada. Charles opposed a military takeover in Grenada partly because of her own experiences on Dominica.

The islands are home to several species of iguanas. Islands without sandy beaches emphasize "eco-tourism," stressing their natural beauty and wildlife and offering activities such as camping, hiking, and bird-watching.

As prime minister, Patrick John had used the army against opponents, and army officers plotted with John to overthrow the Charles government in 1981. As the year began, the government disarmed and disbanded the defense force, following reports that weapons were being traded for marijuana. Against a background of increasing violence, former officers made two attempts to take power. Troops from the neighboring French islands helped to suppress the uprisings.

A one-crop economy is fragile and susceptible to disaster. Hurricanes destroyed almost the entire banana crop in 1979, 1980, and 1995. Throughout the 1980s, Prime Minister Charles sought to increase foreign investment, improve the infrastructure, and diversify agricultural production. Following agreements with the International Monetary Fund and the World Bank, the government reduced export and import controls, privatized some state-owned companies, and limited wage increases for public employees.

Many on Dominica disliked these continuing austerity measures. Despite this dissatisfaction, Charles and the DFP made inroads among peasant and working-class voters. Farmers benefited from projects that brought roads and electricity into the countryside, and some large estates were divided up among the workers. The Charles government took full advantage of its control over the island's only radio station, and the DFP sponsored an aggressive and well-funded youth movement.

Efforts to diversify the economy enjoyed some success. Tourism was slow to develop because of the absence of white sand beaches. Taking advantage of Dominica's rugged beauty and unique natural history, marketing campaigns emphasized "eco-tourism," mountain climbing, and camping. Visits by cruise ship passengers soared from 7,000 in 1990 to 133,000 in 1995. However, the island has found it difficult to borrow the enormous sums needed to build an international airport.

Just before the 1995 elections, Eugenia Charles announced her resignation after 15 years as prime minister. Partly because Charles gave only tepid support to her successor, the election was won by the United Workers' Party (UWP). Edison James (1943–), a banana merchant who founded the UWP in 1988, pledged to increase economic growth and create jobs. Once in office, James's policies closely resembled those of the preceding Charles governments. James pledged to privatize additional government companies, and he sought advice from the IMF on debt restructuring and additional free-market reforms.

SAINT LUCIA

Saint Lucia, also a volcanic island, is almost as mountainous as Dominica. Bananas became the primary export crop after sugar was abandoned in 1964. Virtually all former sugar land, although not ideally suited to the industry, was devoted to bananas produced by independent peasants on small plots. By the late 1980s, this one crop occupied three-fourths of all arable land, and almost half of St. Lucia's working population grew bananas. However, yields were relatively low. Farmers made a profit only because their output was sold to a guaranteed market in the United Kingdom and Europe. If the 1997 World Trade Organization ruling against such trade preferences were to be enforced, Saint Lucia's banana industry no longer would be viable. Through 1998, however, the European Union nations refused to implement the WTO ruling, despite U.S. threats of retaliatory tariffs against products from EU members.

As in other British colonies, political parties were closely tied to labor unions. John Compton (1926–), who created the United Workers Party (UWP) in 1964, had studied economics in London and qualified as a barrister. Returning to Saint Lucia, he successfully owned and managed a plantation. Under Compton's leadership, the UWP controlled parliament from 1964 to 1979 and again from 1982 to 1997.

The opposition Saint Lucia Labour Party (SLP) favored more governmental support for local entrepreneurs and a foreign policy less subservient to the United States. With union support, Allan Louisy led the SLP to victory in 1979, a few months after Saint Lucia became independent. However, internal feuds within the SLP forced Louisy to resign in 1982.

John Compton again became prime minister as the UWP won the general election in 1982 and retained power with reduced margins in 1987 and 1992. Successive UWP administrations have improved education and public health, and diversified the economy through foreign and local investment in light manufacture and tourism. Compton's government became directly involved in the economy by investing public funds in specific private projects as well as in infrastructure improvements.

Since the late 1980s, politics in Saint Lucia has focused on bananas. The rapidly expanding tourist industry provided sufficient revenues to cover most of the island's import bills. Nevertheless, the banana crop continued to employ thousands who could not easily find other work. In late 1988, the government took control of the producer's association, which purchases crops from individual growers. Disputes over banana prices throughout the 1990s led to a series of strikes, often violent, that disrupted production and shipment of the crop.

Opposition to Compton's government increased in 1995. A commission of inquiry concluded that Saint Lucia's representative to the United Nations, Charles Fleming, had used $100,000 in foreign aid to pay political campaign expenses. Fleming refused to return from the United States, and he insisted that Prime Minister Compton and others knew of his actions. Compton resigned as prime minister in March 1995. Vaughan Lewis (1940–), former director-general of the Organization of East Caribbean States, took over as UWP party leader.

Returning to power after 15 years, the Saint Lucia Labour Party decisively won the May 1997 elections, and Kenny D. Anthony (1951–) became prime minister. Anthony promised to defend European trade preferences for Caribbean bananas while improving the crop through tax incentives based on quality and export performance.

SAINT VINCENT AND THE GRENADINES

Lying at the southern tip of the Lesser Antilles, this chain of some 600 tiny islands stretches from Saint Vincent down to Grenada. The islands are formed from the peaks of a partially submerged chain of volcanic mountains; Mount Soufrière on Saint Vincent is still active. A violent eruption in 1902 killed 2,000 persons and devastated the northern half of the island.

Since Saint Vincent is composed almost entirely of volcanic ash and lava, the soil is extremely porous. Water seeps through rapidly, leaving the surface dry. Nevertheless,

Small country stores supply the needs of islanders living away from the areas frequented by tourists and cruise ships.

agriculture continues to play a major role in Saint Vincent's economy. Since sugar production ended in the early 1970s, the most important exports are bananas and arrowroot—a tuberous root ground into a starch for baby food, biscuits, and computer paper. Many Saint Vincentians earn their living as independent small farmers, so labor unions are less influential than on other islands.

Saint Vincent lacks a large international airport. Although the number of visitors increased in the 1980s and early 1990s, tourism is smaller in scale than in most other Caribbean islands. Primarily concentrated in the Grenadines, tourist facilities cater to yacht owners and wealthy visitors who own property in the islands.

Saint Vincent belonged to the Windward Islands grouping from the mid-19th century to 1959, when it became part of the West Indies Federation. With the federation's collapse, Saint Vincent gained local autonomy in 1969 and full independence in 1979. The People's Political Party (PPP), the first party to gain widespread support, mainly appealed to labor union members. However, the PPP lost much of its following in the 1960s to the Saint Vincent Labour Party (SVLP), which won the votes of the more conservative black middle class. Led by R. Milton Cato (1915–97), the SVLP fought crime and drug abuse, followed a pro-Western foreign policy, and introduced government management of the economy. Cato won the 1966 and 1974 elections, and he became independent Saint Vincent's first prime minister in 1979.

Concern over Cato's advanced age and ill health contributed to his defeat in 1984 by the New Democratic Party (NDP), founded and led by Sir James "Sonny" Mitchell (1931–   ). Mitchell enjoyed four consecutive terms as prime minister. The NDP won all 15 elective seats in 1989 and took 12 of 15 in 1994. In the June 1998 elections, the opposition Unity Labour Party (ULP) won a larger percentage of the total vote islandwide. Nevertheless, Mitchell's NDP still managed to capture eight of the 15 seats in parliament. Although Mitchell had been critical of the United States, he favored the 1983 invasion of Grenada, and Saint Vincent participates in the Regional Security System for the eastern Caribbean.

GRENADA

On Grenada, as on the other English-speaking islands, the personalities of leaders and local concerns influence political choices. Political parties originally grew out of island-wide labor unions led by men with a strong emotional or even charismatic appeal. Some parties have enjoyed their greatest success with agricultural laborers, while others are popular with urban workers and black and colored merchants and professionals. All, however, seek votes from every segment of society rather than from only one economic class.

The marxist dictatorship imposed on Grenada from 1979 to 1983 by the People's Revolutionary Government (PRG) was an aberration. Marxism attracts few islanders in the Commonwealth Caribbean. Most are deeply religious and abhor the militant atheism of marxist ideology. After centuries of British rule, moreover, most island leaders believe in parliamentary democracy and reject calls for armed revolution. On Jamaica, for example, Michael Manley and Edward Seaga strongly attacked the opponent's political philosophy and policies. But neither man tried to keep power through force when defeated at the polls.

In March 1979, the PRG overthrew Prime Minister Eric Gairy, carrying out the only successful revolution in the history of the British islands. Most Grenadians—who assumed the PRG intended to hold free elections—welcomed the revolution because they held Gairy's government in deep contempt. Gairy, who had dominated Grenadian politics since the early 1950s, became the island's first prime minister when independence was granted in 1974. Gairy then seized complete control, staying in power through fraudulent elections, corruption, and violence.

Gairy's regime resembled that of the Duvaliers in Haiti. He controlled the government and made all decisions. Supporters received import monopolies in return for kickbacks, and Gairy built a personal empire of hotels, restaurants, and nightclubs. Opponents were threatened by laws controlling newspapers, restricting public gatherings, and allowing the police to arrest and hold people without charge. Opposition meetings were broken up by the police, the army (called Green Beasts from the color of their uniforms), and various groups of thugs collectively known as the Mongoose Gang. Almost nothing was spent on education, and hospitals lacked medicine, beds, and linen. The economy was in shambles, and unemployment reached 50 percent.

The New Jewel Movement

Shortly after Gairy won the 1972 elections (partly through fraud), several young Grenadians organized groups opposed to his government. Most belonged to the urban middle class and had earned professional degrees at universities in North America and Europe. During their studies abroad, they had become committed believers in a mixture of marxist and black power doctrines. Maurice Bishop (1944–83), a London-educated lawyer, organized a political group in Saint Georges, the island's capital. Unison Whiteman, an economist with a degree from Howard University, attracted rural laborers to his Joint Endeavor for Welfare, Education, and Liberation (JEWEL). The two groups merged in 1973 to form the New Jewel Movement (NJM).

Bishop and Bernard Coard (1944–   ), who joined the NJM in 1976, became the party's most important leaders. Handsome and tall, with a radiant and optimistic manner, Bishop was a mesmerizing orator in the tradition of Jamaica's Michael Manley and Cuba's Fidel Castro. Coard had studied politics and economics at Brandeis University and the University of Sussex. While he totally lacked Bishop's magnetism, Coard was considered an effective manager as well as the party's leading intellectual.

Prime Minister Gairy believed in witchcraft and the invasion of the earth by flying saucers, and he often made decisions based on his dreams. On March 12, 1979, he flew to New York, hoping to convince the United Nations to recognize the existence of UFOs ("unidentified flying objects"). At 4 A.M. the next day, 46 members of the NJM's military wing easily captured the army barracks and state radio station. Gairy's Green Beasts were asleep, and the sentries guarding Radio Grenada fled when they saw the barracks on fire.

The People's Revolutionary Government in Power

The jubilant people of Grenada literally danced in the streets at Gairy's overthrow. If the NJM had held elections, Bishop would have obtained a large majority in parliament.

However, NJM leaders, firmly dedicated to Leninist principles, intended to keep all power in their own hands. They immediately suspended the 1973 constitution and established a People's Revolutionary Government (PRG) under NJM control. The PRG assumed all legislative and executive powers, and it also controlled the judiciary. Existing laws were abolished and replaced by "People's Laws" signed by Bishop.

Maurice Bishop and Bernard Coard shared control of Grenada after 1979, with Bishop taking charge of foreign affairs and Coard running the economy. In 1983, their struggle for power destroyed the NJM and led to Bishop's murder. Both men were committed marxists who deeply admired Fidel Castro, and Bishop named his son Vladimir in honor of Lenin, the founder of the Soviet Union. Because of his more populist manner, observers outside the NJM sometimes regarded Coard as more radical than Bishop. Judging by NJM records, however, there was little difference in their basic beliefs or goals.

The middle-class leaders of the NJM tried, at least in their speeches, to reach out to Grenada's poor farmworkers. But Bishop and Coard never meant the New Jewel to be a mass party. Copying Cuba and the Soviet Union, Bishop and Coard organized the NJM as a tightly controlled Leninist "party of the vanguard." Only sincere communists were welcomed, and members were carefully screened during at least two years of probation. At its high point in September 1982, the NJM had only eighty fully qualified members.

Taking the title of prime minister, Bishop appointed a cabinet with some 20 ministers—a few of whom were not party members—responsible for specific departments of the government. However, all real decisions were made by the NJM. The party's supreme body was a Central Committee with 15 to 20 party members, chaired by Bishop. Normally it met about once a month to decide policy matters and give overall direction. Bishop also chaired the Politburo (political bureau), whose seven or eight members met weekly and implemented the Central Committee's decisions. Since there were few party leaders, each usually held several jobs. Coard sat on both the Central Committee and the Politburo and served as minister of finance and deputy prime minister. Hudson Austin, who led the March 1979 revolution, became commander of the People's Revolutionary Army (PRA), headed two ministries (defense and construction), and belonged to both ruling committees.

As in the Soviet Union, the PRG set up various mass organizations for women, children, and teenagers, as well as "grass roots" groups in each village. These implemented its orders, sought to indoctrinate the people, and might report local concerns. But they had no independent authority, and the PRG immediately moved to head off any opposition to its total control. In March 1979, it authorized Austin's People's Revolutionary Army to imprison anyone, without trial and for as long as it wished. The PRA suppressed opposition newspapers and imprisoned their shareholders. It jailed at least 200 persons suspected of disagreeing with its policies. Some were held for up to four years, and many were horribly tortured.

The PRG's ultimate goal was Soviet-style communism, with the state owning all industry and farms. It immediately nationalized the electric utility and telephone companies, the banks, and some hotels. It also set up state farms and seized the largest private estates. Because it lacked managers, the government temporarily allowed some private ownership of small companies. But it rigidly controlled all exports and imports.

The PRG soon established close ties with Cuba and the Soviet Union. New Jewel leaders virtually worshiped Castro, who now developed a close personal friendship with Bishop. Grenada helped Cuba establish contacts with government and opposition leaders throughout the Caribbean and Latin America. The U.S. government charged that the PRG further assisted Castro in setting up centers of revolutionary subversion. Through its Cuban ally, the PRG became a strident supporter of the Soviet Union. In January 1980, Grenada and Cuba thus were the only nations in North or South America to vote against a United Nations resolution condemning the Russian invasion of Afghanistan.

Cuba and the Soviet Union rewarded Bishop's loyalty with enormous amounts of aid, given both as grants or gifts and as long-term loans. The PRG was so successful in tapping foreign resources that its policies have been called "foreign-aid socialism." The government carefully drew up shopping lists of projects. It then solicited funds from the Soviet Union, other communist countries, and such oil-rich states as Algeria, Iraq, Syria, and Libya. Altogether, these donors gave the PRG at least $81 million between 1979 and 1983. And it further secured an additional $45 million from Western governments and international agencies. Grenada, with fewer than 100,000 inhabitants, thus ranked among the top five aid receivers in the world.

The centerpiece of Cuban aid was the construction, beginning in December 1979, of a new airport at Point Salines, a few miles from the capital of Saint Georges. Castro gave millions in grants, and hundreds of Cuban workers and engineers worked around the clock at the site. With a runway almost 10,000 feet long, the new airport would be available to the largest aircraft—both civilian and military. The PRG claimed that Grenada needed a modern airport to support an expansion of tourism. The United States charged that Point Salines airfield would give Cuba and the Soviet Union a safe base in the east Caribbean. Bishop encouraged U.S. suspicions by refusing to rule out Cuban or Russian military use.[1]

The Collapse of the PRG
and the Murder of Maurice Bishop

The PRG faced serious economic and political problems by the summer of 1983. Despite lavish foreign aid, the government had spent far more than it received. It now ran out of money and could not pay its foreign suppliers, the army, or government workers. Tax receipts were down as the number of tourists fell. Harmed by rigid controls and alienated by the imprisonment of prominent businessmen, private companies stopped investing. The state farms, agricultural factories, and fishing company lost money. Only the construction industry boomed. The PRG had wasted much of its foreign aid. Moreover, since most foreign grants were tied to specific projects, the PRG could not use them to pay day-to-day expenses.

As its economic problems mounted, the PRG became increasingly unpopular. Despite much-publicized Cuban assistance, public services actually decayed, and conditions in the schools and public hospitals remained deplorable. Living standards had fallen under the PRG, and unemployment was rising. The morale of NJM members and the People's Army was low, and most of the party's mass organizations no longer met.

Under the PRG, all decisions were made at the highest level, by the Central Committee and the Politburo. Since he headed both groups, some party members blamed the PRG's problems on Maurice Bishop's ineffective leadership. Bernard Coard escaped blame for party decisions because he had resigned from both governing bodies in October 1982. Moreover, many party members believed that Coard, the party's economic expert, was more likely than Bishop to solve Grenada's debt problems.

A long series of indecisive Central Committee meetings culminated in a three-day gathering between September 14 and September 16. Although they recognized the importance of Bishop's personal popularity, all 15 members joined in criticizing the prime minister's inept management. The Central Committee then voted to create a joint leadership "marrying the strengths of comrades Maurice and Bernard."[2] Bishop remained prime minister and head of the Central Committee, and he continued to represent the PRG at public and international meetings. Coard became chairman of the Politburo, responsible for day-to-day administration of the party and government.

Bishop accepted the joint leadership proposal at a general meeting of all party members on September 25. But, during a 12-day trip to Hungary, Czechoslovakia, and Cuba, he apparently changed his mind and looked for supporters outside the NJM. A combined meeting of the Central Committee and Politburo expelled Bishop from both bodies, and the Central Committee placed him under house arrest on October 13. The following day, Radio Grenada announced Bishop's dismissal as prime minister.

Despite the PRG's failures, Maurice Bishop himself remained popular. On Wednesday, October 19th, more than 10,000 Grenadians (10 percent of the nation's population) gathered at the central market square to protest Bishop's arrest. About 3,000 persons eventually marched uphill from the market to Bishop's house and liberated the former prime minister. Bishop decided to capture the PRA headquarters at Fort Rupert, located atop a high hill south of the market square and approached by only one narrow road. With Bishop and several members of his cabinet in the lead, the crowd stormed the fort. The soldiers surrendered at Bishop's order, and his supporters armed themselves from the fort's arsenal.

After failing to negotiate a compromise with Bishop, the Central Committee sent three armored personnel carriers to retake the fort. Before Bishop surrendered, the resulting battle killed at least 40 of his supporters and three of the attacking soldiers. On the orders of the Central Committee, a firing squad executed Bishop and four of his cabinet ministers. Two hours after this massacre, Hudson Austin, commander of the army, announced the formation of a Revolution Military Council. It would rule Grenada for only six days.

Operation Urgent Fury

The murder of Bishop and his closest associates was universally condemned by both the PRG's opponents and its friends, including Fidel Castro and Michael Manley of Jamaica. On October 21, 1983, representatives of the seven other members of the Organization of Eastern Caribbean States (OECS) met in Barbados.[3] With strong support from the prime ministers of Barbados and Jamaica, they unanimously decided to intervene in Grenada and requested help from the United States and other governments.

Four days later, on October 25, 1,900 U.S. soldiers invaded Grenada in a military action known as Operation Urgent Fury. Three hundred Caribbean soldiers—from

The Invasion of Grenada

Caribbean Sea

• Gouyave

▲ Mt. St. Catherine

Pearls Airport

Grenville •

GRENADA

OCTOBER 25, 1983
U.S. MARINES
CONDUCT HELICOPTER
ASSAULT

South East ▲
Mountain

*Atlantic
Ocean*

⊛ **St. George's**

OCTOBER 25, 1983
U.S. AIRBORNE
TROOPS ATTACK

*Point Salines
Airstrip*

N

| 0 | | 5 | | 10 Miles |

| 0 | | 5 | | 10 Kilometers |

Antigua, Dominica, Saint Lucia, Saint Vincent, Barbados, and Jamaica—accompanied the American forces but did not take part in the fighting. The British government did not permit participation by Montserrat, which is still a Crown colony. Prime Minister Chambers of Trinidad strongly opposed military intervention.

U.S. troops occupied the island within three days. Some 800 Cuban workers building the Point Salines airport were captured and returned to Cuba. Only a small number among the Cubans and the 1,500-man Grenadian army resisted. The militia was largely pro-Bishop and hardly mobilized. Altogether, 18 Americans, 24 Cubans, and 16 Grenadians died in action.

The OECS members believed that the massacre of a prime minister and his cabinet members justified military intervention. The governments of these small islands, which have minuscule defense forces, also believed that Grenada and its Cuban ally threatened the security of the entire eastern Caribbean. The U.S. government said that it had intervened both in response to the OECS request and to protect some

1,000 Americans living on Grenada—including about 600 students at Saint George's University Medical School.

Judging by public opinion polls, both Grenadians and the inhabitants of other nations in the Commonwealth Caribbean approved of the invasion. It was condemned by the governments of the Soviet Union, its allies, and many Latin American states. Britain, France, and Germany also initially criticized U.S. intervention. They subsequently supported it when the Reagan administration produced military treaties between Grenada and Cuba and other documents seized during the invasion. Under these agreements, Grenada would have received large amounts of weapons and might well have become a Cuban military base.

Grenada Rebuilds

The United States removed its combat forces in December 1983. With the help of some 800 U.S. and OECS troops, an advisory council appointed by the governor-general administered the island until the December 1984 election. Except that Grenada did not rejoin the East Caribbean Supreme Court, the 1974 constitution was reinstated.

Even before the PRG coup, Grenada had a comparatively weak tradition of democracy. In some British colonies, labor unions were affiliated with relatively broad-based parties. In contrast, Grenada's union was simply a device Eric Gairy used to gain power for himself. Grenada thus lacked both strong political organizations and strong labor unions. Parties have been small and fragmented; often they have been created merely to serve the ambitions of one man.

Gairy returned to Grenada in January 1984 to lead GULP, and a number of other parties also reemerged. The United States feared that a divided opposition would allow GULP to win a majority in parliament. At a meeting attended by the prime ministers of Barbados, Saint Lucia, and Saint Vincent, Grenadian political leaders agreed to merge their parties into the New National Party (NNP). The NNP took control of parliament, while Gairy's GULP took one seat. No candidate of the New Jewel Party—renamed the Maurice Bishop Patriotic Movement—was elected. Herbert Blaize, a lawyer who had held the office twice during the 1960s, again became prime minister.

Blaize's government relaxed the rigid controls imposed by Bishop's regime. The United States and international bodies provided substantial monetary aid for several years. With foreign help, the island's roads, telephones, and health care facilities were improved. However, Blaize had little toleration for criticism. During 1988 and 1989, the government prohibited the sale of books and magazines that criticized its policies, and it deported journalists and politicians from other Caribbean countries.

Blaize's autocratic style provoked dissent within his own political coalition. In 1987, George Brizan (1943–   ) and two other ministers resigned from Blaize's government and formed the National Democratic Congress (NDC). Brizan had worked for the Bishop regime as an education official. Two years later, Blaize lost control of the NNP to Keith Mitchell (1946–   ), a political moderate who had studied and taught mathematics at Howard University in the United States. Blaize formed his own party but died in December 1989.

New elections in March 1990 brought the left-wing NDC to power. (Despite his dismal record in the 1970s, many farmworkers remained loyal to Eric Gairy, whose GULP came in second.) Nicholas Brathwaite (1925–   ), a civil servant in the Fabian socialist tradition, became prime minister; Brizan served as Trade and Industry Minister. High debts forced Brathwaite's NDC government to cut benefits and raise taxes. Strikes by government and port workers during 1992 and 1993 disrupted the economy and prompted parliament to pass laws restricting work stoppages.

A Grenadian jury tried 14 persons—including Bernard and Phyllis Coard and Hudson Austin—for the murders of Maurice Bishop, his followers, and 40 members of the crowd at Port Rupert. All received death sentences in 1986. While most Grenadians wanted them to hang, Coard and other New Jewel members still had many influential American friends. Repetitive appeals delayed their executions, which Prime Minister Brathwaite commuted to life imprisonment in August 1991.

The NNP trounced the NDC in June 1995. Keith Mitchell became prime minister and kept his promise to abolish the income tax. Mitchell, like other Grenadian leaders, is not fond of dissent. Soon after taking office, he replaced the staff of the government-owned Grenada Broadcasting Corporation with his own political supporters. In February 1999, Grenada's 26,000 voters gave Dr. Mitchell total control of the government, as the NNP won all 15 seats in the island's parliament. George Brizan's NDC was annihilated, and Brizan himself lost the constituency he had held since the 1984 elections.

Grenada's main parties have adopted free-market and export-driven policies. Despite efforts to diversify the economy, Grenada remains dependent on exports of nutmeg, bananas, and cocoa. After Indonesia, Grenada is the world's second largest producer of nutmeg. The two nations have signed cartel agreements to cut production, but their efforts have failed to raise prices.

Grenada has had greater success in encouraging tourism. Ironically, the island owes much of its prosperity to the Cuban-built Point Salines airport, which made possible direct flights from North America and Europe. Lavish resorts dot the former people's republic. The Bishop regime's bombed-out headquarters overlooking Saint George's Harbor was torn down in 1998 and replaced by a luxury hotel and a marina for 500 yachts.

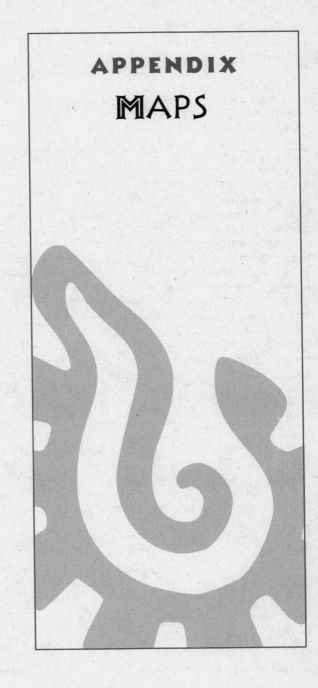

APPENDIX
MAPS

THE BAHAMAS

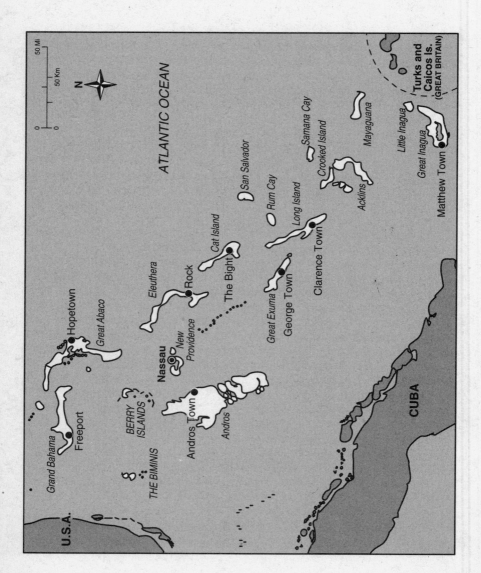

THE CARIBBEAN

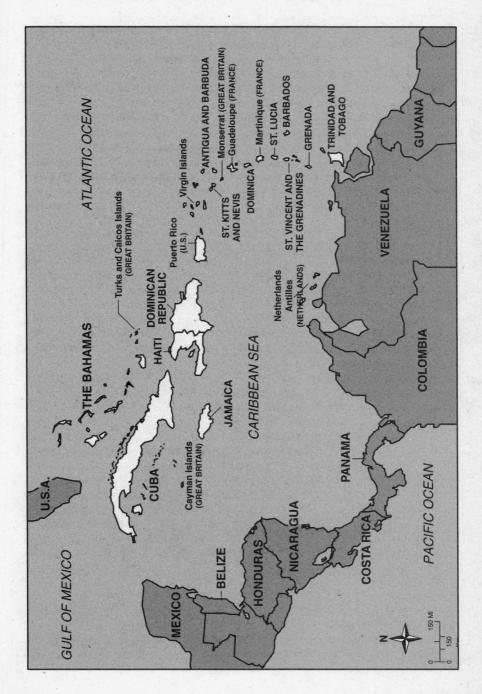

CAYMAN ISLANDS (GREAT BRITAIN)

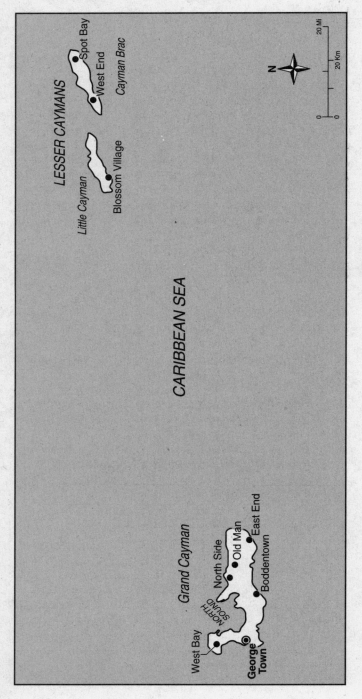

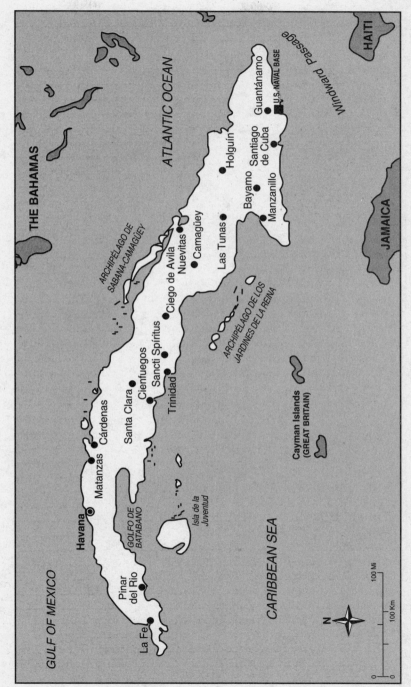

DOMINICAN REPUBLIC

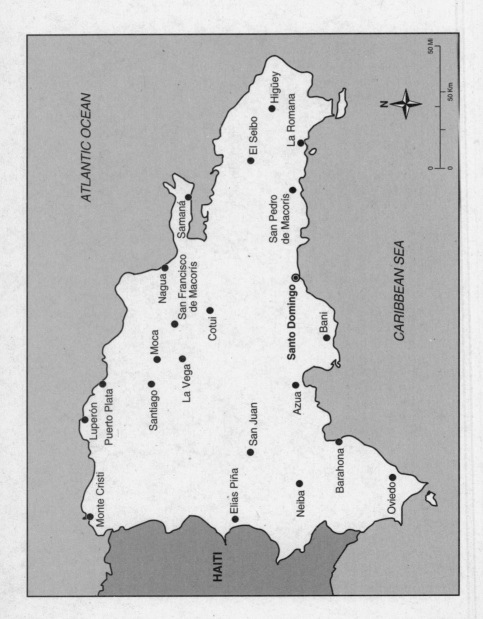

EARLY TERRITORIAL SETTLEMENTS

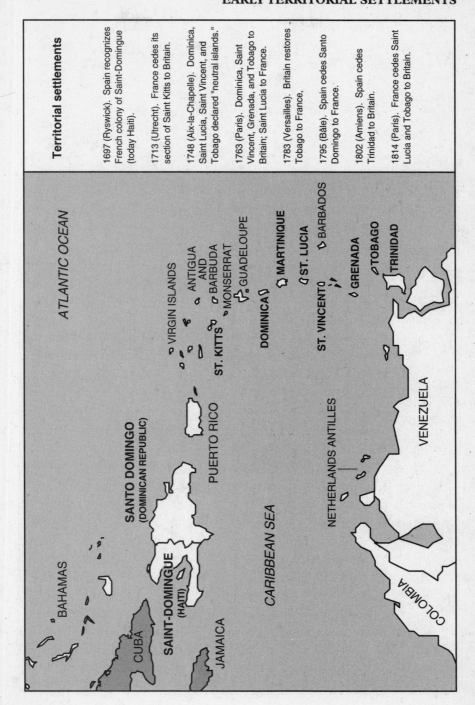

Territorial settlements

1697 (Ryswick). Spain recognizes French colony of Saint-Domingue (today Haiti).

1713 (Utrecht). France cedes its section of Saint Kitts to Britain.

1748 (Aix-la-Chapelle). Dominica, Saint Lucia, Saint Vincent, and Tobago declared "neutral islands."

1763 (Paris). Dominica, Saint Vincent, Grenada, and Tobago to Britain; Saint Lucia to France.

1783 (Versailles). Britain restores Tobago to France,

1795 (Bâle). Spain cedes Santo Domingo to France.

1802 (Amiens). Spain cedes Trinidad to Britain.

1814 (Paris). France cedes Saint Lucia and Tobago to Britain.

ATLANTIC OCEAN

VIRGIN ISLANDS

ANTIGUA AND BARBUDA

MONSERRAT

GUADELOUPE

ST. KITTS

MARTINIQUE

ST. LUCIA

BARBADOS

DOMINICA

ST. VINCENT

GRENADA

TOBAGO

TRINIDAD

SANTO DOMINGO
(DOMINICAN REPUBLIC)

PUERTO RICO

CARIBBEAN SEA

NETHERLANDS ANTILLES

VENEZUELA

BAHAMAS

SAINT-DOMINGUE
(HAITI)

CUBA

JAMAICA

COLOMBIA

FRENCH ANTILLES

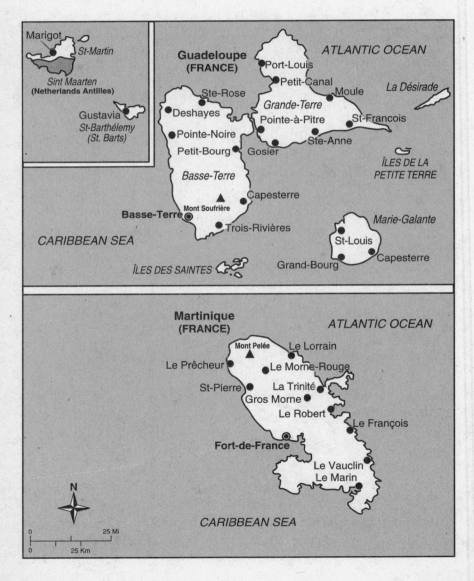

GRENADA

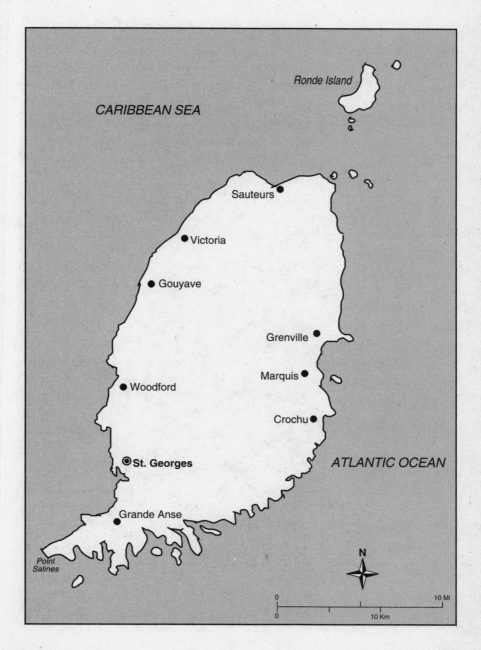

CARIBBEAN SEA

Ronde Island

Sauteurs

Victoria

Gouyave

Grenville

Marquis

Woodford

Crochu

St. Georges

ATLANTIC OCEAN

Grande Anse

Point Salines

N

0   10 Mi

0   10 Km

HAITI

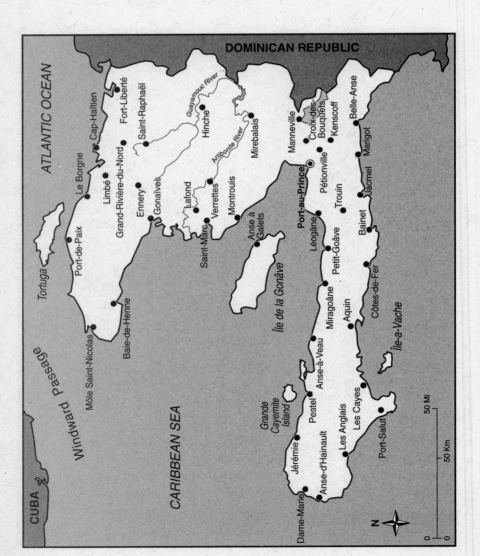

JAMAICA

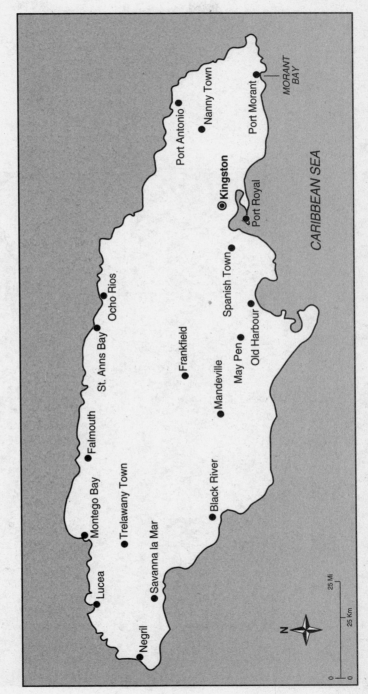

NETHERLANDS ANTILLES

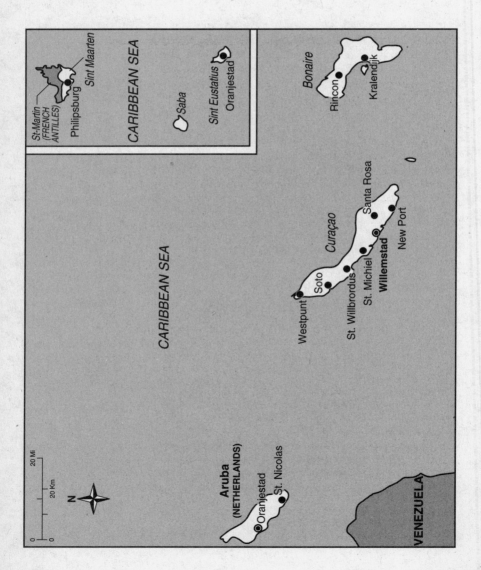

THE NORTHERN LESSER ANTILLES

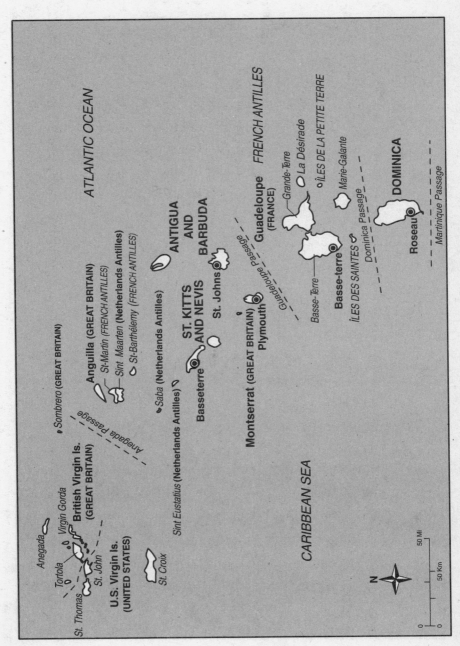

PUERTO RICO

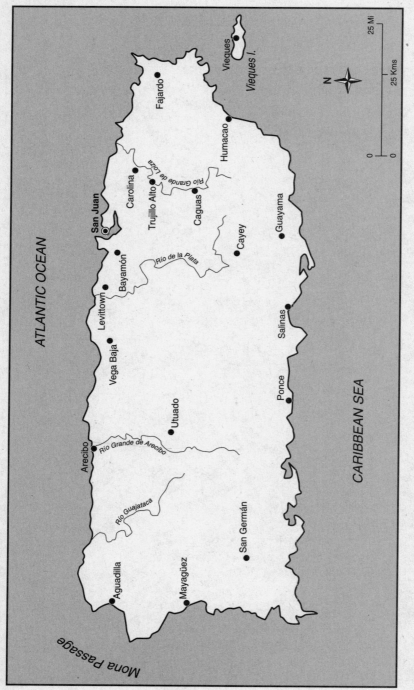

TURKS AND CAICOS ISLANDS (GREAT BRITAIN)

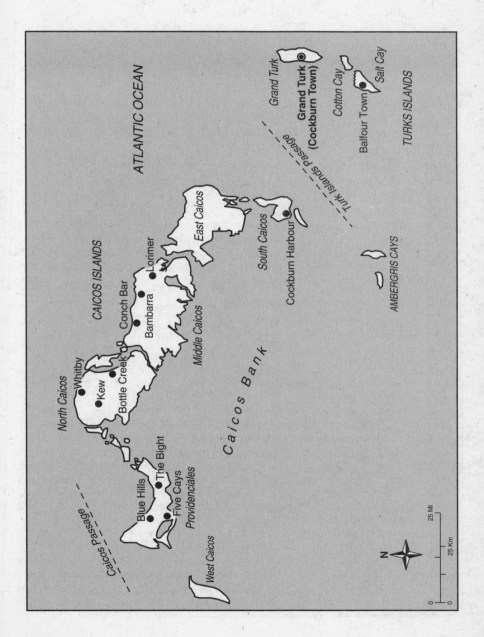

NOTES

PREFACE

1. Some of the significant differences between the Euro-African Caribbean and the Euro-Indian mainland are summarized by Robert West and John Augelli in *Middle America: Its Lands and Peoples,* 3rd edition (Englewood Cliffs: Prentice Hall, 1989), pages 12–18.
2. In Latin America, the term *criollo* originally was reserved for native-born whites. In the Caribbean, *creole* denoted all long-established populations and cultural habits, and it was used to contrast them with recent immigrants.

CHAPTER 1

1. I use the U.S. system of weights and measures throughout. For example, distances are expressed in miles rather than meters, and temperatures are cited in Fahrenheit and not in Celsius units.
2. This first era of mountain building and volcanic activity began during the Cretaceous period and probably lasted into the Eocene epoch. To emphasize its relative age, the geographical region comprising the Greater Antilles has been called "Antillia."
3. Mont Pelée (Martinique) erupted in 1902, Mount Soufrière (Saint Vincent) in 1812, 1902, and 1976. Mont Soufrière (Guadeloupe) erupted in 1956 and showed signs of instability in 1976. The volcano at Chanes Peak (Monserrat) erupted in 1995, devastating the island (See chapter 18.) In addition, there are volcanic vents (called *soufrières*) or hot sulfur springs on Nevis and Saint Lucia as well as in the crater of Mont Misery on Saint Kitts.
4. Also referred to as semi-evergreen, semi-deciduous, and semi-evergreen seasonal forests.
5. Carl Sauer, *The Early Spanish Main* (Berkeley and Los Angeles: University of California Press, 1969), page 68.
6. Yellow fever is unusual outside the tropics because the virus dies out at temperatures below 60°, and the mosquito lapses into a coma at 50°. *Aëdes aegypti,* which lives up to four months, can survive long ocean voyages. Thus sailing ships sometimes brought terrible epidemics to Philadelphia, New York, Boston or even northern Europe. But these plagues invariably died out with the first frost.

CHAPTER 2

1. Carl Sauer, *The Early Spanish Main,* 194.
2. Lyle McAlister, *Spain and Portugal in the New World, 1492–1700* (Minneapolis: University of Minnesota Press, 1984), 82.

CHAPTER 4

1. Throughout, this book uses the words *city* and *town* in the usual American sense. That is, a city usually is larger than a town. The royal grants founding municipalities distinguished between a city (*ciudad*), a town (*villa*), and a peasant village (*pueblo*). The distinction was a matter of honor and was not based on population or economic importance. Generally, only Indian villages were called *pueblos.*
2. Frank Cundall and Joseph Pietersz, *Jamaica under the Spaniards* (Kingston, Institute of Jamaica, 1919), page 12.

CHAPTER 5

1. It is inaccurate to group the islands under national labels—as French, British, Dutch, or Danish—for a second reason. Since the settlers came from only a few regions, the islands were developed by provinces rather than by nations. The first French settlers, for example, came almost exclusively from provinces along the Atlantic coast, such as Normandy, Brittany, and Poitou.
2. A different Turtle Island from the famous buccaneer haunt north of Hispaniola.
3. This is the version given by the French missionary Jean Du Tertre, who came to the region a few years later. According to a less plausible legend, a representative of each group set off from a designated point and walked along the coast until both met again. With the Dutchman drinking gin and the Frenchman wine, this procedure allotted the French the larger share of the island.

CHAPTER 6

1. African slaves did not replace white indentures in British North America until the 1690s.
2. The restrictions enacted in the 1651 Navigation Act served as the immediate cause of the First Dutch War between England and the Netherlands (1652–54). However, this war was mainly fought in Europe, and it did not greatly affect the Caribbean colonies.
3. Including slaves, the king of England had about 73,000 subjects in the West Indies, the king of France about 21,000.

CHAPTER 7

1. In 1656, a former governor of Nevis brought over some 1,400 settlers—including families and children—to Morant Bay in Jamaica. Within a few months, one-half to two-thirds had died.
2. Nellis Crouse shows that Jean Le Vasseur went to Tortuga in 1642—and not in 1640 as

most histories indicate. See Nellis Crouse, *French Pioneers in the West Indies, 1624–1664* (New York: Columbia University Press, 1940), page 86.

CHAPTER 8

1. British pirates tended to prefer Port Royal, while French pirates operated from Tortuga. However, few among the brethren of the sea were staunch nationalists, and pirates of many nations took part in the larger raids.
2. *A General History of the Robberies and Murders of the most notorious Pyrates* (London, 1724–28) describes the final great era of piracy, that based in the Bahamas. Defoe's history is based—sometimes loosely—on the transcripts of pirates' trials and interviews with pirate victims.

CHAPTER 9

1. See pages 73 and 74 for the 4.5 percent tax on goods exported from Barbados and the Leewards. The government rebated part of the import duties on products reexported from Britain to other countries.
2. Altogether, residents of Great Britain and Ireland received two-thirds or more of Jamaica's annual income and profit in the 1770s. Their European rulers probably took as much from other Caribbean colonies, but precise statistics are lacking.
3. Basil Davidson, *The African Slave Trade: Precolonial History 1450–1850* (Boston: Little, Brown, 1961 [published in hardback as *Black Mother*]), page 51.
4. Cited Richard Sheridan, *An Economic History of the British West Indies, 1623–1775* (Baltimore: Johns Hopkins University Press), page 60.
5. V. S. Naipaul, *The Loss of El Dorado* (New York: Vintage Books, 1984 [first published 1969]), pages 124–125.

CHAPTER 10

1. Slaves thus made up a smaller portion of the population on Bonaire, Curaçao, the Bahamas, and the Caymans, which are too arid for cane estates. Orlando Patterson summarizes information about this and other large-scale slave societies in *Slavery and Social Death: A Comparative Study* (Cambridge, Massachusetts: Harvard University Press, 1982), pages 353–364. For comparison, slaves made up only one-third of the population in the American South during the 1800s (Patterson, page 363).
2. As Table 16 indicates, Portuguese traders brought the largest number of African slaves to the New World, carrying almost 4 million to their plantations in Brazil.
3. After the bankruptcy of the first Dutch West India Company in 1674, the government chartered another company under the same name. This second West India Company administered its Caribbean possessions (to 1794) and retained a monopoly of the African slave trade until 1734.
4. Six of every 10 men sent by the Royal Africa Company between 1695 and 1722 died during their first year in Africa—with this extraordinary death rate contributing to the company's failure.
5. Herbert Klein, *The Middle Passage: Comparative Studies in the Atlantic Slave Trade*

(Princeton, New Jersey: Princeton University Press, 1978), page 241.

6. Richard Pares, "Merchants and Planters," *Economic History Review,* Supplement Number 4 (Cambridge, England, 1959), page 23.

7. According to tradition, this device was invented in Sicily in 1449. It remained standard in Europe and the Americas until long after 1800.

8. Studies of the British islands show that planters imported only about 30 pounds of dried fish annually for each slave. Few Cuban and Puerto Rican planters complied with laws requiring masters to give slaves a half-pound of salted meat or fish daily.

9. Table 16 summarizes slave imports into various regions. For the population of the Americas in 1825, see Angel Rosenblat, *La Poblacion indigena y el Mestizaje en America* (Buenos Aires: Editorial Nova, 1954), volume I, chart between pages 36 and 37. For the Cuban population in 1877, see Jack Ericson Eblen, "On the Natural Increase of Slave Populations: The Example of the Cuban Black Population, 1775–1900," *Race and Slavery in the Western Hemisphere,* edited Stanley Engerman and Eugene Genovese (Princeton, New Jersey: Princeton University Press, 1975), page 216.

10. In the British Leewards, for example, about one-quarter of all slaves perished each year during the 1680s.

11. In the British islands, the death rate probably also fell from about 1760 because some planters adopted a policy of "amelioration." As prices rose for new hands from Africa, they began trying to reduce deaths among the slaves they already owned. Amelioration later served as the planters' main response to the abolitionist movement described in Chapter 13. To show good faith, island assemblies amended the laws regulating slave treatment. They outlawed cruel punishments—dismembering, for example—and they decreed minimum feeding standards.

CHAPTER 11

1. After the War of the Spanish Succession, the Treaty of Utrecht (1713) gave the French part of Saint Kitts to Britain.

2. French expeditions devastated Saint Kitts in 1666 and 1706, Nevis in 1706, and Montserrat in 1712. See Chapter Eight.

3. Cited in Richard Pares, *War and Trade in the West Indies, 1739–1763* (Oxford University Press, 1936), page 286. William Beckford, Lord Mayor of London and Member of Parliament, was a member of the wealthiest family in Jamaica; in 1754, he and his brothers owned plantations totaling 42,075 acres (Sheridan, *Sugar and Slavery,* 228).

4. France retained fishing rights off the banks of Newfoundland and in the Gulf of Saint Lawrence, with the little islands of Saint-Pierre and Miquelon as fishing stations.

5. In the treaty of alliance with Spain, the French government renounced all claims to North America east of the Mississippi, but it reserved the right to make conquests in the West Indies.

CHAPTER 12

1. Evidence gathered under torture is untrustworthy. Thus historians believe the planters exaggerated the goals and number of participants in several slave conspiracies.

2. Altogether, the British armies fighting in the various West Indies campaigns lost 45,000 men from 1793 to 1798: David Geggus, *Slavery, War, and Revolution* (Oxford: Clarendon Press, 1982), page 463, note 50.

3. Prime Minister Pitt had personally intervened in Parliament to abolish the slave trade

only 10 months earlier in April 1791. See page 183.

4. Because the Haitian Revolution succeeded, Toussaint Louverture has received more attention than equally courageous rebel slaves on other islands, such as Julien Fédon. History is written by the winners, but failed revolutions also deserve mention, because they too affect subsequent generations.

5. Toussaint was 48 years old in 1791. According to tradition, he had been a slave on the Breda plantation in the North Province. The owner and overseer favored him with unusually good treatment, and he rose from coachman to the important post of steward, responsible for all the livestock on the estate. A devout Roman Catholic, Toussaint was semi-literate and expert in the use of medicinal herbs. Following the slave uprising, he maintained calm on his master's plantation for a month before conveying the whites to safety, and only then joined the rebels. Toussaint himself helped to create this legend. Recent investigations suggest that he was not a slave in 1791, but was instead a freedman who owned both land and slaves.

6. Christophe, who was born in Grenada, preferred the English name Henry to the French Henri.

7. C. L. R. James, *The Black Jacobins: Toussaint L'Ouverture and the San Domingo Revolution.* Second edition (New York: Vintage, 1989 [originally 1963]), 242.

CHAPTER 13

1. Both William Wilberforce and Thomas Clarkson belonged to the Clapham Saints, an evangelical group within the established Anglican Church.

2. A subsequent law (1811) made slave trading a felony both for foreigners trading in British dominions as well as for Britons everywhere. In 1824 Parliament declared slave trading on the high seas to be piracy punishable by death.

3. The Danish Crown had already outlawed the import of slaves into its colonies by an act of 1792 effective in 1802. However, the Danish islands continued to serve as a center for the re-export trade, which shipped slaves to neighboring islands. Interisland sales were the most profitable part of the trade in the Virgin Islands (see page 127). Thus the 1792 Danish law was less rigorous than it might seem. The United States in 1794 already had prohibited American participation in the slave trade to other countries. By an act of March 1807, Congress prohibited the import of slaves into the United States after January 1, 1808.

4. Island legislatures often required colored voters to meet higher property qualifications than white voters.

5. See Table 17, page 161.

6. The network of conspiracies before the Baptist War in Jamaica involved slaves on almost 100 separate estates.

7. As used in Caribbean studies, *peasant* and *peasantry* refers to cultivators with small amounts of money working limited plots of land. Although foreign to American usage, these terms do not have a pejorative connotation in this context.

8. A "task" is a set job—for example, hoeing a fixed amount of land.

9. Britain allowed Jamaican taxpayers to elect the Legislative Council's nine "unofficial members" after 1884. The Cayman Islands, with their very small population, retained a highly democratic system. At first, every free man could choose to attend and vote at an annual meeting. Later a legislature meeting from the 1830s, was elected by all males—without even fixed age requirements. In 1863, Parliament ruled that the governor of Jamaica had to approve Cayman laws, and the governor also appointed a commissioner (from 1898) as a representative on the island.

10. The vestry, which administered local government in each of Jamaica's parishes, included certain elected members and the justices of the peace. The Custos Rotulorum (literally

"keeper of the books") was the principal magistrate of each parish. Appointed by the governor and confirmed by the Crown, he presided over the vestry's meetings.

11. According to an official inquiry, the soldiers and Maroons destroyed 1,000 homes, executed 85 persons without trial, and hanged 354 after a brief court-martial. About 600 men and women were flogged, some receiving hundreds of lashes.

12. Bernard Semmel, *Jamaican Blood and Victorian Conscience: The Governor Eyre Controversy* (Westport, Connecticut: Greenwood Press, 1976 [first published in 1963]), page 41. See also Eric Williams, *British Historians and the West Indies* (New York: Africana, 1972 [first published 1966]), pages 115–118.

13. Circular dispatch signed by the duke of Buckingham on August 17, 1868, quoted by Hume Wrong, *Government of the West Indies* (Oxford: Clarendon Press, 1923), page 79.

CHAPTER 14

1. Giving into British pressure, the Spanish government outlawed the slave trade in 1820, but local officials did not enforce the laws. See page 184.

2. See Table 16. The high point of the trade came just before it was outlawed. More than 96,000 slaves—19,000 per year—were landed between 1815 and 1820.

3. Thus the 1853 tariff law set the tax on a barrel of Spanish flour at $2.90 while taxing a North American barrel at $9.20.

4. See Table 21, page 190.

5. Following a revolution in September 1868, the Spanish republic gave both Cuba and Puerto Rico representation in the Spanish Cortes. The government canceled its grant to Cuba after the Revolt of Yara, but Puerto Rico continued to send representatives to the Cortes from 1869.

CHAPTER 15

1. In return for some concessions in Europe, France transferred the small island of Saint-Barthélemy to Sweden in 1784. Saint-Barthélemy was returned to France in 1870 and once again became (with Saint-Martin) a dependency of Guadeloupe.

2. According to the imperial constitution of 1805, "No white man [*aucun blanc*], whatever his nationality, can set foot on this territory as master or proprietor, and is unable in the future to acquire any property." Subsequent governments generally enforced this rule until the American occupation in 1915.

3. For a short time, the south seceded to form a third state under André Rigaud, and La Grande-Anse formed an autonomous region throughout the entire period of division.

4. Coffee can grow "wild" up to 3,000 feet in the sense that new plants grow from seeds dropped by parent trees. When the French introduced coffee, the slaves carefully pruned, fertilized, and grafted the plants. The Haitians now let nature take its own course, and quality and production both declined.

CHAPTER 16

1. See Hugh Thomas, *Cuba: The Pursuit of Freedom* (New York: Harper & Row, 1971), page 472.

2. The 1940 constitution permitted an ex-president to run again after an eight-year absence from office.

CHAPTER 17

1. Aristide's book *In the Parish of the Poor* (New York: Orbis, 1991) summarizes the main themes of these speeches, including his justification of revolutionary violence.
2. In June 1993, the U.S. Supreme Court ruled by a majority of eight to one that this policy of interdiction and return did not violate U.S. law.
3. As is the case in every nation except the United States, Haiti has one national police force. Some mayors have set up municipal constabularies, but these forces are illegal.

CHAPTER 18

1. *Thieves' World* (New York: Simon and Schuster, 1994), page 21.
2. Cited Arturo Morales-Carrión, *Puerto Rico, a Political and Cultural History* (New York: Norton, 1985), page 189.
3. See Table 21. Although Puerto Rican sugar was protected by U.S. tariffs and quotas, its price was set on the world market.
4. Initially Puerto Rican profits were 100 percent exempt, but the exemption was later reduced. Under the previous law, firms were taxed when they repatriated accumulated profits. Thus, the old system provided an incentive for firms to leave Puerto Rico and transfer their profits away from the U.S. when their tax exemption period ended.
5. Since 1982, beneficiaries receive checks instead of stamps, allowing them to spend the money however they please.
6. In response to the 1990 census, 52 percent of Puerto Ricans reported that they spoke just Spanish and could speak no English at all, and another 24 percent said that they could speak English only with difficulty. In a 1993 public opinion survey, 95 percent said they preferred the Spanish language.
7. See Juan Manuel García-Passalacqua, "The Role of the Puerto Rican People in the Caribbean," *Democracy in the Caribbean,* edited Jorge Domínguez and others (Baltimore: Johns Hopkins University Press, 1993). As García-Passalacqua notes (page 175), Puerto Ricans reject a Caribbean role because they do not want to accept their own "*negritude,* a trait they share with the rest of the Caribbean. The expression of the African soul has survived in the region. Yet in Puerto Rico the elite has lived for centuries under the delusion that it belongs to the 'European,' or white, world, preferring to identify itself with Spanish royalty rather than with Puerto Rico's Afro-American Roots."
   It is not possible to know how ordinary Puerto Ricans view their own racial identities. Beginning in 1950, in deference to Puerto Rican sensibilities, the Census Bureau has not asked islanders the questions on racial and ethnic identification that mainland Americans are legally obliged to answer. Lighter-skinned Puerto Ricans find it easier to get jobs, and parents encourage their children to marry persons with lighter skins than their own. Samuel Betances, "Race and the Search for Identity," *Borinquen: An Anthology of Puerto Rican Literature,* edited María Batin and Stan Steiner (New York: Random House, 1974), page 428. See also José Luis González, *Puerto Rico, the Four-Storeyed Country: The Question of an Afro-Mestizo Culture,* translated Gerald Guinness (Princeton: Wiener, 1993).
8. Suriname (formerly Dutch Guiana) withdrew in 1975, becoming an independent republic.
9. Including the smaller islands, such as Saint-Barthélemy, associated with Martinique and Guadeloupe.
10. Settlers from Saint Kitts colonized Montserrat in 1632, occupied Anguilla in 1650, and moved on to the Virgin Islands at the end of the 18th century. See pages 75–77.

CHAPTER 19

1. *Memorandum on the Closer Association of the British West Indian Colonies* (London, 1947), Part II, paragraph 11.
2. Bridget Brereton, *Race Relations in Colonial Trinidad 1870–1900* (Cambridge: Cambridge University Press, 1972), page 212.

CHAPTER 20

1. Countries with "observer" status in CARICOM included the British overseas territories of Anguilla, Bermuda, and the Cayman Islands, as well as the non-English speaking nations of Aruba, the Netherlands Antilles, the Dominican Republic, Puerto Rico, Mexico, Venezuela, and Colombia.
2. The Rastafarian movement or religion, founded around 1930, emphasized its members' racial origins in Africa and rejected Jamaica's creole society and culture. Using Old Testament language, Rastafarians condemned Jamaica as Babylon, a land that held them in captivity. They sought a new home in Africa and especially in Ethiopia, whose emperor, Haile Selassie, they regarded as divine.
3. During the 1960s and 1970s, the Nonaligned movement was a loose association of political leaders, mainly from Africa and Asia. Although all espoused some form of socialism, they claimed to be neutral in the rivalry that opposed the United States and western Europe (the "First World") to the Soviet Union and eastern Europe (the "Second World").
4. *Economist,* March 21, 1992, page 48.
5. Cited in Selwyn D. Ryan, *Race and Nationalism in Trinidad and Tobago* (Toronto: University of Toronto Press, 1972), page 427.
6. Scott MacDonald, *Trinidad and Tobago: Democracy and Development in the Caribbean* (New York: Praeger, 1986), page 191.
7. *Budget Speech and Taxation Measures,* 12 December 1988 (Port of Spain: Government Printery, 1989) cited by Selwyn Ryan, "Structural Adjustment and the Ethnic Factor in Caribbean Societies" in *Democracy in the Caribbean: Political, Economic and Social Perspectives,* edited Jorge Domínguez and others. (Baltimore: Johns Hopkins University Press, 1993).

CHAPTER 21

1. In a 1980 interview, Bishop said, "Suppose there's a war next door in Trinidad, where the forces of Fascism are about to take control, and the Trinidadians need external assistance. Why should we oppose anybody passing through Grenada to assist them?" Quoted in *Newsweek* March 31, 1980, page 44.
2. "Extraordinary Meeting of the Central Committee NJM," Minutes, September 16, 1983. Printed in *The Grenada Papers: The inside story of the Grenadian Revolution and the making of a totalitarian state—as told in captured documents,* edited Paul Seabury and Walter A. McDougall (San Francisco: Institute for Contemporary Studies, 1984), page 294.

SUGGESTIONS
FOR FURTHER
READING

This list is by no means a complete record of all the works and sources I have consulted. It indicates books that I believe will be of general interest. Thus I have not included works in languages other than English, books long out of print, or articles in journals for specialists.

OVERVIEWS AND WORKS ABOUT SEVERAL ERAS

Aldrich, Robert and John Connell. *France's Overseas Frontier: Départements et territoires d'outre mer.* Cambridge: Cambridge University Press, 1992.

Andrews, Kenneth. *Trade, plunder and settlement: Maritime enterprise and the genesis of the British Empire, 1480–1630.* Cambridge: Cambridge University Press, 1984.

Baker, Patrick L. *Centering the Periphery: Chaos, Order, and the Ethnohistory of Dominica.* Montreal: McGill-Queen's University Press, 1994.

Beckles, Hilary. *A History of Barbados: From Amerindian Settlement to Nation-State.* Cambridge University Press, 1990.

Beckles, Hilary and Brian Stoddart, eds. *Liberation Cricket: West Indies Cricket Culture.* Manchester, England: Manchester University Press, 1995.

Betances, Emilio. *State and Society in the Dominican Republic.* Boulder, Colo.: Westview, 1995.

Blume, Helmut. *The Caribbean Islands.* Translated by Johannes Maczewski and Ann Norton. London: Longman, 1974.

Boyer, William. *America's Virgin Islands: A History of Human Rights and Wrongs.* Durham, North Carolina: Carolina Academic Press, 1983.

Brereton, Bridget. *A History of Modern Trinidad, 1783–1962.* Kingston, Jamaica; Exeter, New Hampshire: Heineman, 1981.

Burns, Alan. *History of the British West Indies.* 2nd edition. London: Allen & Unwin, 1965.

Burton, Richard. *Afro-Creole: Power, Opposition, and Play in the Caribbean.* Ithaca, N.Y.: Cornell University Press, 1997.

Cambeira, Alan. *Quisqueya la Bella: The Dominican Republic in Historical and Cultural Perspective.* Armonk N.Y.: Sharpe, 1997.

Craton, Michael. *A History of the Bahamas.* Revised edition. London: Collins, 1968.

———. *Searching for the Invisible Man: Slaves and Plantation Life in Jamaica.* Cambridge, Mass.: Harvard University Press, 1978.

———. *Sinews of Empire: A Short History of British Slavery.* Garden City, N.Y.: Anchor, 1974.

———. *Testing the Chains: Resistance to Slavery in the British West Indies.* Ithaca, N.Y.: Cornell University Press, 1982.

Craton, Michael and Gail Sanders. *Islanders in the Stream: A History of the Bahamian People. Volume 1: From Aboriginal Times to the End of Slavery.* Athens: University of Georgia Press, 1992.

Curtin, Philip. *The Atlantic Slave Trade: A Census.* Madison: University of Wisconsin Press, 1969.

———. *Death by Migration: Europe's Encounter with the Tropical World in the Nineteenth Century.* Cambridge: Cambridge University Press, 1989.

———. *The Rise and Fall of the Plantation Complex: Essays in Atlantic History.* Cambridge: Cambridge University Press, 1990.

Davis, Darien. *Slavery and Beyond: The African Impact on Latin America and the Caribbean.* Wilmington, Del.: SR Books, 1995.

Deerr, Noel. *The History of Sugar.* 2 volumes. London: Chapman & Hall, 1949–1950.

Dupuy, Alex. *Haiti in the World Economy: Class, Race, and Underdevelopment since 1700.* Boulder, Colo.: Westview, 1989.

Goslinga, Cornelis. *A Short History of the Netherlands Antilles and Surinam.* The Hague: Martinus Nijhoff, 1979.

Hamshere, Cyril. *The British in the Caribbean.* Cambridge: Harvard University Press, 1972.

Heinl, Robert, Nancy Heinl, and Michael Heinl. *Written in Blood: The Story of the Haitian People 1492–1995.* Lanham, Md.: University Press of America, 1996.

Kilson, Martin, and Robert Rotberg, eds. *The African Diaspora.* Cambridge: Harvard University Press, 1976.

Kiple, Kenneth. *The Caribbean Slave: A Biological History.* Cambridge: Cambridge University Press, 1984.

Knight, Franklin. *The Caribbean: The Genesis of a Fragmented Nationalism.* New York: Oxford University Press, 1978.

Knight, Franklin, and Colin Palmer, eds. *The Modern Caribbean.* Chapel Hill: University of North Carolina Press, 1989.

Lewis, Gordon. *Main Currents in Caribbean Thought: The Historical Evolution of Caribbean Society in Its Ideological Aspects, 1492–1900.* Baltimore: Johns Hopkins University Press, 1983.

Morales-Carrión, Arturo. *Puerto Rico, a political and cultural history.* New York: Norton, 1983.

Moya Pons, Frank. *The Dominican Republic: A National History.* New Rochelle, New York: Hispaniola Books, 1995.

Nicholls, David. *From Dessalines to Duvalier: Race, Color, and National Independence in Haiti.* New York: Cambridge University Press, 1979.

———. *Haiti in Caribbean Context: Ethnicity, Economy, and Revolt.* London: MacMillan, 1985.

Ortiz-Fernandez, Fernando. *Cuban Counter Point: Tobacco and Sugar.* Translated by H. de Onís. New York: Knopf, 1947.

Pérez, Louis. *Cuba: Between Reform and Revolution.* 2nd edition. New York: Oxford University Press, 1995.

Rotberg, Robert I. *Haiti, The Politics of Squalor.* New York: Houghton Mifflin, 1971.

Sheridan, Richard. *Sugar and Slavery: An Economic History of the British West Indies, 1623–1775.* Baltimore: Johns Hopkins University Press, 1974.

Suchlicki, Jaime. *Cuba: From Columbus to Castro.* 4th edition. Washington, D.C.: Brassey's, 1997.

Thomas, Hugh. *Cuba: The Pursuit of Freedom.* New York: Harper and Row, 1971.

Thomas, Hugh. *The Slave Trade: The Story of the Atlantic Slave Trade, 1440–1870.* New York: Simon & Schuster, 1997.

Trouillot, Michel-Rolph. *Haiti, State against Nation: The Origins and Legacy of Duvalierism.* New York: Monthly Review Press, 1990.

———. *Peasants and Capital: Dominica in the World Economy.* Baltimore: Johns Hopkins University Press, 1988.

Vertovec, Steven. *Hindu Trinidad: Religion, Ethnicity, and Socio-Economic Change.* London: Macmillan Caribbean, 1992.

Wagenheim, Olga. *Puerto Rico: An Interpretative History from Pre-Columbia Times to 1900.* Princeton, N.J.: Wiener, 1997.

Ward, J. R. *Poverty and Progress in the Caribbean, 1800–1960.* Economic History Society, Studies in Economic and Social History. London: Macmillan, 1985.

Watts, David. *The West Indies: Patterns of Development, Culture and Environmental Change since 1492.* Cambridge: Cambridge University Press, 1987.

West, Robert, and John P. Augelli, and others. *Middle America: Its Lands and Peoples.* 3rd ed. Englewood Cliffs, N.J.: Prentice Hall, 1989.

Williams, Eric. *From Columbus to Castro: The History of the Caribbean.* London: Andre Deutsch, 1970. Reprint, New York: Vintage Books, 1984.

PART I
THE CARIBBEAN UNDER SPANISH RULE

Andrews, Kenneth R. *The Spanish Caribbean: Trade and Plunder, 1530–1630.* New Haven Conn.: Yale University Press, 1978.

Ashburn, P. M. *The Ranks of Death: A Medical History of the Conquest of America.* Edited by Frank Ashburn. New York: Coward-McCann, 1947.

Haring, C. H. *The Spanish Empire in America.* New York: Oxford University Press, 1947. Reprint, San Diego: Harvest/Harcourt Brace Jovanovich, 1975.

Keegan, William F. *The People Who Discovered Columbus: The Prehistory of the Bahamas.* Gainesville: University Press of Florida, 1992.

Lynch, John. *Spain under the Habsburgs.* Vol. 2, *Spain and America, 1598–1700.* New York: Oxford University Press, 1964–1969.

McAlister, Lyle N. *Spain and Portugal in the New World, 1492–1700.* Minneapolis: University of Minnesota Press, 1984.

Means, Philip. *The Spanish Main, Focus of Envy, 1492–1700.* New York: Scribner's, 1935.

Phillips, William. *Slavery from Roman Times to the Early Transatlantic Trade.* Minneapolis: University of Minnesota Press, 1985.

Sauer, Carl. *The Early Spanish Main.* Berkeley and Los Angeles: University of California Press, 1969.

Verano, John and Douglas Ubelaker. *Disease and Demography in the Americas.* Washington, D.C.: Smithsonian Institution, 1992.

Weeks, John M. and Peter Ferbel. Ancient Caribbean. New York: Garland Publishing, 1994.

Wood, Peter. *The Spanish Main.* Alexandria, Va.: Time-Life Books, 1979.

PART 2
NORTHERN EUROPEANS COME TO STAY

Beckles, Hilary. *White Servitude and Black Slavery in Barbados, 1627–1715.* Knoxville: University of Tennessee Press, 1989.

Botting, Douglas. *The Pirates.* Alexandria, Virginia: Time-Life Books, 1978.

Bridenbaugh, Carl, and Roberta Bridenbaugh. *No Peace beyond the Line: The English in the Caribbean, 1624–1690.* New York: Oxford University Press, 1977.

Crouse, Nellis. *French Pioneers in the West Indies, 1624–1664.* New York: Columbia University Press, 1940. Reprint, New York: Octagon Books, 1977.

———. *The French Struggle for the West Indies, 1665–1713.* New York: Columbia University Press, 1943. Reprint, Octagon Books, 1966.

Davies, K. G. *The North Atlantic World in the Seventeenth Century.* Minneapolis: University of Minnesota Press, 1974.

Dunn, Richard. *Sugar and Slaves: The Rise of the Planter Class in the English West Indies, 1624–1713.* New York: W. W. Norton, 1973.

Earle, Peter. *The Sack of Panama: Sir Henry Morgan's Adventures on the Spanish Main.* New York: Viking, 1982.

Goslinga, Cornelis. *The Dutch in the Caribbean and on the Wild Coast, 1580–1680.* Gainesville: University of Florida Press, 1971.

Israel, Jonathan. *Dutch Primacy in World Trade, 1585–1740.* Oxford: Clarendon Press, 1989.

———. *The Dutch Republic and the Hispanic World, 1606–1661.* Oxford: Clarendon Press, 1982.

Pope, Dudley. *The Buccaneer King: The Biography of Sir Henry Morgan, 1635–1688.* New York: Dodd Mead, 1977.

Smith, Abbot. *Colonists in Bondage.* Chapel Hill: University of North Carolina Press, 1947.

PART 3
THE SUGAR EMPIRE

Beckles, Hilary. *Natural Rebels: A Social History of Enslaved Black Women in Barbados.* New Brunswick, N.J.: Rutgers University Press, 1989.

Brathwaite, Edward. *The Development of Creole Society in Jamaica, 1770–1820.* Oxford: Clarendon Press, 1971.

Cohen, David, and Jack Greene, eds. *Neither Slave Nor Free: The Freedmen of African Descent in the Slave Societies of the New World.* Baltimore: Johns Hopkins University Press, 1972.

Dayan, Joan. *Haiti, History, and the Gods.* Berkeley: University of California, 1995.

Frick, Carolyn. *The Making of Haiti: The Saint-Domingue Revolution from Below.* Knoxville: University of Tennessee Press, 1990.

Gemery, Henry, and Jan Hogendorn, eds. *The Uncommon Market: Essays in the Economic History of the Atlantic Slave Trade.* New York: Academic Press, 1979.

Goveia, Elsa. *Slave Society in the British Leeward Islands at the End of the Eighteenth Century.* New Haven, Conn.: Yale University Press, 1965. Reprint, Westport, Conn.: Greenwood, 1980.

Heumans, Gad, ed. *Out of the House of Bondage: Runaways, Resistance and Marronage in Africa and the New World.* London: Frank Cass, 1986.

James, C. L. R. *The Black Jacobins: Toussaint L'Ouverture and the San Domingo Revolution.* 2nd edition. New York: Vintage Books, 1963.

Klein, Herbert S. *African Slavery in Latin American and the Caribbean.* New York: Oxford University Press, 1986.

———. *The Middle Passage: Comparative Studies in the Atlantic Slave Trade.* Princeton: Princeton University Press, 1978.

Kuethe, Allan. *Cuba, 1753–1815: Crown, Military, and Society.* Knoxville: University of Tennessee Press, 1986.

Lovejoy, Paul. *Transformations in Slavery: A History of Slavery in Africa.* Cambridge: Cambridge University Press, 1983.

McNeill, John. *Atlantic Empires of France and Spain: Louisbourg and Havana, 1700–1765.* Chapel Hill: University of North Carolina Press, 1985.

Morales-Carrión, Arturo. *Puerto Rico and the Non-Hispanic Caribbean: A Study in the Decline of Spanish Exclusivism.* 3rd edition. Barcelona: Medinaceli, 1974.

Ott, Thomas. *The Haitian Revolution, 1789–1804.* Knoxville: University of Tennessee Press, 1983.

Pares, Richard. *War and Trade in the West Indies, 1739–1763.* Oxford: Oxford University Press, 1936. Reprint, New York: Frank Cass, 1963.

Patterson, Orlando. *Slavery and Social Death: A Comparative Study.* Cambridge, Mass.: Harvard University Press, 1982.

Price, Richard, ed. *Maroon Societies: Rebel Slave Communities in the Americas.* Baltimore: Johns Hopkins University Press, 1979.

Rawley, James A. *The Transatlantic Slave Trade: A History.* New York: Norton, 1981.

Solow, Barbara and Stanley Engerman, eds. *British Capitalism and Caribbean Slavery: The Legacy of Eric Williams.* Cambridge: Cambridge University Press, 1987.

Stein, Robert. *The French Slave Trade in the Eighteenth Century: An Old Regime Business.* Madison: University of Wisconsin Press, 1980.

———. *The French Sugar Business in the Eighteenth Century.* Baton Rouge: Louisiana State University Press, 1988.

Walvin, James. *Black Ivory: A History of British Slavery.* London: Fontana, 1993.

Ward, J. R. *British West Indian Slavery, 1750–1834: The Process of Amelioration.* Oxford: Clarendon Press, 1988.

PART 4
THE ABOLITION OF SLAVERY
AND THE CHALLENGES OF FREEDOM

Bolt, Christine, and Seymour Drescher, eds. *Anti-slavery, Religion, and Reform: Essays in Memory of Roger Anstey.* Hamden, Conn.: Archon Books, 1980.

Brereton, Bridget. *Race Relations in Colonial Trinidad 1870–1900.* Cambridge: Cambridge University Press, 1972.

Davis, David. *The Problem of Slavery in the Age of Revolution.* Ithaca, N.Y.: Cornell University Press, 1975.

Drescher, Seymour. *Capitalism and Antislavery: British Mobilization in Comparative Perspective.* New York: Oxford University Press, 1987.

———. *Econocide: British Slavery in the Era of Abolition.* Pittsburgh: University of Pittsburgh Press, 1977.

Eiser, Gisela. *Jamaica, 1830–1930: A Study in Economic Growth.* Manchester, England: Manchester University Press, 1961. Reprint, Westport, Connecticut: Greenwood, 1974.

Eltis, David. *The Abolition of the Atlantic Slave Trade: Origins and effects in Europe, Africa, and the Americas.* Madison: University of Wisconsin Press, 1981.

Green, William. *British Slave Emancipation: The Sugar Colonies and the Great Experiment, 1830–1965.* Oxford: Clarendon Press, 1976.

Hall, Douglas. *Free Jamaica, 1838–1865.* New Haven: Yale University Press, 1959.

Heuman, Gad. *"The Killing Time": The Morant Bay Rebellion in Jamaica.* Knoxville: University of Tennessee Press, 1994.

Johnson, Howard. *The Bahamas from Slavery to Servitude, 1783–1933.* Gainesville: University Press of Florida, 1996.

Knight, Franklin. *Slave Society in Cuba during the Nineteenth Century.* Madison: University of Wisconsin Press, 1970.

Moreno-Fraginals, Manuel. *The Sugarmill: The Socioeconomic Complex of Sugar in Cuba, 1760–1860.* Translated by Cedric Belfrage. New York: Monthly Review Press, 1976.

Paquette, Robert. *Sugar Is Made with Blood: The Conspiracy of La Escalera and the Conflict between Empires and Slavery in Cuba.* Middletown, Conn.: Wesleyan University Press, 1988.

Walvin, James. *England, Slaves and Freedom, 1776–1838.* Jackson: University Press of Mississippi, 1986.

PART 5
POVERTY AND PROGRESS IN THE CARIBBEAN SINCE 1914

Abbott, Elizabeth. *Haiti: The Duvaliers and Their Legacy.* New York: McGraw-Hill, 1988.

Azicri, Max. *Cuba: Politics, Economics, and Society.* London: Pinter, 1988.

Balfour, Sebastian. *Castro.* Second edition. London: Longman, 1995.

Baver, Sherrie. *The Political Economy of Colonialism: The State and Industrialization in Puerto Rico.* Westport, Conn.: Praeger, 1993.

Bourne, Peter. *Castro.* New York: Dodd Mead, 1986.

Bryan, Anthony, ed. *The Caribbean: New Dynamics in Trade and Political Economy.* Coral Gables, Florida: University of Miami North-South Center, 1995.

Bunck, Julie. *Fidel Castro and the Quest for a Revolutionary Culture in Cuba.* University Park: Pennsylvania State University Press, 1994.

Chevigny, Paul. *Edge of the Knife: Police Violence in the Americas.* New York: New Press, 1995.

Del Aguila, Juan. *Cuba: Dilemmas of a Revolution.* Revised edition. Boulder, Colo.: Westview, 1988.

Desmangles, Leslie. *The Faces of the Gods: Vodou and Roman Catholicism in Haiti.* Chapel Hill: University of North Carolina Press, 1992.

Dietz, James. *Economic History of Puerto Rico: Institutional Change and Capitalist Development.* Princeton, N.J., Princeton University Press, 1986.

Domínguez, Jorge. *Cuba: Order and Revolution.* Cambridge, Mass.: Harvard University Press, 1978.

Domínguez, Jorge, Robert Pastor, and R. DeLisle Worrell, eds. *Democracy in the Caribbean: Political, Economic, and Social Perspectives.* Baltimore, Md.: Johns Hopkins University Press, 1993.

Dupuy, Alex. *Haiti in the New World Order: The Limits of the Democratic Revolution.* Boulder, Colo.: Westview, 1997.

Eckstein, Susan. *Back from the Future: Cuba under Castro.* Princeton, N.J.: Princeton University Press, 1994.

Edie, Carlene. *Democracy by Default: Dependency and Clientelism in Jamaica.* Boulder, Colo.: Rienner, 1991.

Eriksen, Thomas. *Us and Them in Modern Societies: Ethnicity and Nationalism in Mauritius, Trinidad, and Beyond.* Oslo: Scandinavian University Press, 1992.

Fauriol, Georges. *Haitian Frustrations: Dilemmas for U.S. Policy.* Washington, D.C.: Center for Strategic and International Studies, 1995.

Fernandez, Ronald. *The Disenchanted Island: Puerto Rico in the Twentieth Century.* Second edition. Westport, Conn.: Praeger, 1996.

Findlay, Ronald and Stanislaw Wellisz. *Five Small Open Economies.* New York: Oxford University Press, 1993.

Garcia, Maria. *Havana USA: Cuban Exiles and Cuban Americans in South Florida, 1959–1994.* Berkeley: University of California Press, 1996.

Geyer, Georgie Anne. *Guerrilla Prince: The Untold Story of Fidel Castro.* Boston: Little Brown, 1991.

González, José Luis. *Puerto Rico, the Four-Storeyed Country: The Question of an Afro-Mestizo Culture,* translated Gerald Guinness. Princeton: Wiener, 1993.

Griffith, Ivelaw. *Drugs and Security in the Caribbean: Sovereignty Under Siege.* University Park: Pennsylvania State University Press, 1997.

———. *The Quest for Security in the Caribbean: Problems and Promises in Subordinate States.* Armonk, N.Y.: Sharpe, 1993.

——— and Betty N. Sedoc-Dahlberg, eds. *Democracy and Human Rights in the Caribbean.* Boulder, Colo.: Westview, 1997.

Gunst, Laurie. *Born Fi' Dead: A Journey through the Jamaican Posse Underworld.* New York: Holt, 1995.

Halperin, Maurice. *Return to Havana: The Decline of Cuban Society under Castro.* Nashville: Vanderbilt University Press, 1994.

Hamm, Mark. *The Abandoned Ones: The Imprisonment and Uprising of the Mariel Boat People.* Boston: Northeastern University Press, 1995.

Harlan, Judith. *Puerto Rico: Deciding Its Future.* New York: Twenty-First Century, 1996.

Hinckle, Warren and William W. Turner. *The Fish Is Red: The Story of the Secret War against Castro.* New York: Harper & Row, 1981.

Hintjens, Helen and Malyn Newitt. *The Political Economy of Small Tropical Islands: The Importance of Being Small.* Exeter, U.K.: University of Exeter Press, 1992.

Hughes, Colin. *Race and Politics in the Bahamas.* New York: St. Martin's, 1981.

Johnson, Howard, ed. *The White Minority in the Caribbean.* Princeton, N.J.: Wiener, 1997.

Kincaid, Jamaica. *A Small Place.* New York: Farrar, Straus, Giroux, 1988.

Klomp, Ank. *Politics on Bonaire,* translated Dirk van der Elst. Assen: Van Gorcum, 1986.

Langley, Lester. The United States and the Caribbean in the Twentieth Century. 4th edition. Athens: University of Georgia Press, 1989.

Lewis, Gordon. *The Growth of the Modern West Indies.* New York: Monthly Review Press, 1968.

Lowenthal, Abraham. *The Dominican Intervention.* Cambridge, Mass.: Harvard University Press, 1972.

MacDonald, Scott. *Trinidad and Tobago: Democracy and Development in the Caribbean.* New York: Praeger, 1986.

Mandle, Jay. *Persistent Underdevelopment: Change and Economic Modernization in the West Indies.* New York: Gordon & Breach, 1996.

Martinez, Samuel. *Peripheral Migrants: Haitians and Dominican Republic Sugar Plantations.* Knoxville: University of Tennessee Press, 1995.

Meléndez, Edwin and Edgardo Meléndez, eds. *Colonial Dilemma: Critical Perspectives on Contemporary Puerto Rico.* Boston: South End Press, 1993.

Mesa-Lago, Carmelo, ed. *Cuba after the Cold War.* University of Pittsburgh Press, 1993.

Mintz, Sidney and Sally Price, eds. *Caribbean Contours.* Baltimore: Johns Hopkins University Press, 1985.

Mintz, Sidney. *Caribbean Transformations.* Chicago: Aldine, 1974.

Montaner, Carlos. *Fidel Castro and the Cuban Revolution: Age, Position, Character, Destiny, and Ambition.* New Brunswick, N.J.: Transaction Press, 1989.

Moore, Carlos. *Castro, the Blacks, and Africa.* Los Angeles: University of California Center for Afro-American Studies, 1988.

Morris, Nancy. *Puerto Rico: Culture, Politics, and Identity.* Westport, Conn.: Praeger, 1995.

Pattullo, Polly. *Last Resorts: The Cost of Tourism in the Caribbean.* London: Cassell, 1996.

Payne, Anthony. *Politics in Jamaica.* Revised edition. New York: St. Martin's, 1995.

Payne, Anthony and Paul Sutton. *Modern Caribbean Politics.* Baltimore: Johns Hopkins University Press, 1993.

Payne, Anthony, Paul Sutton, and Tony Thorndike. *Grenada: Revolution and Invasion.* New York: St. Martin's, 1984.

Pérez, Louis. *Cuba and the United States: Ties of Singular Intimacy.* Second edition. Athens: University of Georgia Press, 1997.

Pérez-López, Jorge, ed. *Cuba at a Crossroads: Politics and Economics after the Fourth Party Congress.* Gainesville: University Press of Florida, 1994.

Pérez-López, Jorge. *Cuba's Second Economy: From Behind the Scenes to Center Stage.* New Brunswick, N.J.: Transaction, 1995.

Plummer, Brenda. *Haiti and the Great Powers, 1902–1915.* Baton Rouge: Louisiana State University Press, 1988.

Ratliff, William, ed. *The Selling of Fidel Castro: The Media and the Cuban Revolution.* New Brunswick, N.J.: Transaction, 1987.

Rivera-Batiz, Francisco and Carlos Santiago, *Island Paradox: Puerto Rico in the 1990s.* New York: Russell Sage, 199?.

Ryan, Selwyn. *The Disillusioned Electorate: The Politics of Succession in Trinidad and Tobago.* Port of Spain: Imprint Caribbean, 1989.

———. *Race and Nationalism in Trinidad and Tobago.* Toronto: University of Toronto Press, 1972.

Ryan, Selwyn and Taimoan Stewart. *The Black Power Revolution of 1970: A Retrospective.* Saint Augustine, Trinidad: University of the West Indies, 1995.

Safa, Helen. *The Myth of the Male Breadwinner: Women and Industrialization in the Caribbean.* Boulder, Colo.: Westview, 1995.

Sedoc-Dahlberg, Betty, ed. *The Dutch Caribbean: Prospects for Democracy.* New York: Gordon and Breach, 1990.

Schmidt, Hans. *The United States Occupation of Haiti, 1915–1934.* New Brunswick, N.J.: Rutgers University Press, 1971.

Senior, Olive. *Working Miracles: Women's Lives in the English-Speaking Caribbean.* Cave Hill, Barbados: University of the West Indies, 1991.

Short, Margaret. *Law and Religion in Marxist Cuba.* Coral Gables, Fla.: University of Miami North-South Center, 1993.

Smith, Robert Freeman. *The Caribbean World and the United States: Mixing Rum and Coca Cola.* New York: Twayne, 1994.

Steiner, Stan. *The Islands: The Worlds of the Puerto Ricans.* New York: Harper & Row, 1975.

Sutton, Paul, ed. *Europe and the Caribbean.* London: Macmillan Caribbean, 1991.

Trías Monge, José. *Puerto Rico: The Trials of the Oldest Colony in the World.* New Haven, Conn.: Yale University Press, 1997.

Wallace, Elisabeth. *The British Caribbean: From the Decline of Colonialism to the End of Federation.* Toronto: University of Toronto Press. 1977.

Watson, Hilbourne, ed. *The Caribbean in the Global Political Economy.* Boulder, Colo.: Rienner, 1994.

Weinstein, Brian and Aaron Segal. *Haiti: The Failure of Politics.* New York: Praeger, 1992.

Wiarda, Howard and Michael Kryzanek. *The Dominican Republic: A Caribbean Crucible.* 2nd edition. Boulder, Colo.: Westview, 1992.

Wilentz, Amy. *The Rainy Season: Haiti since Duvalier.* New York: Simon & Schuster, 1989.

Worrell, Delisle. *Small Island Economies: Structure and Performance in the English-Speaking Caribbean since 1970.* New York: Praeger, 1987.

Yelvington, Kevin, ed. *Trinidad Ethnicity.* Knoxville: University of Tennessee Press, 1993.

Young, Virginia. *Becoming West Indian: Culture, Self, and Nation in Saint Vincent.* Washington, D.C.,: Smithsonian, 1993.

Zimbalist, Andrew, ed. *Cuban Political Economy: Controversies in Cubanology.* Boulder, Colo.: Westview, 1988.

Zimbalist, Andrew, ed. *Cuba's Socialist Economy: Toward the 1990s.* Boulder, Colo.: Rienner, 1987.

Zimbalist, Andrew and Claes Brundenius. *The Cuban Economy: Measurement and Analysis of Socialist Performance.* Baltimore: Johns Hopkins University Press, 1989.

PHOTO CREDITS

PAGES 306 and 322. Courtesy British Virgin Islands Tourist Board.

PAGES 6, 11, 16, 41, 65, 136, 153, 218, 269, 305, and 313. Courtesy Caribbean Tourism Organization.

PAGE 8. Courtesy American Airlines.

PAGES 12, 297 and 300. Courtesy Curaçao Tourist Board.

PAGE 25. From Bryan Edwards, *The History, Civil and Commercial, of the British Colonies in the West Indies* (London: John Stockdale, 1794), Volume 1, frontispiece. Print courtesy Archives and Special Collections, Richter Library, University of Miami.

PAGE 37. From Theodore Bry, *Collectiones Peregrinationum in Indiam Orientalem et Indiam Occidentalem* . . . (Franfurt-am-Main, 1590–1634). Print courtesy Archives and Special Collections, Richter Library, University of Miami.

PAGES 69 and 305. Courtesy Saint Kitts and Nevis Tourist Board.

PAGE 72. Courtesy Barbados Board of Tourism.

PAGES 119 and 120. Courtesy French West Indies Tourist Board.

PAGE 135. From a color print published by Montaner y Simon, Barcelona, second half of the 19th century. Print courtesy Archives and Special Collections, Richter Library, University of Miami.

PAGE 157. Engraving from an original painting by Agostino Brunias in Bryan Edwards, *An Historical Survey of the Island of Saint Domingo, together with an Account of the Maroon Negroes in the Island of Jamaica* . . . (London: John Stockdale, 1801, as Volume 3 of Edwards's *History of the British Colonies* [originally published 1796]), between pages 310 and 311. Print courtesy Archives and Special Collections, Richter Library, University of Miami.

PAGE 159. Engraving from an original painting by Agostino Brunias in Bryan Edwards, *History of the British Colonies,* Volume 1, before page 391. Print courtesy Archives and Special Collections, Richter Library, University of Miami.

PAGE 173. From Marcus Ransford, *An Historical Account of the Black Empire of Hayti: Comprehending a view of the Principal Transactions in the Revolution of Saint Domingo* . . . (London: James Cundee, 1805), before page 337. Print courtesy Archives and Special Collections, Richter Library, University of Miami.

PAGE 182. From a pamphlet published in January 1830 with an antislavery article originally printed in the *Westminster Review*. Print courtesy Archives and Special Collections, Richter Library, University of Miami.

PAGE 200. From *Frank Leslie's Illustrirte Zeitung*. Print courtesy Archives and Special Collections, Richter Library, University of Miami.

PAGE 205. A color print by W. A. Rogers contemporary with the events illustrated. Print courtesy Archives and Special Collections, Richter Library, University of Miami.

PAGE 280. Courtesy Clement-Petrocik Company.

PAGE 290. Courtesy Bob Krist for the Puerto Rico Tourism Company.

PAGE 294. Courtesy U.S. Virgin Islands Division of Tourism.

PAGE 299. Courtesy Tourism Corporation Bonaire.

PAGE 302. Courtesy Michael Doneff for the Clement-Petrocik Company.

PAGE 307. Photo by Allen Montaine for Medhurst & Associates.

PAGE 318. A sepia gravure from "Souvenir Views of Trinidad, British West Indies, the Jewel of the Caribbean." Ottawa, Canada: The Photogelatine Engraving Company, no date, [*circa* 1920s or 1930s]. Print courtesy of Archives and Special Collections, Richter Library, University of Miami.

PAGE 332. Courtesy Jamaica Tourist Board.

PAGE 337. Courtesy Trinidad and Tobago Tourist Office.

PAGES 343, 345, 356 and 358. Courtesy Bahamas Ministry of Tourism.

INDEX

Entries are filed letter by letter. Page numbers followed by the letter *t* refer to tables; the letter *f* indicates an illustration.

A

ABC terrorist group, 230
abolition of slavery, 179, 180*t*
  and apprenticeship/*patronato* systems, 186–87, 203
  and British abolitionist movements, 180–85, 182*f*
  in British colonies, 179–81, 184
  in Cuba, 203
  in Danish Virgin Islands, 215
  in Dutch colonies, 213–14
  in French colonies, 168, 211
  slave revolts related to, 185–86, 211, 215
Abu Bakr, Yasin, 338
ACS. *See* Association of Caribbean States
Adams, Grantley, 316–17, 321, 323
Adams, J.M.G.M. "Tom," 340–42
adelantado, 24, 47
adventurers, 60
Africa: Castro's Cuba and, 244–45, 248
  diseases in, 129, 384
  slave trade in, 126, 128–30
Africans. See also slaves
  Coromantees, 163–64
  Dahomets, in Haiti, 217
  and diseases, 18, 20, 73, 130, 142
  as indentured laborers, 192, 211
  slave revolts by, 160, 163–64
  term, xvii
aid: from home countries, 279–80, 297, 302
alcaldes ordinarios, 48
ALP. *See* Antigua Labour Party
Americas: European discovery of, 22–24
  Spanish claim to, 35
Amis des Noirs, 166–67
Amory, Vance, 354–55
Anegada. *See* British Virgin Islands
Ango, Jean d,' 38
Angola: Cubans in, 244, 248
Anguilla, 281, 304, 306
  drug trafficking in, 282
  political status of, 323
  population of, 5*t*
  and Saint Kitts-Nevis, 353
  settlement of, 77

wars affecting, 100, 147
animals
  domestic, gone wild, 87
  introduced, 50
  native, 13
Anthony, Kenny D., 358
Antigua
  Bird family rule in, 310–11, 319, 349–53
  drug trade and crime in, 283, 283*t*, 352–53
  emancipation on, 187
  foreign debt, 328*t*
  illegal weapons trade in, 350, 352
  independence of, 310, 323, 347
  Maroons in, 156
  population of, 5*t*, 76*t*
  rebellion in (1710), 103
  in Second Dutch War, 97
  settlement of, 75–76
  slave revolts on, 161*t*
  sugar aristocracy on, 115
  tourism in, 348, 350
Antigua Labour Party (ALP), 350–51, 353
Antoneli, Juan Bautista, 42
apprenticeship, of former slaves, 186–87, 203
Arawak Indians, 13, 15–17, 28–30, 51, 54, 124
  agriculture of, 14–15
  descendants of, 32
  extermination of, 31–33
Araya Bay, Venezuela: and Dutch salt trade, 42–43, 64
arid climate, 10
Aristide, Jean-Bertrand, 255, 272–77
Arthur, Owen, 342
Aruba, 4, 65–66, 214, 279, 295
  drug trafficking and, 282, 299
  economy of, 298–99
  map of, 378*f*
  oil production in, 295, 297*f*, 298
  population of, 5*t*
  in 20th century, 279, 296–99
asiento, 52
assembly industries, 270, 278–79, 287, 340
Association of Caribbean States (ACS), 330
attachés (Haiti), 273, 275
audiencia, 29, 46–48
  of Santo Domingo, 29, 47–48, 53
Austin, Hudson, 361, 363, 366
Ávila, Pedro Arias de, 30
Avril, Prosper, 272
Ayscue, George, 74
Azar, Jacobo Majluta, 260

B

Báez, Buenaventura, 222
Bahamas, 4, 5*t*
  British settlement of, 91–92
  drug trade and crime in, 282–83, 283*t*, 344
  economy of, 326, 328*t*, 343–46
  geology of, 7
  independence of, 323
  map of, 368*f*
  pirates in, 92, 98, 103–4
  population of, 5*t*, 188*t*, 329*t*
  slave revolts on, 161*t*
  in War of Jenkins' Ear, 153
Balaguer, Joaquin, 255, 257–62
Balboa, Vasco Nuñez de, 30
bananas, 348
  EU preferences for, 348, 357
  in Saint Lucia, 357–58
Barbados
  Adams in, 316–17
  and Carlisle grant, 70
  depression of 1930s in, 314
  economy of, 326, 340, 342
  and English wars, 74, 88–89, 151
  federations and, 75, 198
  foreign debt, 328*t*
  indentured servants in, 72–73
  independence of, 323
  island assemblies in, 194
  Maroons in, 156
  planters in, 115–16, 198
  population of, 5*t*, 71*t*, 115*t*, 188*t*, 329*t*
  riots during 1930s in, 314
  settlement of, 68, 70–72
  since independence, 340–42
  slaves in, 141, 161*t*, 185
  sugar production on, 68, 71, 109, 113–16, 190, 340, 342
  trade regulation of, 74–75
Barbados Defense League, 198
"Barbadosed," 73
Barbados Labour Party (BLP), 317, 340–42
Barbados Workers' Union, 317
Barbuda, 347, 350, 353
  population of, 5*t*
Barceló, Carlos Romero, 290
Barrington, John, 148
Barrow, Errol, 317, 340, 342
Basque, Michel le, 93
Basse-Terre: as town name, 79
Batista y Zaldívar, Fulgencio, 226, 230–34
Batraville, Benoit, 265
Battle of The Saints, 152–53
Bay of Pigs expedition, 237–38
Beckford, William, 146
Bell, Philip, 74, 91